Nationalism
and the State
Second Edition

In memory of my mother and father

Nationalism and the State

Second Edition

John Breuilly

Manchester University Press

Copyright © John Breuilly 1993

Published by Manchester University Press
Oxford Road, Manchester M13 9PL, UK

British Library Cataloguing-in-Publication Data
A catalogue record for this book is available from the British Library

ISBN 0 7190 3800 6 paperback

Reprinted 1995, 1998

Printed in Great Britain
by Redwood Books, Trowbridge

Contents

Preface to the first edition

The scope of this book is ambitious. Clearly no one person can understand in detail more than a tiny fraction of so vast a subject. But if there is to be any general understanding of nationalism it is essential to go beyond what one knows in detail. During the process of planning and writing I became sharply aware of an important gap in the literature. What had never been undertaken was a general investigation of nationalism as a form of politics using the method of comparative history. There were general works by sociologists, political scientists and other kinds of social scientists. These had insufficient and often poorly organised information with which to work. Specific historical studies were frequently organised in different ways which made direct comparisons difficult if not impossible. Furthermore they did not need to define general terms such as nationalism particularly carefully because their main concern was not with nationalism as such. There were broad chronological surveys which treated nationalism as but one aspect of modern history. But these failed to make clear the distinct contexts which generated nationalism. Nationalism may be modern but modernity is not nationalism. There were general works with rather clearer analysis but they tended to define nationalism as a set of doctrines, ideas and sentiments. These left obscure the reasons why it frequently became politically significant. Finally there were a few – very few – good comparative historical studies which concentrated on a particular region and period. These partially filled the gap, but by virtue of their specific focus on region and period they could do no more than that. A more general application of this comparative historical approach seemed to me essential.

My intention was to provide a systematic description of nationalism as a form of politics. This took longer than I had originally planned, and the book grew in size. I had to come up with a clear definition and to construct a useful typology. Then I had to do more reading and thinking in order to select, analyse and compare cases within each of the types I had constructed. At this stage I was sceptical of 'theories' of nationalism.

I saw my task as organising the data rather more effectively than hitherto and, at best, indicating the shortcomings of some of the existing general approaches to the subject.

However, as I worked on the book a central theme did develop almost imperceptibly. This is the key role played by the modern state in shaping nationalism. In part the idea is a product of the approach: by concentrating on nationalism as politics I was compelled to consider closely the political context in which it develops. The modern state is the most important feature of that political context. In part what I moved towards was less a theory than the placing of nationalism in a wider framework. It is not so much that the modern state causes or produces nationalism as that nationalism makes eminent sense in some of the situations that are shaped by the modern state.

It is because this wider framework became clear to me only in the course of writing the book that is is made most explicit in the conclusion. To develop the idea fully would require a book on the development of the modern state. My reading so far suggests that there is a gap in the literature on the modern state equivalent to that which I have indicated for nationalism. But that is another story.

I have contracted innumerable intellectual debts on the way. Books such as this can only be written on the basis of a wide reading of the secondary literature. The university library at Manchester has provided me with invaluable help in getting what I needed on the cases considered.

But for the existence of the undergraduate course from which the book arose I would not have put in the initial work which made it possible. Writing and re-writing lectures, running seminars and marking essays on nationalism have sharpened my thinking on the subject. I was fortunate to join a lively modern history section at Manchester where there was a good deal of discussion about history and how it should be taught at university and attempts, as in the course 'Themes in Modern History', to put into practice some of the ideas that were discussed. Generally a large yet compact department has made it easy for me to pick the brains of colleagues on a very wide range of historical matters.

I would like to thank Constantine Brancovan, Judith Brown, Kenneth Hyde and Arthur Mawby for their comments on drafts of particular passages or chapters. I am especially grateful to Ian Kershaw and Terence Ranger for their detailed comments as well as discussions of drafts of various chapters. These led to some extensive rewriting and, I hope, improvement. Comments by Anthony D. Smith on drafts of the introduction and conclusion were of great value. The general appreciation by Peter Worsley of a draft of the whole book was heartening and his many criticisms were invaluable when I came to revise that draft. Above all I am grateful to him for insisting on the need for a more extensive and ambitious conclusion than I had originally intended. I am, of course, alone responsible for the defects that remain.

Finally my thanks to my wife, Liz, who has helped me in more ways than I can say.

Preface to the second edition

Since the publication of the first edition of this book in 1982 both the world and the author have moved on. However, I have not felt it necessary to engage in a fundamental re-writing for this second edition. The main reason for this is that I still hold to my principal argument: that nationalism should be understood as a form of politics that arises in close association with the development of the modern state. Apart from that, it is simply not possible to keep abreast of historical reinterpretations in all the cases on which the book touches. I have in some cases - for example that of Indian colonial nationalism - corrected what appeared to me to be unbalanced features of my original interpretation. I have tried to be clearer and more consistent in treating nationalism as politics which is only, if necessarily, defined in terms of a particular idea. Apart from that my main concern has been, so far as the chapters of the original book are concerned, to clarify and tighten my arguments, to make changes where informed criticism has convinced me of the need to do so, and to take account of more recent literature where this seemed appropriate.

In addition to that there are some substantial changes from the first edition. A large part of the original Introduction which critically surveyed other approaches to nationalism has not only been thoroughly revised but also shifted to a separate appendix. I realise now that I had plunged the reader into quite complex critical arguments before I had developed a positive case of my own. I think it is better to develop my own argument first and then leave it to the reader to decide if s/he wants to consider my views of the arguments of others.

The two chapters that made up Part III of the original book now, in revised form, constitute Part I of this edition. Some critics of the first edition seemed to think that my relegation of the social and ideological features of nationalism to the end of the book indicated my view concerning their relative unimportance. I would stress that although I consider nationalism to be a form of politics and, therefore, that political analysis provides the key to a general understanding of nationalism, I am well aware that no nationalist politics can be understood without a consideration of its social composition and the ideas which it takes up. I hope that moving these chapters to the beginning of the book will make that clearer.

Finally, I have added an additional chapter on nationalism in contemporary east-central Europe. The collapse of the USSR and its communist satellites in 1989–91 is something that no serious commentator, including myself, envisaged in 1982. A decade later anyone who claims to have developed a general framework which assists in the analysis of nationalism must show how that can work in contemporary east-central Europe. That is the purpose of the new chapter 17.

John Breuilly, *Bielefeld, November 1992*

1

Introduction

1 Basic arguments

This book outlines and applies a general procedure for the study of nationalism. It treats nationalism as a form of politics. It creates a typology of nationalist politics and then uses the method of comparative history to study particular cases. The argument, which is systematically developed on this basis, is that nationalism is best understood as an especially appropriate form of political behaviour in the context of the modern state and the modern state system.

I would make two claims for this book. First, it treats nationalism primarily as a form of politics. Although many studies of individual cases of nationalism do this, general studies and more theoretical works tend to focus on other aspects of nationalism. Nationalism is treated as a state of mind, as the expression of national consciousness, as a political doctrine elaborated by intellectuals. Probably the most commonly-held assumption – shared by these various approaches – is that nationalism arises ultimately from some sort of national identity or that it is the search for such an identity. I hope to show that this is a very misleading idea. The other common approach is to regard nationalism as the expression of something 'deeper' such as class interest or an economic or social structure or a cultural formation. However, although *particular* nationalist movements can be illuminated by reference to this or that class, economic development, programme of modernisation or cultural achievement, I do not think such ideas help one understand nationalism *generally*. To focus upon culture, ideology, identity, class or modernisation is to neglect the fundamental point that nationalism is, above and beyond all else, about politics and that politics is about power. Power, in the modern world, is principally about control of the state. The central task is to relate nationalism to the objectives of obtaining and using state power. We need to understand why nationalism has played a major role in the pursuit of those objectives. To understand that we need to examine closely how nationalism

1

operates as politics and what it is about modern politics that makes nationalism so important. Only then should we go on to consider the contributions of culture, ideology, class and much else.

The second distinct contribution of this book resides in the method of analysis. I do not develop a general theory and then apply it to cases: I am sceptical about the use of such a procedure in historical investigation. I do not outline a general argument which uses examples in a very brief, illustrative fashion. Such examples are usually unrepresentative and are removed from their historical context. A general framework of analysis is only acceptable if it permits, and is shown to permit, an effective analysis of particular cases. This requires two procedures. First, it is necessary to develop a typology of nationalism. The internal variations within nationalism are too great to allow of a single method of investigation and so one must begin by identifying various types of nationalism which can be considered separately. After such a consideration one can seek to locate underlying similarities between those types. Second, each type must be investigated by the comparative historical method. Within each type I select a few cases. I analyse these cases using the same methods and concepts, which also enables me to compare and contrast them systematically. Only in this way can one move on to draw general conclusions from the case studies.

In the rest of this chapter I will provide a definition of nationalism which focuses upon its political character, and then develop a typology of nationalism.[1] The chapters in Part One of the book consider the social and ideological aspects of nationalism.[2] The main sections of the book are Parts Two and Three in which the typology of nationalist politics is developed through the comparative analysis of a range of cases. The arguments of these parts of the book are used to support my conclusion, which is that the modern state and the modern state system offer the key to an understanding of nationalism.

2 Definitions and classifications

The term 'nationalism' is used to refer to political movements seeking or exercising state power and justifying such action with nationalist arguments.

A nationalist argument is a political doctrine built upon three basis assertions:

(a) There exists a nation with an explicit and peculiar character.

(b) The interests and values of this nation take priority over all other interests and values.

(c) The nation must be as independent as possible. This usually requires at least the attainment of political sovereignty.[3]

This 'core doctrine' differs from that advanced by Smith[4] mainly in eliminating all propositions involving *explicit* generalisations beyond the particular nation to which the nationalist appeals. Often nationalists do see their own nation as simply one amongst many. Certainly such a recognition would appear to be implicit in nationalist doctrine. But nationalists do not necessarily behave fairly, and one cannot apply logical standards to political ideologies. For example, Smith is led to deny that German National Socialism is a form of nationalism because its creed of racial inequality is incompatible with the nationalist vision of a plurality of unique and free nations.[5] The distinction is an important one, both morally and politically, but it is absurd to exclude Nazism as a form of nationalism. It drew upon earlier nationalist ideas and movements, insisted that the supreme values were those of the national community, and couched much of its appeal as well as receiving much of its support in terms which drew upon earlier traditions of German nationalism.

Smith is rightly concerned to distinguish nationalism from ethnocentrism. A vague definition of nationalism which includes any statements about nations or ethnic groups would create an impossibly large subject. That can be avoided by including only statements which make the idea of a peculiar nation explicit; make this assertion the foundation of all political claims; and which are the central ideological statements deployed by a political movement or organisation. One can see how this enables one to exclude many statements with an ethnocentric character from the category of nationalism by considering the debate over the modernity of nationalism.

The debate is often based upon different assumptions and definitions. I do not quarrel with historians who claim that a national consciousness existed in medieval Europe or that there were patriots active in the sixteenth century. I would simply argue that such phenomena should not be labelled as nationalism. To justify such an argument I would cite a couple of examples.

Two of Dante's works are 'On Vernacular Language' and 'On the Monarchy'. In the first of these Dante sought to locate an Italian language. He recognised that there were larger categories such as the East European, Germanic, and Romance language groups and also smaller categories such as the numerous dialects spoken throughout the Italian peninsula. However, he claimed to have discovered an Italian language between these categories. Armed with this discovery (or invention) Dante went on to identify the Italian nation with this language. He urged Italian poets to use Italian, to defend its purity and increase its expressive capacities.

'On the Monarchy' was a plea for a universal emperor. Monarchy, Dante argued, was the only political system that could secure harmony within a society. For universal harmony one required universal monarchy. In that condition of harmony men could devote themselves fully to the duties they owed to God.

3

What is striking is that the arguments of the two works move in independent spheres. Dante's concern with language and nationality is purely cultural; his concern with universal monarchy is purely political. The monarch has no 'national' task. Even the subordinate authorities which Dante envisages working under universal monarchy are not related to peoples or regions which might be regarded as national.

Furthermore, Dante is quite unselfconscious about this absence of a connection. He does not seek to defend this absence because it did not occur to him, or to his contemporaries, that a connection should or could be made. Dante is clear proof of the existence of some kind of national consciousness and concern with national language and cultural identity in late thirteenth and early fourteenth-century Europe. He is equally clear proof of the non-existence of nationalist consciousness.

Again, Shakespeare provides ample proof of such 'national' consciousness. But generally, as in *Henry V*, the 'national' refers to the customs and manners of the common people; it does not shape the values and actions of those who hold power. The Spanish army in the Netherlands was divided into 'nations', each with an associated stereotype. But what matters is that the different nationalities on the eve of Agincourt serve Henry, and that the different nationalities in the Netherlands serve Spain.

One can continue this argument with reference to Marcu's study of 'nationalism' in sixteenth-century Europe. In a chapter on Italy, Marcu considers the 'nationalist' statements made by a number of writers. Most of these writers lament the success of the French invasions of Italy which began in 1495.

> Who can find words to describe our shame? The Gallic king has come and oppressed region after region, so that the whole country now lies in tears and pain.[6]

Few of these writers, however, developed any political programme on the basis of this feeling of shame. Calling upon God to avenge Italy's servitude, as Domenichi did, does not amount to such a programme. Two other writers appear more political. Donato Giannotti, writing in 1553 and now preoccupied with the Imperial threat, called upon the Papacy, aid from France or England and co-operation between Italian princes. However, this was envisaged as a way of responding to an immediate threat and not as the basis for reorganising Italy along national lines. Muzio Justinopolitano did try to specify the way in which Italian princes could co-operate with each other, citing the Swiss cantons as a model. In a very strained way this might be regarded as pointing to some idea of an Italian polity, and thus as a form of nationalism.

However, Marcu has selected the strongest evidence for her case. Even then, most of these writers were not nationalist as defined here. They had little influence over princes and never organised or associated with any political movement which might have tried to put their ideas into action. The most coherent image of 'Italian independence' one can derive from this is one which would include the Spanish king as one of a number of legitimate rulers in Italy. Foreign rule as such was not the object of attack, but rather foreign rule of a particular kind imposed by invasion. The concerns of an Italian patriot are to be found alongside or (more often) subordinate to other values such as the maintenance of legitimacy or order or the interests of particular city-states or territorial princes. Marcu has achieved a great deal in the way of identifying and describing certain sorts of national consciousness in sixteenth-century Europe but this should not be confused with nationalism.

So the definition employed here can avoid the danger of being too vague and all-embracing and, among other things, draws attention to the modernity of nationalism.

The definition also excludes from consideration political movements which demand independence on the basis of universal principles. The term 'nationhood' is often used to describe the achievement of such independence, for example, in the creation of the United States of America. However, the leaders of that independence movement made little reference to a distinct cultural identity to justify their claims. They demanded equality and, failing that, independence, and justified these demands by appealing to universal human rights. Parts of North America were simply the areas in which these rights were being asserted. Admittedly a sense of national identity developed after the achievement of independence but by then nationalism had taken on a rather different character – for example in the conflicting visions of nation that clashed in the Civil War or in the 'melting pot' idea of the relationship between new America and old Europe.

There are problems about excluding such 'universalist' movements from consideration. The conditions which give rise to them are closely connected to those which lead to nationalism. This is considered in chapter 3. Furthermore, one of the roots of nationalism is the idea of the nation as an independent group of citizens, an idea which played a central role in the political language of the American independence movement. I consider this further in chapter 1, where I argue that such ideas only become nationalist when combined with other ideas about a distinctive cultural identity.

It is often difficult to distinguish between universalist and nationalist elements of certain movements. For example, the German National Assembly which met in Frankfurt am Main in 1848–49 to form a nation-state did not claim that all ethnic Germans should live in that state. One could argue that this was not merely a question of pragmatism, affected by the desire both to include other ethnic elements in a united Germany and to avoid the problem of over-ambitious claims, but proof that the parliament was not committed to the values of ethnic nationalism.[7] Much of the case for a nation-state was made in terms of human rights which have universal application.

Yet one could not argue that the Frankfurt parliament simply applied the universal principles about human rights and constitutional government to an area which happened to be called Germany. To begin with, this does not suffice to justify the claims of unification nationalism. Separation from a larger state or reform of the existing state can be justified by pointing to discriminatory or unjust treatment, and this can be phrased in terms of universal values. But to justify unification one has to go further and identify some entity which needs to be unified. In this case the entity was the German nation. It is difficult to estalish precisely what, in the absence of the ethnic criterion, members of the Frankfurt parliament meant by the German nation. But one can work out what might be called an historical-territorial concept of the nation which was very different from an ethnic conception. Such a conception tends to transfer the criterion of identity from people (the ethnic conception) to places. Many nationalisms do this. The place, the national territory, becomes a shorthand term for a complex network of ideas concerning the nation. What these ideas are can only be worked out by considering the claims that are made in relation to the national territory. Many of these claims will be couched in universal terms.

The same problem of distinguishing between 'universalist' and nationalist movements arised from what might be called the 'voluntarist' or subjective view of nationality. Its most famous expression came in Renan's definition of the nation as a twenty-four-hour-a-day plebiscite. As soon as people ceased to think of themselves as members of the nation, the nation would cease to exist. The implication is that that nation has no 'objective reality' even for nationalists if they take this view. To base national identity upon individual choice would seem to involve abandoning any notion of group identity which distinguishes one group from all others. Such a view of nationalism would, therefore, surrender the idea that the nation was a cultural entity and hence make it impossible to identify any specific nation.

But pushed this far Renan's view ceases to make sense. The constant reiteration of the statement 'I am French' is empty unless linked to some notion of what being French means. In turn, that meaning can become politically significant only if shared by a number of people with effective organisation. It is the shared meanings and their political organisation that constitute a form of nationalism rather than the purely subjective choices of individual Frenchmen. Of course, this does not meant that the national has an objective reality: we are still referring only to the shared views of nationalists. But at least it means that we can refer to a set of common ideas which can be analysed and their origins and purposes explained. Thus one can work out, even for those nationalists who share Renan's position, a nationalist case which rests upon views about a distinct national identity.

It is also difficult to distinguish universalist from nationalist claims in the language employed by many modern anti-colonialist movements.[8] On the one hand, claims to independence for territories such as Tanganyika or Nigeria could be grounded upon an appeal to universal human rights and it is difficult to construct a plausible account of some cultural identity one might call the nation in these cases. On the other hand, cultural themes have loomed much larger in the language of anti-colonial movements than they did in American resistance to British or Spanish rule. Modern anti-colonial movements have seen themselves in relation to an allegedly superior Western culture and have sought to counter it by elaborating accounts of their own, non-western cultures. This conception of an indigenous culture is used in part to underpin political claims. Such cultural ideas tend to operate on a fairly sweeping level: Arab, African, Indian, Chinese. But there have also been more specific reponses which may or may not be integrated into anti-colonialism. These are what have been variously called 'sub-nationalist' or 'tribalist' movements, which have often made statements referring to ethnic identities. The most effective form of anti-colonial nationalism – that operating at the level of the colonial territory – finds itself in-between these very broad anti-western and very specific ethnic claims. However, although this can lead to conflict, more often such nationalist movements incorporate these cultural claims into their own case, referring to their own society as a rich mix of sub-cultures and themselves as being part of a larger project such as Pan-Africanism or Arab nationalism. These matters are considered in detail in Part Three.

The attempt to construct a cultural or ethnic identity at the level of the colonial territory can have a degree of plausibility if there is some real continuity between the peoples and territories of the pre-colonial and the colonial eras. However, in many cases such a construction looks quite artificial because of the sharp break in continuity introduced by colonial rule. However, even in these cases, apart from the idea of the nation as a body of citizens claiming independence on the basis of universal human rights, one also encounters the idea of the nation as a project, a unity to be fashioned out of the fight for independence and in the new era of freedom. In this respect, as well as the others I have mentioned, universalist themes of human rights and political self-determination are inextricably tied to nationalist themes of cultural identity in modern anti-colonialism. For this reason such movements need consideration whereas I leave aside the independence movements of North and South America, Canada, New Zealand and Australia where such a cultural dimension does not figure so centrally.

I consider *significant* nationalist movements. By this I mean movements which posed a serious challenge to the state. Obviously one must consider the origins of such movements, for example the role of founding intellectuals, before they achieved such significance. However, I do not consider nationalist movements which may have developed quite elaborate doctrines but never became significant politically; whereas I do consider other movements with much less elaborate doctrines but which were politically significant.[9] Political significance tells us something important about the nature of a movement and also alters the role of ideology within such a movement. The use of nationalist ideas are used to identify a movement as nationalist, but it is politics rather than ideology which has the central attention in this book.

Most of this book considers nationalist oppositions to the state. There is also state-led nationalism but defining governmental nationalism is more difficult. The term nationalist in this context often means no more than particularly offensive and aggressive policies pursued by national governments. In this sense Hitler was a nationalist, but not Stresemann. However, this tends to be a moral rather than an analytical distinction, having its place within a tradition which contrasts nationalism as a 'bad thing' with patriotism as a 'good thing'. However, to regard all policies of self-interest undertaken by national governments as nationalist would be to empty the term of any specific meaning.

More usefully one could confine the term 'governmental nationalism' to two specific situations. Externally it could refer to policies aimed at extending the territory of the state into areas which the state claims as belonging to its nation. Thus Hitler's claim to the Sudetenland or to Austria could be regarded as having a nationalist underpinning in a way that would not be true of his claim to *Lebensraum* in the east. Internally, one could describe as nationalist actions taken against specific groups or individuals and justified on the grounds of the anti- or non-national character of these groups or individuals. The official nationality policy of Nicholas I of Russia or the anti-semitism of the Third Reich could be described in these terms.

Nevertheless, I am sceptical as to the value of investigating these situations in a comparative way with the aim of arriving at a general understanding. Foreign policy framed in nationalist terms is usually just part of a larger framework within which such policy is formulated. Particularly if that policy is rather detached from the internal politics of the state, it is more likely that a general understanding will be provided by models of international relations rather than through the concept of nationalism.

Clearly the internal function of governmental nationalism is more closely and obviously related to the position of the government *vis-à-vis* those it claims belongs to the nation, and continues the politics of earlier oppositional movements from which that government originated. However, the very assumption of state power tends to mean that a political movement acquires new sorts of power and is subject to new sorts of influence and considerations. Whereas the organisation and ideology of a nationalism movement are central to its activity when in opposition, this becomes less the case once it acquires state power. Consequently I consider governmental nationalism as a distinct subject only when the links to an earlier nationalist opposition phase are especially evident or when the government conflicts with a nationalist opposition claiming to speak for another nation. Aspects of governmental nationalism are considered in chapters 11, 13, 14, and 15.

I do not consider nationalist pressure groups. Although committed to nationalist ideas, such groups do not seek to control the state. Usually this is because they regard the existing state as national and wish merely to influence its policies. It can be because they feel they lack real power, though pressure groups can change into movements seeking control of the state if either they acquire more support or if they become alienated from the state. It is with such movements that this book is concerned, that is, significant political movements, principally of opposition, which seek to gain or exercise state power and justify this objective on nationalist grounds.

Although this narrows the range of relevant subjects, it still covers a great deal. To manage this one needs to subdivide into different classes. Classifications are simply sets of interrelated definitions. Empirically they are not right or wrong; rather they are either helpful or unhelpful.

The focus here is with nationalism as a form of politics, principally opposition politics. The principle of classification will, therefore, be based upon the relationship between the nationalist movement and the state which it either opposes or controls. A nationalist opposition can seek to break away from the present state (separation), to reform it in a nationalist direction (reform), or to unite it with other states (unification).

Furthermore, the state which is opposed may or may not define itself in national terms. If it does, conflict may arise between governmental and oppositional nationalisms. Such conflict is very different from that between nationalist oppositions and states which do not regard themselves as national.

These distinctions yield six classes, which are set out here with relevant examples:

	Opposed to non-nation states*	Opposed to nation-states
Separation	Magyar, Greek, Nigerian[10]	Basque, Ibo
Reform	Turkish, Japanese	Fascism, Nazism
Unification	German, Italian	Arab, Pan-African[11]

* A rather clumsy term but I can think of nothing better

9

These categories provide the basic rationale for the organisation of Parts II and III. Part II deals with nationalist movements in non-nation-states and Part III with nationalist movements in nation-states. However, some additional distinctions are also required.

First, I have separated the treatment of nationalism in 'western' states (that is, states in Europe and in areas of predominantly European settlement overseas) from non-western states.[12] Although comparisons can be made, the differences berween these two types of situation are so great that they need separate treatment. Modern anti-colonialism, in particular, is a very special form of nationalism and receives extended treatment in Part II.

Second, I argue that there was no such thing as reform nationalism in Europe until the creation of nation-states. So there is no chapter on this subject. However, there were what I term 'national' oppositions in European states which had similar purposes to reform nationalist movements. In order to understand something of the background to nationalism proper and of the distinctive situations which transform a national opposition into a nationalist one, it is necessary to consider these precursors of nationalism. This is the subject of chapter 3. Unification nationalism outside Europe is considered in Part III although it has a history which antedates the establishment of nation-states in those areas. Unification nationalism in Europe after 1871 is of little importance and, therefore, is not considered, with the special and partial exception of the role of nationalism in German reunification in 1989–90 considered in chapter 17. In addition to a consideration of nationalist opposition I also look at governmental nationalism in the new nation-states in chapter 13. With these qualifications, the subject matter of the various chapters in Parts II and III is based directly upon the categories outlined above.

There are problems with this system of classification and alternative categories have been advanced.

One problem is deciding where to place a particular case. Any classification based on general principles is bound to encounter this problem. Its utility will, in part, depend upon whether particular placings seem perverse and whether there are too many 'difficult' cases. I deliberately select an especially difficult case: that of 19th century Polish nationalism. A Polish populist nationalist would have wanted to separate Polish territory from the control of the three partitioning powers of Austria, Russia and Prussia; to unify these territories into a single Polish state; and to do so in a reformed version very different from the aristocratic Polish kingdom of the 18th century. Finally, in post-1871 Germany such a nationalist would be opposed to a nation-state, but in the Habsburg and Romanov dynasties would oppose non-national states. So this case could go in all six categories!

Yet the six categories draw attention to important differences within

Polish nationalism. The separatist movements, though each oriented to a future Polish state, took different forms according to the different situations in which they found themselves. This largely defined the nationalist movement because opposition to the respective partitioning powers was the first and most urgent task. The Russian-based Polish nationalism, and therefore the anti-Russian strain within Polish nationalism, predominated up to the 1860s. Furthermore, there were tensions between 'restorationists' and 'reformers' with the former concentrating on gaining international support and the latter on mobilising a popular movment. Both kinds of nationalists could only distance themselves from the particular issues of separation when in exile. Finally, the Polish movement in Prussia changed character when Prussia itself shifted from predominantly dynastic, non-national character to becoming part of the German nation-state. Something similar happened when the Tsartist state shifted to a Russian ethnic nationalist policy. So although Polish nationalism *as a whole* can be placed in all six categories, the categories point to important distinctions within Polish nationalism.[13] So one can defend this classification even in relation to such a peculiarly difficult case.

A second problem is to decide whether one is dealing with a nation-state. I base this decision upon the case the state itself makes in relation to nationalist opposition. Thus between 1860 and 1870 the Prussian/German state shifted to a German national position against its Polish subjects. The Spanish government has opposed Basque and Catalan nationalisms on nationalist grounds. Although this opposition was more repressive and intolerant of any cultural autonomy under Franco than today, the opposition is still a national one. In Britain there has been a tendency to separate the concept of nationality as citizenship from that of nationality as culture, claiming that it is possible to be British and Scottish, British and Welsh at the same time. However, if the distinction is challenged, as it is by Scottish and Welsh nationalists, defenders of the integrity of the United Kingdom usually resort to an historical, territorial, and civic conception of British nationality which underpins the present state and sets limits to the claims made on behalf of 'merely cultural' nations. Yet this has always been somewhat incoherent and faces a real problem in defining the English/British relationship. In so far as an English nationalism develops in response to Celtic nationalism it could actually undermine the ideological defence of the United Kingdom.[14]

I define modern anti-colonial nationalism as separatist. Such movements claim independence for what was already a separately administered territory in a different part of the world from that of the colonial power. Clearly, separation means something different in these cases from those which involve boundary changes such as those demanded by separatist movements in the multinational dynasties of Europe. However, the nationalism of the Muslim League in the Indian subcontinent did involve separatism of the latter kind, and this preceded the formation of an independent state. So this was separatist both in relation to colonial rule and to Indian nationalism.

Another difficulty arises when a nationalist movement in a particular territory seeks a political union with its 'own' nation-state, for example, the German nationalists of Bohemia, later the Sudetenland region in Czechoslovakia. This can be seen from three angles: as part of the drive towards German unification; as an expression of governmental nationalism on the part of the German government; and as separatist nationalism amongst the Bohemian/Sudeten Germans. Actually, as with the Polish case discussed earlier, these are very real distinctions within German nationalism. Given the particular interest of the book in nationalist opposition, my principal focus will be upon the separatist aspect – treating the demand for unification and support from its 'own' nation-state as resources which help shape the character and achievements of such a separatist nationalism.

This classification is wholly political. That is not to say that the socio-economic situation or the ideological character of nationalism is regarded as unimportant. One needs to pay attention to these matters in considering every case. However, a focus on nationalism as political action should define and classify its subject in terms of political action. To add further qualifications, whether in terms of social base or political doctrine, would multiply the categories in a way which would undermine the whole point of classification.

Furthermore, classifications based upon these other principles have severe drawbacks. To define and classify nationalist movements in socio-economic terms confronts the problem that all significant movements bring together different social groups within a particular territory and also deny that they are to be regarded in socially exclusive terms. Clearly some social interests play a greater role than others in nationalist movements, but this is something to take account of in specific analyses, not in the preliminary act of classification.[15]

A similar criticism can be applied to classifying nationalism in terms of political doctrine.[16] First, one has to identify the nationalist ideology and decide about its classification. Hayes, for example, sought to align nationalist ideology with more general political values. Thus he identified, amongst others, Jacobin, traditional and liberal nationalist doctrines. Kohn was particularly concerned with the distinction between 'western' and 'eastern' forms of nationalism, contrasting doctrines which emphasise citizenship and individual choice with those which stress cultural identity and group membership.

In practice it is very difficult to apply such distinctions. I have already challenged the attempt to distinguish nationalism from fascism on intellectual grounds. In mid-nineteenth century German nationalism one can identify strands which variously emphasise liberal constitutionalism with-

12

out ethnic discrimination, language as the bearer of national values, and race. Although one or other of these ideas has more centrality at a particular phase, most broad nationalist movements contain doctrinal mixtures at any one time. What is more, changes in the political situation can bring about rapid shifts in the balance of doctrines and languages employed in a nationalist movement.

It also is not helpful to argue that some doctrinal variants of nationalism are not 'really' nationalist at all. We have already encountered this argument with respect to fascism. It is used also in relation to liberalism which is often regarded as both logically and morally incompatible with nationalism. This incompatibility is adduced as a major reason for the disintegration of movements which sought to combine the two doctrines. Such an argument often concludes that fascism, far from being incompatible with nationalism, is its logical culmination. In arguments of this kind doctrine does not merely define nationalism; it actually shapes its historical development.

However, ideology is not a logical mode of thought and history is not logic. Some Germans, Italians, Hungarians and others in mid-nineteenth century Europe regarded themselves as both liberals and nationalists and were so regarded by their opponents. They combined nationalist and liberal claims in some form or another and constructed political movements which tried to realise those claims. As a consequence liberal nationalism does exist, as does also romantic nationalism, linguistic nationalism, ethnic nationalism, and various other doctrinal positions with a nationalist component, and all their overlapping and interrelated positions. This means both that one must take nationalist doctrine seriously (see chapter 2 below) but one cannot make it the basis for classifying nationalist movements. It may be the case that the 'ultimate' objectives of nationalism and liberalism are incompatible, and this will undoubtedly set limits on possible achievements. But within those limits, and most history operates within such limits, the historian has to respect the way people do subscribe to different mixtures of ideas.

Another danger of this approach is that it can make too much of nationalist doctrine. Nationalist ideology matters, not so much because it directly motivates most supporters of a nationalist movement, but rather because it provides a conceptual map which enables people to relate their particular material and moral interests to a broader terrain of action. Excessive focus on doctrine tends to exaggerate the role of nationalist ideologues and to see the expansion of nationalism in terms of the conversion of people by the ideologues.[17]

Another method of classification – combining political with social elements – focuses upon the different types of movements or organisations.[18] One may distinguish between elite and mass nationalism, constitutional and illegal nationalism, peaceful and violent nationalism.

Organisation may take the form of party or secret society; nationalist parties may be closed and undemocratic or open and democratic. There are numerous possible variations in organisation. That, indeed, is a major drawback to such a principle of classification: one is liable to end up with too many categories. What is more, the categories apply equally well to all other political movements and organisations. Finally, as with doctrines, most significant nationalist movements combine different principles of organisation at the same time. The Indian Congress movement, for example, consisted of many different organisations of different kinds by the 1930s. Although such differences were sometimes due to different views of nationalism, sometimes they were no more than a product of temporary tactical disagreements and sometimes of the need to have different organisation for different groups or regions. What is important, however, is that almost all those involved remained loyal to the central nationalist goal of independence and to Congress as the heart of that nationalism. In organisational terms Congress is unclassifiable, but it *was* Indian nationalism. This organisational diversity only makes sense in relation to the political context in which Congress developed and operated and the problems in the way of achieving independence. The key element in that context was the relationship between Congress and the Raj. That takes us back to the type of classification that I have proposed.

3 Conclusion

In the appendix I critically review a range of approaches to nationalism which emphasise some non-political element such as class interest, economic objective, cultural identity, or psychological function. Readers interested in theoretical issues may want to read that before proceeding to chapter 1. The argument of that appendix as well as the approach I have outlined in this introduction all point in one direction.

Nationalism is a form of politics. Before trying to theorise about the 'real' purpose or cause of this form of politics – before trying to go 'behind' nationalism in search of some non-political base which supposedly gives rise to nationalism – one should try to work out precisely what is the form of politics we call nationalism, its political context and its political modes. Most general studies of nationalism neglect this task, preferring varieties of non-political theorising. Historical studies of particular cases put politics at their centre but do not seek to relate this to the central issue, which is the general significance of nationalism in modern times. The *only* starting point for a general understanding of nationalism is to take its form of politics seriously and to study that politics in a way that does justice to the complexity and variety of nationalisms whilst seeking to locate common patterns. The *only* way to do this is by means of comparative historical investigation. The purpose of this introduction has been to

14

outline the procedures for defining and classifying nationalism, to enable a comparative investigation of this kind to be undertaken.

That investigation is the task of Parts II and III of this book. However, it is important to understand the typical ways in which different social groups can support or oppose nationalism and also to understand why and how nationalist ideology has developed and its typical roles in nationalist politics. This will be considered in chapters 1 and 2. Finally, in the conclusion I will try to draw out the underlying patterns which the arguments of the book point towards, namely that the key to an understanding of nationalism lies in the character of the modern state, which nationalism both opposes and claims as its own.

Notes

1   In the first edition of this book the introduction included a section critically reviewing other approaches towards nationalism. I have now moved that, revised, section of the book into an appendix.

2   In the first edition of the book these chapters came at the end of the book. This conveyed the impression to some reviewers that I did not regard the social bases and ideological appeals of nationalism as important. I have concluded that it is better to introduce these general themes in advance of the comparative analysis of nationalist politics and so these two chapters now make up Part I of the book.

3   Some nationalist movements demand less than this but usually because they recognise that full independence is either unattainable or liable to be dangerously short-lived, because the new independent nation will be exposed in a way that it was not within a larger political structure. The Czech demand for increased autonomy within the Habsburg empire was pragmatic in this way.

4   Anthony D. Smith, *Theories of Nationalism* (London, 1971), p. 21.

5   Smith elaborated the argument in a later book *Nationalism in the Twentieth Century* but only by dint of arguing that fascism was unlike nationalism. However, that argument only worked by excluding the possibility that fascism is one type of nationalism, although different from all other types. Those other types also differ from one another: it is Smith's definition which places fascism in an entirely different category, not the descriptive account of such differences.

6   E. D. Marcu, *Sixteenth Century Nationalism* (New York, 1976), p. 34 quoting Geronimo Frascastoro.

7   The 'ethnic nationalist' case was put strongly by L. B. Namier in *1848: the revolution of the intellectuals* (London, 1944). F. Eyck, *The Frankfurt Parliament, 1848–49* (London, 1968) is an important corrective. See now D. Langewiesche, 'Germany and the national question in 1848', in *The State of Germany*, edited by J. Breuilly (London, 1992), pp. 60–79; and also further below, pp. 105–9.

8   See Thomas Hodgkin, 'A note on the language of African nationalism', in

St. Anthony's Papers, no. 10 (London, 1960), pp. 22–40.

9   See, for example, chapter 16 which includes consideration of the culturally elaborate but politically weak Welsh nationalism and culturally less elaborate but politically much stronger Scottish nationalism and Ulster Unionism.

10 Modern anti-colonial movements could be said to be opposed to nation-states such as Britain or France. But really they are opposed to these states as imperial powers, not as nation-states. That still leaves complications, as with the way in which French Africa was defined as overseas France or the way in which inhabitants of Portugese Africa were defined as Portugese. This is a real issue which had consequences for the way nationalism developed in these colonies.

11 These movements existed prior to the establishment of independent African and Arab states but I am particularly concerned with their significance later on.

12 This applies even to the Ottoman empire, where I consider its European and Middle Eastern territories separately, although I also make comparisons between them. See below, pp. 154–5.

13 For more detail on Polish nationalism see below, pp. 115–20.

14 For the emergence of English claims to Scotland and Ireland in the 17th century (Wales never being considered a national problem) see below, pp. 84–8. For Celtic nationalism in the 20th century see below, pp. 320–32.

15 The typical roles of major social groups is considered in chapter 1. The problems with approaches to nationalism which focus on its socio-economic character are considered in the appendix.

16 For examples of this approach see Carlton J. Hayes, *The Historical Evolution of Nationalism* (New York, 1931); Hans Kohn, *The Idea of Nationalism* (New York, 1967); and Anthony D. Smith, *Nationalism in the Twentieth Century* (Oxford, 1979).

17 I pursue this argument of nationalist ideology as a conceptual map in chapter 2. The danger of focusing on the contribution of ideologues or intellectuals in studies of nationalism is considered further in the appendix.

18 See, for example, K. Symmons-Symonolewicz, *Nationalist Movements: a comparative view* (London, 1970); and, more briefly, *id.* , 'Nationalist movements: an attempt at a comparative typology', in *Comparative Studies in Society and History*, 7 (1964–65), pp. 221–30.

Part I

Social and intellectual bases of nationalism

1

Social bases of nationalist politics

1 Introduction

In this book I argue that one cannot develop a general understanding of
nationalism by means of class or any other kind of socio-economic analysis. The enormous social diversity of modern nationalist movements rules
out such approaches. Nevertheless, in nationalist movements as in all other
political movements, there are social and economic interests. One can
identify some typical relationships between broad social groups and nationalism, though I would stress that these do not exhaust all possible and
actual relationships and do not in any sense 'explain' nationalism. In this
chapter I will begin by considering the general processes which bring about
nationalist politics and broadly defined social groups into some relationship. Then I will consider how communal conflict can be related to
nationalism. Finally I will consider typical relationships between major
social groups (as well as some other collectivities such as Christian churches and Islam) and nationalism.

2 Mobilisation

Even if nationalist movements do not have active popular support they
claim to speak for the whole nation. In this sense nationalist politics is
always mass politics. In many cases nationalism involves the organisation
of mass support for political purposes or the management of large groups
which have suddenly intruded into a previously exclusive political arena.
In practice it is difficult to distinguish these two kinds of mass politics –
'from above' and 'from below' – from each other.

   One can identify various general changes which make it possible or
necessary for politicians to forge links with large parts of the population
hitherto uninvolved in politics. These processes I will call mobilisation. By
this I mean changes which make it possible for politicians to establish
contact with large numbers of people or which can create the expectation

and capacity on the part of large numbers of people to insist on some sort of political representation. Nationalism is one way of coping politically with this mobilisation, although it also serves other purposes.

The most basic changes are economic ones. In the countryside the penetration of market relationships break down local isolation and the control of local elites. This can provide a point of entry for outside political groups as well as compelling some of the people affected by the intrusion of markets to turn their attention outwards.[1] The formation of an urban working class is, of course, the best known of the ways in which economic change creates a new capacity for mass political action. Labour migration, that is the extension of the labour market into the countryside, can have as great a mobilising effect upon rural populations as can the development of rural industry and of commercial agriculture.

There are also political changes which can break down local barriers or a general attitude of non-involvement at popular level. Conscription, for example, can create new contacts between state and the lower levels of rural society which may lead to support for new kinds of politics. In revolutionary and Napoleonic France, in Ireland during the First World War, and in many parts of Africa during the Second World War, it was conscription which first made many people take a political interest in the world beyond their locality. It may be resentment against the state, as in Ireland, or the revelation of a wider world which was then taken back to the villages, as in much of British West and East-Central Africa – the central point is that it extends and politicises attitudes.

More directly war itself not only provides new experiences and contacts but often breaks down traditional controls and leads to a search for alternative sources of authority. Peasant mobilisation in China upon which the communists as well as the nationalists could build was hastened by the Japanese invasion of the country in the 1930s. More generally the breakdown of control, of which war is the ultimate expression, provides an entry point for new sorts of leadership. The abrupt withdrawal of the Belgian government from the Congo had a mobilising effect in this way.

However, war, invasion, and political collapse are as old as humanity whereas nationalism is modern. These types of crisis need to be placed in the context of broader and more modern political change. The key to this is the impact of modern state centralisation upon existing patterns of authority. The imposition of imperial rule, for example, usually involved some diminution of existing authority and also contributed to the formation of new, indigenous types of authority. This could mobilise elements of the subject population. Conflict between different elites might involve a resort to nationalist opposition and attempts to exploit popular sentiment against rivals. This process could be accelerated if the imperial power sought to undermine existing opposition by itself extending political participation downwards, as was the case in India. Political opponents to the imperial power would have to respond by turning to the new entrants into the political arena. This may, indeed, be the challenge issued by the imperial state in order to ensure the creation of a movement to which state power can be stably transferred. More generally the extension of bureaucratic control into the localities – for example by imposing elementary education or welfare provision, by introducing new taxes, by attacking traditional practices such as polygamy, or by breaking down local forms of privilege and discrimination – compelled people to consider how that bureaucracy could be resisted or controlled. The development of electoral politics provided one means of achieving this.

Changes of this kind in one area can have a 'demonstration' effect upon other areas. The rise of mass parties in the more developed coastal region of Nigeria, along with the prospect of political independence, forced the Fulani rulers of northern Nigeria into creating their own political party to defend their interests. The leaders of the Baganda were stimulated to mobilise their people more effectively in the face of a Ugandan nationalist movement and the prospect of independence. Landowners in East-Elbian Germany and elites in the Muslim majority regions of British India responded in similar fashion.

Once such processes are set in motion they are not easy to stop. Where such processes are purely political, unaccompanied by major economic and cultural changes, then such mobilisation might have little impact on traditional authority. Fulani rulers and the Kabaka of Buganda, the Catholic church and large landowners in much of inter-war Spain or central Europe did not compete for votes 'democratically': they instructed those traditionally under their control to vote for particular candidates. Nationalist movements often spread by gaining the support of local notables who can deliver votes and other kinds of backing in this way. Sometimes a nationalist movement has genuine mobilisation in one region but support based on elite co-ordination of this kind in another region.[2] The resources of nationalist parties are often small, and the vote they manage to secure on polling day often reflects this kind of politics as well as a brief effort of will, after which politics relapses back into local and non-democratic forms.[3]

There are also cultural changes which undermine established and exclusive political patterns. The introduction of popular, state-controlled education in Europe or of extensive mission education in colonial territories can have a major impact on popular attitudes. Mass literacy, 'print capitalism', and the construction of a 'standard, national culture' provide the basis for new popular political attitudes and demands.[4] The development of new methods of communication and improvements in the structure of communications make possible the transmission of ideas – as well as altering the nature of those ideas – on a scale hitherto unimaginable. I do not consider that these developments by themselves explain the emergence

21

of nationalist movements, but without them it is difficult to see how many nationalist movements could have acquired the support and influence that they did.

All these processes do not simply alter the situation and interests of people; they change people. Most dramatically, the move into a city is for many people a move into a new world in which their old ways of thinking, acting, being are brought into question. To make that move successful, people need to redefine themselves, their interests, and their ways of acting. Nationalism can play an important part in this process of redefinition. In the city new political contacts are made. In the city nationalist politicians can most easily organise new events such as rallies, demonstrations and mass oratory, and can deploy symbols and sentiments in a new way. Again, I do not consider that the modern city and the search for new identities directly gives rise to nationalism, but they are important elements of the context in which many nationalist movements develop.

3 Communal conflict and nationalism

Apart from providing mass support for nationalist movements aimed against the state, towns have also been the main centres of communal conflicts which have become closely linked to rival nationalisms. As such communal conflict cannot be analysed simply in class terms, I will consider it before looking at class involvement in nationalism.

The starting point for urban communal conflict is when immigrants come to compete on a group basis with one another and/or with members of the 'host' community. Such competition can be over a wide range of issues. It may be material resources, such as jobs, housing or education. It may be concerned with religious practices such as the treatment of cattle (a major source of Muslim-Hindu conflict) or forms of public worship. The range of issues over which conflict can occur as well as the factors determining whether different groups gradually assimilate to one another or draw even-sharper distinctions between themselves are almost infinite. It is difficult to imagine what general theory could grasp such variety. I will simply single out a few of the factors which seem to favour communal conflict and its transformation into nationalism.

There must be some distinguishing characteristic which can mark off one community from another. Language, religion, skin colour and other outward marks of genetic difference, and place of origin are the most frequently encountered characteristics. 'Objectively' the mark of distinction may appear quite trivial. However, unless there is some prior pattern of strong community organisation (for example, Jewish ghettoes) there is probably a point beyond which a distinction would be too slight to be usable.

The meaning conferred upon this distinguishing mark and the uses

22

to which it is put have little to do with the distinction itself. People vested with a common identity by virtue of their place of origin may have had no common identity whilst in that place. Many of the 'tribal' groupings of modern Africa arose through this categorising process, which began in towns and was then extended back to the places from which the immigrants had come. Once created, such distinctions are not merely imposed but accepted and used by those to whom they are applied.

Even when the distinction had been consciously made earlier, it was transformed in the urban context. Popular Protestantism in Belfast took on very different forms in the nineteenth century in response to Catholic immigration from those it had assumed before, either in the countryside or in Belfast itself. The notion of being an Ibo was not only made more intense outside Iboland but it was associated with new stereotypes born out of the process of communal urban conflict. The explicit and intense character of these marks of distinction are due to the fact that they are not simply parts of a broader way of life. Rather they are substitutes for such ways of life, and they serve to provide, from a fairly narrow base, principles for constructing new ways of living.[5]

Such constructions can point to assimilation rather than conflict. The Jewish modernist who defines religion as a private affair and insists that Jews can take a place in public life in just the same way as citizens with other religious beliefs is engaged in precisely the same sort of rethinking of Jewish identity as is the Zionist or the anti-semite who redefines Jewish identity in national or racial terms. Each is dissolving traditional ideas of what it meant to be a Jew and replacing it with a more explicit and specialised idea. The modernist, however, is aiming at assimilation – at least in public affairs – whereas the Zionist and the anti-semite are aiming to provide a new communal identity for the Jew which will have political consequences. What all have in common is that society – in this case the identity and place of the Jew, and the Jewish community in that society – is not 'given', an implicit routine which one simply lives, but is changing in ways which require people to think out more explicitly who they are and how they should behave.[6] It is when situations make these sorts of demands upon people that political ideology can become relevant. At one level such ideology is a means of dealing with puzzlement. (See chapter 2 for an elaboration of this argument.)

It is difficult to specify the conditions in which this will lead to communal conflict. Much depends on the capacity of immigrants to adapt to the demands of the host community, which in turn will depend upon the values and social situation of both immigrants and hosts. Much also depends upon the capacity of the urban economy to meet demands for jobs, housing, education and other resources without seriously undermining the position of the host community. Competition for such resources, especially when they are very scarce, is a major ingredient in creating and

23

sustaining communal conflict.[7]

Such conflict can take two broad forms. One is where none of the groups involved achieve much success. Although conflicts using marks of distinction will be intense, this will not be reflected clearly in the occupational structure of the city. In early nineteenth-century Belfast Catholics and Protestants competing for textile jobs, especially in linen, were in this situation. Work was unskilled, labour plentiful, and competition amongst many small employers was intense. This made it impossible for one group to carve out a position of privilege. The first large-scale sectarian clashes which date from the 1830s were fluid, sporadic, unorganised and focused on the maintenance of boundaries between predominantly Protestant and Catholic residential areas.[8]

This conflict could be exploited by nationalists but it was a difficult and dangerous resource, unstable and difficult to control. Unless political elites are in desperate straits they will be unwilling to unleash energies of this kind. Sometimes they do so inadvertently. In the early decades of this century Muslim and Hindu elites were appalled at the devastation caused by large-scale communal riots in Calcutta for which their own conflicts bore some responsibility.[9] The links between nationalism and this kind of communal conflict are loose and incapable of generating an organised mass political movement.

The situation is very different when the distinctions used to identify communities are associated with divisions in the occupational structure. By the later nineteenth-century the economy of Belfast had shifted towards an emphasis upon shipbuilding and related industries. Limited labour competition, large employers, and some high-skill occupations made it possible for Protestants to control certain sectors of the labour market. Catholics were forced into less attractive jobs. As in New York at the same time, different ethnic and religious groups came to be occupational as well as residentially distinctive. In the mining regions of South Africa and Bohemia distinctions of race and language respectively have been used to reserve better jobs for one group.

In these situations communal conflict becomes more continuous and organised. Clear patterns of leadership emerge, especially from the more favoured community, where it is linked to the reserved occupations. Conflicts shift from being sporadic disputes over boundaries and other group symbols to a focus upon the resources at issue. Trade union and electoral politics and the application of pressure upon governments, especially city government, acquire prominence. Identity is still expressed and reinforced through marches and demonstrations and anniversaries, but even these taken on a more organised and systematic form.

Conflict of this kind offers a more predictable and controllable resource for nationalist politicians once they can establish understandings with community leaders. However, the understanding must be paid for. At times of crisis and external threat the community may simply want the security of more extensive political ties and not press its particular interests. At other times it will insist upon recognition of its own concerns. Working-class support for Ulster Unionism, for example, is not simply the product of manipulation. Protestant workers had constructed community organisation before the rise of Unionist politics and this enabled Unionist politicians to mobilise mass support very quickly. However, that largely working-class Protestant community then pursued many of its own interests through Unionism, both before and after partition.[10]

Such communal conflicts do not directly lead to nationalism. Often they tend towards the urban 'machine' politics of Tammany Hall in New York. Belfast politics was taking on this shape by mid-nineteenth century. It was only a wider political crisis over Ireland which forced urban communities in Belfast to link themselves to wider political divisions, thereby incorporating communal organisations into nationalist movements. Those broader nationalist movements are about much more than communal divisions as we will see in parts II and III.

4 Nationalism and class

The categories used here are very general and would be modified and refined in particular cases. They suggest no more than certain general and typical responses to nationalism. Under the heading 'ruling class' I include what are as much political as social groups. 'Traditional' is also a vague term, something which can often be used to advantage by nationalists claiming to represent rather than challenge tradition.

(a) The traditional ruling class

(i) Introductory remarks. Nationalism redefines the nature of legitimate authority. Nationalism is frequently associated with political change which favours new elites. Nationalist politics are typically crisis politics, and crises threaten the *status quo*. Consequently one would expect to find an established ruling class opposing nationalism. That is, in fact, usually the case. Therefore, it is worth identifying the typical situations in which this is not the case.

(ii) The nobility. In Poland, Hungary and Japan some of the nobility, especially of the middling ranks, used their local power to oppose the existing state in the name of the nation. In Poland and Hungary the great magnates stood by the state. In Japan, although the lords of Choshu and Satsuma were involved in the events leading to the Meiji restoration, the impetus came from middling samurai on their domains. In all three cases an important support role was played by the large poor nobility.

25

In each case the nationalist argument was framed in terms of tradition: the restoration of the historic kingdoms of Poland, of St Stephen, and of the Meiji Empire. The nobility ran their own estates and local affairs, handling disputes with peasants with little resort to the central state. No other social group, apart from the peasantry, was in a position to challenge noble pre-eminence. Where peasants could act independently, as in the *jacquerie* in Galicia in 1846, it had the effect of bringing noble-led nationalism to an end in the region.

In these cases the state was organised through links between central government and noble landowners who possesed formal political rights as well as substantial local autonomy. The nobility *was* the state in the locality. It was the attempt by the central government to undermine this situation which often provoked noble resistance. This was most marked in Poland where the partitioning powers substantially reduced the political authority of much of the nobility. It was a feature of the Josephine reforms in Hungary. The Tokugawa regime's rather milder centralising reforms also aroused resistance.

To resist effectively these nobles had to develop new political ties amongst themselves and with other elites, and even upon occasions to mobilise popular support and appeal to powerful outsiders. Nationalism helped in these tasks. It papered over internal divisions such as those revealed by the Meiji repression of rebellion in Satsuma or the differences between Kossuth and Gyorgey in 1848. During a political crisis, in which the authority of central government had broken down, such conflicts were played down and nationalism helped unify a variety of interests in a common movement. These very specific situations provided the right combination of threat and opportunity to push elements of the nobility into such nationalist politics.

(iii) Traditional states. By this I mean states which limit political participation to traditionally privileged groups. A few states of this kind have managed, at least partially, to transform themselves into modern nation-states with an industrial base and mass political institutions without too much political pressure from internal opposition below the privileged groups. The best known cases are those of Prussia and Japan.

One needs to distinguish the state from the traditional ruling class. Bismarck's policies between 1864 and 1871 were not actively supported by many Prussian nobles. Indeed there was much criticism of Bismarck for his abandonment of tradition and he relied principally upon liberal support for a crucial period. The Meiji government forced through reforms which undermined the position of many samurai and which provoked some domain lords into revolt.

Yet one can argue that such reforms maintained the position of that ruling class and preserved many privileges more effectively than failure to reform would have done. The problem with the idea of the traditional state reforming itself out of existence is that it calls into question the very notion of a traditional state. In both cases political reform long preceded the dramatic events of the 1860s and 1870s. One might indeed argue that the traditional state had aleady largely disappeared and that the German unification and the Meiji restoration should be seen as revolutions from above which completed the transformation of the state and actually relocated class power.[11]

However, in both cases effective political power remained confined to a minority, one overwhelmingly drawn from the traditionally privileged. Certainly the state presided over major changes which shifted the basis of economic power and transformed its own institutions. This is precisely the problem: one cannot think the problem away by saying either that nothing essential changed or by calling the change a 'revolution from above', a phrase which simply empties the term 'revolution' of any useful meaning it retains. The task of the historian is rather to pinpoint precisely how change was handled, change which presented itself not in an abstract way but as immediate political problems to which the existing state was able to find constructive responses. That state was not a static institution suddenly confronted by 'change', but an evolving political structure which had constantly been adapting to pressures towards market economics and constitutional accountability. In Prussia and Japan elements of the political elite carried through dramatic reforms, involving the use of force, which markedly altered the nature of the state but retained power in the hands of that elite. Reforms such as the introduction of a national, democratically elected parliament in Germany or the abolition of the domains in Japan carried a high-risk with them and had to be justifed both in conservative and nationalist terms. What needs to be explained is how and why such high-risk policies could be implemented.

In both cases the traditional state was under severe pressure. The Perry expedition and the subsequent trade treaties imposed upon Japan revealed the superiority of the West and the dangers this involved and also sparked off internal dissent as to how to respond. In Prussia Bismarck faced a constitutional crisis and growing strains with Austria over policy in Germany.

It was important that the reformers within the elite believed that they could control and restrict the changes needed. The economic gap between these states and more advanced economies was not so vast that only radical transformation could close it. The strong local position of the nobility meant they could adapt to a crisis of central government. In both cases the initial acts of force – wars against Austria and France, removal of the Shogunate – did not seem seriously to threaten the traditional state, and indeed could be seen to strengthen it. In both cases challenges from reformist opponents outside the ranks of the privileged was weak and, as

27

with much of the Prussian liberal movement, could be incorporated by state-led reforms. In neither case did political crisis or war spark off popular action which threatened the state. Nationalism, therefore, legitimised institutional changes and the use of force, helped incorporate some reformist opponents, and maintained very substantial powers in the hands of an hereditary emperor and those traditionally privileged groups which surrounded him and staffed the higher ranks of the state service.

Some historians have argued that this type of nation-state formation produced a 'deficient' nation-state because there was only limited change under authoritarian control and not closely linked to the development of a genuine national consensus. This critique, reacting against the original nationalist celebrations of Imperial Germany and Japan, goes on to connect those deficiencies to later problems, such as the pursuit of aggressive policies abroad by fascist or militarist regimes.[12]

Such interpretations raise many issues which cannot be explored here, such as the relationship between political and economic change, and the idea of 'deviation' from some pattern of normality.[13] However, one point does need to be made. These critical accounts, like the positive national images they challenge, do see nationalism as a major force contributing towards the formation of nation-states. One could expect Germany or Japan or Italy to become a nation-state. The only problem is that the wrong kind of nationalism gave rise to the wrong kind of nation-state, or put differently a pseudo-nationalism gave rise to a defective nation-state. However, it remains to be shown that some 'alternative' nation-state, created by some other kind of nationalism, was ever a credible possibility. It is necessary to demonstrate the existence of such historical alternatives as real forces at the time, not simply constructs of the historian's imagination. It is difficult to see such alternatives in the German, Japanese and Italian cases. And more generally, I will argue in this book that it is rather state structures which shape nationalism than the other way around. This does not mean that one should regard each nation-state formation as a unique accident and nationalism as no more than the ideology used to justify that accident. However, it should encourage scepticism towards the idea that there is a 'normal' path towards nation-state formation, and that in some way Prussia/Germany and Japan failed to take that path.

(iv) Traditional rulers in colonial society. Many 'traditional' rulers who operated within the colonial collaborator system were hardly traditional at all. However, where an individual or an elite had previously had some degree of authority and the colonial state had supported or reinforced that authority, the term seems reasonable. Generally such rulers would oppose nationalism as it challenged the colonial state with which their authority was linked and might also support local threats to their immediate power. However, this generalisation needs qualifying in various ways.

Nationalists might themselves act as collaborators at certain times.

This blurs the distinction between 'traditional' collaborators and 'modern' nationalists. Where nationalist are influential collaborators, or where they appear as likely successors to imperial power, traditional rulers might well seek alliances with them. In this way, for example, the modernist elite which took the lead in developing political organisation and identity among the Yoruba of western Nigeria also managed to bring many local chiefs into the movement.[14] It may also be that traditional rulers will adopt the rhetoric and even, to some extent, the organisation of nationalism to ensure a position of strength against the original nationalist movement. Whether this defence takes the form of federalism or domination (both forms apply to some extent to the Fulani rulers of northern Nigeria) or separatism (as in Buganda) is a tactical matter.

Little more than these weak generalisations can be hazarded, above all because the imposition of colonial rule so undermines existing systems of authority that the notion of traditional power under colonialism has only a very limited validity.

(v) Traditional religious authority. By and large, traditional religious authorities have been hostile to the radical and secular creed of nationalism. However, again one must add qualifications. Much depends on the position the nationalist movement takes towards established religion. Where, as in Turkey, nationalism identified traditional Islam with the traditional state and both as its enemies (an identification reciprocated by Islamic leaders) there was clear conflict. But where religious authority is itself opposed to the traditional or established state, the situation is more complicated. Such situations are likely to occur where there is a general view that religion and politics are distinct spheres of activity although the boundaries are in dispute. In such situations religious authority and nationalists can find themselves opposing the same enemy. The Irish, Rumanian, and Greek resistances to the British, Habsburg and Ottoman governments respectively could all, from one angle, be regarded as movements of oppressed religious minorities. Nationalist definitions of the nation were often suffused with religious terms. The clergy might play an important part in the nationalist movement. The population at large might come to regard religion and nationality as inseparable. This feeling would be made more intense in cases, such as those under the *Kulturkampf* in Prussian Poland, where the government persecuted the Catholic church as a bastion of the nationalist movement.[15]

Usually, however, there were both organisational and ideological distinctions between religious authority and nationalist movement and a good deal of mutual suspicion. Rabbis in eastern Europe might support some form of Zionism because of the increased pressure on Jewish communities in the later nineteenth century. But only among a minority of rabbis who moved towards a religious modernist position was this support regarded in any more than a pragmatic way. Again, Irish republican nationalists and the Catholic church, though both mainstays of the Home Rule movement, have regarded each other frequently as rivals, even opponents. Religious authorities are always aware that nationalism poses a potential, if not an actual, threat to their own position and beliefs.

I have not touched upon the most important type of relationship between religion and nationalism, which is the part played by non-traditional religious groups such as independent churches and millenarian movements. This is too complex and vast a subject to deal with here.[16]

(b) The middle classes

(i) Introductory remarks. The term 'middle class' is extremely vague. Even the sub-groups into which one can divide it vary in character and solidarity from one case to another. I will simply refer to certain of these broad sub-groups and draw a basic distinction between their situation in pre-industrial and industrial societies.

In the higher reaches of the middle class – the bourgeoisie – there are broadly businessmen (merchants, bankers, owners and managers of large firms) and the leading professions (including state officials where these require professional qualifications). In the lower middle classes there are broadly the 'old' groups of craftsmen, shopkeepers and petty merchants and the 'new' groups of white collar workers such as clerks and teachers. The distinctions between these groups are often blurred, and there are many important conflicts within these groupings but they do enable us to identify broad patterns of response to nationalism. Here I will consider the business class and the petit bourgeoisie, leaving aside the professional/state official group as this raises special problems considered under the heading of nationalism and intellectuals.

(ii) Businessmen. The image of the capitalist businessman as an achiever seeking to break down traditional social and economic restrictions and acting to displace the dominant classes of pre-capitalist societies from power is one widely shared by Marxists and non-Marxists alike. Nationalism in nineteenth-century Europe was often understood from this perspective. Marx, who did not pay much attention to nationalism in any general or theoretical way, saw the major nationalist movements in progessive terms. Their objective was to replace a patchwork of traditional states by a few large, modern constitutional states. The unification of Germany and Italy and the restoration of Poland and Hungary would sweep away a myriad of small states, destroy the immobile, reactionary Habsburg empire, and strike a blow at Russian despotism. It would also create large internal free-trade areas which would favour rapid industrial capitalist development. The liberal form taken by nationalism would en-

sure that in the liberal constitutional state the capitalist class could play the leading role, which would mean government policies favouring capitalism. All this would hasten the growth of the working class and the ultimate crisis and demise of capitalism in favour of socialism and the classless society. Liberals agreed with the short-term perspective but believed that nation-state formation, capitalism and constitutionalism would bring about the end of history.

There were other kinds of nationalism – illiberal and/or separatist – which did not fit this model. But Marx and liberal nationalists condemned and rejected such nationalisms, especially when taken up by 'non-historic' peoples who challenged the national claims of the leading or 'historic' nations.

However, if we take the four major cases on which this understanding is based, it is already clear that businessmen are of no importance in the Hungarian and Polish cases. It would also be far-fetched to see the noble landowner leadership within these movements as agrarian capitalists striving for a transformation of the rural economy. The argument does look plausible for Germany and Italy. Certainly many businessmen did favour greater unity.

However, they did little about this in practical terms. By 1848 there was only one business lobby in Germany on a national scale, that of the sugar beet processors whose concerns were protectionist and highly sectional. Other, less well organised business groups did favour greater free trade. This division between free-traders and protectionists weakened business influence. In crisis periods many businessmen seemed either indifferent or concerned more about returning to stability than pursuing the dangerous goal of unity. Business interests played a role in funding the National Associations set up in Italy and then in Germany but, as we shall see in chapter 4, these made only a limited contribution towards unification.

If the links between business and nationalism are so weak even in such favourable cases, it is not surprising that they are even weaker or non-existent or negative in many others. In colonial societies businessmen often opposed nationalism for fear of its impact on established economic relations and the possiblity of anti-business policies by a new regime. However, businessmen anxious to displace foreigners from particular economic niches might support nationalism. Such support, usually indirect in the form of financial help, both sustained and constrained nationalist movements, as seems sometimes to have been the case with Indian Congress. However, such support did not mean a directive role for business interests. Often it was little more than belated assistance to a prospective or actual victor in the struggle for state power. Until business interests are well established and organised, that is until an advanced industrial economy has been created, one cannot really expect much more than this kind of political involvement. One might still claim that particular nationalist movements 'represent' capitalist business interests, but 'represent' tends to become a rather intangible notion.

There are some cases of very direct business involvement in nationalist movements in societies with little industry. These seem to occur where business groups support nationalist resistance to a central state which is seen to pose a direct threat to business interests. Catalan and Basque nationalism in the early decades of this century seem to fit this pattern.[17]

These cases suggest two general points. The first is that such support is pragmatic and, therefore, tends to be discontinuous as circumstances alter. But a nationalist movement cannot be turned on and off like a tap. In order to be available for discontinuous and pragmatic uses, it must have a more permanent and committed basis. But that also means that businessmen cannot simply manipulate nationalism. Rather nationalism develops as a form of political action towards which business interests may then take up a definite stance. The second point is that definite support will tend to be related to immediate and narrow concerns. These will most likely take the form of the defence of established positions. This suggests that the model of business interests shaping a political movement which is seeking to implement any long-term and general interest of the capitalist class is a myth. There may be such political movements, but they cannot be understood as expressions of actual business interests.

Some of these points seem also to be borne out by the relationship between big business and fascism, the one case of business-nationalist links in industrial society which I will consider. This has been closely studied for the examples of Italy and Germany. I summarise what seem to me to be the main findings for both the periods of fascist opposition and fascist rule.

At certain times under Weimar the Nazi party received financial support from particular businessmen and firms. Fascist leagues in Italy received similar support, as did the Falange in Spain. However, such support was also provided, and usually on a larger and more organised scale, to other, more conventional right-wing political groups. Furthermore, business support for fascism tended to increase at times of political crisis, or in the phase just before the fascists took power. This suggests that business groups felt unable to control the political process directly and sought to secure favourable access to those who might be able to exert such control. Fascism offered a possibility of political control, but one that had already been worked out and made credible on other grounds than that of business support or involvement. Naturally, fascist oppositions tempered their policies in order to gain such support (and also to weaken possible right-wing opposition to themselves). It is also important to understand why businesses can come to take extreme anti-democratic positions. But fascist oppositions cannot be understood as instruments of capitalist interests.

32

Only two fascist movements took power, so generalisations are limited. However, the relationship between industry and fascism was what one would expect, given the relationship that had existed during the period of opposition. Mussolini and Hitler preserved a capitalist economy and disappointed many of their more radical supporters by coming to agreements with business interests. The destruction of the political and economic organisations of the working class and the taking-over of any autonomous cultural associations workers had constructed strengthened greatly the position of employers. Certain foreign and rearmament policies benefitted particular business interests. However, those policies as well as the appropriate economic and financial measures to implement them, were determined by the regime. Businessmen responded pragmatically to those policies. In the more extreme case – Germany – those businessmen increasingly had to play a role through political institutions like the SS (Schutzstaffeln = Protection Squads) if they wished to maintain and extend their interests.

This seems to typify the relationship between business and politics. Business interests are incapable of producing any general policies or powerful ideology. The calculation of self-interest defined economically seems resistant to such expressions. Therefore businessmen are incapable of controlling changing, crisis-ridden political situations in which such policies and ideologies, organised through political movements, are necessary for such control. Of course, one can still argue that fascism was the only solution available to save a certain sort of capitalism, and that the pragmatic responses of industry in a capitalist society had the effect of shaping government policy, but these are rather intangible arguments and it is difficult to know how to put them to the test.

(iii) Petite bourgeoisie. This is the first of the numerically large social groups to be considered. Nobles, traditional rulers, businessmen and clergymen can furnish leaders and financial support to a nationalist movement, but if it is to have a mass character it must obtain this from other, larger social groups.

In the societies of large parts of western and central Europe since at least the mid-nineteenth-century, and in other parts of the world in the twentieth, the petite bourgeosie have been an important political force. In these societies there has existed a substantial commercial and manufacturing sector, much of it concentrated in towns, but as yet few large-scale capitalist enterprises. If the latter do exist, it tends to be as isolated giants in the economy. In such societies the petite bourgeoisie can make up a substantial part of the population, especially in towns. Broadly speaking, members of this class such as craftsmen, small merchants, and shopkeepers have been hostile to the growth of large and unregulated markets, large-scale units of production, commerce and retailing, new technology, and the expansion of a class of unskilled wage-earners. Among their major concerns have been the exclusion of competitors and the maintenance of small, local, controlled markets. The concentration of such groups into towns, including capital cities, as well as traditions of organisation and collective action through guilds or urban governments, meant that such groups have often been able to play a major role in popular political movements.

Such people naturally grativated to political creeds which played down class identity. Within urban society they encountered above themselves a fairly small and privileged set of officials and rich businessmen, and below, an ill-assorted collection of mainly casual and unskilled workers. The only effective labour organisations were largely found amongst skilled craft workers who shared many of the values of the petite bourgeoisie. Popular political action tended to be focused on the towns until the development of more organised mass politics in western Europe towards the end of the nineteenth century. Such petite bourgeois groups could easily dominate this popular politics. There was a natural tendency for that politics to express itself in populist rather than class terms. Even socialist ideas were formulated in terms of the 'small man' or the 'producers' versus the rich and idle. This kind of political language could easily be assimilated into the language of nationalism with a natural identity being made between the 'people' and the 'nation'.

For this to develop into nationalism proper requires further conditions. One is a cultural division between more modern economic groupings and the petite bourgeoisie. Sometimes this division does not lend itself to a nationalist interpretation – for example in many German towns where there was a Protestant/Catholic divide along these lines. In this case it was a confessional rather than a nationalist party which took up many petite bourgeois concerns. Another condition would be where a government controlled by other ethnic interests pursued modernising policies which damaged the position of petite bourgeois groups. Generally speaking these ethnic divisions were not very important in western Europe. Consequently, populist opposition to such threats was phrased in democratic populist terms rather than nationalist terms. This could in turn fuel a powerful national movement if such populists assumed power and were threatened by other states, as can be seen in the character of *sans culottes* politics in Paris in the 1790s.

In east-central Europe, and in some colonial societies in the twentieth century, these economic tensions have been reinforced by ethnic divisions. In Bohemia, for example, the boycott movements led by Czech nationalists against German businesses were enthusiastically supported by Czech craftsmen and shopkeepers. Such movements were a direct attack on more advanced and larger-scale German competition. They were also part of a more general resistance to a government which sought to centralise political control and liberalise the economy in a threatening manner. In parts of west Africa market traders and small producers have played a leading role in nationalist movements, especially in urban areas. The removal of large European and Asian trading companies could be seen to benefit such people. In all these cases a genuinely populist and democratic politics could be given a nationalist form.

One should not exaggerate the 'reactionary' character of such politics. Industrialisation, especially if associated with per capita growth, gently rising price levels, and an increase in consumer spending, benefits many small shopkeepers, craftsmen and merchants. Such people might just as easily be found supporting moderate liberal or conservative politics as forms of radical nationalism. However, in urban areas the petite bourgeoisie ceases to be the dominant element in popular politics as larger numbers of wage-earners begin to develop their own organisations. Furthermore, the petite bourgeoisie itself develops greater complexity and internal diversity. Alongside the (changing) groups of shopkeepers, craftsmen and small merchants and traders, there also grows a 'new' lower middle class based on the expanding tertiary sector. These people – clerical workers, school teachers, lower level managers and supervisors, etc. – are dependent employees but clearly their work and their sense of status is very different from that of blue collar workers.

This internal diversity, along with the rise of a powerful labour movement, can lead to lower middle class support for a rather different kind of nationalism. There is a greater sense not merely of threat but also weakness. This tends to produce a more defensive political response than earlier. Order rather than change; consensus rather than conflict; threats from below rather than above: these become the central concerns.

There is also a marked decline in the ability to participate in the political process in an independent manner. Lower middle class groups can generate small, sectional pressure groups, often in conflict with one another, but not more generalised forms of political representation. Consequently such groups tend to require strong and unifying leadership from elsewhere. The nationalist leagues and parties which have drawn upon lower middle class support tend to be authoritarian in organisation and ideology, even if they also rail against the political establishment. The ideology which appeals is negative, stressing the absence of social division, of class identity and of class conflict and disorder. At times of political crisis, particularly if such fears cannot be expressed through a broad-based conservative party, this can lead to support for fascist or similar movements which place great emphasis upon these kind of appeals. Nationalism can take on a more direct and ethnic character if these conditions are also associated with working-class urban immigration drawn from groups culturally distinct from the host lower middle-class population. However, this is not necessary to lead to petite bourgeois support for radical right nationalism.

(c) The working class

It has often been assumed, especially by historians with left-wing sympathies, that there is some conflict between working class interests and values and nationalism. Given the importance of working class support to any popular politics in industrial societies, this is an assumption that needs to be carefully examined.

There are four situations in which working-class support for nationalism needs consideration. One is where workers are asked to support their nation-state in conflict with other states. A second is where workers within a particular territory divide on national grounds and support conflicting nationalist movements. A third is where there is working-class support for a nationalist movement seeking political independence. A fourth is where significant sections of a national working-class support radical nationalism.

Working-class movements in western Europe mainly developed within already existing nation-states in which they occupied a subordinate political position. In so far as such movements were committed to class politics and radical change, they opposed the existing nation-state and tended, consequently, to be suspicious of nationalist arguments. There also developed internationalist labour organisations with a nominal membership of millions which opposed nationalism and declared that workers would oppose their governments if they pursued imperialist policies or declared war on other states. The Second International, founded in 1889, grounded this position on the idea that the working-class had a supranational identity. However, in 1914 the major labour and socialist parties affiliated to the Second International supported their respective states when Europe was plunged into war. Trade unionists quickly accepted the need to co-operate in the war effort. There was little working-class resistance to conscription, the shifting of economies to a war footing, and the suspension of many political rights. There was much evidence of working-class enthusiasm for war, as expressed in demonstrations and volunteering for military service. The response to 1914 – something which deeply shocked many internationalist socialists and labour activists – had a major impact on how the relationship between workers and nationalism was understood.

Basically there are three views. One is that workers were always devoted to the nation, although perhaps that devotion had been concealed for various reasons before the crisis of 1914. Another is that working-class leaders had succumbed to nationalism by 1914 and that this prevented working-class opposition to the war from forming. A third is that by various means the working-class, or at least important sections of it, had been brought round to a nationalist position within the major nation-states. I will briefly review these approaches, focusing on organised labour for which we have the most reliable evidence.

The first argument can cite in its support a long tradition of radical nationalism within the organised labour movement. In the Paris Commune or among the small groups of organised workers in Germany in the 1860s this kind of radical nationalism does appear central. The radical tradition from which it drew assumed that there was no conflict between such nationalism and internationalism. Such workers criticised the new states of Germany and Italy or the French Third Republic as not being 'truly' national. The constant emphasis upon opposition to the existing nation-state and the way that state itself appropriated the language of nationalism could conceal this underlying national commitment. This would fit in with the way in which labour leaders, even when condemning their own government's foreign policy, distinguished between the true national interest and that represented by the government.

This argument merits serious consideration. However, it is necessary to plot an essential continuity between the early radical nationalist phase of mid-nineteenth century and the mass support for national governments in 1914. There is a major difference between the sentiments of radical nationalism and those of national defence. The argument plausibly points to the nationalist element at the heart of the early labour and radical movement, but does not make clear how or why these should continue (although often in a concealed form) to influence the mass working-class organisations of industrial society.

The second approach is richly represented within the marxist, particularly the Leninist, tradition. Labour leaders are seen as becoming obsessed with piecemeal advance and with defending the organisations and the gains they have already achieved. In these ways they come to identify their interests with the state of which they have become a subordinate part. The routine forms of class conflict and the institutions through which that conflict takes place come to be treated as prized possessions which must be defended against external threat. Sometimes the argument takes the even cruder form of alleging bribery and corruption as explanations of the behaviour of working-class leaders. The basic outcome is either that workers are unable to express their 'natural' opposition to the war or that alternative, more radical kinds of working-class leadership are prevented from mobilising opposition to the war.

Again there is much to be taken seriously in this argument. Many labour leaders were anxious to preserve their organisations and influence. Indeed, they often treated the war as an opportunity to join the political establishment. This was not always the case – there are interesting cases of reformist labour figures such as Eduard Bernstein or Ramsay MacDonald opposing the war and conversely of radicals such as Hervé supporting it.

However, the main problem with this argument is to demonstrate that such labour leaders were opposing, even suppressing, very different sentiments amongst their members. One might argue that this is a sign of just how effective those leaders were in blocking the formulation of radical alternatives but such an argument tends to compare the actual behaviour of workers against some ideal standard. It is the mirror image of the nationalist claim that workers are naturally patriotic and, if they are not, this is because of some kind of manipulation.[18]

The third argument can be applied either to a part or the whole of the working class. In the first variant, usually one or other version of the idea of a 'labour aristocracy' is invoked, showing how certain privileged sections of the working class are brought round to an acceptance of the nation-state. A more general argument is that the working class as a whole was well on the way by 1914 to being positively 'integrated' into state and society. Rising levels of consumption and changing patterns of strike action and collective bargaining are cited as evidence of the 'acceptance' of capitalism. Welfare provision, franchise reform, political influence, and legal security for working-class organisations all contribute to the acceptance of the political *status quo*. Finally at a cultural level the growth of mass media, often projecting national values, as well as compulsory, state-controlled elementary education, could contribute to making working-class people feel a part of the nation.

This seems to be the most promising approach, although one must not simply lump all these processes together or generalise too much from evidence of adaptive behaviour in one or another sphere of life. What little evidence there is, for example, suggests that jingoism had little appeal to organised workers in England and that too much, therefore, can be made of those aspects of working-class culture which seem to reflect such attitudes.[19] Advances in economic or political power could lead, after all, to greater conflict with employers or the state. What is 'integration' from one angle (a cosy idea emphasising how workers are domesticated) can be seen from another angle as the making of concessions to the steady advance of working-class power. This ambivalence suggests that it would be useful to distinguish between nationalism, nation and class as objects to which workers can attach certain values.

A particular example can show the value of these distinctions. During the First World War miners in South Wales went on strike. Naturally this was denounced as treasonable in parts of the press and brought miners into conflict with both employers and the state. South Wales was a region which had seen a growing intensity of conflict between workers and employers before the war. In this conflict the state had become involved on the side of the employers. Workers had shown some support for radical creeds such as syndicalism. All this might indicate a high degree of class consciousness that would reject nationalist appeals. On the other hand, volunteering rates for the army were high in the mining valleys and there is no reason to suppose that the volunteers did not reflect more general sentiments in the region. One seems to confront contradictory behaviour in which commitments to class and nation both exist. However, there is no necessary contradiction. The miners' strike was provoked by the failure to bring in controls on the price of coal and the profits of mine owners. The miners took the view that the war demanded sacrifices from all classes. If government did not insist on this, then the miners would do so themselves. This sentiment was of importance during the war – in Germany and France as well as in Britain. What one encounters here is an integration of class and national loyalty which conflicted with prevailing nationalist sentiment.

I do not think it possible to say where loyalty to class or nation 'comes from'. One can simply use these terms to describe certain social categories and the values attached to them. What one then frequently finds is a view of the nation which does not deny class divisions but insists, from a distinct class perspective, upon greater justice and equality between classes. It puts that insistence above the pursuit of the national interest as defined in conventional nationalist terms. More precisely, it proposes a modified view of the national interest which reflects a particular class vision. This can be seen as a product of the economic and political advances mentioned before. The latter can lead to a closer identification with the 'nation'. But it is an identification made in class terms and from an increasingly powerful position. Whether this attitude can be reduced to the rather bland terms of 'reformism' or 'integration' is debatable.

From this point of view the distinction the Second International drew between defensive and offensive wars can be seen to have a genuine meaning for many workers. It could be seen as a tactical device by leaders anxious to ward off radical demands for definite action in the event of war. It certainly was a distinction which had little objective meaning. In the July crisis one government after another could plausibly point to the aggression of others, and even manipulate the situation to produce at least the appearance of such aggression in order to elicit working-class support. Nevertheless, the distinction had a moral sense within working-class movements. It can help explain the indifference or even hostility of many English workers to the Boer War or of the German labour movement to navy-building; the great anti-war demonstrations of the year or so before 1914; and the growth of anti-war sentiment from 1916 onwards when the slaughter was clear, governments seemed unwilling to negotiate peace, and suspicions grew that war aims had always been about much more than defence. If one assumes that loyalty to the nation and loyalty to the state were potentially complementary as well as conflicting, and complementary in a way which opposed dominant forms of nationalism, then a consistent intepretation of these events can be offered. Such an interpretation, I would argue, becomes even more applicable after 1918.

The second situation concerns national conflict within the ranks of the working class of a particular territory. The example of Austria-Hungary before 1914 is instructive because it enables us to consider the views of Otto Bauer who made the most important and convincing attempt amongst Marxists of the period to understand nationalism.

One aspect of this conflict took the form of communal antagonism between Czechs and Germans in parts of Bohemia. Eventually it gave rise to independent parties drawing upon ethnic working class support and each adopting the title 'national socialist'. I have already discussed the roots of such communal, if principally working class nationalism and will not repeat that.[20]

Another type of national distinction between Czech and German was made within the ranks of the Austrian Social Democratic Party. This explicit recognition of nationalism and of nationality as having some legitimacy is especially interesting in a party which claimed to subscribe to Marxism. Initially the party had insisted that class and national loyalties were incompatible. However, its attitude changed as nationality conflict increased and began to affect labour organisations. First, it recognised nationality distinctions on a territorial basis. Later recognition took a personal form: a Czech worker could remain in Czech sections of trade union and party organisations even when living in predominantly German areas. These successive positions corresponded to shifts in the attitude of the party towards political change in the empire. The party began with the idea of realising socialism under a unitary state; moved to a concept of federalism based on territories; and then subscribed to a complex notion of political organisation and national autonomy in which the personal concept of nationality would play a role.

In part these shifts were responses to the pressure of events, but they were also associated with some rethinking of the Marxist position on nationality. Otto Bauer, the central figure in this process, argued that national culture, rooted in common experience which was embodied in language and thereby transmitted from one generation to the next, was an objective reality. The nation was, to use his term, a 'community of fate'. In order to relate this to the other 'reality' of class, he pointed out that national culture was shaped by the contribution of various classes. In a socialist society national identity would no longer be distorted by class divisions, and the members of the nation would be able to participate in the national experience in a more intense and widespread manner than ever before. This did not mean that national conflicts would continue. Antagonistic relations were based upon class divisions. The distinctions between nations, once class divisions were removed, would give rise to co-operation and coexistence. Nationality conflict had to be related to class divisions, and it was on this basis that Bauer analysed Czech-German conflict. The conclusion he drew was that it was essential to separate national (cultural and non-antagonistic) from class (economic and antagonistic) issues. This could be achieved if each nation was given national autonomy, thereby leaving conflict to focus, in a clear and direct way, around class divisions.

In practice the distinction proved impossible to sustain. The orthodox Marxist conclusion was that Bauer was wrong to accept the notion of an objective culture, of a social reality irreducible to the level of class. To accept this objection would be to return to the blind alley of trying to reduce everything to the level of class interest and struggle. I would argue that Bauer's principal failure was not to recognise that nationality distinctions, from the outset, were associated with particular forms of politics. They were not pre-existing cultural realities and movements which particular classes then proceeded to exploit for their own purposes.

Working-class nationalism proper, concentrated in Bohemia, was related to communal competition over scarce resources. This took nationalist form when linked to elite political conflicts over state power in a way which will be later considered.[21] Even then, working-class nationalism remained rather apart from other forms of nationalism. Nationalist conflict of this sort led in turn to modifications in the structure of the state. For example, nationality distinctions were introduced into the voting system and there were changes in official language policy. Labour politics, like all other politics, had to adjust to such changes. As a result, nationality distinctions within the Social Democratic Party crystallised. In part this was based also upon divisions – linked to skill, occupations and income – *within* the working-class. However, it was the political adaptation which then provided the basis for such interests to articulate themselves in terms of nationality.

These adaptations by the party demonstrated its determination, as a party of the whole empire, to preserve the Habsburg empire territorially. In this sense a similar process of 'integration' or the advancement of working-class interests was taking place in Austria-Hungary as has been described already for western European nation-states. However, this could not express itself in terms of national loyalty because the state was not a nation-state. At the same time the Austrian Social Democrats could not deny any notion of national identity and loyalty, as such notions were being incorporated into the structure of the imperial state and political competition for control of that state. In order to cope with these problems Bauer resorted to the two-level treatment of apolitical cultural nationality and political class loyalty. In doing this he ignored the fact that nationalist politics are not reducible to pre-existent cultural identities and class divisions which are unfortunately confused with one another. We must pay attention to the way in which state power is exercised under modern conditions, how groups organise to pursue state power, and how all forms of politics, including working-class politics, have to adjust to these broader political developments. Only a small part of this adjustment took the form of outright working-class nationalism, and that can be seen primarily in terms of communal conflict over scarce resources.

A similar procedure could be used to understand nationality-cum-religious conflicts within the Ulster working-class. Once again the two extremes – nationality/religion as the 'objective basis' of divisions or as a fiction manipulated by class interests – are inadequate. Communal conflict in the city provides part of the answer.[22] However, another part of the answer is to be found in the development of a modern, participatory state and the ways in which labour groups connected to political elites and state institutions. Where the state cannot credibly be controlled by an ethnically or religiously defined grouping – for example in the USA – similar communal conflicts amongst workers do not give rise to nationalist politics. Where the state can be so controlled, what often began as much less clearly defined ethnic or other cultural distinctions give rise to more sharply defined nationalist political conflicts – as in many new post-colonial states.[23]

The third issue to be considered is the relationship between organised labour and anti-colonial nationalism. Usually organised labour is a rather small, if well-placed, interest within a largely non-industrial colonial society. Often unionisation begins among groups such as clerical employees of the government or in particularly large units of employment such as railways, docks and mines. This pattern of development is very different from that of nineteenth-century Europe.

Labour movements could be of great importance to nationalism because of the relative scarcity under colonial conditions of any popular organisations that could be politically mobilised. Very often the concentration of unionised workers in the capital or the regions of most economic significance to imperial interests gave them a vital political importance. There are various examples of early positive links between such labour movements and nationalism. The nationalist party in Tanganyika, TANU, had some of its roots in white-collar trade unionism and later worked closely with dockers in Dar es Salaam. Sekou Touré came to power in Guinea through the trade union movement. Tom Mboya founded his political career on the class links between trade unionism, especially in Nairobi, and the nationalist movement; his union career began with employment in government service concerned with agriculture. In Tunisia the trade unions provided a cover for nationalist activity when open politics was banned. In the rather special conditions of South Africa (different because the white population is relatively large and fixed and the industrial development of the country advanced) the African National Congress draws much of its support from unionised workers; its present Secretary-General Cyril Ramaphosa first came to prominence as a trade union leader.

However, on the other hand, there have been many cases where organised workers stood aloof from or were even hostile to the nationalist movement. The Indian Congress had limited support from industrial workers. In some places, for example among mill workers in Bombay, communists had already made inroads before independence. In Nigeria the labour and nationalist movements largely went their separate ways.

This suggests that there were conflicting pressures involved, producing very different relationships in various cases. If one views colonialism as a form of economic exploitation in which political control is particularly prominent, it might seem natural for labour movements to work with nationalists. This is what often happened – particularly where government was the employer (as on the railways and docks) or very closely implicated with the employers (as in the copper mines of central Africa). However, organised workers often held a relatively privileged position within colonial society. The achievement of independence might endanger this if the new state insisted, in the national interest, on wage restraints and limitations on collective bargaining. In any case, trade unions were often flimsy affairs, and union leaders had too many problems of their own to want to take on the added dangers and complications of involvement with nationalists. Very often, nationalist movements drew on support from other social groups whose interests ran counter to those of workers. For all these reasons, which apply only to that tiny part of the working-class population which was organised in unions and in other ways, workers might be less than positive in their response to nationalism. The only conclusion that one can draw is that there is no typical relationship between organised labour and colonial nationalism. As for the mass of unorganised workers, there is too little evidence and they are so difficult to define or delimit as a class that no generalisations at all can be hazarded.

Finally there is the question of working-class support for radical nationalist or fascist movements. Let me be clear about this question. I am not concerned here with the support of fascist regimes when they engage in war with other states: the issue of supporting one's 'own' state has already been dealt with and goes beyond questions of the particular political complexion of the government in power. Neither am I concerned with nationality conflicts within the working class with which I have also dealt. Rather the concern here is where large numbers of workers in an ethnically fairly homogenous society support a radical nationalist movement in its competition for state power with other political groups such as communists, social democrats and moderate nationalists.

The major example of this is the rise of Hitler and the National Socialist movement to power. For a long time the conventional view was that National Socialism drew its mass support from the urban lower middle classes and the peasantry, as well as receiving support and co-operation from groups higher up the social scale. Working-class support was regarded as marginal in two ways. First, less support was provided from working-class quarters than from other social groups in absolute terms. Second, a lower proportion of workers supported national socialism than of other classes, and these workers were in some sense 'marginal' to the working class as a whole.

More recent research has severely undermined these ideas. A significant proportion of workers – if by this term we mean manual wage-labourers in the secondary sector of the economy – supported the National Socialist movement both in terms of voting and also membership. (Many, however, preferred to join the paramilitary wing of the movement, the Sturm Abteilung (SA) or Storm Troopers, popularly known as the Brown Shirts.) Unfortunately, most of this research has confined itself to the level of statistical analysis and not proceeded to offer much in the way of alternative explanations.

One type of explanation would continue to stress socio-economic interests. The unemployed were more likely to vote National Socialist (but also communist) than the employed; so too were the non-unionised, workers in small towns, and employees in small workshops compared to the unionised, those working in large cities and in large factories or mines. Clearly the capacity to organise independently which is associated with these different characteristics matters a good deal.

However, one must also take account of the particular political crisis which engulfed the state in late Weimar. Inexorably rising unemployment, endemic political squabbling, and governmental paralysis meant that people looked in desperation for new political solutions without asking many questions about the particular social or economic policies that would accompany such solutions. In such a crisis class has a limited explanatory value, although it should be borne in mind that the communist party drew overwhelmingly on working-class support, that the vote of the SPD (German Social Democratic Party) remained fairly stable, and that in relative terms urban lower-middle class and peasant support for Hitler was far higher than that of workers.[24]

(d) Peasants

I use this term to refer to groups in which family farming predominates; where the cultivation of land is the main or sole source of livelihood; where there are community restrictions upon innovation; and where there is usually a fairly close system of political and economic control exercised by other groups.[25] There are problems in applying the term in this way, for example, to some parts of Africa where one might prefer the term tribal to that of peasant society. But by and large I am concerned with peasants as defined, and not with landless labourers, businessmen farmers, or other forms of communal agriculture, even if this is beginning to generate a recognisable peasantry.

The integration of peasant support into any extensive and enduring political movement, including nationalist movements, is something which has only happened in this century and which has been of particular

44

importance outside Europe. Peasant action obviously played a crucial role in the French and Russian revolutions but one cannot see it as part of an organised political movement, let alone a nationalist one. Traditional leadership by gentry or clergy of peasant movements which have subsequently been seen as precursors of nationalism – for example the Spanish insurrection of 1808 against Napoleon – were short-lived. In any case, it is a moot point how far these altered the patterns of peasant organisation or values and to what extent they should be seen in nationalist terms. In places such as France after 1848 one can observe the development of more organised links between radical politicians and peasants, but usually specifically nationalist issues were not involved. One major exception to this was in Ireland, where nationalist politicians such as Parnell did organise mass support for their party, although traditional institutions such as the Catholic church also played a major role. Towards the end of the nineteenth century one also finds some nationalist movements in east-central Europe starting to tap peasant support. However, it is the independence movements of twentieth century Africa and Asia which have made the question of the relationship between peasants and nationalism such an important one.

The first question one must ask in looking at these cases is how it is that peasants come to be involved in *any* extensive and enduring political movement which challenges the established political arrangements both of the central state and within the locality. The processes which make peasants available to such movements have already been discussed under the heading of mobilisation. What needs now to be understood is how that process of mobilisation can take place under nationalist auspices.

One matter which needs some attention is the character of conflict within the peasantry and the local political community and how this can be related to the wider nationalist movement. It may be, as in the case of the support for Chinese communists against both the Japanese and Kuomintang, that there is a communal advantage involved. In that case nationalism can be expressed simply as hatred for outsiders. But in many colonial situations things have not been so straightforward. In part, new groupings such as commercial peasant cultivators have been anxious to establish more extensive political contacts in order to combat external pressures from buyers, from European farmers or the adverse policies of the colonial state. Equally, if not more important, have been internal conflicts such as that between chiefs and clan elders among the Kenyan Luo or chiefs and coffee growers among the Chagga around Mount Kilimanjaro.[26] In these cases links with a nationalist elite can represent one way of combatting a rival element within the peasant community which has achieved an important collaborator position. Nationalism then becomes something rather more complex than xenophobia or simple anti-colonialism. The heterogeneity of the peasant community and the nationalist leadership requires a more abstract presentation of what nationalism means, and this a more elaborate nationalist ideology can provide.

It is in colonial situations that conflicts of this sort are most likely to take nationalist form. In other cases attacks upon groups that have close links with the existing state cannot be focused upon an alien presence and therefore tend to stress corruption rather than nationality.

The implication of these remarks is that the relationship between peasants and nationalism is particularly contingent and variable. The refusal of Chinese peasants in some areas under Kuomintang control to take a 'nationalist' view of affairs is connected to their way of forcing nationalism into a very narrow mould in which Kuomintang policies were as much under criticism as was the threat from the Japanese.[27] This view of peasant nationalism as something narrow and contingent upon specific peasant interests is very different from that of Fanon, who sees in peasant nationalism a repudiation of the whole system of inferiority and subordination to which colonialism subjected the peasantry.[28] This is a twentieth-century myth rather like that of the nineteenth century which saw in the rise of the working-class with nothing to lose but its chains the basis for an absolute rejection of the status quo. Just as an effective labour politics is linked to the pursuit of specific interests and an adjustment to a broader and pluralist political environment, so too is any effective peasant involvement in nationalism.

The appeal of peasant nationalism, therefore, is related to the internal as well as the external conflicts involving the peasant community. The relative weight of these conflicts can vary from case to case, and hence the type of nationalism which is supported will vary. In colonial situations support for nationalism will be closely linked to the way in which the colonial state develops its collaborator system. It will also be related to the capacity and willingness of the nationalist elite at the centre to make an effort to represent and co-ordinate various peasant interests. The demand by the colonial state that the nationalist movement demonstrate extensive support or the attempt by the state to undercut nationalist support by seeking to extend its network of peasant collaborators, often provides both the incentive and the means for peasant mobilisation under nationalist leadership. But much of the attention must shift away from the role of the peasantry to that of the nationalist elite. This brings one to the question of whether nationalism, which has variable meanings for the major social classes, can be seen as an expression of the needs of some distinct group. This in turn raises the question of the role of intellectuals in nationalism.

(e) Professionals and the role of intellectuals

A distinction needs to be drawn between the part played in nationalist movements by members of the professions as a social group and the contribution made by those loosely described as intellectuals to the leadership of nationalist movements.

(i) The professions. Members of the professions, including those involved in government administration, tend to be more closely associated with public affairs than members of other social groups. They tend also to belong to the most highly educated sections of society. These characteristics can help account for the very distinctive links between the professions and nationalism. Professionals, especially those in government service, can come to see themselves as the embodiment of the public interest as well as members of particular occupational groups and social positions. Such an ethos of being 'above' sectional interests can be found, for example, in nineteenth-century Prussian bureaucracy and in the Indian Civil Service under the Raj. Such officials tended to regard government as a disinterested and efficient matter carried on without regard for private concerns and making no allowance, except on practical grounds, for divisions of class, colour or creed. They tended also to subscribe to meritocratic principles of recruitment and promotion within the professions and the civil service.

Such ideals naturally appeal most to those who benefit from their (supposed) application. But they can also have very different meanings for others. The refusal to take account of cultural distinctions which affect levels of competence, such as might be involved in the choice of an official language, and the way that choice is applied could stimulate nationalist responses.[29] Conversely, deviation from the ideal practice, for example at the top of the Indian Civil Service, where there was a 'whites only' category, could produce charges of hypocrisy and the demand for counter-discrimination.[30] More generally, the failure to compete effectively can be blamed on the operation of hidden forms of discrimination, and one can either demand counter-discrimination in order to restore genuine competitiveness or an abandonment of the whole notion of meritocratic procedures which ignore cultural distinctions. Both of these positions can be expressed in a nationalist way. Particularly in the professions and government service, where the values of fairness and impersonal justice are most quickly absorbed and where disappointment at their imperfect operation is most keenly felt, this nationalist reaction is likely to take a sharp and early form. Furthermore, professional people have specific skills which can be used in political matters (e.g., lawyers in relation to constitutional negotiations and government officials on matters of administrative reform) as well as high status within their society. More generally they are usually skilled in the arts of communication essential to effective political action under modern conditions.

It is not surprising, therefore, that nationalism, particularly in earlier, elite phases, tends to draw a very large proportion of its support, and even more its leadership, from the professions. This is reflected in the membership of such bodies as the German National Assembly of 1848–49 or the early Indian National Congress. It is also reflected in concern with issues such as recruitment to public service, educational facilities and official

47

language policies. Distinctions within nationalist movements between more radical and more moderate groupings can often plausibly be related to distinctions between the lower and the higher, the less and more secure reaches of the professions and public service.

One can take the argument further. One might see members of the professions as occupying a rather ambivalent position between state and society. Such people are frequently educated in the values professed by a modern state but not shared by most of the society which that state controls. The very security and social status of many professional people often turns upon the position they can come to occupy within state institutions – in schools, courts, and administrative bodies. Exclusion from expected positions can be seen as a betrayal of principles concerning merit and as a simultaneous expulsion from a firm position in state and society. Nationalism can provide a new identity which contains and fuses images of an ideal state and an ideal society in which these people will have a secure, respected and leading position. I do not wish to repeat criticisms I make in the appendix concerning psychological theories of nationalism: rather I understand 'identity' here to refer to the political and social interests which commitment to a nationalist ideology and politics can promote among members of the professions.

(ii) Intellectuals. There is no general support for nationalist movements from professionals. Most members of the professions and of government service are, almost by definition, defenders of the *status quo*. They have obtained their positions by operating effectively within the political, educational and other established institutions. Many remain aloof from overt political activity – whether because of self-interest, lack of interest, or a sense that this is the proper, disinterested position to take. In any case, one must distinguish between the degree of participation furnished by different social groups and the social origins of nationalist leaders. The fact that a nationalist political leadership might be drawn overwhelmingly from the professions does not amount to saying that nationalism is the politics of the professions. The social characteristics of political leaders do not make them representative of those social categories in either the sense of being typical or of promoting the interests of those categories.

To some extent one can explain the prominence of intellectuals[31] in the leadership of nationalist movements in similar ways to that of the involvement of professional people. Like professionals, intellectuals possess skills such as literacy, administrative and legal training, participation in activities such as speaking and journalism which can fit them for political leadership. Engaging in constitutional negotiations with a foreign government, drafting statements for the press or addressing a public meeting, or adapting nationalist ideology to particular circumstances are activities for which training in the professions can be particularly valuable. What is

48

more, members of the professions often have the sort of job security, good income and flexibility of hours which enable them to take part in time-consuming, poorly or even unpaid, and often insecure political activities. However, these points apply to any kind of political activity. Lawyers are over-represented in just about every major political party. The argument that nationalism in some special way is the politics of the intellectuals has to go beyond these general points. It can do so by pointing to particular characteristics of nationalist intellectuals, and to the role of ideology in nationalist movements.

The typical nationalist intellectual can be seen as an unsuccessful professional. Failure is relative. An Indian who does not make it to the top of the Indian Civil Service is different from an unemployed graduate, who in turn is different from someone who has completed his secondary education and cannot obtain a much desired teaching post. In some cases failure means not getting the respect, influence and salary thought appropriate to a professional position; in others it is simply failure to get the position. But clearly all these situations are very different from that of a successful and respected barrister who becomes an M.P. for the British Conservative Party.

From this position of failure, one can argue, the intellectual responds in a number of ways. Alienated between a modern state and a traditional society, the intellectual tries to appeal to society to press his case against that state. The intellectual comes to see himself as the vanguard of society seeking to impose upon the state the justice he has been denied. The intellectual scheme of social and political transformation places the blame for failure elsewhere and provides a vision of personal success in an ideal future. The formulation and pursuit of such abstract visions may be regarded as peculiarly the work of intellectuals detached either from the concrete concerns of the principal social classes or the practical problems of those actually running the government. This detachment enables the intellectual to offer, in the form of nationalism, a purely abstract and self-contradictory 'solution' to the problem of how the state can 'represent' society.[32]

One can then go on to argue that there are certain situations which tend to produce substantial numbers of such intellectuals. For example, if educational institutions train more people for the professions and government service than there are places available, then there will be an increasing number of failures. Some analyses of nationalist or socialist radicals in nineteenth-century Europe, or of the sequence of nationalist movements in twentieth-century Africa have drawn particular attention to the formation of an 'intellectual proletariat' and the varying educational policies of colonial states.[33] Once this surplus of intellectuals exists, then the right intellectual and political context can move them towards elaborating nationalist ideas and forming nationalist movements.

49

However, there is a second argument following on from this one which invests this politics of the intellectuals with a very special significance. This is the view that intellectuals who lead nationalist movements are not subject to the kinds of constraints from their supporters as apply to many other political leaders. Disraeli may have been an intellectual like Nkrumah but the British Conservative Party was more firmly controlled by particular social interests than the Convention People's Party. Nationalist politics are frequently elite affairs conducted in politically fragile states. Nationalist leaders appeal to the disenfranchised, often disoriented masses who they can bring on to the streets but who themselves lack well-defined interests or organisations. The autonomy of the intellectual leadership is often stressed and the question of who precisely that leadership represents is seen as less important.

A third argument, which again relates to the preceding two, stresses the importance of ideology in nationalist movements. Unlike political movements which appeal to specific interests, the essential element of nationalism might be regarded as its claim to represent the whole nation. This is a highly abstract claim even if it is decked out with spuriously concrete appeals to language or colour or history or custom. The concern with ideology can once again be seen as something peculiar to intellectuals, suggesting both a good deal of autonomy on their part and some sort of failure of more pragmatic interest-group politics. This in turn predisposes the observer to see nationalist ideas in irrational and manipulative terms.

To all these arguments a whole range of, in my view persuasive, objections can be raised. First, there are a large number of nationalist movements in which intellectual leadership is not particularly marked, especially when one looks at local levels of leadership rather than focusing entirely upon the central figures. Second, there are often clear links between intellectual leadership at the central level and specific social interests. Political leaders retain a good deal of autonomy, but that is a general condition of successful political action. It can be seen in cases where leaders actually believe (or come to believe) that they are above society. Nkrumah, seeking to detach himself from the various interests which had helped bring him to power, and claiming to act on behalf of the nation, ended up undermining the limited basis of his own authority. Observers can be misled by the formal apparatus of nationalist parties and of one-party states, with their authoritarian character and stress on leadership, into imagining that these leaders enjoy a much stronger political position than is really the case.[34] Much greater weight should be given to the many informal ties which constrain nationalist leaders but which do not appear in public. Finally, one can argue that a politics which has to co-ordinate a diverse set of elites, or to mobilise extensive popular support, or to provide legitimacy in the eyes of important outside political forces has to couch its messages in fairly abstract terms. All modern politics – not just nationalist politics – involves the public deployment of abstract ideas. It would be wrong to regard this political language as simply manipulative. But equally the abstractness and often, on the surface, irrationality of such language does not mean that they have nothing to do with more limited and hard-headed interests. There seems to be no good reason why ideology and in turn the role of those who formulate that ideology, should be assigned priority in the treatment of nationalism. Instead one should try to locate the sorts of political situations in which nationalist politics, with its attendant ideologies, becomes effective. The idea, I would conclude, that nationalism should be seen primarily as the search for identity and power on the part of failed intellectuals is a gross exaggeration, even if that is what it may mean to many intellectuals in nationalist movements.

Those we might loosely call intellectuals have certain skills which can be employed in the formulation of political ideas and in the organising of political movements. These skills are of particular importance in those nationalist movements in which ideology plays a prominent role and from which most of the leading social classes remain aloof. However, this leadership by intellectuals is subject to all sorts of constraints from its constituencies, which in turn are drawn from a very diverse range of social classes that vary greatly from case to case. Nationalism cannot be seen as the politics of any particular social class. Neither can it be regarded as the politics of the intellectuals.

Notes

1 For some examples see above pp. 132–3, 137–8, 143, 191–2. For a good comparative study of the relationship between market penetration and the emergence of nationalism in central Europe see M. Hroch, *Social Preconditions of National Revival in Europe: A Comparative Analysis of the Social Composition of Patriotic Groups among the Smaller European Nations* (Cambridge, 1985).

2 See the consideration of Italian Fascism in chapter 15.

3 See, for example, A. Zolberg, *Creating Political Order: the party states of West Africa* (Chicago, 1966), pp. 12–36.

4 The impact of 'print capitalism' and 'print culture' is considered in B. Anderson, *Imagined Communities: reflections on the origins and spread of nationalism* (London, 1983); and on the development of a 'standard national culture' by E. Gellner, *Nations and Nationalism* (Oxford, 1983) and, more generally, *Plough, Sword and Book: the structure of human history* (London, 1988).

5 I base this argument not upon the general idea of an 'identity need' but more narrowly upon the idea of a possible need, in new and strange situations, to find new principles on which to base new kinds of collective action.

6 See, for example, D. Sorkin, *The Transformation of German Jewry 1780–*

1840 (Oxford, 1987).

7   E. Gellner, *Thought and Change* (London, 1964) chapter 9.
8   Peter Gibbon, *The Origins of Ulster Unionism: the formation of popular Protestant politics and ideology in nineteenth-century Ireland* (Manchester, 1975).
9   J. H. Broomfield, *Elite Conflict in a Plural Society: Twentieth-Century Bengal* (Berkeley, 1968), pp. 117–24.
10 Patrick Buckland, 'The unity of Ulster Unionism, 1886–1939', *History* (1975).
11 See the general argument of Perry Anderson, *Lineages of the Absolute State* (London, 1974).
12 A similar, though less developed, critical tendency exists in Italian historiography, especially associated with the work of Antonio Gramsci.
13 On the relationship between industrial development and political change see now Francis Fukuyama, *The End of History and the Last Man* (1992), especially Part II 'The Old Age of Mankind'. I consider the issue of 'deviation' for the German Second Empire in 'National Peculiarities?' in my book *Labour and liberalism in nineteenth-century Europe: essays in comparative history* (Manchester, 1992), pp. 272–95.
14 R. L. Sklar, 'The contribution of tribalism to nationalism in western Nigeria', in *Social Change: the colonial situation*, edited by Immanuel Wallerstein (London, 1966), pp. 290–300.
15 The term *Kulturkampf* refers to the campaign against Catholics prosecuted mainly in the 1870s against Catholics at both German and state level within Germany.
16 See S. Baron, *Modern Nationalism and Religion* (New York, 1960) and A. D. Smith, *Nationalism in the Twentieth Century* (Oxford, 1979), chapter 2, 'Nationalism and the millenium'.
17 R. Payne, 'Catalan and Basque nationalism', *Journal of Contemporary History*, 6/1 (1971); J. Harrison, 'Big business and the rise of Basque nationalism', *European Studies Review*, 7 (1977). I am grateful to Dr. Harrison for advice on nationalist movements in Spain.
18 I criticise this kind of argument in the appendix.
19 Richard Price, *An Imperial War and the British Working Class: working class reactions to the Boer War, 1899–1902* (London, 1972).
20 See above, pp. 22–5.
21 See below, pp. 131–5.
22 See above, pp. 22–5.
23 See below, chapter 9.
24 On the more general political explanation of the success of radical nationalism in Germany and elsewhere, see below chapter 15.
25 See the introduction by the editor in T. Shanin (ed), *Peasants and Peasant Societies* (Harmondsworth, 1971), pp. 14–17.
26 See below, pp. 189–92; and John Iliffe, *A Modern History of Tanganyika* (London, 1979), pp. 490–4.
27 See below, chapter 11.
28 Franz Fanon, *The Wretched of the Earth* (London, 1965).
29 See below, pp. 131–5.

30 See below, pp. 171.
31 The term is a vague one, although some writers have tried to give it a definite meaning. The work of Kedourie, *Nationalism* (London, 1960), and his introduction to excerpts from nationalist writings edited by him, *Nationalism in Africa and Asia* (London, 1971), is particularly concerned with nationalism as the work of intellectuals.
32 I consider these features of nationalist ideology in detail in chapter 2. Wilhelm Riehl used the term 'intellectual proletariat' of the radicals of the 1848 revolutions. His style of analysis was taken up later by L. B. Namier, *1848: The Revolution of the Intellectuals* (London, 1944). On varying educational policies in Africa see the section 2b, 'Westernisation' in chapter 7.
33 See below, pp. 157–8.
34 See below, chapter 13.

2

Sources and forms of nationalist ideology

1 Introductory remarks

Ideology must, first and foremost, be understood as an intellectual phenomenon. People may use it as a form of emotional compensation or as a political weapon. However, it cannot be reduced to the level of a cry of pain or a tactic. Ideology relates people's problems to society as a whole: that is why it can serve the emotional and political functions it does. However, ideology has its roots in an intellectual attempt to solve some puzzle about society as a whole. Because such puzzles and related predicaments are shared generally, the answers offered at a fairly sophisticated level by intellectuals can, in a simplified form, be adopted by others as ideology. So one must begin by examining the sorts of puzzles, and the initial non-ideological responses they provoked, which could give rise to nationalist ideology.

Ideological statements often appear to be descriptive statements about the world. In so far as they do involve descriptive statements about matters such as racial differences or events in the history of a nation they can be subjected to tests by disciplines like human biology and history. But the core of a political ideology is its commitment to some ideal and the actions prescribed in order to achieve that ideal. That core can be criticised only in terms of inherent plausibility, internal consistency and a view of its underlying values. One cannot 'disprove' it. However, ideological statements often take on the appearance of normal descriptive statements but with some feature which makes them arbitrary or immune to refutation. Attention should be drawn to these features.

Ideology, derived from disinterested attempts to understand the world, can have a political impact only if presented in simplified forms and embodied in symbols and ceremonials. It is in these forms and embodiments that one can gain some understanding of its role in a political movement. On the basis of that understanding one can in turn work out what features of an ideology account for its use in particular situations and

54

its appeal to particular groups.

These very general remarks set the pattern for the rest of this chapter. First, I will look at how the notion of the community could be employed in response to some problems of modernity. Then I will examine the typical ways in which this notion of community, particularly in terms of the idea of the nation, could be translated into ideological forms. The next step will be to examine the simplification of these forms and their rendering into symbolic and ceremonial forms. Having tried to estimate its impact within nationalist movements, I will draw some conclusions about the particular features of nationalist ideology which make it so attractive in modern politics.

2 Intellectual sources

A major problem in modern political thought concerns the relationship between state and society. Each seemed on its way to becoming a self-contained sphere. The growth of a free-market economy extending beyond individual states gave rise to ideas about society as a 'private', largely self-regulating set of activities. The growth of bureaucratic absolutism gave rise to the idea of an enlightened state detached from society which it ruled according to rational norms.[1]

This is a very different problem from that concerning the relationship between a government and its subjects. Such a relationship is set wholly 'within' the sphere of politics. One conception of the nation – that is, of the nation as the body of citizens – remains inside that wholly political framework, even if some implicit reference to cultural identity is involved.[2] However, the problem of the relationship between state and society concerns the nature of the connection between politics and non-politics. Obviously state and society are not really separate from one another and they are abstractions employed to make sense of complex human affairs, but they seem unavoidable in the modern world. They have to be given definition and content, and the nature of their relationship with one another has to be established. One way of doing this is to subordinate one of the categories – state or society – to the other. The most influential accounts, liberal and Marxist, tended to subordinate state to society. The nature of the state and of political conflict was derived from society through concepts such as the social contract or the class struggle. Others, such as Hobbes, sought to deny that society had any independent structure without political order or, like Hegel, regarded the state as the realm of universal values far beyond the petty and sectional concerns of civil society. But, except in certain utopian visions, the sense of an enduring distinction between the two spheres of state and society, and of the problem of their relationship, could never be set aside.

All these various approaches to the problem accepted the distinction and the difficulties it raised, and tried to provide general, rational answers. But from a conservative position the attempt at a general and rational understanding of human affairs itself came under attack. This attack was taken up in a polemical form by Burke in his objections to the pretensions of the French revolutionaries. He believed that their claims to be able to outline an ideal social and political order on the basis of universal reason and then to act politically in order to realise it were based on a false view of what human beings could understand and do. Burke insisted that each society is particular and highly complicated. Human understanding was limited, and, therefore, deliberate interference in the complex web of human affairs which had built up imperceptibly over a long period of time should also be limited. 'The nature of man is intricate; the objects of society are of the greatest possible complexity; and therefore no simple disposition or direction of power can be suitable either to man's nature or the quality of his affairs.[3]

This set a limit on human reason which went beyond the traditional conservative ideas about man's moral failings. But the advance of 'reason' and the great claims made for rational forces such as the modern state, or the market economy, required an even stronger rebuttal. Burke had simply argued that society was opaque. Far more radical was the argument that each society was unique. From this argument the distinctive features of nationalist ideology were to be derived.

I shall call this idea of uniqueness historicism. A brief review of one German writer, Herder (1744–1803), will supply the principal features of this argument. This is not to suggest that Herder was the first or the only one to advance these ideas, or that he was himself a nationalist. In fact the historicist case had been put earlier and more originally by the Italian writer Vico. Other German thinkers of the late eighteenth century developed historicist ideas. Herder's own political values, such as they were, if anything contradicted his historicist position and cannot be described as nationalist. However, he developed historicist ideas in a particularly striking way and linked them firmly to a particular concept of the nation. Furthermore, his ideas had a direct influence upon those who, during the nineteenth century, began to develop elaborate nationalist ideologies.

Herder grew up in an intellectual environment which was putting increasing emphasis on particularity and variety in human affairs and in which history was developing as a critical discipline. Germany itself was a land of contrasts, with many petty states alongside large and powerful ones. But the ideas, and the states, were under pressure, regarded as embodiments of fragmentation and backwardness. Progress and reason suggested an ever greater uniformity and an end to the myriad of small states. Herder reacted strongly against that which he regarded as both condescending and threatening, and sought a firm ground from which to defend variety in human affairs.

A good place for seeing what form this defence took is his view of language. His starting point is very simple: only language has made men human.[4] The notion of 'pre-linguistic man' is, for Herder, meaningless. Man is defined by his language capacity. What is more, language can be learnt only in a community. It is synonymous with thought. Every language is different from every other. These points, to which most people today would assent, were not considered beyond debate at the time Herder wrote. Some argued that the origins of human language lay in human invention. Herder rejected this view. But from this position one could go on to make some more far-reaching claims.

If language is thought, and can be learnt only in a community, it follows that each community has its own mode of thought. Furthermore, to go on to argue that languages are unique could lead to the conclusion that each language is not simply a particular way of expressing universal values. Rather, it is the manifestation of unique values and ideas. Understanding of a language comes not by translating it into the terms of 'universal reason' or into another language but by learning it. Language is the property of the community, but it stretches beyond any one generation. It may be modified and adapted according to the needs of the community but it cannot be radically transformed. Moreover, language does not only have continuity through time, but, in its vocabulary, grammar, sounds, etc., has a unity. A language is not an arbitrary collection of utterances. Finally, no language is superior or inferior to any other, as there is no general scale against which all can be measured.

These views are of major significance simply because language is so important in human society. But the arguments can be extended much further if all other human activities are understood as sorts of languages. Dress, architecture, customs, ceremonial, song, law: all these and many other activities can be understood in the same way. Ultimately 'community' is understood as the sum total of these modes of expression. Furthermore, this sum total is itself more than a collection of items and must be grasped as a complex unity. The ambition of the student of any society must be to grasp this unity by learning all the ways of the society in question. Each element in a society only makes sense in terms of the whole, which, in turn, is manifested only through these various elements. Understanding a society is rather like learning a language.

The major form such understanding took was that of history. History has been given a greater or lesser role in the understanding of human affairs from other perspectives, but for historicism history is the only way to understand a society. History is not 'evidence' on which theories could be tested or a charter drawn up from which to justify present decisions. It is not a constraint on the present or a rich profusion of the various forms human nature has assumed. Rather it is the only way to apprehend the spirit of a community; it is the principal way of learning the language of a particular society.

There were various elements within this historical approach. The study of language itself was regarded as particularly important. So also was the study of ordinary people, who were regarded as the core of a society. A concern with folklore which is more than simply antiquarian is largely derived from historicist concerns. Finally, in more modern times an ahistorical approach has been added to these forms of understanding. Certain types of social anthropology insist on the need to understand the whole community, and in its own terms. However, this understanding has little historical dimension. The notion of wholeness tends to be expressed through the idea of every activity having a function within the community.

It is not an accident that the focus of historicist attention in *modern* societies (which leaves aside much of functionalist anthropology) is upon 'culture'. Modernity involved the separation of state and society. Within the sphere of 'society' writers like Adam Smith had identified a particular sphere of activity – the economy – which could also be analysed in general and rational ways, abstracted from the particularities of power or culture. Indeed, rational analysis required that institutions and activities be understood in terms of single purposes such as maintaining order or maximising profits.

Only in the – in consequence attenuated – sphere of 'culture', therefore, could any sense of particularity and community be found. The idea of culture was difficult to define and use – partly because it was in danger of becoming a residual idea, partly because of the tension between generalising claims and particular description. It was a big jump from the collecting of folk songs to grasping the 'spirit of the nation'. However, modernity helped to solve the problem it had created. Modernisation produced the institutions and practices – such as periodicals and newspapers, schools and 'cultural' societies – one of whose tasks it was to adumbrate that sense of culture. The people who ran these institutions – pastors and journalists and teachers – could see themselves as the vanguard of that culture. Their audiences – the extensive and anonymous readerships of newspapers, the membership of choral societies with similar repertoires, the pupils of schools with similar curricula – seemed to embody the idea of a cultural community. In these ways one should see the rise of historicism not simply as a reaction against the generalising and rational features of modernity, but also, with its specialised concern with culture, as one aspect of that modernity.[5]

There are serious problems about the historicist approach. The rejection of universal standards of reason raises problems about the rationality of the terms of analysis that are employed. The need to apprehend the spirit or the 'wholeness' of a society which is central to the historicist position tends to express itself in the form of intuition. It is not relevant to go into these problems or to deal with the major ways in which historicist work has developed. Only in so far as these matters are reflected in the ideology derived from historicism will they be considered.

3 Translation into ideology

Strictly speaking it should be impossible for historicism to give rise to political value judgements. At most it could insist that it is wrong to apply one's own judgements to another society. But the intrusion of certain extra ideas into the historicist position could change this.

The most important is what I would call the idea of authenticity. One can see this idea being introduced in Herder's own writings and used to back up his own rather liberal political values. Herder denied that government could be understood as the product of a social contract or divine agency. Neither has any historical basis. Both require one to make a jump from a society without government to one with government. Both are used, in fact, not as an historical claim but as a way of evaluating government by some universal standard, as Kant made explicit in his subscription to the idea of a social contract. Herder, however, insisted that the emergence of government should be seen as a real historical development, even if we cannot provide evidence for the process. He argued that society began as a number of families. In this situation no formal system of government was required. But as families joined together to form more extensive societies it became necessary to develop new forms of leadership which took the form of government. The conquest of one society by another also can introduce a separate system of government.

Thus far Herder seems to work from within the historicist position. It is when he evaluates this development that he moves beyond it. Conquest is regarded as the disruption of the natural development of a particular society.

> Nature produces families; the most natural state therefore is one people (Volk) with a natural character. . . . Nothing seems more obviously opposed to the purposes of government than the unnatural enlargement of states, the wild mixing together of different human species and nations under one sceptre.[6]

Herder particularly objected to large, impersonal 'machine' states such as the Prussia of Frederick the Great, which he saw as the artificial product of war and conquest.

A somewhat similar version of this approach, in more elaborate form, can be found in the work of the Czech historian and nationalist, Palacky. He took over from Herder the idea of the Slavs as a peaceful group of peoples subjected to oppression and exploitation by various robber peoples such as the Magyars and Germans. The Czechs, identified as a language group, began with their free, 'natural' societies; clusters of families with an informal, democratic system of government. Palacky goes on to describe the various conquests. Resistances to these conquests are focused upon as high points in the national history. The Hussite movement is interpreted in this way. The various activities of the Czechs are seen as manifestations of their national spirit. Palacky hoped that his history would help restore a keen sense of national identity which was, in turn, a necessary condition for a reassertion of Czech rights.

This distinction thus drawn between what was natural and unnatural in history is paralleled in the other major areas of historicist concern. Fichte, for example, in the field of language went much further than an aesthetic concern with purifying language. For him language mirrored the national soul, and to purge the language of alien impurities was to defend the national soul against subversion by foreign values. The Germans, he argued, unlike other Teutonic groups, possessed a continuous and 'living' language. But its life required constant protection. Fichte regarded Latin as a dead language, and for him 'dead' took on a powerful, literal meaning. He argued that to take abstract, lifeless Latin terms into German would have a deadening effect. The German language was more concrete. The importation of Latin words would lead Germans to ascribe some of the alien values associated with them to their German 'equivalents'. Gradually the values for which the German words originally stood would be lost. The defence of the living language was simultaneously a defence of the values of the human group using it.[7] In a similar way the racist currents of thought developed in the nineteenth century identified a pure racial group and then sought to protect its purity from outside influences. At this point, however, the idea of 'natural' was linked to a view of human 'nature' which went beyond history and culture and grounded its justification in an appeal to the 'science' of biology. In this sense modern racism goes beyond historicism. But it deploys similar notions of purity and impurity and, in the way it uses ideas of nature and science, should be seen as much as an aspect of as a reaction against modernity.[8] In both the language and race arguments, defence of the national culture could take the form of a purge of impure elements in order to return to the pure, 'natural' state of affairs.

In the field of social anthropology similar ends could be reached through the employment of the concept of 'equilibrium'. Changes introduced from outside into a 'tribe' (itself largely a product of historicist intellectual values and colonial practice) could be seen as upsetting the state of equilibrium. Everything in that society could be justified as contributing to the equilibrium. Jomo Kenyatta, having studied in London under the functionalist anthropologist Malinowski, produced an account of the Kikuyu which employed these sorts of ideas.[9] For example, his defence of female circumcision argued that it was not only arrogant of Europeans to condemn the practice as barbaric, but also mistaken. That condemnation rested on the attempt to apply some universal standard to all social practices. But the practice only had its meaning, its rationality, in the context of a unique community. Within that community this meaning was associated with the way in which the passage from female adolescence to womanhood was marked, and that passage in turn was a major element of the social and sexual structure of Kikuyu society. It was only from within that frame of reference that judgements could be made.

One could multiply examples of this sort many times. The basic assumption is that one can identify a particular human unit – the Czech people, the German language, the Aryan race, the Kikuyu tribe – and establish what is natural within it and use that unit, in its natural state, as the source of value judgements. Deviations from that natural state are, of course, unnatural, and what is unnatural is bad. In this way the historicist concern with understanding society as a unique totality can be transformed into a way of making value judgements about historical change in terms of the way unnatural developments undermine a natural state of affairs.

However, the units identified are necessarily more or less arbitrary ones. Groups and languages can be categorised in many other ways. It is difficult to understand why war and conquest, such frequent occurrences, should be regarded as unnatural. It is difficult to see how the historicist can be reconciled to not being able to understand the many 'unnatural' societies which exist, and how one understands historical change. Finally, of course, the 'return' to the natural situation can be understood only in a very general and vague way, that is, as a return to the spirit of that past. The Czechs Palacky studied did not and could not have produced Palacky himself or the complex and changing society of Bohemia which gave rise to Czech nationalism. The 'traditional' Kikuyu whom Kenyatta described were heavily Christianised and many of them opposed female circumcision, and Kenyatta could never have arrived at his conclusions if he had remained a 'natural' Kikuyu. These arbitrary judgements, justified by the contrast of natural with unnatural, are an essential ingredient of nationalist ideology.

The notion of a return to the spirit of the past was often accompanied by an historical perspective which read the appropriate trends into events. Figures in the past became instruments of the national destiny or obstacles in its path. Thus Heinrich von Treitschke, the German nationalist historian, could defend the actions of the eighteenth-century Prussian state because it was seen as the vehicle of later unification. On the other hand the Habsburg empire, as a multi-national state, and the smaller German states (particularly the allies of Napoleon) were subjected to a much more critical treatment. Associated with this, von Treitschke came to emphasise the role of Protestantism in the German national spirit and to deny the centrality of the Catholic religion in German society. Again, this is arbitrary and inconsistent with a proper historicist approach. So too is the

61

identification of figures from the 'national' past in terms of current political disputes. In the disputes between supporters and opponents of the internal settlement in Zimbabwe there were rival claims to be the true heirs of the participants in the disturbances of 1896–97 in Southern Rhodesia. The movement led by Sithole used populist language; that led by Mugabe used class language; but in both cases the ideological use of history was the same.[10]

The final, and most important, ideological ingredient is the way in which the historicist concept of community is linked to political demands. The demand for a nation-state with many of the features of other nation-states seems hard to reconcile with the justification that a unique nation needs its own special form of independence. Some consistent cultural nationalists have indeed resisted the demand for national self-determination on the grounds that it is an imitation of the West,[11] but this is exceptional. Usually what happens is that nationalist ideology operates with three notions which are mutually incompatible but, if not properly examined, can seem powerfully persuasive.

First, there is the notion of the unique national community, now in a degenerate condition but capable of being restored to its natural, authentic state. Second, there is the idea of the nation as a society which should have its own state. But in this understanding the basic distinction between state and society is accepted in a way that contradicts the historicist view of community as a whole. Finally the nation is thought of as the body of citizens – that is, a wholly political conception – and self-determination is justified in terms of universal political principles. Nationalist ideology never makes a rational connection between the cultural and the political concept of the nation because no such connection is possible. Instead, by a sleight of hand dependent upon using the same term, 'nation', in different ways, it appears to demonstrate the proposition that each nation should have its nation-state. Nationalist ideology can superficially appear to have provided an answer to the problem of the relationship between state and society, both accepting the modern distinction but also claiming to reject or transcend that division.

There are numerous variations upon the basic themes I have outlined. The nation can be defined in a great variety of ways, and this can give rise to conflicting claims about who belongs to which nationality. The values of the nation, its true 'spirit', are matters of even greater dispute in which the various claims made have in common only the fact that they can be subjected to no rational tests. The manner in which the contrast between natural and unnatural is drawn also varies widely. These variations will depend on a combination of intellectual tradition, inherent plausibility and political need. Thus the initial impulse behind the categorising of many African societies as tribes can be located in European intellectual traditions. They were adapted to social reality in various ways but retained an inherent plausibility because of the small-scale nature of many African societies. They could be sustained both because their advocates had the power virtually to project their own ideas about social identity on to colonial subjects and because it suited elements in indigenous society to manipulate these categories to their own advantage. Such categories, enshrined in various forms of 'indirect rule', hardened and shaped much political action. In their turn they have shaped territorial nationalist movements – both by forming part of their political material and by forcing nationalists to relate cultural diversity to the claim for territorial rather than 'tribal' independence. The ideology is not, therefore, a gloss upon some pre-existent social reality but a constituent of that reality.[12]

Nationalist ideology is neither an expression of national identity (at least, there is no rational way of showing that to be the case) nor the arbitrary invention of nationalists for political purposes. It arises out of the need to make sense of complex social and political arrangements. But that need is itself shaped both by intellectual traditions and the sorts of responses which any intellectual scheme evokes when it is activated in some way or another. At the highest intellectual level anthropologists or scholars of the Orient or political thinkers carefully work through what they regard as the relevant evidence in order to test their ideas. At a practical level administrators, traders, missionaries and others work with particular assumptions about social arrangements and values in order to achieve their own objectives. In so far as they do achieve them they will tend to take these assumptions as true.

The same point can be made about nationalists. They also begin with a fund of intellectual assumptions about what society is and how it is organised. They relate these assumptions to their own political projects. In fact they argue that those projects are determined by their assumptions; that they are the spokesmen for the nation. However, their precise political projects and the manner in which these are carried through are the product of certain political situations rather than the expression of national needs. Nevertheless, the proclamation of such needs as the basis of their politics is an essential ingredient of that politics. Precisely because their assumptions about national identity and need are not purely arbitrary they have a more or less plausible connection with existing social arrangements and needs, with actual beliefs and with often widespread political grievances. Of course the ideology is more than a reflection of those things; rather it incorporates them into a broader vision which transforms their significance. The ideology also provides nationalists with a cause in which not only they themselves but many others genuinely believe, often including opponents who have been brought up with similar intellectual assumptions and values. In so far as nationalist objectives appear relevant to the interests of various political elites and social classes, so far will nationalist ideology be enhanced by the way in which members of these groups can

63

agree that they are part of the nation. In this way nationalist ideology actually brings into being an imitation of its own ideas. In so far as nationalism is successful it appears to be true. That, of course, is its ultimate form of plausibility.

However, I have only considered the intellectual origins of nationalist ideology and its translation into ideological form at a fairly sophisticated level. To work effectively as a popular political ideology it needs simplification, concreteness and repetition. It is because nationalist ideology is particularly adaptive to these processes that it can have great popular appeal. Simplification involves above all the construction of stereotypes. There are stereotypes of the nation in terms of history or racial characteristics or cultural practices as well as stereotypes of enemies. Repetition through speeches, newspaper articles, rallies, songs, etc., is an essential part of the work of a nationalist party. The turning of these simplified and repeated themes into concrete form is achieved primarily through symbolism and ceremonial. It is upon this aspect of the popularisation of nationalist ideology that I will concentrate because it is here that nationalist ideology has characteristics which distinguish it from other popular political ideologies.

4 Symbols and ceremonies

Nationalist movements, like all mass movements, make use of symbols and ceremonies. These give nationalist ideas a definite shape and force, both by projecting certain images and by enabling people to come together in ways which seem directly to express the solidarity of the nation. Nationalist symbolism is able to do this in particularly effective ways because it has a quality of self-reference which is largely missing from socialist or religious ideology. Nationalists celebrate themselves rather than some transcendent reality, whether this be located in another world or in a future society, although the celebration also involves a concern with transformation of present reality. It is upon this self-reference quality that I will concentrate.

One can see this easily in comparing the way in which leaders are treated in nationalist and socialist movements. Nationalist leaders have been used as a symbol of the movement during the phase of political opposition, whereas the 'cult of personality' in communist movements tends to occur only when the movement is entrenched in power. The cult serves very different purposes in these two situations. Socialism can find the image of what it seeks in rational models of the classless society. Nationalism finds such rational projections of its ideal more difficult to achieve. The focus upon the leader can provide a better way of making this projection, as well as giving it a very concrete form and strengthening the existing political movement. For example, Gandhi, with his asceticism, non-violence and concern with tradition, embodied the national ideal for which he strove. The leader as symbol is particularly important in the case of badly divided nationalist movements which would find it difficult to produce a more substantial expression of their unity.[13]

Self-reference symbols such as the blond, blue-eyed men and women of Nazi posters are prominent in nationalist propaganda. Signs of the national ideal such as the spinning wheel symbolising a return to the 'authentic' India helped establish Gandhi's vision of independent India. At a more abstract level great attention is paid to the colours of flags or motifs such as the swastika.

One could spend a long time analysing nationalist symbols, propaganda, and ceremonials, and there is a good deal of literature on the subject. Fascist ceremonial in particular presents a rich variety of ways of promoting solidarity around the nationalist cause. I will take rather different examples of nationalist ceremonies, both because they are less well known and also because they can be used to convey a great deal about the appeal of nationalism generally. The examples come from Afrikaner nationalism. They are the Geloftedag (Day of the Covenant) and the Ossawatrek. Some background information is needed before these ceremonials can be considered.

On 16 December 1838 a battle was fought between some white trekkers and Zulus at Blood River. Before the battle the whites vowed that if God granted them victory they would celebrate that day every year. The battle was won. However, the vow of one particular group of whites in a disorganised migration had little impact in following decades. It was only with the emergence of republican nationalism during resistance to the British annexation of the Transvaal in 1880 that the vow was recalled. In the course of the resistance it was refined into a ceremonial with a special Covenant Oath which declared:

> Brothers and fellow countrymen, we stand here before the Holy God of Heaven and Earth to make a vow that, if He will be with us and protect us and give the foe into our hands, we shall ever celebrate the day and date as a Day of Thanksgiving like the Sabbath in His honour. We shall enjoin our children that they must take part with us in this, for a remembrance even for our posterity. For the honour of God shall herein be glorified, and to Him shall be given the fame and honour of the victory.[14]

When the Union of South Africa was established in 1910 and the major party division went through the Afrikaner community after 1918 the celebrations seemed to lose their point and declined. By some people they were taken to symbolise the rightness of white supremacy. This, with the implication of solidarity between English and Afrikaans-speakers, rather went against the original anti-British message of 1880. It was only in the 1930s when, for a variety of reasons, there was a renewed emphasis on

65

the identity of the Afrikaaans-speaking community that the Blood River celebrations became prominent again. They helped transcend party political divisions between Afrikaans-speakers.

This sense of identity was dramatically reinforced when the Ossawatrek was instituted. The idea began with Heinrich Klopper, a founding member of the secret nationalist association, the Broederbond and leader of a mass Afrikaner cultural organisation among railway workers. The purpose of the Ossawatrek was to commemorate the centenary of the battle of Blood River in a particularly striking way. This would be fulfilled by means of a dramatic re-enactment of the Great Trek. The idea caught on, and in 1938 a number of ox wagons were taken along carefully selected routes. At each town and village people gathered to celebrate. Special ceremonies were held at places of historic importance such as the grave of Cilliers, who had composed the Covenant Oath. The ceremonies culminated in celebrations at the site of the battle and of the newly established Voortrekker museum in Pretoria on 16 December.

Two contrasting points can be made about the impact of these events. The first is that they undeniably awoke a sense of identity in many Afrikaners, even if it was only short-lived. The second is that it did not, in the short term, assist the cause of Afrikaner nationalism. In the election of 1938 the specifically nationalist party gained twenty-seven seats, compared to 111 for the United Party, which embraced both English and Afrikaans-speakers. This was, admittedly, before the peak of the Ossawatrek. But even afterwards, despite nationalist protests against participation in the second world war (which led to breakaways from the United Party), the reorganised nationalist party could gain only forty-three seats. A basic sense of Afrikaner identity was a necessary but by no means a sufficient condition for the rise to significance of Afrikaner nationalism.[15]

At this point, however, I wish simply to concentrate on the cultural and ideological aspects of the matter and not the ways they could be turned to political account. These ceremonials contain, in a very powerful form, a number of features which nationalist symbolism generally exhibits.

There is the re-enactment of a moment in national history. History provides identity within the historicist frame of reference; symbolic history provides an intense and summary view of that history. The most favoured events are times of heroic resistance to aliens. In this case it is the resistance to both the British (intruding into the Cape) and the blacks; in Palacky's, to the Hussite movement against the 'German' state; at the premiere of an opera by Verdi in 1849 in the embattled Roman Republic, it was the 'Italian' resistance to Frederick Barbarossa in the twelfth century. In Germany in 1944 Goebbels invested much effort into producing a film of the resistance of the fortress of Kolberg led by Gneisenau to Napoleon's troops in 1806. That Dutch-speaking migrants, Bohemian heretics, the citizens of the city-states of northern Italy, and Prussian soldiers had no political consciousness of themselves as Afrikaners, Czechs, Italians or Germans does not matter. It is the contemporary effectiveness that is important.

This effectiveness – if the propaganda and ceremony was indeed effective – displays a number of characteristics. First, one must stress the intellectual and organisational effort involved. The Ossawatrek, for example, was well organised. Its imagery was vivid and a solemn sense of occasion was retained throughout. But above all – and this gives nationalist imagery a special power – people were being asked to celebrate *themselves*. Dr Malan, leader of the Afrikaner nationalist party in 1938, caught this meaning in his speech of 16 December:

> The Trekkers heard the voice of South Africa. They received their task from God's hand. They gave their answer. They made their sacrifices. There is still a white race. There is a new People. There is a unique language. There is an imperishable drive to freedom. There is an irrecusable ethnic destiny . . . . Their task is complete . . . . The struggle with weapons has passed . . . . Your Blood River is not here. Your Blood River lies in the city.

> I scarcely need tell you that Afrikanerdom is on the trek again . . . . It is not a trek away from the centres of civilisation, as it was one hundred years ago, but a trek back – back from country to city. In that new Blood River, black and white meet together in much closer contact and a much more binding struggle than when one hundred years ago the circle of white-tented wagons protected the laager, and muzzle-loader clashed with assegai. Today black and white jostle together in the same labour market.[16]

The message is clear. The heroes of the past are joined by ties of blood and language to the men of the present. That link is a sort of guarantee that the men of the present can rise to their challenges as their ancestors did. The ceremonial itself manifests this possibility in miniature and holds out the promise that much more can be achieved. This achievement is written in the destiny of the nation.

Allied to specific concerns – for example, the problem of the Afrikaans-speaking immigrants into the cities after 1918 – the sentiment can have a powerful effect. It was, in fact, propagated by elites which felt excluded from positions of power and influence in a liberal state, where English culture was particularly objectionable because it was not buttressed by any formal system of discrimination, and where English figures dominated the economy.

The combination of such elite resentment and potential communal conflict is one we have encountered frequently. But to succeed it was necessary not simply to make appeals to self-interest. It was necessary to bind together a variety of elites and to mobilise poor Afrikaner support in the cities. The self-reference symbolism of the Covenant Oath and the Ossawatrek played a major role in this.

The central message, conveyed through anthems, rallies, speeches,

67

elaborate ceremonials, is of an embattled people. The aim is to return to the heights of the past, though in a transformed fashion. If the political circumstances are appropriate and the objectives of the movement can be connected to specific interests, this appeal can become a force in its own right without which success is impossible.

Having said that, it is important to bear in mind the limitations of ideology and imagery. People will tend to respond only if they are not merely accessible but if the message has relevance, and that will depend on their prior views of their situation. The Kolberg film, for example, was broadcast at a time when many Germans knew that the war was going to be lost, just as Prussia had lost the war of 1806–07. Given this prior view, the film could actually deepen the sense of pessimism instead of stimulating a sense of defiance. The current sense amongst most Afrikaners that settlement with the black majority cannot be avoided has diminished the relevance of apartheid ideology, which had been an integral part of Afrikaner nationalist ideology, and has even led to the playing-down of white supremacy ideas. People are not, for the most part, deliberately taking up or dropping certain ideological themes, rather their changing situation leads them to highlight or neglect particular themes amongst many.

Furthermore, the ideology/imagery contains many different messages, and it is difficult to know which evokes a chord. Moodie, for example, in evaluating the significance of nationalist ceremonial among Afrikaners, insists on the need to distinguish between '. . . a sophisticated theological interpretation of God's acts in Afrikaner history with an explicitly republican eschatology;. . . [and] . . . a far more inchoate sense of generalised feeling of 'Afrikanerness' with emphasis on common language.'[17]

The first sort of appreciation plays an important part in the actions of small elites; the second in the sentiments of much of the following. In the same way the supporters of German National Socialism had a range of perceptions, from systematic ideology to a vague sense of the need for strong leadership and an end to disunity within the nation.[18] These vague ideas can, in turn, be linked to what are strictly non-nationalist, even anti-nationalist, ideas such as devotion to a particular church. Without underestimating the role of nationalist ideology, one can see that it can only supply the most general orientations and that the creation of specific objectives, forms of action and bases of support must be understood in terms other than the appeal of the proclaimed values of the nationalist movement.

One can, though, argue that the self-reference quality of nationalist propaganda and the theme of the restoration of a glorious past in a transformed future has a special power which it is difficult for other ideological movements to match.

5 Conclusion

I have argued that the central motif of restoration of a past state in which the nation was most fully itself has an enormous appeal and in part accounts for the impact of nationalist ideology and symbolism. But one needs to go somewhat further than this, and to return to the problem of the relationship of state and society. The nationalist 'solution' to the problem is, on the surface, quite simple. Societies (= nations) are unique. Government by alien societies can only do violence to the unique national spirit. Therefore each nation must have its own government. That government is the nation-state. This is not merely an abstract ideal. History can be understood only in terms of the achievements and frustrations of the nation. The demand for statehood is rooted in the national spirit, even if inarticulate and repressed, and the nationalist simply speaks for that spirit.

However, the identity of the nation is provided in arbitrary ways. The leap from culture to politics is made by portraying the nation at one moment as a cultural community and at another as a political community whilst insisting that in an ideal state the national community will not be 'split' into cultural, economic and political spheres. The nationalist can exploit this perpetual ambiguity. National independence can be portrayed as the freedom of the citizens who make up the (political) nation or as the freedom of the collectivity which make up the (cultural) nation. Nationalist ideology is a pseudo-solution to the problem of the relationship between state and society, but its plausibility derives from its roots in genuine intellectual responses to that problem.

The appeal of this pseudo-solution is that it enables the nationalist to construct from a wide variety of practices and sentiments prevailing among the population of a particular territory the idea of a national community, and to transform this into a political claim. By seeming to abolish the distinctions between culture and politics, society and state, private and public, the nationalist has access to a whole range of sentiments, idioms and practices which hitherto had been regarded as irrelevant to politics but are now turned into the values underlying political action. It would be wrong to see nationalism as the expression of pre-existing national values and practices in political form. That view is tantamount to accepting the self-assessment of nationalists. Nationalist ideology works on existing values and practices in a new way, and it operates on a great variety of levels. Furthermore, it selects from those values and practices in ways designed to enhance their political significance. The general point is that this emphasis on cultural distinctiveness and identity has particular advantages in a situation where it is possible to mobilise mass support or co-ordinate a wide variety of elites in a bid for territorial independence. It is also of value in an international situation where the claim to state power is regarded as legitimate only if it is couched in the form of national self-determination. Cultural appeals add to that legitimacy and also help provide the basis of support for a nationalist movement which gives its particular claim to state power credibility. The claim to uniqueness is ultimately used to justify the claim to have a state just like any other.

Nationalist ideology has its roots in intellectual responses to the modern problem of the relationship between state and society. This response, above all in the form of historicism, was a serious attempt to deal with the problem and to rebut what it saw as the falsehoods of analysis based on allegedly universal standards of reason. It was turned into ideology by means of notions such as authenticity and teleology. It was also combined in a powerful but illogical way with purely political values, especially those associated with democracy. The net result was to transform certain important ways of understanding human affairs into a type of political ideology which is beyond critical examination. At the same time the historicist concern with history and popular culture was channelled into various symbolic and ceremonial forms. These had a particularly powerful appeal because of their quality of self-reference and the way they took existing sentiments and actions and transmuted them into political ideology. This appeal in turn was grounded upon the claim to link cultural distinctiveness with the demand for political self-determination. Such claims had to be related to specific interests and only worked in particular sorts of political situations. Furthermore, no particular element within this ideology can be automatically regarded as decisive among supporters. But, with these qualifications, ideology can still be regarded as a powerful force which was essential in the work of co-ordination, mobilisation and adding legitimacy to what was carried out by a nationalist movement.

Notes

1   I will return to this central feature of modernity as a key to understanding nationalism as a political movement as well as an ideology in the Conclusion.
2   As in the English and French cases considered in chapter 3.
3   Edmund Burke, *Reflections upon the French Revolution*, edited by Conor Cruise O'Brien (Harmondsworth, 1969), pp. 152–5.
4   For Herder's views on language see *J. C. Herder on Social and Political Culture*, translated, edited and with an introduction by F. M. Barnard (London, 1969), especially 'Introduction', pp. 17–32, and 'Essay on the origin of language', pp. 117–77.
5   For the contribution of newspapers and their readerships to the construction of the idea of a national community see Benedict Anderson, *Imagined Communities: reflections on the origins and spread of nationalism* (London, 1983). For the way in which modernity helps in the construction of a 'standard national' culture, see Ernest Gellner, *Nations and Nationalism* (Oxford, 1983).

70

6   J. C. Herder, *Ideen zur Philosophie der Geschichte der Menschheit*, in *Sämmtliche Werke*, edited by Bernard Suphan (Berlin, 1887), vol. 13, p. 384.

7   See especially the fourth address in Fichte, *Addresses to the German Nation*, translated by R. T. Jones & G. H. Turnbull (Chicago & London, 1922).

8   See Zygmunt Bauman, *Modernity and the Holocaust* (Oxford, 1991).

9   Jomo Kenyatta, *Facing Mount Kenya* (1938).

10   Terence Ranger, 'Rhodesia – the propaganda war', *New Statesman*, vol. 97, no. 2518, 22 June 1979, p. 922. Since becoming Prime Minister of Zimbabwe Mr Mugabe has played down his earlier emphasis upon class division.

11   The Zionist ahad Ha'aman, for example, raised this sort of objection to the aim of achieving an independent state of Israel and stressed instead the need to develop an authentic cultural national identity.

12   A similar argument for the way in which the concept of the 'Oriental' has shaped relations between the West and societies of the Middle and Far East has been advanced with great force and subtlety by Edward Said in his book *Orientalism* (London, 1980).

13   See below, chapter 15, in the cases of Hitler and Mussolini.

14   Quoted in T. Dunbar Moodie, *The Rise of Afrikanerdom* (London, 1975), p. 179.

15   On the election results and their significance see Neville Stultz, *Afrikaner Politics and South Africa, 1934–1948* (Berkeley & Los Angeles, 1974).

16   Quoted in Moodie, *op. cit.*, p. 199.

17   *Ibid.*, p. 97.

18   See below, pp. 310–7.

Concluding remarks to Part I

Nationalism, like all significant modern political movements, must appeal to a variety of social and economic interests. One can identify typical ways in which major social classes and other interests can be brought into support of nationalist movements. However, there is no necessary relationship between nationalism and any particular social or economic interest. Just about every major social interest has supported one or another nationalist movement. The most successful nationalist movements build upon a coalition of such interests. Many of these interests can be found supporting other kinds of politics, often opposed to nationalism. Therefore, although one must always pay attention to the social character of nationalism, to understand nationalism generally one has to look elsewhere than to its sociology.

Nationalist ideology is based on important responses to modernity and, when deployed in symbolic and ceremonial forms, can have a very real power of attraction. In certain ways nationalism is more appealing in the modern age of mass politics than most of its ideological rivals. Nevertheless, nationalist ideology can only work when it appears to be appropriate to the political situation and relevant, in terms of their given situation and concerns, to those who support such ideas. Furthermore, such ideas have to be simplified and made concrete, and then repeatedly projected to their target audience. That requires political commitment and organisation.

This suggests that the key to a general understanding of nationalism is to be found in the sphere of political action and organisation. That is **not** to say that politics is more important than social interests and ideology in any or indeed all particular cases. It is only to argue that the search for the common features underlying all nationalist movements should focus upon the political context. In Parts II and III of this book, through a series of cases studies, that is where the focus will be directed.

72

Part II

Varieties of nationalism
(i) In a world without nation-states

3

Prelude to nationalism: religious and national oppositions in early modern Europe

1 Introduction

In this chapter I consider the ways in which the power of the state increased in early modern Western Europe, and how this in turn shaped political opposition to the state. I consider how opposition employed religious dissent in new ways and compare this to subsequent nationalist movements. Then I turn to the more general forms political opposition could assume and how the national idea could be developed within that opposition. The two cases of England and France are considered in order to show how the development of national opposition was closely related to a new political context created by expanded monarchical power. The ways in which this could converge upon nationalism are briefly considered towards the end of the chapter. The general conclusion is that the development of the idea of the nation is best understood in terms of new ways in which political oppositions must confront a new type of state.

I do not, at this stage, consider the arguments which have been advanced as to why monarchical power increased so dramatically in early modern Europe.[1] Nor do I consider in any extensive way how this new type of state differed from earlier types.[2] These are issues which are taken up in the more general concerns of the conclusion. Here I am concerned rather to provide an account of patterns of political change in early modern Europe and how they helped generate types of political opposition which had a close and indispensable influence upon the subsequent development of nationalist movements.

It is generally agreed that the roots of modern nationalism are to be found in the territorial and monarchical states of Western Europe in the early modern period. As these states extended their authority over their subjects and diminished that of other institutions such as churches, estates and guilds, and as they came into increasing and more intensive conflict with one another, so they took on the character of nation-states. That is to say, the idea of the 'nation' achieved a limited political relevance.

These states did not, however, justify their actions in nationalist terms and were not so judged by their critics. That would have implied that the state, in some way or another, was an expression of the society it governed. Such a notion would have been offensive to those in authority or routinely participating in politics. In the political rhetoric of the period the idea of the nation, if it appeared at all, was subordinated to religious and monarchical principles. The English cause at the time of the Spanish Armada was symbolised by the person of Elizabeth I and the Protestant religion. Louis XIV could declare with little fear of contradiction: 'In France the nation is not a separate body, it dwells entirely within the person of the King.'[3] National historiography of the sort promoted by the Tudor, Valois and Bourbon dynasties, when it was not simply boosting the monarchy, extolled the nation in terms of its landscapes and resources rather than the character of its inhabitants.

The process of state-building helped create the political context within which nationalism could develop and the national sentiments which nationalists could subsequently exploit. It was not, however, itself justified in nationalist terms. It was rather in political opposition to those increasingly powerful monarchical states that something approaching nationalism can be identified. Although adopting a political rhetoric in some respects similar to that of the monarchical state, within such opposition movements the appeal to the national idea came to take on a more prominent role. This had a direct bearing upon the later development of nationalism.

To understand this one must first grasp the way in which new sorts of political opposition were formed in early modern Europe. One way of doing it is to look at religious-cum-political opposition. The comparisons one can make between this sort of opposition and later nationalist oppositions are illuminating. From that argument one can go on to show how the political concept of the nation was shaped by the relationship between monarchical state and political opposition.

2 Religious-cum-political opposition

One aspect of the growth of state power in early modern Europe was the changing relationship between church and government and, more generally, between religion and politics. Governments wished to secure greater power over the Catholic church in order to reduce papal power, to provide government with greater resources, and to create closer links between religious and political loyalties. Between 1486 and 1523, for example, the Spanish monarchy extended its control over many church appointments, from newly conquered Granada to its lands in the New World and finally to the historic Spanish territories. This last agreement of 1523 was modelled upon the Concordat of 1516 between Francis I of France and the Papacy, which secured many church appointments to the crown and reduced the rights of appeal to Rome. The eventual outcome of these agreements was to produce national churches whose leaders were loyal to the monarchy.

This encroachment upon church autonomy often exploited as well as promoted national sentiment. Henry VIII based assiduous propaganda on this national theme in the 1530s. The background to Luther's success in Germany included sentiments such as those expressed in the late fifteenth century pamphlet entitled 'Reform of Sigismund' which attacked papal and foreign corruption. Luther expressed such sentiments himself. The major beneficiaries of this attack upon Rome were the princely states of northern and central Germany. In these ways monarchical, religious and national sentiments were closely linked to one another. The process was unique to Europe. In some societies, such as those of the faith of Islam, religion and politics could not overlap in this way because they were not initially separated from one another. In other societies religion was a private affair, as with many of the Greek and Roman cults, and could not attain political significance. In Europe the Catholic church had come uniquely to combine religious and secular functions and had largely survived the political system of empire in which it had first developed. As the territorial monarchy became the central institution within a new sort of political system, so it became necessary to redefine the relationship between church and government. This was a gradual process which long antedates the Reformation. Up to the time of the Reformation the process of redefinition had been largely framed in institutional terms, and this confined the dispute to manageable proportions. The French and Spanish examples which have been cited could be regarded as continuations of this process. Except for isolated examples such as the Hussite movement, heresy and a political challenge to the Papacy did not go hand in hand. It was with the Reformation that institutional and doctrinal challenges to the Catholic church converged in a general way. This could come about either through a challenge over doctrine being taken up by the secular authorities (as was the case with the Lutheran reformation) or through a challenge to the institutional authority of the church leading to doctrinal disputes (as with the English reformation).

Another development gave the Reformation a novel character. It coincided with the advent of 'print capitalism'.[4] It now became possible to mass produce books and pamphlets. The Protestant stress upon direct access to the word of God, and that word increasingly as the written word, could only be carried through the medium of print. Luther's pamphlets and his Bible translation were among the best sellers of their day. Yet these were not 'privately' consumed. Bible readings and discussions stressed the shared character of beliefs. At the same time, extensive circulation of religious literature in vernacular languages created a sense of the audience as a language community and democratised access to the word of God.

77

The Catholic church was thereby challenged in fundamental ways which went beyond doctrinal questions.

When such a challenge was organised and led by the government it could serve to link monarchical, religious and, possibly, national loyalties more closely together. But this closer connection between religion and politics could also be reflected in opposition to existing monarchy. If the monarch claimed to be head of the church he could brand a political challenge as heresy and see a dispute over religious doctrine in terms of rebellion. But this could in turn push these different sorts of challenges together. Heretics or sectarians could see in the state an instrument for religious change. Political opposition could see in religious dissent a defence of its own actions and a means of broadening support for itself. The most important examples of this convergence of religious and political opposition came with the Calvinist challenges to monarchy in France and the Netherlands. However, where government embraced reformed religion, political opposition could be associated with a militant Catholic movement.

The Huguenot church, the form taken by Calvinist opposition in France, had a clear hierarchical structure which built up from the individual church with its disciplinary committee to the national synod. Sermons, bible readings and 'self-criticism' provided the means to spread propaganda and maintain discipline as well as supply the essential organisational backbone to the Calvinist movement in France. The church brought together into a single organisation groups which had not traditionally acted together: urban artisans and men of letters, impoverished local gentry, and great magnates with their peasant followings.

In all these ways the Huguenot church could be seen as a new sort of political movement. However, it could act effectively only when provided with leadership from within the established political class. Aristocratic and gentry participation furnished essential peasant support and military skills. Men such as Coligny and Condé supplied the necessary political leadership. Popular religion and organisation were not themselves enough. Anabaptism, which was much more than a movement of religious cranks, was branded as such and brutally crushed with the agreement of all established interests, partly, at least, because it raised the prospect of social change. Once even so well organised and effective bodies of religious militants as the Catholic League in France (above all in Paris) or the Calvinists of Antwerp had been abandoned by their aristocratic allies, they were quickly suppressed. The Lutheran reformation in the cities of southern Germany, where it received the most popular support, made little headway for lack of a widely based political class prepared to support it, and only later succeeded with princely support in areas where its popular impact seems to have been rather less.

Yet religious movements had an appeal that extended beyond the interests of oppositional elements within the established political class, and therefore offered those elements a resource which could be of crucial importance. The appeal to religion could justify the fearful act of rebellion. It could provide essential bonds of sentiment and organisation among what was otherwise a very disparate opposition. It could enable political opposition to mobilise groups not directly interested in the concerns of that political opposition. To understand why an appeal of this sort was of particular importance in early modern Europe it is necessary to consider how the growth of state power had altered the position of any potential political opposition.

This growth placed an increasing amount of patronage at the disposal of the crown. Factions competed with one another for a share in it. Only if faction leaders at court could obtain enough patronage were they able to sustain their support in the localities and among a myriad of followers. Only if provincial and local interests had good court connections could they pick up cherished appointments to financial or judicial offices and other valuable resources. With the increased state control of patronage, which itself was constantly expanding, the spread of factions building upon earlier ties between lord and vassal, and upon networks of local and provincial institutions, spread and enveloped whole regions. Monarchy found it increasingly difficult to maintain a balance between competing factions, although quite unable to govern without recourse to them. Under Philip II of Spain and during much of the time when Catherine de Medici effectively ruled France, some interests in the Netherlands and in France came to feel that the balance had swung too far in favour of a particular faction. The favoured factions were identified as the Spanish party (which immediately imparted a national flavour to the struggle) and the Guise faction respectively. Dissatisfied factions looked to more drastic ways of recovering their position. They might attempt to bring the monarchy under their control, a policy pursued by the Huguenots in the 1560s. They might look to separation, the eventual aim both of the Calvinist rebels in the Netherlands and of the Huguenots. But such drastic moves could hardly be justified in terms of patronage squabbles, which in turn could hardly mobilise the support of large parts of the population over extensive areas. The distintegration of the various Frondes of mid-seventeenth century France and the fizzling out of the rebellion of the Earl of Essex in 1601 show clearly the weakness of self-interested opposition without a unifying and inspiring cause. So religious and political oppositions had need of one another as well as sharing a common hostility to an increasingly powerful state. The precise ways in which these two sorts of opposition came together is a matter of detailed investigation which cannot be undertaken here.

There are a number of similarities between these opposition movements and many later nationalist oppositions. In both cases a movement with clear political objectives led by elements of the established political class has a creed which can create popular support and unify a wide variety of groups. The creed offers an alternative focus of loyalty to the monarchy and can be made available to a variety of groups which are territorially defined and brought together by the power of the state to which all are opposed. The penetration of the state into areas previously left alone by government both necessitates and makes possible the development of opposition calling upon the alternative principles embodied in the religious or nationalist creed. This creed is disseminated through a well organised system of communication and employs powerful symbols and ceremonial activities which increase the spirit of solidarity. The organisation which expresses the new creed binds together groups in new ways that go beyond the more limited traditional solidarities. The elaboration of the creed is carried out by a section of the intelligentsia – in the early period notably drawn from the church, later more often from the professions. Militant attachment to the new creed (especially from urban groups) can create internal tensions because it conflicts with the more moderate (and usually more purely political) goals of the leadership. This tension must be controlled if the movement is to hold together, and this is often done by avoiding any clear commitment on social change and emphasising shared values which transcend social distinctions. The major objective of both sorts of opposition is to gain control of the state, either by taking over the existing state or separating from it.

There are equally instructive differences. Nationalism is explicitly political. It appeals to people in terms of their rights and their own identities rather than in terms of their shared beliefs. These identities already abstract from social distinctions. All this makes nationalism more immediately political and appropriate to mobilising and organising a variety of territorially bounded groups. Furthermore, nationalism developed within a general context where mass political activity could be undertaken in a more continuous and sustained way than had been possible in early modern Europe. For all these reasons nationalist opposition has usually been much more effective politically than religious movements.

These comparisons do not involve any judgements about motives. No suggestion is intended that people with limited political interests cast around for a cause with which to bolster their pursuit of power or that those with religious grievances search for effective political connections. Certainly this did happen, but not always. Rather the two processes were linked by the manner in which monarchical power increased. In a similar way, as we shall see, state power altered the meanings attached to culture as well as making political uses of cultural identity particularly attractive.

Generally one can observe that the pursuit of state power by effective and extensive political oppositions linked to popular and organised religious movements occurred in very specific circumstances and ways in early modern Europe. The central feature of these circumstances was the changing character of the state. These oppositions can also be instructively compared with later nationalist movements, which in turn must be related to the changes in the state to which they were opposed. In this sense, therefore, it is possible to endorse the saying attributed to Namier that religion was a sixteenth-century word for nationalism.

3 National opposition

(a) General remarks

The growth of monarchical power in early modern Europe exhibited four interrelated aspects:

(i) *Centralisation.* As the state took more and more resources from those it governed, in such forms as increased revenue, conscripts and legal powers, so it reduced the importance of local and provincial institutions as places where decisions were made and enforced. More and more people realised that it was to the central government that they must direct their attention in order to get things done, or to stop things being done.

(ii) *Collaboration.* Collaborators were required on an increased scale both to undertake necessary services on behalf of the state and to tie significant groups and interests to the state. In the absence of modern technologies of communication, coercion and information processing, increased state power required more state servants. Legal interventions required more lawyers in the service of the state. New powers of taxation meant more tax collectors. Expansion of armed power called for more officers and soldiers and more elaborate support services to provide weapons, food, clothing, fortresses, ships, etc. All these new functions had to be supervised by a more elaborate and extensive administration.

Yet these functions could not be undertaken by completely new groups and institutions. Local and provincial assemblies and interests had to be won over in order to impose and collect new taxes effectively. Official powers were frequently sold, simply to raise revenue or because previous efforts to carry them out directly had proved ineffective. In this way the state was supported by and virtually identified with a growing, complex and heterogeneous network of collaborators located in a variety of institutions. Various groups competed with one another for the increased patronage at the disposal of the state. This patronage was itself a major form of state power which prevented powerful interests cutting themselves off from the crown. The state was not embodied in a public bureaucracy and could not call upon an ethic of public service to sustain itself.[5] But at the same time this competition could get out of hand.

81

Conflict could take various forms: factional competition, outgroups against in-groups, conflict between different types of collaborators (such as venal and non-venal officials, or officers of royal institutions and those of other institutions). A further complication was that this new structure of collaboration had to build upon or partially displace earlier, strongly entrenched systems of local and social privilege which had previously constrained and defined the sovereignty of the state. All this makes it very difficult to identify some central institutional feature of 'ancien regime' states. As I shall argue, this in itself has important implications for the recourse to the concept of the nation by political oppositions.

(iii) The image of the state. As the state intervened more and more in the affairs of its subjects, so, paradoxically, did it come to appear more detached from them. More precisely, the nature of its detachment changed. The state was less and less a distant, almost another, world which had little to do with those it notionally controlled. Indeed, its control came closer and closer. But this looming presence appeared as something far above its subjects. The state seemed to acquire a life of its own. To use a spatial analogy, 'horizontal' distance from most of its subjects was increasingly being replaced by 'vertical' distance above them.

Monarchy was elevated to a new and more glorious level. The claim to 'absolute' sovereignity established an impassable divide between the one agency that made the claim and everything else that became the object of the claim. This claim led to a vision of the state, or rather of the crown, as a 'public' authority standing for some general principle or interest over and above the myriad 'private' interests which made up society. The apparent separation of state from society then raised the problem of how they were connected to one another. In trying to answer that problem the idea of the nation acquired a particular importance.

(iv) International rivalry. The growth of state power occurred within the framework of an increasingly international economy and took the form of conflict between states, no one of which was indisputably dominant. Each state responded to threats from other states by increasing its military power and seeking to define some political and economic region as its sole possession, as well as forming coalitions with other states. The process was an escalating one, and something akin to an arms race took place. Intensive conflict between a number of states which increasingly resembled one another and which seemed increasingly detached both from 'private' society beneath them and a broader set of economic relationships beyond them involved a permanent tension between the idea of the state as the source of absolute power and the reality of the state as something limited both from below and beyond.

The response to threats from other states had limits and was varied.

England, with the protection of the sea, had less need of large land forces than continental states. Some small states could, by skilful diplomacy, commercial wealth or luck, negotiate between the major powers. Others, both large and small, could not do this and could not respond adequately in military terms. Poland's fate, for example, vividly illustrated the price that could be paid for failing to keep up in the arms race. Naturally military expansion was closely associated with the other three aspects of the growth of state power. Wars were increasingly costly and compelled the search for new sources of revenue and manpower. In this way they could have a much greater impact upon the mass of the population than had usually been the case before. This could intensify political identification with or against the state.

This is a fairly abstract description of the growth of state power in early modern Europe. I do not, at this stage, wish to explore possible explanations of this. Instead I want to examine the political implications of these changes, particularly with regard to the emergence of national opposition.

At first monarchy was able to handle the growth in its power. But, as the number and variety of those involved in politics increased, so did the scope of political conflict and the difficulties of managing it. It became increasingly difficult for the crown to remain aloof from conflict or to avoid becoming identified with particular groups or institutions. This was particularly unfortunate given the new image of the crown serving the general interest. It could force opposition groups, which were becoming something more than small factions, to look to alternative general principles by which to justify their challenge to the crown. We have already seen the part religion could play in this. The idea of the nation represented another option. The very success of the centralising monarchy in conflict with other monarchies had encouraged the sense of a plurality of societies, each with its own unity but different from the others. This idea could be emancipated from its subordination to monarchical principle. Political opposition which claimed to represent the interests of the nation could insist that these interests had implications for the staffing, policies and structure of the state. The idea of the nation offered a general framework within which a variety of interests could be accommodated. It could be used to suggest that the purpose of the 'public' state was to express and defend the identity and interests of the 'nation'. In these ways society ceased to be regarded as a fragmented cluster of private interests unified only by the state above it, but was seen rather as a unity whose essence was expressed in the concept of the nation and which should then shape the state.

At first political language which used the term 'nation' in these ways was still imbued with the more traditional concerns about religion and legitimate authority. The national idea did not necessarily involve an attack upon monarchy as such. When national opposition did find itself opposed

83

to monarchy it often encountered great difficulty in working out an alternative principle of government better suited to the needs of the nation. Even in its most radical forms the invocation of the nation against monarchy did not go so far as to become nationalism. It did, however, prepare the ground for nationalism. It is time to turn from the abstract to the concrete. Attention to the cases of England and France should provide more substance.

(b) England

English monarchy, unlike many of its continental counterparts, was unable to create a large standing army. Although control of such resources as trading monopolies and tax collecting rights were important to the crown, they were not nearly so extensive as in France and Spain. The revenue derived from the sale of offices and the venal bureaucracy this created were of minor importance compared to France. So too were the scope and size of royal officialdom operating directly under the control of the crown. Unlike France and Spain the English crown did not have to deal with local or provincial institutions of any importance. English monarchy had, although with limited powers, constructed a centralised system of government much earlier than its French or Spanish counterparts. By the early modern period this process firmly included Wales. With the Act of Union of 1707 the process began to be extended to Scotland, although certain institutional differences were respected. The great exception was Ireland to which the 'absolutist' model of political control is more appropriate, and which, of course, generated a very different kind of nationalism. (In the following account I will use the term England, rather than Britain, though neither is satisfactory.)

What this meant was that England did not travel as far along the road to absolutism as many continental monarchies. Absolutism can be regarded to some extent as an effort to overcome enormous threats to unity from within and sovereignty from without, and the comparative weakness of such threats in England by the early modern period had decreased the need to respond in this way. It also meant that in England the major institution through which collaboration was secured for further centralisation was a central representative assembly, Parliament. It was through agreements with Parliament and informal links with local – above all, gentry – interests that the Tudor monarchs reduced noble and church power. This sort of political evolution had two major consequences for the subsequent development of national opposition. First, the centrality of a single institution in the collaboration required to increase royal power provided an immediate central focus for subsequent opposition to the crown. National opposition could develop more quickly than in other states where the collaboration system was more complex and disparate. At the same time, the close relationship of Parliament to a monarchy which did not acquire the same degree of detachment from society as did the absolutist monarchies of the continent meant that this national opposition centred on Parliament did not face the problem of overcoming an impassable gulf between 'state' and 'society'. As a consequence, the idea of the nation was not radically distinct from the idea of the state to which it was opposed. The implications for subsequent political events were enormous. These points can be brought out by considering the role played by the idea of the English nation in the civil war and its aftermath.

As a consequence of its regular collaboration with monarchy in the sixteenth century, Parliament developed firm procedures and conventions. It brought together a variety of local interests and was the only institution that could link these interests together in ways which could match the power of the crown, though that power was articulated through as much as against parliament. Increasingly Parliament could appear as the only effective institution through which to channel grievances against the crown.

Why disputes within the state came to take the form of conflict between crown and parliament and led ultimately to the outbreak of revolution is a complex and controversial matter which cannot be dealt with here.[6] There were a range of conflicts over economic, political and religious matters. They were largely confined to a small political class which it is difficult to characterise or divide in social class terms. What is important is that these different sorts of conflict converged. In the process the new and internally diverse opposition looked to Parliament as a means of organising and expressing itself. Parliament came to provide both an ideological and an organisational function for this opposition.

Pocock has argued that an institution creates an historical image of itself which mirrors its present objectives. Elton, discussing English national consciousness in the sixteenth century has observed: 'National consciousness required embodiment in working institutions in order to acquire enduring reality.'[7] Taken together, these statements provide the key to understanding the crystallisation of an English national idea around parliament. The issue was parliament's power and prerogatives. To defend that power it was necessary to make the nature of the constitution explicit. In an age to which the notion of natural rights was foreign (and such a notion was, in any case, too far-reaching for the sort of conflict involved) the constitutional rights of Parliament had to be based upon historical precedent. Parliamentary lawyers such as Coke defended common law against formal legislation and Parliament as the highest court of appeal and a necessary agent in the making of new law. Defence of common law automatically based itself upon history and opposed arbitrary innovation. Defence of Parliament required an historical account of that body as court and legislature. In its clearest form this account was expressed in the notion of the Norman yoke, although this radical form of the historical argument was only developed in the 1640s.[8] This argument envisaged parliamentary monarchy and the rule of common law as properties of the free Anglo-Saxon nation. The Norman conquest had begun the erosion of those rights, liberties and practices in favour of strong monarchy.

Such an argument had many attractions. It suggested that absolutism was a continental phenomenon, both because it had advanced further on the continent and because its threatening existence in England had its roots in the conquest. It was also very easy to associate absolutism with Catholicism and, therefore, the cause of parliamentary liberty with true Protestantism. In these ways an ideology could be created which centred on Parliament and incorporated national, religious and anti-absolutist themes. To regard Parliament as the expression of the political rights of the nation also limited the scope of the national idea. The nation comprised not all the inhabitants of the country but only that section of them represented in Parliament. Property rights, limited participation in politics and the continuation of substantial inequality were permitted within this idea of the nation. In all these ways the national idea cannot be described as nationalism. The nation is understood in a political rather than a cultural sense; it has limited scope; it is closely associated with religious justifications for opposition; and initially that opposition did not challenge monarchy as such.

There were two major weaknesses in this ideology. Although it helped to bring about the open clash with the crown and the execution of Charles I, it did not develop an alternative political principle to that of monarchy. Parliament was too entangled with the established system of government and the contrast between 'state' and 'society' was still too blurred for a national idea based upon Parliament to be able to generate a clear alternative. One reason for the various failed experiments in different forms of government during the interregnum was this ideological incoherence. Second, and related to this, the early development of a national opposition based on Parliament meant that it was initially adapted to the limited nature of political participation. However, the radicalising effect of the civil war itself and the way it brought new groups into politics meant that this limited conception of politics and government soon came under challenge. So much is clear, for example, in the disputes over the rights of property and people in the famous Putney debates. These radical challenges could lead, in an intermittent and partial way, to a broadening of the concept of the nation beyond the established political class. However, such challenges were more often couched in religious than in national terms. This, along with the practical failure of radical movements in the interregnum, meant that concepts of the nation based on natural rights did not play an important part in politics.

The restoration and, above all, the revolution of 1688–89 provided an answer to these two weaknesses. The nation was now regarded as the balanced combination of royal and parliamentary power. Piecemeal adjustments to this balance were permissible through the extension of the electorate or changes in constitutional practice. But the emphasis upon gradualism within a set of unique and largely unwritten conventions came to be regarded as the essence of the national political culture and, indeed, of the nation itself. When radical concepts of the nation were posed at the end of the eighteenth century as a means of criticising this image and justification of English politics, the image was given a new and particularly forceful defence by Burke in a way which points to something akin to nationalism, albeit of a conservative sort.[9] By and large the political rhetoric of gradualism and unwritten convention has survived. Since the beginning of the eighteenth century political opposition has either accepted the rhetoric (claiming that it represented the next step forward in the progressive evolution of English politics) or has gone beyond the national framework to appeal to universal principles. This is part of the reason for the absence of any distinctive English nationalist ideology. Not only has there been no foreign presence which could generate nationalist opposition but, prior to the advent of mass politics, a limited revolution had already created a national framework for the state. The response of new groups entering the political arena has therefore been to demand adjustments of this national framework rather than to suggest that they embody the spirit of the nation against a non-national or anti-national state. For example, it was Macaulay's case for a peculiarly English history of progress which provided the major intellectual justification for parliamentary reform in 1832. Alternative arguments based on universal principles of either utility (e.g., the case put by James Mill) or natural rights were marginal, and the appeal to history simply did not figure in the discussion.

Of course, the way in which this political rhetoric has developed and the parallel development of the political system itself cannot be explained purely or even primarily in terms of the rhetoric itself or an English gift for compromise. Many features of the English situation – its island position, its commercial empire, its early industrial growth – all helped make it possible to resolve conflicts in ways which were beyond the reach of other countries. Of course, if one looks beyond England to the British Isles the picture changes. The politics of compromise hardly describes the character of British government in Ireland. An English national idea had implicit implications of subordination for those who were not defined or did not wish to define themselves as English within the British Isles. How this contributed to the development of anti-English forms of nationalism is considered in chapter 16. There is also the complex shift from an English to a British national ideology in the eighteenth century. This took up the anti-Catholic theme, but now directed it increasingly against the Spanish and then the French. The increased scope of warfare, and the formation of an overseas empire, first in the Americas and then in Asia, helped integrate Scottish and Welsh elites into the ruling order. What developed was an Anglo-British, Protestant and imperial idea. However, these external stimuli to nationality have to be linked back to the internal framework – above all that of parliamentary monarchy – within which the national idea was institutionally rooted.

(c) France

The growth of monarchical power in France took a very different form from that found in the English case. The French crown found that seeking collaboration from a central representative assembly was pointless, as that assembly did not have the power to carry out its side of the bargain. The Estates General was not called between 1614 and 1789. Instead the crown negotiated with a variety of local and provincial institutions, representative and judicial. At the same time new offices proliferated, both through the sale of state powers and related titles on a large scale and through the creation of a set of royal officers directly responsible to the crown who sought to oversee the disparate set of arrangements through which the state operated. One institution which might have provided a focus of national opposition, the church, was strongly loyalist, at least at the top of the hierarchy. More than in any other state the French crown enlarged its control over the internal resources of the country while at the same time having to come to terms with a cluster of entrenched social and local privileges.[10]

The result was the creation of a complex and heterogeneous network of collaborators which both buttressed and inhibited royal power and which had a particularly large impact upon the subject population. Political conflict revolved around the competition over collaborator positions and spoils. If the crown sought to alter some part of the network, for example by reducing the extent of venal office or attacking fiscal exemptions, it encountered strong but often disunited opposition. The fragmentation of opposition reflected the heterogeneity of the political structure and the absence of a suitable central alternative institution through which opposition to the crown could be organised. For example, the Frondes of the mid-seventeenth century, taken together, represented a formidable challenge. But, without a dominant and central institution through which to express that challenge, they were defeated largely in isolation from one another.

For a long time afterwards there was little overt resistance to the crown. This was partly due to tacit and mutual respect for its prerogatives and those of its collaborators. Without leadership from important elements within the political class (that is, from the collaborators) the serious discontents created by war and famine in the later part of the reign of Louis XIV could pose no threat to political stability. In so far as there was a political concept of the nation it was expressed in terms of this ramshackle set of political arrangements. The description provided by the *Avocat-*

Général, Segurier, for the benefit of Louis XVI in 1776 is characteristic:

> The clergy, the nobility, the sovereign courts, the lower tribunals, the officers attached to these tribunals, the universities, the academies, the financial companies, the commercial companies, all present, and in all parts of the State, bodies in being which one can regard as the links of a great chain of which the first is in the hands of your Majesty, as head and sovereign of all that constitutes the body of the nation.[11]

During the eighteenth century the crown sought to undermine some of these arrangements. The reasons for these attempts at reform lay in international relations and the threat to the country posed by other powers. The failure of reform and its consequences need to be related to the major social and economic changes which had taken place in eighteenth-century France, particularly affecting the situation of the peasantry. A full account of the origins of the French revolution would need to look at these levels of action. Here I can only concentrate at the intermediate level on how reform, its failure and the opposition it created were shaped by the institutional character of the state itself and how this in turn shaped the development of the national idea.[12]

The attempts at reform made by the crown could have had only limited success because they involved an attack upon the very foundations of the state. But the conflicts and crises stimulated by these attempts led to the development of the idea of the nation in a number of new ways. First, the crown placed an ever greater emphasis on its role of being above society and came to stress the way it served the general interests of society against the various sectional and privileged groups that sought to block its reform attempts. This image of the state was elaborated by various writers who constructed a model of an all-powerful but enlightened monarchy leading society along the path of progress.

Second, opposition to the attempts at reform attacked royal despotism. The remonstrances published by the various Parlements, for example, defended historic privilege as an expression of the liberties of the nation. In the publicist war between advocates of reforming monarchy or the liberties of the subject, those who attacked the crown probably came off best.

It is difficult, if not impossible, to estimate the effects of these conflicts and the language in which they were conducted upon the mass of the population who were not involved. The defence of 'liberty' probably helped create a public opinion favourable to political reforms designed to reduce royal power and any sort of arbitrary authority. The attack upon 'privilege' may have encouraged the general resentment of privilege which seems to have been increasing, although historians differ as to how much and why this was the case. It may also have helped spread the idea that the state should represent the interests of the whole of society and not just

89

small parts of it.

The opposition to yet another set of reform proposals in the 1780s precipitated a crisis which led to the calling of an Assembly of Notables in 1787. This provided an opportunity for the opponents of reform to express themselves through a single institution whilst also providing the crown with the chance to come to terms with a single institution. Both sides in the conflict recognised the need to conduct negotiations centrally and, if compromise had proved possible, a more uniform and centralised set of arrangements would have given the state a new strength. Unlike the English Parliament, however, this assembly had no historic identity, established procedures or solidarity which would have permitted effective negotiation and agreement. This was unfortunate for both sides. The calling of the assembly made clear the depth of the crisis. It suggested that only through some central body would a solution be found. The assembly was unable to find that solution. All this increased the pressure to call a national assembly which might be able to negotiate more effectively and by means of which the crown might be able to undercut the opposition of entrenched privilege. The Estates-General, which met in 1789, was legally a revival of the institution which last assembled in 1614. Actually it was quite new, given the enormous changes that had taken place since. In the crisis conditions of its election neither crown nor established political opposition had been able to control the issues raised or the men chosen. The membership and support for the Third Estate in particular (though the same, in more limited ways, applied to the other two estates) clearly did not belong to the political nation as previously defined. This was recognised by the Third Estate when it distinguished between the 'legal' and the 'real' nation. The liberties of the legal nation were based on historic privilege; those of the real nation upon natural right. It is difficult to see from what other source the Third Estate could have derived a justification for its claim to power.

The crisis of 1787–89 had led to an outflanking of both crown and established political interests. Elements of the political rhetoric of reforming monarchy and privileged opposition could be combined in a new and radical way in the Third Estate. The very existence of this body within the Estates-General (soon transformed into the National Assembly) provided a concrete expression of the new conception of the nation that had been developed. With the establishment of the National Assembly the 'real' nation came to be regarded as the source of legitimate political power. The Declaration of the Rights of Man and of the Citizen (1789) stated: 'The Nation is essentially the source of all sovereignty; nor can any individual, or any body of men, be entitled to any authority which is not expressly derived from it.'[13]

But it is quite clear, from the rest of the declaration and from the subsequent constitution of 1791, that this idea of the nation did not refer to a special group of people with a common cultural identity. The nation was the sum of the citizens, whose rights were based upon their common humanity. France was simply the place in which these universal principles of humanity were first being proclaimed and realised. It was constantly asserted by French governments during the wars of the 1790s that they sought not the extension of French power but the implementation of universal values.[14]

Within the framework of competing states that then existed there were three ways in which this position could move closer towards nationalism.

First, there was a conservative reaction against the French revolution. One intellectual form this could take was to deny that universal principles could be applied to different societies. The argument could be backed up by the assertion that each society was unique and that its political institutions must be understood in that light. This had no direct or immediate impact upon politics but it was an important intellectual influence upon the development of nationalist ideology, as I have argued in the previous chapter.

Second, the conflict between France and other states could lead to a shift of emphasis to French achievements and interests rather than the principles supposed to animate the revolution. In doctrinal terms this did not amount to nationalism in the full sense of the word but it came close to it in practical political terms.

Third, regional revolts against the new government in Paris could promote and combine both of these responses in a new way. Conservatives could see in this regionalism the expression of the traditional and varied values which made up the true French nation, although it would take another century for this to be elaborated into an effective, right-wing national ideology. Radicals could see in it a denial of true French culture, which was committed to universal reason and liberty. In this way cultural attributes could be seen as relevant to the principles of the revolution. Barère, a radical member of the National Convention, applied this argument to language: 'We have observed that the dialect called Bas-Breton, the Basque dialect, and the German and Italian languages have perpetuated the reign of fanaticism and superstition, revered the domination of priests and aristocrats, and favoured the enemies of France.'[15] The French language, a uniform system of administration and law, and a highly centralised government could all come to be regarded as embodying both universal values and national spirit. The French had the peculiar national mission to proclaim, practise and extend a system of government based upon natural rights. Throughout the nineteenth century radicalism in France took up this position and, although highly patriotic, cannot therefore be regarded as properly nationalist.

91

(d) Conclusion

In both these cases the content of national ideology was closely related to the institutional framework within which political conflict took place. But, because the established framework was more capable of organising effective opposition and of handling newly aroused discontents in England, it was there that the idea of the nation remained much more closely bound up with existing institutions. Historic rights (the sort of rights emphasised in the opposition to royal attempts at reform in France) were central to the case made out by the opposition, and these rights were related to historic institutions, above all to Parliament. In France, although the idea of the nation that had been formulated in 1789 built upon earlier political debate, it also went far beyond it. By basing itself upon natural rights it eliminated the need to relate those rights to historical institutions and justified the project of establishing a totally new system of government. Of course, the reasons for the greater radicalism of the French revolution have to be related to the depths of the social crisis which exploded in 1789 as well as to the highly charged international situation that preceded and accompanied the revolution. Nevertheless, the failure of the crown to cope with the initial crisis and the ways in which conflict was conducted and justified at political level were closely related to the institutional character of the state.

In both cases national ideology was primarily political in content and references to cultural identity played a very subordinate role. The concern of political opposition was with rights granted to society by the existing state. The identity of that society was not in question. All that was in question was the content of the historical and natural rights which should be recognised and how they could be incorporated into the system of government. Non-institutional ideas of ethnic identity may well have existed in these, and earlier societies, based upon family and community. However, these could not be institutionalised at the level of extended political action. Only churches or monarchies, and institutions which both collaborated with and opposed monarchy, could provide the institutional basis on which a national idea could be crystallised and transmitted from one generation to the next.[16]

Both cases put the language of nation and national interest into circulation, and it could be adapted in ways that took it closer to nationalism. Furthermore, nationalist ideology and movements later developed in political contexts which can be compared to those that existed in England and France. However, in the situations which lead to nationalism the cultural identity of those involved in political opposition becomes relevant in addition to the rights proclaimed by that opposition. Consequently the principles of historic or natural rights which were developed in the constitutional conflicts of the English and French (as well as American)

92

revolutions are applied to these new situations in a distinctive way.

4 General points

It would be useful at this stage to introduce three ideas which can be applied to the cases already considered and will play an important part in the analysis of further cases. They relate to three different functions which ideology can play within a political movement. I call these functions co-ordination, mobilisation and legitimation. Co-ordination is the part ideology plays in bringing together a set of diverse political interests into a single movement by providing them with a unity of values and purpose. Mobilisation is the part ideology plays in bringing new groups into politics and providing them with political objectives and justifications. Legitimation is the part ideology plays in presenting an acceptable image of a political movement to outsiders.

These ideas do not imply that ideology actually brings groups together, mobilises popular political action or persuades outsiders to provide sympathy or support. It might do such things, but it might equally well rationalise actions of these sorts which were already being undertaken. In fact, it is impossible to treat ideology as either the cause or the effect of 'non-ideological' action. Rather it is one element within a broader pattern of activity, as I argued in the previous chapter.

The evaluation of a particular nationalist movement depends upon the relative importance of these three roles which nationalist ideology can play. For example, if ideology primarily relates to obtaining external support and seems to have no part to play in the internal mechanics of a nationalist movement, this will clearly be a very different sort of nationalism from one in which ideology is closely related to obtaining and organising popular support.

Useful comparisons can be made between the English and French cases on the basis of these three functions. In neither case was the function of legitimation important, primarily because the arguments employed were new and far more likely to arouse the hostility than the sympathy of the only significant external forces, namely foreign governments. In the English case the mobilisation function was of minor importance. Popular involvement came about largely as a consequence of revolution and was, if anything, critical of the ways in which national ideology had been formulated. In the French case the elections to the Estates General meant that politics had extended beyond established boundaries even before the crisis of July-August 1789 touched off mass movements on a far larger scale. The ideology of natural rights and of the real nation had already played a part in those elections. Subsequently revolutionary leaders were concerned as much to manage as to arouse mass participation in politics. National ideology, particularly when the revolution was threatened from abroad,

93

played its part in this. Finally, in both cases national ideology was of crucial importance in promoting and justifying co-operation among a variety of interests already involved in politics. To convert the diverse interests within Parliament or within the Third Estate into a single cause which seemed to explain what those institutions should do and which could even justify moves towards revolution, it was necessary to construct some general view of what those interests stood for. As we have seen, the appeal to the nation played an important part in the construction of this general view.

Notes

1   For two very different approaches within the Marxist approach see Perry Anderson, *Lineages of the Absolute State* (London, 1974), which focuses upon internal class conflict; and Immanuel Wallerstein, *The Modern World System: capitalist agriculture and the origins of the European world economy in the sixteenth century* (New York, 1976), which concentrates on the beginning of a global division between developed and underdeveloped societies.

2   For a suggestive typology see Gianfranco Poggi, *The Development of the Modern State: a sociological introduction* (London, 1978).

3   Quoted in Hubert Méthivier, *L'Ancien Régime* (Paris, 1971), p. 82.

4   The term is from Benedict Anderson, *Imagined Communities: reflections on the origins and spread of nationalism* (London, 1983).

5   To some extent such an ethic did become effective in Prussia, even if modern historical accounts have exaggerated this. As a consequence, to some extent the Prussian bureaucracy became a vehicle of a national consciousness which went beyond simple monarchical loyalty.

6   See Lawrence Stone, *The Causes of the English Revolution, 1529–1642* (London, 1972); and, for a more recent treatment, A. Hughes, *The causes of the English civil war* (1991), and C. Russell, *The causes of the English civil war* (Oxford, 1991).

7   J. Pocock, 'England', in *National Consciousness, History and Political Culture*, edited by O. Ranum (Baltimore, 1975), pp. 98–117 (especially 100–101). G. R. Elton, 'English National Self-Consciousness and the Parliament in the 16th Century', in *Nationalismus in vorindustrieller Zeit*, edited by O. Dann (Munich, 1986), pp. 73–82 (77).

8   On Coke and the defence of parliament in the 1620s see Stephen D. White, *Sir Edward Coke and the grievances of the commonwealth* (Manchester, 1979). On the radical historical case see Christopher Hill, 'The Norman Yoke', in *Democracy and the Labour Movement: Essays in honour of Dona Torr*, edited by John Saville (London, 1954), pp. 11–66.

9   See also above, chapter 2, pp. 55–6.

10   In western Europe the resources available for centralisation in the other major absolutist monarchy, Spain, were furnished from abroad to a much greater extent, though a similar analysis as for France could be developed,

especially for Castille. In eastern Europe local privilege was less institutionally entrenched, and therefore did not supply both the basis and the
potential opposition to the growth of royal power.
11   Quoted in E. N. Williams, *The Ancien Régime in Europe* (Harmondsworth,
1970), pp. 28–9.
12   For an analysis of the French revolution based explicitly on this distinction
between three levels of action – society, state, inter-state – and linked in
turn to an illuminating comparison with the Chinese and Russian revolutions, see Theda Skocpol, *States and Social Revolutions: a comparative
analysis of France, Russia, and China* (Cambridge, 1979).
13   Article III. The Declaration is conveniently published, in an English translation, in *Revolutions*, edited by Merryn Williams (Harmondsworth, 1977),
pp. 96–9.
14   For the nature of the original national argument and then its shifts in
France during the period of the revolution, as well as for the way the
national idea was developed in other countries in reaction to France, see
the essays collected together in *Nationalism in the Age of the French
Revolution*, edited by Otto Dann & John Dinwiddy (London, 1988).
15   Quoted in Carlton Hayes, *The Historical Evolution of Nationalism* (New
York, 1931), p. 65.
16   For an attempt to document these types of ethnic identity in societies of
the ancient and medieval period, and then to connect them to the development of the national idea, see Anthony D. Smith, *The Ethnic Origins of
Nations* (Oxford, 1986). I have criticised this approach at some length in
a review of this book in *English Historical Review* CIII/407 (April, 1988),
pp. 414–18.

4

Unification nationalism
in nineteenth-century Europe

I will consider the three cases of German, Italian and Polish unification nationalism. The German and Italian cases can be taken together because they share many characteristics. Both involved war against Austria-Hungary, the unification of a number of nominally sovereign states, leadership from a particular state (Prussia and Piedmont), and an appeal to history which had to go back a long way to find any sort of plausible justification. Both succeeded. The Polish movement was very different. It occurred in areas occupied by foreign states and therefore when it employed violence it was in the form of insurrection rather than war against other states. Its historical justification had only to refer back to the kingdom of Poland of the eighteenth century, and much of its strength derived from the direct connections that still existed with that kingdom. It failed. Yet, I shall argue, in many ways nationalism was a more powerful and significant movement in the Polish than in the Italian and German cases. Most of the chapter is concerned with establishing this point and considering its implications.

1 German and Italian unification

Nationalism was more important as a product than as a cause of national unification. There was a limited nationalist movement in both countries. Their major contributions to unification were to provide legitimation for unity in the eyes of outsiders and essential elite co-ordination for the effective running of the new state once the initial act of unification had been carried through. The crucial interventions of Prussia and Piedmont were not inspired by nationalism. Nationalism had little popular appeal. What nationalism there was of political significance was rather different from the romantic, linguistic and ethnic ideas which intellectual historians have emphasised.

These severe limitations upon Italian and German nationalism up to the period of unification have been obscured by the success of unification. Success itself seems to point to the central importance of nationalism. It has also led to a historiography which seeks to show that such was indeed the case. This historiography at first approved of unification from a nationalist perspective and turned figures such as Bismarck and William I, Cavour and Victor Emmanuel into nationalist heroes. But even critics of the new nation states have perpetuated an exaggerated view of nationalism. The excesses of the fascist period have led historians to search for nationalist roots of fascism in the nineteenth century. Historians who sympathised with liberal or democratic nationalism have sought to show how its failure in the nineteenth century (a view which implies some prospect of success) meant that the actual nation-states which were established were in some way flawed. The flaws are then related to various problems which beset the new states. Above all, even historians who regard national unification as a kind of an accident in which national sentiment played little role, usually conduct their argument within a subdiscipline called 'German' and 'Italian' history, a subdiscipline which deals with the period before as well as after nation-state formation. However, if one argues that nationalism was not really central to the process of unification, then all these perspectives have to be abandoned, and a comparative, non-national approach has to be adopted. To sustain these apparently implausible arguments it is necessary to begin with the impact of the Napoleonic conquests upon Italy and Germany.

National sentiment played no part in the resistance within Italy to French domination under Napoleon. What publicist resistance there was hardly went beyond the traditional expression of regret and despair at the impotence of the Italian states in the face of foreign aggression, something I discussed in the Introduction. Some governments and established interests did resist because their position was under threat, but equally, Napoleonic control could only be established because of the widespread sympathy and collaboration with the political reorganisation of Italy. If anything, Napoleon positively developed a sense of national identity not merely by his manipulation of the politics of the peninsula (a time-honoured French as well as Habsburg pastime) but through the creation of political entities such as a Kingdom of Italy.

The situation was a little different in Germany, where military resistance, particularly from Austria, was far more important and where the existence of the Holy Roman Empire (it was only formally dissolved in 1806) provided some slight institutional support for expressing resistance in national terms. But Austria herself was naturally not sympathetic, as a European rather than simply a German power, to an emphasis upon the national argument.

However, an argument of this kind was developed and, in the work of someone like Fichte, undoubtedly came to take a nationalist form. It is for this reason that some historians can insist that nationalism was first invented by German intellectuals at the beginning of the nineteenth century.[1] I have considered the intellectual case for this argument in chapter 2. The combination of an intellectual response against Enlightenment rationalism and a political response against French successes certainly did lead to the production of novel and authentically nationalist ideas. But the principal concern here is with nationalism as effective politics, and from this angle nationalism appears much less important. To begin with, the romantic, linguistic and ethnic nationalist ideas that were elaborated between 1800 and 1815 remained on the margins of practical politics. As a consequence their advocates had little in the way of political organisation and failed to develop any precise political objectives. Politically they were no more than the vague ideals of isolated intellectuals. The major organisations in which these views were embodied were militia groups committed to the expulsion of France from Germany, gymnastic societies and student fraternities which engaged in physical and literary activities supposedly representative of national traditions. The military contribution of the militia groups, as of volunteer forces generally, was insignificant: Napoleon was defeated by professional armies loyal to their various dynastic states. In turn, Napoleon's armies included German contingents from states which had willingly collaborated in the reorganisation of large parts of western Germany under French auspices.

Commitment to the cause of 'Germany' rather than of Austria or Prussia or Bavaria did exist outside the ranks of romantic and ethnic nationalists, and was of greater political importance. Stein, the reforming chief minister of Prussia in 1808–09, for example, was committed to the German cause and carried out his anti-French activities in the service of Prussia, then Austria and finally Russia as opportunity and the requirements of the situation changed. But Stein's view of Germany was very different from that of Fichte or Arndt or Jahn. For him Germany was an historic territorial unit expressed in the form of the Holy Roman Empire, which he wished to see continued in some reformed version linked to Prussia and Austria. His own origins as an imperial knight may have led him to take such a view detached from the interests of any territorial state in Germany.

However, men like Stein only became effective in the service of such states. Stein's reform programme in Prussia may have had a German dimension so far as he was concerned, but most of those who worked with him saw matters rather in terms of regenerating Prussia and placing her in a position to throw off French domination. Indeed, the reforms which Stein and his colleagues partially realised in Prussia did more to promote a sense of Prussian patriotism than of German nationalism. The subsequent growth of a demand for national reform at a Prussian level can be analysed in similar terms to those used for the cases of England and France in the previous chapter.

The existing states were prepared to make use of the talents of men such as Stein and even the rhetoric of a German cause, although in a very limited way. However, their aims were framed in terms of state interests and they maintained firm control over the conduct of the war against Napoleon and the diplomatic agreements which followed his defeat.

As for Italy, it was a Napoleonic figure, Murat, who had been installed as king of the Two Sicilies, who first tried to use the idea of a national cause to mobilise resistance against the advancing Austrian and British forces. The appeal had no success, although it was a pointer to the Francophile sentiments of much subsequent Italian nationalism.

The principal contribution of the Napoleonic experience to subsequent 'national' developments should be sought elsewhere than in the resistance movement to the French. Napoleon reorganised the Italian and German lands along the lines of a reduced number of more rationally administered and territorially bounded states. The modern-minded men who oversaw this transformation sought to defend these new creations as best they could, sometimes collaborating with Napoleon and sometimes opposing him. Generally speaking these men and their political creations survived Napoleon's defeat. Within this new political framework ideas of German and Italian nationalism were formed, standing in both positive and negative relationships to the new territorial states, in ways which would have been inconceivable under the patchwork *ancien régime* order.

The Congress of Vienna, which formulated the post-Napoleonic settlement of Europe, has frequently been portrayed as reactionary and anti-nationalist. But as nationalism had never played an important role in the events leading up to the Congress and as the results of the Congress were, in many ways, to confirm rather than undo changes that had taken place since 1789, these judgements seem to be misplaced. The Congress accepted the Napoleonic simplification of the German and Italian lands into tens rather than hundreds of states, and its neglect of the Catholic interest, especially in refusing to restore ecclesiastical principalities (except for the very special case of the Papal states), was particularly striking. It did not take action against leading collaborators in and beneficiaries of Napoleon's control over Germany and Italy, such as Bavaria, Baden and Württemberg, or in central Italy. Although governments, led by Metternich in Vienna, moved swiftly against romantic and radical nationalist groups after 1815, the settlement also provided for more effective national organisation than ever before, in the German case. This constitutes the major difference between the German and Italian experiences.

The German Confederation, with all its limitations, was a much more effective institution than the old Holy Roman Empire. Provided that the two dominant states within the Confederation, Prussia and Austria, were in agreement, it provided an effective way of pursuing all-German policies and was used to intervene in the internal affairs of other German states. The reasons for the contrast with Italy are instructive. First, there was a different geo-political problem. Sandwiched between France and Russia it was essential for the German states to develop some limited unity of action to prevent the kind of division into spheres of influence which had taken place after 1807 and was only ended when France went to war with Russia. Second, there were *two* major powers in the region. They required some institutional framework through which to manage their joint hegemony over the German lands. In Italy the Habsburgs were unchallenged and could use a more informal set of arrangements. Finally, in the German case the Holy Roman Empire had shaped a political culture in which statesmen such as Stein, Hardenberg, Metternich and the German princes had grown up. Ironically, the vestigial 'imperial' idea could now be put to much more practical use because of Austro-Prussian dualism and the enhanced capacity for political co-ordination through a reduced number of modernising, territorial states.

The increased effectiveness of the Confederation, in fact, was one of the major stimuli to a national opposition after 1815 of far greater importance than the intellectual concerns with romantic and ethnic nationalism. Political opposition in the smaller German states was rather more advanced than in Prussia and Austria, partly owing to the impact of French reforms and influence. What is more, the limited constitutional concessions of the immediate post-1815 period provided these opposition groups, made up of small collections of liberal officials, some liberal nobles and businessmen, and some professional people, with opportunities to express themselves. This helped create a limited public opinion sympathetic to liberal reform as well as a much smaller circle espousing more radical ideas. At first these reforming groups were not nationalist and concentrated their attentions upon their particular states. But the use of the Confederation as an instrument for intervention against any constitutional reforms in any German state forced reformers to recognise a national dimension to their activity. Tentative connections were taken up between reformers in different states as well as in exile. Effective organisation beyond individual states had very limited success before 1848 but it did exist and it provided the leadership of a national movement in 1848. One component of this nationalism were minority interests, regional and confessional, created through the construction of larger territorial states – such as the Protestant region of the Rhenish Palatinate ruled by Bavaria or the Catholic population of the new Prussian province of the Rhineland. Given there was no direct route back to the old order, a national state could be seen as a defence against the alien state capital. The increased powers of territorial state interference intensified this perception.

The other major source of a national movement in Germany prior to 1848 was political opposition within Prussia. Although the king of Prussia had not granted his subjects a constitution after 1815, the government did pursue a range of policies which favoured the emergence of a state-wide liberal opposition movement. Policies of administrative and economic liberalism helped create clusters of liberal-minded businessmen and officials. The establishment of a system of provincial diets provided such groups with a limited platform upon which to develop limited co-operation and more precise political objectives. The calling of a United Diet in 1847 took this process one stage further. The liberal movement supported many aspects of Prussian policy, such as the creation of a customs union which bound together most German states by the early 1840s. However, they saw this customs union as the institutional base on which other forms of co-operation could be created, and they believed policies with these ends in view would be better carried out by a liberal, constitutional Prussian government. Equally, they could see in Prussia's increasing involvement in other parts of Germany a further stimulus to the liberal cause within Prussia. This liberal movement, therefore, looked forward to a gradual advance towards liberal institutions and social arrangements in which the Prussian and German levels of action would work together in a mutually reinforcing way. The major differences between liberal opposition in Prussia and that in the smaller German states was the much more positive evaluation by Prussian liberals of the role of the Prussian state.

Finally, the more effective territorial state system raised new expectations. The Customs Union more clearly delimited an economic 'Germany' from the external world and encouraged a sense of economic nationalism. The increasingly effective and co-ordinated way in which the states controlled the movement of artisans or imposed censorship, stimulated a strong negative sense of Germany as a land of un-freedom amongst journeymen and writers forced into exile. One should emphasise, however, that all these views were still in the process of formation by 1848, were confined to small elites, were held by people who were only loosely organised, and coexisted with many other currents of political thought in which the national dimension was absent.

In Italy this combination of liberalism and nationalism was much weaker and more localised. There was no equivalent of the German Confederation which could represent an existing national level of political action and at the same time stimulate opposition to move towards that national level. On the other hand, resentment of Austrian domination of Italy was particularly strong in the areas directly occupied, Lombardy and Venetia, and its influence was resented elsewhere, especially where it had directly interfered in defence of the status quo. But one should not over-emphasise the degree of opposition to Austria; above all, lack of organisation and internal division weakened it. For example, the liberal Lombard nobility, which played a leading role in criticism of Austria prior to 1848 and then in the revolution of 1848–49, looked to leadership from Piedmont and to the creation of an expanded Piedmontese dynasty in northern Italy in which they could play an important role. Liberal opponents of Austria

101

in Venice were enthusiastic about the liberal policies of the new Pope, Pius IX, but could also think in terms of restoring the republic which had been abolished in 1797. Indeed overall there was a strong 'restorationist' sense to opposition to the more modern and extended state of Lombardy-Venetia and some old elites could see in national opposition a chance to return to more localised forms of rule. This was also to be true of opposition movements in the south of Italy. Radical opponents of Piedmont, Austria and the Catholic church often thought in terms of reform at the level of the individual states and, if they conceived of any type of Italian political organisation, saw it in federal terms which best fitted in with Italian political traditions. Each oppositional element – whether restorationist, liberal or radical – tended therefore to think in local or state terms, lacking a larger political structure within which to organise. Piedmont, so much weaker relatively than Prussia, could hardly generate strong national leadership.

The weakness, internal division and loose organisation of any kind of national movement in comparison with Germany helped highlight the role of radical nationalism in Italy. This was expressed, above all, in the views and actions of Mazzini. Mazzini stood for an authentic nationalism. He believed that Europe was divided into a number of distinct nationalities and that the establishment of a series of nation-states expressed both the will of God and the will of the People (a word he usually capitalised). He worked tirelessly and courageously for his nationalist objective. Before 1848 much of this work consisted of conspiratorial activity, often with groups who were rather more opposed to particular restoration states than committed to a united Italy. His inspiration did bring into being a small band of devoted followers and a wide reputation but his direct influence upon Italian politics should not be exaggerated. His view of nationality as expressing the will of the people alienated figures such as Pope Pius IX and Charles Albert of Piedmont. Yet at the same time Mazzini never formulated any practical economic programme prior to 1848 which might have attracted middle-class support, or any programme of social reform which might have made his cause attractive at a popular level. Indeed, his strong anti-socialist views and his constant emphasis upon obligations rather than rights were criticised by radicals. Finally, his commitment to unification without outside intervention removed one means of bringing pressure to bear upon Austria-Hungary. Precisely because his pure nationalism had no diplomatic, dynastic, liberal or popular appeal it could not become the central element within a significant political movement. But in situations of uncertainty or despair, as in Milan in March-April 1848 or in Rome from November 1848 to June 1849, his influence could become much more important. Even then, his was only one political voice, as the arguments between him and other political activists in Milan in March/April 1848 demonstrates.

The sudden political breakdown of early 1848 had very little to do with nationalism. Certainly anti-Austrian feeling in Lombardy and Venetia was of major impòrtance, but subsequent events were to show just how difficult it was to channel it in a positive nationalist direction. However, the political breakdown did create a temporary power vacuum. Those with nationalist objectives now had the opportunity to try to fill the vacuum. What is striking is the very limited degree of success they had.

In Italy the separate states largely went their own different ways. No all-Italian political organisation was established. The fusion of Lombardy and Venetia with Piedmont was the one exception, but its (extremely short-lived) achievement was hardly related to nationalist purposes. From the point of view of Piedmont it was partly a matter of dynastic expansion and partly a concern to clamp down on radical tendencies in Lombardy and Venetia. In Lombardy and much of Venetia the local ruling class also accepted it in these terms and because to fight the Austrians by means of the Piedmontese army (and other regular forces such as those from the Papal states and from Naples) was less dangerous than some sort of *levée en masse*, with all its radical implications. Radicals in Lombardy and Venetia opposed fusion for precisely the same reasons, but they had very little political influence and the plebiscites overwhelmingly endorsed the fusion. The radicals in Milan were also dismayed by Mazzini's advice in April to accept Piedmontese leadership of the revolution and not to proclaim a republic in Lombardy. But Mazzini had hoped that political questions could be deferred until northern Italy was militarily secure. Charles Albert's pursuit of political fusion was seen, therefore, as a betrayal of the national cause by Mazzini, but by that time, with the radicals less influential than they had been during the insurrection in Milan in March and immediately afterwards, there was little that could be done to stop it. As it was, the military hopes that were invested in Piedmont soon proved illusory.

The other possible radical nationalist centre in northern Italy was Venice. But the leader of the Venetian revolution, Daniele Manin, although a genuinely popular figure and a republican, also acquiesced in the military leadership of Piedmont. The revolution in Venice took little account even of the needs of Venetia and soon became isolated. Later there was little co-operation with the republic in Rome, partly because Manin disliked its social radicalism and partly because of his hopes for some diplomatic solution in which France would take the initiative. The Roman republic, therefore, carried out its own revolution in isolation from other Italian states. In the Kingdom of Naples there was no co-operation between opposition groups on the mainland and in Sicily. In fact, liberals in Naples supported the suppression of what was regarded as a Sicilian separatist movement. In a peninsula which had never experienced political unity since the Roman Empire, in which the only really extensive political influences thereafter had been either externally controlled empires or the Papacy, and where the nationalist movement was unrelated to important or popular interests, this is hardly surprising. All that is surprising is that some observers subsequently have thought nationalism was of major importance or have regarded its failure as requiring elaborate explanation. That is not to say that the failure of revolution in Italy, which could have reduced the number of states, was inevitable: it certainly was not. The Austrian regime in the summer of 1848 seemed on the verge of dissolution, and even members of its own government regarded Lombardy as lost. But the force of Italian nationalism was not one of the reasons for that crisis, and it was not the defeat of nationalism in Italy that was important to the success of the counter-revolution.

In Germany nationalism achieved rather more because it was possible to build upon existing national institutions and the ties of political opposition they had stimulated. The liberal and radical elites which had been formed before 1848 were able to organise elections throughout the Confederation to a national parliament, which met in Frankfurt am Main in May 1848. Its task was to draw up a constitution for a German state. The majority of the parliament were liberal in their views, although there was considerable diversity within this liberal majority. These liberals had not fought the elections in any organised way; rather they were clusters of notable opposition figures who were returned as such to the parliament. They developed little in the way of party organisation during 1848. They tended to see their task as one of drawing up a constitution and implementing it by means of co-operation with the new regimes in the various German states, particularly Prussia and/or Austria. They were suspicious of mass politics and did not seek to create a popular following which would have given their views some independence from state governments. The radical minority tended to see the implementation of a constitution through popular pressure coming from below and went some way further towards creating popular political organisations. But most of this was organised at regional and state rather than national level. Generally there was little attempt to develop national political organisation from Frankfurt, and the immense moral authority which the assembly had initially commanded was allowed to slip away. It is problematic, therefore, to what extent the Frankfurt parliament was the centre of any nationalist movement as opposed to being a forum for the expression of views on the national question.

While matters were in flux in Prussia and Austria during the summer of 1848 the liberal majority in the parliament felt that it could not act effectively because the appropriate instruments – state governments – were not yet available. The simultaneous recovery of both Prussia and Austria in the autumn had the effect of splitting the liberal majority between policies which would appeal to Prussia or to Austria. The radicals supported the 'small Germany' solution of pro-Prussian liberals which would have excluded Austria from the new nation-state and made a hereditary German emperor out of the Prussian king. But this support was bought at the cost of incorporating radical features into the constitution on matters such as the emperor's rights of veto and the franchise for election to the lower house. These, along with fears of war with Austria, led Friedrich Wilhelm IV, the King of Prussia, to reject the constitution. Liberal advocates of the constitution, deprived of state support, gave up. Some of the radicals belatedly led resistance in favour of the imperial constitution in Saxony and south-west Germany but it was fairly easily put down by Prussian troops.

As in Italy it was not simply divisions between radicals and liberals that damaged the nationalist cause. New regimes in different states tended to concentrate on their own particular problems even to the extent of rejecting the views of those with similar general values in the Frankfurt parliament. So long as the control of armies lay with state governments their decisions were the ones that counted. What is more, members of the Frankfurt parliament divided on issues not simply in terms of direct differences over how radical or liberal the new nation-state should be. Other values such as those of religion or state influenced them: Austrian radicals as well as liberals in the assembly, for example, rejected a 'small Germany' solution.

There is an important difference of opinion among historians as to the sort of nationalism the parliament represented. For a long time the liberals in the assembly were regarded as unrealistic and/or as expressing a set of values sharply at odds with those displayed by the national regimes which were subsequently established in Germany in the form of the Second Empire and the Third Reich. In 1944, however, Namier argued that the Frankfurt parliament stood for nationalist values centring upon language and power which made it a precursor of those later forms of nationalism.[2] As I have argued that up to 1848 the sorts of nationalism emphasised by historians on account of their later significance were of no practical importance in Germany, to accept Namier's position would be very difficult. It is important, therefore, to look closely at this argument.

When one looks at the debates and decisions of the Frankfurt parliament in 1848/9 a number of things become clear. First, the greater part of the assembly's time and energy was devoted to the constitution. The central questions raised by the constitution were what rights should be enjoyed by the citizens of the new state and what political structure the state should have. The assembly was also concerned with the political questions posed by Prussian and Austrian rivalry. Second, there was a question mark about the boundaries of the new nation-state. Clearly the dispute over 'small Germany' and 'large Germany' arose less from differences over what was Germany proper than over the question of whether one inclined to Prussian or Austrian leadership in a united Germany. To opt for the 'small Germany' choice did not make one any less a nationalist.

The view of the assembly throughout its debates and as expressed in the final constitution was that, as a general principle, the boundaries of the German Confederation could be taken as the boundaries of the new German state. Nationality within that state was defined in terms of citizenship. The existence of language minorities (though their members would be Germans in the political sense of the word) was recognised and special educational concessions were made to them.

In other words the ways in which the boundaries of the new state were largely determined, and the rights enjoyed by members of the new state, made no reference to language or ethnic criteria. Germany was envisaged as an historic territorial unit with an already functioning if imperfect political system. German culture was recognised by members of the assembly as having played an important role in creating this state of affairs, but the new state was not regarded as the political expression of that cultural identity, however defined.

If this were all that was relevant to the matter it would be fairly easy to dismiss Namier's position. One could enter into a debate about the political realism, commitment and courage of German liberals, but that is not strictly relevant here. It is the quality of their nationalism that is relevant.

Two issues seem to support the argument that the nationalism of German liberals in 1848 was not really liberal: the disputes concerning Schleswig-Holstein and Posen. In these cases the Frankfurt parliament supported claims on the part of German-speakers in areas which were outside the Confederation. The fact that it did so and the manner in which some members of the assembly lauded German rights, German culture and German power can be used to support the case for an illiberal nationalism within the assembly. As the dispute over Posen also involved drawing a line of partition on the basis of language – an exercise rather commonplace in the twentieth century, when language and nationality have frequently been equated – it is on this case that I shall concentrate.

The Grand Duchy of Posen covered much of the area of the former state of Poland which Prussia had acquired. The majority of its inhabitants were Polish-speaking. In the western parts of Posen, however, and in many of the towns, there were German-speaking majorities. Some of these towns, especially the fortress town of Posen, were located in areas where there was a Polish majority in the surrounding countryside. Posen had been governed without regard for language differences up to 1848 and with the assistance of Polish magnates.

Many Prussian liberals sympathised with the demand for the restoration of the Polish state. Since the defeat of the uprising of 1830–31 in Congress Poland, which was under Russian control, the Polish cause had become a popular one among liberal and radical circles in western Europe (see next section on Poland). In the spring of 1848 the new liberal Prussian government allowed some autonomy to Posen in the hope of contributing to the cause of restoration. At this point the existence of German speakers in the Grand Duchy was not raised. Language was not seen as having any relevance to politics, and nationalism was understood in historic territorial terms. Equally these Prussian liberals did not see the Polish cause as putting into question Prussian rule in East and West Prussia, where there were substantial groups of Polish-speakers. It is worth remembering that the initial cause of the problem in Posen in 1848 was the commitment of Prussian liberals to non-ethnic Polish nationalism.

For various reasons the Prussian government soon backed away from support for the restoration of Poland. This left the Grand Duchy in something of a limbo. What is more, there were pressures demanding the re-incorporation of Posen into Prussia. German-speakers in the territory protested against their transfer to a Polish state. Others argued for the strategic importance of the fortress of Posen against Russia, especially if no Polish state was created which could act as a buffer. Yet others opposed what they regarded as a soft-minded and dangerous policy which had needlessly given up Prussian territory. Only the first of these pressures can properly be described as a form of German nationalism, and it was of subordinate importance.

In these circumstances the idea of partition represented a compromise between the original policy and the subsequent objections to it. It was in this way that the idea of a partition based on language came to be applied. The language criterion was in fact abused (although the urban German-rural Pole division made it impossible to apply properly anyway), and the small amount of territory left to the Poles was smaller than it should have been and was quite incapable of independent existence. Later, with the success of the counter-revolution, Posen was simply brought back as a whole into Prussia.

So far the policies described were those of the Prussian government; they related to Prussian rather than German interests and can be understood without introducing the issue of German nationalism. However, the Frankfurt parliament debated the matter and came down finally in favour of partition. Whether this had any practical import is questionable. But in the course of the debate some speakers did defend partition in nationalist terms. The speech of Wilhelm Jordan was particularly eloquent on the superiority of German culture in the eastern parts of Europe, on the civilising mission of Germans in the east, and on the rights due to power. It was a powerful if unattractive speech which mocked many cherished liberal values. Finally partition was approved. Much of Namier's argument is based upon sentiments expressed in the debate, such as those of Jordan, and the ultimate decision of the assembly.

However, Jordan's views were hardly typical. He had begun as a radical but had moved more and more to the right. In consequence he was something of a rogue figure in the assembly. Most of the radical left opposed partition, and it was one of their number, Robert Blum, who spelt out quite clearly the contradiction between the ethnic and the historic-territorial principles of nationality. Many of the deputies on the centre and the right voted for partition because they did not wish to go against declared Prussian policy. In any case, as Posen did not belong to the Confederation, it was felt that its treatment did not strictly affect the issue of the boundaries of a German state. Later, in September, when the question of Schleswig-Holstein was raised, it was the radical left which was most 'nationalist' and the right which was least so. But now Prussia was on the anti-nationalist side of the question and the principle was debated in terms of law and history, not in terms of language. Rather, therefore, than ascribing a single dominant nationalist sentiment to the assembly one must recognise the varied principles involved, the pragmatic aspects of the use of language and the support of that use with regard to Posen, and the restricted role these issues of disputed territory played among the concerns of the assembly.

The Posen affair was unique. The idea of using language as the basis of national boundary decisions was not raised elsewhere in 1848 and was not to be employed again until after the First World War. To raise it to the status of a general principle and to regard the views of men such as Jordan or the sentiments of borderland Germans in Posen and Schleswig as typical in 1848 is misleading.

In neither Germany nor Italy does nationalism appear to have had much popular appeal in 1848–49. This is difficult to demonstrate in the Italian case because there were fewer opportunities for the mass of the population to express their views. But there were some pointers. The plebiscites in Lombardy and Venetia in support of fusion with Piedmont were poorly supported, and the reasons for acceptance seem to have been based on the concern of local notables to obtain Piedmontese support against Austria and avoid any radical moves in the regions. The Italians who deserted in large numbers from the Austrian army in March 1848 seem to have done so not out of national loyalty but because the opportunity to break away from hated military service suddenly presented itself. By July some of the peasantry in Lombardy seemed to welcome the return of Radetzsky.

In Germany there were originally high hopes of the Frankfurt assembly, but they seem to have centred on the idea that parliament would impose popular social and economic policies on state governments or at least reduce the hold of those governments over regional and confessional minorities. As the assembly made its liberal position on social and economic questions increasingly clear and as, by contrast, state governments pushed through measures which met some of the demands made by peasants and artisans, so support for the assembly seems to have waned rapidly. The number of petitions sent had declined rapidly by mid-summer 1848 and by-elections were often more poorly supported or candidates were returned with narrow local interests mainly in mind. The campaign for the imperial constitution in May and June 1849 received limited support, and that more because of its radical than its national features. The radicals, who were best able to mobilise popular support, frequently depended upon tapping local interests and symbols to achieve this, and this also hindered their capacity to organise any widespread movement.

The failure of nationalism in Italy and Germany in 1848 was due to its limited appeal and its divided character rather than to the strength of the counter-revolution. The failure of revolution generally is another matter, because issues other than nationalism played a much more important part. This conclusion should hardly be surprising if one does not regard nationalism as a natural sentiment or a heady brew which people find irresistible when they taste it. To a largely agrarian population, with limited communications, little participation in politics, and divided among a multiplicity of states many of which were themselves new and best by regional divisions, it is difficult to see why the issue of national unification should have had any appeal or organised backing beyond particular opposition groups. And even then such groups were loosely organised, divided, and concerned with issues other than national unification alone.

The 'failure' of 1848 did, however, clarify matters. It underlined the incompatibility of Austrian interests with any policy of unification. This had always been clear to Italian nationalists, but not to Germans because of the dominance of Germans within the Habsburg empire. It also made clear to many the limitations of the nationalist movement and the great, if previously hidden, reserves of strength available to particular states. Some turned their attention to reform at state level. Some put their hope in some sort of popular movement, although they could not express this in practical terms. But many liberal nationalists drew the realistic conclusion that to be effective they had to gain support from Prussia and Piedmont. Only those states could confront and defeat Austria, and compel other states to join a national polity. They did come to play that role, but liberal nationalists were not primarily responsible for the fact.

1848 also led to increased tension between Austria and Prussia and the formulation of new policies to control their overlapping spheres of influence. The temporary prominence of a credible bid to establish a German state had provoked reactions amongst the spokesmen of non-German speaking cultural groups such as Czechs (see next chapter) and also stimulated national sentiments amongst 'borderland' Germans. Finally, repression of revolution altered the political situation. Again, a major difference between Germany and Italy needs to be noted. Repression was more effectively co-ordinated on a national level in the German case. At the same time concessions to moderate liberalism, especially in Prussia and Piedmont, provided a platform from which a national and liberal political movement could be built.

In Germany radical nationalists were bitterly opposed to any unification under the leadership of an unreformed Prussia which also excluded the Austrian parts of the Confederation. The result would be seen as Prussian imperialism rather than the true expression of German nationalism. Former radical nationalists like Wilhelm Liebknecht turned to socialism as a way of fighting the new state and were branded as unpatriotic. Liberal nationalists outside Prussia were often enthusiastic about obtaining Prussian support, because they could see no other way of bringing unification about. But although they could affect the policies of governments such as Baden this had little influence on the policies adopted by Prussia or their outcome. The most important positive nationalist influence on Prussian policy was that of Prussian liberals. As before 1848, they envisaged a liberal Prussia leading the way to unity. At the end of the 1850s they had exploited the imposed constitution of 1848 to create a genuine popular movement, by the standards of the time, which from 1858 had a majority in the lower chamber. The conflicts this created between crown and parliament finally led in September 1862 to the appointment of Bismarck as Minister President. The liberal opposition were appalled. Bismarck was regarded as a reactionary who stood in the way of liberal reform and who could play no positive part in the national question. They were confident he could not last long. His famous speech about solving issues by means of 'blood and iron' was received with incredulity and amusement rather than awe. As a consequence, the policies Bismarck pursued up to the war with Austria in 1866 were largely opposed by the liberals, although they led to national unification. By the time liberals recognised and acclaimed his achievement the only task that remained was to organise and complete the new state. Their role in the process was important because Bismarck's policies had alienated many former conservative supporters who could not approve of the violent destruction of the peace settlement of 1815.

Bismarck had not acted as he had because of any commitment to German nationalism. His actions were based on Prussian interests as he perceived them. The dualism between Austria and Prussia kept Prussia weaker than necessary. Since 1815 many things had tended to tip the balance of power in favour of Prussia. The international situation permitted limited use of Prussian power to turn this change to political advantage, provided it was justified in German rather than Prussian terms. The existence of liberal nationalist organisation throughout the German states played an important part. Bismarck also realised that Prussia's internal constitutional crisis could be settled by satisfying liberal opposition on the national issue.

In two respects Bismarck's much vaunted 'realism' was based upon an acceptance of modernity and led to the adoption, in some form, of the national idea. First, he rejected the idea of shared sovereignty over the German lands as a nonsense – the last vestiges of the old imperial ideology were thereby discarded. For Bismarck the powerful, territorially concentrated state alone could exercise power. Therefore the German lands must be divided between Prussia and Austria – the question was simply how this was to be achieved and where the dividing line would be drawn. Second, he recognised that the extended political class of a modern society, as Prussia was rapidly becoming in the early 1860s, could only be effectively handled through a constitutional system. To both justify Prussian expansion and to give it constitutional form, the national idea was essential. At the same time Bismarck did not see this in ethnic terms (wishing to preserve the Habsburg empire with its dominant German elite and to maintain a German cultural presence in other states, such as Russia). It was the territorial and constitutional changes envisaged which took Bismarck to the national idea.

As for the liberals, they were never prepared to mobilise popular opposition to the Prussian government and make the crisis an open conflict. Faced with a *fait accompli* on the national question, many of them accepted it. They justified acceptance with the arguments that there was no point in rejecting the indubitable progress Bismarck had made and that the unstable character of his achievement would push the new Germany further in a liberal direction. Bismarck's dependence on liberal support in the first decade of the new state seemed to confirm as much. This acceptance of a state which was not as liberal or as unitary as that envisaged in the constitution devised by the Frankfurt parliament in 1848–49 was more widespread among liberals outside Prussia, especially in the territories annexed in 1866–67, who were particularly dependent on Prussian initiative, than among 'old-Prussian' liberals, who could not easily forget the bitter conflicts with Bismarck between 1862 and 1866.

There is no evidence to suggest that national unification under Prussian leadership was popular. Most German states were on the Austrian side in the war of 1866. The Prussian case was put in terms of Prussian rather than German interests in the war manifesto. In the elections to the customs parliament which Bismarck convened in 1869 candidates firmly opposed to an extension of unity under Prussian control were returned from the south German states which remained outside the North German Confederation Bismarck had established in 1867. In that Confederation and in south Germany it was radical nationalists and, above all, anti-Prussian Catholics, as well as regional anti-Prussian groups, that commanded the most popular support. There was popular enthusiasm, it seems, for the war against France in 1870–71, though it must not be exaggerated. But enthusiasm for a war against a powerful foreign state which had been plausibly depicted as the aggressor was not the same thing as positive national support for the new Prussian-German state. Subsequently the two mass parties which developed in the Second Empire, the Catholic Centre Party and the Social Democratic Party, were both persecuted by Bismarck as anti-national.

The situation was not much different in Italy. Cavour, the moderate liberal Prime Minister of Piedmont during most of the 1850s, represented that brand of Italian 'nationalism' which looked to the creation of a north Italian state under Piedmontese control. There did exist a National Association (on the same lines as its German liberal imitator) with branches outside Piedmont which Cavour hoped to put to diplomatic use, but it proved disappointing. As in the German case its main contribution was to furnish a political leadership outside Piedmont for the new state, as well as to help legitimise that new creation by managing the referenda conducted in the central Italian states on joining with Piedmont in a Kingdom of Italy. However, far more important in the extension of Piedmontese control in north Italy in 1859–60 was French support in the war against Austria.

Cavour was even less prepared to bid for popular support for endorsement of his policies than Bismarck. This is not surprising: in the mid-nineteenth century moderate liberals were far more suspicious of mass electorates than were cynical conservatives like Bismarck who believed the illiberal sentiments and accessibility to conservative influence of the mass of the population could work to their advantage. Furthermore, the French alliance restrained Cavour from making any alliance with radical nationalism. Although some radical nationalists had always favoured French support, this had been envisaged as support from a radical regime in France, not from the plebiscitary dictatorship of Louis Napoleon. Cavour would have spurned such a radical ally, just as he so feared the radical role of Garibaldi, and he declared in 1860 that he would like to have Mazzini hung as a traitor.

The major problem with this interpretation is that Garibaldi did make a significant contribution to the cause of Italian unification in 1860. His intervention in Sicily ensured that unity was extended into central and southern Italy. Piedmont was compelled to invade the Papal states and to move south into the kingdom of Naples in order to bring Garibaldi's new regime under its control. This can easily be interpreted from a nationalist angle as demonstrating the popularity of the national cause in 1860. Cavour can be seen as a partner in the same cause as Garibaldi, or as the unwilling instrument of the national cause, or as the man who sought to suppress a popular radical nationalism.

None of these interpretations fits the facts. Cavour did not support Garibaldi's expedition to Sicily, which sailed from a Piedmontese port. Cavour knew that to prevent it would have caused trouble. There is dispute as to whether the Piedmontese navy made a serious attempt to intercept the expedition once it had set off. But in any case it seemed to have little chance of success. Certainly it is not necessary to assume any tacit collusion between Cavour and Garibaldi.

Garibaldi's amazing success in Sicily was due to the decrepit state of the Bourbon regime on the island. The speed of his invasion made it possible for both popular opposition and the propertied elements hostile to the regime to see in him an ally and a means of overthrowing the government. Only this general support could have enabled the pathetically weak military force under Garibaldi's command to take over the island. The support had nothing to do with the nationalist cause, which was weaker in the south, particularly in Sicily, than in any other part of Italy. It was purely to do with the domestic problems of the Bourbon regime. Indeed, it is reported that when the cry of *Viva Italia!* was raised during Victor Emmanuel's entry into Naples some natives thought it must refer to his wife. It was Garibaldi's willingness to give way to the Piedmontese thrust from the north in the name of Italian unity that took a domestic crisis into national politics.

This raises a general problem concerning the relationship between nationalism and more general political conflict. No nationalist movement is based on pure sentiment. All nationalist movements build upon a variety of interests. This is not to diminish the role of nationalism. It would be naive to imagine that any powerful political movement can be based entirely or even primarily upon sentiment, or commitment to ideology. One might then argue that it is wrong to dismiss the role of nationalism in the Italian case, in particular the role of Garibaldi, because that involves comparing what actually happened with some ideal and impossible image of a movement fuelled entirely by commitment to the nationalist vision. Since no such nationalist or indeed any significant political movement has ever existed, one could argue that the comparison is unreasonable.

However, a more reasonable comparison can be made. Ideology – and this applies to nationalist ideology – can play an important part in co-ordinating actions among political elites, mobilising popular support and legitimating the actions of a political movement. Such an ideology is not the sole reason for the nationalist commitment but it does provide inspiration and clarity, without which effective political action would be impossible. In performing such a role ideology becomes an integral part of a political movement, relating its ideas to the particular political conditions of the time. This is very different from a situation in which a nationalist movement intervenes effectively in a political conflict in which it has played no previous role and where its ideology is not closely related to the form taken by that conflict. This distinction is of practical importance. Where a nationalist movement has helped shape the language of political conflict it will continue to play an important role once the particular crisis has been

113

settled, even if the alliances which the nationalist movement helped construct break down. But where the link between supporting interests and the nationalist movement is purely external and contingent this will not be the case. With the end of the particular crisis which the nationalist movement catalysed or exploited the movement will quickly fade away, and the pre-existing interests and political languages will reassert themselves.

That is precisely what happened to Garibaldi. Despite his undoubted popularity there was no Garibaldian movement after 1860. It was not simply because he was a poor politician or because he was outmanoeuvred by Cavour and others, though such was the case. Nor was it because he was reluctant to play a part in Italian affairs after 1860. He was elected to parliament, expressed strong views on Italian affairs, and played an important part in bringing Rome into Italy by seeking to invade it on a number of occasions. But these arguments make too much of personality. More precisely, they fail to relate personality to situation. Garibaldi was a 'bad' politician because he had never been engaged in the construction of a political movement: he was not a political leader. Given that, there was no political movement after 1860 to sustain him. The concern with Rome was a continuation of the purely sentimental commitment prior to 1860 and no more of a contribution to constructing a political movement. Indeed, even radicals after 1860 recognised that obsession with unity was no substitute for building up a popular movement to challenge the political interests that gained from unity. But, conversely, it was precisely Garibaldi's lack of concern with political matters that explains his success. No 'realistic' politician would have embarked on the ventures he devised. Equally, such adventures were not the stuff of which political movements are made. The inability of radical nationalists, for example, to channel southern resentment of the policies of the new state is a sure sign of just how unimportant radical nationalism was as a political movement in contributing to Italian unity.

Historians have overestimated the chances of radical nationalism leading the way to unity in Germany and Italy. But nationalism was never a popular idea before unification, and the obstacles in the way of radical nationalism were insuperable. The only important functions nationalism could play were in helping to co-ordinate the efforts of various liberal elites to establish the new state in the first years of its existence and to legitimate the formation of that state in the eyes of foreign governments such as Britain and France and their influential public opinions. To analyse Germany or Italy as 'flawed' nation states because they did not possess the features considered appropriate to a 'proper' nation-state is to apply an impossible standard. It is alright as a purely moral judgement, but historians can apply critical standards only in the light of what was reasonably possible. Only if an existing state had been prepared to lead unification from above would it have been reasonably possible, and nationalism must, therefore, be evaluated in the light of its contribution to promoting such a policy.

However, it would also be wrong to see 'nation'-state formation as accidental or purely the result of statecraft and traditional territorial ambitions. In both the Italian and German cases the need to bring modern elites together to help run the new state required that a constitutional order be created rather than simply a system of annexation, and either the imposition of the conquering state's institutions or confirmation of those of the conquered province. Those options were also unacceptable to the modern states of Britain and France whose support or at least neutrality was essential. The language of nationality was central to the task of fusing the principles of territoriality and constitutionalism. However, in particularly backward areas such as the Italian South, the major purpose of the constitutional order was not to help introduce modern principles of politics, but rather to impose as much control as possible. This would markedly affect the extent to which a common sense of national identity, still a prospect for the future rather than a present reality, could be developed. The major differences between Italy and Germany in this regard can still be discerned in the contrasting forms taken by fascism, as we shall see in chapter 15.

2 The Polish case

The nationalist movement to restore the old Polish state was most important in those areas and among those groups with the closest connections to the historic kingdom of Poland, which had only been finally laid to rest in the later eighteenth century. The group with the closest connections was the nobility. This was a very large and diverse element in Polish society. It was the lesser and middling nobility who were of particular importance. The great magnates could find political positions under the partitioning powers, but not many of the rest of the nobility could. At the same time many of this class had not suffered economically. The most important legal changes which might have undermined the control of the nobility *(szlachta)* over the land had been the introduction of the Code Napoléon. It continued unmodified in the Russian-controlled area, Congress Poland, from 1815 to 1846 and was interpreted in a way which favoured the *szlachta*. In the areas brought back under Prussian and Austrian control after 1815 the French code was replaced with other legal codes but these were hardly less favourable. Rather more control was exercised politically by central government in these two cases, and there were some moderate land reforms but not such as to undermine the position of the bulk of the *szlachta*. So this group remained, resentful over the loss of political importance but still capable of playing a prominent part in affairs. It is a general truth that it is not the repressed who lead political oppositions; the story of Poland (= all Poles) as a repressed people is a myth and, if it had been true, there could have been no nationalist opposition of the kind that did take shape in the mid-nineteenth century.

There were also important political continuities from the eighteenth century. With the establishment of the Grand Duchy of Warsaw Napoleon had provided the *szlachta* with a new political role. This was not brought to an end in 1815. Although Russia absorbed some of the territory formerly belonging to the Polish kingdom into her own western territories, the bulk of it was organised in the form of a separate kingdom, commonly known as Congress Poland, which was joined to Russia by personal union. This kingdom had its own constitution, its own university, even its own army, and was granted a remarkable degree of autonomy in the years immediately after 1815. Posen and Galicia, the areas under Prussian and Austrian control respectively, were brought much more directly under the central government, although also retaining separate political identities in the form of a Grand Duchy and a Kingdom respectively. The city of Cracow, nominally free until 1846, was brought under Austrian control after the failed uprising of 1846.

Political control in all cases was secured by obtaining the collaboration of the great magnates, who in turn had networks of clients among the lesser nobility. But with the support they received from central government the magnates did not need to pay too much attention to maintaining their networks in good condition. Hence among the middling ranks of the nobility were people with the capacity and inclination to seek a restoration of historic Poland.

The focus of such opposition was in the areas with the greatest autonomy. The rising of 1794 came from the rump state of Poland which remained after the first two partitions. The insurrections of 1830–31 and 1863 were centred in Congress Poland. Other parts of historic Poland played a much less important role. In those areas absorbed into western Russia nationalist *szlachta* were able only to follow initiatives taken in Congress Poland. In Posen the nationalist movement flickered ineffectively in 1846. In 1848 it was more owing to support from outside, above all from Prussian liberals, that it achieved anything.[3] The limited autonomy of Cracow up to 1846 helps explain its pre-eminence in the nationalist movement. Finally, the szlachta in western Galicia, with considerable assistance from exiles, did spark off an insurrection in 1846. This was the major nationalist action outside Congress Poland. However, the social base of the movement was so narrow that it was destroyed by a peasant *jacquerie* in which over a thousand landowners were murdered, especially in eastern Galicia where peasants did not even share the Polish language with their masters. Restoration nationalism ceased to be important in Galicia thereafter. The Galician episode was to haunt nationalist landowners. It could also be brandished as a possible governmental response to nationalism, although the Habsburgs had not pursued that policy in 1846 and, until the 1863 insurrection, no other government was prepared to do more than threaten to exploit the peasants' hatred of their lords, in order to enforce good conduct on nobles. As we shall see, when governments did act in that way, they secured political stability in the short-term but created the conditions for a peasant-based nationalism in the longer term.[4]

So far one could argue that the political movement for the restoration of Poland can hardly be seen as particularly modern. The type of social and national consciousness it represented had long existed among the Polish *szlachta*. The 'nation' was defined in narrow terms, and the movement can be seen simply in terms of privileged nobles seeking, through restoration, to reassert their political position. However, successive defeats of this aim led to the adoption of an increasingly radical programme by a minority of the *szlachta*. Only popular support, it was felt, could provide the force to achieve success. The idea of extending limited political rights and making economic reforms, above all on the issue of land tenure, extended the national idea beyond the ranks of the *szlachta*. Particularly for those forced into exile, or for the small urban intelligentsia in towns such as Warsaw and Cracow, these sorts of programmes presented no great conflict of interests. The bulk of the nationalist *szlachta* remained a good deal more cautious about the promises that were made to win support but remained tied to the general aim of obtaining autonomy, at least, and inhibited from collaboration with the occupying powers. What is more, the Catholic clergy were also prepared to support action against non-Catholic powers such as Prussia and, above all, Russia. So nationalism could be broadened to bring in a range of interests beyond the *szlachta*.

At the same time there is no doubt that after 1815 the development of romantic and radical nationalist ideas in western Europe did have an impact on the ideology of Polish nationalism. The idea of Poland as a single nation with a mission to redeem itself had become commonplace by the 1830s. However, this feeling was rarely expressed in terms of ethnic or linguistic characteristics. Such criteria would have contradicted the objective of restoring historic Poland, a kingdom which incorporated a number of different language and ethnic groups.

Nationalism, therefore, radiated out from the *szlachta* groups with the most direct links to the historic kingdom of Poland and with the capacity and inclination to lead an effective movement. Such a capacity was greatest in those areas with the greatest political autonomy. The claims of this szlachta group had been broadened and radicalised by the adoption of a properly nationalist programme after 1815 but that group remained of central importance to the whole movement. These points can be examined concretely by looking briefly at the insurrections of 1830–31 and 1863. Then one can compare the Polish with the German and Italian cases

117

and draw some general conclusions about unification nationalism in Europe.

In 1830, following the news of the July revolution in France, radical elements in Warsaw were able to create disturbances in the city. The lack of Russian intervention and the taking over of the resistance by moderate and better known figures drawn from the nobility sustained the momentum of this movement and extended it beyond Warsaw. Now a szlachta-led movement called together a diet which was also dominated by *szlachta*. True to Polish traditions, the diet was divided and failed to act in any decisive way. No serious attempt was made to obtain popular or international support. The Russians restored control fairly easily once they had decided to intervene. What this episode showed was that important elements from the szlachta were prepared to defy Russian control. They could turn a limited, urban disturbance into a more significant challenge. At the same time, the moral obloquy associated with collaboration with the Russians inhibited any effective prevention of this resistance from within Polish society. Yet once resistance had been initiated the *szlachta* leadership was not prepared to give the movement the organisation or programme necessary if it was to have any chance of success. This political irresponsibility on the part of the *szlachta* was to dog the nationalist movement throughout the period that this class remained the leading element. One should also note the international features which sustained Polish nationalism in this period. There was the assumed connection between revolution in France and the Polish cause, as evidenced by 1830–31 and again in 1848. There was also enthusiasm for the Polish cause in France, Britain, and the German states, which was expressed not merely in radical circles, but, for example in the British case, amongst influential Whig groups. This in turn stimulated great fear in the governments of the partitioning powers, as was again made particularly clear in 1830–31.

Re-imposition of control by Russia was remarkably mild in the circumstances. Political autonomy was reduced and independent institutions such as the army and university were abolished. But separate constitutional existence continued and the economic basis of the *szlachta* as a whole was not attacked. The focus of the nationalist movement shifted into exile. There two distinct currents can be discerned. The more moderate elements, associated with the dissident magnate Czartoryski, sought international support from France and Britain. Liberal sympathy for them was strong in those countries and their cause was well publicised. More radically-minded exiles tried to work out an agrarian programme which would secure peasant support. These exiles were very popular among radical and early socialist circles in France and Britain and elsewhere in western Europe. But they had little effect upon events in Congress Poland. Only internal changes could favour further action there, and that only came in the 1850s. The cautious programme of reform undertaken after the Cri-

118

mean war and the death of Czar Nicholas I in 1856 provided the necessary conditions. Elements of the Polish nobility were drawn into consultation over reforms, above all those touching the emancipation of the peasantry. At the same time as this was happening, a more radical movement, building upon exile programmes and with some popular support among the depressed intelligentsia and artisans of Warsaw, sought to force events further. They succeeded in organising popular demonstrations in the city. Again the szlachta, although not a party to the movement, felt pressured by it into raising their own demands and to begin retreating from the prospects of co-operation with a Russian-inspired reform movement. Initially the Russian response was to rely upon Polish collaborators led by the magnate Wielopolski. But his attempts to push through a limited programme of reform in 1862 received no united support from either *szlachta* or clergy, who remained anti-Russian and concerned not to appear compromised as traitors. In Warsaw the radicals continued to build up their organisation. Matters came to a head when Wielopoloski and the Russians decided to take repressive measures against the radicals. This sparked off an insurrection and forced members of the *szlachta* to choose sides. Many decided to assist the insurrectionary movement. This brought them immediately into the leadership. It made the insurrection politically more significant but led at the same time to a moderating of the agrarian programme originally adopted by the radicals. The insurrection, in fact, received only limited peasant support and in some cases nationalist guerillas executed peasants suspected of co-operating with the Russians. The insurrection lasted as long as it did mainly because of the initial reluctance of the Russian government to incur the international odium which would follow military repression. Once its reluctance was overcome the repression proceeded fairly easily.

Subsequent Russian policies destroyed the basis of restoration nationalism. Political autonomy was drastically reduced. Above all the Russians pushed through a land reform and peasant emancipation programme far more radical than anything undertaken in Russia itself. The result was to destroy the *szlachta* as a class and bring to the fore in the countryside a class of peasant proprietors. In the short run this eliminated any prospect of a challenge to Russian control and certainly meant that any subsequent challenge would not be motivated primarily by the desire to restore historic Poland.

However, this also meant that the system of 'indirect rule' which could be pursued through separate constitutional arrangements and a class of noble collaborators was at an end. More direct methods of government were required. This and a later, related Russification policy stimulated new nationalist responses far more popular and radical than anything the *szlachta* was able to inspire. But it had only rhetorical connections with the older form of nationalism; was very different from what existed in

119

Posen and Galicia; and is better understood as simply a form of separatist nationalism aimed against Russia. These events also show why, apart from a commitment to the values associated with noble pre-eminence, the Austrian and Prussian governments were wisely never prepared seriously to challenge the economic position of local nobilities, no matter how big a nuisance nationalist elements within that nobility might prove.

What was unique about restoration nationalism in Poland was its close and concrete links with what it sought to restore. This, as well as the *szlachta* leadership, gave it its political significance. Political autonomy, as it existed in Congress Poland, enabled this leadership to mount a challenge to the occupying power. Nationalism brought in other groups which made important contributions (especially the radicals in exile and in Warsaw) but the movement never really succeeded in breaking beyond its original social confines in the countryside. The common social leadership in the different occupied areas, the co-operation in exile, and the close connections to the historic kingdom, meant that the movement never simply broke up into separate parts although it had very different characteristics and opportunities under the various occupying powers. However, with the destruction of its social position in Congress Poland, the heart of restoration nationalism was destroyed and henceforth it was specific conditions in the different states which shaped Polish nationalism.

3 Conclusion

These nationalist movements were confined to fairly small social and political elites. The few attempts to create a popular basis for them were ineffective. Although radical nationalism could have an important effect as a catalyst of change, this could be channelled in a positive direction only by more moderate nationalists. All three movements had a good deal of sympathy from governments and public opinion in western Europe. Nationalism was identified with the search for liberal constitutional government against the illiberal regimes of Austria and Russia and, to a lesser extent, Prussia.

The objective of unification was remote from popular interests. Such interests could often obtain reform through the existing states. The numbers of those within the ranks of the nationalist movement prepared to bid for popular support were limited. The nationalist movements were primarily elite movements. Given the variety of conditions in the different political units this is to be expected.

In Germany and Italy the liberal elites which subscribed to the programme of national unity were fragmented and lacking in social or political authority. This led them to look to existing states for support. Gradually they became entangled in the concerns of those states which pursued the objective of unification for their own ends. But the legitimating

120

function of nationalism in the eyes of France and Britain as well as the support these liberal nationalists could provide to the new nation-state were of importance to the success of unification. Generally speaking, the co-ordination function was rather more important in the German case and the legitimation function in the Italian case.

In Poland, especially in Congress Poland, the *szlachta* elite which supported restoration nationalism was more unified and had more authority than the elites which took up the national idea in Germany and Italy. The *szlachta* also had to act against rather than with the governments which controlled them. This made nationalism more effective but at the same time presented it with much greater problems.

All three nationalist movements tended to define their objective in historical-cum-territorial terms: the German Confederation, the peninsula south of the Alps, the historic kingdom of Poland. These areas included linguistic minorities. But that was not felt to be a problem. Nationality simply was not thought of in such terms. The minority groups in question had barely begun to assert their own claims. The nationalism of the Poles and Germans and Italians came from dominant cultural groups, to whom, therefore, cultural divisions seemed invisible or unimportant.

This also meant that such a nationalism represented a transition from older to newer forms of politics. In Lombardy and in Poland the leading role in nationalism was taken by liberal nobles. The demand for constitutional government could be seen as a new way of seeking the sorts of local noble political power which such groups had possessed at some point in the eighteenth century. It was a response against a government which had undermined that power and which was increasingly drawing a sharp distinction between economic privilege and pre-eminence on the one hand and political power on the other. At the same time the support from western Europe for political justifications couched in liberal and national terms, as well as the radicalising effects of earlier failures, pushed these movements towards a new rhetoric, new alliances with urban interests and, less successfully, with peasants – and, therefore, into a more properly nationalist movement. This was partly the case in Germany as well. Here state reform, especially in Prussia, in Bavaria, in Baden and Württemberg, had also drawn a sharper distinction between economic privilege and political power. Although the leading figures in the moves towards unity were bourgeois, one must not forget how well supported the Prussian liberal movement was, for example, among landowners in eastern parts of the state in the 1850s.

This points to a final characteristic of unification nationalism. Such a nationalist movement must be both effective in individual states as well as extending beyond them. This is very difficult. Increasingly conditions will come to favour the development of the nationalist movement in one state rather than another. Gradually the nationalist movement will come

121

to mirror conditions in that state. It will tend to become the ally of a particular state (as with Piedmont and Prussia) or the opposition to it (as in Congress Poland) or a mixture (as in Lombardy) of the two. To understand why this happens one must understand that conditions in such states both necessitate and permit a new sort of political action. In that political action nationalism – though often in ways which link it to older objectives – can come to play a part.

The new nation-states of Germany and Italy lacked much of what we would understand by the term 'national'. The more dominant role of Prussia and prior developments towards a national economic and political system meant that Germany could adopt a rather loose, federal structure in which state rights and particularist identities were respected. The new state acquired new powers but more for immediate functional purposes than as part of a 'nation-building' programme. These powers and the extensive system of political participation encouraged political organisation increasingly to develop a national focus. In this way a process of national integration took place, even if many of those political organisations opposed the actual regime, which found it difficult to accept many of the implications of national integration.

In Italy, by contrast, the weak position of Piedmont and the highly regionalised and often backward character of politics led to a highly elitist politics of centralisation, in a desperate attempt to inhibit the centrifugal forces at work. However, such policies exacerbated rather than overcame regional differences, especially in the south. By the end of the century it was clear that, though an Italian state had been formed, the project of making Italians still had a long way to go.

Notes

1   E. Kedourie, *Nationalism* (London, 3rd ed., 1966) argues this case forcefully.
2   L. B. Namier, *1848: the revolution of the intellectuals* (London, 1946). This was a greatly expanded version of the Raleigh Lecture in History given in London in 1944.
3   See above, pp. 106–8.
4   A comparative study of these governmental options would be worth undertaking. Radetzsky threatened such a policy in northern Italy after restoring military control in 1849, but did not actually carry through the radical land reform programme that must be at the heart of such a policy. Metternich and Vienna had occasionally threatened such a policy in Hungarian Diets before 1848 but pursued a pro-magnate policy in economic terms after the Hungarian revolution was repressed. The key question is: was either the dynasty or the national nobility prepared to play the peasant card?

5

Separatist nationalism
in nineteenth-century Europe

1 Introduction

In this chapter I consider a number of separatist nationalist movements in the Habsburg and Ottoman empires. Many other such movements, for example in Britain, Scandinavia and Russia, are not taken into account. However, not only do these two multi-national empires offer a fairly comprehensive range of case studies but also comparison between them is of special value. Apart from certain basic and important differences and similarities, the two empires bordered on each other and both included members of the same 'nations'. Consequently one can see, through controlled comparison, how important was the common factor of nationality in the way nationalist movements developed in them. The analysis of these cases supports two central arguments. First, there is a general tendency for the initial nationalist response to come from culturally dominant groups. These nationalist movements express their case in historic territorial terms. They tend to promote, as a reaction, nationalist movements among culturally subordinate groups which express their case in ethnic and linguistic terms.

Second, there was a fundamental difference between the nationalist movements in the two empires. In the Habsburg empire the internal functions of co-ordination and mobilisation were of particular importance and the ideology of nationalism was highly developed. In the Ottoman empire the external function of legitimacy was of particular importance, and much of the ideological justification of the movement was taken over from elsewhere, especially the nationalist ideas elaborated in the Habsburg empire. Yet, although its internal functions were more weakly developed, nationalism in the Ottoman empire was more successful than in the Habsburg empire, at least until 1918. These basic differences are related to a range of differences between the two empires in the conclusion to the chapter, but the central difference, it is argued, was between the structure of the state in the two cases.

The basic similarity between the two empires is that they included a great variety of different cultural groups. Members of some of these groups, such as the Turks (or, more accurately, Ottomans) and the Greeks, the Magyars and the Germans, occupied a superior position. Others, such as the Czechs and the Bulgarians, were subordinate and were wholly located in one or other empire. Yet others, notably the Serbians and the Rumanians, occupied subordinate positions and were located in both empires. It is on the basis of these different situations that the cases considered in this chapter are selected. From the outset one should remember that, until nationalism became important, the cultural distinctions were often vague and were not always seen as national distinctions.

There were some important basic differences between the two empires. Most of the European subjects of both were Christians, principally Catholic, Greek Orthodox and Uniate,[1] as well as significant Protestant minorities in the Habsburg Empire. The bulk of the Catholic, Protestant and Uniate groups were in the Habsburg Empire; of those who followed the Greek Orthodox faith, most were in the Ottoman Empire. The Habsburg government was a Christian state dominated by Catholics; the Ottoman government was Muslim. However, in the European parts of the Ottoman empire the Greek Orthodox church played an important part in government.

The Habsburg state could broadly be described as a feudal one which subsequently developed absolutist and constitutional features.[2] The Ottoman Empire could not be epitomised in this way, although alternative shorthand labels such as 'decaying military despotism' or 'centralised bureaucracy' tend to miss important features of the state such as its use of religious identity and institutions and the type of informal collaborator system it operated in many areas.

With these broad comparisons in mind (others will be made in the conclusion) a range of cases can be examined. I look at seven in varying detail under five groupings: the Magyars; the Czechs and Croatians; the Serbians and Rumanians; the Bulgarians; the Greeks. These groupings correspond to the distinctions made earlier between dominant and subordinate positions, and to whether the subordinate group was divided between the two empires or not. Two important cases are not considered: those of the Germans and the Ottomans. As the dominant cultural group in each case, separatist nationalism had little appeal for either, and a sense of distinct national identity was related to the need to maintain imperial power. I do consider Turkish nationalism from a different perspective in chapter 11.

124

2 Case studies

(a) The Magyars

Hungary had been brought under Habsburg control in the early modern period. By the end of the eighteenth century the historic kingdom of Hungary was split into a number of areas. There was Hungary proper, Transylvania, Croatia, parts of south-east Hungary occupied by Serbians with some degree of autonomy, and the military border areas which were controlled directly from Vienna.

In the eastern (transleithian) half of the empire by the mid-nineteenth century the Magyar-speaking population was larger than any other language group but made up only about a third of a total population of some 13.5 million. Magyar-speakers were in an absolute majority in Hungary proper, where most of the peasantry were Magyar-speaking. Elsewhere the Magyar-speakers were found predominantly in the higher, non-peasant parts of the population.

Hungary proper was bound to the Habsburgs legally by the Pragmatic Sanction of 1723. It had its own constitution and a Diet which could propose legislation to the emperor (or rather the king of Hungary, as he was officially in Hungary). The diet was dominated by the Magyars: the upper house by the great magnates and the lower by the numerous middling gentry. The diet had interests that extended beyond Hungary proper. For example, the Croatian diet sent delegates to the Hungarian diet. Magyars also occupied positions of power outside Hungary itself. Membership of the Transylvanian diet, for example, was divided between the three 'nations' of the Magyars, the Saxons and the Szekels. Within Hungary proper, and to some extent elsewhere, Magyar gentry had considerable authority in local affairs and ran the county governments.

The Magyars, especially the nobility, had a good deal of power at both local and national level, particularly in Hungary proper, and occupied a privileged position in the eastern half of the empire. Many Magyar magnates welcomed the ties with the Habsburg Empire, which provided them with protection against possible Russian and Ottoman threats. Magyar nationalism was hardly a response to oppression in the usual sense.

Its impetus came from above. It was the product of attempts at reform by the imperial government which encroached upon the privileged. Joseph II (1780–90) was the most extreme example of the attempt by a monarch to transform society and state on the basis of rational principles. His efforts threatened the Magyar position, particularly that of the nobility, in a number of ways.

Joseph attempted to make German the official language of government throughout the empire. It was the natural choice if there was to be one official language, as the rational principle of efficient government suggested there should. Naturally it was resented by Magyar-speakers, who

125

regarded it both as an affront and as a measure which put them at a disadvantage in relation to native speakers of German. This led them to lay greater emphasis upon the Magyar language. Magyars had originally used Latin in the proceedings of the Hungarian diet. Faced with the threatened use of German, they riposted by pressing for the replacement of Latin by Magyar. This in turn aroused the hostility of the Croatians, who sent deputies to the diet. In this way a reform motivated by universal principles contributed to an intensified concern with vernacular languages and the divisions between language groups.

Joseph also sought to interfere in the relationship between lord and peasant. He wished to end the onerous system of Robot or labour services, which he believed depressed agricultural productivity and hence the tax revenue of the state as well as rendering the peasantry less fit for military service. Peasants welcomed the reforms but threatened to take things further. The nobles resisted, feeling threatened both from above and from below – particularly where the divisions between lord and peasant coincided with divisions between Magyars and non-Magyars and could thus add fuel to the flames of any nationalist movement.

Joseph also pressed for church and educational reforms, which could have had the same effect. He wanted to see children educated in their vernacular language, which would have meant placing a much greater emphasis upon the use of non-Magyar languages in the eastern part of the empire. He wished to reduce the degree of subordination suffered by the Greek Orthodox and Uniate churches, and this again could be seen as a threat to the Catholic and Protestant Magyar communities.

As a consequence of these attempts at reform, Magyars, particularly those with privileges, felt threatened both from above and below. For some the appropriate response was little more than a narrow defence of traditional privilege in established ways. But others concluded that a new and more serious menace required new and more effective resistance. The sort of conclusions such men could arrive at can be illustrated by considering the ideas and actions of Stephen Szechenyi (1791–1860) and Louis Kossuth (1802–94).

Szechenyi was a great magnate and a man of learning with a highly cultured, cosmopolitan understanding. He was able to look at the problems confronting Magyars in a new way. He was haunted by Herder's prediction that they were a doomed people, threatened by Germans from above and Slavs from below. Only progressive adaptation, he believed, could save them. In a number of influential books he urged that the Magyars – above all, the nobility – should take the lead in introducing economic reforms. Labour services, entail and the virtual caste division of labour were inefficient and under increasing pressure. It was therefore in the enlightened interest of the noble landowner to end these practices by means of voluntary agreements with his peasants. Thus a transformed

Magyar nobility could preserve much of its position. In this gradualist way (with many other economic reforms also suggested) Szechenyi approved of much of the Josephine reform programme and envisaged such progressive reform taking place in the context of a political partnership between nobility and imperial government.

By the 1820s his ideas were beginning to have some impact. More enlightened noble landowners did see that a free labour force could serve their own interests better than a tied one and that some reform was in any case unavoidable. The imperial government had retreated from the headlong pace of reform set by Joseph II. It seemed that matters might now proceed in a gradual, liberal and negotiated manner. Szechenyi optimistically believed that in the eastern part of the empire the cultural superiority of the Magyars would transform and assimilate non-Magyars as they acquired greater freedom and advanced in society. To ensure this, however, it would be necessary to develop Magyar culture to the highest degree. Szechenyi was one of the founders of the Hungarian Academy of Science, which set itself this task. Given this optimism, he was not averse to granting some degree of local autonomy to other language groups.

But his optimism proved unjustified. Many Magyar landowners, unable to take the risks of adjustment which large magnates could contemplate, opposed agrarian reform. The imperial government under Metternich blocked the path of gradual change for fear of its revolutionary consequences. This failure (although the diets of the 1830s and 1840s did achieve a good deal) stimulated more radical ideas which were typified by Kossuth. A minor noble, lawyer and political journalist, he believed that the Magyar elite had to mobilise popular support if it was to preserve its position. He advocated a sweeping land reform programme, other grandiose but vague economic projects, and political changes which would have made government in Hungary more independent and more democratic. His main support came from the lesser gentry, who felt excluded from political power by the partnership between imperial government and magnates. Kossuth never moved, before 1848, to a position more radical than would serve the interests of this class. But there was also some urban support for his views, especially among the small intelligentsia of Pest and Buda.

This more radical approach could lead to conflict in two directions. It might provoke opposition from a conservative imperial government, magnates and even elements of the lesser nobility. Already by 1847 it looked as if the imperial government might ally with a conservative reform party to head off political threats. Such rapid change could also bring many non-Magyar-speakers into political participation. To guard against the first possibility Kossuth tried to stimulate Magyar political opposition, focusing particularly on the gentry control of county government. To avoid the second he proposed a strong defence of Magyar culture, for example by insisting on the use of Magyar in schools and government.

127

Although the differences between Kossuth and Szechenyi had become clear by 1848, they both worked within the same broad set of assumptions. Neither envisaged Hungary gaining independence from the Habsburgs or the planned reforms undermining the leading position of the nobility. Neither really created what could be called a political movement. Their different ideas were supported informally by various groups in the periodically convened meetings of the diet. Szechenyi helped organise a new type of political meeting, the Casino, where discussion could take place. As a journalist and editor Kossuth became the nearest thing there was in Hungary to a professional opposition politician. But both exerted their influence through personal contacts and public advocacy of their ideas rather than through the medium of a political organisation.

In 1848 this political opposition was quick to exploit the general breakdown of authority in March 1848, though the most violent confrontations to the Habsburgs had come in Milan and Vienna. A new Hungarian government passed a series of reform measures, known as the April Laws, which were approved by the emperor Ferdinand in his capacity as king of Hungary. The April Laws provided for the abolition of labour services, with state-aided compensation, the integration of Transylvania into Hungary (Croatia would enjoy limited autonomy) and the transfer of most political authority from Vienna to Hungary. In short it envisaged the establishment of a liberal, constitutional version of the historic kingdom of Hungary bound to the Habsburgs only by personal union. Vital provisions concerning control over finance, foreign policy and the armed forces remained ambiguous and left it uncertain how much power would really remain in Vienna. At first, in the general crisis of the spring of 1848, the imperial government had little choice but to accept Hungarian demands and a government was set up under the leadership of Batthanyi, with Kossuth and Szechenyi in the Cabinet.

But the instability of the settlement had to be decided one way or another. During the summer of 1848 the imperial government began to regain confidence, and tensions between it and the Hungarian government deepened. In any conflict with the Magyars the imperial government had a number of resources. The Magyar nobility had no desire to engage in revolution, and as long as possible sought to emphasise their loyalty. When the situation became one of outright conflict many Magyars abandoned the nationalist cause, and those who remained were divided between moderates defending the April Laws and radicals who believed it was necessary to go much further. This radicalism was itself weakened, however, by the interests of the gentry, which precluded reforms that would destroy its own position. In addition the Habsburgs continued to command fairly substantial bodies of loyal troops. Finally, the Magyar cause was opposed by many non-Magyars, in particular the Croatians and the Rumanians.

128

This last point is of particular interest. The new government was adamant in its insistence on the use of Magyar as the official language and as the medium of education. It insisted too on a single government, and not a federated system. To non-Magyars, particularly outside Hungary proper, where they were in the majority, all this could appear as a way of ensuring Magyar dominance. In addition to the many individual rights created by the April Laws these groups began to insist on certain collective rights based on nationality. They in turn were condemned by the Magyars as illiberal and nationalist. At the same time the Habsburg government held out a vague prospect of greater autonomy in various parts of the empire to attract non-Magyar support.

It is worth noting the different Magyar attitudes to these different national claims, and the results. Demands for autonomy in Croatia were regarded as valid, since the country had an historic identity, its own diet and a native nobility. Yet at the same time the Croatians were the most vehemently opposed to any sort of Hungarian state, and it is difficult to see how their antagonism could have been avoided. On the other hand, the Rumanian claim to autonomy and national recognition was rejected by the Magyars. It came from non-noble groups who had no institutional authority, made up overwhelmingly of peasants, and without any recognised historic identity.[3] It was couched primarily in linguistic terms. The view of the Magyars was simply that political claims could not be justified in this way. Yet the Rumanians did not begin with so intransigent an opposition to the Hungarian cause as the Croatians, and a more conciliatory approach could perhaps have prevented the moves towards Rumanian military action against the Hungarian army. The important point is that this view was not just a matter of 'interest'; rather it showed how interest was defined by certain intellectual assumptions.

For all their divisions and ambivalent loyalties the Magyars managed to assemble sizable armies and establish their authority over an extensive area, the only revolutionary movement to do so in 1848. This was because they were part of the regional ruling class and, as army officers and county administrators rather than as members of discussion circles, were able to exercise military and other kinds of power. The principal agents of the repression of the Hungarian nationalist movement in 1848–49 were imperial and Russian troops. Defeat was followed by harsh persecution of the leaders and the imposition of a system of highly centralised control from Vienna throughout the 1850s. Yet the economic pre-eminence of the Magyar nobility was not seriously undermined (though the liberal land reforms remained in existence), and provided a basis for renewed attempts at greater political authority on the national level. However, the goal was now sought through negotiation rather than resistance. This can be seen by looking at the views of Deak, the main architect of the so-called Compromise of 1867.

Deak sought a settlement on the basis of the Pragmatic Sanction of 1723. He wanted to establish a dualist state with fairly centralised institutions in the eastern half of the empire. The authority of the Hungarian government and the pre-eminence of the nobility within it reflected much of what had been envisaged in the April Laws, only now the problems of control over finance, foreign policy and the armed forces were settled in favour of central government. At the same time, however, the pressures and defeats (1859–60 against France and Piedmont; 1866–67 against Prussia) which forced Vienna into agreement meant that the Hungarians could play a much larger role in central government than had seemed possible in 1848.

The response to the claims of other nationalities resembled that of Magyars in 1848. But now the counter-claim was much stronger and had a rather different, more authoritarian significance. Deak's view was reflected in the report of the majority of the Committee on Nationalities established by the newly recalled Hungarian parliament in 1861:

> From a political point of view, all Hungary's citizens, whatever language they speak, form but one nation, the unified and indivisible Hungarian nation corresponding to the historical concept of the Hungarian state.[4]

The consequences were clear. A nationalist nobility was forced to recognise the authoritarian character of its interests in order to arrive at an enduring settlement of its claims. The ambiguities of 1848 had given way to the realism of 1867. The significance of this can be appreciated by considering how Kossuth's views developed after 1848. Kossuth was convinced that the imperial government remained hostile to the autonomous and democratic Hungary which was his objective. But the failure of 1848 indicated new ways of combating that hostility. First, the imperial government must be attacked when its position was weak and Russia could not intervene. Such occasions might occur at times of international crisis, and the opportunities created by the Crimean war, the war with France and Piedmont in 1859–60 and with Prussia in 1866 were all explored with this end in mind. Of course, precisely the same pressures pushed the imperial government into a conservative compromise which deprived Kossuth of any significant following among the Magyars themselves.

Second, and particularly interesting, Kossuth recognised that a very different policy from that of 1848 would have to be pursued in relation to non-Magyars. He was prepared to abandon any claim to Magyar superiority and to concede that language differences could justify political distinctions. The final shape of his thinking was to envisage a Danubian confederation in which Hungary, Transylvania (assuming it opposed union with Hungary), Croatia, Serbia and possibly other south Slav areas would be joined together as equals. The notion was, of course, hardly realistic but it serves to show that after 1848 commitment to democratic values

130

and the historic territorial concepts of nationality was no longer possible in the eastern half of the Habsburg Empire.

It also shows that in the effort to sustain democratic values greater recognition is given to the claims of ethnic nationalism. This association of democracy with the right of self-determination on the part of linguistic groups was particularly derived from the situation in the Habsburg empire and, in its impact on western public opinion, was to give ethnic nationalism a powerful source of legitimacy.

In conclusion, we can see that Magyar nationalism was based on a defence of the considerable political autonomy and socio-economic privileges enjoyed by Magyars, particularly the nobility. This defence tended to polarise into a conservative and a radical form. It worked with an historic territorial concept of the nation, although the radical view, as expressed by Kossuth, eventually moved beyond that position. This defence organised itself around existing institutions such as the Diets, the county administrations and the army. Eventually it was as a political elite bargaining with a weakened imperial regime that Magyar claims were granted.

There were two major reasons why this defence took a nationalist form. Reform from above could be seen as a German threat to the Magyar position. Demands for greater rights from below could appear as a Slav and Rumanian threat. Defence of political autonomy and economic privilege became identified, therefore, with defence of Magyar culture and identity. It also provided the basis on which to justify new political demands and to bring Magyar-speaking peasantry into a common movement. Given their position of authority, elements of the Magyar nobility were able to act effectively in this direction. But for most of them the claims of nationality combined with, and did not replace, the claims of class or even dynastic loyalty. The hardening of a nationalist position (and one should remember that for some decades the precise meaning of national identity and how it should be applied was in flux) helped promote and intensify ethnic nationalist responses from subordinate non-Magyar groups. Increasingly in the eyes of international public opinion these responses came to be identified with democratic values.

(b) The Czechs

As with so many other 'small nation' nationalisms,[5] Czech nationalism was preceded by a scholarly preoccupation with Czech culture. It was not difficult to restore a Czech literary language, as Czech culture had flowered during the period of the Protestant Reformation in Bohemia. The revival of interest in this culture and its re-formulation as a national achievement tended to come from figures such as enlightened clergymen in the late eighteenth and early nineteenth centuries. It was part of a shift of intellectual attention towards language, folklore, customs and local history which provided important instruments for later nationalist movements.[6] After

1815 it extended among Czechs to some government officials, nobles and students.

It had no political relevance at the time. The Czech (though the more appropriate terms would be the Bohemian and Moravian) nobility was loyal to the empire and politically dominant. What little pressure there was for local autonomy was expressed in terms of the traditional privileges of the estates and the diets of the provinces of Bohemia and Moravia. Two impulses worked to transform this concern with Czech culture into nationalism: conflict with the imperial government and local economic change. In some ways the two were closely related.

Before 1848 limited economic change had produced a small class of artisans and professional people who were dissatisfied with present arrangements, particularly with German economic dominance in the towns and in government service and the professions. Attempts to enforce German as the official language increased their resentment, and attempts at centralisation generally alienated locally dominant nobles. By 1848 students and artisans in Prague and a few other towns were taking an interest in the cultural revival and supporting ventures such as a Czech trade school and the Bohemian museum. Many of the students came from humble origins which may have enabled them to stimulate interest in this cultural movement among the lower orders.

The events of 1848 suddenly politicised the movement. At first Germans and Czechs in Prague co-operated in framing liberal demands. But Czechs reacted sharply against demands for elections to the Frankfurt parliament. Bohemia and Moravia belonged to the German Confederation but Czechs had no wish to become part of a united Germany. Such a move cut across traditional loyalties and, in the light of the cultural revival and existing conflict with German-speakers, could hardly appeal as a new political loyalty. Their response was to reiterate traditional loyalty but, in reaction to the historic conception of Germany, to combine it with an emphasis on Czech identity.

This point of view was expressed in the famous declaration of the Czech historian Palacky. He insisted that the Habsburg empire should continue but in a way which took account of Czech identity. Palacky is a classic example of the transition from cultural to political nationalism. He had begun working for the Bohemian Museum in the 1830s and his great project, the history of the Czech people, was originally financed by the Bohemian diet. In the 1840s his increasingly anti-German feeling caused him to switch from German to Czech in the writing of this history. The German threat of 1848 pushed him into politics.

One could see this as another instance of the historic territorial nationalism of a dominant cultural group (the Germans) stimulating an ethnic nationalist response from a subordinate cultural group (the Czechs) in the same way that Magyar nationalism gave rise to Rumanian and Slav

132

nationalism. However, it took a while for Czech nationalism to frame its political objectives in ethnic terms. Palacky initially sought federalist reform of the Habsburg empire, but in relation to historic provinces, not language groups. The Czech movement, with its well-placed elites and somewhat distinctive culture, remained aloof from a general Slav movement in 1848, as its distance from the Slav Congress held in Prague in June demonstrates. The most telling comparison is with the Croatian movement, which also, unlike the Rumanians or Serbians, did not move to an ethnic position but worked from its existing institutional basis.

However, the federalist ideal, as embodied in the Kremsier constitution, came to nothing as the counter-revolution pursued a policy of absolutist centralisation. This policy was seen, reasonably enough, as a German policy in which the German upper middle class as much as the nobility, church and court were involved. This pushed the Czechs towards a stronger and linguistically based nationalism.

At the same time economic change in the form of liberal land reform and the growth of capitalist manufacturing generated potential support for a nationalist movement. Czech migration into towns previously dominated by German-speakers could increase ethnic tension. A newly emancipated Czech peasantry came into conflict with a German merchant and financial class. Small Czech merchants, retailers and manufacturers objected to liberal economic policies which seemed to favour larger German competitors. As early as the 1840s, in fact, the patriotic movement was strongest in those parts of eastern and central Bohemia where market penetration was most advanced.

Without political leadership these various conflicts would have remained fluid and largely apolitical, perhaps taking the form of peasant protests against debt and prices and commual conflict in some of the towns. But at the very time when a range of social groups had grievances which could be related to their ethnic identity, the policy of centralisation forced the small Czech elite of professional people, scholars and students into an opposition which could also be related to an ethnic identity.

This process was intensified by the emergence of an overt German nationalism. Again this had both political and economic roots. Until 1848 Austrian Germans were committed to an empire which they dominated, although there was a vague support for German unity provided it did not threaten to undermine the empire. The events of 1848 showed clearly that German and imperial ambitions were incompatible. Most Austrian Germans opted for imperial loyalty. But soon afterwards the German position within the empire itself came under threat. The wars of 1859–60 and 1866 with their attendant crises led to constitutional change which reduced the Germans' role. Hungary acquired greater automony; northern Italy was lost; a limited system of federal rights was created in the western half of the empire. Austrian Germans seemed to be excluded from a united

Germany for the foreseeable future. From the 1870s imperial ministries were no longer under German control. The Habsburg dynasty itself shifted its centre of support away from Germans to other groups. At the same time, in Bohemia especially, the newly mobilised Czechs in countryside and town were perceived as a threat to the German position. German miners, for example, reacted sharply against Czech-speaking workers prepared to work for lower wages. Threats were one problem. Concessions to Czech demands were seen as an even worse one. When, for example, Czechs were granted linguistic parity in Czech majority areas there was a violent German reaction. The creation of language-based electorates at the turn of the century institutionalised these lines of conflict. Yet the nationalism of the Germans was never unified: many remained committed to non-national parties; and the pan-German demand for unification with Germany received only minority support. Nationalist movements of both Czechs and Germans received little working-class support; in the worst affected borderland areas the response was rather to set up organisations to defend the specific interests in German- or Czech-speaking workers. Although national identity shaped much of domestic politics in the decades up to 1914, it often did so in non-nationalist ways. For example, the Austrian Social Democratic Party repudiated the idea of political self-determination or automony but aimed for cultural autonomy and organised itself on national lines, something already discussed in chapter 1. Finally, it is worth noting the inability of Czech nationalists to undermine seriously the Habsburg war effort between 1914 and 1918. National independence came about as a result of military defeat and the way in which the Czech nationalist movement was able to put a strong and plausible case to the victorious allies.

Czech nationalism can appear as a typical case of cultural revival becoming political nationalism. It is worth pointing out that cultural revival did not necessarily move in that direction. For example, among Slovaks (principally clergymen) it had come earlier than among the Czechs, who often regarded the Slovak resurgence with hostility. A leading figure in the Slovak movement, Jan Kollar, who constructed the concept of a 'Czechoslovak', regarded himself politically as a Hungarian. The Slovaks were a small group (at most two million people) surrounded by economically, culturally, politically and numerically superior groups of Poles and Magyars. There was only a tiny elite, principally clerical, and even this was split between Catholics and Protestants. There was no type of economic development which might have either produced new elites or mobilised elements of the peasantry in support of a nationalist movement. There were no functioning political institutions around which a political concept of Slovak nationality or forms of national political action could crystallise. Slovaks were divided between the western and eastern halves of the empire. All these things blocked any move towards political nationalism, both

134

ideologically and practically. After 1867 the hesitant moves towards nationalism were blocked by Magyar policies in the newly autonomous Hungary.

Similar points could be made about the Slovenes in the south-west. It may be that, under certain conditions, close proximity to superior groups of another language stimulate cultural revival but at the same time the overwhelming character of that proximity prevents it becoming nationalism. On the other hand, a nationalist movement such as that of the Croatians was less directly tied to cultural revival than the Czech movement but, with leadership from a native nobility, took a much stronger political form.[7] Finally, one must remember that the national categories which were formulated by various writers in the Habsburg empire were fluid and often mutually contradictory. Nationality was not some natural phenomenon which was easily identified but something which had to be constructed. The ways in which some constructions but not others came to underpin a nationalist movement cannot, therefore, be derived from their intellectual validity but only from a context in which it makes political sense to use them in the pursuit of state power. In the cases so far considered the common factor was the impact of imperial policy on existing or emerging political elites. Such elites were driven to new types of political defence, although the latter were for some time combined with dynastic loyalty of a sort. Nationalism allowed varied elites to combine together (particularly in the Czech case) and, in association with liberal economic reform and development, provided a means of tying newly mobilised popular groups to this political movement. The appeal to outside forces, the legitimacy function, was of little importance in the emergence of the nationalist movements, although externally triggered crises (1866, 1918) were vital to their success. The actual way these nationalist movements developed in the Habsburg Empire can be more clearly illustrated by the Rumanian and Serbian cases.

(c) The Rumanians and the Serbians

Nationalist movements among these groups developed in both the Habsburg and the Ottoman empires. A comparison, therefore, would be particularly useful for identifying the significant factors which conditioned a particular type of nationalist response. The argument that will be pursued here is that the context – above all, the political context – within which the movements developed in the two empires was different in crucial ways which pushed the nationalist movements in completely different directions.

The Rumanians were found predominantly in Transylvania in the Habsburg Empire and in the semi-autonomous principalities of Moldavia and Wallachia in the Ottoman empire. In Transylvania the Rumanians were a majority of the population, with a distinctive language. They were an overwhelmingly peasant people. They had no political rights, as membership of the Transylvanian diet was restricted to the three 'nations' of the Magyars, Szekels and Saxons. Their two churches, the Greek Orthodox and the Uniate, did not enjoy the same rights as the recognised Catholic and Protestant denominations. Indeed, tithes paid by Rumanian peasants went to these 'foreign' churches.

Church leadership of a cultural revival in the eighteenth century, coupled with the rise in expectations aroused by the Josephine reforms, encouraged the development of a national movement. A famous petition of 1792, on which Uniate and Greek Orthodox church leaders co-operated, identified the Rumanians as a nation with a continuous history extending back to the Roman Empire and asked for equal rights to be granted them on both an individual and a national level. This set the pattern for future development. The ideological and political leadership was supplied by churchmen, although secular, professional people began to play an increasingly important role, particularly as the movement grew more radical. The issues of religious inequality and agrarian reform provided the basis of popular support.

Events of 1848 were particularly important in raising expectations. At first Rumanian nationalists expected to co-operate with Magyars. But Magyar policies, particularly the insistence on the integration of Transylvania into Hungary and on the use of Magyar as the official language, frustrated the possibility of co-operation. Rumanians increasingly turned towards the imperial government, with its vague promises of autonomy for Transylvania and an improvement in the Rumanian position. Although the guerilla bands which operated against the Magyars in 1848–49 were not, perhaps, important from a military point of view, they had immense political significance in symbolising a shift in the tactics of Rumanian nationalism.

The period after 1848 was one of frustration. The centralist policies of the imperial government provided the Rumanians with none of the hoped-for autonomy. The compromise of 1867 made things even worse, as Magyar dominance was confirmed. The creation of a Rumanian state out of the Danubian principalities of Moldavia and Wallachia in 1881 provided a possible focus for a separatist nationalism. Yet the main aim for several decades was still towards full equality within Transylvania. A free peasantry and a growing Rumanian middle class (overwhelmingly in the professions) still hoped for help from the imperial government. Besides, the situation in the state of Rumania was hardly one which attracted many Transylvanian Rumanians. Yet, particularly after the rejection of a petition drawn up with popular support in 1909, the hope of internal improvement receded. With the defeat of Austria-Hungary in 1918, incorporation into an enlarged Rumanian state was accepted, but not without great misgivings.[8]

The nationalist movement and its situation were very different in

Moldavia and Wallachia. Economic division here did not correspond largely to language divisions as it did in Transylvania. There was a Greek-speaking elite ruling the principalities, drawn from the rich Phanariot quarter of Constantinople. But it was principally an official elite. Divisions between land-holders and peasants were largely within the Rumanian-speaking population. Furthermore religious division could hardly become a basis for a Rumanian nationalist movement. The Ottoman government granted great political privileges to the Greek Orthodox church, to which most Ottoman Rumanians belonged. The conflict on religious lines would then pit the bulk of the Greek Orthodox population against their nominal Muslim rulers. But this was not a major conflict and it was not a national division. There was conflict within the Greek Orthodox community on national lines. Local Rumanian notables resented the privileged position of the leadership of the Orthodox church and the Phanariot rulers. But this was a conflict confined primarily to the upper levels of society. When Greek Orthodox and Phanariot leaders attempted to lead the principalities into action against the Sultan in 1821, the move was ignored by the Rumanians and indeed helped to provoke a peasant uprising. Both were crushed, and the major beneficiary was the Rumanian nobility who came to furnish the new rulers (hospodars) from their ranks. They were interested in national claims only in a narrow way, namely as a means of increasing their political freedoms. Students returning from the west, as well as the effects of reforms introduced during the period of Russian control in the 1830s, stimulated some nationalist rhetoric but it never extended very far. Its limitations were revealed in 1848 and afterwards, when attempts to express nationalism in reform terms were defeated. Nationalism thereafter principally expressed the manoeuvres of the native nobility in its attempts to exploit foreign influence in such a way as to maximise local independence. By 1881 these manoeuvres had resulted in the creation of a 'nation' state, though it had to be supplied with rulers from foreign royal families. This nationalism acquired a popular basis only in the form of anti-semitism. The Jews formed virtually a substitute middle class in Rumania and were the object of bitter hatred among the peasantry.

Although the details are different, a broadly comparable picture emerges from a consideration of Serbian nationalism in the two empires. The Serbian cultural revival centred upon the autonomous region of the Voivodina in the Habsburg empire. It was supported by an emergent class of traders in the region. It was stimulated by cultural contacts with the larger cities of the empire. Discrimination against the Greek Orthodox church provided an institutional focus for action. The favoured position of Catholic Magyars in land-holding gave a nationalist movement some economic support. Historically Serbians could point to promises made by the Habsburg rulers in the seventeenth century to grant them political rights, promises which had not been kept.

In all these ways – cultural, economic, religious – the Serbians could develop a quite effective cultural nationalist movement. In 1848, like the Rumanians, they turned against the Magyars. Furthermore, from the 1830s they could look to an autonomous Serbia within the Ottoman empire for inspiration and contemplate the possibility of incorporation into Serbia.

The area which became Serbia presents a strong contrast to Serbian nationalism in the Habsburg empire. It made no notable contribution to the Serbian cultural revival. Indeed, it largely borrowed from what had been done in the Habsburg Empire. The leaders of the movement that created an autonomous Serbia were not clerical or professional people but poorly educated local notables with little, if any, interest in nationalist ideas. If there was division on religious matters it was within the Greek Orthodox church where there were demands for a special Serbian autonomy, demands which the Ottoman empire was quite happy to accommodate.

The Serbian state was created not by nationalist pressure from within but by the need to respond to the weakness of central government. By the end of the eighteenth century the authorities were unable to protect the inhabitants from the depredations of the janissaries, the Ottoman soldiers. The consequent anarchy reached a peak in the first decades of the nineteenth century. The janissaries were reacting against Ottoman attempts to curb their power. Local resistance was finally provoked when the janissaries massacred Serbian notables and many others. It began with appeals to Constantinople to restore order. When it became obvious that the government could not do this the only alternative was to impose control locally. This was achieved with support from outside powers such as Britain and Russia. In this way Serbia had established limited autonomy by the early 1830s.

Only then did western influence push the country towards limited reforms. Nationalist ideas developed within the Habsburg empire could be employed to legitimise the Serbian authorities in the eyes of foreign backers and public opinion, as well as serving to justify attempts to gain greater independence and further territory. Nationalism never served any important internal function in the phase of opposition and was used after power had been achieved primarily to legitimise action to outsiders.

Provisionally one can conclude that Serbian and Rumanian nationalism in the Habsburg empire was a response to local subordination in economic, religious and political affairs. Cultural revival made national ideas available, and economic change created new elites and mobilised popular groups whom nationalism could bring together in a common movement. The centralising and modernising reforms of the imperial government, by provoking Magyar nationalism, led in turn to the development of counter-nationalist movements from the subordinate groups.

In the Ottoman empire these groups were not subject to local discrimination, religious or economic. Nationalism was less a response to central government or a dominant cultural group than a narrow reaction on the part of local notables to unpopular agents of Ottoman government such as the Phanariot rulers or the janissaries. Often Constantinople was happy to promote this local but narrow resistance, as it was unable to control its own agents. The stimulus to such resistance came about primarily through the failure of the central government to exercise effective authority. Its first objective was for local notables to establish a new authority in their own hands. Apart from the national dimension of insisting on national autonomy within the Greek Orthodox church, the principal function of nationalist ideology was to legitimate foreign backing for these resistance movements. Popular support was nonexistent and the leading elites involved were small and homogeneous. As a consequence the functions of co-ordination and mobilisation were much less important than in the Serbian and Rumanian nationalist movements of the Habsburg Empire. The general implications will be taken up at the end of this chapter. It now remains to consider a couple of nationalist cases wholly within the Ottoman empire.

(d) The Greeks and the Bulgarians

Here again external intervention and Ottoman weakness were of major importance in bringing into existence and sustaining the Greek national independence movement. Ottoman weakness was particularly apparent in southern Greece, favourable terrain for guerilla warfare and where it was very difficult to maintain communications with central government. Various forms of support for the Greek cause, above all from Britain, France and Russia, both official and unofficial, played a major role in keeping the movement going during the 1820s. The Greek state which was eventually created was largely under British control (although French influence was also important) and imported its ruler from a cadet branch of a German royal family.

Nevertheless the role of nationalism was much more apparent in the Greek than in the Serbian and Rumanian cases. There was a sustained conflict with central government which called for organised resistance of much greater proportions. The particular image of Greek nationality and what the struggle for national independence was imagined to be about played a very great role in the response of public opinion in Britain and France to this conflict. A wider range of elites were forced to co-operate with one another than in the Serbian and Rumanian cases. On the face of it, Greek nationalism was a far more 'genuine' movement than its Serbian or Rumanian counterparts in the Ottoman empire and, in that regard, more akin to some of the nationalist movements in the Habsburg empire. To see if this is the case it is necessary to consider the Greek movement in some detail.

Ottoman rule in the Greek peninsula was similar to the type of government practised in other parts of the empire. The Christian – that is, the Greek Orthodox – faith was tolerated, and local religious leaders were granted extensive powers. Much of everyday life was regulated by ecclesiastical law. A vigorous system of communal government existed, and it was not only religious leaders who played an important role in it. Unable or unwilling to impose direct military control in a difficult terrain, the Turkish authorities could maintain order only with the help of local notables. Since these notables, or chiefs, were in perpetual conflict with one another, a complex and shifting politics was the outcome as different groups competed with one another and entered into collaboration with or resistance to the Ottoman government. In such circumstances there was little clear perception of a sovereign state existing over and above the variety of local political arrangements.[9]

In the Greek case local autonomy was reinforced by the special position enjoyed by the Greek Orthodox church throughout the European part of the Ottoman empire. The Ottoman government had granted far-reaching powers to the church. It had abolished a number of local church authorities, as in Serbia and Bulgaria, and brought the Christians in these areas under the control of the Greek Patriarch, who resided in Constantinople. The Patriarch and his officials combined religious and secular powers over the Greek Orthodox population. For example, they had powers of taxation which enabled them to finance the large contributions the Patriarchate made to the government.

Greeks had other powers as well. They had special responsibilities for commanding and manning the Ottoman fleet. They dominated the merchant marine. A Greek traditionally acted as Dragoman to the Porte, a position which might roughly be translated as Foreign Secretary for European affairs. The rich Greek families of the Phanariot quarter of Constantinople supplied the official personnel of the church and the rulers of Moldavia and Wallachia.

The prominent and powerful role of Greeks in the Ottoman empire had a number of consequences. Many Greeks were able to think in broad terms about the future of the empire. Their ideas took a variety of forms. One thing they all had in common: Greek interests and values were understood not merely in relation to the peninsula or in terms of speakers of the Greek language. Greek was thought of in terms either of the Hellenic heritage (which even in the simple terms of settlement extended beyond the peninsula to include western Asia Minor) or of the role of Orthodox church as the instrument for the reorganisation of the European part of the empire. Even Greek-speakers were spread far beyond the peninsula.

Among these varied ideas were ones of western origin, though notions about democracy and freedom claimed in turn to be expressions of classical Greek values. The elite members of the Greek Orthodox community had ready access to these ideas, either through study and travel abroad or in the well stocked libraries such as those the Phanariot rulers of the Danubian principalities maintained. Furthermore, people in these positions were bound to turn their minds to the future form political organisation would take in a decaying empire. It was a secretary to the Phanariot rulers in Moldavia and Wallachia, a man called Rigas, who adapted western ideas, particularly the constitutional thought developed in France at the time of the revolution, to produce a constitution for his vision of a Balkans under Greek rule. Here Greek was a broad Hellenic notion, not a narrow ethnic idea. Moreover it was an aide to a former Phanariot ruler, Ispilantis, who tried to raise a Greek (i.e. Greek Orthodox) insurrection in the Danubian region in 1821. Although it received little support there it did spark off the rising in the peninsula.

In this rising external support was crucial, and it was ideas of a restored Hellenic civilisation which most appealed to outside opinion. This in turn affected the internal character of the independence movement. Ispilantis, after his failed insurrection, was able to recruit many local notables to his organisation, the Filiki Eteria (Friendly Society), owing to a belief that it had Russian support. As European financial and military backing was channelled into the peninsula it provided the focus for common action on the part of local notables, both chiefs and religious leaders. It was essential that they acquiesce in the public leadership of figures who expressed the objectives of the struggle in terms acceptable to the outside world.

Yet these local figures, and others, had very different concerns. Religious leaders looked towards something like a restoration of Byzantium. Indeed, it is difficult to see how church leaders could contemplate a restoration of the Hellenic spirit with any pleasure. Local chiefs, many of them bandits (i.e. local notables not in Ottoman favour at the time), were concerned only to exploit the situation in order to expand their influence. They also needed to find resources to replace the declining authority of the Ottoman government and the collaborator system it had sustained. But it is doubtful whether the very notion of a sovereign state, national or otherwise, would have made sense to such people.

These groups all conflicted with one another. Local chiefs and religious leaders were in competition for local influence. Both regarded Phanariot and other outsiders with suspicion but had to allow them to assume leading roles because of the precious resources they brought. The merchants and seamen made another, almost independent, contribution. In terms of military conflict popular support was mobilised through established channels of authority, not by means of new sorts of political organisation and ideology. The only exception was the communal violence in the towns which led to massacres of those in Turkish settlements. This had in part been provoked by the massacre of the Patriarch and many

141

other Greeks in Constantinople following news of the first risings in the peninsula. But these communal conflicts were not welded into any broader nationalist organisation or ideology.

The competing elites were never able to co-operate in a single movement. What fragile unity there was frequently depended upon direct help from outside. External intervention saved the day on a number of critical occasions, as when combined British, French and Russian action prevented Mehemet Ali from moving against the rebels. When the Turkish threat receded somewhat in the mid-1820s the 'national' movement degenerated into a series of local faction feuds. Only a renewal of the Turkish threat forced the factions to bury their differences temporarily. Yet western Europeans continued to cleave to the Hellenic ideal, even when, as was the case with Byron, their own specific experiences contradicted that ideal.

With the defeat of the Ottoman government it became necessary to find a positive content for the idea of a Greek state. The first constitution presented a facade for western consumption which masked the anarchy that existed. National political institutions only began to acquire real authority because of western pressure. The first president of Greece, Kapodistrias, failed to overcome factional disputes and was assassinated. The Bavarian Otto, who became king in 1831, soon had to give up his attempts to construct modern state institutions. In fact, the idea of establishing a sovereign state was not a commonly held objective. It was beyond the imagination of local chiefs; objectionable to church leaders; too narrow for those who dreamed of a Hellenic Balkans. Kapodistrias, one of the clearer thinkers on the matter, thought that some form of provisional autonomy would be best, as it would make it easier to press for expanded frontiers at some later time. But Britain, France and Russia insisted on 'national independence' and their word was final. Once this state was formed it was able to generate an ethnic nationalist ideology which legitimised its own existence and justified attempts to expand into the north of the peninsula. Later it was to underpin claims in the western part of Asia Minor which were to help stimulate a violent Turkish nationalist response.[10] But ethnic nationalism was the product rather than the cause of the Greek nation-state. By the standards of nationalist movements in the Ottoman empire the Greek movement was exceptionally strong and popular, but the external function of legitimacy was still the major one. By the standards of nationalist movements in the Habsburg empire it was ideologically confused and highly disorganised. Its historic and institutional justifications were hardly nationalist and were glosses either upon the universalist principles of western Europe or the ambitions of the Greek Orthodox leadership. Its ethnic justifications were a product of independence rather than opposition. However, the dominant position of the Greeks in the Ottoman empire did enable them to formulate some sort of nationalist case before other European groups, which in turn developed much of their nationalism against the Greeks.

This can be seen in the Bulgarian case, which will be considered very briefly. The Bulgarian national movement took shape around resistance to the Greek patriarchate in Constantinople. Members of the Greek Orthodox church in Bulgaria became dissatisfied with this central control and sought to establish an independent authority for the church in Bulgaria. They could appeal to historical precedent for this. The appeal could, in turn, be used to build up a conception of a historic Bulgarian national identity. A rich class of Bulgarian merchants in Constantinople linked to an expanding trade in Bulgaria itself provided the social support for the development of this idea into practical political forms. The Ottoman government was quite happy to support demands for a separate church authority. That enabled it to exploit rivalries within the Greek Orthodox church and also fitted in with some of the reform ideas which were then circulating.

Nevertheless these disputes were religious rather than nationalist. They did, however, enable Bulgarian elites, both clerical and secular, to provide themselves with a collective sense of identity and to reject the definition of Bulgarians as Greeks (i.e. Greek Orthodox) which had hitherto prevailed. Once a separate church authority was established it provided an institutional basis for the further elaboration of nationalist ideology and organisation. It is doubtful whether this Bulgarian movement could have achieved more than limited religious autonomy by its own efforts. But, as in the Serbian and Rumanian cases, a mixture of Ottoman weakness (weakness which was not primarily due to nationalist challenges) and external intervention – above all, Russian and Austrian – played an important part. The policy of foreign powers in establishing client states in Ottoman Europe once more required some justification, and the limited Bulgarian nationalist movement was able to supply it.

3 Conclusion

I have argued that the three functions of co-ordination, mobilisation and legitimation provide a useful means of analysing the role of nationalism in a political opposition. The cases considered in this chapter suggest that co-ordination and mobilisation were of particular importance in the nationalist movements of the Habsburg empire and that legitimacy was most important in those of the Ottoman empire. The reasons for this basic difference are related to major differences between the two empires as a whole. These can be analysed on four levels: international relations, state structures, economic relationships, and the position of the various Christian denominations.

The Habsburg empire, except for a brief period in 1848, was regarded as a stable unit in the international community. This was particularly so after it had adjusted to the setbacks of the 1860s and reorganised itself. With the possible exception of Russia, the major powers of Europe had no wish to exploit internal tensions within the empire in a way that would undermine its stability. Nationalist opposition within the empire, therefore, had to concentrate upon developing internally effective movements. Appeals to outsiders would be of far less importance. By contrast, the Ottoman empire was regarded as a highly unstable and decaying unit within the international community. The establishment of client states in place of Ottoman authority was more attractive than the alternative options of propping up the empire or taking direct control of particular regions. Nationalism offered a credible justification for this policy. This was of particular importance in Britain and France, where a liberal public opinion had an important influence upon foreign policy for much of the century. At the same time, central government weakness forced local notables in some areas such as Serbia to consider pressing for autonomy in order to preserve local stability. To achieve this task, however, new types of political organisation or ideology were not necessary.

The Habsburg empire of the eighteenth century could be described as a feudal state. The basic feature of such a state was that it exerted control over the population at large through a privileged class of noble landowners. The nobles were granted formal and fairly exclusive political rights which were embodied in a variety of institutions and exemptions. These institutions existed at local, provincial, national and imperial level. They varied in importance according to the ways in which Habsburg power had been extended into a particular area. Thus, for example, they were of little importance in the military border area, where the Turkish threat had required a more immediate form of authority, or in Venetia, where the dominance of the city-state of Venice had prevented the development of an important territorial land-owning nobility with which the imperial government could come to terms. Again, the counter-reformation in Bohemia and Moravia had undermined the position of a local nobility and made it difficult for subsequent generations of nobility in the two provinces to think in national terms. By and large, imperial authority was stronger and more immediate in the western parts of the empire. The 'purest' system of feudal authority was to be found in Hungary.

From the late eighteenth century the Habsburg dynasty came to see this mediated system of authority (to which one must add a semi-autonomous and privileged Catholic Church) as a major weakness and by a series of reforms sought to undermine it. The consequences were twofold. First, the institutions which came under attack formed the bases of an effective resistance to the reform programme. The more important the institution the more effective was the resistance. So it was Magyar noble resistance that was particularly strong and which would be formulated in national terms, that is, in terms of the historic rights of a national nobility which were connected to its rights in the former kingdom of Hungary. At the same time, the reform programme suggested that, in place of a chain of privileges and mediated authority which spread outwards and downwards from the imperial government, there should exist on the one hand a sovereign state and on the other a series of private arrangements, over land, religion or education, which could all be summed up as constituting society. As resistance took on new forms it came to accept something of this idea and abandoned the narrow defence of privilege. Now the 'nation' was regarded as the source of state sovereignty, which should be expressed in constitutional, not absolutist, form.

These two points – elite entrenchment in 'old' institutions and the modernising process which created the new public-private distinction – also furnished the bases of the nationalist organisation. Political elites organised themselves through institutions such as county administration and the Diets. Their ideas were elaborated through the emergent cultural associations of 'civil society' – the discussion circles, the newspapers and periodicals. The elaboration of national ideas involved a constant interaction between these two institutional matrices. In part the ideology served to explain novel developments of the period to participants in the national opposition movement, and not just to furnish them with political goals and justifications.

This national opposition was first developed through privileged groups and expressed in historic territorial forms. But it was an opposition particularly beneficial to particular language groups. Such opposition itself came, therefore, to emphasise the importance of language and cultural identity. That in turn stimulated counter-nationalisms from subordinate language groups which, deprived of institutionalised privileges through which to express their ambitions, came to base them simply upon language, religion and other forms of cultural identity. The organisational basis of these movements was much simpler. They appealed to a territorially more concentrated group and lacked the elite diversity or economic development of the more dominant cultural groups. Again the ideology, with its greater concentration upon history and language, appeared to reflect and help the self-understanding of the developing national movement. It also depended much more on popular support and this tended to make a land reform programme and appeal to democratic principles more central.

The Ottoman state was organised in a completely different way. A system of bureaucratic and military control from the centre combined with a series of informal agreements with local interests. (The role of religious authority in the state will be dealt with in a moment.) As the bureaucratic-military authority decayed, so these local interests sought to buttress their authority from other sources. They did so in the same informal ways as they had collaborated with (or resisted) the Ottoman authority. Thus Serbian politics both before and after 'national independence' was largely based on feuds between local notables with just a few major kinship groups playing the leading role. The Ottoman government did make some attempts to reform its political institutions, but they were weak and unsuccessful. They were more likely to precipitate a breakdown of authority in a particular area (as with the attempted disciplining of the janissaries in Serbia) than to form the basis of new forms of political action, whether in support of or resistance to the reforms. There were no local institutions which could give political resistance a clear focus. There was no system of government reform which could force upon political movements new ideas about the nature of the state and how a distinct sovereign state should be organised and legitimised. There were no local divisions on language lines, so local attempts to secure autonomy had no need to emphasise such issues and in turn stimulate counter-reactions from other language groups. For all these reasons a new political language was not required to bind political elites together, mobilise popular support or underpin the novel political project of creating a sovereign state. But because that political language had already been elaborated and accepted in other parts of Europe it could serve to legitimise the local movements abroad.

In the Habsburg empire economic and language divisions often coincided. So long as these relationships remained stable this could not lead to nationalism. The response of privileged groups to political reform could stimulate a nationalist reaction from elites within the subordinate language groups, such as church leaders. But the prospect of economic change which the reform programme of the government created, as well as the reality of alterations in lord-peasant relationships in a liberal direction, could affect far larger sections of the population. Nationalism could become a way of integrating their new social ambitions concerning land ownership or urban employment in a more extensive political movement. In the Ottoman empire ethnic divisions had little to do with economic divisions. In any case, there was no clear system of privileged land ownership, nor as in the Habsburg empire, such good prospects for agricultural change aroused by market opportunities. Generally, therefore, there was no important economic impetus to popular action which could be or had to be organised by a nationalist movement. Only among certain economic elites – Serbian dealers in farm produce, Bulgarian merchants, Greek ship owners – did nationalism become important and play a limited co-ordinating function.

In the Habsburg empire religious divisions overlapped with economic, political and language ones. This was particularly important for subordinate language groups because church leadership concerned initially with equal church rights could play an important part in elaborating ideas of national identity and furnishing a national movement with organisation in its early days. In the Ottoman empire in' Europe division by religious denomination and faith was less important. The Greek Orthodox church occupied a privileged position and was cautious about opposing the government in Constantinople. Opposition which did develop from this basis would be framed in non-national terms: Christian against Muslim. This did have indirect national connotations, as 'Christian' meant Greek Orthodox, and that in turn was related to the legacies of classical Greece or Byzantium. Such ideas, barely national and in some cases anti-national, were effective because they could build upon existing privileges and institutions in Ottoman-controlled Europe. It was the reaction against them among the Christian community that led directly to nationalism. The demands of Serbians and Bulgarians for autonomy from the Patriarchate could be made the basis of an argument for national autonomy. Again, the resentment of Rumanian notables at Greek Phanariot rule could encourage a superficial nationalism.

This conflict between Greek and non-Greek in the Ottoman empire has interesting parallels with the conflict between Magyars and non-Magyars in the Habsburg empire. In both cases the conflict was more directly related to nationalism than resistance to the central state. In both cases the most effective political movements were constructed by the privileged group, which framed its demands in the rather large and institutional terms which its privileged position involved. The response of subordinate groups, often with the assistance of central government, was to claim national autonomy against the privileged group. In the Habsburg case the other factors enumerated in this conclusion meant that the claim resulted in powerful and effective nationalist movements, in the Ottoman case the claim could be only weakly reinforced from other sources.

The most interesting general point to emerge from these comparisons is that the development of an internally effective nationalist movement (i. e. one in which the functions of co-ordination and mobilisation are particularly important) is related to the structure of the state to which that nationalism is opposed. It is not too fanciful to compare the way in which nationalism developed in the Habsburg empire to the ways in which national opposition developed in England and France. In all three cases one can observe a basic three-way interaction between a state which is threatening major institutions, privileged groups entrenched within those institutions, and the non-privileged population. But there are two major differences between England and France on the one hand and the Habsburg empire on the other. First, in the Habsburg empire this threefold division had ethnic dimensions. Second, given the extent and diversity of the empire, the only way to secure state power was by separation rather than reform. So in this case the goal is separation rather than reform, and the language used to justify it is couched in terms of cultural identity and not simply in terms of historic or natural rights.

These internal functions are of much more importance than the external function of legitimacy in the understanding of nationalism. If the legitimacy function dominates, this merely indicates that there is nothing in the character of the opposition movement which would itself develop a nationalist ideology. The reasons have to be sought outside the opposition movement. But for that movement to be able to use such an ideology it must have been developed and become acceptable elsewhere. The legitimacy function is a secondary one, dependent on the prior success of nationalism in terms of its other two functions. Any political movement can use the language of nationalism to impress outsiders, and little can be learnt about such movements on that basis. But where nationalist ideology is used to construct an effective political movement by binding diverse elites together and mobilising popular support, then there is a much closer relationship between the use of ideology and the political movement generally. The comparisons drawn in this chapter suggest that the political context – above all, opposition to a modernising state – is particularly important in creating such a close relationship.

Notes

1   The Uniate church was a break-away from the Greek Orthodox church. It retained much of the Greek Orthodox form of worship but recognised the spiritual supremacy of Rome.
2   For a general treatment of these terms see G. Poggi, *The Development of the Modern State: a sociological introduction* (London, 1978).
3   See below pp. 135–9.
4   Quoted in G. Szabad, *Hungarian Political Trends between the Revolution and the Compromise, (1849–1867)* (Budapest, 1977), p. 113.
5   I take this term from the title of the book by Miroslav Hroch, *Vorkämpfer der nationalen Bewegungen bei den kleinen Völkern Europas* (Prague, 1968). There is now an abridged English version published under the title *Social Conditions of National Revival in Europe: A Comparative Analysis of the Social Composition of Patriotic Groups among the Smaller European Nations* (Cambridge, 1985).
6   For further details on these kinds of intellectual events, as well as the role of the Czech nationalist historian, Palacky, see above, pp. 55–64.
7   There were other forms of Croatian nationalism with a more elaborate cultural basis but the dominant form in 1848 was that led by the native nobility and justified in historic and institutional terms.
8   The implications of this for another form of Rumanian nationalism, the fascist movement of the period from the end of the First World War into the Second World War, are considered in chapter 15.
9   This analysis can be compared to that provided on the Mughal Empire. See below, pp. 219–23.
10   On Turkish nationalism after the break-up of the Ottoman empire see below, pp. 244–7.

6

Separatist nationalism
in the Arab world

Arab nationalism can be considered as one sort of modern anti-colonial nationalism. This is investigated in chapters 7–10. Since the achievement of independence by a number of Arab states it can also be considered as one case of unification nationalism. This is dealt with in chapter 14. Here I wish to conduct a much more limited analysis. I will compare Arab nationalism in the Ottoman empire with European nationalism in the Ottoman empire. I will also compare that same Arab nationalism with early Egyptian nationalism from about 1890 to 1919. The first comparison will help pinpoint more precisely the reasons for nationalist resistance in the Ottoman empire. The second will help elucidate further the importance of the difference between state structures of empires for the way in which nationalist opposition develops. Any such exercise requires a consideration of Arab and Egyptian nationalism up to 1918–19 and two sets of comparisons. This will be fairly brief, as Arab nationalism in the Ottoman empire was poorly developed and Egyptian nationalism is considered only in contrast with Arab nationalism.

1 Arab nationalism in the Ottoman empire

A more plausible case can be made for Arab nationalism as the product of intellectuals and the search for cultural identity than is the case with many other non-western nationalisms. There exists a common language and, to a degree, a common cultural and political heritage. Nationalist intellectuals have been able to build solidly on this promising foundation. Such intellectuals have played a prominent part in Arab nationalist politics. The founding figure of the Ba'athist party, which has long dominated Syrian and Iraqi politics, was Michael Aflaq, a leading nationalist intellectual. Sati 'Husri, the 'Arab Fichte',[1] occupied high office in Iraq and Egypt before and after the Second World War and helped develop an educational system designed to inculcate nationalist values into Arab youth. These and many other figures testify to the importance of nationalist intellectuals in Arab nationalism. Their importance can be traced back to the origins of the movement in the Ottoman empire.

The task of doing this was first undertaken by George Antonius.[2] He located the beginnings of Arab nationalism in Christian intellectual circles in Beirut in the 1880s. These groups were the product of mission schools established in Syria and the Lebanon.[3] Helped by European teachers, a Christian elite was able to standardise a written form of Arabic and to elaborate ideas of Arab national identity. Through this elite western values of progress and democracy were introduced into the Arab world. Put into a nationalist form, such ideas could be harnessed to a growing discontent with Ottoman rule which culminated in the resistance movements of the First World War. After the war nationalist resentment turned against the British and the French when they went back upon their promises of political autonomy for the Arabs. There was a shift of emphasis away from democratic and liberal concerns towards a collective concern with Arab cultural identity and its political expressions. This has continued to play an important part in Arab politics even after various parts of the Arab world achieved statehood.

In a simplified form this is how the 'intellectual' interpretation of Arab nationalism goes. It can be related to a focus upon the plight and role of a westernised intelligentsia in a backward and exploited society. The creation of a nationalist ideology can be seen as a way of creating an effective political opposition to alien governments. It can also be related to the personal difficulties of members of this intelligentsia. Antonius himself, for instance, can be represented as an example of a convert to western ways who suffered from racial discrimination and turned to nationalism in consequence.[4] But not only was the exposure to western ways of little importance in the Ottoman empire (Antonius worked as a government official in the British administration of Egypt), so also was any form of racial discrimination.

This observation already suggests the limited use of the 'intellectual' approach for an understanding of the origins of Arab nationalism in the Ottoman empire. Criticisms of this approach can go much further than this. To begin with, there was little resistance to Ottoman rule until just before 1914, and it is difficult to characterise much of what there was as nationalist. An Arab congress which met in Paris in 1913, for example, did little more than call for some decentralising reforms. It refused to extend its claims to other parts of the Arab world outside the empire.

The intellectual origins of Arab nationalism can, in fact, be under-stood in another way. The Maronite Christian community on which it was centred could use the concept of nationality as a way of overcoming its separation from the Muslim majority surrounding it. Yet this attempt at integration (an attempt by a community rather than by intellectuals as such) received no support or sympathy from Muslims, and the society

150

which first propagated the idea was soon disbanded.

To understand the limited success of nationalism before 1914 one must consider the situation of the Arab subjects of the Ottoman empire. To begin with, Arabs were tied to their ruler by a common religion. Some intellectuals did try to 'nationalise' the Islamic faith, but this was an obviously artificial exercise which went against the whole outlook of a major world religion. For so long as the Ottoman empire was seen to embody the Islamic faith there was a strong body of loyalty to it. The break-up of an Islamic power into a number of smaller units would have been regarded as retrograde.

The traditional practice of government also inhibited the growth of nationalism. A great deal of local autonomy was left to traditional notables, and government was managed on informal collaborator lines. (I discuss the idea of collaboration in the next chapters dealing with anti-colonial nationalism.) Some areas were fiscally exploited, such as Syria; but others probably benefited financially from Ottoman rule, such as the Hijaz, with its holy cities. Apart from a few areas close to the Mediterranean there was little economic development that could give rise to new elites which might be attracted to nationalism.

Traditional, local and Muslim values were dominant. When Mehemet Ali briefly occupied Syria and the Lebanon in the 1830s and introduced various western-style reforms such as individual property rights they were accepted only by the Christian minority. Most of the Muslim peasant majority rejected them and welcomed the return to a strong, traditional Islamic state. In such a state terms of national identity were unknown. 'Arab' was a word applied to desert nomads; 'Turk' referred to Anatolian peasants.

The major impulse to nationalism came about through reform attempts by the Ottoman government, which are dealt with briefly in chapter 11. They involved a tightening up of central control which alienated traditional collaborators, who saw their local autonomy endangered. Other reforms, such as those introducing an official language, smacked of Turkish nationalism and could help stimulate a counter-nationalist resistance. Reforms which aimed at a partial secularisation of government offended Islamic sentiments.

Resistance was not confined to established political interests. Groups such as army officers and Christian merchants had initially welcomed the reform programme. But as the reforms took on a Turkish rather than an Ottoman colour, and an autocratic rather than a liberal form, even these groups within the Arab world moved towards opposition. In the circumstances nationalism could help co-ordinate action among diverse opposition elites.

Before 1914, however, such a process of co-ordination had barely started. The attempts of central government to strengthen its control over

151

Arab areas during the war did intensify the sentiment of resistance. The British and the French were willing to back resistance in the Arab world, and this resistance was rendered respectable by being framed in terms of national liberation. One only has to think of the myths woven by and around the figure of Lawrence of Arabia. However, resistance to the Ottomans was always under the control of traditional authorities who had been the least susceptible to nationalism before 1914. Had the area been granted autonomy after 1918 the probable result would have been the division of the region into units under these traditional rulers. The establishment of a modern colonial system of control under British and French mandates was a vital condition for the development of an effective Arab nationalism.

2 Arab nationalism and Egypt

The Egyptian situation was quite different. Since the invasion of Napoleon Egypt had been increasingly removed from Ottoman control. Under Mehemet Ali and his successors the country was subjected to a massive series of reforms designed to enable it to emulate the western powers. This general project was justified not in nationalist but rather in statist terms. New military technologies were imported. A reformed administration was created. Modern manufacturing enterprises, especially arsenals, were set up. Foreign traders were encouraged to settle. Individual land-holding was introduced. The cultivation of cotton as an export crop was promoted and irrigation schemes were pursued. Much of this required numerous trained personnel. Consequently western-style educational institutions were established, and many western European works translated and published. At first the concentration was upon technical subjects but it proved impossible to limit attention to them for very long.

All this was pushed through in an autocratic style. The penetration of reforming autocracy into society unbalanced existing political relationships and called for adjustments in all walks of life. This had barely begun to be apparent when Ismail's bankruptcy in 1876 brought the financial affairs of the government under Anglo-French control. Limited military resistance escalated into a major rebellion against the government in 1882 and led to British military intervention. The rebellion was not itself nationalist, although both its memory and its dynamics could contribute to later nationalist resistance.[5] From then until 1923 Egypt was effectively a British colony. The British administration continued many of the policies pursued earlier, but they were conducted within a less autocratic framework. This enabled some Egyptians to develop new ideas and forms of action.

Two particular adaptions are of interest here. The first concerns the adaption of the Islamic faith to modernity. A number of intellectuals tried to reconcile Islam with principles such as modern science, utilitarianism and human rights. At the same time they remained committed to basic ideals such as the unity of the Islamic community, an ideal which was not compatible with the principles of either Arab or Egyptian nationalism. The Pan-Islamic sentiment (not necessarily in a modernist form) certainly had popular support in Egypt. It culminated in an extensive protest against the abolition of the Caliphate by the Turkish government in 1923.[6]

The other response was that of Egyptian nationalism. It was based firmly on liberal nationalist principles taken over from Europe. It was embodied in parties seeking support in the limited representative assemblies that were established. It tended to be vague on what constituted the national identity of the Egyptian people, although references to the pharoahonic period played its part. It also tended to be ambiguous or silent on the tension between the ideas of the nation and of Islam as the ultimate source of authority and the ideal form of a political community. This evasiveness continued after 1923 because nationalist politicians were aware of the limited appeal of secular nationalism and did not want to confront basic Muslim tenets any more than was necessary. In none of this did Arab nationalism play a part. One of the leading nationalists, Mustafa Kemal, for example, subscribed both to Egyptian nationalism and to pan-Islamism. This has been explained partly in terms of his failure to appreciate the ultimate tensions between the two sets of ideas.[7] But on both counts he was hostile to Arab nationalism: it put in question the integrity of Egyptian nationalism and it threatened the position of the Ottoman empire, the major Islamic power and a useful thorn in the side of the British.

Nationalism in Egypt prior to 1919 appears, therefore, to have been a movement of certain educated, urban elites, confined to the larger cities, building upon a largely political conception of the Egyptian nation, combining with religious modernism and pan-Islamism, and hostile or indifferent to Arab nationalism. From this point of view one must admit that the uprising of 1919 is something of a mystery. It was certainly not nationalist in the sense that most of its participants were motivated by nationalist principles. Economic hardship and religious resentment of an alien government were of far greater importance. But popular sentiments in mass nationalist actions are rarely inspired directly by nationalist ideology. However, the nationalist movement does not appear to have sought to organise widespread grievances on a large scale before 1919 or to have sparked off the uprising. How mass resistance acquired the momentum it did and how the nationalist movement was able to pose as its leader are questions not easily answered. So far as I know the type of historical research into Indian nationalism, which might help to explain the Egyptian case, has not yet been carried out.

What it is important to note here is that by 1919 Egyptian nationalism was able to co-ordinate elite political action to a fairly high degree, had a clear ideological case on the basis of western political principles, and seemed capable of leading mass action even if it could not initiate it. At the same time it was indifferent or hostile to Arab nationalism. There were later debates over the reform and standardisation of the language, but these were not couched in linguistic nationalist terms. There was some sympathy for the plight of other Arab communities when brought under French and British control, but Egyptian politicians had their own problems to confront. This aloofness from Arab nationalism continued throughout the period of the monarchy up to 1952. Subsequent Egyptian involvement in the Arab nationalist cause under the leadership of Nasser was therefore a departure from tradition and is considered in chapter 14.

3 Conclusion

A comparison between European and Arab nationalism in the Ottoman empire suggests a number of points. In both cases the internal forces favouring nationalism were weak. This was particularly so in the Arab case, where there was no separate Christian majority whose general subordination and internal disputes could give rise to a limited nationalism. The efforts of the Christian community in the Lebanon were based upon different considerations and had little impact.

Another major difference was the relative strength of the Ottoman government in the two areas. In Europe, where conflict with the major powers was more serious, the Ottoman government had been breaking down by the beginning of the nineteenth century. Reform attempts merely hastened the process and forced local interests to devise alternative arrangements. These interests could also look west for support – both from kindred but more developed nationalist movements such as those of the Habsburg empire, and from the governments and public opinions of major European powers.

In the Arab regions central control was much stronger. The existing collaborator system was fairly stable and there was no need to explore alternative political arrangements. Before 1914 western governments had little interest in fomenting autonomist movements in the non-European parts of the Ottoman empire and there were no linked nationalist movements to which Arab nationalists could look. When the Ottoman government did embark on reform shortly before 1914, its greater control compared to European areas meant that the impact was marked. It stimulated some resistance which was co-ordinated around vague nationalist ideas before 1914. With the outbreak of war the burgeoning resistance movement could now use nationalist arguments to help legitimise support it received from the Allies. The limited development of nationalism by 1918 was the product of modernising reforms by the Ottoman government in the decade before 1914 and political instability and interference generated by the war itself.

Programmes of modernisation were much further advanced in neighbouring Egypt. As a result, a territorial nationalist movement was able to develop to a fairly advanced stage by the time of the First World War. But the territorial focus of this nationalist movement cut it off from Arab nationalism. The comparison here suggests that the modern colonial state was particularly conducive to the development of territorial nationalism; whereas a decaying empire like that of the Ottomans could only produce nationalism either as a way of legitimising successor states or in response to its own desperate attempts to modernise. In all cases there once again seems to be a close relationship between the development of an internally effective nationalist opposition and the project to create a modern state and society.

The particular significance of the modern colonial state has been touched upon in this chapter. It is clearly of such importance for an understanding of twentieth-century nationalism that it calls for more systematic treatment. This is the subject of the next four chapters.

Notes

1   Bassam Tibi, *Nationalismus in der Dritten Welt am arabischen Beispiel* (Frankfurt a. M., 1971), p. 110.
2   George Antonius, *The Arab Awakening* (London, 1938). Note the title, implying that there had always been an Arab nation: it had merely been 'asleep' for some centuries.
3   I use these terms for the period before 1918 although they did not then refer to precisely the same territories as today.
4   E. Kedourie, *Nationalism in Africa and Asia* (London, 1970), pp. 86–7. This is but one example of Kedourie's general approach. Analytically there are many affinities between Kedourie and Antonius, although where Antonius sees a vanguard of the nation, Kedourie discerns uprooted ideologues.
5   For the contribution of 'pre-nationalist' resistance to subsequent nationalism see the following chapters dealing with anti-colonial nationalism.
6   The Caliph was the supreme Islamic authority on earth. Although Muslims in many countries opposed particular actions of the Caliph, such as declaring the Ottoman conflict with the Allies in 1914 a holy war, they were committed to the maintenance of the office. For the Muslim response in India to the abolition of the Caliphate see below, p. 175 and pp. 207–8.
7   Nadav Safran, *Egypt in Search of a Political Community: an analysis of the intellectual and political evolution of Egypt, 1804–1952* (Cambridge, Mass., 1961), pp. 85–90.

7

Approaches to anti-colonial nationalism

1 Introductory remarks

Anti-colonialism is one of the main forms of nationalism. It has developed in a vast range of societies and its successes have transformed the political map of much of the world. The few cases I consider represent only a fraction of the whole. Hence this chapter first considers various approaches which the reader should be able to relate to the cases I consider as well as to others. The criticisms of these approaches in this chapter as well as the findings of the case studies and comparisons are combined in the general interpretation advanced in chapter 10.

In this chapter we are dealing with no more than abstractions. Not all general interpretations fit into the categories outlined. Historical studies, if they are any good, are much more than the application of a general approach. But the categories do point to certain general understandings of the subject which have shaped interpretations of particular cases of anti--colonial nationalism. These categories are primarily concerned with the colonial situation. Only if one can provide some general account of that situation can one go on to offer a general interpretation of the nationalist movements which opposed and abolished it.

2 Political approaches

(a) Domination

At its simplest colonialism can be seen as conquest and nationalism as the means by which that conquest was brought to an end. Colonial domination can be seen to encompass every sphere of life. If domination is so total, its ending can only be seen in terms of the withdrawal of imperial power. This may come through weakness (e.g. due to wars with other great powers) or farsightedness (e.g. the desire to bring colonial societies to independence). The approach centres entirely upon imperial power, and colonial society is seen simply as the object of that power. Some nationalists have, in fact, subscribed to this general picture in order to stress the immensity of their achievement in overcoming the status of victim, but such an argument generally involves a barely credible jump from total subordination to effective resistance.

This very simple account caricatures the approach. But even if nationalist resistance is assigned a role in bringing about independence, it tends to be as just one of a number of pressures upon a calculating imperial power. This is the great weakness of the approach. In fact imperial powers were often reluctant to conquer, frequently established control by agreements with elements in the indigenous society, constantly modified their policies in response to pressure from colonial society, and in many cases left because they could no longer control such pressure. These considerations underpin other approaches. However, it is possible to go too far in rejecting the degree of imperial domination. The problem really is how to relate it to other features of the colonial situation.

(b) Westernisation

This approach starts from the recognition that colonialism enabled many non-European societies to acquire European characteristics. It goes on to argue that nationalism was one of them. From this basis it concentrates on how the transference of nationalism took place. Usually central to this is the way in which a class of western-educated natives was created. Nationalism could provide a general as well as a more specifically political identity for elements of this new class, and enable them to mobilise more widespread resistance to colonial rule. The degree to which such a western-educated class is developed in a particular case can be regarded as the key to understanding how nationalism could develop.

For example, it has been argued that different educational policies were pursued by the British, the French and the Belgians in tropical Africa.[1] The net effect was to produce a large westernised elite in British West Africa with limited employment opportunities; a rather smaller elite in French West Africa; and hardly any western-educated elite in the Belgian Congo. Very crudely these differences can be correlated with the development of nationalism: earliest and strongest in British West Africa and latest, if at all, in the Belgian Congo. The rise of Indian nationalism can also be written in terms of the growth and fortunes of a westernised elite or set of elites.[2] The approach involves a very specific definition of nationalism to set it off from other forms of resistance. It offers a plausible explanation of why nationalism so often follows a period of quiet and collaboration: that was when indigenous elements were learning western values. It can link different imperial policies to different situations, such as the presence of a large settler class (which would inhibit the creation of indigenous westernised elites).

The role of popular support in nationalist movements is usually

157

understood in negative terms. The disruptive effects of colonialism in such forms as war, urban growth, labour migration and Christian penetration make many people available to a new political movement which offers them new hopes and identities.[3]

This approach became prominent in the 1950s when the successes of the British West African and Indian nationalist movements engaged attention. It seemed to fit these cases well. It also tied in with the absence of nationalism in less 'westernised' areas such as the Belgian Congo, southern and east-central Africa. It was elaborated upon by political scientists who paid particular attention to the formal organisation of nationalism, especially the political party, with its programme, organisation and leadership which all seemed very western. It concentrated on the prominence of large towns in providing mass support. Nationalism was seen as a form of politics which spread from the most advanced into the less advanced areas of colonial society.

One difficulty with this approach is the contrast it draws between westernised and traditional groups. In practice it becomes very difficult to apply the distinction. What is more, it is difficult to assign typical roles in the nationalist movement or the system of collaboration with the imperial power in terms of this contrast. These problems have become particularly apparent as investigation has extended beyond the central leadership of nationalist movements, including the cases of British West Africa and India. A second difficulty arises out of the negative treatment of popular support. Strong positive interests can be related to popular support. Ideology, from this perspective, becomes less important as a source of identity and commitment for bewildered masses, and more important as part of a process of political organisation. Finally, with the development of clearly nationalist movements in less 'western' forms, other approaches have been required which can, in turn, lead to new general interpretations.

(c) Collaboration

It has often been recognised that imperialism works effectively only if it is accepted by much of colonial society and if it actually operates through a network of indigenous collaborators. However, this has often been regarded as of secondary importance compared to the impact of imperialism in the form of either domination or westernisation. But such recognition can be made central to an understanding of the colonial situation and the nationalist challenge.

This approach makes a sharp distinction between political control and economic exploitation. Satisfactory economic exploitation can co-exist with formal political independence, as in the case of China. Areas with little economic attraction to an imperial power can be brought under its formal control, as in the case of Tanganyika. Obviously in each particular case economic and political relationships interact. But what is important is

158

that no general relationship can be established. If that is the case, the reasons for the establishment of 'formal empire' have to go beyond the desire to exploit an area economically.[4]

One reason may be to forestall other powers. This case has, above all, been argued for the 'scramble for Africa' between 1880 and 1900 which transformed most of the continent from formal independence to formal subordination.

But the significance of the transformation is contained in the word 'formal'. Annexations on paper did not necessarily change the substance of politics to any extent. Such changes depended upon the sort of collaboration which the imperial power and the indigenous society could negotiate. If a particular system of collaboration broke down the imperial power might be compelled to intervene more directly. When, for example, the Egyptian regime was threatened by military and popular rebellion the British government was forced into a takeover. Such interventions were undertaken reluctantly because of their cost, a reluctance that could be exploited by indigenous elites if they became aware of it. As soon as possible the imperial power would set about establishing a new and more effective system of collaboration. But in this it was dependent upon the capacity of indigenous society to respond in the required ways. In many cases the imperial power had to modify its requirements accordingly. Thus, although some colonial officials wanted to introduce direct taxation into parts of British West Africa, it was delayed until well into the present century for fear of alienating important collaborators. 'Indirect rule', seen from this perspective, was not a European technique of administration but a rationalisation of dependence upon collaborators.[5]

Resistance to imperial power can be looked at in terms of how it led to modifications in the collaborator system. The military resistance of the Fulani emirates in northern Nigeria suggested to Lugard that their authority was vital to effective government in the area. Once the resistance was overcome the emirs became collaborators in one of the first experiments in indirect rule. In other cases resistance might at least force the imperial power into a more conciliatory approach. This was the effect of the Maji-Maji rebellion of 1905 on the German authorities in Tanganyika. It was the Hut Tax revolt in Sierra Leone in 1898 which, although itself defeated, helped the British government decide against introducing direct taxation into other parts of West Africa.[6]

Resistance can be linked with collaboration in other ways. Both can be seen as alternative tactics available to those with significant resources. That this could be seen in tactical terms is shown by instances where certain leaders and groups switched from one relationship to the other. More important than the distinction between collaborators and resisters is that between indigenous societies with bargaining power and those without. But, of course, the ability to strike a bargain depends on what the other side wants. The higher the demands of the imperial power, generally speaking, the less likely that potential collaborators would be both able and willing to co-operate. In this sense one can envisage that beyond a certain level of economic demand, for example, direct political control would become necessary. Conversely, once a high level of political control was established for some non-economic reason (e.g., in the wake of repressing a rebellion), it might then appear worthwhile introducing sweeping economic changes because there was no need to worry about undermining patiently negotiated forms of colloboration. So at a certain point where the collaborator argument becomes inapplicable, economic and political relationships perhaps do tend to converge.

Nationalism can be related to the breakdown of the collaborator system. Robinson puts it succinctly:

> . . . when the colonial rulers had run out of indigenous collaborators they either chose to leave or were compelled to go. Their national opponents in the modern elite sooner or later succeeded in detaching the indigenous political elements from the colonial regime until they eventually formed a united front of non-collaboration against it. Hence the inversion of collaboration into non-cooperation largely determined the timing of decolonisation.[7]

There is a problem with the phrase 'sooner or later', which suggests but does not define some basic weakness in the collaborator system that brings about its downfall and leaves the role of the 'modern elite' rather ambivalent as agents or beneficiaries in this process. But the approach places the development of nationalism firmly within the political structures established by colonialism rather than seeing it as an assault on those structures from outside. This creates a strong sense of continuity. On the one side it is not easy for the nationalist regime to break with the political structures of colonialism because it is so closely shaped by them. As Robinson concludes:

> . . . since anti-colonial movements emerged as coalitions of non-collaboration out of the collaborative equations of colonial rule and the transfer of power, the elements and character of Afro-Asian national parties and governments in the first era of independence projected a kind of mirror image of collaboration under imperialism.[8]

On the other side the colonial system of government was also constructed out of existing political relationships and earlier informal agreements. Formal empire becomes a phase in the complex and continuous politics of indigenous societies.

The approach is subtle, flexible and ingenious. It is generally truer to the reality of the colonial situation than either the domination or the westernisation arguments. Nationalism is no longer simple resistance, or a form of imitation, but one aspect of the politics of colonialism. However,

160

there are problems.

First, the notion of a collaborator is a formal and general one. Second, investigations of collaboration have been pursued most effectively in the very early phase of colonialism. These two weaknesses go together. It may be that colonialism undermines specific patterns of collaboration and therefore introduces certain types of discontinuity and instability into the situation. Until the notion of collaborator is broken down into types of collaborators, and the possible phasing of these types within colonial politics examined, the idea remains generally uninformative. It is in the early phase of colonialism that indigenous society might most clearly compel certain accommodations upon the imperial power. There would seem to be an important difference between collaborators manufactured out of colonialism itself and those who existed earlier. This, in part, is what the westernisation approach is seeking to locate and the collaborator approach is liable to obscure.

It is also difficult to see how a 'modern elite' comes to lead a set of 'non-collaborators' in a nationalist movement. The breakdown of collaboration is not to be equated with the rise of a nationalist movement which fills the vacuum. The chaos of the Belgian Congo is a vivid example of what happens when this 'mirror image of collaboration' is not created at the time independence is achieved. One must ask what are the specific conditions which enable an effective nationalist movement to be constructed.

Finally, this approach runs the danger of missing the wood for the trees. 'Formal empire', as the very term suggests, introduces new forms of political authority. Even if the issues and interests involved in political conflict change only gradually, this change of form has important consequences for the ways in which conflict is understood and organised. This is of major importance to an understanding of the rise of anti-colonial nationalism.[9]

(d) Resistance

The concern with resistance can be linked with collaboration, as was argued in the preceding section. Both emphases are part of the movement among historians to 'recover the initiative' displayed by indigenous societies in the creation, operation and abolition of the colonial situation.[10] But there are distinct reasons for stressing resistance rather than collaboration.

First, nationalist movements naturally wish to associate themselves with some tradition of resistance to the imperial power. This can take the form not only of an historical argument making such connections but also of those connections actually being invoked in the popular ideology of the nationalist movement. Furthermore nationalists can seek to integrate or otherwise exploit contemporaneous resistance movements which originally had nothing to do with nationalism.

Studies of resistance can also lead to a re-evaluation of mass support for nationalism. Nationalism can be seen as a form of politics appropriate to the extended sort of resistance needed to challenge imperial power effectively. However, the bases of this sort of resistance may be located outside nationalism. Earlier cases of popular resistance to colonialism could create forms of non-traditional and widespread political action upon which nationalism could build. For example, some of the resistance movements which arise shortly after the imposition of imperial authority have a scale and character which is new. The Maji-Maji rebellion brought about loose co-operation between many different societies in Tanganyika. Some of the leadership was new, particularly that provided by religious figures. Local values concerned with matters such as the magical creation of invulnerability to bullets were phrased in more general terms which enabled similar responses in different societies to be linked together. In these ways the rebellion took on a 'national' character. Again, a good deal of attention has been paid to African adaptations of Christianity which led to the establishment of independent churches or millenial movements and, in some cases, open rebellion. These broke with established patterns of political action and leadership and ideology.

The relationship of these novel and extensive resistance movements to nationalism is a complex subject. In some cases they can be seen to create a pattern of co-operation which nationalism later took over, either by integrating or replacing them. In other cases, if they continue in various forms, they could be indifferent or even hostile to nationalism. One can also point out that earlier forms of resistance contribute indirectly to subsequent nationalism by compelling changes in the character of colonial rule which in turn condition the rise of nationalism. But by then one is running the danger observed in the collaborator approach of ending up with a highly formal argument which registers the existence of one complexity after another but provides no real general illumination. As with the collaborator approach, it is necessary to ask whether there are specific phases in the forms of resistance to colonialism and what it is about nationalism that makes it such an appropriate means of bringing the colonial situation to an end.

The approaches emphasising collaboration and/or resistance were developed in order to make sense of the rise of nationalism in areas such as east and central Africa as well as to extend understanding of nationalism in British West Africa and India to the positive roles played by popular support and more traditional elites. In such cases it was not very helpful to think in terms only of westernised elites leading the movement or urban areas providing the main bases of mass support mainly for negative reasons. Historians and social anthropologists who took up these lines of enquiry were concerned to penetrate the formal labels of party and ideology to the 'real' politics below. They were influenced by a wider trend in historical writing towards an emphasis on the contribution of those who are ruled to the making of history. Their concern with substance rather than form led them to note continuities between the pre-colonial and the colonial era. The disappointments of the first nationalist regimes in Africa and Asia suggested that independence did not break so completely with the colonial past as had sometimes been thought. All these considerations underlay the new approaches to nationalism, which could be extended to anti-colonial nationalism generally. The dangers are that they may over-look general patterns of change, emphasise the 'substance' of politics at the expense of the 'forms', and forget the simple fact that some people do have far less initiative than others.

3 Economic interpretations

The general problem with most economic interpretations of imperialism is that they tend to by-pass the political level or reduce it to a set of economic relations. Economic imperialism can hold sway with or without formal empire. Nationalism may or may not challenge it. One may distinguish between those nationalisms which present a challenge and those which do not, and seek the difference in, for example, different class bases. But that tends to leave aside the possibility of any general understanding of anti-colonial nationalism, even if it produces some worthwhile results.[11] Consequently the historian of anti-colonial nationalism can find it difficult to take up any position with regard to disputes about whether imperialism be understood essentially as a process of economic modernisation or of systematic underdevelopment of colonial societies. What he can do is insist that no economic interpretation should lead us to conclude that the development of nationalist politics is somehow not significant, that human agency must give way to the force of various structural imperatives. In some accounts the responses of colonial society seem to be prejudged as a realistic adaptation to or a futile struggle against these imperatives. Not only does this reify economic forces, it fails to do justice to the complexity of colonial situations, falling into the same trap as the domination and westernisation theses. Such approaches may provide useful general contexts but they do not help us understand the details of the process, the political choices and values involved. When they are adapted or abandoned in the attempt to understand particular cases it may be possible to find in them some useful ideas for the study of anti-colonial nationalism.

One useful emphasis comes in what might be called the economic equivalent of the collaboration argument. Hopkins, for example, links the establishment of formal empire in parts of west Africa to the strains that developed in existing patterns of economic co-operation.[12] African responses to new opportunities continued to shape the economic situation under formal empire. This observation is taken from an area in which African cash crop farming assumed considerable importance and helped prevent the emergence of either plantation or settler agriculture. But even where European penetration was more direct there was often a vital degree of indigenous collaboration. Iliffe has pointed out how the development of plantation agriculture in parts of northern Tanganyika was conditional on the ability and willingness of African farmers to adapt their agriculture in order to supply the plantation labour force with food. The plantation workers, who had to be drawn from farther afield, were often attracted by wage levels and conditions of work. They made a choice rather than simply being coerced to work on the plantations.[13]

Obviously the degree of choice varied. Labour recruitment to the mines of central and southern Africa hardly left much room for 'collaboration', except for those Africans who acted as recruiters. But in other cases such collaboration and choice were of much greater importance. And this is a process which has never stopped: there is no final state of underdevelopment, no point at which indigenous initiatives cease to arise or can only take the form of resistance.[14] Equally, of course, there is no final state of modernity at which the general pressures of the dominating and developed economies of the world cease to constrain the degree and type of choice available to the members of colonial societies.

Indigenous initiatives place constraints upon colonial government. The ability of African farmers to produce food or export crops has to be balanced against European demands for a monopoly of profitable agriculture or for non-agricultural production to be given unconditional priority. Moreover, as on the political level, this also gives rise to conflicts in the indigenous society over valuable collaborator positions. At the same time European interests come into conflict with one another, for example, settler farmers in dispute with monopoly buyers of cheap African agricultural produce. From all this a complex picture emerges in which the colonial state can no longer be understood simply as the agency of economic exploitation or development and in which one can no longer simply juxtapose the interests of indigenous society against imperialism.

An interesting attempt to put this picture in a Marxist frame has been made by Lonsdale and Berman.[15] By providing a theory of the colonial state, they lay the foundation of a specifically Marxist understanding of anti-colonial nationalism.

The crucial theoretical notion employed is that of the 'relative autonomy' of the colonial state. This is seen not merely as a fact of political life but as a necessity if the state is to be effective. The state has to protect the interests of the 'dominant mode of production' at both an economic and a political level. In order to operate as 'the legitimate authority for the pattern of class domination and subordination peculiar to each social order'[16] it must be seen and must see itself as representing the whole social order. If it is seen or sees itself simply as the instrument of the dominant class it will be unable to command the consent of subordinate classes and will become unstable as a result.

Within this general framework one can note tensions between various functions of the state. It may have to act against elements of the dominant class in the general interests of that class. There may be tensions between the state's economic and political functions. In the case of Kenya there seems to be, at least as Lonsdale and Berman present it, no single dominant mode of production, which must further complicate the policies of the state. Within this complex general framework they provide a compelling account of events in colonial Kenya. A general picture emerges of a colonial state adjudicating between the demands of African peasant and European settler modes of production and favouring the dominant groups within these two modes: the chiefs and their kin and the large European farmers. This in turn sets up opposition from subordinate groups such as squatters, the poorer inhabitants of the native reserves, and the clan groups outside the favour of the chiefs. These resistances can be regarded as the basic elements on which a nationalist opposition could build. Elsewhere Lonsdale has outlined a framework for the analysis of the political processes which can lead to nationalism.[17]

The approach is illuminating. It can, however, be improved if stripped of the Marxist terminology in which it is presented. It is difficult to see what explanatory force 'relative autonomy' has even generally, but there are very specific problems when one applies the notion to a colonial state.[18] In some senses, of course, it is not a state at all but a political instrument of the imperial power. On the one hand this reduces the autonomy of the colonial state. On the other, by providing it with an external basis of support it helps insulate it from internal pressures and hence increases the degree of autonomy. The same points apply at an economic level. The colonial state could be used as an instrument of economic interests outside its power; equally it could help produce new economic activities and relationships. In Kenya the political system of indigenous collaboration contributed to the formation of a class of favoured chiefs and their kin. The desire to reduce the cost of colonial control contributed to the encouragement of European settlement and farming. Obviously, once certain situations have been created they will exert a pressure on the colonial state, even if that state was their principal cause in the first place. But one can develop an analysis which recognises this interaction between an 'autonomous' colonial state and various economic interests in colonial society without adopting the notions of relative autonomy or dominant modes of production employed by Lonsdale and Berman.[19] Such an analysis, which would accept many of the specific interpretations they advance, can lead in turn to a very different general perspective. In this perspective it is not so much the colonial state as the instrument of imperialism and class domination which is central as the way in which colonial rule and the development of capitalism create a sharp distinction between economic and political levels of action. Even if political activity is primarily influenced by economic considerations this distinction has its own influence on the forms taken by political opposition to the colonial state. This point will be taken up in the case studies of chapters 8 and 9 and in the general observations made in chapter 10.

4 Cultural interpretations

As with economic interpretations, an approach which emphasises the cultural aspects of imperialism can by-pass the specific level of politics. The main insight of such an approach (which can also have its domination/westernisation/collaboration/resistance variants) is the suggestion that the real crisis in colonial society is not so much about political control or economic exploitation as about a confrontation of values. From this perspective nationalism can be seen less as a way of ending political or economic subordination than as a way of constructing a new identity which overcomes this crisis of values.

It could be seen as just one of a number of ways of doing this. Perhaps of greater importance would be the complex religious adaptations that have taken place in colonial situations. In part these are a response to Christianity. More fundamentally they can be seen as a response to western values which are incompatible with those of traditional religion. In this context nationalism may be seen as a substitute for religious values, appropriating western ideas but simultaneously embodying them in values derived from the colonial 'nation'. The plight and contribution of intellectuals in this process have been particularly closely studied, and this approach fits in well with the general westernisation approach.[20]

At another level one might regard nationalism as a means of constructing a new political identity.[21] This is undertaken not for narrow political purposes but in order to construct a genuine political community. One might see as a general weakness of the modern colonial state its inability to create such a political community. In this sense nationalism points to a specific deficiency in the colonial state.

These ideas are illuminating, though they are rarely expressed in the systematic and general forms in which political and economic interpretations are often couched. They are also difficult to relate to practical politics. For example, many nationalist ideologies are deficient both in a purely intellectual sense and in the appeal they have to the society for which they claim to speak. But it is difficult to see how far that really affects the strength of a nationalist movement. So one wonders how important explicitly political values and the construction of a coherent and plausible sense of identity are to the pursuit and exercise of political power.

166

Again, it is clear that western views on matters such as personal relationships, property rights and legal procedures are incompatible with the traditional practices and values of many colonial societies. Explicit changes are required. But it is not obvious that these various conflicts either can or need to be solved in some general ideological system in order to create a political movement, and subsequently a political community, to which the bulk of the community can commit itself. As with economic and political relationships, these are complex matters which are negotiated between indigenous society and the representatives of western values. The negotiations are always in movement and there is no final solution. One of the great illusions of nationalist ideology is precisely that such a final solution can and must be found, and this is furnished by the nationalist vision. The sense that such solutions are 'needed' can make both contemporaries and historians more credulous than they should be in responding to the particular 'solution' proferred by nationalism.

So to see nationalism as the answer to crises of values and identity is to ask for too fundamental an understanding of what is essentially an attempt to obtain state power. On the other hand, ideology is something more than a matter of practical politics, taken up or abandoned according to pragmatic criteria. I will try to show nationalism's role as provider of an alternative political community to that offered by the colonial state in chapter 10. The more general role of political ideology in nationalism was considered in chapter 2.

5 Conclusion

All the approaches considered offer some important insight into the nature of the colonial situation and of the nationalist challenge to it. Together they demonstrate the complexity of the subject, which cannot be contained within a specific explanatory theory. But for an understanding of colonial nationalism a certain general framework can be derived from them. It would be pointless for this to be no more than a 'balanced' combination of the various ideas presented here, if only because some of them are incompatible. First, I will focus on political interpretations, because, as I have pointed out, the cultural and economic interpretations can do little more than indicate certain limits within which nationalism operates. The specific institution shaping political choice is the colonial state. This state operates within a general context of external political domination but seeks to establish a public and autonomous character in its dealings with colonial society. The extent to which it succeeds in doing this varies greatly. The changes in the forms of political conflict which flow from this bear directly on the rise of nationalist opposition. This approach seeks to combine the 'substance' of the collaborator approach with the 'form' of the westernisation approach. It is the construction of a collaborator network within the institutional framework of a public and autonomous state which provides the optimal conditions for the rise of an effective nationalist opposition to imperial power. The detailed working through of this argument is contained in the case studies of the next two chapters; its general formulation in chapter 10.

Notes

1 The argument was originally advanced by Thomas Hodgkins, *African Nationalism* (London, 1956). For a more recent re-statement which summarises much subsequent research see Henry S. Wilson, *The Imperial Experience in Sub-Saharan Africa since 1870* (Minnesota, 1977), pp. 230–43.

2 Anil Seal, *The Emergence of Indian Nationalism* (Cambridge, 1968), takes this line.

3 The general critique of this approach to nationalism is outlined in the appendix, pp. 415–21.

4 This argument, and the search for other reasons for establishing formal empire, was first advanced by Ronald Robinson and John Gallagher in *African and the Victorians: the official mind of imperialism* (London, 1961). The shift in approach this book introduced led on to the concern with collaborators.

5 As argued by Robinson in 'European imperialism and indigenous reactions in British West Africa, 1890–1914', in *Expansion and Reaction*, edited by H. Wesseling (Leiden, 1978), pp. 142–63.

6 *Ibid.* , for the effect of the hut tax revolt. A synthesis of work on the Maji-Maji rebellion is provided in John Iliffe, *A Modern History of Tanganyika* (Cambridge, 1979), pp. 168–202. For the argument as to its effects which links this with the importance of resistance generally see Terence Ranger, 'Connections between 'primary resistance' movements and modern mass nationalism in East and Central Africa', *Journal of African History*, IX (1968), pp. 437–53, 631–41.

7 Ronald Robinson, 'Non-European foundations of European imperialism: sketch for a theory of collaboration', in *Studies in the Theory of Imperialism*, edited by Roger Owen and Bob Sutcliffe (London, 1972), pp. 117–42 (139).

8 *Ibid.*

9 See below, pp. 218–22.

10 I take this phrase from Terence Ranger, 'The recovery of African initiative in Tanzanian history', The University College, Dar es Salaam Inaugural Lecture series, No. 2 (Dar es Salaam, 1969).

11 I make this general criticism of Marxist approaches, in so far as they focus on the economic level of action, in the appendix.

12 Anthony G. Hopkins, *An Economic History of West Africa* (New York, 1973), pp. 124–66.

13 Iliffe, *op. cit.* , pp. 301–17.

14 A point made by Terence Ranger in a review article, 'Growing from the

roots: reflections on peasant research in central and southern Africa', *Journal of Southern African Studies*, 5, no. 1 (October, 1978).

15 J. M. Lonsdale and B. Berman, 'Coping with the contradictions: the development of the colonial state in Kenya, 1895–1914', *Journal of African History* 20 (1979).

16 *Ibid.*

17 These are cited in the analysis of Kenyan nationalism in the next chapter.

18 For a brief and lucid discussion of the idea see Ralph Milliband, *Marxism and Politics* (Oxford, 1977), pp. 74–90.

19 Iliffe, *op. cit.* , provides many brilliant accounts of these sorts of relationships in Tanganyika without resort to the terminology employed by Lonsdale and Berman.

20 A particularly brilliant account I would cite of this approach, especially because it is applied in a case where formal empire was not established but the crisis of values was acute, is R. Levenson, *Li'ang Ch'i Ch'ao and the Mind of Modern China* (Berkeley and Los Angeles, 1967).

21 This idea is developed with great subtlety in Nadav Safran, *Egypt in Search of Political Community: an analysis of the intellectual and political evolution of Egypt, 1804–1952* (Cambridge, Mass. , 1961).

8

Anti-colonial nationalism:
two case studies

1 Introductory remarks

In this chapter I consider the two cases of India and Kenya. Nationalism
took very different forms in very different circumstances in these two cases.
In the next chapter I consider cases where territorial nationalism either
failed to develop before the achievement of independence or was subjected
to a powerful 'sub-nationalist' challenge. These positive and negative
examples will be used to develop general points in chapter 10, which also
takes up certain general points raised in the previous chapter. The cases
are examined in some detail in order to bring out the complexity of
anti-colonial nationalism and to avoid the criticism that particular cases
are seen as simple expressions of an overall model of anti-colonial nationalism.

2 Indian nationalism

Indian society is so vast and diverse that there would seem to be no
obvious economic or cultural base for a nationalist movement to build on.
Yet through the Indian national Congress there was constructed an organised, nation-wide nationalist mass movement. As a consequence historians of Indian nationalism have been particularly aware of the need to
examine the political determinants of nationalist opposition. They have
been able to draw on a large body of sources as a basis for such an
examination. This may account for a particularly satisfactory blend of
conceptual and empirical argument on the subject of Indian nationalism.
It is this approach, often known as the 'Cambridge school' which informs
much of what follows, although I try to take account of the critical
comments I made in the previous chapter on the collaborator approach,
and also the valid criticisms of the Cambridge school made by historians
of India who wish to lay more stress on colonial repression, the role of
ideas, and the autonomous contribution made by popular movements.[1]

170

The westernisation approach seemed plausible, particularly during the elite phase of Congress up to about 1920 when western-educated figures such as lawyers, government officials and merchants dominated the nationalist movement. The elite of western-educated Indians was large. Where the British did not supply sufficient education Indians founded their own schools and colleges. The moves to nationalism could be associated with the frustrations of those acquiring or seeking western education and the failure to achieve the employment opportunities that such education promised. The moderate nationalist Surendranath Banarjea, for example, turned to opposition after dismissal from the Indian Civil Service. The Rowlatt report of 1918 stated that extremist nationalism, which took the form of acts of terrorism, found its main basis of support among higher-caste Indians of student age.[2]

At the same time one could associate imperial loyalty with less favoured groups in society. Most notable was the Muslim community, elements of which opted for close links to the British and improvements in their own position under imperialism in order to be able to challenge Hindu elites.[3] There were also cases of low-caste Hindu groups co-operating with the Raj in a common opposition to high-caste Brahmins with western education and nationalist sentiments.[4] Subsequent divisions between nationalists and non-nationalists could be traced back to these earlier divisions in terms of access to western education.[5]

The government liked to see nationalism in this way because nationalists could be depicted as relatively privileged, self-serving and unrepresentative. By contrast the Raj and the loyalist groups with which it dealt could be presented as more representative of the whole community. Such views seemed to be confirmed by the actions of nationalist elites. For some time from its establishment in 1885 Congress leaders seemed to be obsessed with issues such as procedures for administrative appointments and the provision of higher education, hardly matters with popular appeal. At times nationalist politicians blocked social reform measures proposed in various provinces when these threatened the interests of the groups from which nationalists were drawn. The government liked to believe that there was no single group which could represent Indian society as a whole and that an impartial authority above the clusters of interests and cultures was the best guarantee of good government.

Even when nationalists took up 'traditional' concerns this too was regarded as manipulative rather than as expressive of any genuine traditional solidarity or value system. For example, when in 1892–93 the nationalist politician Tilak opposed a bill to raise the age of consent for sexual intercourse for women from ten to twelve years it was regarded by many observers as a bid for popularity, even if he could cite ancient sacred Hindu texts in support.[6] The Hindu and Bengali revivalist movements of the early twentieth century likewise could be seen as the work of those

171

educated elites most cut off from any living source of traditional values.

Continuing with this approach, one could also view divisions within the nationalist movement in terms of divisions among the westernised elite. For a number of reasons elite politics varied from one province to another. Up to 1920 nationalist politicians were tied to particular regional bases. National politics appeared as weak alliances between these regional leaders. Tactical differences in the early nationalist movement also seemed to reflect internal elite divisions. Moderates wished to exploit the reforms wrested from the British in 1909 and 1918. These reforms provided for participation in legislative councils and then the exercise of certain executive functions at provincial level. For these moderates the principal concern was to be effective enough in these institutions to maintain support from the highly qualified and limited constituencies which elected them. They were seeking incorporation into the structure of imperial government as a new type of collaborator. On the other hand the extremists condemned such methods and took individual terrorist action in the hope of pushing the government into further concessions. Support for this extremism came from the lower reaches of the educated elite.

Both tactics, council entry and terrorism, were forms of elite politics and their practitioners were suspicious of popular politics. The mass protests against the partition of Bengal had badly frightened the nationalists. When Gandhi advocated the organisation of a mass-based non-co-operation movement in 1919–20 it was almost as objectionable to the extremist politicians who dominated Congress as it was to moderates. It took a year for his approach to be accepted by C. R. Das, who led the nationalist movement in Bengal, although regional hostility (Gandhi was from Gujarat in western India) may have played a part as well as fear of mass action.[7]

It seems plausible, therefore, to discuss Indian nationalism up to about 1920 in terms of the concern of a westernised elite. Earlier mass action, such as the Mutiny of 1857 and the communal riots in early twentieth-century Calcutta, and the numerous tribal, communal, caste, religious, and labour protests seem to have little to do with the nationalism of Congress.

This fits in well with a historiography which focuses on elites and indeed is often biographical in its approach. Although Congress up to 1920 involved only a 'microscopic minority'[8] the approach works by considering politics the affairs of elites and nationalist politics, in particular the affair of Congress elites. It can be broadened slightly by a partial abandonment of the westernisation approach, whereby provincial and even local elites of any kind are drawn into links with Congress. It certainly has been made clear in various local studies that 'traditional' elites were closely involved in nationalist politics even before 1920.[9] In many cases nationalist politics were connected to local and provincial faction conflicts which defy more general terms of analysis. All one could conclude from this is that colonial politics depended upon elite collaboratlon up to about 1920. This political system, heavily biased towards locality and province, created conflict among political elites. Collaboration and nationalism were associated with this conflict and were largely elite phenomena up to 1920.

Generally I would accept this approach provided that it is qualified in a number of respects.[10] First, one must not forget that the Raj was a *British* institution, and that even (in certain respects perhaps especially) the most highly placed Indians confronted racism and subordination as a constant experience. Even moderate 'loyalists' could exult at Japanese successes in 1905 or the humbling of the British by Boer farmers. The concern with religious and linguistic revivalism was as much an expression of cultural alienation from the British as it was of manipulation of popular sentiments or rootlessness. Second, one must not forget that the British had major economic and strategic interests in maintaining control of India. These both ensured a limit to how far collaboration could be extended and also could underlie quite broad currents of anti-British feeling within Indian society. Both these elements give a unity and commitment to nationalism which can be neglected by the focus on the narrow interests of particular elites within the colonial political structure.

Finally, historians in the last decade have drawn attention to the continuation of many kinds of popular protest against the existing order, both as embodied by the Raj and various entrenched Indian interests. These protests, of course, did not use the language of nationalism and rarely rose above a particular regionalised communal, caste, or other interest. However, they formed both a pressure upon and an asset for nationalist politicians even before 1920. Their own dynamics are still not well understood, nor have historians worked out a systematic method of relating them to organised politics, but that does not mean they should be ignored. These mass movements also placed constraints upon the British and other opponents of Congress and conditioned changes made to the political institutions of the Raj.

However, I do not believe the elite approach can in any easy way be replaced or even complemented by a 'class' approach or a 'history from below'. First, it is wrong to search for some 'essential' identity which can be seen as either the building or stumbling blocks of a nationalist movement. Muslim and Hindu, caste and class, are as much constructed and changing identities as is that of nationality. The focus here is upon the changing context within which a political movement which stressed national identity developed. Popular movements, different identity constructs, shifts in government policy, in the international situation – all these condition the way a nationalist movement develops. Above all, the changing political institutional framework is closely linked to this development. It is upon this level of action that I will focus attention.

Up to 1920, therefore, Congress can best be understood as primarily a co-ordinating agency within a system of elite politics. Co-ordination was weakly developed at national level because the important resources in the system, at least so far as the activities of Indian politicians were concerned, were still located at local and provincial levels. But nationalism did not stop at that stage. By 1920 nationalists had not yet achieved provincial self-government and had no rights at all at a national level. Furthermore, reforms such as those of 1918 were accompanied by the repression of extremist activity and policies of fiscal restraint which undermined the moderate strategy of collaboration, by giving collaborators too few resources with which to cultivate support and by removing the most significant powers concerned with finance and order to the centre.

The non-cooperation movement of 1920–22 took Indian nationalism into a new phase in which mobilisation became as important as co-ordination. The movement strengthened national leadership. It brought in extensive Muslim support. It organised mass action on a much greater scale than had been the case before. From then on Congress and Indian nationalism went through phases of agitation, repression and negotiation which progressively advanced their organisation, their political power, the extent of their support, and their objective of supplanting the Raj. The three phases are roughly 1920–28, 1929–35, 1936–47. The last culminated in independence, an achievement flawed by partition of the subcontinent.[11]

How did the limited nationalist organisation of 1920 manage to lead and control these massive campaigns and resistances and conduct hard constitutional negotiations over this period of twenty-seven years? The nationalists have a simple answer. Over this time larger and larger sections of Indian society became nationally conscious, and as they insisted on their rights as a nation so Congress became increasingly militant and popular. By means of repression and by whipping up religious divisions the British managed to hold on for a decade or so longer than they otherwise could and in so doing poisoned the nationalist achievement. The Muslim nationalist argument would agree up to a point but would see religious division as the expression of two nations (not one split by communalism and British manipulation). However, the argument is simply untenable where it is not untestable. One cannot merely equate the rise in nationalism with the rise in national consciousness (whatever that might be), and if one does one can hardly argue that the one caused the other. In fact a great deal of historical research has shown just how complex, changeable and faction-ridden Indian politics was throughout this period. This is not to deny the importance of mass resentment (especially on economic issues) and cultural alienation which underpinned much opposition to the Raj, but only to insist on the need to take account of the internal tensions within Indian society and their changing character and to pinpoint precisely the autonomous political characteristics of the nationalist movement.

174

One can point to a number of problems confronted by the idea of a steady rise in national consciousness and nationalist commitment. For example in the Punjab, Congress only became the dominant Hindu political organisation after 1938 and only then by abandoning the secular nationalism of the All-India Congress. After 1926 and the death of Das the nationalist movement in Bengal went into precipitate decline because its obstructionist politics had ended up by putting so much power in Muslim hands. Yet as late as 1942 Hindu communalist politicians in Bengal were prepared to serve in Muslim-dominated governments. As for Muslim nationalism, it had barely taken shape by 1940. In the elections of 1937 the Muslim League did very badly.[12] On the other hand, the degree of Muslim involvement in Congress never recovered from the level it had reached during the Khilafat[13] movement of the early 1920s.

There was no steady rise in nationalist sentiment, and unity was always very fragile. This had already been shown in the non-cooperation movement of 1920–22, which had engaged only sporadic mass support. The tactic of rent refusal aroused hostility from landlord supporters of Congress. The withdrawal from participation in schools and courts soon proved too much for many of the elite employed in those institutions and this part of the campaign was already crumbling before Gandhi called it off. Afterwards the Muslim Khilafat movement faded and Muslim affiliation to Congress slumped. Nominal membership of Congress dropped from perhaps more than two million in 1922 to less than 200,000 by March 1923.

The picture this conveys – and taking the story further in time confirms it – is one of discontinuity in terms of level of support and in terms of the social, regional and religious bases of that support. Investigation of the internal politics of Congress reveals enormous factional conflict. Factions moved in and out of Congress because of local and provincial disputes. Yet the demolition of the argument that Congress expressed some sort of solidarity – be it of class, nation, religion or anything else – by itself makes it appear incredible that Congress could have achieved what it did. Two possible explanations pinpoint the roles of ideology and personality. An ideological commitment, vital among the activists, could be regarded as the bond unifying the movement as a whole. In this sense the continued repressive and racist character of the Raj furnished a common object of hatred, even if there were vast differences between secular and religious ideas, between Hindu and Muslim and Sikh revivalisms, and many other ideological currents in the Indian politics of the day.

Particular leaders, above all Gandhi, could inspire affection and support where explanation in terms of objective interests would not suffice. Gandhi has lately been subjected to a 'hard-headed' approach which focuses on his political skills, on the way in which he built up networks of political 'subcontractors' through his various campaigns, and the manner in which

175

the doctrines of non-violent protest and economic self-sufficiency could channel mass support in ways which would not alienate business and other elite support.[14] This is a welcome corrective to Gandhian hagiography but it can be taken too far. There is no doubt that Gandhi evoked sentiments at a popular level which we as yet barely understand. His extreme difference from other Congress leaders – his dress and life-style, his 'non-political' image (if one employs western notions of politics) all contributed to making him appear as a saviour figure to many of the poorest people. And in turn it was this popular appeal which gave Gandhi such power in relation to those 'normal' Congress politicians who were immured within local and factional conflicts.

Nevertheless, personality and ideology could only work to produce a mass national movement if underlying them were national process which both pushed politics upwards to focus on taking over the Raj itself and pushed that politics downwards to mobilise mass support. The obvious place to look for these processes is in the Raj itself. This can be done in two ways. First, there is the economic and military context within which the Raj operated, and the way this affected Indian society. For example, the expansion of mass support in the first non-cooperation campaign of 1920–22 cannot be understood without reference to the impact of the First World War upon India. It led to changes in economic and fiscal patterns which both generated a more powerful business community and increased the tax burden upon many Indians. Both these elements meant that the two key social groups in Congress in the inter-war period – businessmen and the better-off peasantry – could play a more important political role. The Second World War had similar effects on business developments and the earlier Depression had increased economic resentments. At the same time, the desperate situation of the British by 1942 led Congress into its last and most massive campaign, the 'Quit India' movement. This was repressed (and the Muslim communalist movement deliberately favoured by the British as another method of control) but at great cost which made Congress intent upon gaining independence and which convinced much of British political opinion that old-style colonialism was a thing of the past. British weakness after 1945 as well as pressure from other quarters such as the USA are an essential part of the context in which independence was finally achieved. So on the one hand one has to look at events on a large scale, not only at an all-India but also at a global level. However, that does not adequately explain the precise way in which Congress, and later the Muslim League, developed. To do this we have finally to look at the internal evolution of the Raj, seeing it not only as an enemy of the Indian nation, a negative focus of nationalism, but also as the linchpin of a complex and changing collaborator system which positively shaped the nationalist movement. This is not a separate development. The administrative reforms of 1918 are closely linked to the repression embodied in the

Rowlatt Bill and expressed in the Amritsa massacre of April 1919. The Government of India Act of 1935 which laid the foundations of Congress electoral success in 1937 was born out of a phase of repression in the early 1930s. One should never forget this broader context when looking at the 'positive' way in which Raj institutions were developed and how this shaped in turn the development of Congress.

In looking at these changes three related ideas can be examined: the 'nationalisation' of factional conflict;[15] the contest for the allegiance of the 'dominant peasant';[16] and the view of Congress as the step-by-step replacement of the Raj.

The key element in factional conflict was the way in which collaboration with the British was conducted. From the very beginning British administration was based on large-scale collaboration. It began with finding people to operate the system of rural taxation, the financial prop of government. It spread to the use of urban groups such as lawyers, merchants and clerks who would help run the expanded administration, the trading networks and the increasing number of legal interventions in which the administration was involved. The provision of western education was closely linked to these essential collaborative roles, without which imperialism in India would have been inconceivable. Access to highly prized collaborator positions became a matter of competition, though it must be remembered that western education was not necessary for many of them. This competition was for some time confined to fairly small groups at local and provincial level. Policy-making and little else was pursued at a national level until well into the twentieth century, and this could be conducted by the small European-only elite at the top of the Civil Service. At lower levels competition might be related to caste or religious or class differences, but there seems to have been no general pattern.

The demand for collaborator positions expanded faster than the supply. Congress became concerned with such demands at a local and provincial level. The administration responded in a number of ways to the problems of managing the collaborator system. It tried to repress some of the disaffection which was created. It tried to expand participation in the system in order to undercut those who opposed existing institutions. Thus the reforms of 1909 provided for greater participation in legislative councils, with native representatives being voted in by various carefully defined constituencies. It was hoped that this would meet the demand for involvement in government and also balance various group interests against one another. However, fiscal restraint meant that access to influence over provincial budgets, for example, proved disappointing. Such restraint was also associated with a greater degree of central control over finance. Again, as collaborator power by 1918–20 moved firmly up to a provincial level – with an expanded elective element (though only some one to three per cent of the total adult population) so it seemed to find that real power was

177

receding further upwards to the national level. The basic reasons for this development lay in economic and strategic concerns, but the insitutional reform response shaped the character of Congress development.

The electoral aspect of these reforms altered the manner in which politics was conducted. As constituencies expanded it became necessary to employ better propaganda and more formal political organisation. When the electorate was extended into the hinterlands of the Presidency capitals, politicians had to move out to the provinces as a whole. In Bengal, for example, after 1918 both Muslim and extremist nationalist politicians quickly realised the need to build up better contacts in the molfussil towns, that is, the local centres of administration and justice. Until then elections in very limited constituencies could be won through informal contacts and pressure. Politicians representing small elites were very conservative on local issues, although they could sound quite radical on provincial and national issues. But the reforms began to break down the insulation between the various levels of political action. The uniformity of reforms meant that this was a national process. Where it did not take place, in the princely states outside British India, nationalism did not become significant until much later, and then largely because of interventions from outside.

Politics therefore was becoming both more organised and extensive at its lower levels and increasingly focused upon national institutions at its upper level. The co-ordinating function of Congress could adapt to the moves from provincial to national focus. It was much more difficult to adapt to the new function of mobilisation which became so important after the reforms of 1918. This was where Gandhi was to play so vital a role, especially where this mobilisation extended well beyond the new electorates. At this point, however, it is with the factional character of nationalism that we are concerned. Reform itself did not transform the pattern of politics. In the Punjab, for example, Hindu political elites managed to maintain their position without recourse to national politics until after the elections of 1936. Then they found that the new provincial ministry under Muslim control which had support from the government and contacts with the Muslim League was no longer matched by their resources at a provincial level. Accordingly Punjabi Hindu politics moved to establish links with Congress. That in turn increased the communalist emphasis within Congress. It was not merely the extension of political activity downwards but the nationalisation of provincial politics which increased this communal element. This communal element in nationalist politics was, therefore, as modern and as much a product of institutional change as was the earlier more secularist emphasis within Congress. The essentialist approaches of either the 'one-nation' view (unity being poisoned by British manipulation) or the 'two-nation' view (Muslims only belatedly waking up to the dangers of Hindu domination) are equally misconceived.

The shift of focus in Punjabi Hindu politics provides a clear example of how the expansion of the collaborator system compels out-groups to associate with a centrally focused opposition to the Raj and its existing collaborators. Congress was the opposition. Just as the collaborator system was itself highly diverse and changing, so was Congress, its mirror image. This diversity was reflected in Congress organisation and policies. Congress decisions were not binding upon the membership. Gandhi himself recognised that only on central bodies such as the All-India Congress Committee was it practicable to demand acceptance of majority decisions. Congress was constantly splitting and re-forming as, for example, when Motilal Nehru and C. R. Das established the Swaraj Party in the early 1920s in order to contest elections to the legislative councils. Personal followings played an important part in internal Congress politics. Jawarhalal Nehru constantly deplored this, as when he noted in August 1934:

> Might not the dominant part of the Bengal Congress be called today 'the society for the advancement of Mr. Nalini Ranjan Sirkar' . . . and the other part probably a similar society for a similar laudable object?'[17]

In such circumstances the tactics of council entry and non-cooperation possessed a certain negative similarity. Neither threatened the heterogeneous structure of Congress in the way a more direct and violent resistance might have done. One reason why Gandhi called off his campaigns when he did was his realisation that large-scale violence, which he deplored in principle, could destroy Congress from within as well as calling down upon it greater repression. Indeed, the internal threat was probably the greater. With important financial backing from rich businessmen, Congress could not afford to become involved in labour unrest in any organised way. Indeed, it never did acquire significant support from urban workers. Likewise its agrarian programmes never were very radical, and rural support, although massive, probably did not extend much beyond the better-off or 'dominant' peasants. Gandhi's politics of non-violence were certainly sincere but one has to see how well they fitted the problems Congress faced when mobilising mass support to realise just how appropriate they were even for politicians who regarded them as no more than a tactic. Again, Nehru and others of a vaguely socialist inclination criticised Gandhi when he extolled the virtues of poverty and the rights of property but their views, if acted upon, would have undermined the fragile unity of Congress. Nehru realised this and distanced himself from 'left' challenges to Gandhi's authority within Congress. Apart from his real popularity among the populace generally (especially among groups such as the Untouchables whom he championed) Gandhi has to be seen as a consummate politician who played a vital role in co-ordinating a very diverse set of factions, as well as mobilising mass support in ways which did not serious threaten the elite co-ordination role of Congress.[18]

One response of the British to the nationalist challenge was to try to undercut it. Electoral reform as well as expanded powers for elected representatives had that purpose in 1918 and 1935. The new electorates of 1918 were hardly massive and the later non-cooperation campaign reflected the limited penetration of the reform. Labour and peasant actions, for example in the tea estates dispute in Assam in 1921, were marginally involved. Even then they were fairly obviously manipulated by nationalist politicians, rather than being treated as a means of extending the scope of organised support to a more popular level.[19]

Mass mobilisation became even more important in the late 1920s and especially during the civil disobedience campaigns of 1930 and 1931–32. Congress took up the issue of rents and taxes in some areas such as the United Provinces. Here the effects of the depression upon agricultural prices had made such payments a matter of great concern to those of the peasantry prosperous enough to be making them. Resistance had already occurred before Congress became involved. The great advantage of its involvement was the limited room for manoeuvre open to the government. The authorities could and did try to reduce assessments in cases of special hardship and danger. But it was dependent on land revenue and was, in many areas, tied to a network of collaborators equally dependent upon rent or tax collection. Yet Congress itself could not take the matter too far, for it included in its own ranks people who depended upon such revenues, especially rents. It tried to distinguish between taxes and rents (an unreal and pointless distinction so far as many peasants were concerned) and insisted that it would be wrong to withhold payment completely. There was anxiety lest non-payment lead to violence, which might damage its position. Nevertheless Congress was still better placed to exploit the issue than was government. Congress never moved to a radical platform on agriculture, not only on account of its support among rent-collecting groups but because this would have alienated the more prosperous peasantry to which it increasingly made an appeal.

The government response to this outflanking of its own position was twofold. It repressed Congress with mass arrests in 1931–32. Then it pressed on with its own reforms, worked out fairly independently of any Indian opinion, which would enfranchise most of the more prosperous peasantry, the 'dominant' peasantry. This was one feature of the Government of India Act of 1935. The basic idea was to shift the system of collaboration on to stronger ground in the hope that nationalists, tied to their own specific social and economic interests, would not be able to match this bid for popular support. Most important of all was a greatly expanded electorate for the purpose of electing provincial ministries.

In some areas the idea of raising up rivals to Congress bore fruit. Where Muslim or low-caste Hindu elites had effective political organisation it led to the rise of mass-based parties opposed to Congress. This happened in the Punjab and Bengal. If the new provincial ministries which were formed under the 1935 Act were allowed to push through measures of social reform beneficial to this mass electorate the position of Congress could be weakened still further. The main danger in these areas was that popular Muslim politics could push Hindu communalist organisations beyond the provincial level towards Congress. This could lead to tensions which could make some areas virtually ungovernable. In the next chapter I will consider the reasons for this popular Muslim politics and how far its success could be seen as another attempt by the government to fight back against Congress advances.

Elsewhere, where Congress was stronger, had developed some sort of a popular base in 1931–32, and communalist parties could not match its popularity, there was another way the British could hope to blunt the nationalist challenge. First, the prospect of gaining influence through electoral participation tempted Congress to come back into legal and permitted political activity, which in turn tended to put the 'right' within Congress into a stronger position. Then, success in those elections, by letting Congress take over provincial ministries, meant that the government could hope to incorporate Congress into the collaborator system. This policy seemed to be having some success by the time of the 1937 elections, held under the provisions of the 1935 Act. Nehru was dismayed to view from prison what he regarded as the takeover of Congress by conciliatory figures. He had hoped and believed that the repression of 1931–32 had eliminated such people from its ranks.[20] Rather it had put the militants behind bars, and the concessions of 1935–36 had brought moderate or opportunist figures increasingly to the fore.

The electoral reforms required Congress to cultivate the dominant peasantry constituency much more effectively than earlier. It could build upon its record in the campaigns of 1931–32 in order to do this and came out the overall victor in the elections of 1937, winning most of the provincial ministries. But although this induced moderation it also had the effect of making the party too formidable a collaborator. From 1937 onwards Congress *was* the government at provincial level in most of British India. This position stabilised Congress by providing it with new resources which tied supporters to it. As successive reforms had brought it into the administration of the country it was largely modelled on the institutions of government. In many ways it was simply the organised exploitation of the changes introduced by the Raj into its collaborator system. This is why so much of the conflict between Raj and Congress seemed, to shrewder observers, like a form of shadow-boxing. The term is peculiarly appropriate: in many ways Congress was the shadow of the Raj. From 1937 its assumption of state power was inevitable, although miscalculations of its own strength and the last attempts of the British to find countervailing collaborators (which were also the efforts of other groups to find British support to balance against Congress) were to poison its inheritance.

181

Congress was both a challenger to and a part of the Raj. Its nationalist ideology was linked to this two-edged position. On the one hand this ideology provided an inspirational vision of Congress as the expression of a nation challenging foreign rule. Given its mass character and its lack of serious indigenous rivals it seemed to many who were involved that this was all that Congress could possibly be. The problem was finding words and images to express it. Nehru recognised that no words, no images were really appropriate:

> India becomes Bharat Mata, Mother India, a beautiful lady, very old but ever youthful in appearance, sad-eyed and forlorn, cruelly treated by aliens and outsiders, and calling upon her children to protect her. Some such a picture rouses the emotions of hundreds of thousands and drives them into action and sacrifice. And yet India is in the main the peasant and the worker, not beautiful to look at, for poverty is not beautiful. Does the beautiful lady of our imagination represent the bare-bodied and bent workers in the fields and the factories? Or the small group of those who have from ages past crushed the masses and exploited them, imposed cruel customs on them and made many of them even untouchable? We seek to cover truth by the creatures of our imagination and endeavour to escape from reality to a world of dreams.[21]

Nehru is too honest (and too socialist) to be completely taken in by his own imagery. Yet his experience of the growth of Congress, its fairly united and national character, pressed such imagery upon him. What else could Congress be if not the political expression of the Indian nation? No doubt one can locate the intellectual origins of this way of looking at a political movement as the expression of the nation in Europe, and in chapter 2I considered these origins. One could argue that in part such ideas helped shape Congress. But the truth would be nearer the reverse of this. The construction of Congress as a political reality out of the pressures created by the colonial state actually pushed nationalists towards the imagery of nationalism. Congress *looked like* the image of nationalism. It was difficult to see how Congress politicians could explain and justify their political activity, except in nationalist terms.

One function of nationalist imagery is to provide the ideological basis of the claim that the nationalist movement is simply an expression of the peculiar and paramount needs of the nation. This could be linked to the mobilisation of mass support for Congress which that imagery both promoted and reflected. The other function of the case made by Congress concerned the form of government appropriate to the nation. Again one can locate the intellectual origins of the commitment to democracy and self-determination in Europe and see colonialism in terms of westernisation, transmitting these ideas to colonial society. Again there is some truth in it. But in many ways what Congress called for was a democratised Raj, a Raj in which the lower elements of the existing political system would be dominant. The idea of a political community which these univer-salist values of democracy and self-determination projected was closely linked to the political community formed within the institutions of the Raj, the political community expressed through Congress.

The two images fused: a society (the Indian nation) demanded a democratic and independent state (the nation-state). Congress both ex-pressed the needs of the nation and the form, in miniature, which the new state should take. In chapter 2 I argued that this fusion of indigenous cultural identity with universal political values is typical of nationalist ideology. In Congress, as major opponent of and major collaborator with the Raj, the fusion had a very special force. The function of legitimacy no doubt played an important part in Indian nationalism (for example, the response of the United States of America to the demands of Congress) but the functions of mobilisation and co-ordination (for the idea of Congress as a political community was linked to the ways it collaborated and bound together its diverse factions) were far more important. The reasons can be sought, above all, in the way Congress opposed but also accepted the structures of the Raj.

Other cases of anti-colonial nationalism were not usually able to combine these components of opposition and acceptance to the same degree. In India the scale of collaboration required to run the colonial state was particularly large, given the size of the sub-continent and the popula-tion, its internal diversity and the small number of Europeans who lived there. The very western structure of the state shaped the collaborator system and the opposition to it in very western ways. Mass support induced the belief that the nationalist movement must represent the needs of a whole society, the nation. Belatedly the challenge of Muslim nation-alism made it even more important that the cultural identity of this single nation and its expression through Congress be spelled out. Rarely do we find all these elements present to the same degree. But it is possible to use the Indian case as a norm. If it indicates the optimal conditions for the rise of an organised and massive nationalist movement, other cases can be measured against those conditions. I shall do this with the Kenyan case below. In the next chapter such optimal conditions will be shown to be even more notable by their absence in cases where territorial nationalism failed to develop. The challenge of 'sub-nationalist' movements should throw further light upon the determinants of anti-colonial nationalism.

3 Kenyan nationalism

(a) Narrative

Kenya was formally taken over by Britain in 1896 as part of the East Africa Protectorate and became the colony of Kenya in 1920. Much of the administration was conducted through Africans appointed to such posts as paramount chief, chief, sub-chief and headsman. By 1910 this was known as the Native Authority system. It was further developed and formalised in the 1920s, when Local Native Councils were established at district level. The system was limited by the special political, administrative and judicial rights granted to European and Asian immigrants in the towns and in reserved lands.

Apart from political institutions colonialism had other effects on the African population. A wide range of Christian denominations set up mission schools and churches throughout the colony. In the absence of much higher education they were the main source of education on western lines. White reserved lands were worked on by squatters and, increasingly, wage labourers. At the same time more Africans were crowded into the land left for their use. On this land there was some differentiation as African farmers began to cultivate food and export crops for sale. Urban growth provided new employment opportunities. The African population of Nairobi, for example, grew from 40,000 in 1938 to 95,000 in 1952. By 1948 perhaps half Kenya's African wage labourers worked outside agriculture.

These changes had the greatest impact upon the Kikuyu, the major language group. Their territory straddled the Rift Valley, the centre of white reserved land. Nairobi was in Kikuyuland. The bulk of the Kikuyu elite were rapidly Christianised. It is not surprising, therefore, that formal political opposition to colonialism started amongst them. In the early 1920s a Kikuyu, Harry Thuku, formed the Kikuyu Central Association (KCA), which was critical of the existing collaborators, land alienation and the lack of African representation on the Legislative Council. The KCA had limited success and support, and Thuku was imprisoned for some time. But it continued to exist through the 1930s, maintaining solidarity with the help of adaptations of the traditional oathing practices of the Kikuyu. When, in the late 1930s, the government began clearing squatters off white reserves and moving them into crowded native reserves the KCA (banned in 1938) could become the focus for the grievances that resulted.

The Second World War boosted the economy and increased demand for African labour whilst leading to a political tightening up. After the war a more aware African population ran up against all sorts of obstacles to their advancement. An African was nominated to the Legislative Council (Legco) in 1944, but this was more than offset by political concessions to European settlers. The increased concern with 'development' on the part of the government affected more and more Africans, often adversely, but as objects rather than participants in the development process.

Generally the international situation seemed to favour demands for greater rights for Africans. The United States of America and Russia were both critical of European empire overseas. Britain had been weakened by the war and by 1947 compelled to concede Indian independence. The United Nations represented a public forum to which demands could be addressed and legitimised in the language of nationalism. But the British government did not regard east and central Africa in the same way as India or even British West Africa. Settler influence was far stronger. The presence of settlers had blocked the formation of a well-educated African elite and this was used as a justification for not granting political rights to Africans. In any case, autonomy was thought of in multi-racial terms. The area, apart from any intrinsic economic value it was thought to possess, was considered strategically important for the protection of shipping movements through the Suez Canal. So conditions favoured the increase in nationalist demands but tension rose as these demands were rebuffed.

The effect was to push elements in the nationalist movement to more extreme opposition culminating in violence. As we shall see, it was linked with factional disputes and directed as much against African collaborators as against white officials or settlers. In October 1952 the government declared a state of emergency and mounted a large-scale operation to destroy what became known as the Mau Mau movement, which was confined to the Kikuyu. This involved moving Kikuyu into special villages to isolate them from 'terrorists'. Mau Mau fighters were forced into the forests. By 1954 the military effort had followed them. By 1955 the Mau Mau threat had effectively been overcome, though in 1963 some fifteen hundred Mau Mau fighters came out of the forests, once promised an amnesty.

At the same time the government entered into a series of negotiations and reforms. African participation in Legco was expanded over the years and nominees admitted to the Executive Council (turned in 1954 into a Council of Ministers). A land reform programme was pushed through, designed to build up loyalist bases of support, especially among the Kikuyu.

After 1956 and the Suez crisis British commitment to the maintenance of colonies in east Africa was in doubt. The election of Africans to Legco (1957) and expanded representation on Legco (1958) provided African politicians with a legal way of registering support for their demands. The whole process of decolonisation accelerated with Macmillan's appointment of Iain Macleod as Colonial Secretary in 1959. From then on the main issues concerned timetabling and whether provisions for multi-racial and/or federal rights should be embodied within the new state. This question divided the Africans, but the major political elements among the largest groups, the Kikuyu and Luo, pushed for a unitary state without provisions for racial groups. The party representing this policy achieved a decisive majority in elections of May 1963. The veteran nationalist leader Jomo Kenyatta became Prime Minister of the internal government on 1 June 1963. Full independence was achieved on 12 December.

This is the bare sequence of events. It is now necessary to analyse the role and character of Kenyan nationalism within it. The principal concern will be the way in which the political context shaped the development (and non-development) of nationalism. In order to explore this I will consider three issues: the role of the Kikuyu; the relationship between them and other major African groups, especially the Luo; and the part played by Kenyatta. From these considerations some general conclusions can be drawn.

(b) Analysis

(i) The role of the Kikuyu. The Kikuyu people in pre-colonial times could not be described as a tribe if by that term is meant a society with a common system of extended kinship and political authority. Rather it was a language group divided into many smaller segments. The unity and group consciousness of the Kikuyu were a product of the colonial period. Various European elements had identified them as a group. Mission education used (and thus codified in written form) their language as a vehicle of instruction. The administration used them as a political unit for certain purposes. Migration to Nairobi from different regions of Kikuyuland and contact there with Europeans, Asians and Africans speaking other languages provided a series of daily experiences to which the notion of Kikuyu identity seemed appropriate. In these and other ways a sense of being Kikuyu came to matter. It was, of course, linked with a sense of racial identity which colonialism particularly rubbed in.

At first this identity could be put to political use by the elites that collaborated with the colonial authority. However, it might acquire an oppositional character if the position of those elites was eroded or challenged. This could lead either to members of the elites themselves turning to opposition or to new elements in Kikuyu society challenging the dominant collaborators. A number of examples of how it could happen may be cited. For example, in the early 1930s there was a campaign by some missionaries against the Kikuyu custom of circumcising adolescent girls. It was supported by many within the Kikuyu Christian elite. It could be opposed by those critical of the collaborator system, such as the KCA, who could mobilise popular feeling against interference with traditional customs and values. Subsequently this particular issue was taken up by Kenyatta and fitted into what was really a highly developed theory of Kikuyu cultural nationalism.[22]

Even more important was the question of land. Alienation to whites caused resentment. Internal conflicts were particularly related to what happened on the land reserved for African use. Commercial opportunities and a rapid increase of population there led to increased conflict over its control and use. Chiefs and their kin could be seen as manipulating their

186

collaborator positions to their own benefit. Some of the factional conflict which could develop expressed itself through the Local Native Councils, but as these were captured by particular factions so others were forced to find alternative channels of protest.

The position of the collaborator groups was weakened in two crucial ways. First, pressure from white settlers (and to a lesser extent Asians) prevented the extension of African collaboration beyond rural district level outside white reserved lands. This meant that any attempt to engage in political action beyond rural district level involved moving outside colonial institutions, a move collaborator politicans were reluctant to make. Secondly, the same restrictions (for example, settler pressure on economic policy) limited the resources available to collaborators through co-operation with the colonial authority and, therefore, the extent to which they could bind an extensive following to themselves and maintain local dominance. One of these limitations was the question of reserved land for whites. Another was the insistence of white farmers on favourable conditions for labour supply to their holdings and the removal of effective African competition. Another limitation concerned the execution on native lands of conservation schemes which offered few direct benefits to many of those recruited as communal labour for such schemes. Indeed, it often appeared that collaborator elites secured their own narrow interests within these limitations at the cost of reduced control over the indigenous population and the emergence of challenges to their authority.

Co-ordination through Nairobi and the existence of a common set of problems soon allowed these challenges to extend beyond the local level and, necessarily, outside colonial institutions. The KCA was the first clear example. Opposition was confined to the Kikuyu and was regarded as illegitimate by the colonial government and its collaborators. The problems this situation could create were intensified after the Second World War. The rise in expectations coupled with increased government intervention to 'develop' the economy pushed elements in Kikuyu society into more determined opposition. The problem the militants faced was how to co-ordinate and control an extensive movement of opposition in the absence of institutional channels of expression. The answer was found in an adaptation of the practice of oathing.

It has already been mentioned that this practice was taken up by the KCA in the 1930s in order to sustain solidarity. Its revival after the war had, at first, limited objectives. It was used by ex-KCA officials, some Kikuyu elders and Kenyatta to promote and maintain solidarity among those already involved in oppositional politics. But the pressure of circumstances forced matters further. Within a year or two after 1945 in at least one area where squatters had been newly concentrated the oath had taken on additional meaning.

The next step came when radical Kikuyu politicians in Nairobi, men involved in trade union or independent church activity,[23] decided to compensate for lack of unity and effectiveness by using the oath to mobilise greater support. In a variety of ingenious ways the oathing movement was extended and its impact strengthened by making it a more intense experience and by linking it with more extreme demands over land and independence than had hitherto been raised. However, the militants could not control the movement they had begun. The pent-up frustrations it channelled and intensified began to break out in local conflicts. Much of the violence was directed against other Kikuyu who were seen as collaborators and beneficiaries of the colonial system. It was this sort of violence, culminating in the assassination of a leading Kikuyu politician, which provoked the declaration of the state of emergency. Some of the worst incidents under the emergency seem to have been not so much the work of the Mau Mau as the result of local disputes, usually about land, on the assumption that the Mau Mau would be blamed. Equally, however, many people joined the Mau Mau because of local conflicts with better-placed collaborator figures. Only this makes sense of the fact that the great majority of those killed on the 'loyalist' side during the emergency were civilian Kikuyu. A movement directed primarily against whites, both settlers and government officials, would lead one to expect a very different pattern of casualties.

It is interesting to analyse the various options confronting Kikuyu politicians up to the declaration of the emergency. Some of the Nairobi militants have claimed that with the oathing campaign they were simply building up a more resolute nationalist movement than had hitherto existed. Given another year, they could have created an extensive and effective movement which would have included non-Kikuyu.[24] This was seen as imperative, given the failure of either collaboration or moderate opposition to improve the situation of the Africans. As it was, the government's precipitate military action forced them into fragmented guerilla activity. This analysis is debatable. It seems to have been their failure to control the mobilisation process they had initiated that led to outbreaks of violence and the emergency, rather than the actions of the authorities pushing the militants into violence and fragmentation. Moreover, the oathing movement seems to have had very little impact beyond the Kikuyu.

It was these sorts of considerations – controlling mobilised groups and co-ordinating action with non-Kikuyu – as well as a concern to avoid repressive activity by the authorities that turned Kenyatta towards a more moderate path. He did not wish to alienate all Kikuyu loyalists or to split the Kikuyu openly between extreme nationalists and collaborators. He had used oathing to co-ordinate rather than mobilise. This was a policy with more relevance to non-Kikuyu groups, who were not so badly affected by colonial policies. It is interesting that one way in which he tried to prevent the slide towards extremism within the leadership of the Kenya African

Union[25] was by seeking to place non-Kikuyu in important positions. The militants resisted this: not because they were 'tribalist', whatever that term means, but because at the time their policies were only really accepted among Kikuyu.

After the emergency the polarisation of the Kikuyu intensified. The land reform programme and the creation of safe villages on the one hand created a particularly strong collaborator system. The military action against the Mau Mau on the other created a particularly repressive and violent confrontation with extreme nationalists. Local conflict deepened. As a fragmented guerilla movement under intense pressure Mau Mau failed to preserve clear political unity and goals. This, as well as its oathing practices and the violent acts which always accompany this form of warfare, have led to depictions of the movement as a form of barbarism, a relapse into 'primitive' behaviour – contrasted with 'civilised' loyalism and, later, constitutional nationalism. The argument is untenable and it makes a mystery of the way in which Kenyatta, the 'leader into darkness',[26] also emerged as the leading figure in the negotiated process of decolonisation. The people who had begun the Mau Mau movement were nationalists. Even under the most extreme pressure its leaders remained committed to Kenyan independence and tried to keep some kind of overall political organisation going. Structural deficiences – acting outside recognised institutions, building on local grievances, running up against collaborator enmity – compounded by the declaration of the emergency prevented the movement acting in terms of its leaders' objectives and cut it off from other forms of nationalist action.

Furthermore Mau Mau helped to shift colonial policy towards granting some sort of autonomy. However, the framework for negotiating this excluded the Mau Mau, and it was non-Kikuyu as well as Kikuyu loyalists who led the way in the negotiations. Not surprisingly, after 1963 many 'freedom fighters' and their sympathisers took the view that the Mau Mau had made all the sacrifices which enabled the loyalists to gain all the prizes.[27] Certainly one must remember that nationalism among the Kikuyu can be understood only in terms of the internal conflicts induced by colonialism and that, at its most extreme during the emergency, it led as much to civil war amongst the Kikuyu as to a determined assault upon white settlers and the colonial government.

(ii) The role of the Luo and the Luyia. The Kikuyu make up about 19 per cent of the African population, followed in numerical importance by the Luo (about 14 per cent) and the Luyia (13 per cent). These groups, again hardly to be described as tribes, inhabit south-western Kenya up to Lake Victoria. Were significant elements among them to join with Kikuyu in a nationalist movement, this would dominate African politics in Kenya. This was what happened, and as it is the key to the success of African

189

nationalism in Kenya it is these non-Kikuyu groups which need the closest consideration. There is a particularly good secondary literature on them.

As elsewhere in Kenya the region in the south-west called Nyanza Province had been brought under a system of native authority by about 1910, with the inevitable competition for collaborator positions. Again, the collaborator system could be weakened if it imposed too much on the indigenous population without providing services in return and if local elites formed which were excluded from participation in the native authority institutions. Again, the issues of land and labour were central to this process, although trading also played an important role.

The block of good land preserved for white use, the so-called White Highlands, extended into Nyanza Province. The railway to Uganda was completed by 1910 and could encourage both European settlement and African cash crop farming. For a time both could develop without too much conflict and primarily at the expense of a growing class of Africans who worked for others in both sectors. But beyond a certain point conflict became serious. At times, and increasingly, labour for farmers, for governmental purposes such as wartime service, and for schemes of conservation, could not be obtained without resorting to some form of coercion. Chiefs often helped in obtaining labour both for their own interests and because of pressure from above. This encouraged local opposition to them and weakened their local bases of support. The problem became particularly acute when disputes arose over the use of land in native reserves. Some groups opposed measures such as the registration of individual holdings or terracing to conserve land because they feared that those in authority would manipulate the changes to their own benefit. It was this rather than opposition to 'progressive' reforms which motivated them: later, when they controlled the reform process, such former opposition figures would push such measures through enthusiastically. Opposition of this sort could be quite effective at a local level by building upon lineage groups excluded by the chiefs and their kinfolk from the benefits of collaboration.

Pressure from European settlers provided another stimulus to opposition. Attempts to restrict commercial agriculture among Africans in order to preserve a European monopoly aroused bitter resentment. The setting aside in 1931 of a recent land ordinance concerned with native reserved land when gold was discovered in north Nyanza made clear the weakness of the collaborator system and the favoured position of European interests in the colonial state. Another focus of opposition concerned the Asian traders, who were resented by African traders, who in turn felt that many chiefs as well as Europeans preferred to deal with the Asians because they gave better service. Finally, extensive mission education might produce new elites who could not find a place in the collaborator system and would move into opposition, where they could provide leadership for all the other diffuse opponents of the status quo. The expectations of this opposition could be raised by the nearby example of the Baganda in Uganda who had obtained much greater autonomy under colonial rule than any group in Kenya.[28]

In all these ways there was pressure on the existing political arrangements. To some extent local collaborators might provide some support for the pressure in order to maintain their own position and to try to persuade the government to extend their authority. The government could make limited responses in this direction. For example, the introduction of the Local Native Councils in 1924 seems to have incorporated some mission elites into a wider collaborator system. But there were strict limits, and the responses could themselves give rise to further problems. For example, the Luyia in north Nyanza had a paramount chief, unlike the Luo to the south. The establishment of the Local Native Councils tended to switch the major emphasis of collaboration towards the councils and away from the paramount chief. Consequently, when new opposition developed over land issues and could not gain control of the councils it demanded the restoration of an effective paramount chieftancy. This ploy offered the opposition a chance of institutionally extending its organisations and claims beyond local to regional level and of undercutting the position of the established collaborators. Later, in the 1950s, it appears that the paramount chief was brought back into the collaborator system, abandoned his oppositional stance and so forced his former supporters into other forms of action. One of these was to take up links with the Kikuyu in national level opposition to the colonial state. This had begun to happen in the 1930s but, with more local options remaining to be explored, had been of limited importance. Twenty years later one finds some of the people active in the earlier period taking up contacts with the oathing movements.[29]

Another path for opposition beyond the local level was through trading networks and links with Nairobi. Luo who settled in Nairobi began in the inter-war period to set up welfare associations which could become a focus for supra-local action. The use of trading contacts to develop a wider sphere of political action is epitomised in the career of Oginga Odinga.[30]

Mission education had early given Odinga access to a wider outlook than he would otherwise have had. In the 1930s an opposition group, based on African trading interests, established a pressure group in central Nyanza. It employed a full-time official who travelled round the province building up an organisation and helping with various welfare projects. Odinga travelled with him and gained his first taste of political activity at an all-Luo level. Subsequently his further education and work as a teacher broadened his horizons and increased his resentment at European superiority and racial prejudice. However, he was not in a position to express this in effective political terms. The opportunity to do so came when he abandoned teaching and set up as a merchant. In 1946 he established the

Luo Thrift and Trading Company. This put him with the African trader opposition in central Nyanza. It also provided him with a network of contacts which extended to Nairobi. The heightening of tension after the war provided such opposition with greater potential local support. At the same time the extension of Kikuyu political activity could link up with Luo opposition. In 1951, as part of his efforts to extend support for the Kenyan African Union beyond the Kikuyu ranks, Kenyatta went on a countrywide campaign tour. He visited Kisumu, the main town in central Nyanza, and it was on this occasion that Odinga joined the KAU.

The reforms and negotiations initiated after 1952, along with repression, provided a focus for activity on the part of opposition politicians from outside Kikuyuland. Indeed, in part they had to represent Kikuyu interests, as political activity was severely restricted among the Kikuyu. The trading networks and pressure groups provided an important local base for these politicians. They could be turned to institutional use when the first African elections to Legco were held in 1957. Odinga contested and won the seat for central Nyanza. From this point on he occupied, under the transitory institutions established in the process of decolonisation, a political base which linked local, district and national levels of political action. From that position he was able to play a leading role in the constitutional negotiations which led to independence.

One can see that the development towards genuine nationalist politics moved along completely different routes among the Kikuyu and the Luo. The polarisation created by the collaborator system among the Kikuyu ended up in virtual civil war. The process of reform this helped to initiate meant that loyalist elements among the Kikuyu could advance their position while Mau Mau was repressed. But even the loyalist or moderate opposition groups were kept out of explicit political activity during the emergency. Nationalism was divided and inchoate among the Kikuyu. In the case of the Luo and Luyia, especially the former, opposition did not reach such intense levels as among the Kikuyu. The leading opposition figures, therefore, instead of encountering repression or apolitical reform, were able to develop their bases into the transitory institutions of the decolonisation period. The problem was how the divided nationalism of the Kikuyu and the more institutionalised nationalist movement among the Luo could be co-ordinated to create a united movement which could dominate the negotiations for independence. Kenyatta played a vital part in answering this problem.

(iii) The role of Jomo Kenyatta. Kenyatta's early political career was essentially that of a Kikuyu politician. He became Secretary General of KCA in 1928. He was aware of the need to make contacts beyond the Kikuyu but circumstances did not permit much to be done before the Second World War. He came to Britain in 1931 and stayed, apart from

trips to Europe, until 1946. Most of his practical political work during this period was undertaken in Kikuyu interests, for example, on problems of land ownership. His book, *Facing Mount Kenya*, which represented a form of cultural nationalism, was about the Kikuyu and raised questions about the relationship between cultural nationality and territorial nationalism.[31] When he returned to Kenya his practical activity until shortly before his arrest in 1952 was as a Kikuyu politician, although it extended into such things as the independent schools movement. He was just beginning to extend the work of the KAU beyond the Kikuyu when the emergency and his arrest brought him to an abrupt halt.

Kenyatta had also been closely involved with the pan-African movement. This undoubtedly widened his horizons and provided him with contacts and a prestige that was far greater than that of any other black Kenyan politician. Yet it was never a substitute for effective political activity at a Kenyan level. Both Kikuyu and pan-African sentiments were couched in cultural terms and came to be overshadowed by the more political focus of Kenyan nationalism. What needs to be understood is why Kenyatta was able to emerge from prison in 1961 as undisputed leader of the nationalist movement.

Part of the answer, of course, can be provided in terms of his prestige and martyrdom and his charismatic appeal throughout Kenya. But that alone does not suffice. Here I want to concentrate on his role in the light of the structure of nationalism in Kenya as analysed in the previous two sections.

To recapitulate the conclusions of that analysis, there were two major divisions within Kenyan nationalism. One was between Kikuyu and non--Kikuyu opposition politics, which had developed in very different ways. The other was within the Kikuyu, where internal conflict was particularly savage: as a result there were directly opposing contributions to Kenyan nationalism among the Kikuyu. Little progress had been made beyond this situation by 1952. Kenyan nationalist leaders were people bound to particular local constituencies. Kikuyu politicians were unable to represent adequately any sort of Kikuyu opinion during the emergency. So although important advances were made at that time it was impossible for any active nationalist politician or group to achieve leadership within a united movement. Negatively, at least, no one was able to pre-empt Kenyatta's leading position while he was in prison.

The conflict within the Kikuyu, even among opponents of the *status quo*, stopped any Kikuyu politician active during the 1950s becoming undisputed leader of Kikuyu opposition. Up to 1952 Kenyatta had carefully avoided becoming identified with the more extreme or more moderate elements among the Kikuyu opposition. For example, although in his book he had launched an uncompromising defence of female circumcision, eight years earlier when the controversy raged his position was much more ambiguous and conciliatory. His recognition of internal divisions among the Kikuyu themselves on the issue is rather at odds with his subsequent account, which presents female circumcision as an integral part of an organic and consensual Kikuyu culture. His exile after 1931 removed him from much of the internal conflict which developed in the 1930s, especially as KCA became more intransigent. After his return in 1946 he sought to avoid being captured by the conflicting elements within KAU. His role in activities such as the independent schools movement kept him in the forefront of opposition without directly aligning him with those who differed over how opposition to colonialism should be conducted. However, as conflict among Kikuyu opposition mounted up to 1952 the demands on him to identify with one or another party became insistent. Europeans condemned him as a terrorist because he would not openly disavow violence; the Nairobi militants distrusted his ties with moderate figures and his failure to support them more fully. By the time of the emergency Kenyatta was moving towards a disavowal of Mau Mau while probably becoming aware just how direct were the links between KAU and the Mau Mau leadership. It is difficult to see how he could have avoided a definite commitment much longer. Ironically his arrest, trial and imprisonment enabled him to preserve his neutrality whilst making a martyr of him. It was precisely his absence from the divided politics of nationalism over the next decade that uniquely qualified him to paper over the divisions in the nationalist movement. Once he had committed himself to the unitary and constitutional nationalists from the Luo and the Kikuyu who came together in KANU (Kenya African National Union) that party was assured of domination of African politics. For a British government concerned to find a successor regime it was apparent that KANU was the only practical choice.

(c) Conclusion

The divisions within Kenyan nationalism can be seen as a product of the weaknesses of the collaborator system and of the ways in which the colonial state responded to them. Because of the constraints of strategic assumptions before 1956, and the settler presence, the collaborator system could not be expanded to provide national institutions in which Africans could act effectively. Deprived of the means of either opposing or taking over Kikuyu politicians, the first nationalists, moved away from the co-ordination of oppositional factions, both Kikuyu and non-Kikuyu, to the mobilisation of popular support. But they had been compelled to do this before they were in a position to control that support or even maintain unity among oppositional elements within the Kikuyu. The result was to push the most extreme nationalists into the dead-end of guerilla warfare. The reforms and negotiations which also developed in the 1950s did little to allow national-level politics to form before 1957, and even then it was only really allowed among non-Kikuyu. When nationalism's function became increasingly to demonstrate to the British the capacity to form a legitimate successor state (mainly after 1959) Kenyatta played a crucial role in binding together elements of the divided nationalist movement.

In general terms, of course, the simple existence of the colonial state and of privileged racial minorities was the fundamental condition for the development of nationalism in Kenya. Practical politics had to accept the territorial unit as the basis for the pursuit of state power. The notion of a state power which was the ultimate objective of the nationalist movement was then the *sine qua non* of a territorial nationalist movement. But the specific character of that movement was intimately related to the precise structural features of the colonial state. The collaborator system was sufficiently developed to allow effective forms of opposition to build up from local conflicts within the various African populations. But it was sufficiently restricted to force much of that opposition outside the institutional channels of action provided by the colonial state. The tactics of co-ordination and mobilisation came into conflict with one another up to 1952; the nationalist movement polarised under the emergency. The combination of collaboration with restraints upon the levels to which it could develop served to produce a powerful but flawed nationalist movement.

4 Concluding remarks

The general conclusions to be drawn from these case studies will be developed in chapter 10. Here I will simply make some broad preliminary observations.

Anti-colonial nationalism is closely related to opposition within indigenous society to the collaborator system established under the modern colonial state. It cannot, therefore, be seen in simple nationalist terms of colonial society against imperial power. The cultural identities to which it appeals are functions of the forms taken by opposition politics. As there is never unity among the various language and other cultural groups which are identified in nationalist ideology, one can hardly see such group identities as the ultimate source of the nationalist movement.

The collaborator system can be weakened in a variety of ways, above all by having to face too heavy demands on it. To maintain control the colonial government has to continually repair and modify the system. The limitations on the process of modification directly determine the ways in which nationalist opposition develops in colonial society and state. There are external factors shaping colonial policy, and nationalism is, in part, an appeal to outsiders as well as to the imperial power itself once it has decided upon decolonisation. But they cannot be related to the internal dynamics of anti-colonial nationalism because they extend beyond the colonial situation. When looking at those internal dynamics the concepts of co-ordination and mobilisation can prove useful.

The Indian case provided optimal conditions for the combined co-ordination of diverse nation-wide interests and the mobilisation of mass support. This, along with the challenge of Muslim nationalism, was related to the development of a nationalist ideology which both reflected and promoted co-ordination through colonial institutions and the mobilisation of popular support. The Kenyan case provided more flawed conditions for such development. Mobilisation and co-ordination, especially among the Kikuyu, conflicted with one another. The cultural underpinnings of opposition politics were pitched either at the sub-national level (especially among the Kikuyu on matters such as oathing and female circumcision) or at the pan-African level. An all-Kenyan nationalist movement was structurally flawed and, therefore, had a rather poor ideological expression. This movement and its accompanying ideology primarily served to legitimise the succession to the colonial state.

The existence of a distinct state power under foreign control is the general condition for the development of anti-colonial nationalism. The latter therefore accepts the territorial units provided by the colonial state. The institutions through which the collaborator system works, and modification of those institutions in the face of opposition from indigenous society, provide the initial determinants of the way in which the nationalist movement develops.

Notes

1 These concerns are responsible for most of the revisions I have made to the original version of my interpretation of Indian nationalism. I am especially indebted to advice from Rudra Mukherjee during his period as Simon Fellow at Manchester University.
2 I owe this reference to Professor Judith Brown, who provided very helpful comments upon the original draft of this section on Indian nationalism.
3 See below, pp. 206–14.
4 For an example in Madras see Crawford Young, *The Politics of Cultural Pluralism* (Wisconsin, 1976), pp. 102–3.
5 For examples in Bengal see J. H. Broomfield, *Elite Conflict in a Plural Society: twentieth century Bengal* (Berkeley, 1968), especially pp. 1–41.
6 On Tilak see Gordon Johnson, *Provincial Politics and Indian Nationalism: Bombay and the Indian National Congress, 1880–1915* (Cambridge, 1973). Kedourie in his introduciton to the nationalist extracts which he edited, *Nationalism in Africa and Asia* (London, 1970), takes this view of Tilak.
7 I owe this reference to regional hostility to Professor Brown.
8 The phrase was used in a speech by Viceroy Dufferin in November 1888 and is cited in Sumit Surkar, *Modern India 1885–1947* (2nd ed., London, 1989), p. 94.

196

9   Broomfield, *op. cit.* ; C. A. Bayly, *The Local Roots of Indian Politics: Allahabad, 1880–1920* (Oxford, 1975).

10   Much of what follows is indebted to the arguments put forward in Sarkar, *op. cit.*

11   For this periodisation see D. A. Low's introduction to the volume of essays he edited under the title *Congress and the Raj: facets of the Indian struggle, 1917–1947* (London, 1977), pp. 7–12.

12   On the formulation of the Pakistan idea and its achievement, see below pp. 213–4.

13   This was the protest movement against the attack upon and ultimate abolition of the Caliphate, for which see above, p. 155, note 6. For its role in the non-cooperation movement see Judith Brown, *Gandhi's Rise to Power: Indian Politics, 1915–1922* (London, 1974), pp. 190–229.

14   These ideas have been developed most thoroughly in Judith Brown's study of Gandhi.

15   For this idea I have been particularly influenced by the essay by Anil Seal, 'Imperialism and nationalism in India', in *Locality, Province and Nation: essays on Indian politics 1870–1940*, edited by J. Gallagher, G. Johnson, and A. Seal (Cambridge, 1973), pp. 1–28.

16   For the use of this term see Low, *op. cit.* , pp. 1–2. Even Sarkar, *Modern India*, who is critical of much of the Cambridge school finds himself accepting the key role of this group within inter-war Congress, as well as the way in which Congress was *becoming* the Raj. 'This was not just a question of party organisation throttling lower-level spontaneity; what was involved was the gradual establishment of a kind of hegemony (never absolute or unqualified, however, as we shall see) of bourgeois and dominant-peasant groups over the national movement'. [254]

17   Quoted in Broomfield, *op. cit.* , p. 299.

18   On the other hand, Gandhi's anti-industrial views could only have limited appeal to business groups within Congress. The stress on economic independence could help such business interests, but in many ways Nehru's 'developmental nationalism' fitted their interests more effectively in the long-run, especially once Congress had acquired power.

19   In the original version of this chapter I underestimated the extent and autonomous character of many of the popular movements that were loosely linked to the Non-cooperation campaign. For a corrective see Sarkar, *op. cit.* , especially pp. 178–226.

20   Jawarhal Nehru, *An Autobiography* (London, 1958), pp. 504ff.

21   *Ibid*, p. 431.

22   See also above, pp. 60–1. Kenyatta sought to undermine the idea that the practice was 'irrational' by arguing that it had a function within Kikuyu culture. He sought to undermine the idea that the practice was 'immoral' by arguing that moral values were internal to a particular culture, not some universal (= western) code which could be applied to all societies. The problem was – as with so much nationalist discourse – that Kenyatta was fabricating an essential, consensual Kikuyu 'culture' in order to sustain this argument.

23   One leader, Fred Kubai, was involved in trade unionism. Another, Bildad

Kaggia, played a leading role in an independent religious movement. Both had been deeply affected by their war service.

24 These claims were made in interviews conducted by John Spencer and contained in his unpublished paper 'KAU and the 'Mau Mau': some connections' (1975). I have drawn greatly upon this paper in my account of the oathing movement.

25 The Kenyan African Union (KAU) was founded in 1946 and Kenyatta became its president in 1947.

26 A phrase used by the Governor of Kenya, Sir Philip Mitchell, when declaring that Kenyatta would not be released from prison and allowed to lead the national movement.

27 The use of the term 'freedom fighter' and the disputes, both practical and historiographical, over the credit due to the Mau Mau are dealt with in R. Buijtenhuis, *Mau Mau Twenty Years After: the myth and its survivors* (The Hague, 1973).

28 See J. M. Lonsdale, 'Political associations in western Kenya', in *Protest and Power*, edited by Robert Rotberg and Ali Mazrui (New York, 1970), pp. 598–638.

29 One man, John Adala, is mentioned in *ibid.* , p. 625 (for the 1930s), and in Spencer, *op. cit.* , (for the 1950s).

30 For this account I draw upon Lonsdale; and Odinga's autobiography, *Not Yet Uhuru* (London, 1967).

31 I have already mentioned this. See also above, pp. 60–1.

Sub-nationalism in colonial states

1 Introductory remarks

In the previous chapter I sought to show how the structure of the colonial state shaped nationalist opposition to that state. The major concern was with the development of territorial nationalism, that is, nationalist opposition which accepted the boundaries established by colonialism. I did not devote much attention to what might be called cultural sub-nationalist or tribalist movements.[1] In particular I did not consider these movements as obstacles to territorial nationalism. This is not because such movements have been unimportant. Indeed, they have been of major importance, and for that very reason they need explicit analysis. In this chapter and in chapter 12 I will provide this analysis. The major argument in these chapters is that the determinants of these sub-nationalist movements are the same as those of territorial nationalist movements.

It is important to realise what this argument is directed against. There is a common and widespread assumption that in the modern colonial state territorial nationalism is 'artificial', whereas sub-nationalism or tribalism is 'natural'. This is because the territory is itself the product of modern colonialism, whereas sub-nationalist movements can base themselves upon enduring identities which preceded it. One might argue that territorial nationalism is a practical acceptance of colonial realities and that it can only flourish given particular conditions, such as the formation of a westernised elite and institutions through which to organise at a territorial level. However, the argument might continue, such movements will always be weak because there will exist at the same time loyalties to sub-national or tribal units.

In a way this argument perpetuates the nationalist approach.[2] Genuine nationalism – that is, nationalism which springs from the sense of belonging to a particular cultural group – is located at a level other than that of the territorial state. In order to counter this approach one must demonstrate that such sub-nationalist movements are no more or less the product of cultural identity than territorial nationalist movements, and that there is no inherent conflict, or at least incompatibility, between political movements operating at these different levels. Of course, once a political movement within the territory of the colonial state wishes to make claims to autonomy or independence it has to go beyond universalist anti-colonial arguments to arguments about distinct group identity within colonial society. But we have seen enough so far to realise that the language nationalists use cannot be taken as a guide to the real basis of nationalist politics. In this chapter I will consider the actual bases of sub-nationalism under colonialism. In chapter 12 I will look at sub-nationalist challenges to newly independent states.

The three cases considered in this chapter are different in important ways. In the Belgian Congo there was no territorial nationalism of significance at the time the region acquired formal independence. In the case of Uganda a particular group, the Baganda, had a clear sub-national identity and set of political claims long before independence was granted. In the case of India Muslim nationalism emerged only shortly before independence to challenge a highly developed territorial nationalist movement. I take such different cases in order to avoid developing general conclusions from too narrow a basis.

2 The Belgian Congo

At first glance the case of the Belgian Congo (contemporary Zaire) suggests that there is some validity in the fundamental distinction which is often made between territorial nationalism and cultural sub-nationalism. To begin with, the colonial state did very little to introduce such changes as would have enabled a nationalist movement to infiltrate the collaborator system and to build up from local to national level. No provision was made for formal African participation in the administration until changes were suddenly brought about in the 1950s. Members of the rather poorly developed western-educated elite, the *évolués* as they were significantly called, were not granted important rights which could have brought them into an organised relationship with the colonial state.[3]

Consequently when reforms were introduced there was no territorial nationalist leadership or movement available to exploit them. The result was chaos. The holding of elections in the major towns in 1957–58 was accompanied by the first major ethnic conflicts. The latter, in turn, weakened colonial control, arousing expectations of fundamental political change. The next step was the spread of these expectations into the countryside. This occurred in a regionalised way, in what might be called a series of 'political fields'.[4] Conflict within these fields was based upon the original ethnic conflicts of the period of the first urban elections. As a result the first government under Patrice Lumumba was an uneasy alliance of regional factions resting upon ethnic bases and with very little collective discipline or authority. Many more provinces were created than under the colonial regime in order to meet various particularist claims. This led, in turn, to a realignment of ethnic conflicts which culminated in the rebellions of 1964–65. The defeat of these with external assistance, as well as general exhaustion after years of disorder, enabled Mobutu to re-establish central authority. Although the state of Zaire is not necessarily stable (Mobutu has had to call on European aid to deal with an invasion of Shaba province from Angola and more recently has faced severe internal challenges), and is certainly very corrupt and inefficient, one can, after about 1966, refer to it as a state rather than a fictional authority.

A wide range of issues underlay the disorders of 1957–60 as well as the renewed breakdown of control in 1964. There was imbalance and tension between richer and poorer regions. This helps account for the secession of copper-rich Katanga in the first phase and its centralist position in the second phase. There was intervention by outside interests such as the white mercenaries who fought for Katanga. There were the excessive, often literally millenial, hopes associated with independence. These made political organisation difficult and, when independence failed to come anywhere near to fulfilling them, produced renewed unrest. There were severe economic crises which began in the late 1950s, got worse with the upheavals of independence, and contributed to further political conflict. But although these issues are important they do not provide a general key to the forms political conflict took at the time. Above all, they do not themselves explain the lines of ethnic conflict which emerged throughout the country.

The 'nationalist' view of sub-nationalism would seem to provide such an explanation, which could take one of two forms. The first would be the argument that ethnic conflict was so fundamental, both in itself and as a way of expressing conflicts over other matters, that it prevented the development of territorial nationalism. The second would be that territorial nationalism might have developed if it had been given time: the brevity of the transition from colonialism to independence did not allow it to take firm shape. As a consequence, political organisation had to build upon the established ethnic identities, which were destructive of stable territorial government. The implication of this argument, as of the first, is that ethnic politics or sub-nationalism is not dependent upon a particular process of political reform, of political organisation under the colonial state, as is territorial nationalism. The plausibility of these arguments rests upon their association of ethnic conflict with cultural sub-nationalism, and the underlying view that ethnic ties provide the natural basis for political competition in indigenous society once freed from the constraints of colonialism. We will examine the argument that the ethnic labels themselves are a product of colonialism and that their use, when unconnected to political structures developed by colonialism, signals rather fragility and instability. To reiterate what is the major theme of this book: there are no 'natural' bases to politics; stable political identities are developed out of political processes; the belief in 'natural' bases to politics is grist to the nationalist ideologue but destructive of any enduring politics.

To test these arguments one must examine the ways in which ethnic conflicts came about. Urban growth seems to have been particularly important, since much ethnic conflict originated in the towns and then extended into the countryside. For the urban origins of the conflict the sort of explanation put forward by Gellner seems appropriate.[5] One can see this by looking at the conflict between Lulua and Luba in the Luluabourg region.

The terms Lulua and Luba seem to have had very little significance as late as 1890. A group identified as the Lulua were picked out by early colonialism as collaborators and this led to a confirmation (or creation) of a favourable position for Lulua elites in rural society. Disfavoured groups, subsequently categorised as the Luba, were readier to migrate to the growing towns. There some of them acquired the limited western education and new sorts of employment, as clerks, orderlies, caretakers, that colonialism made available. When new types of cultural associations began to form, along with some articulate criticism of the colonial regime, Luba tended to play a leading role. This led to resentment among those Lulua who had subsequently moved to the towns and occupied an inferior position compared to earlier Luba migrants. Identities formed and hardened in the towns could then be exported back into the countryside. The colonial government began to worry about the potential opposition from *évolués* and to shift the collaborator system firmly back towards the 'traditional', 'authentic' Africans. This undermined effective administration of a rapidly changing economy but made sense in terms of maintaining political control. Naturally it was welcomed by Lulua elites in the countryside, and it contributed to making the Lulua–Luba contrast sharper and more tense. The limited political identities which were created were produced by a combination of colonial intellectual assumptions, administrative practice and indigenous response.

As governmental authority rapidly eroded in the late 1950s Lulua elites became disturbed by the prospect that the better equipped Luba elites might dominate the region in an independent state. The sudden collapse of colonial rule deepened their concern and also precluded the possibility of common action against the imperial power. Once electoral politics moved into the countryside Lulua elites were assured of victory over the urban-based Luba. With popular backing for their position the Lulua, in concert with other non-Luba groups, forced through mass expulsion of the Luba from the region. Huge numbers of Luba moved southwards, where their presence caused other forms of instability.

One could argue that some such pattern of events, if in less extreme form, happened in other regions of the Congo. Two different processes – elite division due to the manner in which the collaborator system was installed, and conflict arising out of competition for scarce resources in towns, both associated with new ways of identifying friends and foes – combined to produce ethnic conflict which dominated political competition in the period immediately before and after the collapse of imperial power.

Clearly this conflict was not based on age-old group identities and divisions. Not only that, but the group identities in question had barely been elaborated upon by intellectuals before they were put to political use. There were cases of such elaboration. Among the Bakongo of the lower Congo basin a cultural identity had been constructed by indigenous intellectuals in alliance with missionaries. It was reinforced by the creation of a standardised written language and expressed through historical works on the Bakongo. Subsequently the Bakongo were a major unit in the political conflicts of the independence era. But this was a highly exceptional case. There was rarely such a degree of European concern with a particular ethnic/language group or a class of indigenous intellectuals able to build upon it. Even in the case of the Bakongo, their regional opponents had a more fluid and ramshackle sense of identity built up mainly in reaction against Bakongo pre-eminence.

Linked to this one finds that ethnic identity, at least in relation to political conflict, was in constant flux. Over the period 1957–65 the ethnic bases of political conflict kept shifting quite rapidly. This makes it difficult to see them as the primary source of political conflict. After all, if ethnicity is supposed to supply the principles of the political map by which people orientate themselves, it is hard to know what principles underlie the redrawing of the map over the course of a decade.

The basic answer is simple. On the one hand there was the major objective of political action from about 1957: seizure of resources abandoned by the colonial authority. On the other hand, given the poor development of the collaborator system, there were few means of pursuing this objective effectively. Competing political factions were compelled to devise instruments as best they could. One was alliance with powerful foreign interests, both governmental and economic. Another was popular support. What one must remember is that political factions did not actually mobilise popular support: mobilisation was rather the consequence of political breakdown. In the uncertain situation which ensued mobilised groups, especially in the countryside, were as much in search of leaders as leaders were in search of followers. The way in which the alliance was sealed is well described by Young:

> The new political class, compelled by the electoral timetable to develop a
> rural clientele at breakneck speed, necessarily relied on the ethnic linkages.

The political lexicon which developed was heavily laden with ethnic terminology because the infinite complexity and incomprehensible fluidity of
both provincial and national politics could be diminished by the application
of ethnic labels to contending groups. The inaccuracy inherent in this
process could in turn be reduced by the self-fulfilling prophecy: once labels
became current, groups often tended increasingly to resemble their stereotypes.[6]

To this should be added one qualification. If factional competition altered
for any reason, such as the discovery of new resources, this could lead to
a rapid alteration in the ethnic labelling process before it became fixed.
The main way of 'fixing' the labels was turning them into a principle for
the control of major political institutions. It was precisely the absence in
the first place of indigenous political institutions which could be used to
gain control over the colonial state that enforced dependence upon ethnic
labels but simultaneously made those labels fragile and changeable.

Such conflict can hardly be termed cultural sub-nationalism if the
term is to denote politics based upon fairly fixed and elaborate and
long-established group identities, upon 'natural' or 'primordial sentiments'.[7]

Two other general implications follow. The first is that the idea of
'national integration', in so far as it denotes a policy designed to achieve
harmony within the territory of the state by ensuring the cultural homogeneity of the inhabitants of that territory, is ineffective and indeed obscures an understanding of the policies which actually do create stability.
I take this issue up in different contexts in chapters 12, 15 and 16. The
second is that where one does encounter a genuine cultural sub-nationalist
movement under colonialism, its basis is not some natural cultural identity
different from that operating among other indigenous groups. Rather the
basis lies in the structure of the colonial state and the ways in which that
structure shapes collaboration and opposition within indigenous society.
To demonstrate this is the major concern of the next two sections of this
chapter.

3 Bagandan sub-nationalism

Before Uganda became independent in 1962 it was obvious there was
going to be a major problem over the position of Buganda in the new state.
In 1960 Bagandan leaders had submitted a memorandum to the British
government demanding virtual independence from the rest of Uganda.
When these demands were not met the boycott of the elections leading to
independence was so effective that, in Buganda, only 2 per cent of the
electorate voted. Tensions continued until the President, Dr Milton Obote,
in 1966 dismissed the Kabaka of Buganda from his position as Vice-presi-
dent and imposed what amounted to one-man rule. A new constitution

was subsequently drawn up which ended all autonomy for Buganda.

Uganda comprises a multitude of ethnic groups which some observers put at about twenty-eight. None of the other groups have made such extensive claims as the Baganda. In many cases ethnic identity did not seem to have a fixed and constant meaning. Consider, for example, the following passage:

> A Kisi (Kenyan Bantu) commiserated with a semi-skilled Luo in Swahili about the discrimination in employment against Kenyans in Kampala. Together they blamed members of the local tribe, the Ganda, for this discrimination. Next day the Kisi went to the house of an influential Soga, who had a temporary Ganda wife, to ask him in Luganda if he could get him a job as a messenger in the Post Office where he (the Soga) worked as a clerk. The Kisi stressed the fact that he was Muntu (singular of Bantu) and urged the Soga to regard this as more important than his not being a Ugandan.[8]

Ethnic labels were thus switched according to context and purpose. Individuals could use a variety of labels in their everyday life. This fluidity in itself probably inhibited the use of ethnic labels for political purposes. It is these purposes which will account for resort to a particular ethnic label, rather than some especially deep-rooted sense of identity which will give rise to certain patterns of political action. What matters, then, is the special political purposes the identity of Baganda served rather than the existence of some especially intense cultural sense of identity among the Baganda. One finds this in the colonial history of the country.

When the British came, in the late nineteenth century, to impose control in what is now known as Uganda they sought, as was normal, indigenous collaborators. In the Baganda they encountered a society with a well organised state system whose leaders were willing to co-operate. Co-operation did not merely take the form of preserving traditional authority, although the position of the ruler of Buganda, the Kabaka, was improved and fixed by the British. The Baganda also converted to Christianity in large numbers and came to dominate entry into mission schools and institutes of education beyond the primary level and into the new, favoured forms of employment created for Africans under colonial rule. Bagandan co-operation extended to helping the British impose their rule outside Buganda. One writer has gone so far as to refer to Bagandan 'sub-imperialism'.[9] What is more, Bagandans even supplied the British with the ethnic terms by which to categorise and control other societies in Uganda.

The special status of the Baganda as collaborators was recognised formally, and they were granted an extraordinary degree of authority in a treaty of 1900. Subsequently their leaders would invoke this treaty in support of the view that their society was independent of and equal to the

British and that the treaty was subject to the principles of international law. This was a gross exaggeration of the original meaning of the treaty, especially so far as the British were concerned, but it does indicate the particularly favourable position of the Baganda in Uganda and the effective way in which they have combined autonomy with collaboration, traditional authority with an openness to western values and opportunities.

Naturally this favourable position was evident to the non-Baganda elites which began to form under colonial rule. These groups, as they developed political organisation through colonial institutions (particularly Christian denominations), could see in the Baganda a common political enemy. The British also came to find it inconvenient to have such a favoured and powerful single collaborator group: it inhibited the development of a territorial collaborator system. Consequently, in a gradual and complex way, political pressure both from above and below began to build up against the Baganda.

It reached a critical point in 1953 when the British took a hard line against them and deposed and deported the Kabaka. Many Baganda had been moving towards territorial-level politics, but this arrested such movement. The action suddenly posed a threat to the political position of the Baganda and could be used to buttress those traditional authorities which had most to lose in the face of such a threat. The chiefs used their established authority to mount a campaign for the restoration of the Kabaka, the symbol of Baganda identity and autonomy. So effective was it that the Kabaka returned in 1955 to an ecstatic welcome. From then on, whilst territorial politics built upon factional linkages organised around Christian denominations, the major political concern in Buganda was communal and sub-national. This conflict was compounded by the fact that it had been clear for several years, especially after the Suez crisis, that independence was only a matter of time. Attention switched from effective action either with or against the British to internal conflict over the form the new state should take and which groups, therefore, would dominate it. The special political identity of the Baganda, established through colonialism, ensured that they played a distinct, sub-nationalist role in this conflict. How this role continued in the post-independence period is considered briefly in chapter 12.

4 Muslim nationalism in India

This case poses more difficult problems for the argument I have been developing in this chapter. One cannot argue that the political structure of the colonial state inhibited the emergence of territorial nationalism as it did in the Belgian Congo. The existence of Congress and the results of analysis of Congress in the previous chapter refute that argument. Nor can it be claimed that Muslim sub-nationalism was the result of some special

206

autonomy within the colonial state as was the case with the Baganda. Muslims did have certain corporate rights but nothing like territorial autonomy prior to 1947, and Muslim nationalism as a significant or-ganised movement hardly goes back more than a decade before 1947.

Superficially, therefore, the obvious explanation of Muslim national-ism would be to see it as a sudden reaction against the prospect of Congress (i.e. Hindu) rule. The basis of the reaction would appear to be a natural sense of Muslim identity, or at least the overriding importance of religious identity and division in Indian society. Precisely because the argument is so plausible it is necessary to go into some detail in order to show that it is wrong.

In the elections of 1937 Muslim politicians acted in a fragmented and largely provincial way, and the Muslim League in particular did badly. In the next elections of 1945–46 the Muslim League dominated the Muslim vote. It emerged as the 'third force' in Indian politics apart from Congress and the Raj and presented a new demand for a separate state of Pakistan to be made up out of the six Muslim-majority provinces, five in north-west and one in north-east India. Eventually the League had to accept partition of the Punjab and Bengal, but a substantial proportion of its demands were met. What needs to be examined here is why this political movement was able to achieve such a degree of importance so quickly.

It is hardly possible to refer to the Muslims of India as a community. They were (and are, but there have been important changes since 1947) spread over a large and discontinuous territory and a wide range of social groups. In Bengal the mass of Muslims were poor, illiterate peasants. In the United Provinces there was a substantial Muslim elite which 'western-ised' as effectively as high-caste Hindus. In the Punjab Muslim peasant resentment of Hindu moneylenders was shared by Hindu and Sikh peasants and formed the basis of common action against urban creditors. In some western provinces such as the Sind the Muslim majority was so large and internally divided that there was no way in which they could find some non-Muslim group against which to develop a common sense of identity. Instead, in this and other Muslim-majority provinces, the divisions among Muslims were of central importance. One might conclude that this only serves to demonstrate how overwhelming was the importance of religious identity, since it overcame such obstacles. But that endows religious senti-ments with a barely credible power. In any case, even among the Muslims there were very different ways in which Islam was interpreted and prac-tised. The notion of a sense of religious community which overwhelms any other ties pointing to different group identities should be used only as a last resort to explain Muslim nationalism.

Until the 1930s Muslim politics was largely confined to the provincial level. Those elites which did try to develop it beyond that level were divided among themselves. Jinnah, the 'founder' of Pakistan, had been

207

closely associated with the Khilafat movement which co-operated with Congress in the early 1920s. Even after the collapse of the Khilafat movement there remained a substantial if diminished Muslim involvement in Congress. Muslims were unable to respond in any united way to the constitutional inquiries conducted by the Simon Commission (established in 1927) or to the work of the conference which was held in London in 1930–31. Some, including Jinnah, were prepared to support a sketch of a constitution worked out in Congress,[10] but others rejected it. Most of the discussion, even among Muslim politicians, assumed a single successor state to the Raj.

The idea of Pakistan was mooted only in the 1930s and adopted as official policy by the Muslim League only in 1940. Even then it was interpreted in different ways. Some, including Jinnah, envisaged Pakistan as a secular state founded upon a claim that the Muslims of India made up a civilisation and a people separate from the Hindus. Others envisaged Pakistan as an Islamic state, embodying the true faith and taking up links with other Islamic states. The division between a nationalist and a religious view of Muslim identity has continued to be important since 1947. Others saw the demand for Pakistan as a tactic to press Congress into concessions on the form of the successor state rather than as a legitimate objective in itself. This was particularly the view among Muslim politicians from Muslim-minority provinces who dominated Muslim nationalist politics into the 1940s. For these minorities autonomy within a single successor state was preferable to a partition which would abandon them to a non-Muslim majority.

Lack of community or of unified and national-level politics makes it difficult, therefore, to see the demand for a separate Muslim state as an expression of a distinct Muslim interest or sense of identity. To explain this it is necessary to examine at least five matters: the origins of a separate Muslim politics; the role of Muslim-minority provinces in leading this politics at a national level; the extension of this politics into the Muslim majority provinces; the role of communal conflict along religious lines in this politics; and the circumstances leading to the adoption of the demand for Pakistan.

Until the last decades of the nineteenth century the British government had not quite accepted the view that there was a distinct Muslim interest in India, although obviously it recognised the significance of religious differences and their association with other differences.[11] In a general way – though without deliberate political intent – British colonialism was responsible for constructing the idea of a single Hindu religion and identity which covered most of the regions and inhabitants of the subcontinent. The point is well made by Bankimchandra Chattopadhyay (1838–94), a Calcutta intellectual:

Search through all the vast written literature of India, and you will not, except in modern writings where the Hindu as sought obsequiously to translate the phraseology of his conquerors, meet with any mention of such a thing as the Hindu religion . . . There is no Hindu conception answering to the term 'Hinduism', and the question .. what is Hinduism, can only be answered by defining what it is that the foreigners who use the word mean by the term.[12]

Identity is created by the outsider with particular intellectual and political interests. The power of the outsider in the colonial situation ensures that the identity is taken up in various ways by the 'Other' so identified. By the late 19th century this identity could be employed in various ways – in the form of Hindu revivalism, for example – or could be opposed in various ways, for example by secular nationalists and by Muslims. What mattered is that the notion of such an identity, and its corollary that the Muslims represented the major minority community, was established under colonialism.[13]

The next stage was to invest such identities with active political meaning. The growth of Congress, even in its early stages, set the government looking for alternative or additional sources of support. The failure of Curzon's strategy of providing disinterested government which refused to note the special claims of various indigenous political elites compelled the government to search further for political collaborators. To find such collaborators and tie them to the government required reforms. One way, already considered in the previous chapter, would have been to introduce reforms designed to incorporate moderate nationalists into the collaborator system. Another was to try to incorporate non-nationalist groups.

Certain Muslim groups had already displayed strong sentiments of loyalism. This was based primarily on the realistic assumption that the British would be ruling India for the foreseeable future and one might as well adapt to that reality. These self-selected Muslim elites could present this adaptation in terms of the Muslim interest. Inevitably that interest was interpreted in rather narrow terms related to the preoccupations of those elites. The concern with education and access to administrative positions resembled the concerns of the contemporary Congress leadership.

When this rather modernist and loyalist approach was combined with claims to stand for the interests of the Muslim community as a whole it appeared to the British to offer a very useful collaborator group. The leading exponent of this point of view, Sir Sayyid Ahmad Khan (1817–1898), set the tone of an adaptive Muslim loyalism by the end of the century.

In accepting the offer of collaboration the British also accepted the image of the Muslim community that came with it. This represented the Muslims as a backward group in need of corporate concessions to protect them from the more advanced Hindu nationalist elite. The image benefited

209

the Muslims. It also justified British recognition of special Muslim interests in terms of the imperial mission of promoting the interests of all subjects. This argument was used against those who saw no more than classic divide-and-rule policy, and also to buttress the charge that the nationalist elite was an unrepresentative and self-serving interest. (Interestingly the Muslim collaborator elite could be taken as representing all Muslims, but the same claim by the Hindu nationalist elite was rejected.)

Some recognition of corporate differences had been registered in the 1880s with the setting up of communal electorates for local boards. The crucial step came, however, with the establishment of the Muslim League in 1906. Lord Morley, Secretary of State for India, announced in that same year his readiness to embark upon reform of the government of India. Minto, the Viceroy, in October 1906 received a deputation of thirty-five Muslims who asked for corporate status in a reformed system. The government accepted the representativeness of these politicians with very little inquiry. Minto used this acceptance as a justification for the creation of communal electorates for the provincial Legislative Councils which were established in 1909. From that time on Indian politics was forced to organise along religious lines. As the electorate was enlarged by a series of reforms so this politics began to develop a popular base. However, it would be wrong to see here simply a success for divide-and-rule imperial policy. It is necessary to take a closer look at the Muslim interests to whom the concessions had been made.

The bulk of the leadership of the Muslim League in its early years came from United Provinces. Sir Sayyid Ahmad Khan based his activity upon the college of Aligarh in United Provinces. It was this college which was the centre of the initiative to send a deputation to Minto. In the United Provinces there were important Muslim elites of landowners and government officials. Muslims were a more urbanised group than the Hindus. So the Muslim community and its leadership were rather unlike the image of the Muslim community in India which the Muslim League projected and used to justify the demands for special treatment.

The Muslim elites in United Provinces were subject to various pressures. The growth of commerce and the extension of the influence of various traders and moneylenders into landownership had hit some landowning groups hard. This pressure was particularly acute in the eastern half of the province. The reforms of local government provided rich resources for factional conflicts associated with these developments. In the east of the province the common interests of the beleagured landowning class meant that its members co-operated among themselves into the 1930s irrespective of religious differences. It was only the links which Congress formed with elements of the peasantry in the elections of 1937 that finally undermined this solidarity.

The situation was rather different in the west of the province. Here there was a small Muslim elite of professional people which had little scope for influence in local affairs and was at loggerheads with the conservative landowning Muslim elite. The professional group hoped to exploit the reforms of 1909 which tied local and provincial politics together by allying with Congress. This forced the conservative Muslim elite into defensive responses which included trying to exploit communal Muslim feeling. It demanded separate and over-proportional representation for Muslims in the provisions of a new bill to reform municipal boards. Even after some gains had been made in this direction by 1916 the conservative elite continued to be critical and to demand more, playing the communal card in support of its politics. Hindu politicians had to oppose its demands because concessions would have undermined their control of municipal politics which was the springboard for participation in provincial politics.

Although Muslim elites opposed one another in western United Provinces the communal structure of politics established from 1909 in the electoral system benefited the conservative elite. Some local politicians in Congress advocated making concessions to Muslim demands in order to establish co-operation between the communities. But their dependence upon Hindu support, which was hardening in its attitude towards Muslim communalism, limited the amount of ground they could yield. Increasingly, therefore, politics took on a religious communal form in western United Provinces. Where a Muslim conservative elite was not so interested in such politics, as in eastern United Provinces, such a politics was much more weakly developed. However, western United Provinces was richer, more urbanised and more populous than the eastern half of the province. As a consequence the communal politics of western United Provinces gradually came to predominate at provincial level. This helps explain the leading role of United Provinces politicians in the leadership of the Muslim League, something still reflected in the composition of the Working Committee of the Muslim League as late as 1946.

The emergence of provincial Muslim politics in United Provinces shows that there was unquestionably a religious dimension to social and political conflict but that there were other conflicts which cut across religious divisions. Furthermore, there was only a limited degree of communal conflict on religious lines which was expressed in political form. What seems to have been the case is that religious identity was one possible resource for competing political elites. The creation of communal electorates, part of the extension and modification of the collaborator system, increased its value enormously. At the same time reforms pulled local and provincial levels of political action closer together. In this way elite conflicts in which religious identity was employed as a resource could come to overshadow other forms of political conflict at provincial level. This process by which conflicts within indigenous society are shaped by colonial institutions and become increasingly interlinked and extensive resembles the way Congress itself developed. Since the use of religious identity as a political resource made sense only where certain Muslim elites were under pressure, the process was at first confined to Muslim-minority provinces.

The extension of Muslim League influence into Muslim-majority provinces came much later in the 1930s. The main reason was the impressive performance of Congress in the elections of 1937. Until then provincial politics in Punjab or Bengal had been little concerned with national issues. Parties often combined Muslim with low-caste Hindu interests and did not need to invoke religious identity in order to be effective. For the same reason Congress could make few inroads into Hindu groups. Partly this was because such groups often worked with Muslim interests; partly because, where communalism did develop, Hindu parties could not agree with Congress policies. In Bengal, for example, former Congress politicians were disgusted at what they saw as over-generous treatment of Muslim and low-caste Hindu interests which placed them in a position of political subordination. They rejected the readiness of Congress to concede a degree of special treatment in order to preserve co-operation across religious and caste divides. The perspective of Congress, like that of the Muslim League, was derived from the situation in the Muslim-minority provinces. So for a long period politics in the Muslim-majority provinces remained detached from the issues raised in national-level politics. Yet these were the areas where communal religious conflict was to be most violent and which formed the basis of Pakistan.

The assumption of power by Congress in all Muslim-minority provinces in 1937 frightened Muslim political interests in those provinces. Loyalism was no longer adequate because its major assumption, the continuation of British rule, now looked very shaky. Muslim loyalists would have to find another policy. Equally, the provincial government in the Muslim-majority provinces had to face the possibility of a Congress government at national level. The two needs complemented one another. The Muslim League needed greater support and the Muslim-majority provinces needed national leadership. But this combination also transformed the pattern of politics in both sorts of province. It 'communalised' politics in the Muslim-majority provinces in a new and very intense way. Non-Muslim groups which had supported provincial governments could no longer do so if they became tied to the Muslim League. These groups in turn would have to seek countervailing power at a national level and could do so only by association with Congress. However, in doing so in a consciously anti-Muslim way (which implied an emphasis on Hindu identity) they increased communal interests within Congress. This process meant that communalism of a new sort was imported into the politics of both the League and Congress. At the same time the Muslim league had to adapt its political demands to the needs of the Muslim-majority provinces in which territorial autonomy rather than minority safeguards was of paramount importance.

There can be no doubt that communal conflict on religious lines underpinned the rise of the League. Religious revival movements had led to clashes in many regions. Communal conflicts were often associated with economic divisions, especially in urban areas where religious differences could easily become the basis of communal tensions and conflicts. Religion often proved a better way of tying together disparate interests than secular nationalism, which had only elite appeal. So it is hardly surprising that nationalism at a popular level in India was suffused with religious values and linked with religious divisions. But these divisions were too fluid, and other divisions too crosscutting and regionally varied to give rise themselves to organised political conflict. Communalism became a positive political force only when linked with elite conflict. It only did this when, in a particular political context, the appeal to religious identity became an important resource for some elites. This context was created by the way in which certain Muslim elites, not necessarily representative of the Muslim community as a whole, combined with the government to create special communal forms of political action within the collaborator system. The way in which successive reforms pushed local, provincial and national levels of politics together – gradually in the Muslim-minority provinces and suddenly in the Muslim-majority ones – accounts for the way in which communal conflict turned into a struggle between competing nationalisms.

Even then Muslim nationalism was ambivalent and uncertain in its views and aims. Many Muslims opposed the demand for Pakistan and insisted instead on an all-India constitution which would provide substantial protection for provincial and religious rights. This approach was shared by some of the most traditional elements among the Islamic religious leadership. Jinnah raised the demand for Pakistan in 1940 in order to secure Muslim League leadership in the Muslim-majority provinces.[14] Nevertheless it was phrased vaguely, so as not to raise too many fears on the part of Muslims in other provinces. It was essentially a tactical manoeuvre. By this time the British had virtually conceded to Jinnah the power to veto any all-India agreement between themselves and Congress. The dramatic demand for partition served notice on Congress of the concessions they must make to the League if an agreement with the British was not to be vetoed.

It is not possible to consider here the complex train of events between 1940 and 1947. The main characteristic was the way in which relations between the British and Congress deteriorated, to Jinnah's benefit. It became harder for Congress to work out an all-India agreement and to control the more impatient among its own ranks. The progress of the war, especially by 1941–42, made British collapse appear inevitable and imminent. This emboldened Congress to embark on its 'Quit India' movement, the largest one it mobilised. However, the British repressed this very

213

effectively, if at great cost. This served to strengthen Jinnah's position; to harden Congress attitudes as well as increasing its dependence upon popular support, often now mobilised on a Hindu communal basis. Yet at the same time British imperial power was fatally weakened by the war and the British were determined to avoid any repeat of the costly repression of the Quit India movement. The movement for independence was pushing at an open door after 1945. A confident Congress movement would not concede too much to the Muslim League. In response, especially with the increasing importance of the Muslim-majority provinces in Muslim League policy, the Pakistan option became more important. The British increasingly had no wish to compel the competing Indian movements to negotiate the terms of a single-successor state or even to stay long enough to ensure an orderly transfer of power. The final and tragic outcome is well known. The communal conflicts led to massacres and large-scale population transfers. A minor consequence was the creation of two successor states which would, in various ways, support the construction of conflicting schools of historical interpretation which employed the terms 'Indian', 'Muslim', and 'Hindu' in equally dogmatic if opposed ways and which could all serve to obscure the more complex way in which conflicting nationalist movements had come to take shape.

Three ingredients went to make up Muslim nationalism: factional conflict, communal divisions on religious lines, and the creation of a collaborator system which provided special rights for Muslims. The third provided the means of bringing the other two ingredients together. To take a different metaphor: without the catalyst of this sort of collaboration the reaction between communalism and factional conflict which produced Muslim nationalism would not have taken place. The form this reaction took differed in Muslim-majority and minority provinces. National-level Muslim politics developed out of the minority provinces. However, it took the form of a nationalist demand for an independent state, only with the sudden entry of the majority provinces into national-level politics. This sudden entry was due to the realisation that the collaborator system that was the Raj was close to falling into the hands of interests outside those provinces. In this way Muslim nationalism was shaped – indeed, produced – by the structure of the collaborator system established by the colonial state. Communal religious identity was an essential part of the content of that nationalist politics but the nationalist form this politics took was based upon the forms of political action which were permitted within and channelled through the colonial state.

5 Conclusion

A simple and crude contrast can be drawn between the Belgian Congo and Uganda. In the former the sort of large-scale economic change and urban growth which can generate ethnic conflict was far more important than in Uganda. In Uganda the creation of a collaborator system which secured special political rights to a particular group was far more important than in the Belgian Congo. In the Belgian Congo ethnic politics were fluid, a desperate recourse to poorly developed group labels at a time of crisis which acted as a substitute for organised politics developed through the institutions of the colonial state at either territorial or sub-national level. In Uganda a well developed cultural sub-nationalist movement emerged among the Baganda. This suggests that it is the structure of the collaborator system which is of paramount importance in shaping both an effective territorial nationalist and cultural sub-nationalist movement prior to the creation of an independent state. The focus on economic change and urban growth can be connected directly to ethnic conflicts but only indirectly to nationalism.

Muslim nationalism in India differs from Bagandan nationalism in that it developed much more rapidly and over a much wider area. As a consequence it had to make its appeal to communal identity in a way detached from existing political identity and organisation. It also combined a much more diverse set of interests which were subsequently to prove more difficult to control than those within Bagandan nationalism. But Muslim nationalism could achieve what it did only because the collaborator system of the Raj had allowed Muslim politics a distinct role. The subsequent development of Congress as part collaborator, part successor to the Raj then pushed diverse Muslim collaborators into a single intransigent opposition to all-Indian nationalism.

The lack of a well-developed collaborator system constantly being reformed to incorporate indigenous interests meant that in the Belgian Congo indigenous politics could not acquire a fixed and organised character at either territorial or sub-national level. Ethnic politics developed outside the institutions of the colonial state. As a consequence it was uncontrollable and unpredictable. It would be wrong to see the construction of a collaborator system which gives rise to effective nationalist opposition as a way of undermining colonialism if it is imagined that the absence of such a system preserves imperial power. The Belgians, after all, did have to leave the Congo. But it is not always nationalism which compels decolonisation. Only in very special cases is it both possible and desirable for the colonial power to dispense with substantial indigenous collaboration. In the short term the results, primarily those of vicious economic exploitation, may be gratifying. In the long term the result is the chaos that marked the Belgian withdrawal. Nationalism, it should be remembered, is in many ways a very controlled and advantageous way of bringing colonial rule to an end. This is because it is positively shaped by the colonial state, and thus a controlled political conflict can be conducted within the institutions of that state.

However, the collaborator system and the conflicts in indigenous society to which it gives rise can also undermine a single challenge from a territorial nationalist movement. The challenges posed by cultural sub-nationalist movements are based upon particular features of the collaborator system and its related conflicts rather than upon the simple existence of sub-national group identities. One can locate many more tribal or sub-national identities than there are sub-nationalist movements. What is more, territorial nationalist movements do not so much override distinct interests and identities at lower levels as build upon them. Why in some cases this building process breaks down and leads to a sub-nationalist challenge rather than a contribution to territorial nationalism can be understood only by considering the ways in which the collaborator system itself built linkages between different groups in colonial society. Cultural sub-nationalism, like territorial nationalism, is determined by the structures of the colonial state which it both opposes and seeks to possess.

Notes

1   I take the term 'cultural sub-nationalism' from the title of the book edited by Victor Olorunsola, *The Politics of Cultural Sub-nationalism in Africa* (New York, 1972).
2   See below, appendix, especially pp. 406–7.
3   Roger Anstey, 'Belgian rule in the Congo and the aspirations of the évolué class', in *Colonialism in Africa, 1870–1960*, vol. 2, *The History and Politics of Colonialism, 1914–1960*, edited by L. H. Gann and P. Duignan (London, 1970), pp. 194–225.
4   For the definition of this idea and its application to the Belgian Congo see Thomas Turner, 'Congo-Kinshasa', in Olorunsola, *op. cit.*, pp. 195–284.
5   See below, appendix, especially pp. 417–8.
6   M. Crawford Young, 'Rebellion and the Congo', in *Protest and Power in Black Africa*, edited by R. Rotberg and A. Mazrui (New York, 1970), pp. 969–1011 (983).
7   The term is taken from Clifford Geertz, 'The integrative revolution: primordial sentiments and civil politics in the new states', in *Old Societies and New States*, edited by Clifford Geertz (New York, 1963), pp. 105–57.
8   David J. Parkin, 'Social structure and social change in a tribally heterogeneous East African city ward' (PhD. thesis, University of London, 1965), quoted in M. Crawford Young, *The Politics of Cultural Pluralism* (Wisconsin, 1976), p. 245.
9   Michael Twaddle, ' 'Tribalism' in eastern Uganda', in *Tradition and Transition in East Africa*, edited by P. H. Gulliver (Berkeley, 1969), pp. 193–208.
10   This constitutional draft was known as the Nehru Report, as it had largely been drawn up by Motilal Nehru.
11   For a closely argued case along these lines see Peter Hardy, *The Muslims of British India* (Cambridge, 1972), pp. 1–115.

216

12   Quoted in Partha Chatterjee, *Nationalist Thought and the Colonial World: a derivative discourse?* (London, 1986), pp. 75–6.

13   The way such identities are constructed and projected are important and go beyond the day-to-day manipulations of politics. There is a danger, however, in the approach of writers such as Chatterjee and also of Edward Said in his book *Orientalism* (London, 1978) that such identities are seen purely as western constructs. One danger is that one embraces the notion that *any* way of trying to characterise human groups is just one projection amongst others, one form of discourse. The second is that to identify the source of a discourse as 'western' is taken to discredit it. My own view is that some ways of characterising groups fit better with the evidence than other ways and is not purely a matter of discourse, that the source of such characterisations is less important than the tests to which they can be subjected, and that the construction of identity in the colonial world involves active and often very effective contributions from indigenous sources.

14   For the 'Pakistan resolution' of 23 March 1940 see Hardy, *op. cit.*, p. 231.

10

The colonial state and nationalism

Modern colonialism has involved an intense interaction between western and non-western society. The essence of this interaction can be seen in terms of domination, westernisation or collaboration and can be studied at the political, economic and cultural levels. The economic and cultural levels of the interaction can occur outside areas of formal empire. They have, therefore, no specific relationship to the forms of political action which develop under colonial states. Of course, these societies can develop their own forms of nationalism, in part directed against what they regard as economic or cultural colonialism, but these take somewhat different forms than those developed in colonial states. For one example, see the case of China dealt with in the next chapter. If, as I shall argue, politics in colonial states does have a specific form, its determinants must be sought at the level of political interaction. That is not to deny the importance of economic and cultural relationships in particular cases (indeed, in all particular cases) but simply to insist that in general and conceptual terms these different levels of interaction have to be considered independently of one another.

In chapter 7 the political variants of the domination, westernisation and collaboration approaches were outlined and criticised. Briefly, the domination approach pays too little attention to the content of colonial politics, while the collaboration approach pays too little attention to the form of colonial politics. Both these deficiencies can be met by a modification of the westernisation approach. This has tended to concentrate too much on the creation of western groups, practices, institutions and values, understood in economic and cultural terms. If, however, one focuses upon the creation of western forms of political action into which collaborators are drawn under the colonial state, then the notion can be used more effectively. It also means that one does not have to take up a position on the question of whether colonialism promoted or impeded modernisation as a process of total societal transformation. The modernisation concept is focused narrowly upon political institutions.

The key idea involved in this modified application of the concept of westernisation or modernisation is that of the colonial state as a new type of political authority. The degree to which this new type of authority is realised in particular colonial situations will determine the form and extent of nationalism.

The importance of the distinction between form and content in political action which this involves can be demonstrated with regard to India. In a fascinating and elegant essay Heesterman has outlined the way the Mughal empire functioned before the establishment of British control.[1] A central feature was the absence of a 'public domain'. For example, Heesterman points to the importance of what he calls the 'inner frontier' in the Mughal empire. One might interpret this term to mean an area under the nominal control of the government but where it did not have effective authority, that meaning such things as control of policing and the enforcement of law. The problem with stating the issue in this way is that it implies that the government perceived itself as normally or ideally having such effective authority. If, however, the government of the Mughal Empire did not see things like that it is difficult to see how such a view of political authority can legitimately be used in an analysis of its politics. The use of the idea in this manner implies that the government is a state (or at least a would-be state) in the modern sense of the word – that is, an authority with sovereign power throughout the territory claimed to be under its jurisdiction. Max Weber, for example, included within his definition of the state the monopoly of large-scale means of violence. However, many pre-modern 'states' claimed authority over areas where they did not have such a monopoly. Where such a clear and distinct claim to power and sovereignty within a particular territory was not made, there was no need to have the sharply defined boundaries we associate with statehood. Thus the Mughal empire was not a state in the modern sense of the word and did not possess 'boundaries' but instead had varying amounts of authority within its 'inner frontiers'.[2]

The normal method of government in the Mughal empire was the exploitation of local divisions, making alliances with some local groups against others. This description resembles the account given by advocates of the collaborator approach of how European control was 'imposed' in various parts of Africa. Not surprisingly, therefore, indigenous societies often saw nothing new upon the arrival of European powers but treated them as one more factor to be taken into account in the normal equations of politics.

As Heesterman points out, one feature of this sort of politics is the bewildering way in which shifts occur which seal alliances with or against the central authority. Yesterday's bandit is today's government servant. What is a power of taxation on one occasion is highway robbery on another. The seeming unimportance of terms denoting allegiance to or

219

against the government has led advocates of the collaborator approach to move towards a close analysis of the specific issues which make sense of these shifts.

European penetration often involved taking part in this politics. But it was not the only choice available, as Heesterman points out in relation to officials of the East India Company. They could choose:

> . . . either to involve themselves and their resources at local level, to manipulate and arbitrate competition and conflict – as the Mughals had been forced to do – or to withdraw as far as possible from local conflict in order to pool and reserve the Company's power and resources.[3]

Heesterman concludes that eventually Company officials opted for the second alternative. He points to certain disasters following from illegal private trading as one reason but does not take the matter further. One could perhaps argue that these incidents were regarded as disasters because the Company was accountable to London. The western terms of reference which found involvement in local politics a form of corruption and de-manded accountability to London helped push the Company towards the second choice. The notion of corruption itself was specifically modern, implying as it did a public sphere of activity in which public morality rather than private interest should govern conduct. The decision to with-draw from local politics:

> . . . found its clearest expression in the Permanent Settlement of 1793. Whatever this momentous decree may have done for the introduction of full private ownership of land protected by law, its main thrust was the reservation of power and the use of force as well as the refusal to get involved in local affairs. This meant now that a public realm, the state, was decisively set apart from the web of competing social forces, which were left to cope with their local situations, as many new-style landowners found to their grief.[4]

One can see here that the claim to govern within sharply defined boun-daries was closely tied to the modern idea of sovereignty. The state now could not be seen as just one agent among others, but as an institution which imposed a final will upon all others. To do so required not merely setting apart but also a clear definition of territory upon which this final will was to be imposed. The idea of the nation as a single, geographically bounded group derives from the idea of the state as a single, geographically bounded territory.[5]

I would stress that my concern here is the public aspect of the Permanent Settlement. It has been persuasively argued that as a systematic arrangement of land tenure there was nothing modern or modernising about the Permanent Settlement. It re-classified a class of rent-collectors as landowners and conferred privileges upon them. In many ways this in-hibited the energetic and innovative development of agriculture which might have been better served by giving more rights to as least some of the actual cultivators of the soil. Indeed, some have gone so far as to argue that this was a clear example of colonialism having a reactionary effect, preserving if not actually creating a class of quasi-feudal landowners.

I am not qualified to make any judgement on this debate. My concern, however, is with the other aspect of this settlement, namely the construction of a public realm based upon a polity/property distinction. The Permanent Settlement can, in this way, highlight what is perhaps a central problem for colonial nationalism, that is making connections between localised and often exploited, even 'de-modernised' societies and the more extensive, modern political institutions of the colonial state.

The advocate of the collaborator approach with its concern for the 'substance' rather than the 'form' of political action might question this emphasis in a number of ways. The first would be that something like the Permanent Settlement may have been imposed in parts of India but not in many other territories. Zealous colonial officials did call for the introduction of direct taxation or European law not just to raise revenue or eliminate customs but also in order to register the existence of a new, public authority. But this would conflict with control understood in terms of collaboration with existing indigenous groups. Iliffe has neatly summed up the tensions in colonialism which Heesterman discussed in terms of a choice. 'Control required powerful allies with obedient followings. Administration required efficient agents who could impose uncongenial innovations'.[6] One might, therefore, argue that in some cases one choice was made and in some cases the other. Where administration led to the creation of new agents of colonial rule (including those drawn from the indigenous society) one would have a clear case of a 'public' colonial state. Where control led to alliance with well-established indigenous interests colonialism would mean very little. In addition, the advocate of the collaborator approach might even seek to explain why particular cases moved to one extreme, stayed at the other or came to rest somewhere in between in terms of the availability of collaborators.

However, the problem with this response is that almost every case would have to be considered an 'in-between' one. After a while colonial officials would be bound to want to innovate or modify the existing patterns of political collaboration. They might be responding to economic pressures from traders and others, or cultural pressures from missionaries, or to directives from their political superiors. In any case, no society is static, so from within indigenous society there would also be pressure leading to changes. What then mattered was that the colonial state was alien, that its ultimate source of power and motives for action lay outside the colonised society. This meant that shifts in patterns of collaboration would always require sanction from above. Politics, therefore, would never remain frozen into the patterns it had assumed when Europeans first encountered the colonised society. As a consequence, after some time the collaborator system would appear to be the product of colonial rule, and the collaborator system would have to orientate itself to the notion of a state over and above factional interests, above 'society'.

This change in the form of politics and of political authority, and consequently in political attitudes within indigenous society, can change without a wholesale upheaval of the system of alliances made at the time colonial authority was established. Attention to the occupational or socio-economic bases of collaborator politics can obscure this fundamental change. Heesterman, for example, points out that in many practical ways the Permanent Settlement did not change things a great deal. The old style of 'corrupt' politics continued. Taxes were re-defined as rents and revenue collectors as landowners but the content of such claims and the holders of such titles remained largely unchanged. Moreover the new definitions were often difficult to apply to particular cases and officials were constantly required to adapt them to the 'realities' of the situation. But in a telling passage Heesterman points to the essential, if intangible, change which had been introduced:

> The British Raj, like any colonial regime, was perpetually pulled in opposite directions by the need to leave the ruled-over society alone and the equally pressing need to deal with it in an effective way. However, not only the rules of the game, but the game itself had changed. By way of a metaphor one might say that the traditional game was the balance of the internal frontier, which demanded 'horizontal' involvement and dispersion; the new one, on the other hand, was that of an equally precarious balance, but now between 'vertical' involvement and withdrawal.[7]

To continue the metaphor, the creation of a 'public realm' above society was complemented by the creation of a 'private realm' below the state. One feature of the Permanent Settlement was the introduction of a system of private land ownership. In many cases colonialism was associated with the introduction of notions about land or goods as private property, religious beliefs as a matter of private conscience, and the family as a private institution.

However, I would argue that this was more often the unavoidable corollary of the attempt to construct a public realm than part of a drive to modernise all social institutions in colonial society. Indeed, a seemingly contradictory aspect of colonialism was the attempts that were often made by the colonial state to preserve traditional forms of land holding, marriage and inheritance patterns and even religious beliefs. Partly this was intended to maintain stability. Partly it was due to intellectual convictions about the relativity of social norms from one society to another, convictions which were then taken up by various forms of cultural revivalism and national-ism. However, the very contradiction between modern colonial political authority, which claimed a monopoly of 'public' control and corporate practices such as communal land-holding or caste divisions undermined such attempts to shore up 'tradition'. When chiefs within the system of indirect rule were perceived as low-level bureaucrats, as was almost bound to happen over time, the source of their authority was altered even as they maintained it effectively. When colonial governments sought to preserve communal land owning or insisted upon 'traditional' education, their efforts were often rejected because they were seen as a means of preserving inequality and preventing the indigenous appropriation of the real re-sources which were to be obtained through the market place or by means of literacy.[8] 'Custom' came to be confined to ever-narrower spheres of activity, taking on an increasingly ornamental role, something brought out for visiting notables. Even then colonialism often interfered either directly or indirectly through the way in which custom was interpreted by local officials. Thus at all levels, and particularly that of politics, the notion of distinct spheres of activity – of public affairs, economic affairs, domestic affairs – was introduced and steadily undermined the earlier ways in which various activities were organised.

In this way the colonial state could not but help introduce pressure for modernity into colonial society. Even when it undermined local manu-factures or preserved archaic and inappropriate patterns of land-holding, it did so by modern administrative methods. Also, such policies provoked modernist criticism within colonial society. The 'failure' to modernise – and in many ways colonialism did 'under-develop' society – could only be perceived as such from a modernist perspective. Even when indigenous groups responded critically in the opposite direction, for example by seeking to revive 'traditions' such as a lower age of consent (Tilak in Bengal) or female circumcision (Kenyatta in Kenya), they did so in a self-consciously modern manner, and always in conflict with more overt modernists within indigenous society. Modern colonialism is suffused with the idea of modernity even, perhaps especially where, it is failing to deliver on this idea in the field of social and economic development.

The colonial state was a public realm above the society it governed. One implication of this was that it was not obviously the instrument of particular interests. As Lonsdale and Berman pointed out, its 'relative autonomy' was an indispensable element of its authority, and one can accept this even without accepting the implications of the term 'relative autonomy'.[9] Where the colonial state was clearly the instrument of par-ticular interests, as in the Belgian Congo, it was difficult to conceive of, let alone practise, politics in terms of influencing the state or seeking to take it over. Rather the colonial state became something to be removed along with the interests which dominated it. Nationalism found it difficult, if not impossible, to develop and operate effectively in such circumstances.

If the state was the public realm, then activities devoted to influencing or taking it over were public activities. Politics was a specialised form of action with distinct organisation, objectives and rhetoric. Of course in many cases such activity was severely restricted and had to be expressed in other ways. Nationalism could, in such circumstances, lose its identity (as happened with the Mau Mau) but, more often than not, such other forms of action were considered in instrumental terms. When nationalism could become well developed politically, therefore, it transposed the idea of the autonomous state into a national framework. The colonial state was condemned precisely because it could not rule society justly and efficiently as it was ultimately not accountable to that society but to its imperial master. On the other hand, the nation-state would be able to represent fully the national interest and could direct the nation along the path to modernity and social justice.[10]

Not all opposition activity under colonial regimes can be regarded as nationalist. Nationalism has particular features. First, the focus of nationalist movements is upon taking over the state. Even effective sub-nationalist movements develop only in response to the prospect of a territorial nationalist movement taking over state power and they claim, instead, some of that state power for themselves. To achieve its objective it is essential for the nationalist movement to develop one or both of the two internal functions of co-ordination and mobilisation. Co-ordination is closely linked with the way in which the colonial state adapts its collaborator system to pressures from indigenous society. Particularly important are the ways in which this adaptation draws local, provincial and national levels of political action together. This also shapes the conflict which takes place within indigenous society between collaborators and non-collaborators. Thus, for example, the existence of a paramount chieftaincy or a communal electorate has a major impact on how opposition politics, as well as collaborator politics, is organised.

Mobilisation is also closely related to the structure of the colonial state and the changes it undergoes. Fiscal and economic policy can make the actions of the state a matter of increasing concern for more and more people, as happened in India in the early 1930s, for example. It can force local politics up to a national level. Attempts by the state to extend its support downwards by devices such as the extension of the franchise force nationalist opponents into more popular politics. There are, of course, all manner of non-political changes which can mobilise large segments of the population, but they cannot be considered here.[11]

There is a tension between this mobilising function of nationalism and the way the nationalist movement organises itself in relation to the colonial state. Precisely where the introduction of modern political and administrative institions has not been accompanied by modern class formation, but rather where local and pre-modern social and economic arrangements continue to prevail, this tension is an acute one which

224

nationalism has to work hard to overcome or at least control. One can see this in various ways – the large-scale and specialised political relationships favoured by the colonial state as counterposed to the small-scale and unspecialised relationships at a social level; the relationship between state and society; the relationship between the modernist style adopted by nationalism in the political sphere and the populist, often overtly tradition-alist style adopted when seeking popular support. In turn one might analyse this tension in class terms – for example, the problem a bourgeois nationalist leadership seeking control of the state has in trying to convince tribal, peasant, caste and religious groupings that they should follow its lead. Or one might instead draw attention to contrasting styles of political leadership – for example, the populist appeal of a Gandhi counterposed to the modernist rationalism of a Nehru. Nationalism has to negotiate some, if only temporary resolution, of these tensions. A socio-economic analysis can cast some light upon the interests involved in such tensions. An ideological analysis can pay attention to the creative as well as necessarily ambivalent character of nationalist ideas and imagery. Both approaches, however, are in danger of avoiding the dimension of political action which is where, above all, this resolution has to take place. Here I am trying to relate the efficacy of such political action to the political forms assumed by the colonial state.

The legitimacy function of nationalism also plays an important role. Decolonisation is closely associated with the weakening of the European imperial powers through war and the rise of the new powers of the United States of America and the Soviet Union, which opposed European empire. Nationalism provided a legitimate alternative to empire, although usually a universalist ideology sufficed to demonstrate legitimacy. In part this claim to legitimacy was directed at the new powers of the USA and the USSR. However, in order to pose this claim credibly nationalism usually needed to have achieved some degree of real internal development in order to be able to claim that it could form a successor state. Sometimes, however, that development was very limited and in part the product of a tacit collusion between imperial power and nationalist movement designed to achieve a stable transition to independence. In these cases the claim to legitimacy was one directed as much at the imperial power itself, or perhaps the public opinion of the imperial power, as it was to any external power.[12]

Where the colonial state as a public realm was poorly developed or where indigenous political activity had not been fundamentally shaped by the collaborator system, then nationalism was also poorly developed. The lack of specialised political action devoted to the taking over of state power also damaged the appeal of nationalist ideology. This ideology uneasily fuses together the ideas of nation as society and nation as state, but it can operate like this only if it begins with clear and distinct ideas of society and state.[13] Hence also the absence of nationalist ideology in states where it is control of the 'inner frontier' rather than the enforcement of sovereignty within clearly defined boundaries which characterises the political process: in such cases there is no strong distinction between society and state and, therefore, no need for an ideology which seeks to bridge it.[14]

This ideology relates in different ways to the different functions of nationalism. Where the nationalist movement has been able to co-ordinate diverse elites and/or gain mass support the ideology of the movement refers to its membership and support in national terms. The movement can easily claim to be, and to believe itself to be, the political expression of colonial society as a whole. Clearly, when there is no internal nationalist challenge (as opposed to conflict with pro-colonial collaborator groups) the ideology does not need to integrate cultural identity too explicitly into its political demands, though it may need to use cultural indigenous styles and concerns as ways of mobilising popular support. Sub-nationalist challenges or even splits in the territorial nationalist movement (for example, over federalism in Kenya) can lead to cultural identity being more strongly emphasised.

When the nationalist movement has organised itself through as much as against the institutions of the colonial state and is concerned to take power at the territorial level, then it will also have a clear idea of itself as the future state. As is clear from the case of Congress, the more this is so the more the idea of the future state resembles a democratised and fully autonomous version of the colonial state itself. Such an idea is also, of course, appropriate to legitimise the nationalist claim to power in terms acceptable to the imperial power and other western powers for whom the democratic nation-state represents the ideal and normal unit of political community.

Such a situation as this, where a highly developed nationalist movement has an ideology fusing images of colonial society and state into a transformed ideal for the future, is the optimal one, though even here one can discern in the ideological and organisational fragilities of the movement some of the problems that will present themselves once independence has been obtained. However, a situation such as the Indian one can be used to measure the development of nationalism. The problems of coordinating action in the Kenyan case can be evaluated against this model. That can be linked to the failure of the colonial state in Kenya to provide appropriate political channels to cope with the pressures coming from indigenous society. And at a certain point the inapplicability of the model, with its concern with the public state and the extensive collaborator system, will be associated with the absence of nationalism. That is not, to repeat an earlier point, the same thing as a lack of resistance. Colonial rule can be destroyed, and partly from within, without the existence of a nationalist opposition, as the example of the Belgian Congo shows. But the absence of such a nationalist opposition is related to the form colonial rule took.

There is a final and fundamental point to be made about anti-colonial nationalism. The specialisation of functions and relationships, of which the state as public realm is one aspect, is at the heart of modernity. In this way the scale of human action can be enormously expanded. Nationalism can be seen as both a response to and a further expression of this extension of scale.[15] The extension has a very special character in the modern colonial state, where a system of political authority appropriate to the extended scale of modernity usually faces a collection of small-scale societies with relatively unspecialised relationships. The forms this encounter can take are numerous, but eventually, if a stable situation is to be created, or if a politics capable of taking control but also maintaining some control over society is to develop, the two must adapt to each other. The concepts of domination and collaboration are ways of avoiding this conclusion by collapsing one or the other side of the relationship. Westernisation, in a modified form which focuses on the political institutions of the colonial state, can take account of the adaptation process. Nationalism is one form this adaptation can take. It can be seen as a struggle to express certain ideas and actions which join the two very different spheres of activity together.

On the one hand it develops from the 'upward' movement of a variety of local conflicts within indigenous society and the collaborator system to the territorial level of the colonial state. On the other, it develops from the 'downward' movements of the colonial state through its collaborator system and a variety of interventions into colonial society. Nationalism develops specialised political forms which enable it to negotiate with the colonial state: in these ways it takes on a political character appropriate to politics in the modern state. Its claims to statehood are derived from this. At the same time it invests its politics with images and idioms which enable it to claim to stand for the interests of indigenous society. In this way it seeks to preserve its hold upon indigenous society by insisting that it is not simply a modern political movement aiming to take state power. Nationalism thus always combines the incompatible concerns with modernity (in the form of statehood) and tradition (in the form of expressing the unspecialised culture of indigenous society).

There is nothing inevitable about this development. It is an inherently fragile achievement, masking as much as resolving contradictions. Colonial authority may work to impede it and may break down before an effective nationalist movement has developed. The 'tribalism' which so often ensues is not so much a reversion to pre-colonial political relationships which have persisted under the colonial state as a desperate search for bases of political action in the absence of those appropriate to taking over the colonial state. Yet nationalism is not incompatible with lower-level political ties which might disparagingly be called factional, tribal or sub-national. It is upon such ties that a territorial nationalist movement has to build. To counter-

227

pose 'modern' politics with 'traditional' politics is to miss the fundamental point that nationalism is a way of fusing the two. The fusion is often not very stable in terms of either organisation or ideology. That is because the numerous small-scale relationships of indigenous society constantly block the extended scale of nationalist action. The problem can become particularly acute on the assumption of independence, when both a common enemy and many of the resources which maintained a central position for the colonial state become much less important, problems which will be considered in chapter 12. Also the balance between collaborators and nationalists breaks down with the assumption of independence, and this can set in train new sorts of instability. But precisely because it is so difficult to fuse these different spheres together in the form of a political movement the effort to do so must be taken seriously and the creative ideological and organisational achievements properly appreciated. It has become fasionable to depreciate the significance and achievements of anti-colonial nationalism. But such nationalism has frequently overcome huge obstacles to a relatively stable adaptation between the western state and non-western society. The achievement deserves recognition. The costs of failure, as in the Belgian Congo, are enormous. It is the way nationalism overcomes these obstacles in the sphere of politics that gives modern anti-colonial nationalism its specific character.

Notes

1 J. C. Heesterman, 'Was there an Indian reaction? Western expansion in Indian perspective', in *Expansion and Reaction*, edited by H. Wesseling (Leiden, 1978), pp. 31–58.

2 For a systematic theorisation of the distinction between boundaries and frontiers see Anthony Giddens, *The Nation-State and Violence* (Cambridge, 1985).

3 Heesterman, *op. cit.* , p. 51.

4 *Ibid.*

5 This idea can also be related to the changing views of boundary and sovereignty within Europe. I have tried to work out some of these ideas so far as Germany is concerned in an essay 'Sovereignty and boundaries: modern state formation and national identity in Germany', in *National Histories and European Perspectives*, edited by Mary Fulbrook (London, 1993).

6 John Iliffe, *A Modern History of Tanganyika* (Cambridge, 1979), p. 121.

7 Heesterman, *op. cit.*, p. 52. I have already used these terms 'horizontal' and 'vertical' in connection with the development of European monarchy. See above, chapter 3, p. 82.

8 For examples, see Iliffe, *op. cit.*, especially pp. 552–3.

9 See above, pp. 164–6.

10 This was the position that came to be taken by Nehru, the leading figure

in the most developed colonial nationalist movement – Congress – at its 'moment of arrival'. See the penetrating analysis of his ideas in Partha Chatterjee, *Nationalist thought and the colonial world: a derivative discourse?* (London, 1986), chapter 5, 'Nehru and the Passive Revolution'.

11 See above, pp. 19–22.

12 The subject of decolonisation is a complex one which has generated a historiography all of its own. See J. Darwin, *Britain and decolonisation: the retreat from empire in the post-war world* (London, 1988).

13 See above, pp. 69–70.

14 This was borne out by the analysis of the development, or rather non-development, of Arab nationalism in the Ottoman Empire in chapter 6.

15 For the ideas of extension of scale and specialisation of function which are also applied to African society see Godfrey and Monica Wilson, *The Analysis of Social Change* (London, 1945).

Reform nationalism outside Europe

1 Introduction

In this chapter I consider the cases of Turkey, China and Japan. These three states, although profoundly affected by contacts with the western world, were never subjected to formal political control by western powers.[1] The contacts with the west help produce many of the features associated with anti-colonial nationalism. There is the desire to reform indigenous society along modern lines; to reject various economic controls and western pretensions to cultural superiority; and to link both a reformed and independent state and society to a sense of national identity. Particularly in cultural and economic matters the situation of these countries was often as 'colonial' as that of many formally colonised societies.

Nevertheless the absence of formal political control, and therefore of a colonial state, presented nationalist movements with particular problems. In a colonial state the nationalist movement has to reform society and take over the state. But in these at least nominally independent countries a nationalist movement has to transform state institutions in order to be effective. From the outset this concern tended to give nationalism a more thoroughgoing and practical character than anti-colonial nationalism.

The reform impulse usually originated within rather than outside the state itself. It tended to begin with a narrow focus on military reform which was seen as necessary in order to combat direct threats from western powers. The obstacles to such narrow reforms soon became apparent and pushed reformers into the development of ever more radical objectives which could eventually envisage total transformation. As this might endanger many entrenched interests the impetus tended to move to critics of the existing state. The appeal to national identity provided a basis on which their criticisms and eventual opposition could be justified. Nevertheless the tendency was to see transformation coming about by taking control of the state and then pushing through a national revolution from above. As a consequence nationalism in these countries tended to express

230

itself much more in political than in cultural terms compared with many anti-colonial nationalist movements.

When one looks at Japan, Turkey and China what is most striking is the varying degrees of success enjoyed by reform nationalism. The Japanese case is the most successful adaptation of nationalist values to a non-western state. The relative success of reform nationalism in Turkey proved possible only after the destruction of the Ottoman empire. In China the nationalist movement achieved substantial initial success between 1911 and 1937 but failed in conflict with Chinese communism. However, in some ways that communism itself took over certain nationalist characteristics. In order to account for these varying outcomes I will begin with a brief consideration of each case. I then compare them in the form of three pairs before arriving at some general conclusions.

2 China

Western contacts with China extend back to the establishment of trading links in the sixteenth century and earlier. However, the west only began to have a major impact upon China in the nineteenth century. Attempts to reject its influence, for example in the matter of opium imports, were overcome by force if necessary. The erosion of governmental authority which such action produced helped lead to internal challenges such as the Taiping rebellion. When order was restored it tended to leave effective power in the hands of local military commanders rather than the central government.

Nevertheless imperial authority remained strong enough for western states to prefer to maintain it rather than establish direct political control. The power of the imperial state, however, was severely restricted. It had no control over tariff policy. A system of concessions in some of the richer, coastal regions brought certain areas under virtual foreign control, and foreigners were not subject to Chinese law or authority. The restrictions imposed by outside powers as well as the shift of power towards the provinces made imperial government increasingly feeble. Naturally this, along with the intrusive economic role of western countries, was felt as a bitter humiliation by many Chinese, particularly the better educated and more politically involved. Whatever convictions these people might have had about the intrinsic superiority of their civilisation over that of the barbarians, without effective power that civilisation was in danger of gradual extinction. In working out how to combat the danger many in the late nineteenth and early twentieth centuries were pushed towards some form of nationalism.

Yet the attempts to evolve a nationalist position were beset by great obstacles. At the level of values it was difficult to construct some 'alternative' view of the Chinese state which preserved its claims to superiority

231

whilst accepting the need for radical changes. Even if changes were justified in more pragmatic ways they were difficult to effect. The state's powers were limited, and the attempt to push reforms through would encounter both foreign and warlord resistance. What is more, reform of the government administration meant attacking the examination-based system of recruitment and hence the Confucianist principles which underlay study for state service. The government did finally abolish the system in 1905 only in the face of much opposition. These sorts of obstacles could lead to very assertive forms of nationalist ideology which in practice rejected much of the value system underpinning the existing state but implausibly linked a vision of a new beginning with an appeal to the past. More often it could lead to the wholesale rejection of Chinese 'civilisation' and institutions and a demand for complete imitation of the west. That in turn could lead to an appeal to the Chinese 'people' as distinct from Chinese civilisation. This was the direction taken by Chinese communists and, given the obstacles to a national reform programme, one can see its ideological appeal to many Chinese students who had at first moved into nationalism.

But this was still to come at the turn of the century. By that time reformers were expressing their demands either in pragmatic or nationalist terms. The inability of the imperial government to effect change had pushed many of them into opposition or exile. Some had been educated abroad and, like Sun Yat Sen, found their strongest support among overseas Chinese communities. But they had little power within China. Yet the imperial state itself was in constant crisis owing to the erosion of its power from within and without. It had toyed with the idea of a simple mass uprising to force back western influence, but there was no chance of success and such action might well have made the situation worse. Reluctantly the state acted on some of the reform proposals. But by the time it came to do this the effect was simply to weaken it still further. The outcome was its overthrow in 1911. The 'revolution' of 1911 was principally a conservative rejection of the reform programme. Radical nationalists played a minor role in bringing the government down and establishing a republic. But as opponents of the imperial state and nationally known figures some of these nationalists actually found themselves in leading positions in the new republic. Though with little power, nationalists were now in a position to try to work out both an ideology and an effective programme at state level.

The obstacles facing them were huge. They had to bring central government firmly under their control and extend its authority beyond certain parts of the coastal regions of south China. To do this they had to build up sufficient military strength to take action against the warlords. Running government and armies required training, men and resources, most of which had to be organised through a more modern system of administration. With an extension of nationalist authority in these directions, based largely on the idea of developing the institutions of a nation-state which would sustain and express the values of Chinese civilisation, the nationalists would be in a position to take action against outside powers and to tackle the more basic questions of social and economic reform. However, they themselves represented a diverse collection of economic interests and organisations. By 1921 there was a small communist party which was allied to Kuomintang, by now the umbrella nationalist organisation. But Kuomintang also had much support from commercial and manufacturing interests which wanted greater stability and a gradual reduction of foreign influence but not social transformation. As nationalist influence began to spread into the interior and nationalists came to agreements with various warlords so this diversity increased. The result was an increasingly abstract nationalist ideology, and a series of internal disputes which made Kuomintang immobile and were often as vicious as any conflicts with outside opponents. In these circumstances it is not so much the failure of nationalism as the degree of success it achieved that requires attention.

From the mid-1920s Kuomintang began to reorganise for more effective political and military action. It was helped by the Soviet Union, which also insisted upon the full integration of the Communist Party into Kuomintang. Better organisation was built up. Kuomintang began to mobilise greater support from groups such as urban workers and women. In 1924 Whampoa Military Academy was set up to train a cadre of officers. The first military head of the academy was Chiang Kai Shek, the first political head Chou en Lai.

Progress was rapid. From about 50,000 in 1924 Kuomintang expanded to some 400,000 civilian members by the end of 1926. This build-up of support went on in areas under warlord as well as Nationalist control. For example, it was popular organisation and, finally, an uprising in Shanghai in March 1927 that delivered the city from warlord control and into the hands of Chiang Kai Shek. Along with the mobilisation went increasingly effective military action. In 1926 Chiang Kai Shek began the Northern Expedition, designed to bring warlord areas under Nationalist control by means of a combination of force and negotiation.

The Communist Party also benefited from this progress. In early 1925 it had had fewer than 1,000 members. The number had reached some 58,000 by the spring of 1927. Urban workers were prominent in this expansion. It was the Communist Party which led the way in organising workers' and, to a lesser extent, peasants' movements, although the degree of control it exerted in these movements has often been overestimated.

But the process of growth contained an inherent contradiction. On the one hand, the military leadership under Chiang Kai Shek was concerned primarily with territorial gain and the firmer establishment of Nationalist political control. This meant giving social reform a low

233

priority. It also involved taking up negotiations with some war lords, getting financial backing and generally building up support from a very diverse range of groups. Nationalism, in this way, came to be focused outwards, was led by strong, authoritarian means centred upon the army and came to emphasise the co-ordination function in its ideological pronouncements.

On the other hand, the rapid mobilisation of workers and peasants, especially with the involvement of the Communist Party, carried very different implications. These popular movements looked to social change, and in the not too distant future at that. The Communist Party began to emphasise the need to 'consolidate' the successes of 1925–27 (which meant concentrating on social reform) rather than to press on in pursuit of more territorial gains. In any case, the party could argue, the rising in Shanghai indicated that popular movements could achieve more than military action.

This tension was bound to lead to open conflict. Chiang Kai Shek acted first. In April 1927 he turned against the Communist Party and his troops slaughtered thousands of workers in Shanghai. The party was forced underground. Effective communist activity shifted to the countryside, although the official leadership of the party did not come to appreciate the significance of this for a few more years. The way in which the Chinese Communist Party moved towards a strategy based on peasant support and securing control over rural areas is a well known story, and it is not strictly relevant here. What is of concern are the political questions the move raised in relation to nationalism.

First, the initial success of the rural strategy in parts of south-east China was dependent upon the prior absence of state control in the normal sense of the world. China was made up of a series of 'internal frontiers'.[2] Thus it was not too difficult for the communists, with some weapons and some peasant support, to establish local control. However, at the same time Chiang Kai Shek was slowly constructing a modern state which involved the gradual elimination of 'internal frontiers'. It led to the end of this first communist 'experiment'. The communist bases were surrounded and gradually closed down. The Long March of 1934–35 was a retreat to areas beyond the reach of the new state, which turned into the construction of an 'incipient state'.[3]

In terms of political control, therefore, the Chinese communists were the equivalent of warlords. Like the warlords they maintained control over particular areas which were legally part of the Chinese state. Just as warlord power was most quickly overcome by the nationalists in the southern and coastal regions, so too was communist power. Just as warlord power continued in the more northern and inland areas, remote from the nationalist stronghold and less attractive in terms of wealth, so did communist power.

However, there was a major difference between the way in which communist and warlord power operated, even making allowance for some of the more enlightened warlords. The Chinese communists were committed to social reforms which would, at the very least, eliminate gentry control. Because gentry control was so closely tied to the power of the central state (a point to which I return when making comparisons with Japan) the erosion of state power provided the opportunity for anti-gentry groups to take over at a local level. The communist elite was made up largely of intellectuals from the coastal regions, though increasingly, as the party expanded in the north-west, able peasants came to play a more important role. Furthermore, reform was not sought purely for its own sake. It was seen as a basis for taking control of the country as a whole and transforming it along communist lines. The objective of a strong and independent Chinese state was closely linked to the rejection of tradition in so far as the latter was seen to embody the values of exploitative elites. Instead the Chinese 'people' was the force to which the communists appealed.

The link with the Soviet Union gave the communists a unique political resource which increased their power. At the same time their objectives made it more difficult for them to negotiate agreements with the nationalists than it was for many warlords. Their internal politics were also rather different from that of warlord or nationalist areas. The position was fairly simple. A single, concentrated and socially homogeneous elite mobilised peasant support on the basis of social reform and the provision of security against outside forces, be they nationalists, warlords or, later on, Japan. The poor and remote character of the area under communist control made this a perfectly workable form of politics. Nationalism in any positive form played little part in it. There was strong anti-imperialist feeling among the communist elite, but the major concern of the 1927–37 period was the establishment of local bases against the pressure of the Nationalists. Nevertheless, as we shall see, the communist idealisation of the Chinese people could later assume a xenophobic form.

The price the communists paid for this type of politics in the short-term at an all-China level was impotence. Mobilisation and social reform were not the most effective means of reconstructing state power, and such a reconstruction was the prerequisite for attaining further objectives. Above all, it was not an appropriate type of politics in the richer and more complex society of coastal China, especially in and around the great cities such as Shanghai and Canton. There a more delicate type of politics, concerned as much with the co-ordination of a range of interests as with the mobilisation of popular support, was required. It is in this light that the development of nationalist politics after 1927 must be seen.

The moves against the communists in 1927 developed into a general attempt to 'demobilise' many of those who had flocked into various popular organisations in the previous three years. This was justified in

Kuomintang ideology by referring to Sun Yat Sen's idea of a period of 'political tutelage' during which the reconstruction of state power would have to be achieved from above before constitutional and democratic forms of government could be introduced. Trade unions, students', women's and peasants' organisations were either disbanded or placed under greater supervision. The function of the party as a mass institution was increasingly seen in terms of propaganda and purely symbolic political action designed to maintain a sense of solidarity. The party was committed to nationalist reconstruction and was quite prepared to act against either native or foreign capitalist interests where they were considered to be blocking this objective. But not every enemy could be tackled at once, and native capitalists could provide important support for the nationalist cause. Kuomintang took many of its ideas from the nationalist regimes in Turkey and Japan, which were seen as steering a path between communism and capitalism, preserving an economic system based on private property but subjecting it to strong state guidance. The Turkish case also supported the idea of an authoritarian phase of nationalism which would eventually give way to a more democratic era.

One weakness of this approach was that, whereas Sun Yat Sen had seen the nationalist party as the controlling force in such a politics, in practice the party as such came to decline in importance. Dependence upon administrative expertise brought non-party officials into key positions. Above all, the fundamental concern with securing military control meant that soldiers increasingly dominated Kuomintang. This military leadership was in turn divided. Chiang Kai Shek managed to bring various prominent war lords into agreement with the Nationalist regime, but the price he had to pay was their continued dominance in particular regions. As a result the Nationalist regime came to take on the appearance of a military confederacy. This unstable situation led to many factional struggles. At the same time military expenditure, along with the servicing of foreign debt, consumed the great bulk of the government's revenue. It was impossible to cut taxation or to finance reform projects which might have increased popular support, and the regime was tied more closely than ever to economic interests.

There was no easy solution. In consequence Kuomintang has often been written off as a corrupt and paralysed movement with little popularity, incapable of solving the enormous problems it faced. In contrast was the incorruptible communist elite, with its social reform projects and its steady pursuit of long-term ideals. But, as I have argued, the very different conditions under which effective politics had to operate in the richer and more complex coastal regions and in the backward and poor areas under communist control weaken the force of such a contrast.

That does not mean that Kuomintang could not have acted otherwise than it did. At times it went too far in an authoritarian direction. The

236

experiences of 1924–27 had scared many important elements within the Nationalist movement, and some of them tended to associate any sort of popular politics with communism. This led to internal disputes within Kuomintang as some urged the necessity for a popular base whilst others stressed the need for tutelage and the creation of stability before extending participation in politics. A typical example concerned student organisation. More conservative figures in Kuomintang argued that students should devote themselves to their studies and to preparing themselves to make the maximum contribution towards the national interest in the future. Meanwhile they should leave politics to more experienced professionals. This hardly satisfied a generation of students brought up to impatient rejection of the traditional emphasis on age and authority. As a result many went over to the communists after 1937.

But weaknesses such as these can be overemphasised. Between 1927 and 1937 the Nationalist regime actually made quite impressive advances in extending and and strengthening its authority. If there was popular dissatisfaction it did not appear to present a major problem for the regime. More serious seemed to be factionalism within government and the degree to which foreign influence inhibited policy. The probable long-term course of events, without some major change in the situation, would have been the continued reconstruction and extension of state power under the nationalist movement and the creation of an authoritarian and nationalist regime along the lines of Japan and Turkey in which the army and the bureaucracy would predominate. Undoubtedly the social problems that existed in China – above all, that of the peasantry – were far greater than in either Japan or Turkey. But this particular element has been closely examined and, in my view, overplayed.[4]

The outbreak of war with Japan destroyed the possibility of events taking this direction. Many areas under warlord and Nationalist control fell to the Japanese thrusts in the north-east and then against Shanghai and Canton. Chiang Kai Shek was forced to move into central China, where his position was much weaker. The communists remained in control of their base in the north-west around Yenan.

For the next eight years the major objective of both Nationalists and communists was the expulsion of the Japanese. This overriding concern led to the extinction of lesser political forces and left the field clear for a later settling of accounts between the two. There was some co-operation between Nationalists and communists, but only from independent bases of power and in a very cautious and suspicious way. At the same time the situation pushed the balance of power in favour of the communists and enabled them to extend their influence beyond the north-west. To understand how this was possible one has to see why the two sorts of politics already discussed – the communist politics of mobilisation and the nationalist politics of co-ordination – developed as they did in the struggle against Japan.

The communists were able to apply to the Japanese the same methods of politics and warfare which they had used against the nationalists. The Japanese, like the nationalists, were strongest in the eastern and coastal regions. Furthermore, the over-rapid extension of their lines had forced them to concentrate on holding major towns alone. The countryside in many areas was under no single authority continuously. Japanese forces could establish a limited presence only in daytime in particular areas. Many parts of China were criss-crossed by 'armies' owing allegiance to communists, warlords, nationalists, and 'independent' nationalists. In some cases they were bandit or peasant self-defence organisations. The distinctions between the different types of forces and the various allegiances were fluid. Many independent nationalist forces ended up co-operating with the communists against Kuomintang orders because it seemed the most effective form of resistance to the Japanese.

So the communists found their major rural bases, starting in the north-west, defensible against the initial Japanese attacks. From then on their form of politics was particularly suitable to the war which followed. They had developed ways of securing peasant support on the basis of reform (mainly by eliminating gentry and warlord burdens) and, above all, stability and protection. They had access to support from the Soviet Union. They were helped by the failure of the Japanese to install a puppet regime under the leadership of Wang Ching-Wei with any genuine authority which could provide peasants with some protection. Instead brutal retaliation against resistance and lack of reform in Japanese-controlled areas pushed peasants towards communist leadership.

The main concern of that leadership was to mobilise mass resistance to the Japanese. The communists resolutely pursued their established policy as a single elite, whipping up popular support in the pursuit of simple but basic objectives. A vivid example comes from the literacy campaign launched among the peasantry. The campaign itself is proof of the concern with reform and mobilisation. But the content of the material used is also revealing. The following examples are the texts of cards 1 and 20 in a series of graded reading cards captured by the Japanese in 1940.

Card 1

Men. Men and women. All are Chinese. All love China.

Card 20

Reactionary elements. Reactionary elements specialise in making trouble for anti-Japanese armed forces. They kill young men and women who oppose Japan. They destroy anti-Japanese work. They secretly help the Japanese devils and they secretly help Wang Ching-Wei.[5]

This is hardly elaborate nationalist ideology, but that would have been neither appropriate nor necessary. It is interesting that the term 'reactionary' is defined in relation to the Japanese and not in terms of social position. Of course, the two could be linked if it was argued that some social groups were more likely to furnish reactionary elements than others. However, an internal and possibly divisive emphasis was avoided by the communists so far as was possible. Social reform within the peasant community was pursued cautiously. The earlier emphasis on the 'poor peasant' shifted to take account of the 'middle peasant', and in practice policy may have been even more moderate. In this sense mass mobilisation by the communists during the war against Japan can be understood as a form of peasant nationalism.

The nationalists did not, by and large, respond to the Japanese threat in this way. Chiang Kai Shek was reluctant to engage in all-out war if it could be avoided, precisely because of the ways in which it might mobilise and radicalise a popular movement and undermine the careful linkages he had established in an authoritarian fashion. Before 1937 he had avoided direct confrontation with Japan, trying to use international diplomacy instead to reduce Japanese influence in China. Even when the war began it took a little while to move to outright conflict. Only after Chiang had been kidnapped by radical nationalists did he accept the need for open warfare. From then on his position seemed to improve. Many radical nationalists rallied to him, and the regime put up a good military performance. Control over warlords was increased, and a number were executed for treason (a charge they probably found meaningless). Some elements of Kuomintang did favour collaboration with the Japanese. The establishment of a puppet regime under Wang Ching-Wei with the title Kuomintang might have initially confused many peasants. But Chiang forthrightly opposed such collaboration, and most of the Nationalist movement backed him.

Nevertheless he always favoured purely military methods of resistance. Like many other leading nationalists he remained suspicious of ideas such as organisation of the masses into defence corps and the formation of special women's and peasants' leagues. These were favoured communist methods, which made them doubly suspect. Instead nationalism under Kuomintang concentrated on propaganda rather than mass action. But in comparison with communist methods the 'New Life' movement Chiang fostered which emphasised ethical values was thin, uninspiring stuff, abstracted from social experience or interests. This continued attempt to limit the scope of the conflict increased after the attack on Pearl Harbor, as Chiang could now rely on the United States to defeat Japan. But at the same time it could disillusion many radical nationalists within Kuomintang and push some of them towards the communists.

Yet internal disorder or instability in nationalist-controlled areas does not seem to have been too serious. The lack of a popular base became crucial when external forces threatened the Nationalist areas. And here again the nationalists were at a disadvantage compared to the communists. The main problem was that they were forced into the countryside, away

239

from their major power bases in the coastal regions, especially the large cities. This new situation required the development of new forms of politics, which Kuomintang found very difficult. Moreover the Japanese singled out the communists for their major acts of repression, fixing the latter firmly in the minds of many peasants as the real enemies of Japan. Johnson has shown a positive correlation between communist strength and the degree of Japanese repression. Where collaborators had more authority, and more subtle policies of rural pacification were pursued, communists influence was weaker.[6] Of course, it is difficult to work out what is cause and what effect in these relationships.

Resistance to the Japanese came to focus on the communist and nationalist leaderships, each practising rather different sorts of politics and with regional although overlapping concentrations of strength. It was on this basis that a civil war was subsequently fought which ended in the defeat of the nationalists in 1949. I will not deal with that but rather draw some conclusions about the role nationalism played up to the civil war.

Very crudely one can say that, after 1927, the co-ordination function of nationalism dominated Nationalist politics, whereas the mobilisation function, at times taking on a xenophobic form, dominated communist politics. Each form of politics was appropriate to the social and political character of the territories controlled by each movement. The two functions seemed to be mutually exclusive. Mobilisation threatened Chiang Kai Shek's authoritarian policy of co-ordination. Co-ordination, with the compromises it involved, was not a policy the rather purist and concentrated communist political elite was equipped to pursue. Before 1937 it seemed that the nationalist policy had the best chance of reconstructing state power in China. But the Japanese attack tipped the balance in favour of the communist politics of mobilisation. On this basis the communists were in a position to launch a successful challenge for control of state power after 1945 and the carrying through of radical policies of social change.

Elsewhere nationalist movements rather like Kuomintang were more successful, as the cases of Turkey and Japan demonstrate. An examination of these two will make it possible to pinpoint more accurately the particular weaknesses of Kuomintang.

3 Japan

By the middle of the nineteenth century Japan could reasonably be described as a feudal state.[7] Central power rested with the Shogun of the Tokugawa line. He resided in the city of Edo (later Tokyo) and was nominally subject to the Emperor, who lived with his court at Kyoto. The Shogun financed government activity from the yields of his own estates and those of other branches of the family which were vassals of the Tokugawa. Together these families controlled over half the rice yield of the country and were concentrated upon the strategically vital part of Japan around Edo. The bulk of the remaining land was controlled by a number of lords (*daimyo*) in the form of domains. Some sixteen of these were of considerable size and were located principally in the western parts of the country. The daimyo were virtually independent rulers of their domains. They were subject to a number of controls, however, such as enforced residence for part of the year in Edo. Each daimyo controlled a class of soldier-officials (*samurai*) whose members were granted stipends from the rice yield. There was a sharp division in status between samurai and commoners. Status was inherited and social mobility restricted. Land could not be freely bought and sold. In theory, samurai could not engage in farming or commerce. Such is a very bare and somewhat 'ideal' description of the major political relationships in Japan.

Obviously this set of political relationships was different in many important ways from that of any European feudal state. There was no equivalent to the Catholic Church. Towns had little autonomy. There was not the constant conflict between a plurality of states. All this meant that political conflict was not associated with conceptions of liberty as was the case in Europe. Rice cultivation produced different settlement patterns, divisions of labour and population densities than the largely grain-cultivating economies of medieval Europe, though the political consequences of this are a matter of debate. Nevertheless one is struck by the similarities. In both cases the authority of central government was constrained by and dependent upon the local, formal monopoly of power exercised by an hereditary class of landowners (or perhaps land controllers) and their military-official followings. The rest of the population was excluded from political life.

By the nineteenth century this situation and the values which underpinned it were under pressure and had been modified to some degree. Long periods of peace had seen the transformation of the samurai into a heterogeneous class extending from major domain officials to those on very low stipends and often forced into ignoble occupations. Certain sorts of commoners such as rich peasants or merchants could infiltrate themselves or their sons into the lower reaches of the samurai. Such a process probably always takes place, helping to preserve a theoretically rigid society, but beyond a certain point it poses a danger.

That same peace and prosperity had encouraged the growth of castle towns, above all Edo, in which commercial interests came increasingly to the fore. An important group of financiers, for example, specialised in converting domain produce into cash and providing credit facilities to daimyo and samurai. Peasant indebtedness could lead to urban financial penetration into the villages. This, as well as the commercial agriculture encouraged by urban growth, led to the emergence of new social distinctions in the village. Generally a set of financial and commercial interests

241

were becoming more important and were forming influential connections with all levels of 'traditional' society. Also, this economic growth and change varied from region to region, altering the balance of resources between the independent daimyo and those closely associated with the Shogun. One could scarcely argue that Japan was undergoing a quite independent transition from feudalism to capitalism, but changes of this sort meant that there was some predisposition to respond positively to contacts from the west.

Already in the eighteenth century the changes had led to discussion about what form society should take. Some had advocated a return to strict tradition and others thoroughgoing change. Such debates took on more urgency as contacts with the west increased. A few of the contacts were of long standing; the Dutch, for example, had been allowed a toehold on Japanese territory. On the basis of this experience some Japanese scholars had sought, before the nineteenth century, to understand how western societies worked and to relate this understanding to their own society. This too helped prepare a receptive attitude later when the relationship with the west became more pressing.

Japan had been able to resist significant penetration by the west for a long time. By the 1840s, however, the country's rulers were aware that resistance was going to be increasingly difficult. They were well informed about events in China, and the Opium Wars seemed to have particularly ominous implications. There were voices urging reform so that Japan should be able to meet any new challenge from the west. But the demands were largely ignored until the threat became manifest. With the arrival of Commodore Perry's expedition in 1853, and the demand for trading rights, that moment had come.

There were two extreme responses. One was the call to 'expel the barbarian', and it aroused considerable support in some domains. In the 1860s it was to lead to some, such as Choshu, taking military action against the shogunate for its conciliatory policies. The other response was to urge acceptance of the inevitable, the opening up of the country to the outside world and rapid adaptation to superior western ways. The shogunate pursued a middle course. It made concessions to those demands it believed irresistible, but in the most limited and dilatory way possible. At the same time it sought reform in key areas, such as military technology, in order to buttress a more independent policy at some time in the future. One can appreciate the dilemma in which Japan found itself if the logic of these three responses is examined.

Expulsion was utterly unrealistic. It could lead only to the direct entry of the western powers into Japanese affairs, either through annexation, the creation of a puppet regime, or the piecemeal assumption of governmental powers by some system of concessions or special commissions. 'Westernisation' would have led to the incorporation of Japan into a world economy on terms dictated by the developed economies of the west. It would have placed severe constraints upon the government's authority by forcing it to abandon any deliberate policy of control. It might well have led (as even a compromise policy did to some extent) to outright resistance in some domains which would have rendered the country ungovernable and induced more direct western intervention, as in the case of Egypt. One can see why a middle course appeared most attractive to the shogunate. But it could have achieved little more than the preservation of the traditional state in a situation of instability and in thrall to the west for the foreseeable future. The sort of economic growth needed to match the west even in the military field could not be generated out of balance-of-trade surpluses. The shogunate lacked the authority to expand its tax base so as to provide an alternative source of revenue for military and other reforms. To achieve that, radical political change was required.

Of course, the fact that none of these options could have succeeded does not explain why another was adopted. Societies do not make choices, let alone rational ones. Countless non-western countries responded in roughly one or other of the ways outlined above and with roughly the sort of consequences described. Rather this analysis shows just how formidable were the obstacles to a successful reform nationalism. It also provides some measure of the uniqueness of the Japanese achievement in finding an alternative which combined rapid emulation of the west with the maintenance of a strong and independent state.

Nationalism made two general contributions. As an ideology it combined a concern for Japanese identity with the acceptance of the need for extensive westernisation. Japan was identified as a specific nation rather than an incomparable civilisation (a typical Chinese response to the west), a nation whose essence could be preserved through a period of major change. Central to this idea was loyalty to the Emperor. Unlike the Chinese the Japanese did have a traditional alternative to the existing system of government. The restoration of imperial power and the later abolition of the domains could be defended as a return to the traditional arrrangements of an empire divided into provinces which the shogunate had supplanted. The fusion of symbols of tradition with acceptance of radical political change (as was also the case with religious justifications for loyalty to the emperor) played a vital role in Japanese nationalism.

It was able to happen because there was a plausible institutional alternative which could function as a national tradition. But the alternative was not just ideological. The existence of the emperor and the willingness of important figures in his court to co-operate with opponents of the shogunate also provided an organisational focus for the nationalist movement.

This organisation consisted primarily of the co-ordination of action between reform-minded elites in various domains. The innovations in policy planned by the Shogun, such as negotiation of treaties and reforms designed to raise revenue, had called for increased consultation with the daimyo. Regular consultation brought daimyo together more frequently and stimulated them to work out common positions in the absence of central government officials. On this basis, and in alliance with elements of the imperial court, a means of taking political action at the level of central government other than through the Shogunate developed.

At the same time, action at this level could aid reformers in their efforts at domain level. Loyalty to the Emperor and consideration of the national interest could justify reforms, if necessary against the wishes of the daimyo. Naturally such reforms could only be pushed through if there were important interests at domain level which favoured them. Among commercial and other commoner groups there was support for reforms such as the ending of hereditary status distinctions. At the same time, if the actions of these domain reformers were seen as leading to changes in the policies of the shogunate towards the western powers and, perhaps, the replacement of the regime by an effective empire, then they could also receive support from the 'expel the barbarian' traditionalists prominent among the lower ranks of the samurai. In this way the nature of the links between domain and central politics could lead to a temporary and powerful co-operation between ultimately opposed groups. Once the initial stage of the change was completed and the empire had been restored, then reformers found themselves in a position to take further measures. These reformers now controlled central government. Those who opposed measures such as the abolition of the domains could do so only at domain level and had no effective means of co-ordinating resistance among themselves. At the same time reformers continued to have important contacts at domain level. Rather as rejection of the programmes of the French monarchy between 1787 and 1789 paved the way for a far more drastic set of reforms by a more centralised state in the 1790s, so the way in which the mildly reformist shogunate was resisted and overthrown prepared the ground for the more far-reaching reforms of the Meiji governments. The general implications of this process will be taken up again in the comparative sections of this chapter.

4 Turkey

This account will be brief because, strictly speaking, the Turkish case does not belong to this chapter. The equivalent of reform nationalism in China and Japan up to the Meiji regime is reform nationalism in the Ottoman empire. The links between that reform nationalism and nationalism within Turkey after 1918 are complex. Nevertheless the case is worth considering because of particular contrasts which can be drawn between it and the Chinese and Japanese cases.

244

Reform nationalism in the Ottoman empire resembled the Chinese rather than the Japanese case. Theoretically there existed, as in China, a central bureaucracy which ruled fairly directly over a number of provinces. There was little provision for the formal protection or expression of local or regional rights, although, as has been shown,[8] the Greek Orthodox Church held a privileged position in the European part of the empire. Recruitment to government service was, in theory, based on merit, and the exercise of political power was not equated with inherited privilege.

As in China this system had decayed considerably by the nineteenth century. However, the decline took a rather different form. In the Ottoman Empire in Europe the interaction between local elites and external powers led to the establishment of autonomous or independent nation-states highly dependent upon external support.[9] In the Chinese case it had led to the growth of warlord power and, by and large, the bulk of external support went to the central government. China, unlike the Ottoman empire, was not threatened by separatist nationalism because there were no autonomous cultures and institutions such as those of the Christian churches nor any external intervention to which nationalism could appeal for legitimacy. Such a creed had no attraction to warlords, even if much of what they did amounted to separation from central government.

As in China, so in the Ottoman empire some elements within government early recognised the need for change. Likewise reform was originally seen in narrow, practical terms, and it was imagined that it could be divorced from a wholesale transformation of government and society. Military reform was the principal early concern, along with the introduction of more efficient techniques of administration. Some reforms were carried through. The janissaries, the traditional soldier class, were destroyed. Military officers trained in western ideas and techniques were placed in command of new forces, some possessing modern armaments, and some western European officers came to help train these forces. A range of other piecemeal improvements were introduced.

But these steps led to demand for more far-reaching reforms. Access to western military thinking required education in the west, the teaching of foreign languages and the translation of books and articles. New administrations wanted a clear definition of the 'public' tasks they should undertake. Increased expenditure on modernised armies required economic growth and a more effective tax system. This led on to suggestions that initiative be freed in the economy, above all in agriculture, by means of a reform of the system of land ownership and consultation with various important groups about tax reforms. The suggestion could follow that assemblies be established, with formal rights and formal qualifications for people to choose the members. Each step seemed to lead on to another. Yet there was much opposition. In particular many Muslims could not accept the notion of a secular state, to which many of these ideas seemed

245

to point. The government was prepared to consider reform in a piecemeal and pragmatic way, and there were times during the nineteenth century when change seemed practicable. But when the process threatened to destroy the very basis of the status quo, support for it within government rapidly diminished.

However, unlike China and rather more like Japan, reforming groups did come to take control of the state (which remained, in its non-European territories, fairly strong) in the decade or so before 1914. They embarked on a more thoroughgoing programme than had been pursued before. The Young Turk movement pressed towards the establishment of a secular state with greater central power and backed up by an elected parliament. However, its efforts stimulated resistance, as the consideration of early Arab nationalism has already shown.[10] In response, ideas of imperial reform began to turn into a form of Turkish nationalism. But the basis of support for this nationalism was very narrow and it had made only limited advances by 1914.

The First World War transformed the situation. Conflict between government and Arab resistance intensified Turkish nationalist sentiment. The break-up of the empire into its 'national' constituents at the end of the war meant that imperial reform was a thing of the past. Turkish nationalism could now focus on the task of turning Turkey into a nation-state. That state was, from the outset, threatened by the Allied award of Smyrna to the Greeks. The conflict this aroused led to communal strife in the cities of the west coast of Asia Minor. It helped provide a negative, xenophobic base upon which nationalism could build. But xenophobia and communal conflict alone do not make nationalism into an effective political movement. Leadership was required, and there were formidable obstacles within Turkish society to overcome. As before the war, leadership came principally from army officers who were acutely aware of the need for reform and were concerned, at least partially, to achieve something after losing the war. Their attempts, led by Mustafa Kemal (Ataturk), to resist the Allied territorial settlement were disavowed by the Turkish government. Still closely tied to Muslim religious authorities, the government was suspicious of the reformers and sceptical about the possibility of effective resistance to the post-war settlement. Ataturk had to establish a base in the mountain regions of central Anatolia and carry out a revolution against his own government as well as a war against the Greeks. His military success not only regained western Asia Minor but also broke the grip of Ottoman officialdom and Islamic religious leaders over the new Turkish state. Once that was achieved Ataturk was able to push through a series of radical reforms backed up by an elaborate secular nationalist ideology.[11]

This course of events could be interpreted in terms of a shift from the co-ordination to the mobilisation function as the major feature of the nationalist movement. Reform in the Ottoman empire, which was only incidentally nationalist, was based upon the activity of small elites. These were found principally, but not solely, in central government and among Turks. In the last decades before the First World War these elites were broadening the base of their support and taking up closer links with one another, but this was proceeding in a slow and hesitant manner, punctuated by mutual suspicion. The war, the growing importance of the army, and the expulsion of Ataturk into central Anatolia changed the situation. Now reform was explicitly nationalist, leadership was centred on a small and concentrated elite drawn above all from the army. The main job of this elite was to mobilise popular support against the Greeks, where it could build on communal hostilities, and to create an effective army. The destruction of the Ottoman government and the international agreements of 1918–20 had gravely weakened the Ottoman institutions, which had hoped to maintain their sway in Turkey proper. So this militarily-led politics of mobilisation could overcome its enemies and push ahead with further reforms in a fairly radical way.

5 Comparisons

The main comparison I wish to make is between China and Japan. Before doing so I will briefly compare each of these with the Turkish case.

(a) Japan and Turkey

Both countries managed to create nationalist movements which transformed the character of the state and carried through a limited process of modernisation on an autarchic but fundamentally capitalist basis. The ideologies employed were very different. In Japan traditional ideas and images played a very large part. In Turkey nationalist ideology was aggressively secular. It denied the Islamic identification of religion and state, abolished the caliphate, and attacked common practices such as the wearing of the fez. One might argue that the 'traditional value system' in Japan was more adaptable to modern circumstances than in Turkey. However, such arguments are very difficult to mount, let alone prove, because of the intangible and often seemingly arbitrary character of the concept of a 'value system' and also because of the problem of how far such a system of values, in itself, has any demonstrable limits of adaptiveness to new purposes. I would prefer to relate these ideological differences to the different political, above all institutional, contexts within which nationalist politics operated in the two countries.

Japanese nationalism can be described as reformist. The Meiji restoration was itself a very limited and almost bloodless 'revolution'. Continuity was as marked and as important as discontinuity. Very diverse elites ranging from reactionary samurai in the domains to enthusiastic westernisers in the imperial court co-operated, at least for a time, in a common opposition to the shogunate. There was a clear institutional alternative for this opposition to form around within the state itself. Continuity, the confinement of political activity to elites, the diversity of elites involved, and existing institutional alternatives – all were reflected in the artificial, syncretic ideology of emperor loyalty and the restoration of Shinto religion which were used to justify the Meiji restoration and the subsequent actions of the new regime. It is also important to note that in the Japanese case a nationalist takeover of government owed little to war with external powers or indeed any major intervention from outside.

Reform nationalism in Turkey only really became effective in the wake of the destruction of the imperial state it had originally sought to reform. In consequence the nationalist elite was isolated, compelled to radical action, and yet able to succeed because of the way war had undermined existing government. Nationalists had no need to seek compromise with Ottoman officials or with Islam. Instead they could attack officials and religious leaders as part of a great barrier obstructing the building of a strong and independent Turkey. Hence their ideology came to take on a very secular and uncompromising tone.

(b) Turkey and China

In certain ways Turkish nationalism resembled Chinese communism. Both began as part of a wider but weaker reform movement. In the wake of war both built up support from backward regions, with at least some appeal to xenophobic sentiments. Neither, therefore, felt any need to compromise with other elites but determined instead upon an energetic programme of reform once state power had been won through war and revolution.

There were, of course, equally important differences. Turkish nationalism as a popular movement developed suddenly out of a war situation. Its rural base was the product of military necessity and was not linked with social revolution. It did not face the same huge obstacles of foreign intervention, and social conflict and breakdown as in China. Change was conceived of in purely nationalist terms. The central elite came from the army and not from an intelligentsia, and thought in terms of order rather than upheaval. Anti-imperialist sentiment was, quite naturally among an imperial officer class, rather weak. Turkish nationalists did not face competition from other sorts of nationalists, as was the case with the Chinese communists. The two movements operated a rather similar sort of politics but with quite different objectives and justifications and in quite different circumstances.

(c) China and Japan

In purely descriptive terms one can note the different roles played by the co-ordination and mobilisation functions within the nationalist movements in these two countries. In China a nationalist movement briefly took shape in the mid-1920s in which both functions were important. But, after that, politics operating in these two ways tended to part company and characterised the politics of conflicting movements. In Japan reform nationalism remained confined to elites which the nationalist movement successfully co-ordinated in order to take control of the state and introduce a substantial measure of reform. In relation to this description three related questions need to be asked. In what ways did elite co-ordination differ within the nationalist movements of the two countries? Why did mass politics play such an important role in the Chinese but not the Japanese case? What effect did this have upon nationalism?

One can begin by noting that the difficulties facing reform nationalists seem to have been much greater in China than in Japan. To begin with, external constraints were greater. China was a much richer country and so attracted a greater degree of attention and at a much earlier stage. Internal constraints also seem to have been a good deal stronger. Being very much bigger in both area and population, China was much harder to push in any particular direction. Rapid population increase in the nineteenth century had led to extreme poverty, hence the country faced much greater problems in seeking economic growth. It had a much less stable peasantry than Japan. Chinese history is punctuated by frequent peasant revolts, some of the most serious of which took place in the nineteenth century. One could argue that such instability reduced the power of central government to push through any programme of reform and inhibited opposition elites from taking action which might further weaken the government and expose themselves to popular attack. By the time reform was seen as even less dangerous than doing nothing a reform programme had little chance of success.

This argument can be deepened a little. Barrington Moore has compared the two countries in terms of the relationships between lord and peasant.[12] Much of his argument relates to differences between their state structures, and I will return to this point in a moment. However, Barrington Moore also points to characteristic differences in the peasant communities of the two countries which suggest that political control was much more difficult to maintain in China. This would suggest that elite co-ordination politics was bound to be inadequate there. The thesis can also be linked with the further contrast that Japanese nationalism was not challenged by a movement such as Chinese communism. It could be argued that the challenge was itself a product of the weaker political controls which operated in China and, therefore, of the emergence of a politics of mass mobilisation which would eventually defeat nationalism. In other words, the constraints upon reform nationalism were so much greater than in Japan, and the degree of control over the masses – above all, the peasantry – so much weaker that a new stability could be formed only on the basis of a much more radical, mass-based movement.

There is much to be said for this argument. However, it acquires force only when we compare mid-nineteenth century Japan with China in the 1920s and 1930s. More relevant, perhaps, would be to ask why an effective reform nationalist movement did not develop in China earlier in the nineteenth century, when the dangers the country faced were comparable to those threatening Japan in the 1850s and 1860s. Certain points still have some validity but of a much more limited kind. Some, of course, such as the role played by a rival communist movement, do not apply at all.

In seeking an answer to this question I would place particular emphasis on the different forms taken by the traditional state in the two countries. Japanese writers in the earlier part of the nineteenth century did occasionally compare their system of government with the Chinese in order to assess either's capacity to respond effectively to the challenge from the west. Usually they noted in favour of China a centralised system of government and a meritocratic method of recruitment to official positions. In fact, one could argue, these were the most severe disadvantages.

Meritocratic recruitment was based on the principles of Confucianism. Confucianism assumed that the only significant civilisation was that of China. More than that, Chinese civilisation was built upon values of stability, authority, tradition and self-control that were difficult to reconcile with western ideas about change, the merit of innovation, and stress on individuality and self-expression. Of course, value systems at a very general level are rather vague and, in detail, highly flexible. Some Chinese writers sought a more affirmative view of modernity in the works of Confucius and, as is usual in such cases, found what they were looking for. But this value system was developed in a very specific form through the Chinese education system and was deeply rooted in the ethos of those who ran the state. It was very difficult, therefore, for the state to act against such values.

A centralised system of government made the commitment to reform excessively dependent upon those in central government. But the higher one looked, the greater was the attachment of both sentiment and interest to the existing system. In the Japanese case the firm position of the domain and its lord and his officials meant that the reform impulse could start to become effective at a much lower level. In China there was a deliberate attempt to prevent concentrations of power at provincial level. Officials were constantly rotated in order to prevent them becoming closely identified with provincial interests. Naturally a great deal of effective authority was exercised by the gentry at local and provincial levels. But this sort of authority had no organised relationship to the central state. When the latter was challenged or its authority undermined, therefore, local power

250

groups which replaced imperial officials tended to separate themselves from it. Whereas daimyo sought to reform the central state, warlords concentrated on consolidating their position against it. In Japan they were helped by the ideological and institutional alternative to the shogunate offered by the Emperor.

This difference in the organisation of the state is related to Barrington Moore's points concerning the different relationships between lord and peasant. A feudal state is one in which economic and political control are virtually identical. This leads to firm control at the local level, although such control constrains the power of central government. It also means that crises in central government and crises in the localities can, to some extent, be insulated from each other. Yet it also means that the state is articulated through its linkages between constrained central government and dominant local elites. Taken together, this makes it possible for elements of those elites to co-ordinate an attack upon central government without automatically worrying about the implications the resultant crisis might have for their local authority.

One must distinguish between the fear of losing control and the actual loss of control. By themselves peasant communities in Nationalist-held territory were unable to threaten the regime in China seriously. But Kuomintang, as we have seen, was unable to mobilise that peasantry for its own purposes, and indeed feared such mobilisation. But the real weakness would come if Kuomintang was challenged by other political groups which were able to mobilise the peasantry or had access to military power. The weakening of nationalist control in their threatened territories could then lead to increasingly independent action on the part of the peasants. So the lack of control and the failure to mobilise peasant support only became important when war weakened the position of Kuomintang.[13]

The obstacles facing reform nationalists when their states are challenged by western powers are very great. To act effectively they must be ready and able to provoke a political crisis in order to reform government quite radically and yet without fearing that the crisis will get out of control. A political system such as existed in Japan seems much more favourable in this respect than the sort which existed in China.

By the time reform nationalism did become important in China the problem was quite different. The nationalist movement had to reconstruct, not simply reform, the state. There was no firm basis from which to start. Accordingly the progress of the movement was slow and uncertain, its achievements fragile. Establishing political and military order came to take priority over social reform and popular support. Internal and external constraints on nationalist room for manoeuvre were very tight. The measure of success Kuomintang had achieved by 1937 is perhaps more striking than its ultimate failure.

6 Conclusion

Only the Japanese can be regarded as a case of successful reform nationalism. In China such a movement failed and in Turkey its success was based upon the prior destruction of the Ottoman government it had first set out to reform.

Japan resembles European states and societies more closely than any other non-western society. The resemblance has led to a great deal of comparison. It raises the obvious idea of some connection with the country's success in emulating the west. This argument would clearly apply to its successful nationalist movement. I cannot enter here into the complex comparisons which have been drawn. I will focus on one aspect of these comparisons only: that concerning the form of the state.

As in so many states in early modern western Europe and in nineteenth-century central Europe, as well as in numerous twentieth century colonial states, it was possible in Japan for opposition movements to develop at both local and central levels. These different levels were able to reinforce, rather than conflict with, one another. What is more, opposition could use the institutions of the state in its own development and to provide an alternative model of its own objectives. In a similar way to that in which Parliament operated for opposition in seventeenth-century England, for example, so did the Emperor and his court operate in mid-nineteenth century Japan. Of course, the context was very different but the political mechanics were generally alike.

In these situations the state can remain powerful even as its opposition becomes powerful. The reason is that the opposition builds upon rather than seeking to destroy state institutions. Indeed, it is the growth of state power which increases the strength of opposition entrenched in institutions used to promote that growth. In this way the state can appear as a force apart from the groups that seek to control it. More practically, it means that when such an opposition comes to power it has strong institutions through which to work even if they need substantial reform. In political systems such as the Ottoman and Chinese empires, by contrast, a powerful opposition movement devoted to reform rather than separation or a simple transfer of power usually could succeed only if state power was substantially weakened. This meant that such an opposition inherited a state incapable of carrying through its reform programme. Thus the structure of the Japanese state and the degree to which it resembled many western states favoured reform nationalism in a way that was not possible in the states of the Ottoman and Chinese empires.

Notes

1 That is, during the formative period of becoming a nation-state. Japan, of

course, was temporarily governed by the United States of America after the Second World War.

2   For the meaning of this term see above, pp. 219–22.

3   For the idea of an 'incipient state', the closely related notion of 'guerilla action' and the circumstances in which such forms of action can succeed in breaking away from or taking over the existing state, see the general theoretical points made in Alexander J. Motyl, *Sovietology, Rationality, Nationality: Coming to Grips with Nationalism in the USSR* (New York, 1990), especially chapters 7 and 8.

4   As, for example, in Barrington Moore, *The Social Origins of Dictatorship and Democracy: lord and peasant in the making of the modern world* (London, 1969), though this remains a superb piece of comparative history.

5   Quoted in Chalmers A. Johnson, *Peasant Nationalism and Communist Power: the emergence of revolutionary China, 1937–1945* (London, 1963), p. 151.

6   *Ibid.*.

7   For a succinct introduction see W. G. Beasley, *The Meiji Restoration* (London, 1973), chapter 1. The concept of feudalism is explicitly applied to Japan by Perry Anderson, *Lineages of the Absolutist State* (London, 1974), pp. 435–61.

8   See above, pp. 146–7.

9   See above, pp. 135–43.

10 See above, pp. 149–52.

11 However, for a view as to the limitations of these reforms, see below, pp. 270–3.

12 Barrington Moore, *op. cit.*, pp. 162–313.

13 Peasants were not automatically anti-Japanese. Occasionally, as Japanese troops approached, peasants would take the opportunity to turn on Kuomintang soldiers. Peasant 'nationalism' under communist leadership was the product of the material advantages of communist protection and the anti-Japanese sentiments of the communists. This view, which modifies the position of Chalmers Johnson, is lucidly put by Lucien Bianco, *Origins of the Chinese Revolution, 1915–1949* (London, 1971), especially pp. 153–64.

Part III

Varieties of nationalism
(ii) In a world of nation-states

Once a nationalist, or even merely a national, opposition takes control of the state, or, more gradually, the existing state comes to lay stress upon its national credentials, then the specifically nationalist character of politics tends to diminish. Competing groups all proclaim their paramount concern with the 'national interest'. In such a situation nationalism as a specific form of politics becomes meaningless. Again, where all foreign policy is justified in nationalist language it is difficult to identify a specific form of foreign policy which could be called nationalist.

There are, however, certain situations in which a distinctive nationalist politics continues to operate. There are separatist nationalist challenges to the nation-state. There is the pursuit by some governments of 'nation-building' policies which involve an elaborate nationalist justification and an attack upon identities and loyalties which are believed to conflict with national commitment. There are unification nationalist movements which seek to integrate a number of independent 'nation'-states into a wider political unit believed to express the true national spirit. There are radical right challenges to parliamentary nation-states which are based upon a particularly extreme form of nationalist ideology. Finally, there is the recent breakdown of the last remaining multi-national empire – the USSR and its satellite states – which is raising the spectre of nationalist conflict through east and central Europe.

In looking at these cases I treat new states, the nation-states of the developed world, and the USSR separately. The reasons for this will become clear in the course of the analysis. The next three chapters consider separatist, nation-building and unification nationalism in new states. Unification and nation-building nationalism are of little importance in the developed nation-states (except for the very special case of the reunification of Germany which is touched upon in chapter 17), so the three final chapters in this section consider radical right and separatist nationalism in such states.

12

Separatist nationalism in the new nation-states

The matters dealt with in this and the next two chapters are very recent and unfinished. Reliable and comprehensive evidence is rarely available. What is made known to outsiders is often one-sided and apologetic. The subject is too important to ignore but, because of these considerations, theory or polemic often loom larger than hard evidence in the work on it. It is not possible to continue with the method employed so far of comparing case studies which are looked at in some detail. Instead I will outline a more general form of argument and bring in particular cases in a more illustrative way than has so far been the practice. The division between this chapter and the next one is very fine. Attempts to increase the authority of the new nation-state and to challenge that state on the basis of a separatist nationalism are often simply two sides of the same conflict. Nevertheless, from the point of view of general analysis the distinction is worth making.

One can begin by noting two apparently contradictory features of the politics of the new states created by European decolonisation. On the one hand they often appear to be weak and unstable. Among the most important causes of this are the challenges of separatist movements of various kinds. Yet, on the other hand, the new states have largely survived such challenges intact, at least territorially. The creation of Bangla Desh is the only major exception to this generalisation. Part of the explanation can be found in the way international politics operates. No new state is anxious to support any challenges to other new states for fear that this could rebound on itself. In many cases the governments of new states have been able to appeal to important outside powers for help against an internal challenge. For example, the central government received much more external support, including from the former colonial power Britain, than did Biafra during the Nigerian civil war. The exceptional case of Bangla Desh proves the rule in that an external power, in this case India, was finally prepared to intervene against the government of Pakistan which was itself weakened by the physical separation of East from West Pakistan. But international politics offers only part of the answer to this territorial stability. One must also look at the way in which politics operates within the new states.[1]

To do this one must begin by considering the nature of separatist challenges. These are frequently labelled 'tribalist', a derogatory word which is part of the ideological assault to which such challenges are treated. Even if the term is used more neutrally or positively, the implication is that the separatist challenge is based upon an appeal to language or to pre-colonial communal identity which sustains loyalties that are more important than loyalty to the new state. I have already considered some of the weaknesses of such an understanding when looking at anti-colonial nationalism. It is worth reiterating these as well as other objections to such an approach.

First, it is clear that sub-national identities are often as recent as the national identities with which they are supposed to conflict, and indeed both are often the product of the same processes during the colonial period. Second, it is equally clear that effective territorial anti-colonial nationalist movements build upon a series of lower-level conflicts and identities rather than substituting their own, new identities in place of the lower-level ones. It is not that there are relatively fixed identities which tend to conflict with one another but rather that there are a number of possible political roles which may conflict with or complement one another or remain unconnected. Analysis, accordingly, should switch to the determinants of these different relationships rather than trying to discover fixed identities and to measure their intensity or their pedigree. The measurement of cultural homogeneity or heterogeneity is, in any case, at best highly uncertain. People can, if circumstances encourage it, divide on the basis of 'trivial' cultural distinctions. Equally, groups divided by 'fundamental' cultural distinctions can co-operate politically within the same state. Cultural distinctions, therefore, need to be treated as resources for rather than determinants of politics and related to the political system which encourages their use in this way.

One reason for the emphasis on cultural (perhaps, 'non-political' would be a more accurate term) determinants of political behaviour in many new states arises from an inappropriate view of what is meant by politics. Much of the politics of the new states goes on outside the formal institutions of the state. These institutions are, in any case, poorly defined and only loosely separated from one another.[2] But rather than treat instability in terms of how these institutions are overwhelmed by such 'non-political' forces as corruption, nepotism, ethnic divisions and factional conflict, one should seek to widen the definition of political activity within the state in order to include these forces.

The first thing such a widening of perspective points to is how limited are the resources available to many new states. There are, of course, the general constraints upon economic development which vary with the size and wealth of individual countries. But there are also political constraints. As we have seen, the nationalist movement is usually a delicate set of linkages between a number of smaller, usually localised, political groupings. Even after taking over the state the nationalist movement cannot easily emancipate itself from dependence upon these groupings. The state does provide some extra resources; occasionally, as in India, they are very considerable. Victory in the fight for independence can also provide nationalist leadership with immense prestige. But these are assets which can waste rapidly. It is difficult to match the resources of the state to all the claims made upon it by the network of interests constituting the nationalist movement. In matters such as the staffing of the higher levels of the civil service and the army, for example, there is often acute conflict between the demands of administrative effectiveness and short-term political stability. Expectations are often so high at independence that there is bound to be disillusionment with the threadbare reality which actually emerges. This will particularly be the case when a small number of people can be seen to have done well out of independence. Finally, as we shall see in the next chapter, nationalist regimes are prone to waste scarce resources by taking on tasks beyond their capacity.

All these political elements contribute to instability because they involve demands upon the state which it cannot meet. Very soon there has to be some sort of rationing and an attempt to impose it on the population. That is what 'nation-building' is often really about. Separatist nationalism is one way of either manipulating or challenging such a rationing system.

There are three ways an appeal to sub-national identity can seek to alter the distribution of resources. It can be a means of gaining a more favourable position in central government and a bigger say in its decisions. Groups will point, for example, to their under-representation in the distribution of development projects or educational facilities. Given that colonial rule often favoured one community against another, this sort of conflict can emerge rapidly. A second way can be to try to reduce the power of central government through devices such as a federal constitution and entrenched local rights. A third may be to try for total independence, perhaps as a further extension of the second position. If a group has valuable resources in its own locality – such as oil in Iboland or copper in Katanga – one or other of these options can seem particularly attractive. In the case of Bangla Desh it was rather gross discrimination against East Pakistan on the part of the central government that gave rise to demands first for autonomy and subsequently for independence.

But although circumstances may favour one or other of these options, the distinction between them is frequently little more than tactical. Conflict in Nigeria, for example, has taken all three forms. When Ibo elites had favourable access to positions of privilege in central government and the army as well as a political agreement with the dominant groups in northern Nigeria, they were inclined to oppose any sort of explicit ethnic discrimination at central government level. However, to preserve a local basis of power they, and dominant interests in the north and west, all emphasised the importance of federalism. It tended to be minority groups within these virtually autonomous areas that favoured greater centralism. When the position of the Ibo suddenly deteriorated, their elites put greater emphasis on ethnic ties and local autonomy, and ended up demanding a separate state. No doubt the intensity of 'Ibo identity' increased in this later phase, but it was the product rather than the cause of a changed political situation which demanded a new type of politics.

Ethnicity, language or any other criteria used to underpin a claim to sub-national identity can, therefore, be understood as a political resource. Very generally one can argue that such resources are particularly important in situations where resources available to the central government are by contrast very limited, where organisations or groups with political relationships covering most or all of the state territory (such as national trade unions or employers' organisations) are non-existent or of little importance, and where the nature of economic and political change under colonialism tended both to define and favour some communities against others. In these situations political elites have to rely overwhelmingly on localised resources, above all in the form of popular support. Control of central institutions such as the army or the bureaucracy often means little without this local power. The reason why small rebellions in the armed forces of some new states can overthrow a government is that there is very little power at central government level from the outset.

These points require some illustration. I will begin by considering the Indian case. As has been argued earlier, the Indian nationalist movement was based upon the co-ordination of an elaborate set of interest groups in a way closely related to the collaborator system established by the Raj as well as some degree of mass mobilisation. The establishment of Pakistan eliminated one set of contenders for access to the resources controlled by the Indian state. But two major sorts of conflict remained. First, elements outside Congress found themselves without a central body around which they could organise. Second, even within Congress there were tensions over the distribution of resources. Suddenly, it seemed, conflicts almost invisible before the achievement of independence erupted to the surface. One manifestation of this came with the redrawing of provincial boundaries along language lines. Congress had already, in the 1920s, organised itself in this way rather than on the basis of Raj provincial boundaries. But what had been acceptable when Congress represented the 'nation' against a foreign state suddenly became contentious when proposed as a principle for organising the nation-state. In 1948 the government established a Linguistic Provinces Committee. Nehru, who was a member of the committee, expressed his dismay at the demands presented to it:

> [This inquiry] . . . has been in some ways an eye-opener for us. The work
> of sixty years of the Indian National Congress was standing before us, face
> to face with centuries-old India of narrow loyalties, petty jealousies and
> ignorant prejudices engaged in mortal conflict and we were simply horrified
> to see how thin was the ice upon which we were skating. Some of the ablest
> men in the country came before us and confidently and emphatically
> asserted that language in this country stood for and represented culture,
> race, history, individuality and finally a sub-nation.[3]

The interpretation put forward by Nehru, in which national loyalty,
implicitly regarded as modern, enlightened and broad in its vision, is
contrasted with these ancient, ignorant and petty sentiments, somewhat
obscures what was happening. Once it is recognised that Congress was
largely built upon such 'prejudices' and local concerns, much of the
mystery disappears. In fact a whole range of local studies have shown that
the sorts of conflict brought before the Linguistic Provinces Committee
were often new and were a combination of communal cleavage and elite
competition.[4]

But it is also important to note the limitations of this sort of conflict
within India. First, the resources inherited from the Raj, as well as the way
Congress had taken them over step by step, made central government
strong in the face of particular local or provincial challenges. Second, the
sheer variety of language group and/or interest group competition meant
that no one community was ever in a position actually to make a bid for
independence. Also, it was particularly difficult for groups outside Congress to take up links with others in a similar position elsewhere, both
because of their local perspectives and because Congress itself had dominated the process of co-ordinating opposition policies up to the time of
independence. The sheer heterogeneity of Congress certainly inhibited its
capacity to pursue clear policies, but it also tended to make it immune to
open challenge, and forced conflict into informal struggle within Congress.
The inability of Nehru to impose an overriding 'national' loyalty upon the
country or of 'sub-national' groups to go any further than demanding
adjustments in the organisation of the state are two aspects of the same
set of political arrangements.

Much more unstable are new states where colonialism gave clear
pre-eminence to particular communities. The cases of Uganda and Nigeria
provide examples. The special position of Buganda in Uganda has already
been considered for the pre-independence period. It continued to cause
problems after independence. Ethnic demands among non-Baganda groups
tended to concentrate simply upon the distribution of resources by the
central government, but the Baganda, with a special position under the
independence constitution, presented the new state with very special prob-

lems. In February 1966 President Obote effected what amounted to a *coup d'état* and ended the special constitutional status of Buganda. The Baganda responded later that year with an uprising, which was suppressed. Subsequently, particularly after the overthrow of Obote in 1970, conflict shifted into other, more terrible forms. One result was the apparent disappearance of sub-nationalism. A few speculations can be made about this.

Between 1966 and 1970 Obote sought to introduce changes in the political arrangements of the state which were designed to diminish the role of localised political ties. One ingenious idea, for example, was to require parliamentary candidates to gain a certain level of support in three constituencies other than their main one in order to be returned. It was intended that the constituencies should be dispersed about the country and have very different ethnic memberships. The idea was that candidates would be forced to go beyond ethnic appeals or, at the very least, to construct ethnic alliances. The device never came into operation, so its effectiveness was not put to the test. In a moment the possible effect of ethnic alliances will be looked at with regard to Nigeria. Obote also tried to balance ethnic claims against one another in matters such as the distribution of development funds. His was an authoritarian policy of coordination among localised, and ethnically identified, elites, excluding the Baganda. That this was so can be seen in relation to his language policy. He recognised that there were serious obstacles in the way of introducing an African tongue as the official language of government. No single African language is shared by the various elites on which his power rested. The government had to retain English as the official language, but it was only spoken among elites. The policy is effective as elite co-ordination, but it can hardly mobilise popular support. A 'popular' language policy would intensify ethnic divisions. Obote adopted a delicate policy which prevented sub-nationalist challenges by recognising the legitimacy of sub-national claims whilst trying to erode their significance. Under this system the state was able to govern and to maintain conditions for the continuation of existing social and political institutions.

Amin's assumption of control did not help any separatist movement, but this was mainly because his exercise of power was destructive of any form of organised politics. In Uganda the army had, until independence, been officered by Europeans. Africans had got no higher than non-commissioned rank. Consequently military service was ignored by the elites of the privileged communities, above all by the Baganda. Instead the army recruited from peripheral ethnic groups of low prestige. In fact the identity of such groups was itself uncertain, because they played no part in political competition and so had little opportunity to develop any clear identity either for themselves or others. But with independence and the Africanisation of the army some of their members found themselves in important positions.

Amin was typical of this process. He was a Kakwa from north-west Uganda. Poorly educated, he had only reached the position of sergeant by the time of independence, although he was the senior African figure in the army. His English was poor: Swahili is the language of the Ugandan army, which immediately puts it somewhat apart from non-military elites. As a consequence the rule of Amin and troops loyal to him was based on the destruction of any and every elite which could exercise political influence. The growing power of the army was, therefore, accompanied by growing violence and terror and the breakdown of the state as an organised system of rule. Ethnic discrimination was not linked to any positive political objective and the destruction of ethnic elites was not motivated by a clear objective of creating genuinely national institutions. Political conflict was replaced increasingly by diffuse and highly particularistic struggles. This is probably the normal consequence of apolitical military rule.[5] Such activity could not form a basis either for the effective exercise of state power or for opposition to Amin. His system of rule led inexorably to the destruction of those institutions essential for the continued, orderly existence of society. Whether, in the attempt to reconstruct political order and a Ugandan state following his overthrow, sub-national ties will come once more to play an important role remains to be seen.

The case of Nigeria is instructively different. Colonial rule promoted the development of sub-national political identity in the form of the threefold division of Yoruba (south-west), Hausa-Fulani (north) and Ibo (south-east). In the cases of the Yoruba and Ibos political identity was a colonial creation due to the need to create more extensive political relationships than had hitherto existed. In the case of the Hausa-Fulani it was a modification of the Islamic emirate system which had existed prior to colonial rule and which had been preserved through one of the first explicit applications of the principle of Indirect Rule.

This system had a certain stability. All three groups favoured federalism, because none of them could be sure of dominating the central state. Equally, no one group needed to fear domination because it could always ally with the second weakest group against the strongest one. This was a rather more stable situation than where one sub-nation confronts one nation-state, as in the case of Uganda. But a slight shift in power can quickly undermine the system. Such a shift precipitated the breakdown of 1966. The army coup and the suspicious fact that it had spared the life of the Prime Minister of the Eastern province while killing the others, along with the predominance of Ibo officers in the new army leadership, provoked fears of Ibo dominance. These fears and the response were related to other developments. Ibo elites had done well in competition for coveted posts in the civil service, army, professions and elsewhere. Ibo groups had moved into other regions, notably more backward northern Nigeria, where they occupied positions generally more favourable than the bulk of the indigenous population. Ibo interests had also tried to extend their political influence by involvement in minority political organisations in the non-Ibo areas (though they were not the only ones to do so). All this made other people sensitive to the accusation that the Ibo sought dominance. The brutal reaction forced Ibos back into their own locality in ways which started a panic and mobilised the population behind the secessionist move. The fragile system of three-way politics in a federal state had given way to simple and violent polarisation between new state and a sub-nationalist movement.

The break-up of Pakistan is another example of polarisation which cannot be accounted for in terms of modern political identity conflicting with traditional cultural identity. It has already been argued that the Muslim movement itself was internally very diverse and cannot be seen as an expression of 'Muslim identity'. The state of Pakistan faced particularly serious problems. Physically it was split into two territories separated by the distance of a subcontinent. Many of the Muslim political leaders had been drawn from the minority Muslim provinces. The Muslim political elites of what became East and West Pakistan had had no direct political connections with one another. At best, stability would have required allowing virtual autonomy to the two regions. But the leadership, first with its Muslim commitment and then with its increasing base in West Pakistan, would not do that. The attempt to impose Urdu as the official language was perhaps the most blatant instance of discriminatory rule. Although a major language in west Pakistan, it was spoken by less than one per cent of the population of east Pakistan. Bengali elites had already been hard hit by the partition of Bengal, in which the rich centre of Calcutta had gone to India. Resentment would have been hard enough to avoid under the most able political leadership. Under incompetent military regimes political flexibility was non-existent. Gradually elites in east Pakistan came to 'realise' that their national identity was Bengali rather than Muslim. An identity which had become politically relevant around the turn of the century when Curzon had briefly partitioned Bengal was resurrected. Yet even in these circumstances it was not easy to move towards a bid for independence, and the bid succeeded only in a situation of general political crisis and Indian involvement. This suggests that even in particularly favourable circumstances sub-nationalism is difficult to develop into an independence movement.[6] In support of the point I will consider two cases where sub-nationalism has not become very important although on the basis of the degree of 'cultural pluralism' one might have expected it to be.

In Kenya it has often been claimed that the Kikuyu occupy a privileged position. The government party, KANU, has a disproportionately high Kikuyu component. Members of the Kikuyu do particularly well in the take-up of educational positions and more favoured employment. Official statistics provide some support for accusations that development and welfare projects are steered towards Kikuyu areas. Part of the reason may lie in the use of the market to allocate resources, which, for various reasons, favours the Kikuyu, but some of the explanation would seem to be the practice of ethnic discrimination.[7] Yet although this has been a constant undertone in Kenyan politics, sub-national divisions have never dominated politics.

One reason is that the struggle for independence was particularly hard in Kenya, and this helped unify elements from different ethnic groups. The co-operation between Luo and Kikuyu was particularly important, and their continued co-operation has made it difficult for other groups to mount any significant challenge. There were considerable resources to distribute once independence was achieved, which may have reduced the intensity of conflict. There were also important cross-cutting conflicts. For example, the division within the Kikuyu under colonialism[8] continued after 1963. This was expressed among other things, in terms of disagreements about the treatment of members of the Mau Mau.[9] The conflict led some Kikuyu politicians to attack what they saw as a conservative KANU regime based too heavily on what were loyalist groups during the colonial period. These radical elements took up links with non-Kikuyu radicals such as Odinga. At the same time KANU has brought in other non-Kikuyu elements which are more moderate. The country's President, Daniel arap Moi, for example, is a member of the Kalenjin group and was one of the leaders of the KADU federalist movement in the early 1960s. In all these ways the tendency of politics to organise around sub-national ties has been blunted. In the last few years there has developed a corrupt political elite monopolising power in a one-party system in a way which has little to do with ethnicity. This is now crumbling, again partly as the result of external pressure, and the emergence of opposition political groups, especially the Forum for Democracy, transcends the major ethnic divide. Nevertheless, two elements seem to persist from earlier Kenyan politics. First, there is a tendency for Kikuyu politics to divide internally, as seems to be happening within the opposition movement. Second, one element in this Kikuyu politics sees the need for an ethnic alliance with Luo elites. This is also happening, interestingly involving the veteran Odinga, reviving a Luo-Kikuyu linkage in the opposition politics of today. How far these oppositional groups will be able to sustain such ethnic alliances (these words are being written in September 1992) and how successful they will be in their challenge to the present government is something for the near future.

A final example is that of Tanganyika.[10] Here four elements have been of particular importance in preventing sub-nationalism from becoming important. Both in the colonial and independence periods the sheer variety of groups and their regional distribution has meant that no one group has even been able to threaten domination of the state. Second, the nationalist movement did not have to link up local conflicts too tightly for

265

action at the central level because it was never forced into too hard a struggle with the colonial state. So the nationalist movement was not closely implicated in local conflicts nor dominated by any particular group. A third element is the role of Swahili. This was a lingua franca which was widely spread throughout the country and could become the symbol of national unity. No question arose of a choice between English, confined to elites, or a particular African language which would offend all other language groups. This brings one to the fourth element: the role of Julius Nyerere. He has made particular efforts to establish Swahili as the national language, both as a statesman and as a writer.[11] This is only one aspect of his achievement. Precisely because of the weakness of the centre in many new states, stability is closely bound up with the personality and ability of nationalist leaders. Kenyatta was a vital force for unity within Kenyan nationalism. Nyerere has played a similar role in Tanganyika, although the general organisation of politics has also helped him. Outside observers have concentrated on his policies of economic development. From a different perspective it is the maintenance of political order and unity that appears as his major achievement.

To conclude, it is wrong to see sub-nationalism as the resurgence of traditional, particularist identity against modern national identity. It is a mistake to regard local and national (seen respectively as cultural and political) identities as fixed sentiments which are mutually opposed. This is a view which, when taken by the governments of new states, has in fact been counter-productive. An alternative argument put forward by, among others, Heeger and Zolberg,[12] seems much more convincing. It begins by pointing out that the new states have a very weak centre and that formal state institutions cover only a small part of the political arena. Elites engaging in political conflict are often forced to rely on localised resources in the form of popular support. These elites are not so subject to constraints from below as are those in societies where class formation on a national level has taken place. The net result is a very fluid politics.

This elite-directed politics cannot be usefully divided into 'modern' and 'traditional' forms. A trade union or peasant co-operative can overlap with and be as particularist as a tribal or caste association. Equally, any of these sorts of organisation can form part of a territorial political alliance. The study of anti-colonial nationalism is primarily the study of the ways in which linkages are made to form these alliances. A study of sub-nationalism after independence should, in turn, focus upon how and why the linkages break down. Although there are many external pressures which can contribute to breakdown, the forms it takes are a function of the original structure of the alliance.

Independence produces certain changes. The nationalist movement inherits the apparatus of the colonial state. This bolsters its position but can also lead to conflict over the distribution of resources. If particular

266

local elites expect and are able to obtain a substantial portion of those resources, this can lay the foundation for a sub-nationalist response. One can identify at least some conditions which favour such a response.

In some cases the colonial state may have blocked the development of any effective territorial nationalist movement. Sub-nationalism, if the term can be applied in such cases, will be less a challenge to the central state than an attempt to provide a substitute in its absence. Where the number of political units with a sub-national identity is small, the threat any one of them can seem to pose to the new state appears very great. Reaction against that danger may force the political sub-nation into challenging the central government. Finally, political elites can achieve more if they are able to mobilise popular support on the basis of communal cleavages. In the Ibo and Bangla Deshi cases this was of particular importance. It may be that the relative quiescence of the Baganda after Obote put down resistance in May 1966 is due to the fact that this communal politics did not exist in that particular case.

When one or other of these conditions obtains in a new state there are pressures in favour of sub-nationalism. However, in many cases they do not provoke an open challenge. Partly this is because such a fluid political system often prevents any sharply organised politics developing. Partly it is because sub-national claims may be more valuable as a bargaining tactic than as a genuine bid for independence. Partly it is because the pressures of the international system inhibit the movement for independence. Outright sub-nationalism is therefore fairly rare and successful sub-nationalism almost nonexistent.

Finally one should remember that localised politics is not necessarily sub-nationalist politics. A political structure of the sort described can exist in areas of racial, ethnic and linguistic homogeneity. Without a 'cultural' basis political conflict often takes place between regionally based patrons and their client followings.[13] They may justify their actions in terms of policy disputes with their government rather than making ethnically justified claims. These situations cannot be considered here because they do not imply any sort of nationalist ideology. But their similarity to many sub-nationalisms suggests that it is upon political structures rather than cultural identities that attention should be concentrated.

Notes

1 This is true even if the international context is the most important component of any explanation of the success of challenges to existing states. One cannot simply reduce the subject to a 'hard-headed' analysis of power relationships as many political scientists do.

2 This is emphasised in Aristide R. Zolberg, 'The structure of political conflict in the new states of Africa', *American Political Science Review*,

LXII (1968), pp. 70–87.

3   Quoted in Clifford Geertz, 'The integrative revolution: primordial senti-
    ments and civil politics in the new states', in *Old Societies and New States*,
    edited by Clifford Geertz (New York, 1963), pp. 105–57.

4   See, for example, Crawford Young, *The Politics of Cultural Pluralism*
    (London, 1976), chapter 8.

5   A point made by Gerald Heeger, *The Politics of Underdevelopment* (Lon-
    don, 1974), p. 127.

6   The Belgian Congo is not comparable, as 'sub-nationalism' there was really
    a desperate search for a substitute for an effective territory-wide authority.

7   D. Rothschild, 'Ethnic inequality in Kenya', in *The Politics of Cultural
    Subnationalism in Africa*, edited by Victor Oloronsola (New York, 1972),
    pp. 289–321.

8   See above, pp. 186–9.

9   R. Buijtenhuis, *Mau Mau: Twenty Years After. The myth and its survivors*
    (The Hague, 1973).

10 I use this term rather than Tanzania because the remarks do not apply to
    Zanzibar.

11 For example, he translated Shakespeare's *Julius Caesar* into Swahili.

12 Heeger, *op. cit.*; Zolberg, *op. cit.*, and *idem, Creating Political Order: the
    party-states of West Africa* (Chicago, 1966).

13 For links of this sort of politics to ethnic conflict see René Lemarchand,
    'Political clientelism and ethnicity in tropical Africa'; and in an area where
    it is not related to ethnic conflict, James M. Scott, 'Patron-client politics
    and political change in South-east Asia', both in *American Political Science
    Review*, LXVI, No. 1 (1972).

13

Nation-building and nationalism in the new states

A great deal of the work of a nationalist regime in a new state is concerned with the maintenance of order and the promotion of development. Much of this takes the form of practical politics where the notion of national loyalty is an underlying concern rather than an ideological crusade. For example, Obote's proposed electoral reforms were intended to help erode sub-national loyalties, but national loyalty was not invoked as a means of doing this.[1] Rather the idea seems to have been that only structural changes would bring about changes in attitudes. In this chapter I want to consider the reverse of this idea, namely the view that changing attitudes can lead to structural change. The main theme of my argument will be that such attempts to change attitudes directly have had a very limited impact. I will consider this matter in relation to economic development and to the attempt to create a sense of cultural identity.

In considering the links between ideology and development it is necessary but very difficult to distinguish between intentions and achievements, and also between nationalism as a means of promoting, and as a means of coping with, economic development. On the rather problematic assumption that one can make these distinctions in practice, let us consider the argument that nationalist ideology operates as a means of guiding and promoting development. The basic reasoning behind such an argument is that development, usually labelled modernisation, requires the partial or complete abandonment of traditional values and practices. It also produces new, functionally defined and specialised elites. Nationalism can be regarded as a means of binding the latter together and providing a broad identity and purpose for those compelled (or tempted?) by modernisation to abandon tradition. Where nationalism differs from socialism, which from this perspective is usually regarded as the other major ideology of modernisation, is that it builds its case upon an appeal to allegedly traditional features of society, to national rather than class interests. Usually, as well, both nationalism and the imperatives of development have been used to justify authoritarian rule, either by a single party or by the armed forces. It might be useful to cite some examples of the kind of appeal that is made.

Japanese nationalism emphasised the spirit of sacrifice to the Emperor as true patriotism and insisted that adjustment to the modern world was a necessary sacrifice if the country was to remain independent and the Emperor truly ruler of his people. The martial spirit and the notion of patriarchy were extended to underpin the authority of the entrepreneur. In the case of Turkey, the writer Ziya Gokalp provided a rather more elaborate reconciliation of national tradition with commitment to modernity. He separated culture (nationality) from civilisation (which included the modern West), and both from religion. Thus a Turk could practise the Muslim faith and become a modern man without abandoning his national identity. However, failure to make the adaptation to modernity would lead to loss of independence, and this would undermine national identity. It was therefore imperative to accept secularisation of the state and modernisation in order to preserve it.[2] This kind of position, characterised in relation to India as the ideological 'moment of departure' by Chatterjee, tries to steer a compromise between the wholesale rejection of 'western' modernity as embodied in Gandhi, and the equally wholesale embracing of modernity which makes commitment either to the market or the state, rather than to the nation, the central concern. Nehru, with his commitment to the modernising state, was typical of this position.[3]

Clearly a number of newly independent states have tried to justify development within this nationalist framework. The problem is that it is very difficult to know what impact they had on most people. They may have motivated small elites, and this may have been very important. Even then, sentiment may well have been closely bound up with interest. But any wider impact remains difficult to assess and much of the work on the subject is rather speculative. This seems to apply particularly to work which stresses the importance of psychological and cultural attributes in making people receptive to a programme of rapid change. Thus some cultures, such as those of the Japanese and the Ibo, are characterised in terms of their openness or of an 'achievement ethic'. This renders them amenable to change if that is the only way to succeed. Usually such studies draw upon literary sources for their account of the value system, itself an unreliable guide to the views of the silent majority.[4] Often such studies do little more than redescribe the change they purport to explain. Achievement (i. e. modernisation) is the product of the achievement ethic, which is manifested in achievement. Non-achievement presumably denotes the existence of a non-achievement ethic. The argument may be true but it is hardly demonstrable.

A rather different view of the relationship between values, ideology and modernisation can be drawn from Lerner's study of Turkey, although its implications are somewhat opposed to his own arguments.[5] I will deal with this case in some detail because of the interesting points raised by the fact that Lerner returned to his particular case-study village four years after his initial study, thus enabling us to see a process of change over time.

In 1950 Lerner did some research in a village near Ankara. His interviews were designed, among other things, to enable him to evaluate attitudes, which he ranked on a tradition-modernity continuum. For example, some questions were designed to test the capacity for empathy. A person might be asked to imagine what it would be like to be President of Turkey or (partly in order to remove any suspicion of seeking political views, but also to demand a greater imaginative leap) President of the United States of America. A 'traditional' response to these questions might consist of incomprehension or wonder at such presumptuousness. A 'modern' response might consist of a description of the changes one would make if one were President.[6] I should, at this point, make it clear that I do not question the validity of Lerner's methods. They were sensitively employed and the results subtly and convincingly presented. It is with their significance that I am concerned.

In 1950 Lerner could find only one modern achievement-oriented man in the village, a rather unhappy grocer who dreamed of better things such as new layouts and stock for his shop but who was rather isolated from everyone else. At the other end of the continuum was the village leader. He was, however, a 'nationalist'. He listened to radio broadcasts about the Korean war, mainly in order to find out how Turkish troops were doing. He saw the national character in terms of the martial virtues, not openness to change. Incidentally, the way in which radio was used shows that one must beware of presuming that its introduction alone will transform values. The radio was listened to collectively and in a very selective way which seems to have reinforced existing attitudes. Generally Lerner's findings point to a village made up of people with fairly closed and traditional attitudes.

What makes this example fascinating are the results of his return four years later. It was easier to get to the village on the second occasion because a proper road had been built connecting it to Ankara and there was a regular bus service. Many of the villagers now worked in the capital, and this was having a marked impact on the life of the village. It was moving towards the grocer's vision. There was a shop with proper shelves and displays of goods which was introducing new items, for example, in the way of clothes. Unfortunately the grocer had died. The modern shop was being run by the son of the village leader, still alive and well. Many of the villagers now conceded that the grocer had not been quite so wrongheaded as they had once thought. Lerner does not say anything about the capacity of the villagers to empathise on this occasion. It may have been as limited as it was four years earlier. But in some ways at least the villagers were embracing modernity. It would seem that it was opportunity rather than attitudes that mattered.

One can take the example a little further. The new road had been built by a government controlled by the Democratic Party. Franchise reform had extended the electorate and, at the elections of 1950, the five-year-old party defeated the following of Ataturk, the Republicans. The Republican Party had ceased to be identified with the reforming drive of the inter-war period and had become increasingly conservative. The Democratic Party was prepared to take development further and to bid for electoral support on the basis of promises such as those which resulted in a road and a bus service to Ankara for the village. By 1954 the villagers, including their 'traditional' leader, were Democratic Party supporters almost to a man.

This suggests a number of points. The reforms of Ataturk, though impressive, had left many parts of Turkey untouched, including villages not far from Ankara. The regime had been popular in these areas – they were its stronghold – but more in terms of its military achievements, its success against the Greeks, and its creation of a strong, united Turkey. As for modernisation, that was something to be treated in pragmatic terms of material improvements. It was not connected with nationalism and it did not seem to require any particularly receptive set of values.

It is doubtful whether many of Ataturk's most controversial reforms, such as the abolition of the fez and the veil, extended much beyond urban elites already sympathetic to change. Again, in the Japanese case, the Meiji restoration and subsequent reforms were affairs of elites involving little popular disturbance or participation. Nationalist ideology as a creed of reform undoubtedly inspired and to some extent guided the actions of these elites, who also gained from them in various ways. But at lower levels reform was probably seen as something imposed by authority and assessed in pragmatic terms.[7] In both cases one should emphasise the limited degree of change even while recognising its great importance.

Neither in Japan nor in Turkey was the state weak in the ways encountered in the previous chapter. Local and national levels of action were closely bound together in these two cases. The task of nationalist regimes in the two countries was not to balance the claims of locally based elites against one another from a weak centre but rather to co-ordinate the conflicting claims of elites firmly attached to the central government. Nationalism, which incorporated limited reform, played an important role. After some time, however, such nationalism, authoritarian from the outset, became increasingly conservative. One form this conservative nationalism took was concern with military expansion abroad. This sort of nationalism could then be challenged by a more radical party offering the population greater development, as in the case of Turkey, or took the country into expensive military adventures, as in the case of Japan. So the effective use of this type of authoritarian, developmental nationalism would seem to be closely related to a particular phase in a particular type of political system.

It is also instructive to compare these cases with those of China and Russia. The Meiji and Ataturk regimes were run by elites with roots in the ruling class of the old order. To sustain an image of continuity as well as to set limits upon reform such elites found authoritarian nationalist ideology particularly attractive. In China and Russia, with totally new elites in power based on mobilisation for social revolution, it was discontinuity that needed to be stressed. Socialist ideology performed this task more effectively than nationalism. Obviously there was some convergence between the two sorts of ideology. However, it is misleading to discuss them simply as variants on a general ideology of modernisation.[8] They are associated with differently placed political elites with different attitudes towards social change and having to make rather different sorts of economic decisions.[9] Ideology was not produced in some instrumental way to serve particular policies. Rather it had an inspiring, even revelatory, function for these elites because it seemed to describe their situation and to map out their projects so well. But this is rather different from seeing ideology as about something as abstract as 'modernisation' or as a means of transforming the attitudes of large sections of the population. In both cases, for example, one can note the onset of a 'second revolution' a decade or so after the initial takeover of power. In the case of the Stalinist revolution there was a strong emphasis upon economic development, although opposition mainly concerned means rather than ends. In the case of China, the 'Cultural Revolution' cannot be seen in these terms. The common element appears rather to be factional conflict within the party leadership and the fomenting of resentment within the first new generation of the communist era against the failures of the 'old guard'. These sentiments, sometimes also framed with a nationalist condemnation of cosmopolitanism, rather than an ideological commitment to modernity as such, seem to be most important. These cases can also be compared to India. Here the ruling elite did have roots in pre-independence India, but not in the old ruling class so much as the political opposition which, through Congress, had become part of the political system. As a ramshackle political movement tied to its bourgeois and peasant constituencies, Congress could not turn on those constituents in the way the communists in the USSR and China could. On the other hand, as a genuinely popular movement they could not so easily pursue authoritarian nationalist policies, whether used for purposes of development or not, as was the case in Turkey and Japan. The result was a modernist commitment which could not easily translate itself into a distinct policy that attacked those holding back 'modernity', a policy personified in Nehru.

One final example, that of Egypt, can throw light on another aspect of the relationship between nationalist ideology, popular support and development. The Egyptian state, unlike many other colonial and new states, did not have a political system in which localised power was particularly important. The reforms of Mehemet Ali and his successors, including the British; the central position of the Nile and of cotton cultivation; the centripetal influence of the great cities of Cairo and Alexandria: all produced a more centrally focused form of politics. This perhaps explains why the upheavals of 1919 were turned to advantage by the elite nationalist movement instead of leading to uncontrollable anarchy and the breakdown of the country into a series of local political units.

After 1920 Egypt increasingly came to appear as a country in which change got out of control. Cairo in particular exemplified this. It expanded at an enormous rate both before and after 1945. This growth led to the formation of new social groups – white-collar workers, industrial employees, dockers – but above all of a huge pool of casual or unemployed labour. These people were impatient for the fruits of faster economic growth. The economy's dependence on cotton, the price of which began to drop in the 1950s, along with the British control of Suez, encouraged many to see the roots of their problems in terms of foreign control. The centralised nature of politics ensured that these grievances could be expressed through a nationalist movement determined to reform the state and break foreign dominance. In 1952 the army officers' coup put such a movement in control of the state.

Nasser's position was very different from that of Ataturk or the Meiji reformers. He faced the crisis of a rise in population and expectations which economic growth could not match. With a centralised political structure, with the vast urban masses of Cairo and Alexandria, he was also able to build upon popular support in a new way. The nationalist regime he controlled had a strength unique in the Arab and African world at the time. He was able to by-pass elites opposed to his policies and work with popular support. A major sentiment of this support was anti-imperialism. There is no doubt that the expulsion of the British from Suez in 1956 was immensely popular. But such measures did not solve the crisis of rapid growth; nor did any of Nasser's internal policies. Economic expansion was more than absorbed by a rising population. Those seeking social advancement tended to go into the top-heavy professional and administrative sectors rather than into the uncertain and low-prestige entrepreneurial and technical fields.

Increasingly the emphasis in the anti-imperialist fusion of independence and economic development came to be upon independence. The creation of Israel in particular focused the attention of the regime outwards, combining anti-imperialism with Arab nationalism and religious sentiment. The government moved towards policies which required heavy military expenditure and the severing of relations with the United States. These moves impeded any programme of planned economic development. The successive wars and defeats of 1948, 1967 and 1973 also took their toll of the economy.

274

This brief and simplified account suggests a number of points. The centralised political structure and crisis of growth allowed a nationalist regime with a mass basis and a radical reform programme to come to power. Here, one might have thought, nationalism as an ideology changing popular attitudes and promoting development could play an important role. Yet that nationalism increasingly came to turn its attention outwards as though unable to face the vast problems at home. It sought merely to exploit existing popular sentiment rather than to bring about changes in attitudes. At the same time it broke with a traditional, rather elitist nationalism in the way it took up the cause of Arab nationalism.[10] Only under Sadat and then Mubarak, has Egypt turned back to more limited but attainable objectives. However, this has caused problems. On the one hand, it has incurred the wrath of Arab nationalism. On the other hand, the failure to deliver on economic development has discredited nationalism. Increasingly large numbers of people look to some other ideological position and have found it in Islamic fundamentalism. This ideology can help fuel the challenge to authoritarian nationalism, as it does in Egypt, and even more dramatically in Algeria. Whether, once it assumes power (as in Iran) such an Islamic movement can combine its principles with policies of modernisation and the maintenance of popular support is something for the future.

From these cases I would draw one very tentative conclusion. Nationalism as a developmental ideology is effective when promoting cohesion and action among reforming elites in a particular type of political situation. Mass nationalism, facing the crisis of rapid change, is more likely to shift its focus outwards than to stress the sacrifices and adjustments that the population at large must make in order to produce the required changes. This would tend to suggest that 'inwardly directed' nationalism aimed at changing attitudes and behaviour in ways which will assist economic development has only limited effects upon minorities.

Developmental nationalism has had a good run for its money. By now it only commands support where it has commanded success. This has above all been the case in parts of South-East Asia – not just Japan, but also Singapore, Taiwan, and South Korea – and in a more limited way in some of the larger Latin American states. Usually it has involved a combination of free market economics and authoritarian politics – a combination which may have optimal economic consequences.[11] In many parts of Africa, where developmental nationalism has not delivered development, the ideology and the states which subscribe to it are in crisis. In part this is to do with the general discrediting of state-guided economic growth, especially with the collapse of the USSR. That has also removed a major support for many regimes, not just from the USSR but from its western rivals who felt the need to compete with it in the developing world. Above all, however, economic failure has helped stimulate the recent drive to remove such nationalist regimes from power. As one writer has recently pointed out:

> If at the same time of the fall of the Berlin Wall thirty-eight of forty-five sub-Saharan African states were governed by civilian or military one-party systems of greater or lesser authoritarian hue, eighteen months later a handful had actually travelled the road, and over half had committed themselves to competitive multiparty elections and major limitations on executive powers.[12]

Of course, this commitment can be reversed, or a country can slide into civil war and even more terrible problems, as the present case of Somalia demonstrates. Political democracy provides no automatic solution to problems of exploitation, population growth, natural disasters, and endemic political instability. What is clear, however, is that authoritarian nationalism did not have the answers and has failed to convince most of those in whose name it claimed to speak that it does have the answers.

The same conclusion can be hazarded for the much more limited and common endeavour of aiming to create a sense of national identity in cultural terms. Again, it is easier to describe intentions than achievements. This 'politics of cultural engineering'[13] concentrates on education and communication. In the schools, for example, there is not merely an emphasis on the general virtues of obedience and loyalty to the regime but these virtues are linked to some notion of national identity. An interesting feature of this is the history that is taught. In Turkey the comprehensive doctrines of writers like Ziya Gokalp have, in simplified form, become the staple diet of textbooks and teaching. Mazrui has described the way teachers in east African states both in schools and at higher levels of education engage in what he ingenuously calls a process of 'counter-selection'.[14] Under this heading the Eurocentric approach to history which was general in the colonial period is corrected in two ways. First, pupils study the history of their own country rather than that of Europe. Second, within this history stress is placed upon indigenous initiative rather than subjection to the will of Europeans. If possible, attention is paid to those initiatives which can be linked with the present state. At its best, this alternative history can call upon new kinds of approach and innovative research. At its worst – and in the hands of authoritarian nationalist regimes the worst is what one can come to expect – the result is dogmatic myth-making based upon the arbitrary projection of national claims on to the past, and the exclusion of all but the approved interpretations, facts and texts from the syllabus.

Such a curriculum certainly tells us a good deal about the views of governments and, perhaps, teachers. But, as any teacher knows, how much of what is taught gets across at all to pupils, let alone in the ways intended by the teacher, is another matter. To my knowledge, little evidence has

276

been produced on this side of the question. Other things, such as the impact of particular language-teaching policies, can be measured more definitely but they can often be divisive rather than unifying and do not necessarily lead to the acceptance of particular political attitudes.

The growth of literacy and a popular press, but above all the introduction of radios (and, to a lesser extent, television and film), which can be mass-produced fairly cheaply, provide the state with the capacity to project a particular national image to most of its subjects. Under most nationalist regimes in new states the output of the various media is controlled, though this applies more to radio than to newspapers. But once again it is difficult to know what effect it has. The Turkish case just cited shows how radio can be used in ways which prevent it conflicting with prevailing views. The general results of media research in developed capitalist economies suggest that messages have most impact when reinforcing existing values. If the same applied in the new states it would suggest that some sense of national identity must already exist before radio and other media can be used to strengthen it. Furthermore, one must distinguish between popular 'acceptance' of the government's views in areas of remote concern, such as foreign policy in many cases, and in areas of more intimate concern such as questions of wage controls or compulsory military service. Studies of as controlled and accessible a population as that of the Germans under the Third Reich suggest that government propaganda had only a limited positive impact, and that in many ways what really mattered was the ability to prevent people receiving other messages or communicating among themselves.[15] One would expect the impact to be much weaker in developed states with less elaborate controls and a less accessible population. But these remarks can be no more than speculative.

Finally there is the political symbolism with which nationalist regimes seek to imbue the population: flags, rallies, anthems, marches, pictures of the leaders, etc. Once again the impact of all these things is largely unknown.[16] Common sense would suggest that too much of it can be counter-productive and may result in a rather bored, sceptical, apolitical but discreet view of affairs, and certainly that is the general impression one obtains from studies of the Third Reich or what we can now learn of political attitudes in the former USSR and its satellite states. But again, like so much else in this chapter, this is largely speculation so far as the new states are concerned. I am led to the tentative conclusion that, unless there are existing features in the political and economic arrangements of the country conducive to the establishment of a strong sense of national solidarity, the politics of cultural engineering will have very little effect on the population. There would appear to be two major exceptions. First, there are those cadres which are the most intensive target of propaganda and also stand to benefit from what is claimed – for example officers in the armed forces and civil servants. Second, if the symbolism is linked to

277

the pursuit of distinct policies, for example in the Stalinism of the early 1930s or the Chinese Cultural Revolution, then it may engage the commitment of large numbers of people who are given definite tasks and stand to make definite gains. Where the propaganda cannot be related closely to the concerns of particular cadres or the pursuit of a definite policy which will re-allocate significant resources, then one would expect it to have little enduring impact.

This in turn suggests to me the need to keep the idea of 'nation-building' separate from that of 'national integration'. The first term refers to policies deliberately pursued by governments; the second to processes in which deliberate government policy may play little or no part. One aspect of this might be national class formation which ties groups to centrally focused institutions such as trade unions, employers' organisations and class-based parties. Organisations such as these can become tied to the national institutions through which they operate without being in any way ideologically committed to them, especially if these institutions permit participation and provide material benefits such as state welfare or employment. However, the extension of participation and of benefits can only come about as a consequence of economic development and improved state provision of benefits. So even at this level, it is the structural change which underlies the change in attitudes rather than the other way around. In some cases one might find nationalist movements opposing these processes of national integration because of the way they seem to divide the nation on class or party lines.[17] However, the concept of national integration, although useful, needs to be used carefully.[18]

To conclude: nationalism as developmental ideology or as cultural engineering would seem to be of limited importance. In the case of development it can be effective among reforming elites in particular types of political situations. In the case of promoting a sense of national identity it is probably overvalued by nationalist regimes. Its effects in this area are probably confined to reinforcing an existing sense of national solidarity. Indeed, if the policy involves the pursuit of prestige projects which prove to be of little general benefit, it may actually backfire. A sense of national solidarity is more likely to be promoted by processes beyond the control or even the understanding of nationalists. Indeed, they may actively oppose the very things most likely to create an enduring sense of national identity.

Notes

1   See above, p. 262.
2   Ziya Gokalp, *Principles of Turkism* (Leiden, Brill, 1968).
3   Partha Chatterjee, *Nationalist Thought and the Colonial World: a derivative discourse?* (London, 1986).
4   See, for example, D. McClelland, *The Achieving Society* (New Jersey,

1961). The intellectual forerunner of all these studies is Max Weber with his thesis concerning the relationship between the 'spirit' of Protestantism and the development of capitalism. Detailed research on the Weber thesis has tended to shift away from a 'holistic' view of a particular culture, society or religion, and more towards minorities within such cultures, and also towards the context in which such minorities operate as much as the substantive values to which they subscribe. I imagine that there will a similar trend in the search for the cultural roots of modernity outside European or European-settler societies.

5   Daniel Lerner, *The Passing of Traditional Society* (New York, 1958), especially chapter 2.

6   The way in which these attitudes can be related to tradition and modernity were explored, for example, in David Riesman, *The Lonely Crowd* (original edition, New Haven, 1950).

7   From this perspective one should also stress the limitations of Japanese economic development up to and during the Second World War. It was autarchic, authoritarian, closely linked to military ambitions, and with little concern with the consumer sector. It was post-1945 Japan, after a period of institutional reconstruction under American supervision, which has most fully embraced the market and open-ended growth.

8   This is very much the approach in John Kautsky (ed.), *Political Change in Underdeveloped Countries* (New York, 1967), especially in the introduction by the editor.

9   For a trenchant critique of employing an even more specific term, 'industrialisation', to account for decisions taken in the Soviet Union between 1927 and 1935, see M. McAuley, *Politics and the Soviet Union* (Harmondsworth, 1978), pp. 84–91.

10   See above, pp. 152–4.

11   The recent book by Francis Fukuyama, *The End of History and the Last Man* (London, 1992) seeks to argue that liberal democracy not only requires a free market economy but it also the most likely consequence of such an economy. The first proposition seems very persuasive – as yet there has been no liberal democracy in an economy that is not fundamentally based on the free market. The second proposition is much more dubious and Fukuyama is reduced to some rather unpersuasive and somewhat mystical arguments about the desire for recognition in support of this proposition.

12   Samuel Decalo, 'The Process, Prospects and Constraints of Democratization in Africa', *African Affairs*, 91/362 (January, 1992), pp. 7–35 (9).

13   Ali A. Mazrui, *Cultural Engineering and Nation Building in East Africa* (Evanston, Ill. , 1972).

14   *Ibid.* , p. 15.

15   See, for example, Ian Kershaw, *Popular Opinion and Political Dissent in the Third Reich: Bavaria 1933–1945* (Oxford, 1983).

16   On nationalist imagery and ceremonial and examples of its impact, see above, pp. 64–8.

17   This is the main theme, for example, of Eugene Weber, *The Nationalist Revival in France, 1905–1914* (Berkeley & Los Angeles, 1959) though the

term 'nationalist revival' refers to what I would term processes of national integration which were opposed by a declining right-wing nationalism. For examples of how such integration can produce working-class loyalty to the nation-state see above. pp. 36–44

18   See below, pp. 337–9.

14

Unification nationalism and the new nation-states

I will look briefly at the two cases of Pan-Africanism and Arab nationalism and then make some more general comparisons.

1 Pan-Africanism

Pan-Africanism fits very well that view of nationalism which sees it as the product of Westernised intellectuals taking the ideas of justice and equality and turning them, in a nationalist form, against Western societies which do not practise them. The Pan-African movement developed among Western-educated blacks living in west Africa or abroad and received much important intellectual and organisational support from blacks in the United States and in the West Indies. The nature of the movement can be gauged from the composition of the ninety delegates to the fifth Pan-African Congress held in Manchester in 1945. Twenty came from west Africa and twenty-six from African organisations in Britain made up primarily of west Africans. Thirty-three delegates came from the West Indies. The involvement of American blacks had declined since before 1939 as the movement had become more radical. Nevertheless the congress was presided over by Du Bois, who had been prominent in the Pan-African movement since 1918. There were only six delegates from east, central and southern Africa.

Furthermore, west African delegates were overwhelmingly from British colonies. There were only two delegates from French West Africa, both from Guinea. The delegates from other parts of Africa were either from British colonies or from the formerly British territory of South Africa. Whereas some of the delegates went on to play a leading role in the independence movement in various British territories, for their francophone equivalents one should look at deputies to the French National Assembly rather than activists in the Pan-African movement.[1]

Some delegates had no connection with any particular colony. Others were exiled or virtually powerless. Others thought in terms of regional (such as west Africa) rather than territorial independence. From all these

281

perspectives delegates were inclined to take the broad view of African affairs. Their lack of power and their intellectual leanings encouraged sweeping programmes and eloquent debates. To the latter French West African intellectuals made an important contribution, but their political concern with the attainment of equality within a 'Greater France' kept them on the sidelines of the Pan-African movement.

Up to 1945, then, Pan-Africanism was drawn mainly from the English-speaking black intellectual community in the United States, West Indies, Britain and west Africa. It was a lcose and rather eclectic movement with few sources of influence in African society. It received some support from white liberals and radicals. Like so many movements of the kind, with few practical goals, it was beset by internal rivalries in which personality and doctrine played a large part.[2]

After 1945 the fortunes of Pan-Africanism were closely linked with the success of its foremost advocates, especially Nkrumah, in territorial nationalist movements. Their success was grounded in the construction of power bases in those individual territories. In practical terms Pan--Africanism had nothing to do with this. Consequently it came to be dependent upon a series of political movements with very different sorts of organisation and bases of support which focused their attention upon the different colonial states. If only a few of these movements had succeeded they might have been able to claim to represent Pan-Africanism for the rest of colonial Africa. For a short period after Ghana became the first black African country to win independence in 1957[3] it seemed that this might happen. Ghana hosted various Pan-African meetings at which various programmes were drawn up. Nkrumah occupied a uniquely prestigious role in African nationalism.

However, the rush to independence, particularly between 1960 and 1963 [see Chronologies at the end of the book] transformed the situation. Each new state had its own problems and was jealous of any leadership or possible interference from any other. There were differences on general policy. Already by 1961 two rival blocs had formed. In 1963 those committed to Pan-African ideals agreed upon the establishment of the Organisation of African Unity. The OAU has played an important part in co-ordinating the responses of the new African states to common outside pressures, such as the policies to be adopted towards the remaining white-dominated regimes in Africa. But it has been able to do little more than that. So far as the internal affairs of its member states are concerned it remains silent. Nyerere has, quite fairly, called it a trade union for incumbent black African regimes. It has ceased to express, therefore, any definite views on genuine unification.

Pan-Africanism has had a very great ideological significance. It helped black Africans repudiate various claims about the superiority of the West at times when it was not easy to do so. It provided a context within which men like Nkrumah and Kenyatta could look beyond local political horizons and perceive the moral and political fragility of European empire in Africa. In these ways it has had a major impact on the leadership of territorial nationalist movements. But, without a definite political framework within which to operate, Pan-Africanism tended to become vague and unfocused, shifting its attention to cultural issues or general analyses of imperialism. Looked at from a positive point of view, its political programmes appear very thin.

Similar points can be made about regional movements in Africa. Nkrumah's attempts at regionalism in west Africa had some appeal beyond Ghana prior to the emergence of effective territorial nationalisms elsewhere. But when pursued by an independent Ghana such policies of regional integration were quickly rebuffed by other new states like Nigeria. Senghor of Guinea was prepared to make Nkrumah honorary co-president when the latter was overthrown, but this was no more than a sentimental gesture.

2 Arab nationalism

In comparison with Pan-Africanism Arab nationalism appears as a powerful and coherent movement. One explanation may be that the Arabs are a nation bound together by language and, to some degree, religion. Certainly this makes the intellectual basis of Arab nationalism much more plausible than that of Pan-Africanism. But this is a nationalist explanation and, therefore, unacceptable. Once again, it is more illuminating to focus on political arrangements.

Arab nationalism started in the last decades of the Ottoman empire [see chapter 6]. In the inter-war period it remained strong because of a common interest among former Ottoman territories in the removal of British and French control. Nevertheless, continuity of local notable power from the Ottoman period and the different problems which arose in the different mandates had already weakened the unity of Arab nationalism. In Egypt the nationalist movement remained somewhat aloof from Arab nationalism. There was a common sentiment of anti-imperialism, particularly against the British, but little in the way of positive co-operation. From the perspective of this book, which places the emphasis upon states, one would have expected Arab nationalism to recede in the face of increasingly important territorial nationalist movements, especially once these had acquired independence, until it was reduced to a generally applauded rhetoric.

However, two changes after 1945 arrested any such trend. Jewish immigration into Palestine had aroused Arab hostility for some time. It had, however, been largely confined to the areas directly affected. Arab protests had forced the British to retreat from their support for the Jewish cause. However, the terrible events of the 'final solution' in wartime Europe had hardened and strengthened the Zionist determination to establish a state in Palestine.[4] In 1948 Israel was set up with the narrow support of the United Nations. This act outraged Arab states. It could be regarded as a disguised form of imperialism; as a blatant disregard for the rights of Palestinians; and, although the spokesmen of Arab nationalism denied as much, it aroused religious hostility. Israel served the same unifying function for Arab nationalism as did white regimes in Africa for Pan-Africanism. Unlike those regimes, however, it seemed that the new state of Israel could be crushed from the start. Arab nationalism therefore helped to justify the military attacks of 1948. Defeat is an indication of the failure of Arab nationalism to provide any practical co-ordination between the Arab states. But there was a common enmity and, following defeat, a clear need for co-ordinated action against the enemy.

Co-ordinated action requires leadership, which could come only from a particular state. This second condition was met by the rise to power of Nasser. He was willing, from a radical anti-imperialist position, to direct Egypt's energies outwards to a variety of causes.[5] These causes – African nationalism, Arab nationalism, Islam – were rather artificially brought together in his ideas about Egypt's involvement in concentric rings of relationships. In practice the result was a rather opportunist and aggressive foreign policy. This achieved coherence through the steady rise in importance of the Arab nationalist opposition to Israel and the fact that Egypt could dominate this opposition more effectively than any other state. The war of 1956 seemed to confirm to Nasser the identity of Israeli and imperialist interests, and from then until his death he became the undisputed leader of Arab nationalism. His leadership extended to providing closer links between individual Arab states. In 1958 he was able to form, with Syria, the United Arab Republic, which Yemen later joined. It seemed that Arab nationalism might actually be moving to some form of unity.

But differences between individual Arab states remained important. There was great hostility between Egypt and Saudi Arabia. Partly this was due to the differences between a radical nationalist and a conservative monarchist regime. Partly it was a matter of Saudi resentment of Egypt's assumption of leadership in the Arab world. In some ways this hostility almost became an undeclared war. Nasser's attacks on Muslim organisations in Egypt were part of the conflict and can be linked with the general hostility of nationalism in Egypt to Islam as a political movement. There were other differences. Syria, though closer to Nasser in political outlook than Saudi Arabia, came to resent the subordinate position it occupied in the United Arab Republic and left it in 1961.

Above all, the commitment to Arab nationalism conflicted with Egyptian domestic interests. Egypt took the brunt of defeat in the wars of 1967 and 1973. Some of the most radical supporters of Arab nationalism were distant from the front line, and their contributions often did not extend beyond diplomatic and financial support. Not surprisingly, opinion in Egypt became critical of costly policies and resentful of radical critics who made fewer sacrifices. Nasser had been able to by-pass those elites whose nationalism had been primarily territorial in focus, but even at a popular level war-weariness began to erode enthusiasm for the Arab cause. It is this which enabled Sadat to revert to the pre-Nasser traditions of Egyptian nationalism. It required great courage and strong leadership, but its success, so far, is based on the weakness of Arab nationalism at both popular and elite level in Egypt.[6]

Nevertheless Arab nationalism remained very powerful even without Egyptian leadership. A number of states with very different characteristics still continue to subscribe to the cause of Arab nationalism. But precisely because of the differences it has been difficult to co-ordinate action between them. Saudi Arabia, the obvious candidate as leader in place of Egypt, could not easily commit itself to the sort of radical policies (such as withholding oil exports to the USA) demanded by other countries such as Libya. As one state or another take the lead in conflict with Israel, so they claim the mantle of leader of Arab nationalism. However, that frequently brings them into conflict with other Arab states and even the Palestinians. The Syrian involvement in the Lebanon created tensions with Lebanese Arabs, with Iran, and with Palestinians who had established power bases in the Lebanon. Even more striking was Saddam Hussein's claim to lead the Arab nationalist movement in the Gulf War. This claim involved the invasion of another Arab state – Kuwait – and brought the most powerful Arab states, notably Egypt, Syria and Saudi Arabia, into the war against him. Only some smaller states, and much of the Palestinian movement, provided him with any support.

The Palestinians do, however, represent the other unifying element in Arab nationalism. Naturally they are the most determined opponents of Israel. They are also an increasingly powerful force in various Arab states. Palestinians have taken up Western education and values to a greater extent than other Arab groups, partly because of the displacement caused by the establishment of Israel. In some countries they have established virtually independent regions, such as those King Hussein of Jordan eventually attacked in his domain and those in the Lebanon which in turn Syria as well as Israel has attacked. Palestinians also form an important part of the immigrant labour force which, in states like Kuwait, outnumbered the native population (though this has ended with the Palestinian co-operation with Iraq's occupation of Kuwait and the consequent abuse and flight or explusion of Palestinians from Kuwait once the Iraqi presence had been removed). This Palestinian presence constitutes an important pressure on the actions of individual Arab states, although at times it comes into conflict with the interests of those states. Sometimes it is used by those

285

states in their own interests. Furthermore, the Palestinian movement is itself subject to internal conflicts, both between more radical and moderate elements and, perhaps more importantly, between the 'diaspora' Palestinians and those who live in territory occupied by Israel. With current US policy distancing itself from unqualified support for Israeli policy and a Labour-dominated government in power in Israel it may be that negotiations with Palestinians over autonomy in areas occupied by Israel will exacerbate this division and generally undermine the unity and commitment of Arab nationalism.

Generally, since the death of Nasser the aim of Arab nationalism to create some form of political unity in the Arab world both internally as well as against enemies seems to have become more remote. But the oil weapon, the common enmity to Israel and the Palestinian pressure help sustain a much more powerful movement than is the case with Pan-Africanism.

3 Conclusion

Both these pan-nationalist movements have played an important role as intellectual forerunners of territorial nationalism. They have remained important as ways of co-ordinating action against external enemies. But only under one of two conditions can such movements lead to fundamental alterations in the internal arrangements of territorial states, the most extreme being fusion into a single state. The first condition is when one state achieves leadership over others while using nationalism to legitimise its role and to gain supporters in the other states. The roles of Prussia and Piedmont in German and Italian unification are examples. In both cases ideological movements were not nearly enough to achieve unity, and authority had to be imposed forcibly on at least some of the other states. In Africa no state has ever been in a position to do this, even on a regional basis. In a weaker, publicist sense Ghana was able to play a leading role between 1957 and 1960, but that was all. In the Arab case Egypt under Nasser appeared for a time as a more credible candidate for such a role. The failure to defeat Israel in war, however, meant that Nasser was never able to go very far in this direction. No other state since Nasser's Egypt has plausibly been able to claim the leadership of Arab nationalism.

The other condition is the existence of popular movements which accept the pan-nationalist position and can impose it on particular states from below. In the German case this was unimportant. In the Italian case a contingent alliance between popular movements and nationalism did subvert the Kingdom of the Two Sicilies and made a major contribution to Italian unification. In the African case it has had a limited effect, although the residence of resistance movements to Southern Rhodesia in surrounding states did constrain the policies of those states. In the Arab case the Palestinians have acted and continue to act as an important unifying force from below. In all cases, the lack of common experiences (partly because of the lack of a common state) means that there can be no single and broadly dispersed 'national' movement.

Measured by these two criteria, Pan-Africanism is by far the weakest of the unification nationalisms that have been considered. Arab nationalism is much the strongest, because at various times both a leading state and popular pressure have sustained it. Strength is not the same thing as success, however, and the existence of both conditions could weaken unification nationalism by dividing it. In 1848 Prussia partly drew back from leading the movement for unity lest it should push her into the hands of a popular national movement. Sometimes Arab states stand in the same relationship to the Palestinian movement. For success one must also take into account the extent to which international relations inhibit moves to greater unity and the degree of dominance enjoyed by the leading state or a popular national movement. Today the system of territorial states with nominal sovereignty has become very fixed. Only because the two conditions of a leading state and a popular movement have been so clearly evident has Arab nationalism been able seriously to challenge it and at least compel different states to act together in ways which would, in the absence of Arab nationalism, have been inconceivable.

Notes

1 Delegates at Manchester included Nkrumah, Kenyatta, and Hastinngs Banda, who all later became heads of state, as well as many others who played a leading role in various independent states. Senghor and Houphouët-Boigny, who were not present, were members of the French National Assembly before becoming leaders of independent Guinea and the Ivory Coast respectively.
2 On the period before 1945 see Immanuel Geiss, *The Pan-African Movement* (New York, 1974).
3 This excludes Sudan, which became independent earlier, but which it is difficult to characterise as a black African state.
4 I do not include an analysis of Zionism, one of the most extraordinary forms of nationalism. Briefly, its roots lie in a combination of intellectual reaction against the failures of assimilationist liberalism in western Europe and the exclusion of large numbers of Jews from increasingly nationally defined states in east-central Europe, in particular Russia.
5 See above, pp. 273–5.
6 Since Sadat's assassination, his successor Mubarak has been able to continue his policy of agreement with Israel and the USA. What remains to be seen is whether the new Labour government in Israel can make sufficient headway in negotiations to bring the Palestinians and other Arab states on to the same course as Egypt.

15

Reform nationalism
in the old nation-states

1 Introduction

It is essential to distinguish radical right nationalism (henceforth referred to as fascism), which I consider in this chapter, from nationalist movements which might variously be described as traditional, conservative, reactionary or authoritarian. The nationalist movements so far considered, apart from the special type of 'nation-building' nationalism, have all been challenges to the existing state(s). These challenges in Europe have usually been linked with more general liberal or democratic values. Various sorts of conservative nationalist ideas were, however, developed in the nineteenth century.[1]

Some conservative writers, especially after the French revolution, argued that the various and peculiar societies of Europe, sometimes called nations, could not be understood or ruled on the basis of universal principles. From this basis conservatism could move in one of three directions. It might argue that reform was possible but only on a piecemeal basis which did not do violence to the complex structure of the whole society. It might insist that all change should be avoided as dangerous and that the job of government was to protect exactly what existed. It might insist that change had already undermined the values of the nation and that salvation lay only in a return to a past situation where stability and true national identity were to be found. These three forms of conservatism can be called reform, authoritarian and reactionary.[2]

Reform conservatism, whether in nationalist or other forms, is an attitude of mind rather than a distinct political doctrine. It takes its position from the given situation and then develops, in a cautious and pragmatic way, piecemeal policies designed to secure a basic stability. No generalisations about these policies are possible. Again, authoritarian conservatism is dependent on the particular *status quo* in a very rigid way and cannot be analysed as a general political doctrine or movement. Reactionary nationalism is more amenable to general analysis because it is distanced

288

from the particular situation in which it finds itself. The images of reactionary nationalism, however, tend to be very particular and concrete. They are either based on an allegedly historical reality or derived from a combination of different elements from the past. Carlism in Spain, for example, tended to aim not at restoring a particular situation but rather at restoring elements from the past such as provincial powers, traditional monarchy and a strong Catholic church. Very often such a movement was prepared to employ radical means in pursuit of these ends. However, there are two reasons for not considering reactionary nationalism as a distinct form of nationalism. The first is that the concept of the nation tends to be subordinated to concern with monarchy or regional power or the church. Often such movements abandon their nationalist focus in favour of these concerns. Second, and more important, reactionary nationalism rarely becomes very powerful. Usually it has been a subordinate ally of authoritarian nationalism or fascism. So the only distinctive right-wing nationalism I will consider is fascism.

Earlier I argued that once nation-states have been established and the rhetoric of national interest generally accepted it is difficult to identify anything specifically as nationalism. Why, then, should one concentrate on fascism but not on the many other forms taken by political movements which appeal to the idea of nationality in established nation-states? My answer would be that fascism is exceptional in that it cannot be understood outside a nationalist frame of reference and, unlike liberal or radical or conservative nationalism, cannot be seen as a particular application of a more general set of values which could be detached from a nationalist frame of reference.[3] At the same time the character of its view of the nation, although each fascist movement insists on its uniqueness, has a general quality about it which permits comparative analysis. There are other features, as we shall see in this chapter, which also allow of comparative treatment.

Before the First World War radical right nationalism had either been tied to other, less radical nationalist organisations or had seen itself in pressure-group terms.[4] Parties with views which might be called radical right nationalist, above all anti-semitic parties, had fleeting importance and had not developed comprehensive programmes. But after 1918, in the form of fascist movements, radical right nationalism emerged in a number of countries as a force aiming to take state power on the basis of a fairly comprehensive set of claims. Even where relatively weak, as in the case of the Falange, the Spanish fascist party, the commitment to taking power is to be found. Since 1945 political movements of this sort have played no important part in European politics. So in this chapter I will concentrate upon inter-war Europe.

I will also consider fascism only when in opposition. Fascism achieved power only in two cases,[5] and the constraints of government rather blunted its ideological commitments or organisational character. In looking at fascist opposition I will concentrate upon the political context in which it developed and the function nationalism served for fascism within that context. I will pay particular attention to Germany, Italy and Rumania, as these were the most significant fascist movements. But I will draw more general comparisons in order to arrive at conclusions on the subject. Before looking at particular cases it is necessary to propound some general arguments about fascism.

'A radical, anti-bourgeois, anti-liberal, anti-marxist movement of national-imperalist integration'.[6] This definition offers a useful departure point for analysis. One can begin by considering the implications of the terms used.

Radical. Unlike traditional right-wing movements, which may take a nationalist form, fascism does not work primarily as informal elite politics dependent upon the absence of popular participation. Rather, fascism comes into its own at times of intense popular involvement in politics and the breakdown of established political parties. Its own political image is built upon various direct and mass forms of action such as marches, demonstrations and street fighting, and offering itself as something more that just another party for the voter to support. And just as its chosen means seem to be radical, so does its vague vision of a stronger, regenerated nation.

Anti-bourgeois. Fascist leadership is drawn from a variety of groups – intellectuals, ex-soldiers, failed businessmen and professional people – who are usually contemptuous of the routine, stable, anti-heroic lives of established middle-class people. Fascists are also openly hostile to large-scale capitalism, at least while in opposition, with its apparently impersonal and calculating morality.

Anti-liberal. Fascists oppose the idea of the state bound by law and politics organised in a pluralist way through parliament. Legal restrictions on the state appear to them a fictitious and debilitating constraint on what should be the powerful and direct expression of the national will. Party politics appear as divisive and petty, undermining the strength and unity of the nation.

Anti-Marxist. Fascists deny the reality, let alone the primacy, of class conflict and find the rational, materialist approach of Marxism an affront to the emotional, spiritual roots of nationality. Belief in class conflict is seen as the product of Marxist indoctrination. Class loyalty must be exposed as a myth and replaced by genuine national solidarity. Fascists also oppose socialist visions of international fraternity and of a socialised economy as opposed to one regulated in the national interest.

In place of traditional conservatism, parliamentary politics or working-class victory fascists offer the vision of a strong and united nation whose heroic leaders pursue a glorious and expansive foreign policy. This

290

'positive' vision, a very vague one, is the mirror image of the negative views of fascism. The rejection of class, party and elite politics leads to the idea of the nation as a classless, partyless, permanently mobilised organism bound together by blood or language or intuition or some such entity whose values, in some mysterious and direct way, are made known to and expressed through extraordinary leaders. The success of such a crude and absurd view of politics is, in my view, based upon the prior failure of those other views of politics to which fascists are vehemently opposed. These failures can be linked to specific features of the states in which fascism became significant. Once one has analysed these failures, which in part lead to the acceptance of fascism, one can go on to consider its positive appeal.

2 Germany and Italy

Fascism began as part of a reaction against the threats of socialism and working-class organisations. It took organised form during the repression of extreme left-wing and organised labour activity in the period of instability immediately following the end of the First World War. It came to power in the middle of a crisis when the threat from the left could be presented as very dangerous.

In Italy the first fascii were formed in the cities of northern Italy; they engaged in strike-breaking and generally terrorising organised labour, especially during the period of the factory occupations in 1919–20. Fascii also extended into the countryside, into areas such as the Po valley, where peasant and rural labourer organisation had become particularly powerful. Again the same pattern of violence and terror prevailed.

Hitler began his political career as political adviser to troops engaged in repressing left-wing movements in Bavaria. Such repression was also carried out by para-military groups. These para-military groups, as well as the clubs formed by civilians opposed to the threat from the left, provided the major forms of organisation and social support upon which the early National Socialist movement built.

In Italy the fascist takeover followed on fairly directly from the immediate post-war disturbances, which were never really settled. In Germany the Weimar Republic became rather more stable between 1924 and 1928. However, the period 1928–33, especially the last three years, saw a return to political instability. One aspect of this was a sharp increase in votes for the German Communist Party. Again the threat from the left could make the fascist cause appear more attractive.

But alone such a threat could not account for fascist success. First, one must distinguish between appearance and reality. Undoubtedly there was acute social disorder in both countries immediately after 1918, and again in Germany in the last years of Weimar. But in both the left was crippled by internal divisions. The Russian revolution, the Communist

International and the formation of large communist parties in western European countries might have made the left look more dangerous but it also helped divide working-class politics between communists and social democrats. Communist strength was highly regionalised, fluctuated rapidly, and was bitterly opposed even from within, let alone outside, the ranks of socialist and labour organisations.

Second, the threat of communism could appear as great in other countries where fascism did not become so important. In eastern Europe it seemed as important in Hungary and Poland as in Rumania. In France there was a powerful and well organised Communist Party with strong links with unionised workers. One has to go further and look at the effectiveness of non-fascist opposition to the apparent threat from the left. These oppositions can be divided into pluralist and elitist categories. In looking at pluralist opposition we need to examine the nature of parliamentary politics in Italy and Germany.

In both countries there was a rapid move towards the establishment of parliamentary democracy after the war. In Italy universal suffrage had been introduced just before but only became significant afterwards. Furthermore, the switch in 1919 to a system of proportional representation was intended to break down the local and factional politics associated with single-constituency elections and thus to contribute to the development of genuinely national parties. The Catholic party, the Popolari, was a major supporter of this change and seemed to have the best chance of forming a really national and popular party under the new electoral system.

In Germany universal manhood suffrage had been in existence for elections to the Reichstag, the lower chamber of the national parliament, since 1867. But the Reichstag had few powers relative to the executive. Furthermore, considerable power remained at the state and local levels, but many state parliaments and city councils were elected on the basis of a heavily weighted or restricted franchise. The Weimar constitution transformed this situation: by extending the vote to women; by creating parliamentary sovereignty at national level and getting rid of the monarchy; by reducing state and local power; by democratising the electoral basis of state and local assemblies; by harmonising state and national constitutions.

These changes in Germany and Italy had a real effect. In some countries in eastern Europe, and even in some backward regions in Italy and Spain, the establishment of formally democratic institutions did not make much difference to the actual conduct of politics. Landowners, the Catholic church and other powerful interests continued to dominate affairs much as before. But in most parts of Germany and in northern and central Italy the newly expanded and empowered electorate had to be handled in new ways.

One response to this sudden political mobilisation was to seek to channel it into support for parliamentary parties. Partly this could work by getting radical parties of protest – above all, socialist parties – to commit themselves to parliamentary methods. Working-class opposition when expressed through bodies such as the British Labour Party, the post-war German Social Democratic Party or the French Radical Socialist Party did not appear as threatening as when expressed through communist parties or syndicalist trade unions.

It was also important, however, that parties of the right and centre, calling upon support from large, non-working-class groups, held a strong position in the new democratic system. Generally the rapid political mobilisation of these groups in Italian and German politics made this difficult, particularly in times of crisis. However, the failure to hold this part of the electorate took instructively different forms in Italy and Germany. One writer has neatly summarised a major difference as follows: 'Italy's problem was essentially amorphousness while Germany's was that of a multiplicity of powerless but well-defined groups.[7]

Italy's main problem was the need to provide effective party representation for the various social groups between the pre-war political elites and organised labour. The Liberal Party, which had dominated pre-war politics, was unable to adapt to mass politics. It still relied excessively on personal connections. Its chief leader, Giolitti, continued to defend the politics of manoeuvre and personality and advocated a return to single-constituency elections, in which, he hoped, local interests could once more assert themselves. But to the bulk of the electorate this looked like the advocacy of corrupt politics which democratic reforms were supposed to eliminate. Furthermore, Liberal discipline over its parliamentary representatives remained poor and was constantly weakened by internal divisions over matters such as entry into the war. A moderate socialist party was inhibited from moving into an open acceptance of parliamentary methods for fear of losing working-class support to its communist rival on the left. The best chance of creating a popular party of the centre seemed to reside with the new Catholic party, the Popolari. But the Popolari was weakened by its own newness. As a confessional party it tried to represent a very diverse range of social and economic interests. It faced a suspicious Vatican. Pope Pius XI in particular disliked some of the radical causes which the Popolari espoused, although they were essential to its popularity. He was also anxious that the party might become too independent of the church. Deputies from the south tended to be fairly immune from party discipline and were often involved in factional feuds and allegiances. All this gravely weakened the efforts of democratically inclined politicians within the Popolari to build a party with a firm popular base. Only after 1945 would the rise of Christian Democratic movements fill this political gap.

These various failures by the main parties meant that a very broad section of the electorate, including groups such as students, professional people, small businessmen, owner-occupiers, tenant farmers and sharecroppers were not attached to particular parties. This gave the fascists a large social terrain to cultivate and fatally weakened the parliamentary system at a time of crisis. But it also meant that, in cultivating this large field, the fascist movement itself became amorphous. Fascism grew in a rapid and unorganised way in Italy – partly as a parliamentary party itself after its impressive election performance in 1921, partly as a direct form of action replacing parliamentary and legal authority. It took up the interests of a great variety of groups, often themselves with conflicting interests. Such disorganisation and conflict were taken into the movement itself. This helps to account for the fascist emphasis on 'action' rather than 'programme' and 'men' rather than 'parties'. But, though amorphous, fascism did have a loose national organisation and, in Mussolini, a unifying figure to whom all groups could pledge themselves.

Nevertheless, this did make Mussolini's position weak. He preserved the image of forcing himself into power by direct action although the reality was that he had been taken into government by traditional elites. He had a rather ambivalent attitude towards parliament. There were constant and rather confused interactions between different elements in the fascist movement and in various other parties. This blurred the clear opposition which the fascist image of direct action seemed to involve. A shapeless political movement tends to have vague objectives. Mussolini seems to have toyed with the idea of alliances with the socialists or the Popolari before he became Prime Minister. Even after 1922 he sought to work with the Popolari and the Liberal Party. Given the amorphousness of centre politics in Italy, there was nothing inevitable about the formal destruction of the parliamentary system. Indeed in 1924–25 Mussolini could be placed in a crisis because of the response to the murder of a leading socialist deputy, Matteoti, and it took some six months for Mussolini to assert his authority. The speed with which the fascist movement had grown and then taken over power preserved the uncertainty of direction. By the time Mussolini was Prime Minister the movement had had little time to create discipline and unity within its own ranks. It had no clear policies and was based upon no distinct social group or economic interest. It could not provide from its own ranks a political elite sufficiently large, able or organised to subordinate established elites to its power in a short space of time. Certainly the fascist accession to power made a great deal of difference to working-class power and those interested in liberal freedoms and rights. But the fascists were forced to compromise with many groups – such as the monarchy, the army and the Catholic church – and it is difficult to discern any positive alternative arising to the parliamentary system of politics.

The situation developed rather differently in Germany. Long experience of universal manhood suffrage had provided the country with well organised parties drawing upon well defined bases of support. This gave the parliamentary system much better resources for its defence than it had in Italy. Conversely it made much more clear-cut the conflict between parliament and fascism.

There was a well established national, mass Catholic party, the Centre Party, which was independent of the church and prepared to commit itself to the republic at the outset. There was a very large and well organised Social Democratic Party (the whole party had become the largest in the Reichstag at the 1912 elections) which was firmly committed to republican democracy. It had split during the war and many of its members and supporters favoured more radical politics, but it retained a wide degree of support and impressive organisation as well as close links with the bulk of the trade union movement.

There was less clear party representation for Protestant, non-working-class voters. German liberalism had been weakened and divided by the manner of German unification. Many liberal and conservative elites, instead of adapting to mass politics at a national level, tended to retreat into the less democratic politics operating at state and local levels. Increasingly up to 1914 large numbers of non-working-class Protestants were drifting into non-parliamentary forms of political action.[8]

But this weakness was not obvious when the Weimar Republic was set up. At the first elections of January 1919 the Social Democratic Party won a particularly large vote because it was seen by many as the only remaining bulwark against the communist threat. The Centre Party got its usual large slice of the poll. A democratic liberal party, the German Democratic Party, heir to the left-liberal parties of the pre-war period, also did well. There was a firm majority in parliament for parties committed to the republic.

The republic continued to show that it had apparently strong foundations. It defeated the threats from the left in 1918–19, although at the cost of permanent division amongst socialists, now divided into social democratic and communist camps, and compromises between the Social Democrats and various conservative elites such as the army officers. In 1920 the Kapp Putsch, a reactionary right-wing attempt to seize power, was defeated by a general strike which mobilised support from all levels of society and not just the working class. The strike was necessary because the bulk of the army (excluding those active in the Putsch) remained aloof. The lesson to be drawn from this is not so much that the army, or at least its leaders, were anti-republican as that the republic could defend itself against illegal threats from the right without resort to the army. The army could, of course, be used to deal with illegal threats from the left.

Clearly one should not paint too rosy a picture. Many important areas of decision-making remained outside parliament. The army and the police were often beyond interference from democratically elected politicians, and it has been argued that an important opportunity to reform these and other institutions was missed when Weimar was established. Much economic decision-making rested with well organised trade unions and employers' organisations, and the importance of such groups increased during the 1920s. Individual state governments, especially Prussia, retained a good deal of authority, although the fact that the Prussian government remained under social democratic control until a coup removed it in 1932 meant that such autonomy helped the republic. The restraints that all these features of Weimar imposed on the policy-making ability of parliament undoubtedly reduced its effectiveness and this in turn its support. Nevertheless a real challenge to the Weimar Republic could only be mounted through the ballot box, as Hitler clearly recognised after the failure of the Munich Putsch in 1923. And that challenge could only be mounted effectively if voters deserted the parties committed, in varying degrees, to the republic.

The failure of these parties could be explained simply in terms of the gravity of the crisis Weimar faced with the onset of the depression from 1930. There is no doubt that this huge crisis, coupled with the stigma under which it laboured as a product of defeat in war and the hated Versailles peace settlement, was the general cause of the destruction of the republic. But similar problems elsewhere did not lead to the same sort of result. One could counter this argument in either of two ways. First, it could be argued that the problems were far greater in Germany than elsewhere. This is difficult to demonstrate. The unemployment rate, for example, at its height was perhaps three times that of Great Britain, but fascism in Germany was far greater than in Britain, or even in the USA where unemployment and its speed of increase was more comparable with Germany. The argument is a crass one but it shows that the whole notion of explaining fascism in terms of the sheer scale of the economic crisis is a crass one. Why could there not have been some sort of coalition government, such as was tried between 1928 and 1930, or a more authoritarian form of parliamentary government, such as was tried between 1930 and 1933, or some combination of the two? In the case of crises Britain and France in their different ways had moved toward left-centre coalitions (the National Government, the Popular Front). To these arguments there is a counter one, which is that Germans were less disposed to respond to problems in democratic ways than were Frenchmen and Britons. Such arguments, usually supported with a wealth of detail about anti-democratic political thought in Germany or about authoritarian personalities, are inherently undemonstrable. It is more worth while to examine how the parliamentary system of Weimar functioned under stress.

The key to a coalition or authoritarian parliamentary response to the crisis was the ability of parties of the centre and moderate right to retain a large level of voter support. But these parties, excluding the Centre Party, were failing to do that even before the onset of the depression. The German People's Party began to decline almost immediately after the first elections. Both it and the Democratic Party lost ground in the elections of May 1924. The apparent recovery of pro-republican forces in December 1924 was due to a reduced poll, an increase in support for the Social Democrats and a drop in support for various right-wing parties. The liberal parties of the centre made only small gains.

There were also weaknesses in the positions of the Centre and Social Democratic parties. The Centre Party had supported the establishment of the republic in a cautious and pragmatic way, and its votes should not be seen as committed republican votes. The Social Democrats, on the other hand, were weighed down by their pro-republicanism. This could weaken them in competition with the Communist Party when the republic faced a crisis, particularly when the party was in government. Increasingly it tended towards its pre-war habit of putting up principled but democratic opposition to the compromises of government. It did not take part in government between 1924 and 1928 or after 1930. It may have kept the party pure but it helped reduce its power within the republic.

The moderate parties were also incapable of sustained co-operation. In 1925, for example, seven candidates ran for the presidency. Had the pro-republican parties put up an agreed candidate he would have won. As it was, the nationalist idea of putting up Hindenburg in the run-off election worked, as he just defeated Wilhelm Marx of the Centre Party, whom the pro-republican parties belatedly supported. Even then the support Hindenburg received from the Bavarian People's Party, a sister organisation of the Centre Party, was crucial. This points to regionalism, another element which weakened national parties committed to the republic. Subsequently Hindenburg was to play an important part in the events that brought Hitler to power.

Part of the reason for this decline, which accelerated in the last years of Weimar, was that each party tended to act on behalf of tightly defined groups or principles. The electorate tended to regard the parties in terms of interest representation or protest. These political habits go back to the Second Empire, when the lack of parliamentary power turned parties into either negative oppositions or pressure groups. Without the prospect of power there was no incentive, even under a single-constituency system of election, to establish broad-based parties laying claim to the right to govern. The economic fragmentation of the middle classes (more accurately, the Protestant non-working-class) was reflected in political fragmentation. In other countries where these economic interests were just as varied, effective parliamentary government before 1914 had given rise to parties which acted to bind these interests together.[9] Political fragmentation meant in turn that the electorate viewed party choice in narrow interest terms. This narrowly instrumental view of parties in turn produced fluid voting patterns. In addition, proportional representation introduced just after the war meant that parties were not under great pressure to merge in the bid for electoral support, and the fluidity was increased by the addition of women voters and the many new voters of the Weimar period.

The political fragmentation of centre parties and even parties of the right extended into those parties as well. The remaining party of the right in the last years of Weimar was the German National People's Party (DNVP). It split between those prepared to support the policies of Streseman and those determined to join in the campaign against the new Chancellor, Bruning. This enabled the Nazis to co-operate with the more extreme wing around Hugenberg. It also helped make it difficult for the DNVP itself or many of its voters to resist the appeal of a united and even more radical Nazi party at a time of crisis.

The Nazi party exploited the situation very effectively. One could argue that it had created the situation, in that it was the outflow of votes from these various parties to the Nazis that brought about their decline. But the weaknesses of these parties set in before the great Nazi successes and it was only in the light of their weaknesses that the Nazis came to appear as a strong alternative. Even then it is doubtful how positively attractive the electorate found the Nazis: in the last election before Hitler became Chancellor the Nazi vote dropped. It would be wrong to regard Nazism as the destination towards which the Protestant non-working-class electorate of Weimar was steadily moving.[10]

Nevertheless, to take advantage of others' weaknesses called for the creation of a highly organised and national party. Between 1924 and 1928 Hitler had come to recognised this and to construct the required organisation. The party remained deeply anti-liberal, but it was now prepared to defeat Weimar by its own parliamentary methods. The party was unsure of how it was going to do this: for some time it pitched its main appeal to working-class voters. Its first great electoral successes, in places like Schleswig-Holstein with a peasant population, were something of a surprise. Contrary to much received opinion it did not really develop a distinctive propaganda line on matters of substance except for the great pulling power of the figure of Hitler himself and communicating a general image of decisiveness and energy. It was the beneficiary of the failure of other parties, and it was its existence as a single party untainted by power, with a strong-looking leader and a vehement indictment of a political system which it argued produced the weaknesses apparent in Weimar, that led voters to it. And they went, in most cases, out of despair rather than hope.

The final element which needs consideration is the failure of elitist conservatism. Political elites without responsibility to the electorate played an important part in bringing fascists to power. In Italy the monarch played an important role. In Germany the role of Hindenburg and those who advised him was crucial in the last stages of the Nazi accession to government. But the very need to bring fascists into power, whatever views these elites might have held about the balance of power between themselves and the fascists, was a sign of weakness. That this was so can be seen when one considers cases where fascists were not needed.

In the south of Italy a largely backward peasant population was unable to make effective use of the new democratic institutions. Proportional representation here did not lead to national party commitment. Deputies remained tied to particular groups of local clients rather than to the party. As a result the deputies did not act in a collective, disciplined fashion in parliament. That weakened parliamentary resistance to fascism, not only by undermining party unity but also because individual deputies might succumb to tempting offers from the fascists. But it also made it difficult for any central political force, including the fascists, to penetrate the locally based politics of the south. The inability of the left to make headway there meant that, in any case, the particular appeal of fascism as a bulwark against the left was redundant. Established elites had enough direct power at their disposal to deal with such threats without resorting to fascist assistance. Fascism is a national politics and the South was not yet integrated into an Italian national politics.

Consequently, what success fascism had in the south was dependent on its prior success in other regions. Occasionally it could develop on a mass basis in the south, as in Campania under the leadership of Padovani. In such cases fascism might become a radical force and take up connections with other provincial radical elements in fascism which could, together, play an important national role. But the more general pattern was for local notables to ally themselves with fascists if doing so offered the best chance of securing favourable policies from a central government now under fascist control. This elite co-ordination politics could come into conflict with fascism as mass mobilisation. The dominance of factional and patron-client politics in the south meant that it was largely the politics of elite co-ordination that won in this conflict. Here was a case where there was no sudden transition to genuine parliamentary democracy and mass politics and, therefore, where the stimulus to an independent and powerful fascism was weak.[11]

The overall pattern in Germany and Italy was, however, different from this. In northern and central regions of Italy and in at least parts of all major German regions non-democratic political elites were not able to respond effectively to a politically mobilised population. Even where they tried, as in the case of some of the leaders of the German People's Party and the DNVP, the ties with business or the obviously elitist character of the leadership inhibited such parties and reduced their popular appeal. Other institutions such as the monarchy or the army knew full well that they could remain effective only in alliance with political groups that had mass support.

There is no doubt that fascism had some appeal to these elites. Its hostility to the left and to parliamentary democracy largely accorded with their own sentiments. Employers and landowners made financial contributions to fascist parties. The members of the armed forces often sympathised with fascism. But the crucial point was that these groups needed rather than approved of fascists. Financial contributions went to many other parties as well and only became significant for fascism once it was apparent that fascists might take power. The social origins of their leaders, the radical image and methods of the fascists, their paramilitary activity – all aroused, at the very least, distaste among conservative elites. Where fascists were not needed they were not used. Germany had no equivalent of Franco (though Schleicher obviously overestimated the importance of a political general); the Italian monarch did not have the power of a Horthy, Regent of Hungary, or of Carol II, King of Rumania. Fascists were not instruments of conservative elites; rather, co-operation was an alliance of necessity. In consequence, neither before nor after assuming power were fascists under the control of any particular interest or class.

Fascism, then, came to power in circumstances in which its negative response to class, parliamentary and elitist politics corresponded with a situation in which none of these three forms of politics could cope with a crisis facing a political system with a new, politically mobilised population. Much of this population was scared of threats from the left, unattached to or subsequently detached from parliamentary parties and beyond the control of conservative elites. In a crisis fascism, the negation of these three forms of politics, could seem to be the only remaining solution. Why it existed to be turned to at such a point is a matter which still requires consideration. Here, however, one can see that it is a particular political structure that favoured fascism and to which, in a negative way, fascism responded.

3 The Rumanian case

Backward, mainly agrarian countries in eastern Europe obviously experienced a very different politics from those of Germany and Italy. Usually more traditional authoritarian methods prevailed in the face of crisis, rather than fascism. But fascism did become particularly significant in Rumania. It is worth seeing whether the same sort of analysis can be undertaken here, suitably adapted, as for Germany and Italy.

The threat from the left was there, although not in terms of a revolutionary industrial working class. There was an external threat from communist powers, above all the Soviet Union. There were demands for radical land reform and, indeed, peasants in Transylvania were able to use the prospect of Bolshevik 'offers' on land reform to achieve a more substantial reform programme than was offered to the peasantry of the Old Kingdom. In the end Rumanian pushed through the most substantial land redistribution outside the USSR, creating many more smallholdings during the 1920s. However, this did not improve, and indeed may have worsened, levels of peasant debt and poverty, relative over-population, and lack of innovation. This was all to create a special problem of peasant discontent, but that is different from threats from a wage-labour class.[12] There were also strikes soon after 1918 among the small working class, and Codreanu, later the leader of the Iron Guard, the Rumanian fascist movement, was involved in putting some of them down. Already he took the view that repression was not enough: workers had to be converted to a nationalist, Christian and anti-communist set of values. But the threat from the left was hardly a major issue and does not contribute much to an explanation of fascism's importance.

The problems of coping with a new democracy also seem to have been less significant than in Italy and Germany. There was a formal system of parliamentary democracy. The National Liberal regime delayed the first elections until September 1919 in the hope of gaining time for their limited programme of reform to boost their popularity. When it did not, the National Liberals were reinstalled in power by a royal *coup d'etat* in March 1920. Elections thereafter were held in an atmosphere of intimid-ation, corruption, mass disenfranchisement and, later on, a law which ensured a firm majority for any party able to obtain 40 per cent of the votes cast.[13] Only in 1928 was a more democratic party, the National Peasants' Party, able to form a government, and it lasted for only three years. Thereafter various National Peasant and later Liberal politicians headed governments under a system of 'controlled democracy', with sub-stantial powers vested in the recently restored King, Carol II. The net effect was the fragmentation of the two major political parties, the increased personal authority of the king, and the emergence of non-party forms of mass politics – especially those organised by the regime directly as well as by the Iron Guard. When the elections of December 1937 threatened this system Carol installed a minority government and then finally, recognising the logic of the way he had undermined parliamentary parties, he took over directly. He was finally removed, not by democratic means but by German pressure and co-operation between Rumanian army officers and fascists. This followed popular disgust at the failure of Carol's policy of seeking to avoid over-dependence on any one great power which led to his being forced to cede territory in 1940 to the USSR, Hungary and Bulgaria. Incidentally, Rumanian fascism, no more than any other nationalist ele-ment in Rumania, had no desire to become overly dependent on Germany. The nationalist component in fascism is always more important than any sense of kinship with other fascist movements or regimes.

301

At first it would appear that fascism cannot be explained as an attractive alternative way of coping with a mobilised population when parliamentary means have proved wanting, because such means seem never really to have been tried. But the argument does acquire some force when one considers the problems facing conservative elites in Rumania.

Although Rumanian kings (Ferdinand in 1920, Carol in 1938) did flout majority verdicts of the electorate, they could not rule without some form of popular support. There had to be 'confirmatory' elections in 1920. In 1938 Carol was forced first into dependence upon some extreme nationalist elements and then sought to create his own nationalist movement to wrest support from the Iron Guard and other popular right-wing groups. And on three occasions – 1920, 1928, 1937 – the regime could not manipulate elections as it wished and a crisis occurred. There was a good deal of repression, but never the elimination of party competition. There was also a great deal of manipulation by landowners, clergy and government officials as well as attempts to divert attention to various 'foreign' influences. The limitations of this sort of manipulation on the part of conservative elites can help make clear the way in which fascism could become significant.

Rumania was in many ways a 'colonial' economy. Industry was largely financed by foreign capital. Jews, regarded as foreigners even though legally Rumanians, were prominent in the professions, trade and finance. In Transylvania land and business had been largely controlled by German- or Magyar-speakers. Nationalist appeals against these groups had an emotional impact and could also promise some redistribution of wealth. But, because of this, all important political groups were virulently nationalist, which rather diminished the specific value of nationalism to the regime.

Furthermore the regime was inhibited from acting on its nationalist rhetoric. An attack on foreign holdings could lead to a drying up of further investment, on which the economy desperately depended. Discrimination against Jews could be taken further, but it certainly reduced the already low stock of educated and skilled labour; it could, and did from 1939 when the Iron Guard put its 'Romanisation' policies into effect, provoke economic crisis. There was one major exception to these inhibitions: the expropriation of land from Magyar- and German-speakers in Transylvania. But that exception posed the greatest problem of all for the exercise of 'traditional' control.

The regime which held power at the end of the war was that of the Old Kingdom (the Regat), that is, those parts of Rumania which had won independence from the Ottoman empire. In 1913 the population of the Old Kingdom was 7.3 million. In 1919 the population of Greater Rumania was 16.2 million. The bulk of the addition came from Transylvania. The problem of absorbing it was the Rumanian equivalent to the German or

Italian problem of absorbing a mass electorate.

Transylvania was a completely different society from the Old King-dom. Its peasantry were more prosperous and better educated. (The lite-racy rate for the whole country stood at about 57 per cent in 1930; for the Regat at 56 per cent and for Transylvania at 67.3 per cent.) Despite the discriminations suffered since 1867 under the Magyars there was a much more developed Rumanian middle class in the professions and commerce. This peasantry and middle class did not welcome 'national unity' without some reservations. Until shortly before 1914 they had looked west to Vienna for support, principally against Magyar domination, and the national movement was very late in turning to its Rumanian 'brethren'. Already by the end of the war Transylvanians had insisted on some constitutional guarantees and a land reform programme which the regime would not initially grant to its own peasants. Acting on nationalist principles made this peasantry and middle class even more important because it wiped out the traditional source of authority, the Magyar-and German-speaking landowners. To integrate these large groups called for concessions. Concessions in turn raised demands from the Old Kingdom, where peasants in particular disliked the difference in treatment. On this basis a National Peasant Party could emerge.

The National Peasant Party was beyond the control of conservative elites, although like other parties its leadership was drawn from the intelligentsia. But it could not itself push through radical reforms. Partly the reason was that land redistribution had created conservative elements among the peasantry and there was little more to be had from that kind of reform. Partly it was that sub-division of land in so overpopulated and under-capitalised an agriculture often merely led to greater control by landowners as they took over indebted holdings. Partly it was regional disparity and the difficulties of mobilising the worst-off elements in the rural population. Finally, the NPP had the misfortune to take power just as the depression began to bite, drying up markets for agricultural produce. The NPP weakened conservative control, but its own failures created something of a vacuum.

For many Rumanian intellectuals the position looked bleak. They found Jews prominent in the professions. They were being educated to serve in a top-heavy state structure which appeared ineffectual and corrupt. They observed the mass of the peasantry steeped in ignorance and poverty. For some of them nationalism was not enough. Nor was an emphasis on social and economic reform alone. Certainly any solution would include nationalism and socio-economic reform, but more than that was needed.

Codreanu broke new ground in his attempts to work out what the additional factor should be. He found it in the idea of an elite totally dedicated to the regeneration of the Rumanian nation. The elite would be Christian (through Bessarabia the Iron Guard derived many of the Ortho-

303

dox and reactionary ideas of the Russian Kadet movement which had thrived under late Tsarism); it would enjoin a pure life upon its members; it would make any sacrifice, including the supreme one of eternal damnation, for the national cause. These sorts of ideas, of an heroic elite, are commonplace in fascism, but Codreanu and his followers took them much further than any other fascist movement. He tapped an element of idealism which had become frustrated by the almost unique intractability of Rumania's problems. Obviously these ideas were taken up only by a tiny minority, but it could become significant.

There were two phases in the fascist rise. Codreanu began campaigning in parts of Moldavia among an impoverished peasantry largely ignored by the national political forces. It took a great deal of effort and courage for him to break through the administrative and police controls in that part of the country, but when he did he got to politically untapped ground. To the peasants it was probably the almost 'magical' quality of his appeal, a knight in shining armour doing battle with the powers of darkness, that attracted them. However, given their situation, it is difficult to see how they could have generated definite political objectives of their own or furnished the Iron Guard with cadres or other resources. Because of this such groups, although a useful start, amounted to a political resource in little more than simple voting terms.

As fascism began to move beyond this source of support so it found that it had to make more specific appeals. In Transylvania a rather more definite language of social reform was required. When fascists sought to penetrate urban areas and tap support from the small working class they began to take up various corporatist economic ideas. Given the failure of the NPP and the absence of any serious left-wing party, they were able to make some inroads in all these areas. It was the NPP and the small, rural left-wing organisation, the Ploughmen's Front, which first began to appreciate just how important the inroads were. But through the weaknesses of conservative elites and the peasant reform party the fascists had managed to carve out a degree of popular support for themselves amongst increasingly significant and mobilised parts of the population.

The final ingredient needed for success was division among conservative elites or popular parties. The regime was threatened by other extreme forms of nationalism, such as the virulent anti-semitic movement of Cuza with whom Codreanu had earlier been associated. The NPP was concerned to prevent the Liberals winning another majority in the 1937 election and so formed an electoral alliance with the Iron Guard. Officially the Iron Guard picked up about 16 per cent of the votes at the elections, though their real support was probably somewhat greater. The Liberals did not get the majority they had sought. However, the Iron Guard could not participate in government. The king, with his control of the army and the administration, could also exploit political divisions. He formed a minority government out of other, smaller nationalist groupings and watched the various nationalist organisations struggle against one another. Subsequently he imposed direct rule and tried to build up an independent power base. As with Italy and even more so in Germany, the immediate phase before a fascist entry into government saw the breakdown of parliamentary government which left a space for other kinds of political forces. By this time support for the Iron Guard had probably reached its peak. Alone, as in Italy and Germany, fascists could not take power. In this case it was war that brought Carol II down. He wished to maintain some distance from the German government but this policy was undermined first by the Munich agreement, and then by the Nazi-Soviet Pact, and finally by Germany's successes in war in 1939–40. His credentials as a nationalist were destroyed with the annexations of 1940. Germany decided to support an alliance between fascists and the army to topple him. Again, as with Italy and Germany the acquiescence of the army and part of the existing political elite was crucial to the fascist entry into government.

However, the fascist movement which came to power had changed dramatically since 1937. Codreanu had been executed as part of the king's campaign to destroy fascism. Violence had come to play an ever larger role in the activity of the Iron Guard, while the themes of popularity and sacrifice receded. With the prospect of power, recruitment to the Iron Guard had risen but its quality as an elite declined. It began to look like just another nationalist faction striving for power. When it did succeed this appearance was heightened by its corrupt and impatient attempts to undermine the position of the army and carry through 'Romanisation' policies. Inevitably there had to be a trial of strength between army and fascists. By now the Germans had decided they preferred the army as a reliable and disciplined ally to the unpredictable Iron Guard. The Rumanian 'night of the long knives' came in January 1941.[14] With superior force and German backing the army leader, Antonescu, was bound to win. He went on to become a loyal ally of Germany. Fascism in Rumania did not really offer an alternative and necessary form of control to that of traditional authoritarianism. Consequently when it was in government there emerged no 'realistic' element to give up attempts at radical measures in order to compromise with some conservative elites but on its own terms because of its special contribution to the maintenance of order. Traditional conservative control was sufficiently weak to allow a fascist movement to become a prominent, but not the leading, force in government.

Fascism in Rumania was part of a desperate response to underdevelopment. This gave it a special idealist and fanatical quality which was distinctive. The inability of peasant reform movements, conservative elites or pure nationalism to control the new and poorly integrated state of Greater Rumania provided a political opportunity for this quasi-religious appeal to reach large sections of the population. It is worth noting that the lack of integration was principally within the ethnic Rumanian majority of the country; as in Germany and Italy the problem fascism had to address was not primarily that of the 'nation' versus others, but of the failure to maintain political control within the 'nation. But fascism could not begin to solve the economic problems facing the country and could not, in a primitive agrarian economy, maintain the level of mass mobilisation necessary for political success. Broadly, the elements which provide an entry point for German and Italian fascism into politics – the failure to integrate a newly mobilised population by means of authoritarianism, parliamentary government or class politics – operated here but in very different conditions which meant that Rumanian fascism had a different character and a different fate.

4 The limits of fascism

In a very cursory way I will pick out those elements of the political structure of other European states which reduced the appeal of fascism.

In Britain there was no pressure due to defeat in war or to great humiliation or disappointment at the terms of victory. The electorate was considerably expanded in 1918 with universal manhood suffrage and the extension of the vote to many women. But parties had already developed with organisations for mobilising mass electorates and appealing to voters as a potential government. There was a necessary transition for Labour to make in this area, and it took a decade really to establish itself as such a party – but in the form of competition with the Liberals rather than seeking voters without any political traditions. For complex reasons which cannot be considered here Marxism had made little impact on the pre-war Labour Party. Labour managed to avoid a really serious split over the issue of war. Some of its leaders opposed entry into the war, but not radically, and so kept anti-war elements together in the party. Other leaders partici-pated in the coalition government formed from 1916, and so maintained Labour's claim to be potentially a party of government. The party also did not suffer any major internal division over the return to peacetime govern-ment. Its moderate elements were not called upon to play a part in immediate post-war government: a victorious Lloyd George could ensure that. Its more radical elements were not faced with the dangers and temptations of an immediate post-war crisis which could have pulled them out of the party. In Germany, Italy and France divisions of this sort led to the permanent split between communist and social democratic parties. This both made the left seem particularly threatening, and weakened it either as a revolutionary force or as a potential party of government within the parliamentary system. The Labour Party did not face this problem and, despite claims by its conservative opponents, could not become a plausible source of extreme left-wing projects. Hence non-working-class groups felt no attraction to a radical right-wing opposition to Labour. In turn, this was closely linked to the capacity of a popular conservative party to hold together right and centre groups within itself. Consequently, even in periods of serious depression, the lack of a threat from the left and the maintenance of electoral support by the Conservative Party (and, to a lesser extent, the Liberal Party) meant that there was no great political problem of the sort which fascism claimed to be able to solve.

It is typical, therefore, that British fascism developed as a response to economic rather than political crisis. For Mosley fascism was a way of pursuing a new, radical economic policy. But people did not vote for fascists because of their economic policies: they voted for them because there seemed no alternative if political order was to be maintained. Once he had realised that people vote for parties rather than policies (a typical mistake for the intellectual in politics to make) Mosley tried to project a distinct political image. But he failed, not so much because it was imitative and took up themes foreign to British politics, as because the prior failures in the political system needed to make this image appear relevant did not take place.

The French case is somewhat different. There was a strong communist party. During the 1930s, in the wake of a depression which came rather later to France than other countries, there was a process of polarisation. There was disappointment about the outcome of the war, above all a deep fear of Germany and a feeling that the powerful allies of wartime were not providing enough support. A sense of crisis, both internal and external, was strong. In the early 1930s it led to the formation of a variety of fascist organisations with a mass basis. The conditions for a fairly powerful fascist movement existed, as the threat from the left appeared dangerous, as parliament failed to achieve stable majorities and governments, and as it was clear that conservative elites had very limited power.

But there were important limitations, above all in terms of the threat from the left and the decline of parliamentary authority. A system of parliamentary democracy had existed since 1870. Parties with well defined images and bases of support had developed by 1914 and continued to operate after 1918. Voting patterns, as in Britain, did not change dramatically. Rather it was slight shifts in the patterns, expressed through a modified system of proportional representation, that produced different parliamentary complexions. In turn it was different circumstances that led to different coalitions forming governments. Much of the changeability of French government reflected not a volatile electorate or great fluctuations in party strengths but rather parliamentary manoeuvre. This helps explain why in many areas of policy – for example, finance and defence – various governments pursued quite consistent policies. Partly it was also because much continuity was provided by a powerful central administration. Fi-

307

nally it was because the parties of the centre, above all the misleadingly named Radicals, were a constant element in numerous governments. At the same time, parties of the right were not without influence, particularly during the 1920s, and this committed them to parliament. In the 1920s the Communist Party was weak and could not deflect the pro--parliamentary course steered by the socialists. By the time the Communist Party had recovered some of its immediate post-war strength, in the early 1930s, it was concerned to co-operate with socialists and others against the extreme right. This was a policy the Communist International turned to after recognising the folly of its stance in the last years of the Weimar Republic when it had underestimated fascism as the last gasp of capitalism and had continued to oppose common action amongst anti-fascists. It meant that at the time of greatest crisis, in 1936, the Communist Party lent its support to a Popular Front government. In all these ways parliamentary authority was maintained and the fascist alternative, although powerful, was never able to present itself as a necessary means of maintaining order. On the other hand, the strength of anti-parliamentary and anti-left sentiment amongst conservative elites which could not directly secure authority is revealed by the character of the Vichy regime. There were many who could and did introduce fascist values and methods into government. However, indigenous fascism lacked the strength to take power without external interference.

In Spain the response to a political crisis involving the failure of a parliamentary system to cope with mass mobilisation was civil war, leading to the installation of a military dictatorship. The very fact of civil war tends to render fascism redundant, because fascism offers a political solution to crisis. When it appeared that such a political solution was needed fascism did acquire some popular support and financial backing from business. But in the elections of 1936 the Falange took only 0.4 per cent of the vote.

Part of the reason for this failure was the extreme regionalism which existed in Spain. Generally it meant that there was no nationally mobilised population either on the left or on the right. In many cases where local elite control broke down voters turned to left-wing parties. In other cases traditional forces – the clergy, large landowners, administrative officials continued to dominate. In electoral terms right-wing politics became a confusion of local groups with some loose co-ordination from larger groups attached to the church, business or land. But it hardly provided a nationally available mass electorate which needed redirection by a fascist movement. At the same time, this sort of regionalism provided the conditions for civil war which were hardly possible in a more integrated economy and society such as existed in Germany. The contending forces in a civil war need clear regional bases from which to operate.

Civil war in turn meant that, on the anti-republican side, power came increasingly to rest with the army and with Franco, just as the Communist

Party – best organised and with access to Soviet aid – came to pre-eminence on the republican side. Certainly Franco needed political instruments and fascism had its attractions. But it was Franco's instrument and only one of a number. More important was support from the church, from Carlism, and from a whole range of less formal local right-wing groupings. After the war Franco used the Falange to help him govern. But his was not a fascist regime with the ceremonies of mass involvement. Rather he ruled in a simple authoritarian way with the aid, after 1945, of considerable economic growth which blunted discontent with the regime. Unrepentant fascists were to argue, with some plausibility, that such a regime had no popular principle to underpin it and this would turn it into a personal style of government which could not survive Franco, especially if the economy ran into difficulties. The return to monarchy and, through constitutionalism to parliamentary democracy, was proof of the lack of hold of any distinctively fascist style of control or principle of légitimacy. Whether fascism could, either generally or in the particular Spanish case, provide such an impersonal and enduring principle is debatable: no fascist regime has outlived its founding leader.

In east European countries generally, excluding the Soviet Union, traditional authoritarian politics, now with a parliamentary veneer, operated fairly effectively. Rumania was distinctive in being faced with the problem of bringing together two such different societies as the Regat and Transylvania, particularly when one adds to that the manner in which post-war policies eliminated the bulwark of conservative authority in Transylvania, the local land-owning class. The consequent vacuum, which popular parties such as the NPP could not adequately fill, provided a particularly promising entry point for fascism. There were fascist movements in other east European countries but they were never able to become so significant *vis-à-vis* traditional conservative elites as in Rumania.

5 The role of ideology

So far I have stressed a particular weakness of the states to which it was opposed in accounting for the significance of fascism. To this could be raised the objection that fascism has to be understood in terms of class or of a response to particular economic crises or in relation to its positive ideological appeal.

There is no doubt that fascism became significant at times of economic crisis. However, such crises were not peculiar to the countries in which fascism became significant. Economic problems can create political crises but the type of crisis they precipitate and the means available for resolving them vary according to the nature of the political system. This is what I have been concerned with.

Considerations of the class base of fascism have been bedevilled by the question of what 'class base' means. In terms of activist support it is reasonable to argue that fascism draws upon lower middle-class groups, although only upon small minorities within them. In terms of more passive support the term 'lower middle-class' only makes sense if taken to cover every large social group apart from unionised industrial workers. And even then important exceptions, such as south German Catholic peasants, have to be made. It is because fascism offers a solution to a generalised political crisis that it can mobilise temporary support from a very wide range of social groups.[15] Again, the reasons it appears as a solution have to be found in the failings of the existing political system.

One could argue, however, that an important weakness is the lack of commitment to parliamentary democracy, and this can be seen as an ideological weakness. Its mirror image could be regarded as a certain predisposition to fascist ideology. If this is accepted, then a great deal of the explanation of fascism's significance will need to focus on its ideological origins and those qualities in a society which particularly predispose it to an acceptance of fascist ideology. There are numerous studies of the intellectual roots of modern anti-semitism, racism, anti-rationalism and the other assorted creeds which find some sort of resting place in the fascist melting pot. There are studies which emphasise longstanding weaknesses in Italian or German politics or which point to particular cultural or personality types which require or yearn for authority rather than participation. These are taken to weaken the hold of parliamentary democracy.

Such approaches can come perilously close to a nationalist and irrationalist view of history which almost concedes certain fascist principles. At its crudest one can argue that the British, the French or the Americans have democratic cultures and/or personalities whereas Italians, Germans and Rumanians have authoritarian ones. But cultures and personalities are complex and variable, their connections with politics difficult if not impossible to pinpoint. The great weakness of many studies is that in the face of such difficulties they resort to circular arguments. Thus we are asked to accept that any society which accepts fascism is automatically pervaded by authoritarian values and attitudes. One can then raid the historical larder for titbits which support this point of view. If the selective process continues long enough, as it has done in certain sorts of German historical writing, quite a dense and compelling picture can emerge. But it is difficult to know how representative such history is or how it can be connected with the actual choices made in the 1920s and early 1930s that led to the fascist takeover. It is as easy to construct a history of authoritarianism in British history or of democratic and liberal movements in German history. Closer to the actual subject of facsism, the few serious attempts at an empirical investigation of the impact of fascist ideology and the reasons for its appeal make one even more suspicious of general interpretations which stress ideology and its relationship to particular patterns of culture or personality. The core of an objection to this approach is that it confuses conditions for the existence of fascism with conditions for fascism becoming politically significant.

One must begin by drawing a distinction between activists and passive supporters. Naturally this is not a hard-and-fast distinction but rather a continuum. But it seems obvious that someone whose involvement in fascism consisted of a single vote for the Nazis in 1932 has to be seen in a different light from a person who was a member of the party for years. It would seem reasonable to assume that fascist ideology would be more important the more involved anyone was in the movement. The more passive the support, one would imagine, the vaguer, weaker and more general would be the appreciation of and concern with fascist ideas. Thus for example, 'support' for the Nazis could range from full-blooded commitment to the need for a pure Volk, the smashing of the Jewish conspiracy and the assertion of the interests of the German race against all its enemies to a vague feeling that what the country needed was strong government and that it was most likely to come from Hitler and his party. One could hardly link the latter point of view to some specific sort of culture or personality or political attitude. It is 'ideological' only in that it accepts the fascist view of Weimar as a weak and failing system to which the fascists offer the only dynamic alternative. But little can be said beyond that. Further analysis would need to concentrate on the problems which stimulated this indictment of Weimar and the failure of other alternatives.

But perhaps this is to underplay the importance of ideology. It may be that fascist ideology does in fact play a more specific role than has been suggested even for fairly passive supporters. And without the commitment of a core of activists which sustained fascism when it was only a peripheral form of politics, it would have never been in a position to offer itself later as an alternative to other types of politics. Here, at the very least, it would seem, ideology must be important. Moreover it would seem likely that hard evidence about the role of ideology might be available for this activist core.

Many studies do not even go this far. They tend to be concerned either with the forerunners of fascist ideology or with leading members of the movement who expressed their ideas in books, newspapers and speeches. But fascist ideology has precursors in a number of countries and uses ideas in too eclectic a fashion for one to be able to focus on any particular line of thought. Again, the views of leading fascists are eclectic and highly variable. Even if others followed them because of the ideas they represented, it still remains to be established which ideas particularly attracted followers.

The most elaborate study of the ideology of rank-and-file activists that I know is by Merkl.[16] It takes autobiographical accounts of 581 members of the Nazi Party written in 1934 in response to an appeal from an American academic, Theodor Abel.[17] Merkl has subjected these ac-

311

counts to an elaborate computer-aided content analysis. I will briefly take up one or two of his findings concerning anti-semitism which relate to the present argument. I cannot do justice here to the complexity revealed by Merkl's work. But from these examples I will make some general suggestions about the place of ideology in explanations of why fascism becomes politically significant.

One should remember that anti-semitism is a major feature of Nazi ideology. It is a constant and obsessive concern in Hitler's own writings and pronouncements. It crops up in the utterances of other leading Nazis. It received official legislative expression in the Third Reich. By a tortuous route it led eventually to the terrible events of the 'Final Solution'. Although anti-semitism is not of major importance in all fascist ideologies, there can be no doubt of its centrality in official Nazi doctrine.

Table 1   Main ideological themes (while in NDSAP)[18]   +

	Number	Percentage
No ideology worth noting	19	2.6
Strong ideological antisemite	63	8.5
Incidental antisemite (e.g. use of verbal stereotypes only)	38	5.1
Nordic cultist	11	1.5
German romantic	21	2.8
Blood and soil	11	1.5
Revanchist, law and order	42	5.7
Super-patriot, nationalist	166	22.5
Social *Volksgemeinschaft* (solidarism)	234	31.7
Hitler cult	134	18.1
* Multiple responses	739*	100.0

The accounts Merkl examines tend to reveal strong prejudices. This is hardly surprising in the membership of an extremist political party. More interesting is the variety of prejudices involved and the forms in which they are expressed. Merkl provides two tables which rather neatly summarise much of this variety. I think two points stand out. The first is that anti-semitism is the major ideological concern of only a small minority. Taken alone, this would not mean very much. Nazis had many prejudices, and other ones might take priority over those held against Jews without this meaning that most Nazis were not strongly anti-semitic. Nevertheless it is interesting to note that the dominant ideological themes for most respondents are either the general and positive ideas about a strong and undivided nation or simple faith in Hitler.

Table 2   Shadings of anti-semitism

	Number	Percentage
No evidence	146	33.3
Mild verbal projections or party clichés	63	14.3
Sudden *Judenkoller* from cultural shock in 1918	84	19.1
Sudden *Judenkoller* from economic or personal crisis	38	8.6
Relates alleged episodes with Jews	43	9.8
Relates episodes with sexual angle	9	2.0
Preoccupied with the 'Jewish conspiracy' (implying counter-threats)	57	12.9
Total	440	100.0

However, the second table shows not merely that anti-semitism is a subordinate concern for most of the respondents but that it is quite unimportant for something like half of them. When this is taken together with the point that the specific and positive features of Nazi ideology (the *völkisch* identity and the related notions about blood, soil and history) are the main ideological concern of only a small minority this provokes the startling thought that half or more of the activists in the Nazi party had no specifically Nazi ideas at all. Closer consideration of anti-semitic prejudice by Merkl revealed other interesting points. By and large, strong anti-semites belonged to the older generation of members, who had reached maturity before 1914. The younger the membership the less strong seemed to be the concern with any specific ideological questions and the greater the concern with more general matters such as national recovery and unity. In part this would seem to be a matter of intellectual context: political anti-semitism received a fairly clear and specialised political expression in Germany before 1914. Partly it seems to reflect different motives for joining the party. The earlier members would probably be nursing some particular prejudice of an ideological kind when they joined, and many such prejudices would have roots in their pre-war experience. Many later members would tend to think in more practical political terms and link the party with problems such as unemployment or division within government, or even with the desire to do something and contribute to creating an alternative to the crisis-ridden present.

Anti-semites occupied a very high proportion of party offices in relation to their numbers in the party as a whole. Partly this was because they were older and/or earlier members. Partly it was because their commitment tended to be to political work rather than to marching or fighting. Partly it was because they were closest in their thinking and in other ways to the central leadership. This would mean that the anti-semitic theme will tend to become stronger the higher up the party one goes. Within the SA (the paramilitary wing of the party, popularly known in English as the Brown Shirts) and the lower ranks a very different picture emerges.

The second major theme of Merkl's findings is why people have the ideas they do. In much of the literature anti-semitism is seen as a way of finding scapegoats for one's problems, and the need for scapegoats is linked in turn to misfortune as well as to certain ways of looking at misfortune. Yet Merkl's work shows the limited validity of such an understanding. The people coming into the party after 1929 would tend to be particularly hard-hit by economic misfortune. Yet it is in this batch of recruits that anti-semitism or any specific ideological theme seems to be of least importance. Of course, that does not explain why those who are strongly anti-semitic are as they are, but it would suggest that the idea that anti-semitism was a useful political weapon in the sudden rise of the party after 1928 is misleading. Indeed, it does appear that Hitler's speeches and Nazi propaganda more generally, under-played anti-semitism in the period of greatest electoral advance. Rather it seems to be the more generalised, 'non-ideological' perception of the Weimar regime as a failure that appears to be most significant and that this was something which Hitler understood and acted upon.

Merkl also goes on to link his findings on ideology with evidence about personality types and patterns of childhood. The evidence is very slight and dubious in quality, and the conclusions that can be drawn are, to say the least, tentative. If that is the case for such a uniquely rich source of evidence one can conclude that psychological theories of fascism will never be more than speculative.

If this movement away from specific ideological themes on the part of younger members is accepted it would also suggest that the process will accelerate when one moves beyond the party to sympathisers and to voters, particularly those who came to sympathise with or vote for the party in the very last years of the Weimar Republic.

There is no doubt that strong ideological themes are prominent among the early membership of fascist movements. One could argue that some societies will possess a larger reservoir of such themes and potential early fascists than others. Undoubtedly the unsettling experience of war, especially when followed by a humiliating defeat or a disappointing victory, created a large pool of ex-soldiers and others who could not adjust to post-war conditions. Immediate post-war crises ruined and embittered many small businessmen. For these people, and for others such as failed professional people, the new democracy could appear as a sham, something to be opposed root and branch. Such people moved into the early fascist movements as well as many other right-wing organisations. They took up a large and varied collection of nostrums and prejudices and built upon ideologies elaborated before 1914. All this was an essential condition for the existence of fascism and, of course, its existence was a necessary condition of its success.

But in the period between its origins and its rise to power fascism does more than simply expand. It changes its political strategy, its organisation, and its membership also changes. It is impossible to consider the first two points – generalisations are hardly possible and all one could do would be to consider each case. But so far as membership goes one can suggest at least four stages in the German case. First, there is the early activist core drawn in by concerns such as anti-semitism. Second, following on the reorganisation of the party and its absorption of a number of other organisations so that it became a national rather than a Bavarian party, it pulled in new types of members with rather different concerns. It was in the mid-1920s, for example, that the preoccupation with some specific form of socialism and attracting working-class support became prominent. Third, with the crisis which began in 1929 people joined the party because of its image of strength and unity as well as because of Hitler himself. This was strongly related to the way Weimar was seen as a weak political system. The forceful leadership role, incidentally, had a lot to do with the increasing size and internal diversity of the party: it was easier to focus on the leader and the party as a dynamic force than upon specific policies or prejudices. Finally, in the period shortly before Hitler became Chancellor and until mass recruitment was halted in May 1933, there was a large influx of people joining for opportunist reasons. Phase one established a cause; phase two, a party capable of bidding for power. But it was phase three which was crucial – and voter support at this stage can be seen as a weakened version of the views of those joining the party at the time.

What was important for these people was that, independently of the impact of fascist propaganda, the existing political system was seen as weak and divided. It was seen thus because, under the pressure of events, parties committed to pluralist or class politics could not command the stable support of a large part of the electorate. However, the electorate was not prepared to accept the reassertion of pre-democratic forms of authority. The central ideas of fascism – of the united, strong, classless and active nation – are a composite negation of these various and discredited types of politics. It is through their failure that fascism becomes attractive. Of course, fascism makes its own contribution to the failure and helps people perceive it in a particular way. But the departure point of analysis must be an independent explanation of that failure. From the point of view of comparative analysis aimed at understanding why fascism becomes

315

significant (as opposed to particular histories of fascism or a theory which also takes its origins and fate into account) such political failures are rooted in certain aspects of the preceding political system. It is upon these aspects that I have concentrated in this chapter. If one accepts that fascism does become significant in political systems which have these sorts of 'defects', then some progress has been made. It hardly amounts to a full explanatory theory. But it does suggest that fascism should be understood primarily as a particular form of nationalist politics and that its significance can be related to particular features of new parliamentary and democratic states.

Notes

1   For some further considerations see above, pp. 56–9.
2   These distinctions are taken from Klaus Epstein, *The Genesis of German Conservatism* (New Jersey, 1966), pp. 3–22.
3   I would stress that this does not mean that I regard the nationalist ideas as the most important aspect of fascist movements. The nationalist idea is used simply as a way of identifying a range of political movements: indeed that seems the only way in which any movement described in terms of an 'ism' can be identified. Without such a procedure it is difficult to see how one can talk of nationalist or socialist or liberal or conservative politics at all. The means of identifying does not carry with it a commitment to a particular theoretical approach or imply that the ideas stand in some causal relationship to the political movement. I agree with those who say it is important not to confuse nationalism defined in terms of ideas, of collective behaviour, or of culture, but would disagree with the claim that my procedure involves such a confusion. I mention this here because such criticisms have been made in Alexander Motyl, *Sovietology, Rationality, Nationality: Coming to Grips with Nationalism in the USSR* (New York, 1990), chapter 3, especially pp. 48–9. This confusion on Motyl's part between criteria of identification, definition of field, and theorical procedures also leads him to support Anthony Smith's proposition that fascism should not be regarded as a form of nationalism. One might as well, Motyl says, regard National Socialism as a form of socialism. Indeed, at the outset there is no reason why one should not. One could begin by using some definite meaning of the term socialism as an identifier, and then seeing if it enabled one, within the field of the National Socialist political movement, to locate an important range of actions which were accompanied by the appeal to socialism. What one would soon discover is that such actions and appeals were of minor significance, that actions based on appeals to anti-socialism were of much greater significance, and that actions based on appeals to nationalism were of overwhelming significance. Given that, what is the use of an approach which separates nationalism from National Socialism? Finally, Motyl has to break his own absurd taboo by constantly using the word nationalist to refer to organisations (that is, a form of

collective behaviour). Indeed, who would be interested in a book on the problems nationalism poses in the former USSR if nationalism referred only to ideas and not to political movements? It is a strange argument in an otherwise cogent analysis of politics which actually rejects behavourialist approaches.

4   See G. Eley, *Reshaping the German Right: Radical Nationalism and Political Change after Bismarck* (2nd ed., Ann Arbor, 1991).

5   The cases of Germany and Italy. The Rumanian Iron Guard did briefly share power with the army in 1940–41.

6   This is taken from Ian Kershaw whose ideas have strongly influenced this whole chapter. See his book *The Nazi Dictatorship: Problems and Perspectives of Interpretation* (2nd. ed. , London, 1989), especially chapter 2, 'The Essence of Nazism: Form of Fascism, Brand of Totalitarianism, or Unique Phenomenon?'. I prefer this definition to that offered by Ernst Nolte, *Three Faces of Fascism* (New York, 1965), pp. 20–1, which overemphasises anti-Marxism and neglects the anti-bourgeois and anti-liberal features of fascism.

7   W. S. Allen, 'The appeal of fascism and the problem of national disintegration', in *Reappraisals of Fascism*, edited by H. A. Turner (New York, 1975), pp. 44–68 (52).

8   Eley, *op. cit.*

9   I develop this argument in detail – comparing Germany with France and Britain – in 'Conclusion: national peculiarities?', in *id. , Labour and liberalism in nineteenth-century Europe* (Manchester, 1992), pp. 273–95.

10   See James Sheehan, *German Liberalism in the Nineteenth Century* (Chicago, 1978), pp. 279–83.

11   For a telling analysis of fascism in the South of Italy see Adrian Lyttleton, *The Seizure of Power: fascim in Italy, 1919–1929* (London, 1973), especially pp. 188–201.

12   For a convenient summary of land redistribution see the table in Joseph Rothschild, *East Central Europe between the Two World Wars* (Washington, 1974), p. 291. Nearly three-quarters of the population were in agriculture (*ibid.*, p. 285).

13   This electoral law was copied from Mussolini's Italy.

14   The term used for Hitler's murder of leaders of the SA and other political opponents on 30 June 1934, partly in order to come to terms with the army, partly to destroy a threat from radical fascists. In the Rumanian case the army acted directly against fascist radicals and the 'realistic' group of fascists was found not within Rumania but in the form of Hitler's support.

15   There has been a sustained debate over the social character of electoral support for Hitler and of the membership of both the National Socialist Party and the SA. This has largely disproved the contention that the movement and its supporters were overwhelmingly lower middle class. From a large literature see summaries of such work in Thomas Childers (ed.), *The formation of the Nazi constituency 1919–1933* (London, 1986); and Detlev Mühlberger, 'Germany', in *idem*, (ed.), *The social basis of European fascist movements* (London, 1987). In the cases of Italy and Rumania there did not develop so massive and organised a popular base

317

before the assumption of power so such a debate is less important or possible, but see Marco Revelli, 'Italy'; and Raphael Vago, 'Eastern Europe', in *ibid.*, pp. 1–39 and 281–319.

16 Peter H. Merkl, *Political Violence under the Swastika: 581 early Nazis* (New Jersey, 1975).

17 Abel then wrote a book based on this material: *Why Hitler Came into Power* (orig. ed., 1938; reissued, Cambridge, Mass., 1986).

18 Merkl, *op. cit p. 453.*

19 *Ibid.*, p. 499.

Separatist nationalism
in the developed nation-states

1 Introduction

In this chapter I wish to look at a number of separatist movements which
have become particularly important since 1945 in states as different as
Canada, France, Spain and the United Kingdom. These movements have
largely arisen in circumstances which one might think would discourage
nationalism. Various theories about political integration suggest that democratic rights, economic development, the creation of a national pattern of
politics based on class or some other non-national principle, and even, to
some degree, a national mass culture, should all cut the ground from
beneath separatist nationalism. From this perspective the resurgence of
separatism in western Europe and America in the last few decades can
appear as a throwback, as something irrational. But to see it thus is rather
like a nationalist understanding of what is happening, only with the reverse
moral judgement. Actually these new nationalist movements are very different from those of the nineteenth century.

In order to bring out the differences I will consider the case of
Scottish nationalism in some detail. Having looked at a variety of possible
explanations which consider the Scottish case alone, I will complete the
examination by comparing it with other Celtic nationalisms in the United
Kingdom. I will then briefly consider a few other cases. There are certain
distinctive features which join these movements together, although only a
very weak general theory seems applicable. Finally I will consider what
implications these cases have for the idea of 'national integration'.

2 The Scottish case

Perhaps the most remarkable feature of Scottish nationalism is its very
recent rise to significance. In the later nineteenth century and up to 1914
there were a variety of Home Rule movements and some small groups of
cultural nationalists. But these were divided from one another, had no

backing from important elites such as businessmen or landowners, and no popular support. Only in the 1920s did some of these groups come together to form a nationalist party which was the direct forerunner of the present Scottish National Party (SNP). Electoral support for the SNP was limited before 1939 and reached its ebb in the 1950s. There was popular support for the 'Covenant' in the late 1940s – a statement in favour of devolution which received over a million signatures – but the Covenant movement was unable to do anything with this support. The SNP remained a small, rather purist party dedicated to independence.

SNP success began in the early 1960s with improved performances in a number of by-elections. The party did reasonably well in the General Election of 1966. In 1967 came the victory in the by-election at Hamilton, and in 1968 considerable gains in municipal elections. The general election of 1970 was disappointing in the light of these trends. However, the great breakthrough came in the two general elections of 1974. In October of that year the SNP returned eleven members to the House of Commons. This representation was fragile given the difficulties faced by third parties under the British electoral system.[1] In the general election of 1979 SNP representation was reduced to two seats. It remained at two seats in the 1983 General Election, but with voters shifting to the Liberals given Labour's disastrous campaign. It increased to three seats in the elections of 1987 and 1992. In 1992 the SNP obtained just over one-fifth of all Scottish votes, recovering somewhat from the setbacks of 1983 and 1987, but still not back to anything like the performances of the 1967–74 period. However, Scottish nationalism certainly cannot be regarded as a spent force. It has a large and vigorous organisation; it is the second party in many constituencies; and it has established a definite image in the minds of many Scottish voters which appears preferable to those associated with the two main parties or other possible third choices.

This sudden emergence has to be measured against the absence not just of any regional party of importance prior to 1960 but of any distinctively Scottish pattern of political behaviour. Hechter has tried to measure such a distinctiveness in all Celtic areas of the United Kingdom.[2] The measure, called 'peripheral sectionalism', is supposed to indicate the divergence between Celtic voting patterns and the overall pattern for the United Kingdom. What the measure shows, in fact, is a steady convergence of Scottish and national voting patterns. Butler and Stokes[3] show that there are regional divergences in voting patterns but that Scotland falls somewhere between Wales (rather more anti-conservative) and the north-west of England (rather less) and about equal to the north-east of England. These measures take into account different social class proportions in the different regions. So one can hardly see support for the SNP as the latest expression of a peculiar set of Scottish political preferences. This has led to interpretations of the SNP's success as something rather superficial and as unrelated to any particularly Scottish problems. Other interpretations which try to identify a distinctive Scottish dimension to the matter have to explain why this has only revealed itself in a distinctive political form in the last twenty years.

One general approach is to see support for the SNP as a protest vote, as the Scottish version of the general decline of the 'class alignment' in voting which has taken place over the last forty years.[4] Gradually the level of support for the two main parties has been dropping: first for the Conservatives as they were in power between 1951 and 1964; later, with the disappointments of the first Wilson government, for the Labour Party. Nationally the proportion of votes cast for the two major parties had declined from almost 100 per cent in 1945 to about 75 per cent in 1974. The downward trend temporarily stopped with the 1979 Conservative victory, where almost 83 per cent of the electorate voted for the two main parties. But the Conservative percentage dropped and the Labour percentage collapsed in 1983 to a combined figure of 70 per cent. There has been some recovery since (1987: 73.8%; 1992: 76.3%) but there appears to be at least one-quarter of those who vote (and well over one-third of the total electorate) who do not support the two major parties. To that one must add voters who are not committed to either of these parties. Thus third parties have a large reservoir of voters they can try to tap.

The argument can be supported by voting statistics for Scotland. In Scotland support for the Conservative Party began to decline in the mid--1960s. Labour was still able to get half the votes cast at the general election of 1964, but its share had slumped to just over one-third by the election of October 1974. Given the dominance of Labour in Scotland, the phasing of the decline of the Conservatives and then Labour would mean that the shift to third parties would occur rapidly after 1964 rather than more steadily over a longer period of time. This would not necessarily indicate that Scottish voters acted differently from voters elsewhere, but simply that more of them were Labour voters than in many other regions.

But the problem then arises as to why the SNP was the major beneficiary. One can hazard guesses as to the reasons for the general decline in the 'class alignment': a new, socially more mobile generation of voters unattached to party traditions; a pragmatic evaluation of government performance, above all in economic management; and the steadily growing gap from the mid-1960s between what people expect of government and what it has been able to do. But Plaid Cymru did not do so well as the SNP, and the Liberal (later Liberal Democrat) Party could offer itself as a much larger, national political force. Why did the SNP in particular benefit from the shift in voting behaviour?

Partly the SNP pitched its appeal at the right level. Whatever its historic concern with Scottish identity and independence, the message it has put before the electorate has stressed bread-and-butter issues. The SNP

321

argues that, no matter what policies British governments pursue, they will not benefit Scotland, because they will not give priority to Scottish interests. Particularly with public awareness of the importance of North Sea oil from about 1970, this argument has had an impact upon the electorate. Since 1979 the argument has been reinforced by the assertion that the British as a whole vote Conservatives into power, though they are but a minority party in Scotland, and that there is no rescue to be had by voting either for a Labour victory or for Liberal Democrat leverage in the event of a hung parliament. It is the image of 'Scotland first', seen in pragmatic terms, that has brought success to the SNP. This does not mean that the electorate votes for SNP policies. Certainly the SNP, anxious to emphasise its practicality, has produced many elaborate policy statements. But support for parties is based on images rather than policies, and the SNP is no exception. Surveys in the 1970s show that voters put little more stress on Scottish independence than they have ever done and that only about half of SNP voters support it, although it is the party's central objective. The surveys also show that there is little knowledge of specific SNP policies and little concern with nationality in cultural terms. It is the image of 'Scotland first' and the view that this approach will help the Scottish economy which has accounted for the popularity of the SNP.[5]

One still has to ask how the SNP was able to convey the right image to a substantial proportion of the electorate. It is not simply a matter of the special advantage of North Sea oil. Only because of a fairly good showing before 1971 was the party in a position to exploit the discovery of oil. But the economic problems and opportunities in Scotland before 1971 seem little different from those of other Celtic regions as well as some English ones. In looking for an explanation peculiar to Scotland there seem to be four broad arguments.

The first confines itself to a study of parties. Regional parties can do better under the British electoral system than a national third party like the Liberals. So the comparison should really be between the SNP and other regional parties – the major ones being Plaid Cymru and Ulster Unionism. Generally one can note that Plaid Cymru has tended to place a strong emphasis on cultural matters and that the Liberal Party has had much stronger roots in Wales than in Scotland. In Ulster the Unionist Party (now in a variety of organisations, but above all the official Ulster Unionist party and the Democratic Unionist Party) has had immense success but its general policy is the very reverse of separatism (although this can be understood as an especially strong form of nationalism). The SNP has a party organisation extending back several decades; good organisers and industrious party workers. It emphasises separateness and it appeals to the electorate on popular issues such as the rate of employment and economic growth. So one could conclude that of all the third parties (excluding for the moment the National Front or any other specifically English nationalist party) the SNP is best equipped to succeed as a separatist nationalist party. Certainly one must not overlook matters such as organisation and electoral strategy.[6] But it is necessary to go further and ask why a regional appeal could register in the first place and why it takes a different form in Scotland from elsewhere.

One explanation of why a regional appeal works would stress the existence of a national identity. The success of the call 'Scotland first' presupposes some shared idea of what Scotland is and that it makes sense to put it first. A party which argued 'Northumbria first' or 'Lancashire first' or even, as has actually happened, 'Cornwall first' would be dismissed as absurd by the relevant voters. One has to ask what is the difference between the meaning of Scotland and the meaning of Cornwall. An answer might be found by trying to establish a Scottish identity in the form of a common culture or a shared set of values on which a political party can build.

At a purely cultural level it is hard to sustain this approach for Scotland. Even if there was such a sense of cultural identity it appears to have had no political relevance until the 1960s and has had only an implicit relevance in SNP propaganda. It is in any case difficult to specify the content of this silent culture. Many cultural features, for example dialect, exist elsewhere, including English regions. Gaelic has played no role in modern Scottish nationalism, where English was established as the principal language through much of the country in the medieval period, unlike the Welsh language in Welsh nationalism. The absence of a powerful cultural nationalist movement since the nineteenth century has meant that there is no distinctively Scottish literature or art. Hugh MacDiarmid stands out as much because of his isolation as because of his ability. Most of the Scottish 'traditions' in which tourists delight are the product of the first 'tourists', English Victorians; they were kept sentimental and harmless and were celebrated only after the societies of the Highlands which inspired them had been safely destroyed. More plausibly Brand has pointed to something of a resurgence of Scottish national consciousness, for example through the folk song revival which both preceded the rise of the SNP and had some political undertones.[7] But at most one can point to some sort of cultural national consciousness of a very weak and vague sort. In so far as there was anything approaching a 'regional culture' it was, as in so many parts of the United Kingdom, as much an affair of class as of nationality. Finally, to all but the convinced nationalist there is something inherently implausible about the maintenance of a cultural identity over a number of generations which works simply by cultural means and has no political expression. The idea that 'culture produces culture' neglects the point that values and identities are preserved only through action. They are not passive attributes which leave no mark on politics, the economy or the social structure but are conveniently available to be rediscovered at the

323

appropriate moment. Yet these ways of bringing cultural nationality into an account of Scottish nationalism seem to involve just such assumptions.

The argument for the preservation of a distinct Scottish identity is on much stronger grounds at the level of institutions. The Union of 1707 preserved the Church of Scotland and a separate legal and educational system. The clerical, legal and teaching professions may have been unionist in politics but they retained a peculiarly Scottish identity. Industrial labour may have committed itself to the British labour movement but there was a Scottish TUC. The Scottish Independent Labour Party was long associated with the Home Rule movement.

To these have been added the recent creation of what Brand has called a Scottish political 'sub-system' within the United Kingdom.[8] Administrative devolution began with the creation of the office of Secretary of State for Scotland in 1885, and its main office was moved from London to Edinburgh in 1939. In 1907 a special committee of the House of Commons, the Scottish Grand Committee, was established to consider purely Scottish legislation. Other committees with similar functions were set up after 1945 and the scope of their activity gradually increased. Scottish MPs accordingly spend a great deal of their time on these committees and act almost as a separate body in the House of Commons. Post-1945 concern with regional planning has also had a specifically Scottish dimension. During the war a section for economic planning had been formed within the Scottish Office. Its role was expanded from the early 1960s when the Macmillan and Wilson governments took up the cause of regional planning. The creation of the Scottish Development Department (1962) and the Scottish Economic Planning Department (1973), both located in the Scottish Office, have meant that a large amount of public expenditure in Scotland is channelled through Scottish institutions. Naturally lobbies in Scotland wishing to influence these expenditure decisions have focused their attention on the Scottish Office. In all these ways the professions, legislators, administrators and pressure groups have come to work within an institutional framework which is specifically Scottish.

What is more, the regional planning approach has bolstered the SNP's claim that the British government has failed Scotland. It began to do so by defining Scotland as a 'problem'. This was the achievement, for example, of the Toothill report of 1961, which analysed Scottish difficulties and recommended the concentration of regional aid on 'growth points' defined in both industrial and locational (the New Towns) terms. This was not a response to Scottish nationalism. Rather Scottish nationalism was a response to these regional aid programmes, which were a failure by their own standards.

This raises another argument employed by the SNP concerning the particular problems of the 'Scottish economy'. In more or less extreme forms Scotland is presented as a colonial economy subject to and exploited by the English.

There is little to be said for this argument. The Highlands were devastated in the eighteenth century by economic change such as the trend towards sheep farming and deer preserves which were accompanied by depopulation and political repression. Here the view of Scotland as a repressed and exploited society has most credibility. But it has little for other parts of the country. From the eighteenth century the Scottish have played more than their part in the construction of an empire and an imperial, British identity.[9] The industrialisation of areas of Scotland in the nineteenth century was part of the general process of industrialisation in the United Kingdom. Most of it was locally capitalised, and it led to the formation of native working and employer classes comparable to other industrial regions. Industrial development was export-oriented, and the slump in exports after 1918 had a crippling effect on an economy in which engineering, shipbuilding and mining were so important and closely integrated. But it was not due to any colonial relationship but simply to the concentration on heavy industry in that period. If Scotland is colonial on these grounds so too are not only industrial Ulster and south Wales but parts of Lancashire and north-east England. Obviously there are important regional differences, even economic inequalities, and even a distortion of policy within the United Kingdom – especially favouring the south-east of England against the rest of the country – but it is not very helpful to place all this within a model of colonialism or underdevelopment.

Precisely because this was a national problem which had a particularly marked impact on the working class in depressed regions the major political response was support for a national Labour Party, not for a regional party. But when, particularly under Wilson in 1964–70, Labour not only defined Scotland as an economic problem but then failed to find a solution, it was not unreasonable for voters to find a regional party response attractive. At the very least the fear this would create among Labour would force it to take more account of Scottish needs. Labour government policy between 1974 and 1979 testified to the accuracy of this view.

An account such as this, beginning with the general decline of the 'class alignment' in voting, moving to the way in which Scotland was institutionally defined, became a political sub-system after 1945, and has remained an unsolved economic problem for both Conservative and Labour governments since 1960, seems to offer a fairly full explanation of how the SNP could quickly become significant.

3 The Scottish case in wider perspective

There is still, however, something missing. The arguments would seem to have some application to Wales and Ulster. Both those areas would appear to have a stronger sense of cultural identity. In the case of Wales there is a language base for national claims and a far more elaborate cultural nationalism. In the case of Ulster there is a popular Protestantism, which also uses the symbolism of 'super-patriotism'. There is a degree of institutional identity. This is weakest in Wales, although the country has enjoyed a degree of administrative devolution there and has its own Secretary of State. It is particularly strong in the case of Ulster, which until recently had its own parliament, with considerable powers, and now has an equally distinctive state structure embodied in direct rule from Westminster. Both countries have poor agricultural regions. Both have areas of heavy industry which have stagnated since 1918 and which seem to have been going into terminal decline since the 1950s. Both have been the object of regional planning exercises which have had as little success as in Scotland.

Yet the political responses of the three regions have been completely different. In Wales cultural nationalism has been much stronger than in Scotland. There has also been a higher level of 'peripheral sectionalism'. Prior to 1960, in terms of cultural distinctiveness and distinctive political behaviour, Wales would appear to have been a better bet for nationalist resurgence than Scotland. But although Plaid Cymru made some advances in the late 1960s, and particularly in the general elections of 1974, it has been much weaker than the SNP. Furthermore the support for even a very modest degree of devolution was very low in the 1978 referendum, whereas the majority of those voting in Scotland were in favour of the more substantial devolution offered them. Ulster is different in another way. While Ulster Unionism was allied to the Conservative Party one could get a superficial impression of both Unionist loyalty and commitment to a national party. But Ulster Unionism is a quite independent movement. It is also a movement based on a communal rather than a class vote: Ulster voting patterns are quite unique in the United Kingdom. It may be fiercely loyalist, but in ways which are peculiar to Ulster.

To some extent the explanation of the differences in the political responses of the three areas is linked to the degree of dependence, economic and political, upon the United Kingdom as a whole. Ulster Unionism, though not part of a broader national pattern of politics, feels extremely dependent both because of its political fear of Irish unity and because of the level of assistance the economy receives from the British government. In the case of Wales there is also a high degree of economic dependence which inhibits independent political action. 'Nationalism' is often a form of leverage which helps maintain such favourable policies from the centre. Such dependence is not so important in the Scottish case. (The much

326

vaunted figures showing that government expenditure in Scotland exceeds revenue, and the special formulae which ensure higher social spending compared to England do not take into account other elements, such as the regional disparity in tax relief to mortgage holders.) But to give substance to this explanation it is necessary briefly to consider the historical conditions of these different sorts of dependence and the types of politics to which they gave rise. On that basis one can go on to consider the importance of new economic developments, of which the discovery of North Sea oil is just one, though very important.

One can begin in a crude way by dividing each region (taking Ireland as a whole) into an area of subsistence, or at least backward, peasant agriculture and an area of heavy industry. Obviously, these areas were formed at different times. What is clear, however, is that only peasant Ireland was able to generate a significant nationalist resistance to the United Kingdom during the nineteenth century. Peasant Wales and Scotland did not respond in the same way, and this has had an enduring impact on subsequent political development. One might argue that the peasant regions of Scotland and Wales were incorporated into a British state before the age of nationalism, whereas a peasant society still existed in nineteenth-century Ireland which could be mobilised in a nationalist resistance. However, throughout this book I have played down the autonomous importance of ideology and stressed instead the political context. There was no reason why a 'national', if not a nationalist, opposition could not have developed earlier than the nineteenth century. A form of national ideology had arisen in England in the mid-seventeenth century (see above, chapter 3), and to a degree it was used to justify harsh measures in Scotland and, above all, Ireland. The universalist and religious language in which the justification was couched is clear from Cromwell's 'Declaration to the People of Ireland' in 1650.

> We come to break the power of a company of lawless rebels, who, having cast off the authority of England, live as enemies of human society . . ..
> We come (by the assistance of God) to hold forth and maintain the lustre and glory of English liberty in a nation where we have an undoubted right to do it;- wherein the people of Ireland . . . may equally participate in all benefits, to use liberty and fortune equally with Englishmen if they keep out of arms.[10]

There seems no reason why, if it had needed to, a resistance could not have found a language itself, embodying images of nationality, liberty and religion. But there was no need. Defence of legitimacy and the Catholic faith provided a sufficient defence. Just as nationality has a subordinate role in Cromwell's 'English' declaration, so did it in the 'Irish' response. Leaders of peasant resistance did not face new problems of political co-ordination or mobilisation with which an appeal to nationality would

help, or a novel political situation which could not be adequately understood by traditional means. There were no important external powers to
whom a language of nationality would appeal.

What mattered is that Scotland and Wales were on the mainland and
Protestant and were integrated – Wales earlier than Scotland – into the
British state. Generally, after the English Civil War, this state evolved in a
way which did not enable one to make sharp distinctions between a public,
increasingly bureaucratic state and society. Rather the centrality of parliament provided a politics with a strong central focus but without apparently
strong, autonomous centralising institutions. This development meant that
oppositional groups did not usually resort to representing themselves as
spokesmen for a culturally distinct nation against an alien state.[11] In the
case of Wales there was, in any case, no distinct set of political interests
which could have opposed the British state. In the case of Scotland the
Union of 1707 was carried through in a way which blunted the possibility
of regional resistance. The preservation of many Scottish institutions and
the collaboration of important Scottish elites ensured peaceful incorporation, although parts of the Highlands could put up some resistance.

So the political incorporation of Wales and Scotland and the destruction of peasant society in those countries avoided nationalism because it
neither took the form of control by an alien, modernising state nor
provoked hostility from a wide range of elites. But the incorporation of
Ireland took a much weaker form and did not encompass the same
destruction of peasant society. Thus a basis for a later peasant nationalist
movement remained. It was not so much because a peasant society had to
wait for the formation of nationalist ideology and leadership but because
by the nineteenth century the type of political control and the type of state
exercising it had changed in ways that made mass politics possible and
effective.

These different legacies were to affect the political responses of the
industrial areas that developed in nineteenth-century Ireland, Scotland and
Wales.

In Wales there was little sense of conflict between the backward,
rural areas and the new industrial districts. Thus it was possible for many
aspects of 'traditional' Welsh culture to be sustained and developed by
intellectuals from the late eighteenth century without any real sense of
political nationalism being involved. This in turn helped to maintain the
Welsh language in the new industrial regions. The foundations of a strong
cultural but weak political nationalism were thus laid down some time ago.
In Scotland there was a somewhat stronger contrast between the two types
of region. Highland resistance to change continued into the eighteenth
century and helped create strong, rather fearful unionist sentiment in the
Lowlands. In consequence 'traditional' Scottish values were taken up in the
nineteenth century in a much more artificial and sentimentalised form than

was the case in Wales. The absence of a strong cultural nationalist movement can, in part, be explained in this way. It had the effect of making nationalism in the twentieth century a more pragmatic movement than its Welsh equivalent.

The sharpest contrast was in Ireland. In Ireland bureacratic and military rule, rather than parliamentary incorporation, was the form British control took. It is interesting that the first authentic 'nationalist' movement, in the late eighteenth century, was led by Protestants seeking to defend and strengthen the power of the autonomous parliament that had been, briefly, created. It also involved using the radical language of the French revolution. This could help co-ordinate some elites and to legitimate the movement in the eyes of the French, although it completely failed to mobilise Catholic popular action. After 1815 the main thrust of the 'national' movement, focused on Catholic groups, was at first in favour of incorporation – Catholic Emancipation, franchise reform. The British state in Ireland continued to display a more militaristic and bureaucratic face, even when (indeed, often especially when) it was promoting social and economic reforms. This reform process did, however, entail the creation of new state institutions which allowed of greater local participation. In Ireland, as in many other colonial states, the nationalist movement developed as much by infiltrating as by resisting these institutions. Irish nationalism can be understood in terms of the model I outlined in chapters 7 to 10, involving local conflicts between collaborators and non-collaborators which take place within a modernising set of political institutions and in which the nationalist movement increasingly co-ordinates local political responses.[12] Unionism was as much a negative response to this Irish nationalism as a positive commitment. It was a movement not only of land-owning and business elites but a genuinely popular communal movement.[13] Hence it can be seen as a form of nationalism although expressed as loyalism.[14] In the cases of Wales and Scotland unionism in the more developed areas simply provided the basis for steady integration into a national, class-based system of politics, rather than rejecting the emerging national pattern.

One can see how, in the cases of Wales and Scotland, the two sorts of society I have rather simplistically described could not, separately or together, generate a politically significant separatist nationalism. The peasant regions were incorporated politically before modern state structures began to develop; the industrial regions led the way in supporting modern forms of integration. Yet if a nationalist movement could emerge it could draw upon support from both these regions under certain conditions. In the case of Scotland, the Highlands need much regional aid and can furnish the SNP with some of its most telling points about Scotland's heritage and the destructive effects of English imperialism. Traditional industrial regions provide the mass electorate facing serious economic problems which the

SNP knows it must win over from Labour if it is to control Scotland. But by themselves these different regions could not give the SNP the initial boost it required: the first was too weak, the second too integrated. This suggests that we look for what one might call the 'third' Scotland.

Here is Hanham's description of Hamilton, scene of the first great SNP triumph in the by-election of 1967:

> By the time of the by-election all mining had ceased. The town of Hamilton was being modernised. There was a regular electric train service to Glasgow, and since the by-election a fast new road link with Glasgow and other neighbouring towns. Hamilton is being slowly sucked into the new industrial system of greater Glasgow. Meanwhile it is an area which is visibly in course of transition from the nineteenth century cottage life of the coalfield to the twentieth century life of the working class suburbia.[15]

Hanham concludes that the decline of the mining communities reduced Labour's political hold. But it is not just decline that is important. Hamilton is a reasonably successful new development. Indeed, the New Towns policy in Scotland has done as well as, if not better, than in England. There was nothing very much to compare with it in Wales or Ulster. The development of parts of eastern Scotland following the discovery of North Sea oil has continued the process of new development and relocation.

This gave rise to new social groups. There are various middle-class groups – managerial and technical – often working for multinational companies.[16] Many of the workers in these new areas are young, geographically mobile, skilled: little like the communities of labour on which the Labour Party has traditionally drawn. They are the classic material for the 'floating voter'; the social ground on which the decline of the class alignment in voting can take place. It was areas with this sort of population that first began to swing to the SNP. By the late 1960s the initial drive of regional policy was failing, and places like Hamilton, with high expectations, were badly affected. The policy of deflation followed by the Wilson government after the devaluation of the pound in 1967 had its worst effects on the outlying regions of the United Kingdom. The degree of external economic control and the feared transience of the oil boom, could increase anxiety and intensify the search for new political solutions. Such people were ready to turn to the SNP if it couched its appeal in the right pragmatic, materialist terms. The discovery of North Sea oil simply made the appeal even more attractive. Once the party began to 'take off' it could begin to penetrate other areas. At one time it seemed that this was happening and that its second stage of support was growing particularly fast in traditional Labour strongholds.[17] But the first, necessary stage of growth was closely connected with the development of a 'third' Scotland.

Such new regions are less important in Wales and Ulster. In the latter political instability has inhibited regional policy searching for new 'growth points'. If anything it is in Eire that new types of industry are developing. In Wales there is less in the way of resources and the temporary revival of coal mining may have acted as a brake on such new developments in any case. In the 1980s, by contrast, regional policy was pursued more effectively here, during Peter Walker's period as Secretary of State, and against the general trend of central government policy, and this could again make clear the dependency of Wales upon the centre. In a way these comparisons restate the point made earlier about differing degrees of external dependence upon the United Kingdom economy as a whole.

To conclude: the absence of any significant nationalism in either rural or traditional industrial Scotland left the arena free for the rise of a new form of nationalism building on the problems of modernising regions in the country. From this base nationalism had a number of elements around which it could crystallise: the strong and increasing institutional identity of Scotland; the definition of Scotland as a problem area; the failure of successive Conservative and Labour governments to solve this self-defined problem. On these elements the existing nationalist party could, by converting its appeal from marginal, traditional nationalism to a pragmatic and materialist programme, achieve a good deal of success. This combination of circumstances was unique to Scotland, and so the degree of success enjoyed by a new separatist nationalist movement has been greater there than any other part of the United Kingdom. It is, however, in its very pragmatism, a politics highly dependent upon its context, and likely to decline if central government policy proves more satisfactory or other opposition parties can argue more persuasively that they have more chance of altering policy in desired ways than does the SNP.

4 Other cases

Making due allowances for their distinctive features, it also appears to be the role of new social groups in economically more advanced areas that are central to the development of French Canadian and Basque nationalism. Basque nationalist ideology was first formulated at the end of the nineteenth century and came after a long history of regionalist resistance. Particularly under Franco, incorporation into the Spanish state had taken a repressive form involving the denial even of any expression of cultural nationality. This was very different from the situation in the United Kingdom and Canada, where separatism developed within democratic political systems which never denied or repressed cultural nationality.

Basque nationalism has developed in an area economically rather more advanced than most of Spain. Whereas earlier forms of resistance, including the first nationalist phase, were linked with peasant and clerical opposition to the central state, from the turn of the century onwards business and labour groups have been prominent. In Quebec nationalism made few inroads among a traditional Catholic farming population prior to 1945. It has been in rapidly growing cities like Toronto that separatism has developed fastest. But generally Quebec is less economically advanced than some of the English-speaking regions. So the precise situation varies between the Scottish, Basque and Quebec cases, although there are broad similarities.

I will consider the Canadian case in just a little more detail so that generalisations are not derived principally from the cases within the United Kingdom. Quebec was rather isolated from Canadian politics up to 1918. The first hints of nationalism came in reaction to the quickening pace of economic development in the province after 1918. This reaction took the form of anti-modernism and had some support from within the Catholic church. A nationalist gloss was put upon it by a few intellectuals. Particularly with the onset of the depression in the early 1930s, this cultural critique of capitalism had a certain appeal. It was enough to tempt the leadership of the Conservative Party, which had been ousted from provincial control by the Liberals, to enter into an alliance with these anti-modernist and social reform elements. In 1936 they formed the Union Nationale under the leadership of the Conservative politician Duplessis. The new party won the election in 1936 and remained in power until 1939. Fear that Duplessis's hard line against conscription would make compromise with the national government difficult brought the Liberal Party back into power in 1939. But this did not last for long. The introduction of conscription during the war hardened anti-British feeling in Quebec and revived Duplessis's popularity. He was returned to power in 1944 and ruled the province in a corrupt and authoritarian style until his death in 1959.

What is particularly significant about this period is that Duplessis completely ignored the nationalist elements in Union Nationale once he was in power. He was an avid defender of provincial rights and favoured the farming interest. He was also sharply opposed to the connection with Great Britain. But this did not amount to nationalism. He never challenged the unity of Canada. He had no objection to extensive foreign investment in Quebec. Indeed, he believed it to be so essential for provincial economic development that he opposed social reform or labour legislation which might discourage it. As a consequence of his pro-farmer and pro-business policies, as well as the corrupt and authoritarian style of his rule, nationalism began to develop in new directions.

Opposition to his style emphasised the need to create a genuinely democratic system in Quebec. For some, such as Pierre Trudeau, this had nothing to do with nationalism (rather the opposite if Duplessis was regarded as a typical product of Québecois culture), but others saw it as an assertion of the French Canadian people against corrupt machine politics. Nationalism began as a reform rather than a separatist movement.

Its opposition to business associated it with demands for social reform and labour legislation, if nothing more radical. It also popularised the idea that Quebec was the victim of foreign, particularly American, capitalism. This in turn led on to the development of the argument that the province was really a colony within Canada and that only through independence could it bring big business under control and protect the environment from reckless destruction. Finally, the expansion of the role of government increased the recruitment of French Canadians into public service. The use of English as the language of government could cause much resentment and further buttress the nationalist argument. The expansion of government also intensified the conflict over the distribution of powers between central and provincial government and the tax and expenditure rights at each of these levels. The nationalist argument offered a convenient solution to such disputes.

For all these reasons the basis of nationalist support was moving towards professional middle-class and new urban working-class groups. However, there were other political options for these groups. The first was a cleaned-up Liberal Party, which challenged successfully for control of the provincial government in 1959. The Liberals took up many of the popular reform demands and included many who later became nationalists. But the party was handicapped both by the general problem of delivering on all its promises and because its simultaneous control of central government inhibited its actions at times of conflict between central and provincial governments.

Other options included the development of a party of labour. But the sheer size, diversity and newness of Canada prevent the development of a national labour party, and this rather undermined the point of any party of labour at all. There was also a Social Credit movement which appealed to some anti-capitalist elements. But with the failure to develop national-level political organisation, and the problems facing Quebec liberals when their own party was in control of the central state, the various reform elements began to move towards a nationalist position. For many of its supporters this has been a new way of pressurising central government rather than an assertion of national identity and a search for independence. But new groups in the most rapidly developing parts of Quebec have particularly felt the need for this new sort of pressure and have thrown their support behind a nationalist movement. What has developed, as in the Basque and Scottish cases, is a rather tough-minded, frequently radical nationalism which is very different from the anti-modernist, rather romantic nationalist movements of 'peripheral' regions in many nineteenth-century European countries.

5 General points

The distinctive element in these new separatist movements is the leading role played by economically more advanced or more rapidly developing regions. These nationalist movements draw not on peasant or traditional working-class support so much as on a managerial, technical and administrative middle class and a mobile, young, often skilled working class. Once these groups have helped a political movement get off the ground other kinds of support can be drawn upon.

This is virtually the only generalisation that can be made about these movements. I have already shown that the political situations are very different – although generally one can say that nationalism has become particularly important after a period of limited reform. In the Canadian case this was the work of the Liberal Party after 1960; in the Scottish case the work of the regional planning policies of the 1960s; in the Basque case limited reform attempts in the last years of Franco but, above all, the reforms and opportunities provided under the new parliamentary regime in Spain. But the character of this reform and the strength and type of state carrying it through are very different in each case. Accordingly the methods used by nationalists also vary greatly: from the terrorist tactics of extreme Basque nationalists to the parliamentary methods of the SNP. The cultural appeals also vary. They are strong in the Basque and French Canadian cases, having a distinct language and regional culture to which they can appeal, but weak in the Scottish case. A few other generalisations which have been applied to this new nationalism also need discounting.

The nationalists' contention that their territory stands in some form of colonial relationship to the central regions of the existing state has already been criticised in the Scottish case. It hardly applies to Quebec. One can argue about excessive economic control from the United States of America, but that is hardly the same as being a colony of other parts of Canada. Nor is there 'fiscal' exploitation. In fact with both Scotland and Quebec there is much to be said in the opposite direction: namely that they both receive more in government expenditure than they pay in taxes, though that is only part of the story.

The contention may be more relevant to the Basque territories, but only because these have been economically more advanced than central Spain and therefore a tempting prospect for fiscal exploitation. There is also the argument that Spanish economic policies favoured other regions and that a separate Basque fiscal and tariff policy would have been of greater benefit to the region. But again, such arguments are not the same as that which insists upon a colonial relationship. Certainly these nationalist movements have little in common, whatever their rhetoric, with the anti-colonial nationalist movements considered in chapters 7 to 10.

Another argument has been that these nationalist movements are a reaction against bureaucratic centralism. Concerns such as 'small is beautiful', and that government should be 'close' to the people, often figure prominently in their rhetoric. Some of the movements, as in Quebec, have also taken up the ecological theme and linked the idea of participatory, small-scale government with a critique of what is seen as the rapacious and careless destruction of the environment and the waste of precious resources typical of large-scale capitalism (and socialism, for that matter). Of course, such concerns do not have to be expressed through nationalism: there are pressure groups and parties in a number of Western states which develop these themes without any question of separatism or regionalism.

The argument seems rather weak applied generally to these new nationalist movements. First, there is a good deal of variation in the degree of 'bureaucratic centralism' encountered. The Canadian constitution allows provincial rights which opinion surveys indicate would more than satisfy most of the Scottish electorate, including something like half the supporters of the SNP. In turn Scotland has enjoyed a degree of administrative and institutional autonomy that would have been unthinkable in Franco's Spain and which will be difficult to achieve in contemporary Spain. If 'bureaucratic centralism' is to be accorded some independent meaning, rather than simply standing for whatever nationalists care to attack, then these variations would indicate that it plays a very different role in these various situations. Second, the perception that government is over-centralised has little, in fact, to do with the degree of centralisation. Opinion surveys show that the majority of Scottish voters do see government as over-centralised but that a much lower proportion of English voters feel this way. Should one draw the conclusion that Scots are more libertarian or more controlled than Englishmen? It would be more sensible to conclude that, because a regionalist party has been able to present itself to the Scottish electorate in a way that is not feasible in English regions, the arguments that party employs, including the one about over-centralisation, are taken up by the electorate to a greater degree. It is acceptance of the 'Scotland first' argument that leads to the view that present government is overcentralised, rather than the other way round.

A third general argument might link the rise of these nationalist movements to the impact of external crises upon the present state. Basque and Catalan nationalism first became important after the Spanish defeat in Cuba, which in turn led to economic and political crisis within Spain. In the British case the loss of empire and the debacle of Suez were soon followed by the rise of new strains within the United Kingdom. One could argue that the loss of prestige and economic advantage in both cases reduced the commitment of peripheral regions to the central state.[18] In specific cases the argument has a good deal in its favour. A root cause of Britain's economic problems has been her inability to adjust to the loss of empire. It is more debatable, however, whether appropriate adjustments

335

require radical policies from the centre or the continued popularity of break-away movements. The very different ways Ulster, Wales and Scotland have responded show that it is a long and complex route from general economic problems, partially due to external crises, to separatist nationalism. Again, it is difficult to relate the fluctuations in the strength of Catalan and Basque nationalism since 1918 to externally caused crises. And the argument as a whole has little relevance at all to the Canadian case.

It is doubtful, therefore, whether any general theory can account for these various new nationalist movements. All one can do is point to the new and distinctive role played in them by particularly advanced regions and groups. These groups can exploit some form of regional identity to put pressure on central government or to seek greater autonomy for their region. Beyond a committed core of activists, therefore, nationalist support is liable to be pragmatic and volatile. It is support from a sophisticated electorate which has other political alternatives available to it and which takes a rather instrumental view of politics. This can give these nationalist movements a particular realism and effectiveness. But at the same time it makes it difficult to predict even whether such movements will last very long, let alone in what direction they will go.

6 The problem of 'national integration'

One negative implication of these new nationalist movements is that various ideas of political integration worked out by political scientists have only limited value. Progress towards integration tends to be identified as progress towards the ideal Western nation-state. Apart from the general question of whether such a model should be used for states elsewhere, these nationalist movements make one wonder whether it is of much use in understanding the politics of Western nation-states. The United Kingdom, for example, measured by indicators such as economic integration, democratic institutions, absence of regionally peculiar political patterns or very distinctive cultural diversity, would appear around 1960 as one of the most 'integrated' of states. Of course, around 1974, when it appeared in great danger of falling apart, one could identify the various strains at work. But that would amount to little more than a description of the political instability of the time. What does not seem possible is to provide measures of cultural diversity or economic inequality or regional political identity which will enable one to predict the occurrence of such strains and conflicts. If the measures associated with the concept of integration have a very low predictive ability, then the concept is of little use as a means of explaining political events. Its only value is as a way of describing certain political patterns.

This limitation can be explored from the opposite direction, that is, by pointing to stable political situations which, on the basis of measures

336

of cultural, economic and political diversity and separateness, would lead to predictions of political instability. As historians and political scientists tend only to notice these sorts of things when they are required to 'explain' such instability, not very much has been written about them. What we need is a 'counter-factual' literature on the concept of integration which would ask why particular areas did not generate separatist politics. This might be useful, for example, with regard to nineteenth-century Germany. To begin with, there were problems of 'political integration' in the new states set up by the Congress of Vienna in 1814–15. Many of these states were virtually new creations, like Baden, and others had to absorb substantial new territories. The two western provinces of Prussia, Westphalia and the Rhineland, for example, were largely new acquisitions physically separated from the rest of Prussia. The Rhineland in particular would seem to present severe problems of political control. It had no earlier contacts with Prussia. Most of its inhabitants were Catholics, whereas most Prussians were Protestants and there was an established Protestant church. The Rhineland had a different legal system, derived from Napoleon, and a different system of local government. It had a more commercial and manufacturing bias to its economy than did the rest of Prussia. The urban bias was further accentuated by a political tradition of city government, both ecclesiastical and secular. As a consequence there was no territorial nobility of importance, and therefore local elite control was quite different from that in the main part of Prussia. Finally there was recent involvement in the Napoleonic system of the Confederation of the Rhine, which left a legacy of much pro-French feeling. On all these measures one would have thought that separatism in the Rhineland would have been very important. Certainly the Prussian government was aware of the dangers. Yet the region did not turn out to be so great a problem. A clash between central government and Catholic Church in the late 1830s could have proved dangerous, but a satisfactory compromise was reached. Business elites could accept Prussia's economic liberalism and the prospect of a close association with the dominant power in Germany. Aristocratic elites received special concessions from the state. Yet one cannot say that the state practised an astute form of political management. In many ways Prussian administration was inept and insensitive, and created a good deal of resentment. All one can conclude is that significant elites in the Rhineland judged that their interests were better served by remaining within the Prussian state than by the high-risk politics of separatism or greater autonomy. This, coupled with the lack of involvement of the bulk of the population in political affairs, at least up to the revolution of 1848, meant that such an elite acceptance of the Prussian connection was decisive.[19]

Similar arguments could, perhaps, be used to explain why regionalism had little political appeal within the Second Empire after 1871. Apart from some agitation among Danes and Hannoverians, only the Polish movement was at all significant. In 1867 Prussian annexations of mainly Protestant regions in north and central Germany was handled in a way which could best bind more modern-minded elites in those states to the new greater Prussia.[20] Of course, the German Second Empire was far from being a unitary nation-state, and the various states continued to enjoy a good deal of autonomy, especially in south Germany. Nevertheless the absence of such regionalist challenges once again suggests that the concept of integration has little explanatory value. This in turn suggests that political conflict cannot be equated in any direct way with matters such as the degree of cultural diversity or economic inequality or regional political distinctiveness. This is just another way of stating an argument that I advanced in the Introduction: namely that there is no valid explanatory theory of nationalism, only a number of ways of describing and comparing various forms nationalist politics have taken in which the structure and policies of the state need to be given the central role.

Notes

1   Although regional parties such as the SNP are less disadvantaged than national parties such as the Liberal Democratic Party.

2   Michael Hechter, *Internal Colonialism: the Celtic fringe in British national development, 1536–1966* (Berkeley, 1975), pp. 215–33.

3   David Butler and Donald Stokes, *Political Change in Britain: the evolution of electoral choice* (London, 1977), pp. 120–54.

4   *Ibid.*, pp. 193–208, where the phrase 'class alignment' is coined. For a more recent study of the issue see Mark Franklin, *The Decline of Class Voting in Britain: Changes in the Basis of Electoral Choice 1964–83* (Oxford, 1985).

5   On these survey findings see Jack Brand, *The National Movement in Scotland* (London, 1978), especially pp. 144–66.

6   *Ibid.*, pp. 265–92, where these matters are given their proper emphasis.

7   *Ibid.*, pp. 106–26.

8   *Ibid.*, pp. 65–7.

9   Linda Colley, *Britons: Forging the Nation 1707–1837* (London, 1992).

10 Oliver Cromwell, *Letters and Speeches*, edited by Thomas Carlyle (London, 1869), vol. 2., p. 117.

11 On the character of the British state see the ingenious arguments in Tom Nairn, *The Break-Up of Britain: crisis and neo-nationalism* (London, 1977), especially pp. 11–91. I cannot agree with his explanations, not least because they involve an ambivalent concept of 'normality' against which British development is measured. But I am in substantial agreement with Nairn's account of the political effects of the way the British state (on the mainland) operated.

12 I cannot follow this up in detail. However, this approach, which involves debunking much of the republican myth-making, can both explain much of Irish nationalism before 1914, the conservative nature of the nationalist

movement once it took power in Eire, and the ambivalences of Eire towards the Ulster question, where nationalism took on completely different forms.

13 See above, pp. 23–35.

14 An analysis of the language of Ulster Unionism shows just how popular it is (in marches, symbols, even graffiti), how distinctive it is from anything on the mainland, and how it has developed in a close, symbiotic relationship to the peculiar and intense form Irish nationalism has assumed in Ulster.

15 H. Hanham, *Scottish Nationalism* (London, 1969). Hamilton has since returned to Labour with large majorities in every subsequent General Election.

16 Anthony D. Smith, *Nationalism in the Twentieth Century* (Oxford, 1979), pp. 150–65, emphasises the role of these groups in separatist nationalist movements in the developed world. Brand, *op. cit.*, p. 76, points to the high degree of external control over the fastest growth areas in the Scottish economy.

17 Hechter, *op. cit.*, p. 308, note 2.

18 Nairn, *op. cit.*, places a great deal of emphasis upon this argument.

19 And even then, in the Prussian Rhineland, the radical movement, though decentralised in local organisation and ability to mobilise, was more concerned with radical rather than separatist goals. The situation was rather different in the Rhineland territories controlled by Hesse-Darmstadt and Bavaria. See now Jonathan Sperber, *Rhineland Radicals: The Democratic Movement and the Revolution of 1848–49* (New Jersey, 1990).

20 I deal with this in greater detail in an essay, 'Sovereignty and boundaries: modern state formation and national identity in Germany', in *National histories and European history*, edited by Mary Fulbrook (London, 1993).

17

Nationalism in contemporary east-central Europe

1 Introductory comments

In this book I have tried to develop a framework for the understanding of modern nationalism. In the first edition I suggested that nationalism as a specific form of politics was largely finished, at least in the more developed world, though a sense of national identity amongst governments and peoples was clearly of major importance.

I did envisage that in some places conditions were such that they might still give rise to a significant politics of nationalism. To quote from the original Conclusion (written in 1981):

> There are still areas of the world where the sort of situation which originally generated nationalism continues to exist. In eastern Europe one could envisage sections of the political community in countries other than the USSR moving towards a nationalist position, though the degree of political control and the need to use other ideological justifications than those of nationalism make it highly unlikely. (382)

I think this could earn some, but not many, marks for prophecy. Yet if the historian cannot be expected to predict any better than anyone else, nevertheless the claim to have developed a general framework for the understanding of nationalism must be extended to east-central Europe now that nationalism has apparently re-emerged so strongly in that region. In this chapter I try to do this.

Events are too recent and confused to be able to offer considered comparative analyses. Instead I will try to pick out certain major patterns of development and link these to the kinds of argument I have advanced throughout this book.

There are a variety of nationalist movements involved in the breakdown of Soviet power and influence from about 1988. There is the unique case of unification nationalism with the joining of the German Democratic Republic to the Federal Republic of Germany. All other cases are really ones of separatist nationalism.

340

However, these various states stood in rather different relationships to the USSR. First, there are the states which were under communist one-party rule and were somewhat distant from USSR control – above all Yugoslavia, but to a degree also Rumania.[1] Second, there are states which were nominally independent of the USSR but which since the end of the Second World War and especially since 1948 had been firmly under Soviet control. These are the German Democratic Republic, Poland, Hungary, Czechoslovakia, and Bulgaria. In terms of legal sovereignty the movements which have ended communist rule in these countries should be described as reform rather than separatist, but of course they involve both internal transformation and the removal of USSR control. Third, there are those parts of the USSR which were only incorporated into the state after the Second World War – above all the Baltic states of Latvia, Lithuania and Estonia. Fourth, there were those non-Russian parts of the USSR which were incorporated into the state by 1922 following the revolution and subsequent civil war, although the USSR did temporarily lose control of some of those areas between 1941 and 1945. Within those territories I would further distinguish between areas which had official status as national republics within the USSR, such as the Ukraine and Georgia, and areas which were not so distinguished. There were only fifteen republics within the USSR; but the 1989 census officially recognised more than one hundred nationalities and other sources multiply this estimate by as much as eight times.[2]

It is essential to make these distinctions. Much of the contemporary media coverage of developments within the former USSR and its east-central European sphere of influence makes a number of misleading assumptions about what is happening. Before considering developments in a little more detail it is essential to identify and challenge these assumptions.

The first is that the degree and type of subjection within the USSR and its bloc was essentially the same everywhere. The distinctions I have made already indicate that this is not the case. The more independent communist states of Yugoslavia and Rumania, for example, were left comparatively free to elaborate national identities and ideologies of their own, although these in turn took very different forms. In Yugoslavia there was an attempt to construct some kind of supra-ethnic patriotism and delicate balancing of different ethnic interests. In Rumania there was often the exploitation of ethnic Rumanian sentiments directed, for example, against the Hungarian minority. Again, in Poland one finds the communist regime in the 1950s seeking to foment anti-semitic sentiments. At the same time, the ethnic and religious homogeneity of the Polish population both reduced the appeal to ethnic ties in times of crisis and has meant that the Catholic church has had a very powerful, if only implicitly recognised, position within the country.

Again in parts of the USSR with official republican status a degree

341

of cultural autonomy has often been permitted (though this has fluctuated) even if central political control through the Communist Party of the Soviet Union (CPSU) and central economic control through the major planning ministries was retained.[3] However, whenever the stress on cultural autonomy was perceived as a threat to political or economic control, or to the position of ethnic Russians who had settled in very large numbers in some other republics, this was repressed. On the other hand there are regions with, at least, a potential national identity (above all in Soviet Asia) which were not reflected in the republican structure. The USSR was prepared to recognised ethnic variety and even national republics, which theoretically had the right to secede, but with its slogan 'national in form – socialist in content' it sought to divest such recognition of any political significance.

Given, therefore, the different relationships between state and nationality in these various situations, one should expect nationalism to develop in rather different ways.

A second issue is how we understand the epoch of the Soviet Union and its relationship to the development of national identity and subsequent nationalist movements. There are two related dangers to avoid.

The first is to see the history of the USSR in wholly negative terms. The 'triumph of the west' – meaning above all the free market economy and the liberal democratic state – is in danger of uncritical acclamation. We already encounter arguments that only this western combination of economic and political arrangements can both produce efficient economies and satisfy the demand for a degree of autonomy for individuals.[4] The converse of this is that the USSR with its command economy and one-party dictatorship could not provide economic and political goods. Yet clearly the USSR did, in fact, carry through a major task of modernisation. Only during the period of the USSR was an industrial society and mass literacy created in eastern Europe. One might seek to argue that this would have happened anyway, and even more effectively without the revolution of 1917, but that is necessarily speculation and cannot, in any case, deny what actually did happen. Furthermore, the USSR had to bring about recovery from the massive losses of two world wars. Despite this, by the 1970s she had apparently succeeded in achieving industrial transformation, high economic growth, and super-power parity with the USA, something which in itself demanded great technological sophistication. Only with economic faltering from the 1970s and under the enormous pressure of external rivalry with the USA, especially in the field of nuclear weapons innovation, were there set in train the events which led to the collapse of the USSR by the end of 1991.

This negative picture of the USSR also has implications for our understanding of nationalism. Much of the present coverage of nationalism treats it as 'natural' even if irrational. Indeed, its 'naturalness' is sometimes taken to be the main way of explaining its irrationality: people so 'naturally' take up a national identity that they will do so even if this appears to threaten economic stability and growth and to bring grave political and military dangers in its wake. There is an image of the USSR as a kind of deep-freeze which succeeded in suppressing national identity and conflicts between nationalities. Now the freezer has broken down, the constituent nationalities which had lived on in suspended animation can emerge from the subsequent thaw to claim their birthrights. The optimist will think that this may produce some regrettable chaos and violence but will eventually lead to a Europe of nation-states, in which the western European model is generalised to the rest of the continent. The pessimist will think that the sheer number and territorial mixing of nationalities in east-central Europe produces the ingredients for endemic struggle and instability which only imposed supra-national arrangements can avoid. Nevertheless, both assume nationality, the nation-state, and nationalist conflicts as natural and indeed dominating developments in the whole region.

Yet such assumptions are highly misleading. I have argued throughout this book that nationality is a modern construct and that it acquires political significance only under certain conditions. Furthermore, not all the claimed members of the 'nation' are adherents to the nationalist cause (either because they deny membership of the nation or because they do not regard national self-determination as the highest priority). Why that minority who take up the nationalist cause come to political prominence is something requiring careful explanation. Specialists in each particular case are well aware of these problems, but it is essential to place these specialised interepretations within a general framework.

Clearly in one brief chapter I cannot begin to consider the complex story which led to the collapse of communist power in the eastern bloc states in 1989/90 and the collapse of the USSR in 1991, the role of nationalism in those collapses, and the character of nationalism in the new Europe. All I can do is sketch out what seem to be the major features of the story. I will begin by considering the changes within the USSR which created the conditions for state collapse. Then I will consider the role of nationalism within the USSR. Then I will consider the role of nationalism in the eastern bloc countries. I will focus especially on the two states where nationalism has been associated with boundary changes – Germany and Yugoslavia. On that basis I will try to draw some general conclusions and to relate this to the arguments advanced throughout this book.

2 Nationalism and the collapse of the USSR

At the heart of the process which led to collapse was the inadequate economic performance of the USSR. When Gorbachev came to power in 1985 his central concern was not with political reform, the national

343

question, or foreign policy; rather it was with the slow-down in economic growth which had become evident since the 1970s. From the concern to tackle this economic problem there flowed domestic political reforms and changes in foreign policy which came increasingly to take his attention in 1987–88. However, this reform process did not produce economic improvement. Indeed, in the short term at least it had the opposite effect. Furthermore, one consequence of political reform was to unleash a range of forces which had different objectives from Gorbachev and the reformers around him. Attempts to undercut the politico-administrative class which blocked reforms had the effect of giving more power to the national republican institutions. This, coupled with the increasing mobilisation of popular political forces, led to demands for national independence in most of those republics. Those demands, in the context of splits within the regime about whether to halt the reform process as well as popular discontent due to economic crisis led to a major political crisis in August 1991. The failure of the coup in that month quickly led on to the collapse of the USSR. In this process 'nationalism' must be seen as a logical political response to the unravelling of Soviet state power, rather than a 'natural' identity which was chosen by large numbers of people as soon as political controls were relaxed. What is more, there are some instructive differences in the character of 'nationalism' in different parts of the USSR.

This seems to me to be the general pattern of events between 1985 and 1992. It now remains to put a little flesh on the bones of this argument.

By the time Brezhnev died in November 1982 it was clear that there was a lot wrong with the Soviet economy. Official Soviet figures point to the slowest growth rates in peacetime in the late seventies and early eighties, and some Western analysts consider the reality was zero or even negative growth. At the same time the USSR was in serious difficulties in the field of international relations. The USA and her allies had recently installed new nuclear weapons in Europe and Reagan had embarked on the 'Star Wars' initiative which raised deep fears in the USSR. Indeed, for some of Reagan's advisers, one purpose of this technological innovation was to put ever greater pressure on the Soviet economy.

Neither Andropov nor Chernenko were in power for sufficient time to impose any new policy and matters drifted until Gorbachev took power in 1985. His first concerns were with economic reforms of a fairly limited nature. The economic structures were deemed to be too rigid and corrupt. Anti-corruption drives (which had the added advantage of sweeping away many Brezhnev protégés) were one early feature of his policies. Another was the attempt to make economic enterprises more flexible and accountable as embodied in the Law on the State Enterprise (Association) which was published in draft in February 1987 and the measures to increase the role of private co-operative production.

It is quite clear that these measures failed for two basic reasons. First, they did not go far enough. So long as prices were fixed by command and major investment decisions were made centrally, it simply was not possible to generate flexible and accountable systems of production. Co-operatives in part simply became a legitimate version of the black economy, charging high prices for goods which could not be obtained through the state sector. The second major reason for failure was that reforms threatened the position of many entrenched interests – that bloated administrative elite which ran the central ministries, the state enterprises, the huge defence complex and much else. Attempts to reform agriculture towards smaller, more accountable units, for example, ran up against local political elite resistance. Attempts to promote a more rapid growth of private co-operatives encountered resistance from those running state enterprises who felt threatened.

It became clear, therefore, that to achieve economic reform it was necessary to undertake major political reform. Gorbachev and his allies soon moved down this road. There were a number of options they could pursue. The first was to try to replace leaders. Gorbachev sought to put his own men into key positions in the central and republic state apparatuses and in the party leadership. However, those leaders were often only effective by virtue of their networks of clients extending downward into the lower ranks of the administrative class.

The second strategy was to attack this class from below. Gorbachev tried a number of tacks. A more open media – *glasnost* – would expose many functionaries to criticisms and put pressure on them to mend their ways. Attempts to introduce elements of the 'rule of law' would establish a more independent and trustworthy judiciary to which people could turn and which could then correct maladministration. Above all, one could try to purge and limit this administrative class. One method was to try to separate governmental and party activity. Another was to introduce contested elections to both parliamentary bodies (the Soviets from local up to central level) and parties. The idea of having more candidates than there were offices was haltingly introduced, although this was constrained by the role of organisations (including the Communist Party) in nominating candidates and the retention of the one-party system. Gradually there did develop 'platforms' so that voters could choose not just individual candidates but could see those candidates as representing organised points of view, but this was slow because at first such platforms were not permitted, and people tended only to group together *after* they had been brought together in parliaments. In any case, the point of the exercise was not to introduce a multi-party system but rather to cleanse and improve the quality of the administrative class.

These measures of political and institutional reform proceeded with a lot more effect than economic reforms which remained either a dead letter or even tended to have a negative effect on economic activity. By 1988 there were contested elections locally and by 1989–90 this had led on to contested elections to the central parliament, the Congress of People's Deputies, and to national parliaments.

At the same time Gorbachev sought to reduce the pressure on the economy of excessive defence expenditure. His well publicised visits abroad, his four summit meetings with Reagan, and the arms reduction agreements that were concluded, as well as his withdrawal of Soviet troops from Afghanistan all helped make him the most popular Soviet leader ever in western public opinion. *Glasnost* and political discussion in the USSR enabled him to release many dissidents.

However, there were three major problems with this reform programme. The first was that the economy actually got worse. This led many to demand more radical reforms, either in terms of a swift move towards free market economics or in terms of a radical attack upon the bloated administrative elite that seemed responsible for all the shortcomings of the system. The second was that the political reforms and the threatened economic reforms produced a backlash amongst many of the administrative class – indeed, some reformers put economic decline down to sabotage on the part of that class rather than either to misconceived reform or temporary upheaval produced by reform.

But from the point of view of nationalism in the USSR it was the third problem that was most important. This was that economic decentralisation and the introduction of some limited political competition and freedom of expression and organisation unleashed a huge range of social and political forces. Gorbachev had hoped that these forces would support his reform programme, but many of those involved had other concerns.

To understand how this could lead to nationalism we need to understand the nature of the state system that Gorbachev was seeking to reform.[5] This was a state which allowed very little political or economic autonomy. The party effectively monopolised political power. Although a Soviet rather than a Russian institution, the fact that the party had a branch for every republic *except* Russia, indicates the way in which Russian and Soviet control tended to fuse. Again, the network of central ministries concentrated economic decision making in Moscow.

Yet such a system of concentration, although very effective in preventing challenges, actually was very inefficient. So much information was concentrated centrally that it could not be properly processed and made the basis of rational decision making. This enabled local administrations to build up their own power – often constructing informal coalitions across what were theoretically separate institutions and responsibilities in order to prevent uncomfortable interventions from the centre. Under Brezhnev that had led to the development of virtual mafias in many regions.

What is more, these regionalised power bases had a particular feature. The USSR was a federation of republics. Each republic in theory had the right to secede. Above all, each republic had a 'national' character. The reasons for this go back to the manner in which the USSR was formed and the need to appeal to the principle of national self-determination in the revolutionary and civil war period. Although under Stalin the different national regions were treated with great brutality (e.g., the man-made famine in the Ukraine in the early 1930s; the wholesale deportation after 1945 of ethnic groups alleged to have collaborated with the Germans) yet the principle of national republics was maintained. These republics had a shadowy institutional existence. Soviet policy fluctuated in the three areas of cadre formation, economic and cultural issues, but certainly after Stalin's death there was a loosening up in these various areas. In this way 'nationality', at least for the fourteen 'privileged' non-Russian cultural-language groups with a republic named after them and where most members of that group lived, was built into the political structures of the USSR.

This had fateful consequences for the way in which the reforms of the Gorbachev period developed. Both members of the existing administrative class as well as oppositional elements that could now act more freely tended, outside the Russian republic, to concentrate their attentions on building up the autonomy of their own republican institutions.

Within these various republics the national idea had rather different characteristics. Most of the republics are in the western USSR and are in societies which are economically rather more developed than the USSR as a whole. The Baltic republics were especially advanced in relation to the rest of the USSR. They had their own very recent memories of independence; well-developed literary languages in a highly literate and well educated population; and were very open to the west – watching its television, listening to its radio broadcasts, communicating with a large emigré population, and involved in many economic transactions. Everything – cultural identity, aspirations to greater political freedom, and economic self-interest – meant that the effect of the Gorbachev reforms was the rapid growth of demands for national independence, demands which came under the control of nationalist rather than local communist leadership. The only other republic which moved as rapidly in this way was Armenia, though there the growth of nationalism was accelerated by the irrendentist claim to control over Nagorno-Karabakh, and there is also some evidence that the regime itself in 1988 played a part in mobilising national demonstrations as a way of attacking the entrenched regional administrative class.

The situation was a little different in the western republics which had been incorporated into the USSR since 1922 – above all the Ukraine. For a start, the Ukraine mattered more to the centre. Armenia and the three Baltic republics together have a total population (according to the 1989 census) of a bit more than eleven million, the great majority of whom belong to those nationalities (though about one-third of the population of Estonia and of Latvia are ethnic Russians). The Ukraine, by contrast, has a population of about fifty-two million, about one-fifth of whom are ethnic Russians. Therefore, the amount of control from the centre was always much greater and this inhibited the capacity of oppositional movements to develop.

Second, there was in fact far less in the way of a process of cultural homogeneity and national consciousness in the Ukraine. It is a very large territory. The nationalist movement has historically tended to be strongest in the western parts of the territory.[6] It has also gone through many great changes. When the USSR was founded the Ukraine was a peasant society. What national autonomist movements there had been in the 1917–21 period were crushed and then the area was very forcibly incorporated into a centralised Stalinist system in the 1930s. Negative hatred for this system rather than well-developed national feeling accounts primarily for the widespread acceptance and even collaboration with the Germans after 1941. The guerilla movements of the 1944–46 period were ruthlessly crushed but also the population was offered positive benefits in the rapid modernisation of the 1950s and 1960s. Ukrainian economic growth was more rapid than the USSR or even Russia alone, even if this involved much exploitation from the centre. Literacy rates rose rapidly with industrial-urban development. Cadre policy enabled many Ukrainians to acquire party membership and not merely to rise to the top within the republic but to move on to the central level.

Clearly any sense of Ukrainian national identity must alter greatly during this period of transformation. In a way one could say that it increased – as Ukrainians climbed the 'ethnic ladder' so they came into increasing contact with Russians and, in so far as both ethnic discrimination and the use of Russian as the official language of government disadvantaged native speakers of Ukrainian, so this increased a sense of cultural distinctness. This sense was not repressed any more in the Stalinist manner but rather channelled into political and economic rewards. And at the same time there existed the republican institutions around which that sense of nationality could crystallise.

Again, it required the prior breakdown of Soviet state power before such a sense of nationality could be turned into a political form. When it was, it was not emigrés or former dissenters who played the lead role, but rather national communists. The Ukrainian elite had been so thoroughly incorporated into the Soviet power structure that it was able to exploit the shift of power from centre to republic without having to cede power to other, more oppositional groups.

This pattern developed in a number of other republics. In Georgia, for example, although a dissident was the first elected President, there has been a reversion to national communist leadership with the election of

Eduard Shevardnadze to the presidency in 1992.

In all these cases 'nationalism' becomes the politics of inheritance. Motyl puts it very well:

> . . . Party backing of the opposition elites' demands for language and cultural concessions transformed language and culture from symbols of ethnic identity into potential political and economic resources that could mobilise believers of convenience for the nationalist cause.[7]

In other republics or territories which have not had as much economic development (e.g. the central Asian republics) one does not find this politics of nationalism. Even there, however, local communist elites rapidly realised in 1990–91 that the shrinkage of power at the centre had to be compensated by making greater power claims at the republican level. There was the same 'nationalist' conclusion, but without the developed sense of nationality or popular mobilisation. For example, some of the recent conflicts taking place in newly 'independent' republics of what was Soviet Asia (the inverted commas are there because there is still considerable Russian influence) combine ideological appeals, only more to Islam than nationality, with the extreme factionalisation reminiscent of political conflicts in new states of Africa (see above, chapter 12.) In other cases there were inter-ethnic disputes but these only took on a nationalist form when linked to disputes between increasingly independent republics. By that point it was less ethnic identity that structured conflict as state interests. And indeed, one can envisage a series of republican state conflicts which western observers will term 'nationalist' but which will be no different from any other disputes in the field of international relations.[8]

The major historical question which remains is – why did the centre allow these claims to republican independence? I do not believe that that really can be attributed to the strength of non-Russian nationalist movements. Clearly these did have a good deal of support by 1990–91, especially in the Baltic republics. However, the centre was still prepared to act against Lithuania very effectively when she declared independence, and that caused Estonia and Latvia to move much more cautiously. It may well be that by 1991 the centre had decided to let the Baltic republics go, if only because of the western support they could also tap, but was prepared to hold the bulk of the USSR together. The final collapse came because of conflict at the centre itself – above all the botched coup of August 1991 and the role of popular opposition in Russia, especially in Moscow, symbolised above all in the figure of Boris Yeltsin. Even then, after the August coup had failed, Yeltsin sought to retain some kind of a union for a few months. The problem was that his own political base prevented him using the methods of those he had defeated, and by the end of the year he had been forced to concede the move towards a system of sovereign republics. Once that was conceded, Gorbachev's own position became untenable.

In the Russian case there had been no 'nationalist' objective. The fusion of Russian with Soviet institutions has meant that any sense of Russian superiority has been associated with the maintenance of the USSR, not the creation of an independent Russia. However, once the conclusion was reluctantly drawn that Russia had to move in this direction, this did create the possibility of nationalist politics. There are many points of potential conflict between the different republics. These can have an authentically nationalist rather than inter-state character where republics act on behalf of their fellow nationals in other republics. It is then the combination of enclave resistance and republican interference which fuses inter-ethnic conflict with state power which could have a devastating effect. It is noteworthy that the Russian law of citizenship adopted in November 1991 states that it can be applied to those living outside the Russian republic if they request it. In that lies perhaps the seed of the most dangerous nationalist conflict in the successor states of the USSR.

However, the main point I would make is that one should not see the break-up of the USSR in terms of the rise of nationalist oppositions; rather one should see the rise of nationalist oppositions as a rational response to the breakdown of USSR state power, as the 'politics of inheritance' based upon the republics. It is likely that the major preoccupations of these republics will be precisely those that Gorbachev started with – how to revive the economy. And it may well be that these states will then face many of the same problems that were sparked off by the remedies Gorbachev attempted. Already in elections in Lithuania held in late October 1992 the former communists, now national communists, have secured victory over the nationalists who led the state to independence.

3 The collapse of communist regimes in eastern Europe

When one turns to the nominally independent states of East-Central Europe, the changes which came about in 1989–90 clearly can be termed the 'politics of inheritance'. There was one common thread: the realisation that on this occasion attempts to bring about change within the state would not provoke USSR intervention. Whatever their other differences Stalin, Kruschev and Brezhnev had all regarded this buffer-zone between themselves and the countries of the NATO alliance as an area in which Soviet power must be maintained. Even Yugoslavia and, to a lesser extent, Rumania, which had managed to break away from the most direct forms of Soviet influence, nevertheless maintained a one-party communist government which necessarily isolated them from the west and remained at best neutral if not USSR-oriented in their diplomacy. It is no coincidence, therefore, that the final breakdown of communist power in those two countries also came in 1989–90, just as it did in all the other Warsaw Pact states.

The nature of this breakdown was different in the various states and this is of major importance for both an understanding of their recent histories and also making judgements about their possible developments in the near future. In some cases, such as Poland, there had developed mass movements long before 1989 which challenged communist rule (Solidarity) or had acquired a good deal of autonomy (the Catholic Church). In others there was at least a dissenting movement of some importance which could organise the politics of inheritance – for example, Civic Forum and The Public Against Violence in Czechoslovakia. In yet other countries (Hungary, Bulgaria) it was reformist elements within the ruling party which led the transition. In Rumania it was less-organised popular action which violently overthrew Ceausescu. In Germany the transition basically consisted of a takeover by West Germany. The period of transition was very different. In some cases the communists held on to power for part of the transitional phase, for example in Poland. In some cases, notably Rumania and Bulgaria, ex-communists not just individually, but even organisationally, have managed to retain power following popular multi-party elections. Where organised non-communist action had played a key role in overthrowing the old regime, then in the first phase of multi-party politics at least, it was leaders of these organisations who assumed power. Havel's election to the presidency in Czechoslovakia and Walesa's (though following rather than accompanying communist collapse) to that of Poland are emblematic of the respective roles of dissident intellectuals and a mass trade union movement in the transitions in those two states.

However, most of these issues do not in any direct way raise the question of nationalism. There is no question, of course, that each of these states, leaving aside Yugoslavia, has one (in the case of Czechoslovakia – two) leading nationality and that the demand for the independence of the state is linked to the demand for national autonomy. Only in two cases – East Germany and Yugoslavia – was the issue of changing the boundaries of the existing state of central importance. For the other countries the major issues were state independence within existing boundaries, rather than national self-determination, and then how that state should be organised and what policies it should pursue in the difficult circumstances in which independence was achieved. In other words, despite many variations, the overall pattern was what I have described as the politics of inheritance, in many respects comparable to the pattern for many of the USSR republics.

There are potential problems of nationalism in these various cases. Internally the major problem is that of the relationship between Czechs and Slovaks and it does appear that events are moving towards an amicable divorce. I will not consider that case in any detail, though I will return to it in the concluding part of this chapter.

A second issue – not so much of nationalism proper but rather of

351

national attitudes – concerns the treatment of national minorities. For example, the Hungarian parliament has decided it must give explicit representation in parliament to eight distinct minorities (Croats, Germans, Gypsies, Jews, Romanians, Serbs, Slovaks, and Slovenes). Hungarians in turn look to see how Rumania will treat the Hungarian minority in its state. Clearly here is scope (and this is also an inheritance from the communist period) for populist politicians to scapegoat such minorities, for a politics of ethnic oppression, and for the upsurge of inter-ethnic conflict.

However, this could only lead to nationalism proper in cases where the minority in question could raise powerful demands for either federalist arrangements or, most radically, changes to state boundaries. The only possible case I would identify is that of the Hungarian minority in Transylvania. If the Rumanian government were to abuse the rights of this minority and if a populist government in Hungary were to take up the interests of this minority, then one could envisage a genuinely nationalist conflict developing.

But generally other issues are of far greater importance to the new regimes of these states. In most of these countries there are the problems of emancipating themselves from a legacy of an inefficient command economy and an authoritarian political culture. Generalising very broadly it seems to me that two kinds of political currents have tended to emerge in response to these challenges.[9] On the one hand there is a populist politics, drawing upon working class and to some extent rural support, which stresses the need to safeguard living standards and is wary of radical economic experiments. In some cases, such as Rumania, this kind of politics can be taken up by ex-communists who had played a leading role in the old regime. This politics is often rather anti-western and sometimes echoes national themes such as anti-semitism. On the other hand there is a more western-oriented politics which stresses the rapid transition to a market economy as the only real way to solve economic problems, even if in the short-term this leads to many bankruptcies, a rise in unemployment, and price rises. By and large this politics is taken up by the more advanced urban-industrial areas (Bohemia, the Baltic republics, Slovenia) and the big cities, especially the capital cities. Only in Poland, where a mass democratic culture had already been shaped through Solidarity, was it possible for a government based on mass working class support to pursue this painful policy, although even there it has led to tensions and finally splits within the old Solidarity movement. Generally, one can expect continued economic decline to lead to a repudiation of free market reforms and democratic politics, especially as the latter has often been seen primarily as a means of securing economic growth.[10] Within the possible resurgence of authoritarian as well as populist politics, one can expect a nationalist tone to increase, but not really to provide the principal political objectives.

However, except for the chauvinist tone that is sometimes adopted by the populist orientation, the central issue is not nationalism and the division on how to deal with the issues of economic and political reform goes through the major nationalities in these states. (The one possible exception is Czechoslovakia. Bohemia tends more to the western, marketisation line and Slovakia, a less developed region, is more wary. It may be that it is this tension which gives significance to nationality difference, though recent polls indicate that this difference is more strongly represented in political parties than the population as a whole.)

It was not, therefore, nationalism which played a major role in bringing about change in these states, and nationalism is not at present a major issue in the politics of these states with the exception of Czechoslovakia. However, two states clearly present different problems. In the cases of the German Democratic Republic and Yugoslavia the collapse of communism has also led to changes in state boundaries and the formation (or attempted formation) of new 'nation-states'. The two cases, however, are very different – one is a case of unification nationalism, the other of a number of separatist nationalisms, so I will consider them separately.

4 Nationalism and the reunification of Germany

The most important condition of German reunification was, of course, the collapse of any USSR commitment to defending the communist regime.[11] This was made clear at a Warsaw Pact meeting in July 1989. The reform movement already under way in other east European states was putting pressure on East Germany, and one especially proved fatal. This was the removal of the border controls between Hungary and Austria. This enabled Hungary, a favourite vacation resort for East Germans, to serve as an escape hatch. In addition many east Germans sought refuge in West German missions in Budapest and Prague.

The surge in emigration stimulated opposition groups to come into the open in East Germany and the Leipzig demonstrations, which were to prove so crucial in undermining the authority of the government, started in early September. By early October Gorbachev, in a visit to the country, ironically to celebrate the fortieth anniversary of the regime, had made it clear he supported the removal of Honecker and the shift to a reformist policy. By mid-October Honecker was gone and the attempt to pursue reforms had started. But the flood of emigrants could not be stilled and on 9 November came the historic decision to bring down the Berlin Wall.

By the end of November Chancellor Kohl had moved West German policy from simply welcoming all who left East Germany to a programme designed to bring an end to the division of Germany. Though a dramatic step forward it still envisaged unity as the last stage in a step-by-step process of political and economic reform in East Germany and also more general reform in the European Community and between the two major power blocs.

But change moved even more swiftly in East Germany. By now the demonstrations in Leipzig were calling for unification, with a telling shift from the slogan *'Wir sind das Volk!'* (a demand for democracy) to the slogan *'Wir sind ein Volk!'* (a demand for national unity). The new elections held in East Germany in March 1990 were dominated by West German parties and the East German CDU emerged as the largest party, able to command a majority with other conservative groupings. The new government was committed to unity.

Kohl had soon secured the agreements of the two super-powers and the European Community. The economic collapse of East Germany led by May to a treaty between the two governments on monetary, economic and social union which came into effect in July. Political accession to West Germany was achieved on a *Land* by *Land* basis by means of Article 23 of the Basic Law. In this sense the (restored) constituent parts of East Germany formally asked to be taken into the West German state. Formal unification was established on 3 October 1989. On 2 December Kohl and his partner parties won a decisive victory in the first free all-German election since November 1932.

Was nationalism important in this process? If by nationalism we mean an organised political movement seeking state power on the basis of the national ideal, the simple answer is no. It is quite clear that the West German government only put unification on the political agenda once there was a clear crisis and breakdown in East Germany, and even then saw it as a gradual process. In this sense the government was in line with West German public opinion which in early 1990 continued to express scepticism about the wisdom of rapid unification.

In East Germany both the reformist communists who held power briefly between October 1989 and March 1990 as well as the political opposition, such as New Forum, were equally cool about unification. The communists, of course, stood to lose everything. The political opposition were concerned that East Germans should work out answers to their own problems and not simply hand over the whole issue to West Germany. So by early 1990 there were no important political movements deliberately pursuing unification as a political objective.

In retrospect we can see that four things combined to bring about that rapid unification nevertheless. First, the complete bankruptcy of the East German political and economic system created a dangerous vacuum which compelled West German intervention. Second, once most East Germans felt able to express their views freely, they made it clear that they *did* want to hand over all their problems to West Germany, in the clear belief that West Germany knew how to solve those problems. However, it is clear that much of this should not be seen in terms of a national commitment, but rather that unification was the short-cut uniquely available to East Germans for becoming a western society. (Incidentally, it is worth noting that no 'nation' or 'ethnic group' in 1989–90 opted for separating from a clearly richer country from which they benefitted or for joining a clearly poorer country populated by their 'own' nation. There are clear limits to the national commitment.) Third, this option existed because West Germany had enshrined it in its own constitution. A commitment which had meant something very real in the 1950s had become increasingly unreal by the 1990s, with most West Germans coming to regard East Germany as a foreign country. It was by now a sense of obligation rather than a desire for national unity which prevailed. Finally, Chancellor Kohl came to the view that rapid unification was the only realistic option and one which could prove very popular.

One must also recall the euphoric mood in which unification took place. Once most people decide that something should be done, for whatever reason, they possess a great capacity to deceive themselves as to the objections to that course of action. The earlier views that unification should be gradual and that it would be a burden rather than a pleasure were forgotten in 1990. Kohl pushed through a conversion of the East German mark at a 1:1 exchange rate. In the short term this felt good – east Germans acquired purchasing power and west Germans could sell to them. In the longer term it contributed to the complete collapse of the east German economy and thus a greater burden upon west Germany. When the Social Democrat candidate for the Chancellorship, Oskar Lafontaine, raised sceptical questions about the costs of unification in the election campaign in late 1990, the electorate did not want to know, and the net effect was to lose votes. It is clear then that the 'national idea' mattered enormously in 1989–90, but not in the sense of a clear political commitment to national unity, but rather as a 'passport to the west' on the part of east Germans and a painless honouring of an historical obligation to the less fortunate on the part of the west Germans.

At the time of writing (November 1992) the costs of unification are clearer than the benefits. This is having some complex effects upon the national idea in Germany. First, there are the tensions between former east and west Germans. West Germans feel they are paying too much to help (frequently ungrateful) east Germans; east Germans feel they are being treated as second-class citizens. The problem is not simply an economic one. People have become aware that speaking the same language and sharing the same history does not, of itself, actually create common identity. The two German states developed two completely different economic, political and cultural patterns of life over forty years. That cannot be undone quickly. The tendency to denigrate *everything* that happened in East Germany can only make the situation worse; indeed, one finds some (west) Germans talking of a 'lost generation' of east Germans.

Nationalism, as I have argued throughout this book, has no necessary connection to the processes which do in fact create a sense of belonging together in a state or culture. Therefore, the fact that in a way it makes more sense now to talk of 'two nations, one state' than it did in 1989 to talk of 'one nation, two states' tells us nothing directly about what will happen to the national idea.

At present the signs are that the national idea will intensify, but more as a reaction *against* the failure to achieve a painless unity than as an expression of such unity. Unification is a difficult process but it is rendered more difficult by the economic and political problems of both eastern Europe and the major industrial economies. The former leads many to seek asylum in the west, and this has sparked ugly anti-foreigner actions in Germany. Political parties appear as likely to give way to some demands, such as a change in the Basic Law to the clause on the right of asylum[12], as to resist the mood expressed in such demands. Right-radical groups orchestrate attacks on hostels where foreigners live; many ordinary people approve, to a greater or lesser degree, such action; phrases such as 'Germany for the Germans' become more popular; politicians of established parties spend more time 'understanding' the anxieties which give rise to attacks than condemning the attackers and seeking to arrest and punish them. At other levels some observers claim to see a more assertive mood – for example in the drawing of attention to the crimes of Germany's enemies during the Second World War, with the effect (if not the intention) of relativising the crimes of Germans.[13]

At the same time Germany as a major economic power is bound to influence events more than hitherto. It is difficult to see how Germany can agree, for example, to European Community policies which require her to provide massive subventions to the less developed south European member states, while she moves into recession, has to support the ailing east German regions, and is also concerned about western aid to eastern Europe. Given that she cannot agree, she will have to ensure that policies do not move in that direction. Germany is bound to take more and more of the initiatives towards eastern European states, as already displayed in her successfully pressing the European Community to recognise Slovenian and Croation independence.

Put the two elements together – and one can easily construct a disturbing scenario of the kind expressed, for example, by the British minister Nicholas Ridley in 1990 which led to his resignation from the government.[14] One should note that it is Germans themselves who are particularly apt to construct such scenarios.

Historians are no better at predicting the future than anyone else. I do think, however, these concerns should be put into perspective and also linked to the general arguments I have been putting forward about nationalism. First, neither of these tendencies I have identified can be described as nationalism in the sense defined in this book. The first is the kind of ethnic tension that is commonplace in all countries, especially in periods of economic downturn. German racism is not essentially different from French or British racism; but it attracts more attention both because it is, in post-war terms, more recent and because of the nature of recent German history.

The second is the consequence of power relations. It is not a question of Germany 'wanting' to be more assertive. Political analysts who demonstrate the lack of such ambition and who point to the decentralised and un-coordinated nature of much German policy making can make out a good case;[15] but the tendency for Germany to enforce her policies upon others is as likely, indeed possibly more likely, to occur under such conditions. This is because such assertiveness will take place piecemeal and will be seen in relation to the particular issue involved. Policies will develop out of interests and power relations, and only later might they come to be reflected in a new sense of Germany's need to be more assertive and for her enhanced position to be properly recognised by others.

Finally, the two tendencies have little to do with one another. The internal tensions should lead, if anything, to arguments that Germany should have less to do with the outside world rather than more (though that in fact can lead to assertive policies towards others).

What, indeed, is striking is the lack of pride or pleasure in unification; the swing from excessive optimism in 1989–90 to what I would regard as excessive pessimism now. This is hardly 'nationalism' as the term is commonly employed. Probably the key question does not concern national attitudes but rather whether there will be general economic recovery in the near future for the developed industrial countries. If there is, then many of the problems of unification will be settled, ethnic tensions will decline, and German policies will be more easily reconciled with those of other states. If there is not, then the various problems may intensify and sharpen the uses of the national idea in various conflicts. This will not be peculiar to Germany, although given her economic stature it may have more repercussions than elsewhere.

5 Nationalism and the break-up of Yugoslavia

As I write (November 1992) the former state of Yugoslavia is being torn apart by war in which nationalist concerns are dominant. Why has nationalist conflict come to predominate to this degree? Here, above all, ethnic identity of an enduring kind appears to be at the heart of political and military behaviour.

Yugoslavia covers territory which was controlled by both the Habsburg and Ottoman empires in the nineteenth century. I have already argued that Serbian nationalism was a special amalgam of statehood in the Ottoman territory and a more modernist movement in Habsburg territories

357

(see chapter 5 above). At the same time a variety of other national ideologies and politics were constructed in the southern Slav territories of the Habsburg empire. These varied as different social groups came to predominate (for example in the construction of a Croatian national ideology) and some ideologies, such as Illyrianism and then Yugoslavism (meaning south Slavs as a whole) sought to extend beyond the particular language-cum-confessional divisions within the area.

The situation that had been reached by the time of the collapse of the Habsburg empire at the end of the First World War determined the political character of Yugoslavia – a patchwork of different nationalisms attached to the pre-war state of Serbia. That raised the major problem which has beset Yugoslavia ever since – the relationship between its original Serbian core and the attachment of rather more modernised and westernised cultural groupings from the former Habsburg Empire. Amongst these the Croatians have been the most important because they are the largest grouping after the Serbs.

The inter-ethnic conflict this produced was compounded by the way in which Habsburg settlement policies had also established enclaves of Serbian and Croatian communities on the borderland with the Ottoman empire. As we shall see, these policies were in part continued by Tito and they exacerbated ethnic conflict.

Nevertheless, ethnic conflicts were not the only problems that shaped Yugoslav politics in the inter-war years and they cannot be understood without reference to other problems such as regional disparities in socio-economic development and the impact of the Depression. They were also part and parcel of the general problems of east-central Europe in the inter-war years – of the creation of a number of weak nation-states, each with their own minorities or conflicting ethnic groups, each trying unsuccessfully (with the exception of Czechoslovakia) to operate the democratic political arrangements bequeathed to them by the Versailles settlement, and each having to come to terms with the simultaneous resurgence of German and Soviet power in the area while Britain and France retreated from any commitment to defend the states in-between.

The problem of ethnic conflict was both sharpened but also apparently overcome between 1941 and 1945. Hitler ordered the invasion of Yugoslavia in March 1941 after a Serbian-led coup had overthrown the previous regime which had come to an accommodation with Germany. Yugoslavia was divided into numerous political units – some of which were given over to other states such as Hungary and Italy, some of which were given to marginal indigenous political groups, such as part of Croatia to the Croatian fascist movement. In the mountainous regions of western Serbia and Bosnia there developed resistance movements. One, the Cetnik movement, was primarily a movement of Serbians. The other, led by the Communists, came to embrace a range of ethnic groups and was more extreme in its preparedness to court massive reprisals by the Germans and their local collaborators.

The war, therefore, had two consequences. On the one hand it poisoned ethnic relations even further as Cetniks, Partisans, and the Ustaca (the Croatian fascist movement) fought one another. On the other hand, the Partisan movement laid the basis of a powerful and popular communist movement committed to the Yugoslav ideal which was able to take power after 1945. It is interesting to note that in parts of Croatia and elsewhere in the present war, one can often trace the worst ethnic conflicts back to former Cetnik and Ustaca activity and the areas which are slowest to become ensnared back to Partisan activity.

For some time after 1945 the ethnic question therefore appeared to be of secondary importance. The major questions concerned economic development and the assertion of Yugoslav autonomy against the USSR, carried out under the aegis of a powerful one-party dictatorship which had much popular legitimacy, above all in the figure of Tito.

The ethnic problem reasserted itself through economic and political developments. The experiments in forms of 'self-management' socialism backfired. Problems of regional economic disparity began to emerge. Should one try to develop the areas with the greatest economic potential – generally the already more advanced ex-Habsburg regions of Croatia and Slovenia or should one seek to build up the less developed central and southern areas, that is, areas largely under Serbian control? Immediately issues of regionalism and economic development could present themselves in terms of the interests of different ethnic groups – above all Serbs and Croats.

The other problem – one to which I will return in a more general way at the end of this chapter – is that the highly centralised nature of political control in communist dictatorships actually compounds the existing ethnic dimension to regionalism. It does this in two ways. First, negatively, it is not possible to build up other supra-regional connections outside of the enlarged political apparatus. There are no free trade unions or professional associations or cultural organisations of the kind which develop in pluralist societies. All the cross-cutting connections and conflicts which such developments bring with them can reduce regional-ethnic divisions to just one of many differences. Second, as I have already argued in relation to the USSR, in fact the centre cannot handle all the information and decision-making and *de facto* this leads to the concentration of power into regionalised elites.

This was institutionalised in Yugoslavia through the system of six republics (Slovenia, Croatia, Bosnia-Herzogovina, Serbia, Macedonia, and Montenegro) along with two autonomous provinces (Vojvodina and Kosovo) each with a distinct ethnic character and related policies. Furthermore, after the failures of the 'market-oriented' reforms of the late 1960s and early 1970s, in which the Croatians had taken the lead, Tito's restoration of order included the promulgation of a more federalist constitution (1974). In effect the republics became increasingly the source of real power and many politicians did not bother to vacate power here for the weak central institutions. This meant no strong individual or collective leadership could develop at the central level after Tito's death. Politics increasingly was based on the republics and in the two most powerful republics of Croatia and Serbia this was increasingly an ethnically-based politics.

Consequently, when from 1988 Yugoslavia moved to multi-party politics, the most popular parties 'to emerge were oriented to one or another republic. Slobodan Milosevic had already anticipated this development in 1987 by assuming pre-eminence in the Serbian communist party (or League of Communists as it was properly known) on a clearly nationalist platform which focused above all on asserting Serbian interests in Kosovo. Here, in one of the least developed parts of Yugoslavia, there was a large Albanian majority. Serbian influence had poured much investment into the area, though this declined from the 1960s, and this probably raised Albanian expectations. As these were repressed this led to major disturbances and violence between 1981 and 1983. Repression was justified in Yugoslav, not Serbian terms. Though the effect was to accelerate Serbian emigration from Kosovo, Milosevic insisted now on strengthening administrative-military control but arguing the case in Serbian rather than Yugoslav terms.

The next step was for similar nationally oriented parties to come to power in multi-party elections in other republics. The most significant took place in Croatia in April 1990. Like many other western oriented regions (Slovenia, the Baltic republics, Armenia) national parties such as the Croation Democratic Union led by Franjo Tudjman could also call upon funding and personal support from emigrés. His party won emphatically.

So by the summer of 1990 democratisation had brought to power ethnic nationalist parties and leaders in Serbia and Croatia. If each ethnic group had neatly lived only in its 'own' republic one could envisage this also leading to the 'politics of inheritance'. The problem, however, was more complex than that. First, there are large numbers of Serbians in the crescent-shaped republic of Croatia (it stretches along much of northern and much of south-western Yugoslavia). Second, in the central republic of Bosnia-Herzogovina the largest group (around forty per cent) are Muslims whose own ethnic identity has a much more recent history and a more provisional recognition by the Yugoslav regime, and then around forty per cent Serbians and twenty per cent Croatians. Furthermore, these different groups are not wholly concentrated into one place or another but mixed up – both in the cities, especially Sarajevo the capital, and also in villages – with local settlements sometimes mixed, sometimes with predominantly one or another ethnic character.

360

The root cause of the Yugoslav tragedy is how the move to ethnic nationalist power in Croatia and Serbia interacted with the ethnic enclaves both in those two republics and in Bosnia.

In Croatia and Serbia what was being practised was the politics of inheritance. This did involve ethnic assertion – for example as Croatians displaced Serbians from jobs in the administration in Croatia, and this in turn did lead to inter-ethnic tensions and even conflict. So far this was a pattern of the kind one can find elsewhere, for example in Estonian-Russian relations.

This tipped into nationalism when Serbia and, to a lesser extent, Croatia decided to interfere on behalf of 'their' ethnic group beyond republican boundaries. There were two aspects to this.

First, the failure to build up alternative connections – what I would call 'civil society' – meant that the breakdown of central state power left many enclaves isolated from their region. Especially when there was a history of antagonism with roots in wartime conflict and in great socio-economic disparities (for example, between the Serbs and Montenegrin villagers living inland from the Dalmatian coast and the sophisticated, largely Croatian population inhabiting the coastal towns which attracted a lucrative tourist trade) this could lead rapidly to great anxiety. The Serbian government under Milosevic was quick to exploit this anxiety, even paranoia, in parts of Croatia and in Bosnia. The regions of multi-ethnic harmony, such as Sarajevo, were slow to realise what was happening in these 'backwaters'.

At the same time, the statelets which were developing in Serbia and Croatia had access to the weapons, information, organisation and infrastructure which meant that violence would quickly escalate from inter-ethnic riots and pogroms to large-scale war.

The final step came when Slovenia and, more importantly, Croatia claimed sovereignty. There was by now conflict with Serbia which radicalised sentiments in these republics and made them look also to support their ethnic enclaves elsewhere. Once Slovenia and Croatia had been accorded international recognition – and Germany successfully pushed the European Community into taking this step – the issue of what would happen to the other republics posed itself. Glenny sums up the terrible dilemma faced by Bosnia:

> . . . the Bosnian government had only three roads along which it could travel and each led to war. It could have stayed in the rump Yugoslavia and been ruled over by Milosevic and Serbia. It could have accepted the territorial division of Bosnia between Serbia and Croatia, as suggested by Tudjman and Milosevic. Or it could have applied for recognition as an independent state. The Croats and the Moslems considered the first solution unacceptable; the Moslems and the Yugoslavs, the second; and the Serbs, the third.[16]

361

The referendum that was held pointed to the third option, but war followed on inevitably.

What it is vital to note is that only minorities of the different ethnic groups actually wanted that war. The people who live in the capital cities of each of the republics live in multi-ethnic societies: their commitment was to the autonomy of their republic. Many of them wanted to go no further than that, although nationalist parties won majority support. Even most of these voters did not see how their government, in pursuing the policy of republican sovereignty and an element of ethnic assertion (to make up for periods of ethnic subordination) could alienate ethnic enclaves. Nor did they see how extremist leaders, marginal and often regarded as absurd figures in pre-crisis Yugoslavia, could come to dominate the politics of these enclaves and combine with extreme nationalists in the 'home' republic.

The crisis itself creates a new situation. Towns and villages which resisted the moves to inter-ethnic conflict are compelled in that direction, the flight of ethnic groups into safer areas (whether the deliberate result of 'ethnic cleansing' or not) undermines sets of inter-ethnic connections which resist the claims of ethnic nationalists; power moves from the cosmopolitan cities to the army units and the paramilitaries drawing upon rural populations – as is most clear in the fate of Sarajevo. There is a terrible rationality to the process – politicians such as Milosevic, committed nationalists in enclave areas, military and para-military leaders – these all maintain and expand their power in this process – even if the result is destruction and the blighting of the interests of the great majority. It is a very special way in which post-communist state power combines with ethnic conflict which leads to this highly destructive form of nationalism. What is more, one can see many other situations where this combination of state irrendentism and enclave nationalism could break out. The Albanians of Kosovo will surely not put up with their oppression for long, and there is always the possibility of an appeal to Albania itself.

6 Concluding remarks

What general conclusions can one draw from this brief survey of the development of nationalism in the USSR and eastern Europe since 1988?

It is clear that ethnic identity and national consciousness were not obliterated by communism. There are three major reasons for this. One is that cultural identity matters and indeed extensive cultural identities if anything matter more as a society becomes urban and industrial. Urban living, mass literacy and communications help create 'standard cultures'. A second reason is that cultural differences are related to social inequalities. Official language policies, for example, advantage one language group against another. The third reason is that since 1918 states in Europe have either represented themselves as nation-states or, in the case of the USSR, have built the nationality principle into their structures. The kinds of ethnic-national labels achieved by them have tended to become fixed elements in the political process, even if their 'content' has changed dramatically.

However, these developments are commonplace in most urban-industrial societies. They do not lead to breakdown and nationalist conflict in most cases. At worst they lead to endemic inter-ethnic violence; at best to peacefully negotiated dealings of a multi-cultural kind.

Three other elements were required to transform ethnic identity and tension into nationalism. The first was the breakdown of communist state power. The second was the reconstitution of state power at local or regional level. Communist state power always gave rise to regional concentrations of power of a more or less formal kind. In most cases the policy of decentralisation which accompanied the breakdown of central power enabled forms of national communism to take over and these in turn could combine with the rise of national oppositions to construct a new form of state power. This was vital for a non-violent transition to multi-party politics. Communist states did not allow for the development of extensive social connections outside of the political sphere. To some extent the period of *glasnost* did allow this to develop, as did the connections taken up by deputies to elected parliaments, and that has helped integrate political oppositions with national communists. But being able to focus claims to national independence upon republican institutions in the USSR and on the national states in the Warsaw Pact states gave an institutional fixity to nationalism and turned it into the politics of inheritance. The only real danger of violent nationalist conflict in this situation would come about through border disputes. When one looks back to the many border disputes which took place amongst the nation-states of inter-war east-central Europe one might think that created more than enough possible conflicts. Yet those states were the creations of a peace settlement which left clear 'winners' and 'losers'. The present states have seized their own independence and created their own multi-party systems and one can expect that their politics will focus on internal problems rather than border disputes. The major danger will come only if those internal problems include conflict with a powerful ethnic minority, especially if that minority had been privileged under the communist system.

The real danger arises with the third element. In some cases there is not a 'politics of inheritance' but rather a power vacuum. This is because in some situations national identity has not been focused and fixed upon regional political institutions. With the breakdown of power and with the absence of other extensive connections and identities, ethnic identity becomes not one element within a broader set of institutions, but becomes instead a *substitute* for any broader set of connections. And when the two

363

kinds of national identity combine – when a national state takes up the cause of an ethnic enclave in another state – then nationalist conflict can take a violent and uncontrollable form.

No-one can know how politics will develop in east-central Europe in the future. However, it is important to understand that nationalist conflict is not the simple and direct expression of long-standing ethnic identities suppressed under communism. Rather, it is the nature of communist state power, how it broke down, and how successor states developed out of that breakdown which provides the key to understanding how nationalist conflicts could arise.

Notes

1   I leave aside Finland as a rather special case.
2   Stephen White, *Gorbachev and After* (Cambridge, 1992), p. 146.
3   Motyl rather nicely talks of the combination of Austro-Marxism (= cultural national autonomy) and Stalinism (economic and political centralisation). Alexander J. Motyl, *Sovietology, Rationality, Nationality: Coming to Grips with Nationalism in the USSR* (New York, 1990), especially chapter 6, 'The Inevitability of National Communism'.
4   See F. Fukuyama, *The End of History and the Last Man* (London, 1992).
5   For many of the ideas which follow I am especially indebted to Motyl, *Sovietology, Rationality, Nationality* which, in my view very effectively, outlines a framework for understanding the logic of development when one tries to reform a state like the USSR.
6   I cannot embark on a detailed analysis, but it seems to me that a similar type of analysis to that made of the different forms of development of national consciousness and ideology amongst Serbians and Rumanians in the Habsburg and Ottoman empires in the nineteenth century (chapter five, above) can also be developed for Ukrainians divided between Habsburg rule (in Galicia) and Romanov rule. I am indebted to Lutz Häfner (Bielefeld) for advice on this subject and for the sight of an unpublished paper (1992) by him on the subject. On the very limited extent of national consciousness by 1917 see R. Suny, 'Nationalism and Class in the Russian revolution: a comparative discussion', in *Revolution in Russia: Reassessments of 1917*, ed. by E. R. Frankel, *et. al.*, (Cambridge, 1992).
7   Motyl, *op. cit, pp.* 180–1.
8   A good example is the conflict between Russia and the Ukraine over the disposal of the Black Sea navy and the control of nuclear weapons.
9   I am indebted to ideas outlined by Misha Glenny, *The Rebirth of History: Eastern Europe in the Age of Democracy* (London, 1990), especially his chapter on Hungary.
10 See, for example, J. Luxmoore and J. Babiuch, 'Flying from Freedom', *The Guardian*, 2 November 1992.
11 I have developed some of the points made in the following pages at greater length in 'Conclusion: nationalism and German reunification', in *The State*

of Germany: *the national idea in the making, unmaking and remaking of a modern nation-state*, ed. J. Breuilly (London, 1992), pp. 224–38.
12 Even though experts agree that such a change will not really deal with the problem but is more a symbolic move.
13 See, for example, Volker Ulrich, 'Die neue Dreistigkeit', *Die Zeit*, 30 October 1992.
14 See the report of an interview with Ridley, 'Saying the unsayable', *Spectator*, 14 July 1990.
15 Such a case was made out by Professor Willie Paterson (Edinburgh University), a leading analyst of contemporary German politics, at a conference on *Nationalism and Supranationalism in Europe* held in Manchester in October 1992.
16 Misha Glenny, *The Fall of Yugoslavia: The Third Balkan War* (London, 1992), p. 143.

Conclusion

1 General remarks

In conclusion I summarise the major arguments of the book but will also advance some more general ones about the way in which nationalism should be understood. The major idea throughout has been that nationalism should be understood as a form of politics and that that form of politics makes sense only in terms of the particular political context and objectives of nationalism. Central to an understanding of that context and those objectives is the modern state. The modern state both shapes nationalist politics and provides that politics with its major objective, namely possession of the state.

Having summarised the arguments which indicate the centrality of the modern state to an understanding of nationalism, it will be necessary to clarify the meaning of the term 'modern state' as well as certain characteristics associated with it. From there one can go on to examine how the modern state could give rise to nationalist politics. At that point it becomes necessary to examine the strategic relationships between the state and nationalist oppositions which I have classified in terms of reform, separation and unification. Here I shall argue that it is separatist oppositions to the modern state which should be of central concern. After that I will consider the tactics or functions of nationalism, which I have classified in terms of co-ordination, mobilisation and legitimacy.

These arguments focus upon nationalist opposition in a world of non-nation-states. The types of nationalism discussed in Part III raise further issues about the way in which nationalism becomes universalised and loses its distinctive character. But that in turn raises further issues about the breakdown of the modern state itself and how this breakdown affects nationalism. I take up these issues in a concluding section where it becomes impossible to avoid a certain amount of speculation as well as the application of value judgements.

366

2 The modern state and nationalism

Earlier arguments in this book have suggested that there is a close relationship between the modern state and nationalism. The development of the
political concept of the nation was related to the ways in which the
absolutist or would-be absolutist state in early modern Europe shaped
political thought and action (chapter 3). Comparisons between the Habsburg and Ottoman empires suggested that the internal functions of nationalism, that is, co-ordination and mobilisation, which take priority over the
external function of legitimacy, were better developed in the Habsburg
empire (chapter 5). This was related to the more modern state form which
existed in the Habsburg empire as compared to the Ottoman empire. It
was more difficult to argue such a case for unification nationalisms in
Europe, because no single state shaped them and because they were as
much the instruments of particular states as oppositions to those states
(chapter 4). This helps account for their rather weak character – particularly the German and Italian movements – and the important role the
legitimacy function played within them. However, the political modernisation in Piedmont and Prussia as well as in other states where elite nationalism was to become quite strong (such as Baden and Lombardy) can be
closely related to the development of the nationalist movement.[1]

Considerations of nationalism beyond Europe further supported the
general argument. Comparisons between nationalist movements in the
Ottoman empire and Egypt indicated that they were more developed in
Egypt, where a modern state form had been established (chapter 6). A
consideration and comparison of colonial nationalist movements in European empires indicated that these movements were particularly well developed and distinctive where the 'autonomous' colonial state was most
firmly established (chapters 7–10). Finally, a consideration of reform nationalism in non-Western societies suggested that this had the best prospect
of success where indigenous political institutions most closely resembled
those which had, in Europe, given rise to the modern state and national(ist)
oppositions (chapter 11).

The argument became rather more diffuse in Part III. Where states
were defined as nation-states and the language of nationalism had become
universally accepted and employed (as well as for other reasons to be
discussed in the concluding section) it became difficult to establish anything
distinctive about nationalism. However, in some of the new states one
could argue that the failure to concentrate sovereignty in particular institutions, that is, the failure to create a modern state, could continue to give
rise to a distinctively nationalist politics. This could take the form either
of an attempt to turn the weak government into a genuine nation-state
(chapter 13) or of a challenge to that government in nationalist terms
(chapter 12). The newness of these states can also be associated with

367

nationalist movements which seek to transcend them and establish larger 'national' organisations (chapter 14).

The situation in Europe was rather different. In one case the modern state could not cope with the sudden mobilisation of mass groups in particularly unfavourable situations and was confronted as a consequence with a new and distinctive form of nationalism in fascism (chapter 15). The very recent failure of Western states to deliver economic growth has produced political strains which can, under certain circumstances, give rise to nationalist opposition (chapter 16). These two types of nationalism point in different ways to inadequacies in the modern state which originally generated nationalism. In the case of east-central Europe most nationalist movements have focused their aim either on taking over the existing state or creating an independent state out of an existing sub-state unit such as a republic or autonomous region (chapter 17). The scope for further nationalism beyond this is related externally to the continuation of border disputes and irredentism (itself linked to how much stability and strength these successor states manage to develop) and internally to the problems of constructing non-political as well as political institutions around which conceptions of nationality as citizenship rather than nationality as ethnicity can develop. (See the concluding section to chapter 17.) I will take up some of the implications of these current forms of nationalism in the concluding section.

The matters dealt with in Part I also point to the centrality of the modern state in the formation of nationalism. This was not particularly clear in chapter 1, which dealt with the ways in which various social groups were typically mobilised in support of nationalism. That was because various of these groups had been involved in politics prior to the development of the modern state and because all of them had supported movements other than nationalist ones. However, it could be argued that the way in which the modern state defines itself against 'civil society' has meant that groups within that society have required and sought specialised political leadership in order to enforce their claims upon the state. At the same time civil society has been seen by various political elites as a source of support for their various objectives. It is also clear that, in a very general way, capitalism is the major force which both constructs and disrupts 'civil society' and that this development can be closely related to the development of the modern state. Nationalist ideology can be related to the distinctively modern concern about the relationship between state and society, between public and private (chapter 2). This is fused with the age-old concern with the relationship between rulers and subjects. The modern feature of this concern centres upon ways of understanding the modern state in order to transform it.

So the various arguments of the book point to the centrality of the modern state in the formation of nationalism. However, the term 'modern state' has for the most part been used implicitly. To sustain a general argument it is necessary to make its meaning explicit. In doing this, in a rather summary form, I should emphasise that what is being outlined is an ideal type. It highlights certain aspects of state organisation in a way which is arguably illuminating when one turns to look at actual states in the modern period. But there is never a wholly 'modern state' in reality. I should also emphasise that, although I deal with certain other features which accompany the emergence of the modern state, it is not possible to consider various explanations which have been offered for the whole process which gives rise to the modern state.

The modern state is the possessor of sovereignty over a given territory. Sovereignty resides in a specific institution such as monarchy or parliament, and is considered to be, by its very nature, indivisible. The state possesses an elaborate institutional structure which delimits, justifies and exercises the claims attached to sovereignty. The activity of the state is devoted to the maintenance and exercise of its sovereignty against both external and internal threats. Externally the limit upon sovereignty is set by the sovereignty of other states. The political world is made up of a plurality of sovereign territorial states. It has no order other than that created out of the rational pursuit of self-interest which states follow in their dealings with one another. Internally the sovereignty of the state is limited – or, more precisely, divided – by the distinction between the public and the private spheres. In the public sphere the state exercises sovereignty directly; in the private sphere it does no more than provide ground rules for dealings between individuals and groups, rules which can, if necessary, be enforced when broken.

This idea of the state is marked by internal tensions between universality and particularity and between boundlessness and limitation. These tensions are perhaps most apparent in liberal thought in nineteenth-century Europe, when this idea of the state reached its most complete expression both in theory and practice.

The state is universal in that what is envisaged is a world made up wholly of a number of such states. There should be no area or person not subject to the rule of a state. Given that the sovereignty of a state is externally bound only by that of other states, such a situation would be seen as a vacuum which would have to be filled. Someone unfortunate enough to be excluded from the rule of a state, a stateless person, becomes both in theory and in practice a sort of non-person. Yet at the same time there can be no universal state. The very notion of the sovereign territorial state entails the existence of other such states. Without other such states it is impossible to imagine how the state could be bounded or its sovereignty defined. At most a state could defend its existence (rather than its sovereignty) against external forces which were not themselves states. In the absence of the need to defend sovereignty it is difficult to see why the state

369

itself, at least in terms of its external relationships, should continue to exist. So the world is made up wholly of sovereign states with sharply defined boundaries and where the claim to sovereignty is made with the same force throughout the territory so bounded.[2]

This idea of the state is boundless in that it asserts ultimate claims over the lives of those within it. The state is the highest form of human existence in the sense that all other forms of existence are subordinate to it. Yet to define it as a form of existence requires that it be limited and set off against other forms. In liberal theory this is something which can be done only by means of abstractions. Liberals attacked, both in theory and in practice, the concentration of certain powers in particular non-state institutions such as guilds or churches or estates. If such powers were an essential part of public life they should be vested in the state; if not they should be dissolved or extended as rights to all private individuals. So the internal limitations upon the state were not those imposed by the concrete powers of particular groups or institutions – that is privilege. Rather they were limitations within the lives of those who were both citizens and private individuals. The distinction was drawn not between ruler and ruled but between state and society.

To give substance to such limits and distinctions it was necessary to define what was public and what private and to outline the position of the state in relation to these two spheres. To carry through an exhaustive classification in this way was always very difficult but some things could clearly be assigned to one or the other category. Family life, economic dealings, cultural and religious preferences were private matters; forcible attacks on persons and property were public ones. Liberals faced the problem of whether their distinctions were a convenience, confined to a particular historical situation, or a principle, founded upon natural rights or human nature. They also faced the problem of how such distinctions could be defined by any body other than the state and, therefore, how the state could be both sovereign and self-limiting. All manner of devices were set in hand to impose limitation. Certain things were defined as freedoms from the state, though how justified and defended remained a thorny problem. Equally important were the attempts to build freedom and limitation within the state itself. The state was regarded as the association of the citizens. Sovereignty was (usually) vested in parliament, which by means of representation converted the will of the citizens into state power. The successful working of representation was regarded as dependent upon certain freedoms, and on this basis various political rights were outlined which the state could not, or only with great difficulty, breach. Frequently the institutions of the state were structured through written constitutions designed to limit the way in which sovereignty was exercised. Finally, the state was regarded as being bound to observe stringent rules of procedure in the way it operated. The problem of what bound the state remained.

Having accepted the absolute nature of sovereignty and vested it in the state, liberals faced an impossible theoretical task in seeking to limit state power. If the limitations were the product of utility and/or particular historical circumstances, they could not be defended in principle and were liable to be undone once utilitarian calculation or circumstances changed. If, on the other hand, limitation was a matter of principle, there was the problem of how the principles could be defined and enforced against the state without calling its sovereignty into question.

For the most part liberals did not need to face up to these questions because reality seemed to conform to their ideas. For example, the distinction between public and private was reinforced, if not actually created, by the development of capitalism as the dominant economic system in Europe and subsequently the world. This development was accompanied by a body of thought which elaborated on the internal order of the market economy and argued that non-economic interference in it should be reduced to the minimum. The idea that the market economy operated through the exchange of resources between free and rational individuals, each seeking to maximise his satisfactions in a competitive situation, suggested that political power had no part to play in these relationships the way it did in societies where resources were obtained from others by command.

The notion of privacy was not confined to economic relations. Indeed, historically it was the attempt to define other matters as private that first contributed to the notion of the limited public state. The demand for freedom of conscience in matters of religion began by defending itself against the Catholic Church but could easily be turned against the state if and when that came to be seen as the major threat to religious choice. In this way the state could come to be defined as both public and secular, although there is no need to equate these attributes with one another. Equally the notion of the 'private' family whose affairs are beyond the reach of the state cannot be reduced to one aspect of the development of capitalism, although in various ways capitalism has shaped this notion in its more modern forms. Nor can the concern with the cultivation of the 'private' personality and of 'private' friendships which has become so important in the modern period be ignored as another independent source of the notion of a private sphere from which the state should be excluded. One must remember that as much liberal energy in nineteenth-century Europe went into the defence of religious belief or family affairs such as the education of children as private matters as went into the defence of the free market economy.

Nevertheless it would be difficult to argue against the claim that by the nineteenth century capitalism provided the most important element in the notion of a 'civil society'. This had important implications for international relations as well. While political relationships internationally were seen as threatening relationships of power where individuals were repre-

371

sented through their state, economic relationships were regarded as non-coercive dealings between individuals which could operate across state boundaries. The market economy was international and could operate independently of the political system of competing states. In this way it was possible to envisage an international economic order which was not matched by an international political order.[3]

Even where state institutions remained highly authoritarian it is noteworthy that those states also acknowledged the necessity of retreating from economic interference. Indeed, some have argued that such states could more easily do this as well as promoting the appropriate policies than could more participatory states. Prussia, for example, led the way in Germany in state attacks on restrictions on geographical and job mobility and promoted greater freedom of trade through the German Customs Union. Emperor Napoleon III pushed through free trade agreements with Britain and the German Customs Union. Some economic liberals, noting this, assumed that the move towards democracy would also begin the move away from economic liberalism.

Clearly this ideal end-state of a constitutionally defined and bounded state which merely held the ring in activities which were not in the narrowly defined public domain was never actually reached and could only be approximated under certain special conditions. But it provides us with a notion of the ideal form of the modern state as it was being envisaged and pursued in the nineteenth century. It is necessary now to see in what ways these ideas were distinctively modern and how, historically, something approximating to the modern state developed.

The abstract notion of sovereignty long antedates the modern state. The general distinction between public and private found expression in the Roman law division between criminal and civil law. The idea of bounded and competing states was clearly important for the city-states of northern Italy in the Middle Ages. But it was the way in which various ideas were taken from these different sources and used to underpin the claims of territorial monarchs in western Europe that gave rise to the recognisably modern idea of the state. The legacy of Roman law and of papal governmental theory and of city-state methods of diplomacy all helped provide the medieval monarchs of western Europe with the intellectual capacity to define their powers as public ones. The disputes between monarchy and Catholic Church (disputes which it would be anachronistic to describe as church-state conflict) helped shift authority towards monarchs. But still monarchs could hardly enforce sovereign claims over their subjects. Indeed, in a feudal society it was impossible to make the distinctions between public and private or to crush the privileges of various groups in a way which would give some meaning to the notion of a sovereign state. In a few countries, notably France and England, the monarchy was able to press home claims to raise general taxes and to dispense justice, although

372

these were hedged about with numerous practical and theoretical limitations. This was important in the way in which the modern state developed because it meant that the state came to be defined not by means of fiat from above but through negotiations between monarchs and the political community within which their rule operated. This meant that the concept of sovereignty that did develop was always related to notions of rights and liberties. Yet at the same time the forms of collaboration which this negotiation made possible produced more powerful states than had been achieved by conquest alone. So the idea of the sovereign state emerged gradually through a process of negotiation in western Europe.

Significantly this was not the pattern in eastern Europe. There did not develop there either a powerful and privileged class of landowners or autonomous towns with which monarchs had to bargain in order to increase their authority. Indeed, very often privileges were gifts of those rulers in their attempt to help extend their authority downwards and outwards. Privileges so granted could easily be revoked. As a consequence power was detached from social relationships; it had a 'despotic' rather than an 'infra-structural' character.[4] This meant that the extension of state power was not accompanied by a process of negotiations which created political 'liberties'. The lack of autonomy for the political community from the central state was carried over, in a different form, from tsarist to communist governments, and has meant that nationalism developed in a rather different way than was the case in western Europe.

The idea of the territorial state also emerged gradually, as for a long time monarchs did not govern bounded and continuous territories but rather possessed different bundles of powers over different areas and groups. Neither sovereignty nor boundaries were sharply defined attributes of 'public' authority until the eighteenth century. It is significant that it was the 'modern' French state of 1791–92 which objected strongly to enclaves and mixed forms of authority that were associated with *ancien régimes*, and this contributed to unleashing what was in many ways the first national war.[5]

By the early modern period a few monarchies had acquired enough control over matters such as taxation, the church and justice as to be able to conceive of themselves as sovereign in something like the modern sense. Their powers were embodied in specific institutions, and were justified and symbolised by various elaborate means. Such powers had only been achieved through a process of negotiation between the ruler and the political community of the core territory under his sway. As a consequence the monarch's rule was bound up with the institutions of this political community. Only on the basis of some consent from that community, to which various rights and liberties were conceded, was the monarch able to establish and enforce some kind of sovereign power. One of the reasons why consent was forthcoming was the need to defend the territory against the rise of similar states.

In this way the kingdoms of western Europe came to take on the form of national states. The concept of the nation, a concept which related principally to the institutions of the political community that sustained the monarchy, could be turned against the monarchy itself under certain conditions. In this way the process which created the modern idea of the state in its earliest form also gave rise to the political concept of the nation.

This represented the first step towards nationalism. Because the process was confined to a small political community that had developed along with the state, where there was little idea about wider political participation, it could give rise to only very limited national oppositions. However, when the monarchy made more and more claims to represent the public interest the scope for conflict widened. This was reinforced from the eighteenth century by the rapid spread of a market economy which helped clarify the public/private distinction and also provided civil society with new energies and solidarities that could be fed into political conflict. It was now possible for elements within the political community to go beyond their previous forms of opposition and claim to enforce the needs and interests of 'society' upon an unrepresentative state. National ideology began to acquire a mobilising as well as co-ordinating role and a more radical set of political objectives. This was not yet nationalism. New claims were grounded on historic or natural rights, and not the peculiar cultural identity of the ruled society. But the foundations for making that claim had been laid. The modern state was now regarded as deriving its sovereignty from the people, not from God. At the same time the 'people' were a particular set of people, often seen as the members of the civil society which the state ruled, and also as the occupants of the clearly defined territory the state claimed as its own.

Once the claim to sovereignty was made on behalf of a particular, territorially defined unit of humanity, it was natural to relate the claim to the particular attributes of that unit. At first this was confined to certain political characteristics and did not extend, at least explicitly, to cultural characteristics which did not already have some explicit political meaning. But when opposition came from outside the core political community the claim to sovereignty had to shift to new ground. To claim to alter the territory as well as the institutions of the state required some notion of a particular human group with a different territory. Such a notion could be sustained in three different ways. One could appeal to universal principles which were not being observed in a particular part of the state; to particular political rights which applied to only one area of the state; and to a distinctive cultural identity. At first most appeals were couched in largely political terms. The stronger the political opposition the less attractive, by and large, was the need to appeal to cultural identity. Thus American revolutionaries could couch their claims in the universal terms of natural rights, and Magyar opponents of the Habsburg emperor in terms of historic political rights. Where the political opposition was much weaker the situation was rather different. Frequently to establish a political identity and to justify political claims it was necessary to move beyond universal or purely political criteria. It was often necessary to seek support from groups hitherto excluded from political life. Given the existence of certain cultural differences within various regions of the state, it was possible to appeal to cultural identity. At that point politics took on a properly nationalist form.

So the development of the modern state shaped nationalism in various ways. Only under the modern state system could a political opposition see its objective as possession of sovereign, territorial state power and justify that objective in the name of the society ruled by the public state. Only in the context of competing territorial sovereign states could this objective be seen as the possession of a state like other states on the basis of representing a nation like other nations. Yet this claim was also particular: the state concerned had its own special characteristics, so the particular nation concerned also had special characteristics. The idea of the ruled society which might only be definable in terms of its private character, that is, in terms of its 'culture'; of the sovereign territorial state; of a world made up of such states in competition with one another – these are the essential premises upon which nationalist ideology and nationalist politics build. Their objectives may look beyond that situation, above all when they believe they can abolish the distinction between state and society, but they could arise only in that situation and in many ways are tied to it.

These represent the general conditions for the emergence of nationalism. It is the shift of political conflict away from the core political community of the state and also towards sections of society hitherto excluded from political life which provides the particular conditions for nationalism to develop. Only when the existing state is held to have different boundaries from those of the nation are political oppositions liable to move beyond political justifications to arguments that explicitly appeal to cultural identity. The first real nationalist movements, therefore, were movements of either unification or separation. I have argued that separatist movements are the more important and common of the two. But not all separatist opposition to the modern state is nationalist. This means that the question as to when nationalism proper first develops can be phrased quite specifically. In what circumstances will the types of political conflict created by the growth of state power in its distinctively modern form give rise to opposition movements which seek to create separate states and which justify this objective in the name of the nation which is defined in cultural terms? There appear to be two major situations in which this happens: in Europe within the modernising state which has a decentralised political structure and a wide range of cultural distinctions between the populations of different regions; and outside Europe where the modern colonial state has been imposed on peoples of non-European origin. There is little point in recapitulating the arguments about how nationalism developed in these circumstances. Instead I will point to some very general aspects of the way nationalism developed in these types of situation and the major differences between the two types.

The European multinational state pursued a policy of political modernisation for the most part cautiously, as it had no independent basis of power apart from the population it controlled and the historical institutional relationships it had developed with various regions in the process of building up its control. Although making far-reaching theoretical claims about sovereignty and the 'public' role of the state, particularly under Joseph II, the Habsburg state could in fact enforce only limited changes upon the existing political community, which possessed many entrenched privileges and powers. But even these limited changes, along with threats of more extensive ones, could provoke opposition from elements of that political community. The changes, however, appeared necessary, given a threatening international situation. At the same time the advance of private rights in land and in matters such as religion – rights sometimes promoted by the state – helped form a civil society which could be mobilised by oppositional elements within the political community.

In these ways, therefore, the general conditions that have been already noted – international state competition, gradual formation of civil society, new claims to power by the public state, opposition from political groups with entrenched powers and privileges – could lead to the emergence of a 'national' opposition. However, in the case of the Habsburg Empire this opposition was decentralised because of the historically federated nature of the dynasty. Political oppositions in Hungary and Italy could not act together. The only route open to them was to press for greater concessions on a regional basis. The justifications of the opposition came, therefore, to focus upon particular attributes of a region which would support special political claims. Normally such oppositions would refer to the regional political rights that had been enjoyed historically. That was the pattern of early Magyar opposition and even some of the Lombard opposition which resented the introduction of 'German' practices in matters such as noble rankings.

This was similar to cases of regional oppositions which had developed in peripheral regions of France or Spain to centralising monarchy. Given the limited nature of political conflict in the early modern period, that had been all that was necessary. Where such historic liberties, privileges or rights had shallower roots, as in North America, the argument might shift to a dependence on universal values which were not properly being applied in a particular part of the state. But where the state itself claimed to represent universal values, and where it became increasingly apparent that elements of civil society could and should be mobilised in any opposition to the state, then the justification for claiming special political rights could shift towards nationalism. In the case of dominant groups this could take the form of extending the ideas associated with historic rights beyond the privileged who had hitherto been the sole beneficiaries. Thus Magyar and Italian opponents of the Habsburg empire moved only hesitantly towards cultural nationality arguments. Where, however, such dominant groups locally controlled an ethnically distinct population, this could stimulate an explicitly cultural nationalist response. Whereas dominant groups fused the defence of privilege with the claims of historic nationality, subordinate groups fused the defence of equal rights with the claims of cultural nationality. In this way, then, the modernising multinational state could generate authentic nationalist opposition.

In the case of European empire overseas the situation was different because the modern state had an independent base of power located outside the subject population. This meant that it was possible to establish modern state forms before either the general social arrangements (market economy, private family and religious practice, etc.) or political institutional arrangements (representative assemblies, locally staffed bureaucracies) that accompanied the development of the modern state form in Europe could be established. This partly accounts for why 'traditional' patterns of political and social action continue for so long even where the colonial state has a distinctly modern form. Gradually the colonial state did establish some modern institutions through which collaboration could be practised, and it was within these institutions that a nationalist opposition could develop. Nevertheless much of the real political community remained outside these institutions, and at the same time civil society was poorly formed. An opposition that wished to possess the colonial state rather than simply to destroy foreign domination had then to construct an image of the political community and of the society which could 'match' the state it would take over. This was a formidable intellectual and political task and one which could only partially be achieved during the actual struggle for state power. Arguments about cultural nationality played only a subordinate role in the struggle because of the difficulties of matching such arguments with the political claims to take over the state. But it played an important part in the general repudiation of European pretensions to cultural superiority. But it is in the new states that such arguments will become particularly important, because the state will itself monopolise arguments about political nationality, and any nationalist case cannot be grounded upon an implicit contrast between foreigners and natives.

In these ways nationalist movements of real force could develop both within and beyond Europe. Of course it was not their force alone that brought success. The more weakly developed nationalist movements of the

Ottoman empire achieved more than the stronger movements in the Habsburg empire. The nationalist movements of Germany and Italy were more effective than the rather stronger Polish nationalist movement. One cannot equate power directly with success when looking at nationalism. In particular, where the influence of major external powers was crucial and such powers favoured separatist movements, it was often to legitimise independence from a weak imperial state rather than to wrest independence from a strong one that nationalist claims were made. Nevertheless, the rise of nationalist movements in Europe by 1918 and beyond Europe, particularly after 1945, have made a major contribution towards establishing the nation-state as the basic political unit in the world.

In this process separatist nationalism has played the leading role, and in ways which permit of generalisation. The development of effective unification or reform nationalism in non-nation-states is based upon much more specific and, therefore, rarer sets of conditions. I have dealt with such cases in some detail (Germany, Italy, Japan) and there is no need to repeat the arguments. Generally in the two major European cases one can note the advanced form 'civil society' had taken and the advantages unity would secure for important elements within that society as well as the various ways in which political modernisation could give rise to liberal political groups with contacts extending beyond state frontiers. But it was crucial that these groups found a state or states with which they could co-operate. The leading state in this process played the dominant role in such co-operation. In this rather special way interactions between modernising states, civil society and nationalist groups could generate a nationalist movement which could at least legitimise and help run the new nation-state once it had been created.

In the Japanese case the issue was as much about political modernisation as independence. As with 'national reform' movements in Europe, it was necessary to find new social, institutional and ideological bases from which to take over and transform a state which could not be regarded as foreign. It was also essential that these new bases were derived from existing trends or features of Japanese politics rather than being a very new sort of opposition. Much of the argument in chapter 11 comparing Japan with the Ottoman and Chinese empires revolved around trying to show how the conditions which made this possible were uniquely met in the Japanese case. To those arguments I would add a couple of very general points. Japanese reformers did not have to liquidate a 'universalist' set of values such as represented by Confucianism and Islam in the Chinese and Ottoman cases. Japanese reformers possessed in the lapsed institutions of empire an alternative political tradition, peculiar to Japan, around which reform organisation and ideology could build. These conditions enabled them to provide an alternative view of the Japanese state which did not move to new universalist challenges such as those posed by Chinese communists or Turkish secular nationalists. Given that this reform movement developed in Japan in the larger context of Western superiority and threat, it was natural that the alternative tradition was presented by reformers in nationalist terms.

These three nationalist movements and the new states to which they contributed had an enormous impact beyond their own countries. German and Italian unification firmly established the nation-state as the normal political unit in Europe and initiated a new phase of instability and conflict which led to major warfare in Europe and the extension of European conflict throughout the world. Japanese nationalism provided a potent model for many other non-European societies as well as contributing directly to the weakening of European power in the Far East. Nevertheless, although of major importance, these were not typical of the bulk of nationalist movements. It is the relationship between the modern state and separatist nationalism which provides support for a general argument about how nationalism develops in a world of non-nation-states.

On the basis of the preceding argument I would conclude that the development of nationalism as a modern form of politics was closely bound up with the nature of political modernisation in nineteenth-century Europe, and then in areas of European settlement and imperial rule overseas. A number of other points should be noted in order to place this argument into a broader context and to secure it against some possible objections.

First, these political processes that I have outlined could be reinforced by certain intellectual and social-cultural changes. There are those who consider nationalism primarily as an idea and focus on the work of intellectuals in producing and spreading this idea. Clearly political modernisation was often bound up with the creation of a secular intelligentsia. In many cases where such intellectuals were placed in subordinate positions either in peripheral regions or even at the centre, their reflections on modernisation and their role in that process could take ideas of territorial identity and popular sovereignty and go on from that to 'imagine' the nation-state as the political representative of a new kind of community, the nation. Sometimes such an intelligentsia played a major role in nationalist politics.[6]

At the same time the processes of capitalist development and urban-industrial growth, along with the extension of communications, mass literacy, and increased social and georgaphical mobility all created the conditions for what Gellner has termed 'standard national cultures'.[7] This in turn can increase the significance of identity defined in terms of membership of such a culture for many aspects of everyday life. For those who consider nationalism primarily in terms of the growth of such a sense of national identity this is clearly the level of development to which the most attention should be paid.

However, these are distinct even if frequently interrelated processes. Nationalist intelligentsias and populations with a broadly shared sense of national identity are not essential to the development of significant nationalist political movements and organisations. Conversely, such intelligentsias and such populations can exist independently of one another and in the absence of significant nationalist politics. Furthermore, much of the development of 'standard national cultures' took place after the formation of nation-states in western Europe and areas of European settlement overseas.[8] What this meant was that the term nationalism shifted from denoting political movements seeking to create nation-states to denoting either the assertive policies of the governments of nation-states and/or the formation of a popular public opinion which favoured such policies.[9]

Finally, once the most powerful and advanced states have defined the national state as the normative political unit, then this has an enormous impact on political development everywhere else. I have already pointed to the role of 'legitimacy', that is an appeal to powerful outside states, in many nationalist movements. The peace settlement of 1919 rewarded many of these appeals and 'fixed' the nation state as the political norm for Europe. This meant that all kinds of regional or ethnic tensions within states, as well as border disputes between states, would all now express themselves in nationalist terms. This affected political change not merely in western and central Europe but also in the USSR which, although a multi-national state, structured itself on a recognition of some kind of legitimacy to national claims. Naturally, where a nationalist intelligentsia was also formed and/or where urban-industrial development helped shape a 'standard national culture', then the claims of political movements which clustered around these political institutions would have that much more elaboration and appeal. This could help reinforce the power of nationalist politics if and when central state power broke down. But it was upon state institutions which actually paid at least lip-service to some principle of nationality that these reinforcing elements crystallised. The same argument can be developed for areas of European empire overseas after 1945 and the way political oppositions crystallised around colonial state institutions as imperial power crumbled.

In these ways, therefore, the initial conditions which generated very specific forms of nationalism (that is, separatist challenges to modernising states) could, with the formation of nation-states by the most powerful and richest societies, go on to generate an ever more diverse range of 'nationalisms'. The problem is that as the word comes to span ideas, sentiments and politics, and includes state policy, international conflicts, and supportive public opinion, so there is a danger that the term will lose all specific meaning. That, of course, is an indication of its great success.

3 The functions of nationalist ideology

A nationalist movement seeks to bind together people in a particular territory in an endeavour to gain and use state power. The general context for the development of such a movement is supplied by the modern state and the strategic relationships to that state of reform, separation and unification. These matters are best considered primarily in terms of the problems of political practice which nationalists face. But one also has to consider the general relationship between nationalist political practice and ideology.

A number of general observations can be made about the role of ideology in politics. I have already considered the intellectual sources of nationalist ideology and how it can have a particular attraction when simplified and transformed into symbols and ceremonials (chapter 2). To those arguments can be added the point made earlier in this conclusion about how a system of competing territorial states appealing to the idea of popular sovereignty can shape political oppositions which also think in terms of particular, territorially-defined groups striving for independence.

One can add to this further arguments about the general need which exists in the modern world for ideology. Ideology can be regarded as a sort of map. It provides people with the means to identify their own position in the world in relation to others. One cannot take the analogy too far; maps do not actually suggest where one should go, only how to get there. Ideologies prescribe destinations as well as routes. But, like maps, ideologies arise out of the need to make sense of a certain terrain which cannot otherwise be understood. Unlike maps, however, ideology helps shape as well as delineate that terrain. Ideology is constantly ambivalent between the claims of prescribing and describing a state of affairs.

It is difficult to see how in the modern world people could operate effectively without some fairly abstract maps of the world, even if these have come to take the form of apparently commonsense beliefs. The extensive range of dealings in which we are all involved but which for the most part do not appear directly in our lives have to be grasped in some way (at least by some people) if they are to be managed and sustained effectively. Particularly when it appears that a certain state of affairs or set of relationships has to be sustained against the opposition of others, it becomes necessary also to invest these abstract conceptions of the world with values. In this way large-scale conflict is necessarily accompanied by ideology.

Beginning from such premises, one can go on to relate ideology to the general need for identity, a need which in the modern world can only be met by ideological means. From there one can go on to argue that nationalist ideology is a particularly powerful response to this need, given the way it is both abstract and yet offers an apparently concrete repudiation of the levelling and divisive and depersonalising character of modernity as represented, above all, through the development of capitalism, urban life and the impersonal bureaucratic state. At a very general level one can hardly dismiss such arguments, although they are frequently framed in terms which make them impossible to test.[10] But it seems to me to be more important as well as more feasible to place nationalist ideology within a much narrower framework and to link it closely to nationalist politics. The result may seem less profound but at least, I think, it is meaningful.

Consequently I have confined my arguments about the appeal of nationalism to a concern with *political* identity rather than identity in a more general sense. Furthermore I have seen the 'need' for such an identity not as some sort of general human longing but as an essential component of effective political action. Clearly this leaves out a great deal, and I have earlier sought to make it clear that nationalist ideology is not the product of political calculation (chapter 2). But only in relation to the requirements of political action does nationalist ideology tend to become specific, outlining clear objectives and targetting potential supporters. I have classified these requirements under the three headings of co-ordination, mobilisation and legitimacy. The justification for these terms is the assistance they provide in the analysis of the various case studies that have been presented. Here I want briefly to consider the general points which can be made about these three requirements. In doing this one can relate co-ordination, mobilisation and legitimacy respectively to the three levels at which political action takes place: in the existing political community, in society (that is, amongst those members of the subject population who do not routinely participate in political life), and in the international state system. Co-ordination can be regarded as the essential requirement because only by its means does a new type of political opposition – a nationalist opposition – come into existence. Mobilisation and/or legitimacy frequently give that opposition its real force.

Co-ordination is required where a heterogeneous set of political elites seek to act in common to challenge the state. This heterogeneity may take the form of different levels of action – for example, the problem of linking together local, intermediate and national levels of action. Problems of co-ordination in this sense were particularly acute, for example, in British India, where the sheer size of the country and its immense regional diversity presented major problems for the formation of an effective political opposition. The heterogeneity might take the form of divisions between different kinds of elites or elites operating through different kinds of institutions. Thus Kuomintang sought to bind together military, administrative and economic elites; the constitutionalist opposition to the crown in eighteenth-century France sought to bind together a variety of parlements, provincial assemblies and other institutions.

The relationship between such oppositions and the state is a complex

382

one and so, therefore, is the role of ideology in binding together that opposition. It is important to understand first that ideology both shapes and is shaped by the form political opposition takes. Thus the emphasis upon Parliament in opposition to the English crown in the mid-seventeenth century is both a reflection of the role played by Parliament in national politics and an argument about how Parliament should be regarded. In this way ideology appears both as a rationalisation of certain forms of political action and as an instrument of such action. It is this double-edged role which ideology plays in political movements, both promoting and 'reflecting' those movements, that makes it impossible to provide any causal analysis of the relationship between political ideology and political action.

But I have put the term 'reflect' in inverted commas, because even this idea about the role of ideology needs to be qualified. To illustrate this I will continue with the English example. Recently a number of historians have questioned the whole approach to sixteenth and seventeenth-century English political history which concentrates upon the 'growth' of Parliament and which sees Parliament primarily as a curb on monarchical power.[11] There is a great deal that is plausible in the criticisms. Parliament met fitfully at the pleasure of the monarch; it concerned itself with many things other than 'politics' ;[12] much of its work was managed from above; conflict within it was often related to conflict in the royal council and elsewhere rather than between institutions; above all, Parliament was more an instrument for the extension of monarchical power than a limit upon that power. To this have been added some rather narrower arguments about the procedures of parliament and what I would regard as the illegitimate attempt to dismiss what those involved in politics thought they were doing as irrelevant to the study of what they actually were doing politically. Much of this work reminds me of the 'collaborator' approach to modern colonialism.[13] It grasps the detail in a way which is much superior to earlier approaches. It is true to much of the substance of politics. But it misses the importance of political forms. It is in relation to new political forms that new political ideas arise and can be turned to effective use in times of crisis. Just as the collaboration approach stands before nationalism mystified: it is some sort of accident arising out of the breakdown of collaboration – so this new, critical approach in the English case stands mystified before the outbreak of civil war: it is a sort of accident arising out of the war with Scotland. That is hardly adequate, even if it is right to be chary of the view that a nationalist challenge or a parliamentary challenge is just the final expression of some long and steady growth of national or parliamentary institutions and consciousness.

Political opposition develops within the political community, not from outside it. The groups which find themselves in opposition are not permanently opposed to government, because that would render them powerless and would lead to their exclusion from the political community.

In this sense the 'conflict' approach which posits essential opposition between parliament and crown, or between nation and imperial power, misses an essential part of the way politics operates. People do not fight for particular institutions (and the nation can be regarded, in relation to political opposition, as such an institution). Rather, institutions are devices for achieving other ends. An institution can become an effective device in politics only if it actually becomes part of the state. To single out a particular institution as essentially opposition to the state, especially when powerful political groups fasten upon that institution, is therefore to miss its character. It is its grasp of this important point that gives the collaborator approach its strength. It can point to the slides between collaboration and opposition which are perfectly consistent from the point of view of the actors concerned. Only in terms of a subsequent decision that one must be for parliament or against it, for the nation or against it, are such shifts of action seen in terms of fundamental principles. A Congress politician could both sustain and oppose the Raj; a Wentworth could appear as a champion of parliament and then the crown; an Eduard Shevardnadze could function as foreign minister of the USSR and then as President of the newly independent republic of Georgia – without this having to be seen as a matter of changing sides. So far as this critical approach makes us wary of positing essential 'sides' to political conflict (which inevitably leads on to a search for the class or national basis of the sides involved) it is of value. In so far as it enables us to recognise that collaboration is as much a means of realising certain interests as resistance, and that we must not see politics as either one or the other, this critical approach is illuminating.

But that is not enough. Is it an accident that certain institutions, certain forms of political action, become the major vehicle for opposition to government in a particular crisis? The inability of the collaborator approach to deal with the question satisfactorily is its major weakness. What is important is that the political community articulates itself through certain institutions. These institutions provide the channels for political action, be it collaboration with or resistance to the government. It is the way institutional change gives rise to a state which can unify local, intermediate and national levels of political action that is important. This shapes the way in which political conflict is conducted. Parliament is central in the English case because it helped link together these various levels of action in a way that strengthened the state. But that service to the state also meant that it could, at a moment of crisis, provide the institutional basis of opposition to the crown and much of the ideological justification for it. It is the 'growth' of parliament as a national institution of state, not parliament as an effective opposition to government, that is important.

But of course parliamentary opposition could hardly represent itself in this way. Similarly the Indian Congress could hardly represent itself as a complex linkage of factions which had steadily brought together local, intermediate and national levels of political action and which had been able to do this only because its development followed – indeed, was part of – the development of the colonial state in India. Nor could a 'national communist' in a newly independent republic of the former USSR present himself as someone seeking to stabilise and maintain political authority around republic institutions as central state power breaks down. Such a presentation of the case is hardly designed to invest a political opposition with enthusiasm or to provide it with general objectives; and indeed frequently does not chime in with the subjective understanding of many of these political actors for whom selective memory and a constant rationalising re-interpretation of earlier action are vital ingredients for success. A nationalist ideology could become effective only given this prior development of the state and the form political opposition could take in a crisis. That ideology necessarily reflected certain features of that state and particularly of the institutions around which opposition clustered. But it went beyond reflection and transformed that opposition into a cause and sought to provide it with a new sense of unity. Without the sense of a cause and a unity it would have been difficult to keep opposition within the political community together, particularly given the dangers of opposition at times of crisis. In most cases, when there was a real crisis, many elements of the original opposition did draw back, but the sense of unity, as well as an awareness of having gone too far to withdraw again, kept some of the opposition together. Thus although it is wrong to argue that nationalist ideology actually does reflect the nature of political conflict, it is also wrong to see it as arbitrary or accidental or as a convenient fiction. Because parliament had developed in certain ways before 1640, a national ideology which centred on parliament became possible, although the image of parliament contained in that ideology is historically false. Because the Indian Congress did develop in a certain way, it became possible (almost unavoidable) to see it in national terms, although its image of itself as an expression of the national will is unacceptable. Because the republics of the USSR did pay lip-service to nationality claims and have served as a means of preserving political authority with the breakdown of central state power, they can come to be seen as embodiments of the national will, although that is in many ways misleading.

That nationalism operates in this complex way of partially reflecting and partially promoting certain sorts of political action can be shown by relating nationalist ideology to the institutional context in which political action takes place. The English focus on parliament; the Japanese concern with empire; the French emphasis on particular liberties; the links between Serbian and Bulgarian national claims and autonomous units in the Greek Orthodox church; the use of the republican institutions provided by the USSR to organise independence claims: again and again the case studies

385

demonstrate the point. The modern state co-ordinates and specialises significant political action. Political opposition in turn engages in co-ordinated and specialised political action which builds upon the institutions provided by the state. In certain situations, such as political opposition originating from outside the core territory of a multinational empire, nationalist ideology seems best to describe and promote that political opposition.

Much political opposition cannot succeed if it remains confined to the existing political community. The various means by which elements of the population are mobilised politically have been considered in chapter 1. The general processes of mobilisation do not themselves give rise to nationalist politics. They can involve types of conflict in which cultural issues loom large, such as in certain sorts of communal or inter-ethnic conflict, but that is not the same thing as nationalism. So it is upon the issue of how conflicts within civil society can be translated into nationalist politics that one must concentrate. There can be no general formula for dealing with this matter. All one can do is make a few general remarks.

In situations where social groups have created effective ways of representing their interests to government, nationalist opposition will either find it difficult to penetrate such groups or will become simply the representative of one particular group. Thus nationalism as a distinctive form of politics in developed nation-states has largely been overshadowed by other sorts of politics, above all the politics of class. Only where exceptional conditions block the representation of social interests by parties of class or interests (as happened in Italy and Germany after 1918 or in some peripheral regions of post-war Britain) will such groups become free for penetration by nationalism. It is usually when civil society is poorly articulated and where a nationalist group can virtually monopolise oppositional politics that nationalism can become central. For example, among dominant groups in the Habsburg and Ottoman empires political activity was confined to small groups of nobility, clergy and administrators. Magyar peasants or Italian artisans, at a time of crisis, could often only pursue their specific interests through the leadership offered by members of those groups, an offer frequently put in national terms. At the same time one needs to understand what it was that made Magyar peasants or Italian artisans concern themselves with politics and either compelled political elites to consider them or to regard an appeal to them as a way of strengthening political opposition.

In contemporary east-central Europe the problem is rather different. The sphere of 'politics' or the public sphere was enormously expanded, for example through the mass membership of the communist parties and many affiliated organisations. Partly this was necessary as a way of providing some kind of participation to an increasingly well-educated, urban-industrial population. However, the excessive centralisation and monopolisation

386

of power by the party and state meant that here 'civil society' was also poorly articulated, though there was mass political awareness. Groups could be mobilised for political action very quickly, but there were no extensive ties outside of those established in the world of politics – for example, ties created through economic interest groups, professional associations, or organisations of those with the same cultural or other kinds of interests. Instead, the breakdown of state power left many people only with the options of following elements of the political community who now pursued the option of 'national communism'[14] or of orienting themselves to the much more limited, if intensely felt, solidarities of family, friends and locality. Both responses could strengthen two kinds of nationalism – the 'institutional' nationalism which focused on taking over republican institutions and 'ethnic' nationalism which focused on inter-ethnic tensions and fears which increased enormously with the breakdown of political stability.

In many cases in colonial situations changes which would involve social groups in politics had hardly occurred and politics therefore hardly represented social interests at all. In such cases the appeal to cultural identity is often a substitute for the failure to connect politics with significant social interests, or it is aimed primarily at elites in particular regions of the colonial state. Of course the inherent plausibility of many nationalist appeals must be recognised, and one must understand the force which certain ceremonies and symbols can possess independently of any appeal to particular social interests. However, such appeals have little direct political impact in the absence of clear interests within the political community for supporting nationalist objectives and without some means of linking social interests to those objectives. To suggest otherwise is to turn nationalism into an irrational, mysterious force in modern politics, and it has been the major concern of this book to combat that notion.

The final function to which I have referred is that of legitimacy. I use the term in a very restricted sense. For many writers the notion of legitimacy is central to an understanding of any human situation which is characterised by inequality and in which the disadvantaged are not subjugated by simple coercion or other forms of physical control. To understand how people can accept this it is argued one must understand the ways in which the situation can be made to appear legitimate to them. Many different approaches have been devised in dealing with this matter. Clearly nationalism can be analysed in these terms. At one level nationalism in opposition provides a means of criticising the *status quo* and thus challenging the legitimacy of the state. At another level nationalism can be seen as a way of making a particular state legitimate in the eyes of those it controls. I have dealt in some detail with the way in which criticism of the existing state can be channelled into nationalist opposition and there is no need to consider separately why it appears plausible to members or supporters of that opposition. I have also suggested that nationalism as a distinctive ideology has probably been ascribed too great a role in the processes which reconcile the mass of a state's subjects to its rule.[15]

The problem of legitimacy as I define it here is the much narrower one of convincing *outsiders* of the justice of the nationalist case. This is important when an external power is seeking a means of justifying a policy which involves supporting particular oppositions, particularly when that power has to present a case to a powerful and critical public opinion. One must also remember that nationalist opposition frequently emerges at a time of crisis in the existing state in part due to competition with other states. There is, therefore, frequently an intimate link between nationalist oppositions and external states. This intimate link is often sustained and reinforced by emigré communities. Western enthusiasm for the cause of Italy or Hungary in the nineteenth-century was bound up with the images that figures such as Mazzini, Garibaldi and Kossuth could project of their cause. In the twentieth-century emigré communities from the USSR have played a powerful role in shaping public opinion in the west, influencing state policy, and channelling resources back into nationalist oppositions.[16]

Nationalism can also help provide an acceptable formula for orderly political change. In this case it may well be the existing state itself which accepts the nationalist case as legitimate, as happened in much of European empire overseas after 1945. Whether these influential forces actually believe the nationalist case is not a matter with which I will deal in detail. The degree of conviction nationalism conveys to outsiders depends partly on the distance between them and the conflict. Those closely concerned in disputes involving nationalism are more likely to be fully aware of the gulf between rhetoric and reality. Colonial administrators were frequently contemptuous and regarded many nationalist claims as ridiculous. In part this was a reflection of racial and cultural value judgements, but it was also an understandable response to the discrepancy between the values of cultural identity and political self-determination claimed by nationalists and the extent to which these values really seemed to exist within the colonial 'nation'. Generally colonial regimes only became at all uncertain of their right to rule in relation to arguments about political self-determination. The arguments about cultural identity had impact mainly as a way of combating nationalism – for example in the way the British Raj promoted Muslim and lower-caste Hindu interests against a nationalist movement it interpreted as an affair of high-caste Hindus. But more important than the feeling that the arguments about political rights could not easily be rejected were the pressures upon declining imperial powers to find a way of giving up power. Nationalists provided ideologically as well as practically a legitimate alternative. In many cases where the political and social conditions had not been established which enabled nationalism to develop as an effective internal political force, this attitude on the part of the imperial power could play the crucial role in determining how state power was transferred.

European imperial power was destroyed by conflict in Europe and the shift of global supremacy to the United States and the Soviet Union. For both these new world powers the language of nationalism provided an acceptable way of justifying the ending of formal European empire. Again it was the arguments about political self-determination that were of most importance, although cultural ones played a role. To understand why, one has to turn back to nineteenth-century Europe.

There were good reasons for some outside powers to support nationalist claims in the Ottoman empire before 1918. Many such claims could be framed only in cultural terms, given the absence of any distinctive 'national' territory or political rights. Some of the arguments provoked intense responses among the publics of the European powers. Perhaps most striking was the belief in the Greek cause which flourished in France and Britain and the German states in the 1820s and 1830s. Support for the Greek, as well as other causes, also suited French and British governments, which could use nationalist arguments to pursue policies aimed at stabilising particular areas and extending their influence by the establishment of client states. In the case of the Habsburg empire nationalism could plausibly be linked with democratic values, as it was the 'small nations' which, particularly after 1867, could present themselves to European public opinion as oppressed groups. This had little practical effect until 1914 because few European powers were interested in bringing about major political change in the Habsburg empire.[17] From 1914 onwards, however, nationalist arguments could justify the objective of dismembering the Habsburg empire. Nationalism, of course, was much more than that. It is important that nationalism had, in many cases, become genuinely strong in the Habsburg empire and that nationalist claims could be pushed with some force at the end of the war. It is also important from a negative point of view. The absence of any sort of sub-nationalism in Germany made the idea of dismembering the country almost unthinkable. In this sense the universal acceptance of the criterion of nationality (even if employed in many, often mutually contradictory, ways) for drawing the boundaries of states limited the policies that could be pursued after 1918. That was important because it meant that the underlying capacity of a territorially only slightly diminished Germany to reacquire great power status was preserved.

Once the argument for national self-determination, frequently based on cultural identity rather than individual preference, had been applied in Europe it became more difficult intellectually to resist such claims elsewhere. Of course the force of logic was far less important than the actual distribution of power, as Irish and Vietnamese visitors to the Peace Conference at Versailles were to note. But nationalism as a rather unclear mixture of ideas about cultural identity and individual liberty had clearly become an argument which had some force with the major powers and their frequently influential public opinions. At times that force, accompanied by policies of self-interest on the part of major powers, was of more importance in determining the fortunes of a particular nationalist movement than the movement's own capacity to co-ordinate the actions of various political elites and to mobilise popular support.

4 Concluding remarks

Nationalism remains distinctive only for so long as it is unsuccessful. Nationalism is one particular response to the distinction, peculiar to the modern world, between state and society. It seeks to abolish that distinction. In so far as it succeeds in doing so it abolishes its own foundations. Only if there is a distinct notion of the sovereign and bounded public state does the idea of political self-determination make sense. Only if there is a distinct notion of a private civil society which is regarded as the source of sovereignty can one claim that power ultimately rests with the nation defined in 'private', that is, in cultural, terms. If nationalism was true – that is, if there really were such things as (cultural) nations which demanded (political) self-determination and, upon gaining it, could end the modern dilemma of the gulf between state and society – then a distinctive nationalism might continue to operate once it had gained state power. But what has actually happened is very different. One can see this by looking at nationalist movements which have gained power and which have taken seriously the need to bring to an end the distinction between state and society.

One type of this sort occurs in the new states. Here, as I have argued, there is a skewed relationship between modern state forms and an ill-formed civil society. As a consequence the notion of a balanced relationship between state and society is hard to establish. Furthermore, the urgent problems of control and/or development mean that the new states can hardly give priority to the construction of a nation-state on the liberal model. Nor can they content themselves with the limited authoritarian control of European absolutism, either. Instead there is a strong temptation to use nationalism to promote and justify the creation of a nation. The independent state is regarded as the starting point for the construction of this new society, the nation. Of course, the identity of the nation will be related to 'tradition' and to existing cultural practices, but the decisions as to what is relevant and how it should be used in establishing the national identity will rest with the state. In this way nationalism becomes purely arbitrary, because the ideological case of cultural nationality producing certain sorts of politics is in reality reversed. The ideology becomes a sleight of hand which inverts the real relationship between state and nationality. Actually the success of these efforts on the part of the new state is frequently limited and can provoke sub-nationalist resistance. It is no accident that such sub-nationalist responses often bear a closer resemblance to earlier European nationalisms than to territorial colonial nationalism. It is in the new state rather than in the colonial state that cultural identity becomes a way of justifying political opposition to the state, often a state which itself claims to define and express national values. Nationalism remains a distinctive form of politics, therefore, because it continued to challenge the distinction between state and society ('your' state does not represent 'my' nation) and refused to recognise the arguments of the state that it was overcoming that distinction.

More dramatic and significant, however, is the pattern of events in European states in which fascism manages to take power. Here the well developed sense of nationality and the immense power of the state meant that a very serious attempt could be made to abolish the state/society distinction and to put in its place the 'national community' so cherished in fascist ideology. I will look briefly at the case of the Third Reich, in which these ideas received their most powerful expression.

Negatively the fascist notion of a national community in which party or class divisions were abolished and the distinction between 'public' and 'private' eroded was soon put into practice. All parties other than the Nazi party were abolished, interest groups which operated outside the state, such as trade unions, were dissolved. Numerous 'private' associations were 'co-ordinated', that is to say, brought under the supervision of members of the Nazi party. Large-scale repression of dissident elements, control of the media, and the breaking of many organised contacts between people destroyed the chances of effective resistance and the formulation of open and sustained criticism. There is no doubt that the liberal state was abruptly destroyed. The problem, however, is to work out the positive side. How did the new regime actually formulate policy, enforce decisions and establish its authority? In what sense did it elicit co-operation on the basis of a national identification with the regime?

First, one should note that many interest groups continued to exist – in the armed forces, the civil service and the administration, for example. To these were added new organisations and agencies: the Nazi party, the SS, the Labour Front, etc. Some were the product of the period of opposition, others were regarded as 'national' substitutes for organisations such as trade unions, others were brought into being by a combination of power-seeking and policy need under the new regime. The lines demarcating the divisions of responsibility between these various organisations were very blurred. There was no institutional focus of sovereign power. Even the courts were transformed by the new regime with its insistence on extraordinary legislation and its repudiation of the priority of due process in the enforcement of law. It was very difficult for ordinary citizens to predict the behaviour of the organisations which controlled their lives or even to work out which particular organisation or agency was competent to deal with a particular issue.

As a consequence it becomes very difficult to draw a distinction between state and society. The regime seems to have existed as a struggle between competing agencies in which such sovereignty as there was rested with the personal decisions of the Füehrer. As Hitler frequently refused to arbitrate between competing claims, and made such decisions on no formal, rational or consistent criteria, it becomes impossible for the observer to provide any sort of constitutional description of the Third Reich. Why this situation came into existence has been a matter of debate. Some observers regard it as arising out of the very nature of National Socialism, which had no clear alternative to what it destroyed other than power as a struggle in which the strongest survived. Others relate it to Hitler's determination not to be bound by any one institution or agency.

At the same time, however, political participation remained confined to a minority and the grandiose ideas of producing social transformation and permanent mass involvement in public life faded away. Political change certainly hit some social groups more than others – workers were desperately weakened by repression of their major organisations. So there was a substantial shift in the balance of power between classes. But there was no fundamental change in the class structure, and market situation rather than government policy was the major determinant of income distribution. Many social groups applauded by the regime in its rhetoric – peasants, small businessmen – continued to suffer as they had done under the Weimar Republic. Rhetorical praise of the woman who remained at home was undermined by the sharp increase in female employment. The abolition of the public use of class language did not extend to the actual ending of elementary class distinctions. A consciousness of social inequality could not now be publicly articulated, but it remained nevertheless. The National Socialist regime as such was not regarded with great enthusiasm by large sections of the population, although its reduction of unemployment, its successes in foreign policy up to 1938, and the personality of Hitler himself were undeniable assets. However, one should not overestimate their importance: enthusiasm over a diplomatic triumph was short-lived and faded away particularly quickly if it was thought it would demand subsequent sacrifices. As for the great organised expressions of national enthusiasm, these were often devices for keeping otherwise disgruntled activists occupied and, if they did appeal to other sections of the population, it was probably for reasons which had nothing to do with the ideological purpose of the rallies, marches and youth camps.[18]

In other words, the regime failed to put anything distinctive and positive in place of the despised liberal state. The models which have been suggested, either of a genuinely fascist political system or of a totalitarian system, fail to grasp the negativity and shapeless character of the regime.[19] Yet this meant that the regime failed to provide a distinctive form of legitimacy for itself, other than that represented through the person of Hitler. Ultimately the regime was, to use Weber's term, a charismatic regime. In so far as it sought to be more, and also in so far as Hitler himself had immense ambitions extending beyond the repudiation of the Versailles settlement, this involved the regime in expansionist policies, both economic and diplomatic, which pushed it into war. Successes there enabled it to continue to expand, to proliferate its mutually struggling agencies. Society became not so much integrated with the regime as something upon which an irrational and illegitimate political system fed in order to keep going. Whether the Third Reich could, at some point, have halted this process and turned itself into a different, more limited and structured regime with a legitimacy which would have continued beyond the lifetime of Hitler is a matter on which one can only speculate. But the attempt to abolish the state/society distinction produced not an integral national community but arbitrary and irrational political structures in which nationalism became the rhetoric justifying whichever particular policy managed to assert itself against its competitors.[20]

But the erosion of the distinction between public state and private society is not based solely on the nationalist attack upon that distinction, an attack which leaves nationalism itself without any clear focus and hence an arbitrary and shapeless thing. There are processes which more generally and certainly are eroding that distinction.

The central problem is that the liberal model of the sovereign territorial state operating in a competing world of such states, a global economic order based on the free market, and with a strong distinction between state and society, is itself an ideology. It never fully described reality. It was, however, a 'rational' ideology in that under certain conditions the descriptions it supplied bore a close resemblance to what was really the case and actually helped sustain that reality. In the middle of the nineteenth century a peculiar combination of an international market economy related to British supremacy beyond Europe, of a balance of power between the major European powers, and of weak organisation among lower-class groups in the more advanced European economies (to name just the major features) guaranteed the liberal model a certain plausibility. Formal equality among members of civil society disguised their real inequality in the market place. Formal equality among states concealed real inequality among great powers and what were often client states. Free-trade arrangements depended on the inability or unwillingness to challenge British economic supremacy. By the end of the century these conditions had largely ceased to exist. New nation-states such as Germany and Italy upset the balance of power and were not prepared to see their economies develop according to the behest of an international system of free trade. More

393

intense conflict in Europe led to the establishment of formal empire beyond Europe where the imperial power enjoyed privileged economic powers and where the tenets of political liberalism were inapplicable. The growing strength and organisation of lower-class groups, above all of the working class, led to pressure upon the state to regulate and if necessary suppress matters previously left to market forces. Issues concerning welfare and education, previously deemed private affairs, were brought under the purview of the state. Elements within government which had never accepted liberal values were quick to respond to these new social pressures – be it in the form of tariff protection, industrial subsidy or educational provision – and to expand state agencies in order to meet the new demands. By 1914 it was already becoming difficult to draw the sharp distinction between state and society which liberal theory posited. Nevertheless, where a participatory political system and economic growth developed within a nation-state, there did develop a clear sense of national identity. However, this institutionalised national identity was embedded in a range of institutions and was shared by conflicting political groups. This actually prevented the development of a distinctively nationalist politics. Precisely for this reason, it was those who wanted such a distinctive politics who fought against these processes of nation-building – such as Maurras against the French Third Republic and Hitler against the Weimar Republic.

The trend of events since 1914 has accelerated the decline of that liberal theory as a reasonable description of reality. The consolidation of formal empire was clearly illiberal, although the idea of the public colonial state coupled with notions of trusteeship might preserve some semblance of liberal values. World wars led to an enormous extension of government power and an expansion of what needed regulation by the state in the public interest. Such extensions were not easily undone when hostilities ceased. Indeed, they often provided a model for reformers: the 'war' on poverty or unemployment or inequality was seen to require the same sort of effort as that demanded for war between industrial states. After 1918, beyond western Europe, democratic parliamentary government was soon largely removed in favour of governments which suggested that representing the national interest was all that mattered. In eastern Europe, of course, there was not even an interlude between the *ancien régime* despotism of Tsarism and the construction of an all-embracing one-party state. The demise of European empire took place under the shadow of two new powers whose nuclear capacity distanced them from others in an unprecedented way. The sovereignty of many nation-states, old or new, became a hollow sham. Not only was it undermined by informal controls but also formally through treaty arrangements. Many of the nation-states have been drawn into blocs which proclaim allegiances extending beyond the nation-state.

In the non-industrial world the effort to break with dependency and weakness has seemed possible only through state direction of the economy and, except for countries with particularly large resources of population and materials, links with the major power blocs. In the industrial world the demands of business, labour, farmers and growing tertiary groups have led to the concession of special rights to 'private' organisations and to the creation of numerous agencies and powers of intervention which can be regarded as neither public nor private by liberal criteria. Many arguments about these bodies centre not on whether they should exist at all but on what their objectives should be and how they should be controlled. Attempts to throw back the proliferation of these quasi-state powers by liberals (who now call themselves radical conservatives) seem unlikely to achieve much success.

Private 'cultural' spheres of activity are also under attack. I have already dealt with the ways in which new states seek increasingly to define and shape national values, and this involves all sorts of intervention in cultural matters. In industrialising countries based on a command economy the interventions of the state in such matters are equally obvious. But similar processes are at work in the free-market industrial economies. Educational and welfare decisions are removed from the family and instead the state takes upon itself the power to determine what a proper education is, which schools children should attend, and what is permissible in matters of close family relationships. The cultivation of the personality through leisure pursuits is to some extent shaped by various media, much of which is under state control or at least general supervision. At the same time the leisure market attracts the attention of organised capital, which naturally seeks to shape and thereby stabilise the decisions of its customers. Of course, one can easily exaggerate the extent to which people's values and actions are shaped by the media and the various leisure industries. The point I am making is not that this is an 'invasion' of privacy but rather that it involves an attenuation of the very concept of privacy. The exaggerated stress on sexual fulfilment, for example, can be seen both as an intensive cultivation of a clearly private matter or as a further extension of public definitions of human values. The result is not so much that the 'public' sphere expands at the expense of the 'private' sphere or vice versa as that the very notion of a clear distinction between the two is undermined. One can argue that what one observes is state or economic interference in private matters. But the case could equally well be made that what one is seeing is particular 'private' interests – be they trade unions, large businesses or would-be arbiters of taste and morality – intruding on the domain of the state. What is really happening is that the notion of the public and sovereign state is becoming increasingly difficult to employ as a description of reality. The external constraints of alliances as well as multinational companies and the internal erosion of the public/private distinction act to undermine this liberal notion.

395

It may appear that nationalism can adapt quite handily to this situation. Indeed, one could well argue that it is one of the major causes of the decline of the public state, be it in its absolutist, liberal or imperialist forms. The very attempt to abolish the separation between the public state and the civil society it rules is central to nationalist ideology. Consequently the development of highly illiberal forms of nationalism in the twentieth century might be seen as no more than the revelation of the 'true' nature of nationalism.

But nationalism is a parasitic movement and ideology, shaped by what it opposes. A distinctively 'private' society which nationalists can identify as a cultural group, and a public state which nationalists can claim in the name of that cultural group, are the necessary conditions for the development of nationalism as a specific and effective form of political practice and ideology. But when the state comes increasingly to determine the identifiable features of this cultural group and the distinction between state and society is eroded, nationalism becomes either arbitrary (in support of state policy) or mysterious (in support of some sort of cultural identity opposed to that cultivated by the state). The state/society distinction provided the map by which nationalists could find their directions. With the ending of the map any route that is taken can be called nationalist. Anyone can, and does, use some sort of nationalist rhetoric in a world where the nation-state is the basic political unit and where it is difficult to locate cultural groups distinct from the public state. As a consequence nationalism is reduced to mere emotion or pragmatism. The two go together: emotion alone cannot give rise to a specific political movement and ideology; pragmatism needs some emotional basis in which to root itself. It is because of this that many observers have concluded that nationalism is fundamentally irrational, rooted in mass emotion and manipulated by various interests. But it did not come into existence in that form, and in moving in that direction it is losing the qualities which made it specific. In a negative way there are circumstances under which nationalism can be described as a rational ideology.

The reduction of modern nationalism to an arbitrary combination of emotion and pragmatism is clearly shown in many of the separatist movements of the advanced industrial states. In some cases such movements arise from problems similar to those which existed in earlier multinational empires. But in a country such as the United Kingdom the problem is a very different one. Since 1945 the formula which has increasingly commanded popular consent has been one based on the maintenance of full employment and a steady increase in the standard of living. It was adopted in an open political system with mass political organisations based mainly on class alignments. With the possible exception of the Catholic minority in Ulster, where the class alignment did not operate, no important group was excluded from having some influence in this political system. It seemed for a time that in such a society 'ideological legitimacy' was no longer required. Political choice centred on selecting those who could best manage the economy. Whether this argument about the end of ideology ever had any validity when the formula of economic growth worked is debatable. But clearly from the mid-1960s the formula has become increasingly difficult to operate successfully. Yet the very attempt to operate it helped erode the state/society distinction.

As a consequence significant dissatisfaction expressed in nationalist terms had nothing to do with dissatisfaction with a 'foreign' state or even a 'foreign' culture. In the Scottish case one would be hard put to it to give any meaning to such ideas. Politically Scots behaved like British citizens elsewhere; culturally there are no more than certain regional, mainly class-based practices which are no more distinctive than what goes on in various English regions. That is why the SNP appeals not to nationality as a distinctive cultural notion or to political self-determination as a general value which is at present denied to Scots. The appeal lies in the claim to have a way of making the old formula of prosperity work successfully at a regional level, a region which certain institutions enable one to define as Scotland. Sovereignty is not a good in itself but a device for achieving control over oil and management of the economy. As for the preservation of a national culture, beyond a few zealots most of the SNP would be taxed to provide even the thinnest notion of what the term might mean. Nationalism here has become an arbitrary and pragmatic creed. Its basic objectives could well be pursued by other types of politics. Its supporters can pick and choose between a variety of them. There is little resemblance to the situations which originally gave rise to nationalist oppositions. This is not to argue that Rumanian or Indian nationalism was rooted in nationality in a way that does not apply to Scottish nationalism. I have argued throughout this book that nationalism has little to do with the existence or non-existence of a nation, even assuming one can find objective criteria for determining that matter. Rather there were circumstances under the Habsburg empire and the British Raj when nationalism was the most appropriate form political opposition could take. It was a drive to possess state power by elites and social groups which were denied political rights, and in which nationalist ideology appeared not only to promote effective opposition but actually to reflect the nature of conflict by building upon certain cultural features or institutional traditions. That is not the case with the modern separatist movements of the United Kingdom.

There are still areas of the world where the sort of situation which originally generated nationalism continues to exist. In eastern Europe the break-up of the multinational empire that is the USSR has been accompanied by the claims of different groups to national self-determination and, in some cases, to further nationalist conflict between some of those groups. Clearly the problems of possible border disputes and or irredentist claims on behalf of one's 'own' nation – disputes especially likely to be pursued by weak governments seeking to mobilise support around such claims – remain very likely.[21] In many of the new states in areas of former European empire a combination of government weakness and nation-building policies could give rise to sub-nationalist oppositions. The combination of regional disparities in political influence, political elites able and prepared to oppose the present state, the non-involvement of much of the population in other, non-nationalist forms of politics, and the existence of plausible cultural and/or institutional characteristics for a regionally based opposition – all these supply the necessary conditions.

Otherwise what many will call 'nationalism' seems likely to take two major forms. On the one hand there will be strong states with market economies and a 'standard national culture' where people identify with 'their' state in most serious conflicts with other states but otherwise do not expect politics to be about 'national' questions. On the other hand in some parts of the world – possibly parts of the former USSR where a national movement, communist or non-communist, has not re-stabilised power, as well as in parts of the less developed world – there will be much weaker states which cannot contain the bulk of the political community and where there are constant outbreaks of conflict between elements of that community, sometimes making ethnic, sometimes other kinds of factional claims. Stronger states will often intervene in the affairs of these weaker states and the resultant political conflicts might be justified in nationalist terms. But nationalism as a distinct kind of political movement will be difficult to discern in most of this.

Nationalism is not the expression of nationality, if by nationality is understood an independently developed ideology or group sentiment broadly diffused through the 'nation'. If it were we should first encounter colonial nationalism in areas where racial and cultural discrimination is most acute, such as South and east Africa rather than in areas where it was an impersonal colonial administration which was of central importance, such as in India or British West Africa. Nationalism is not a response to simple oppression. If it were we should expect Rumanians to have been nationalist before Magyars, and the inhabitants of the Belgian Congo before those of India. Rather, an effective nationalism develops where it makes political sense for an opposition to the government to claim to represent the nation against the present state. In the various case studies presented in this book I have tried to show how nationalism made political sense and why it was particularly appropriate for certain types of opposition to the modern state.

In doing this I have stressed its rationality even while recognising the ideological and frequently irrational form in which nationalist claims were couched. Too much of the literature on nationalism has tended to ignore its political rationality and sought to find its true meaning beyond politics.

Nationalism comes to be seen as either the instrument of this or that interest (be it a political elite or a social class) or as the expression of some deep human desire which is beyond rational analysis (such as an identity need or national consciousness). The general result is that it appears as itself irrational, whether the emphasis is on manipulation or on non-rational needs. It becomes either a non-rational force which erupts into history or a mask to be stripped away in order to locate the 'real' forces beneath.

To counter such ideas it seemed best to narrow the scope of the enquiry. So long as nationalism is defined in grand terms of a sense of shared identity or an intellectual invention one is almost bound to regard nationalist politics as no more than epiphenomena. By concentrating on nationalism as politics and on how nationalist ideals made eminent sense in certain political situations, it seemed possible to give nationalism a more specific character and to recognise its rational features even while denying the claims made by nationalists themselves.

It is just as important that one recognises the ultimate irrationality of nationalism as a political ideology as it is to see that it is not in itself a particularly irrational form of politics. It is almost a reflex response today to accept that nations should be free and that a united and stable state is in some sense based on national cultural unity. Once one accepts that, then the ability of a political movement to insist plausibly on the existence of some fundamental cultural distinctions within a particular state can mean that the political claims of such a group automatically acquire a degree of legitimacy. New nationalist movements often fail to command sympathy not because the general form of their argument is rejected but because it is believed that their particular case is weak. If a nationalist movement does manage to persuade outsiders that there is a cultural group whose interests it represents, this can become a major political asset. On the other hand, if opponents of the movement can fix other labels upon it, such as 'sectarian' or 'tribal', this can represent a major political liability. The importance of such political arguments is related not merely to the beliefs and calculations of those involved in nationalist politics but also to the way in which nationalist premises have come to permeate modern thinking about politics. For example, to many observers the objective of Irish unity appears a 'natural' one. It is 'natural' for an island to have only one government, and there is an elaborate Irish nationalist ideology which can insist upon an historic and cultural unity as well. Against this the much cruder ideology of Ulster Unionism and the demand to preserve a partition of the island and the maintenance of the connection between Ulster and Westminster can easily be made to appear 'artificial'. One can see how the key idea in nationalist ideology, namely that there are certain natural non-political features on which a legitimate state should be based, are very easily and plausibly introduced into this particular example. Once that

399

broad argument is accepted, the case against Irish unity is greatly weakened. If such acceptance extends to influential groups outside Ireland this can make a great difference to the actual balance of forces in the conflict. The sneaking suspicion that Irish nationalists 'have a case', no matter how detestable the methods some of them might employ, becomes a major political asset.

I would stress that I am not suggesting that Irish nationalists do not have a case; only that it is not the one many of them put. There is no 'natural' basis to politics. There is no cultural or any other non-political unit of humanity which can be regarded as the true basis of legitimate politics. To accept that there is is to abolish the autonomy and limits, and ultimately the rationality of politics. To see that nationalism does not arise from the nation and that it is a specific and effective form of politics only under certain political conditions can perhaps help guard against the idea that there is some natural basis to the legitimate state which lies beyond the public realm, that political movements are and should be no more than emanations of communal feeling.

I also believe that in a world made up of nation-states, especially the developed world where those states are increasingly concerned with the effective management of more or less free market economies, the conditions for the emergence of such nationalist movements largely cease to exist. There may well be inter-ethnic conflicts but for that to become nationalism one would require that a national minority was a regional majority, that there were strong regional economic disparities, that cross-cutting political ties were of minor importance (although those who claimed to represent the minority must have been able to build up a political movement within existing state institutions), that autonomy or transfer to another state could credibly promise economic improvement, and that another state was prepared to risk international conflict for that minority. There are potentially such situations but they are not as common as some commentators who talk of a new age of nationalism and nationalist conflict would have us believe.

Far more commonplace will be tension, sometimes conflict between culturally distinct communities within nation-states but which do not give rise to nationalist politics; and tensions, sometimes conflicts between states which regard themselves as nation-states. In both kinds of conflict the term 'nationalism' will be used, both by participants and observers. However, these are two kinds of conflict distinct both from one another and from nationalist politics, that is political movements which seek to establish national self-determination. Furthermore, the processes which give rise to cultural group identity and conflicts between such groups, as well as the reasons states come into conflict with one another, are extraordinarily varied. To use the term nationalism to cover all these kinds of behaviour (as well as using it to refer to certain kinds of ideas and sentiments) is to

400

ensure perpetual bafflement as to what nationalism is and how one is to account for it.

One can make some progress in understanding, however, by treating nationalism as that class of political movements which make their principal objective the pursuit and assertion of national self-determination. Seen in this light, nationalism is just one particular form of politics. Like all forms of politics it is entangled in a world of material interests, of corruption, and self-seeking rhetoric. Like all forms of politics it has its symbols and ideals, its genuine believers. Like all forms of politics it can rise and fall, and interact with politics that pursue other objectives than that of national self-determination. Like all forms of politics it derives much of its power from the half-truths it embodies. People do yearn for communal membership, do have a strong sense of us and them, of territories as homelands, of belonging to culturally defined and bounded worlds which give their lives meaning. Ultimately much of this is beyond rational analysis and, I believe, the explanatory powers of the historian.

Yet it remains incontestably the case that only in modern times have political movements made an appeal to these kinds of sentiments the basic justification for their objective and ideal – the creation of nation-states. Furthermore such a political objective is just one among many others in modern times. Therefore it is necessary to identify that quality of modernity which gives sense to such a politics, and that combination of factors in modern times which can enable such a political movement to develop and to acquire real power. That can only be achieved through systematic comparison of a wide range of cases. On the basis of such a comparison I have concluded that nationalism is a peculiarly modern form of politics which can only be understood in relation to the way in which the modern state has developed.

Notes

1   I have considered this in some detail for Germany. See 'Sovereignty and boundaries: modern state formation and national identity in Germany', in *National Histories and European Perspectives*, edited by Mary Fulbrook (London, 1993).

2   This compares sharply with pre-modern states with different power claims over different territories and groups and where claims tend to decline as one moves from the territorial core to frontier zones. See Heesterman (note 1, chapter 10); the distinction between frontiers and borders in Anthony Giddens, *The Nation-State and Violence* (Cambridge, 1985); and the highly original study of the changing meaning of boundaries over the modern period: P. Sahlins, *Boundaries: the making of France and Spain in the Pyrenees* (Berkeley, 1989).

3   The novelty and importance of this is stressed in Immanuel Wallerstein, *The Modern World Wystem: capitalist agriculture and the origins of the*

European world economy in the sixteenth century (New York, 1974). For the utopian significance some liberals could derive from the separation of international economic dealings from state interference see Bernard Semmel, *Liberalism and Naval Strategy: Ideology, Interest and Sea Power during the Pax Britannica* (London, 1986).

4   The distinction is made by Michael Mann in *The Sources of Social Power*, vol. 1 (Cambridge, 1986).

5   See T. C. W. Blanning, *The Origins of the French Revolutionary Wars* (London, 1986), and chapter 3 above.

6   This idea is developed brilliantly by Benedict Anderson in his book *Imagined Communities: reflections on the origins and spread of nationalism* (London, 1983). For a more detailed critique of this study, as well as the book by Ernest Gellner, *Nations and Nationalism* (Oxford, 1983) see my review article 'Reflections on nationalism', *Philosophy of the Social Sciences*, 15 (March, 1985), pp. 65–75.

7   *Ibid.* For a further, more systematic development of Gellner's arguments about the changing nature and meaning of culture in the modern age of urban-industrial society see *idem., Plough, Sword, Book: The Structure of Human History* (London, 1988).

8   See, for example, Eugene Weber, *Peasants into Frenchmen: the modernisation of rural France 1870–1914 (Stanford, 1976)*. There is now much agreement amongst historians that the crucial period for the creation of a mass society with national identity in western Europe was 1890–1914, with the world war then creating the most intense 'national' experience to date. For a general overview for Europe see Norman Stone, *Europe Transformed, 1878–1919* (London, 1983); and for the USA see Hugh Brogan, *The Pelican History of the United States of America* (London, 1986).

9   It is actually very difficult to avoid this slippage in meaning, and I have not been completely successful myself. Partly that is because of the pull of common usage of the word nationalism. Partly it is because one can never wholly leave aside the ideas and sentiments that give nationalist politics its principal objective and which can continue to exist even when the conditions for such politics do not exist, for example in the form of pressure groups or inter-ethnic conflicts or just general chauvinism. For example, Motyl makes the valid point that Russian chauvinism did not take nationalist form so long as Russians had an empire to rule. Nevertheless, the rapid switch, once the empire had collapsed, into nationalist politics can only be understood against that background. We need clear definitions and distinctions, but equally we must not forget that these express our analytical needs rather than neatly reflecting the 'real' world. A. Motyl, *Sovietology, Rationality, Nationality: Coming to Grips with Nationalism in the USSR* (New York, 1990), chapter 11.

10   See below, appendix, especially section 6.

11   See G. R. Elton, 'Parliament in the sixteenth century: functions and fortunes', in *Historical Journal*, 22 (2) (1979); C. Russell, 'Parliamentary history in perspective, 1604–1629', *History*, 61 (1976).

12   Although Elton strengthens his case by using the word 'politics' in a very narrow way.

13 See chapter 7 above.
14 This was not the case in certain areas, such as the Baltic states, where for reasons I cannot pursue alternative political oppositions of significance outside of the communist party could quickly come to prominence. However, national communism has made a dramatic comeback at the expense of those who led the way to achieving independent in the October 1992 elections in Lithuania.
15 See above, chapter 13.
16 For an interesting account of emigré communities as one form nationalist opposition has taken in the USSR see Alexander Motyl, *Sovietology, Rationality, Nationality*, especially chapter 9.
17 Kossuth and Garibaldi, for example, were as much cult figures in both liberal and radical circles as were any representatives of the Greek cause. However, the British government made a quite independent assessment of the significance and value of Italian or Hungarian separation from the Habsburg empire and then used such enthusiasm as existed to support policies where appropriate.
18 See William Sheridan Allen, 'The collapse of nationalism in Nazi Germany', in *The State of Germany*, edited by J. Breuilly (London, 1992), pp. 141–53.
19 I think some concept of totalitarianism will be revived in the effort to understand the Third Reich, especially as more information about the former USSR and communist regimes of eastern Europe has to be assimilated into some kind of framework. However, I think this will be more the 'social' model which focuses on the impact of regimes upon subjects rather than the 'political' model which focuses on the institutions of the regime itself. Especially interesting will be to compare the Third Reich and communism in those parts of eastern Germany were there was a fairly rapid transition from one to the other.
20 I think I exaggerated the negative features of the regime in the first edition of this book. There is no doubt that the regime was highly efficient in pursuing many of its objectives. There is also little doubt that both a sense of national identity as well as the power of the regime kept German society working in a very disciplined way until the very end of the war. Nevertheless, there never was (and never could be) a 'national community'.
21 See above, chapter 17.

Appendix: Approaches to nationalism[1]

1 Identifying nationalism

Nationalism is both defined and accounted for in many different ways. In this appendix I will very briefly outline various definitions and explanations in order to situate more clearly my own approach to the subject.

Very broadly nationalism can refer to ideas, to sentiments, and to actions. In the first sense nationalism is understood primarily as the work of intellectuals and the sources historians use are books, essays, and other nationalist publications. In the second sense nationalism is understood primarily as the sentiments, attitudes, values – in brief the 'consciousness' – that characterise a particular culture. Here the historian tends to focus on the development of language and other examples of shared ways of life such as religion and art. In the third sense nationalism is understood as organisations and movements which aim to assert the national interest in some way or another. Here the focus of the historian is upon political action and conflict.

One cannot say that one or another of these ways of identifying nationalism is right or wrong. They are simply different. They also tend to carry with them different explanatory preferences when there are attempts to link the different kinds of nationalism to one another. The historian of ideas concentrates upon the ways such ideas are spread amongst a population and come to influence political behaviour. The historian of cultures argues that eventually these 'folk' ways or the 'standard national cultures' of modern times are taken up by intellectuals and by politicians. The historian of politics sees movements justifying their actions by reference to the ideas of nationalism and exploiting sentiments to attract support.

However, it is essential to bear in mind that there are three very different kinds of subjects involved and that each has a distinct autonomy. There are important connections between ideas, sentiments and politics but they vary in kind and intensity from one society to another. Approaches which insist that nationalism, as a whole, is 'really' the product of intel-

404

lectuals, or cultures, or political activists simply do violence to a complex subject. Many of the approaches I will now consider make this basic mistake.

2 The nationalist approach

The strong, or properly nationalist approach assumes that nationalism is an expression of the nation. The basic level of nationalism, therefore, takes the form of culture and sentiments. The nation, thus characterised, desires independence. Nationalists – both as intellectuals and as politicians – simply articulate and try to realise that desire. Naturally this is the view nationalists themselves take, often with perfect sincerity. It is not a view that anyone else should accept.

To begin with it seems to be impossible to produce an independent definition of the nation which can be correlated in any reliable way with the existence or intensity of nationalism. The definitions provided by nationalists themselves vary enormously and conflict with one another. The Hungarian view is incompatible with the Slovak view; the Nigerian one with that of the Ibo or Biafran. What is more, not all the members of the 'nation' take the same view of the matter; nationalism is usually a minority movement pursued against the indifference and, frequently, the hostility of the majority of the members of the 'nation' in whose name the nationalists act. Nationalists can cope with these difficulties to their own satisfaction by arguing that the nation has 'forgotten' itself (such forgetfulness extending back over most of its history) and that it is their task to bring it back to its true self. An acceptable theory of nationalism can hardly begin from such an inherently undemonstrable point of view.

A weaker point of view is that nationalism is related to some prior development of national identity. One might, for example, trace back conceptions of national or ethnic identity into the past, while acknowledging that such conceptions lacked the full character of nationalist consciousness, above all a concern with legal, economic and political independence.[2] Alternatively, one might argue that although peculiarly modern, nationalism arises from distinct processes of modernisation which produce national cultures and sentiments which are then reflected in nationalism.

The problem with the second argument, as I hope this book has made clear, is that there is no agreed pattern of social, economic and cultural change which can be correlated with the rise of nationalist politics or doctrines.

The problem with the first argument is that nationalism itself takes care to appeal to such histories. There is always some element of truth in such appeals. There is an Italian language; there was a kingdom of Serbia. But to say that that language or that kingdom were bases of modern

405

nationalism, rather than historical achievements (themselves in part constructed and interpreted by nationalists and all with a greater or lesser mythical content) to which nationalists chose to appeal seems very misleading. Furthermore, to use these matters in a nationalist manner is to transform their significance. To be a 'German' in eighteenth-century Germany meant to carry an identity which co-existed with other identities (social estate, confession, and so on). To raise that German identity to a special, political level was both to alter the nature of that identity and also to change the relationship to other possible sources of identity. It is the way in which nationalism constructs identities anew, even if that construction involves appeals to history and culture and sees itself as discovery rather than construction, to which one must pay attention.

I think this suggests something more. The history of cultures, of identities, is a complex one in which no single identity prevails, in which one kind of identity has a meaning only in the context of other kinds of identity. It is better, therefore, to develop an autonomous historical study of the development of ethnic and national identity and to avoid the term nationalism within this branch of history. We can go on to ask whether the development of nationalism as ideas or as politics stands in a particular relationship to such cultural histories, but without seeking to collapse the histories of ideas or politics into the history of cultures.

3 The communications approach

This approach tends to see the 'nation' in terms of a developed system of internal communication which creates a sense of common identity.[3] In a way it is a particular variant upon the 'weaker' nationalist approach I have already criticised.

In two respects the approach is valuable. First, it is arguable that one can only conceive of the different social groups inhabiting a certain territory as having something in common that transcends their many differences with each other (as well as their similarities with groups outside that territory) if they do have regular and intensive communications amongst themselves. Second, it is also arguable that nationalist intellectuals can only spread their ideas, and nationalist movements can only mobilise large-scale support, if they have access to such extended networks of communication. In these ways, therefore, both the form of identity proposed in nationalism and the social reach of nationalism may be related to the emergence of modern systems of communications.

However, there is one crucial weakness in the approach. Intensified communications between individuals and groups can as often lead to an increase in internal conflict as to an increase in solidarity. What is more, such conflict or solidarity might be expressed in terms other than nationalist ones. So one is forced to go further and inquire under what conditions will intensified forms of internal communication lead to increases in conflict or solidarity expressed in nationalist terms. To understand that we need to know something about the types of conflict or solidarity which exist within a particular society and the part nationalism can play in shaping that (both internally and externally). The structure of communications does not directly indicate what those types of conflict are and therefore cannot, in itself, provide us with much idea about what kinds of nationalism will develop.[4]

4 Marxist approaches

Certainly one cannot say that Marxism failed to concentrate upon the issue of conflict. That is one of its central concerns. It is the way that conflict is conceived and related to nationalism that one can criticise.

It is difficult to refer to *the* Marxist approach to nationalism, because there are so many varieties of approach amongst those who regard themselves as Marxists. Broadly, however, one can identify interpretations which stress class conflict within particular societies and those which stress economic conflict between different societies.

Most Marxists would probably agree that nationalism is a modern phenomenon and would probably associate it with the development of capitalism. This development produces new classes and class relationships. These classes, with more extensive interrelationships than had existed hitherto, with a greater degree of physical concentration, and with a system of politics which did not arise directly out of economic relations, had to engage in politics in new ways. Control of the state depended much more than previously upon securing the active support and consent of the majority of the population. As the state did not directly represent the class interests of much of that population, mass politics and its accompanying ideologies had to find alternative appeals to that of class. Nationalism is the major alternative. So far this is fairly general and, as such, neither controversial nor enlightening. Difficulties arise when one tries to account more specifically for the relationship between nationalism and new sorts of class and class conflict.

The approach that focuses upon internal class conflict in a particular society has three options. It can regard a nationalist movement as the work and expression of a single class, with relatively little involvement by other classes. It can regard nationalism in terms of a set of class alliances in which each class has its own rational interest. It can regard nationalism as representing the interests of a particular class but inducing other classes to support that nationalism.

So far as the first kind of nationalism is concerned, it is true that one does sometimes encounter avowedly nationalist movements with a very narrow social basis, but their nationalist ideology is so clearly self-serving

407

that it does not merit serious investigation in its own right. In such cases it is really not necessary to abandon explicit class analysis. Nationalism, at best, can only serve the function of helping that class acquire a greater sense of solidarity and co-ordination.

The second possibility is more important. An example might be the allegedly common interests of the bourgeoisie and the working class in removing pre-capitalist classes from power and setting up a constitutional state in which capitalism can advance at maximum speed. What remains difficult to understand is why such a politics does not organise itself in the form of a set of class alliances, with each class indicating its particular interest in the alliance. Why, instead, should the various classes employ a nationalist ideology and organisation which seems to obscure the rational basis of their politics? Certainly when Marx and Engels themselves called for class alliances they were thinking of alliances between political groups representing the interests of each class.[5]

One answer might be that at the relatively early stage of capitalism in which this alliance occurs the class divisions of capitalism were, as yet, incompletely developed, so that class-based ideology is less attractive than various forms of populism which can take a nationalist form. This, however, comes perilously close to denying the general validity of class analysis. Another answer might be that it is psychologically naive to expect mass politics to proceed in the form of rational alliances, that to mobilise enthusiasm and popular support something more is required, and that can be supplied by nationalism. The problem here is how such irrational elements can be related to the rationality of class interest, which is regarded as the true basis of political commitment. In fact one can proceed from this position to argue that Marxist views about a class acting in its long-term interest by installing a regime which aids another class in the short term are naive and doomed to failure. But then one would have to account for working-class support for bourgeois nationalism in rather different terms from the approach outlined here.

A third answer might be to argue that each class produces its own variant of nationalism – there is no single nationalism in a multi-class nationalist movement – and that nationalism generally is simply the lowest common denominator of such variants. The snag with this answer is that nationalist ideology often stands in clear contradiction to class ideology and organisation. One is still left with the question of why such classes have to resort to nationalism in the first place. Finally, one could argue that the conditions under which such multi-class alliances could be constructed and sustained would seem to be fairly specific (e.g., classes of one mode of production acting in concert against the dominant class of another mode of production). Yet nationalism with multi-class support appears as a general feature of modern politics.

That is perhaps why it is the third option which attracts the most attention. It recognises the multi-class character of many nationalist move-ments and also that such movements do not equally represent the (true, rational) interests of the various classes involved. Therefore much class participation must be understood as the product of some form of manipu-lation which induces classes to act in ways which do not represent (at least fully) their own interests. This might also account for the lack of hard-headed class pragmatism in much nationalist politics and explain why a multi-class movement does not take the form of explicit class alliances.

The approach has its problems. The first is the need to identify the leading class within a particular nationalist movement in order to work out which class interest the movement represents. This is not a simple empirical matter. The debate over the class basis of European fascist movements, particularly the respective roles of the lower middle class and big business, or over the class basis of Bonapartism in the French Second Empire, illustrates the difficulties.[6] The personnel of a political movement do not, Marxists would argue, necessarily represent the interests of their 'own' class, that is, the class to which one would assign them by virtue of their own social origins. The supporters of the nationalist movement are drawn from a variety of classes. Within the Marxist framework the only criterion one can employ is not the direct evidence about their social origins but to note which class interests the nationalist movement serves, particularly when it gains state power. However, this recourse to the notion of class interest raises further problems with which I will deal in a moment.

Let us suppose that the issue of identifying the leading class within a nationalist movement has been satisfactorily solved. The probable result would be that different nationalisms would be assigned different leading classes. One might regard the business and professional classes as the leading class(es) in the liberal Italian and German nationalist movements of the mid-nineteenth century. The lesser gentry would perhaps be taken as the leading class in the Hungarian nationalist mvoement between 1825 and 1867 and in the Polish nationalist movement between 1790 and 1863. One might regard the lower middle class as the leading class in the formative phase of German and Italian fascism. One might argue that the organised Protestant working class provided the leading class in the most recent phase of Ulster Unionism, which can be regarded as a form of nationalism (e.g., the anti-Sunningdale general strike). Each claim would be contested, and the very problem of providing a clear class identity for these various groups (such as 'lower middle class' or 'lesser gentry') would prove contentious. But, assuming each claim could be settled and each class satisfactorily identified, one would expect the diversity of leading classes to remain. This still leaves the problem of why these different classes should all employ nationalist ideology.

One answer might be that it was simply the lowest common denomi-

409

nator for gaining support from other classes. Once that is admitted one can get on with the important business of investigating particular sets of nationalism – business nationalism, gentry nationalism, lower-middle-class nationalism, and so on – without bothering too much about nationalism in general. This is common practice in Marxist analyses, which go on to evaluate different forms of nationalism as good or bad, progressive or reactionary (the terms being virtually interchangeable), according to their various class bases and class objectives. It amounts to a refusal to recognise the necessity of understanding nationalism as such and is a major reason why Marxism has never satisfactorily grappled with the subject.[7]

Alternatively one might devote further attention to the general problem of how a political movement can transcend a particular class base and what role nationalism plays in this process. For example, one might seek to examine nationalism as an ideology and to explain the particular efficacy of that ideology in sustaining political movements transcending class divisions. One would also have to face the unpalatable fact of the frequent success of nationalism in this regard. But to do this one requires some theory of modern politics which will relate nationalism to the pursuit and exercise of state power in the capitalist era. Whether such a theory is possible within the Marxist framework is debatable. However, Marxists have made little effort to develop such a general theory of modern politics, and the question has hardly been pursued at a general level.[8]

In more specific ways Marxism has provided answers to the relationship between nationalism and manipulated class support. For example, concepts of imperialism and the aristocracy of labour have been employed in various ways to account for working class support for the policies of nation-states in Western Europe up to 1914.

Such accounts raise a problem touched upon earlier, namely employing the notion of class interest to account for political action. To argue that a particular class is manipulated implies that there is an objective class interest which is independent of the perceived interest of members of that class. This objective interest can be identified by the observer. S/he can note the discrepancy between the actions which should be taken in pursuit of it and the actions actually taken by members of the class which disclose a different view of their interests. Concepts such as the aristocracy of labour or the role of the mass media can then be introduced in order to account for the discrepancy.

The approach raises a host of problems which can hardly be touched upon here. A number of brief observations can, however, be made. First, the whole point of the notion of class interest in such accounts is its absence. It is a critical device postulated by the observer. It both creates the 'problem' and provides the 'answer'. But if one does not accept the notion in the first place, one does not accept the existence of the problem and, therefore, does not need an answer. Second, one never encounters completely irrational action or the complete realisation of particular class interests. A number of classes can benefit to a greater or lesser degree from a particular set of policies. One can provide this rational explanation for working-class support of their states in 1914 while conceding that many working-class interests were sacrificed. Alternatively, one can point out that even the leading class in a particular political movement is forced to make concessions and give up its maximal interests (e.g., the way in which business interests are compelled to yield the political initiative to fascists). Faced with these balances of interests, as well as the fact that many fateful decisions have to be taken suddenly in situations of uncertainty and incomplete information where all choices carry risks, the historian finds it difficult to identify in any useful way what would be the actions most conducive to the objective interests of a class and thus create a standard by which to evaluate what actually happened. This is not to deny the relevance of the concept of rational action to an understanding of human behaviour or of postulating ideal group interests which are not perfectly realised in practice. It does suggest, however, that the notion of objective class interest as an instrument of historical explanation leaves a lot to be desired.

One frequent result of accepting this notion is that the irrationality of historical figures is exaggerated. For example, many Marxist accounts have overestimated the degree to which workers had been 'incorporated' into their nation-state by 1914 through such means as welfare provision, the mass media, and a collaborationist labour leadership. This is because they have measured the actual behaviour of workers against an abstract conception of the working-class interest, found that behaviour wanting, and then gone on to account for this deficiency in terms of such a process of incorporation. Reform or revolution, acceptance or rejection: simple contrasts like these fail to do justice to the reality of apathetic hostility with which so many workers regarded those above them.[9]

It has partly been difficulties of this sort that have led some Marxists to stress relationships between rather than within societies. Such has particularly been the case with the connection between modern imperialism and nationalism.

Imperialism is seen primarily as a relationship of economic exploitation (although the precise nature of the relationship is disputed). Nationalism in the colonial territory is a response to this relationship. First, nationalists seek political independence. Subsequently they may go on to try to achieve economic independence. It may be that their efforts will be subverted by the ability of imperialism to find allies in colonial society or the newly independent state. On occasion, indeed, nationalists themselves can be regarded as allies of this sort and political independence as a superficial achievement beneath which economic exploitation continues. I will not explore this aspect of the subject any further, however, because it

411

raises the same sorts of issues as those already considered, namely how these nationalist collaborators persuade others to act against their true interests.[10]

But so long as nationalism is regarded as genuine resistance to imperialism the problem does not arise. Anti-colonial nationalism can here be regarded as representing the common interests of different classes in colonial society. Although Marx tended to regard colonialism as progressive, and therefore had little to say in support of such anti-colonial nationalism, Lenin clearly did distinguish such nationalism from nationalism in developed or imperialist societies. Such movements, not merely by virtue of their own action, but for the impact they could have upon the imperialist societies, were to be supported. What is more, there could be different kinds of anti-imperialism – as for example, in the nationalist movements aimed against Tsarist Russia and those aimed against Britain.

Most of these Marxist accounts do not actually examine very closely how nationalism comes to be the key ideological element in such anti-imperialist movements, but content themselves with laying bare the rational class interest at the core of such movements. What is striking about the approach of Tom Nairn is the way he has attempted to grasp the specific appeal of nationalism.[11]

Nairn sees nationalism as, initially, the political response of less developed societies to the problems created for them by the disparities between themselves and more developed societies. Such development extends horizons and raises hopes, but in the less developed societies there are all kinds of obstacles to meeting such expectations. One response is to take decisive political action. The major resource of these societies is their actual population. Nationalism, which in a sense is a glorification of that population, provides a means of mobilising that population behind such political action. As the lines of economic division usually coincide with divisions of language, culture, race or religion, these can be employed to create a common identity to support such action. What is more, they can extend the action from the primary concern with development to such important issues as the presumption of cultural superiority on the part of more developed societies. This nationalism, Nairn argues, can then generate counter-nationalisms in the more developed societies.

Abstractly it is a plausible and impressive argument. However, it does not fit the facts. By placing the initial stages of nationalism within the less developed societies, Nairn inverts the actual sequence of events. Nationalism[12] began in Europe before the establishment of modern empire in most of the overseas areas which generated anti-colonial nationalism and before the development of any non-European nationalist movement. Furthermore, one cannot usefully account for the first nationalist movements in terms of regional relationships of economic exploitation or backwardness. For example, the first strong nationalist movement in the Habsburg empire was

412

that of the Magyars.[13] The Magyars, however, were a privileged rather than an exploited or backward group, and the nationalist movement was led by privileged elements within the Magyars. Admittedly Magyar nationalism was a reaction against what was seen as oppressive control from Vienna, but the nature of that control raised issues of political power and its uses, rather than issues of economic exploitation or backwardness. It was then the nationalism of the Magyars which stimulated counter-nationalisms from among the non-Magyar groups which they dominated and exploited.[14]

Again, the drive to unify Germany cannot really be explained primarily as a response to economic exploitation or backwardness. Certainly some German nationalists of the mid-nineteenth century were concerned, among other things, about the relative backwardness of Germany compared, above all, to Britain and about the contribution which unification could make to economic development.[15] But this was just one concern and German nationalism was mainly directed against internal obstacles to unification rather than external ones, and in this context those nationalists saw themselves as representing the more advanced elements of society. Furthermore, public opinion in those countries which could count as more advanced, France and, especially Britain, was sympathetic to liberal nationalist movements in Germany and elsewhere. So too were governments. Palmerston advocated the separation of Lombardy from the Habsburg empire in 1848. Louis Napoleon, of course, played a crucial role in Italian unification in 1859–60 and broadly sympathised with the moves towards German unity under Prussian auspices in the early 1860s.

Finally, one of the major justifications for the new forms of imperialism which developed in the later nineteenth century was the argument (which though not properly nationalist was closely linked to nationalism) that each nation-state had to protect its interests outside Europe. The national elements in such apologetics for imperialism could help stimulate national(ist) responses from non-European societies. So one could conclude that nationalism begins in the more developed societies and subsequently, often reactively, in less developed societies.

In any case it is difficult to correlate the strength or intensity of nationalism with the degree of economic exploitation or backwardness. Nationalist movements have often developed fastest in areas of the colonial world that were the least exploited or backward. Conversely, where the most naked forms of exploitation took place, or where modern economic and other developments were least advanced, nationalism was frequently of little importance. Nationalism has often been associated with economic stagnation and the careful preservation of the *status quo*, even in the run-up to independence making no radical claims.[16]

Undoubtedly resentment against the economic superiority of other societies has played an important part in modern nationalism. There are obvious connections with the rapid, uneven, interrelated pattern of capitalist development on a global scale. It is when one seeks to go beyond generalities and to locate specific connections that the difficulties arise. To see the specific connection with economic inequality as the basis upon which nationalism arises would mean ignoring many forms of nationalism in areas not directly subject to this economic disparity and the absence of nationalism in many areas where the disparity was most glaring.

To conclude, nationalism is too pervasive to be reduced to the ideology and politics of this or that class or set of classes, at least if one wants to understand it generally. It is too complex and varied to be understood as a reaction to a particular type of economic relationship or disparity which then triggers off counter-nationalisms from the dominating or more advanced societies. As is usual, good marxist history represents the most impressive attempts to provide satisfactory accounts of major modern historical developments, but there appears to be something about nationalism which eludes understanding from within a marxist framework.

5 Psychological accounts

There are many variants upon psychological approaches to nationalism.[17] The usual point of departure is to assume that people need to identify with some cause or group larger than themselves. Under certain conditions, when previous identities have been undermined, people feel the need to find some alternative. At bottom, therefore, it is an answer to a certain kind of psychological problem, although the latter can have causes that extend beyond individuals. The whole point of nationalism, it could be argued, is its insistence on the importance of a special cultural group identity as the bedrock of political claims and action. What is more, it frames this insistence in terms of the recovery of some identity which has always been 'there' but which has been forgotten or abandoned or threatened. So although it may meet new needs, nationalism claims to do so in terms of an 'old' identity. Although it is a novel political doctrine it appears to appeal to precisely that yearning for a firmly rooted identity which is at the basis of its success.

One can portray this identity need, and the way in which it is created and met, in a variety of ways. For example, one can investigate the cultural impact of the West upon non-western societies. A specific concern might be the problems that arise from the formation of a Western-educated elite in a non-Western society. The elite belongs to neither Western nor traditional society. This situation can create an identity-crisis. Such an elite, often called the intelligentsia, can be vulnerable to political ideologies which offer new identities. Nationalism is not the only such ideology,[18] but it does have certain special attractions, particularly to the intelligentsia of non-Western societies.[19] Unlike more universalist political doctrines such as socialism and liberalism, nationalism places cultural identity at the heart of its concerns. Thus a non-Western intelligentsia can construct a new political identity from nationalist ideology which makes the Western claims to independence and freedom whilst at the same time relating those claims to a distinct national identity which is asserted to be of equal value with anything to be found in the West. Within this framework this intelligentsia can literally feel itself 'at home' and can, as nationalists, play a leading role in directing the fight for independence and re-creating the national culture in its fullest form. One might go on to link the actions of such an intelligentsia to other features of their situation: their special skills, which enable them to provide leadership for new sorts of political opposition; the material benefits offered to them by independence; the particular attractions of 'non-material' arguments to intellectuals; and the central role that they would play in constructing a sense of national identity. But the central argument would focus on the psychological problem created by the 'culture shock' of the encounter with the West.[20]

This is a very specific version of the 'identity crisis' approach. Some writers do not seek to go beyond an investigation of the situation of the intelligentsia which becomes the crucial element in the emergence of a nationalist movement. However, working from this point of departure, one could go on to interpret the success of the nationalist intelligentsia in mobilising popular support behind its politics in terms of a more generalised identity crisis.

Such an argument could focus upon the impact of imperialism or modernisation on a traditional society. Major disruptions are engendered by changes such as the transformation of agriculture (moves to individualised forms of cultivation, either by indigenous peasants or large-scale capitalist farmers), the growth of new industries which by means of the market or some kind of coercion pull agriculturalists into new occupations, and through the growth of towns which create new forms of settlement and, in pulling in migrants from the countryside, destroy traditional social patterns. The disruptive effect of political change upon traditional authority and the shock of encountering different cultural values from positions of inferiority mean that the threat to traditional forms of identity is a widespread one. People are plunged into a confusing and alien world, treated as labour power or objects of bureaucratic control, where the various roles people play are separated from one another and the 'whole person' is in danger of disappearing behind these roles.

In such situations nationalism has an obvious appeal. A major concern of modern social thought is the problem of community, of how common identity and a sentiment of solidarity can be created in the face of impersonal, abstract, 'rational' relationships based upon instrumental considerations.[21] Within this body of thought a contrast is frequently drawn between warm, intimate, spontaneous relationships supposedly

characteristic of community, and cold, distant, reflective, calculating relationships supposedly characteristic of society.[22] Nationalism can be regarded as a way of bridging these contrasts. On the one hand it is a
community myth, with its emphasis upon cultural identity and emotional
solidarity. On the other hand, it projects this myth upon large-scale
societies (nations) which it depicts in terms more appropriate (if at all) to
village or small town life.[23] It seeks to exploit the opportunities of modernity, above all by accepting the large-scale mass society which modernity
involves, but at the same time to exploit the sense of loss which modernity
also creates. In a chaotic and rapidly changing world nationalism provides
simple concrete labels for friends and enemies. Because this sense of loss
is at the centre of the experience of modernity, nationalism is more
appealing than the universalist doctrines of socialism, liberalism and
democracy, which share with modernity itself a preoccupation with new
and abstract identities.

Gellner has developed a particularly persuasive variant on this argument which also has the merit of pointing to a specific connection between
identity need under modern conditions and the appeal of nationalism.[24] He
argues that if the process of rapid change that has been briefly described
above removes people from the roles and positions they once occupied –
for example, by compelling them to migrate to towns – they will be unable
to identify themselves in terms of what they do and their social relationships with others. The very move will have left such roles and relationships
behind. Yet there will be, at least to begin with, no new roles or relationships which could make an acceptable basis for a new identity. Instead,
such people will have to fasten upon those attributes they 'carry' around
with themselves, such as language, religion and skin-colour. Gellner goes
on to argue that modern urban-industrial society is marked by perpetual
innovation and social movement, so in fact such cultural definitions of
identity continue to be of importance, especially when promoted by new
institutions such as mass elementary schooling and the mass media. Nationalism bases itself upon an appeal to precisely such cultural attributes,
which are made the bedrock of a whole new identity. So nationalism is
peculiarly appropriate to the shifts in identity which rapid change can
induce.

The merit of such arguments is that they accept the modernity of
nationalism and seek to explain it in terms of problems of modernity. They
tend to focus upon nationalism in the first instance as sentiments, though
of course intellectuals and politicians can play a role in developing and
promoting ideas of national identity. The weaker form of the argument
posits an 'identity need' in terms of the erosion of traditional identity and
sees nationalism as one possible answer to this need. The stronger form of
the argument connects the particular kind of identity need that modernity
creates with the answer nationalism offers.

416

The problem is that the proferred explanation – identity needs under conditions of modernity – covers much more than nationalism. Even if one can show, as for example Mannoni and Fanon claimed to have done in relation to colonialism,[25] what psychological damage has been wrought upon people, one must remember that only a minority of those affected turned to nationalism. Some turned to other ideologies – of class, of religion; some accepted modernity and sought simply to advance their own interests as far as possible; some turned to drink; and about most we know nothing. Nationalism does not necessarily receive its strongest support from those groups which one would imagine to have been most damaged, psychologically as well as materially, such as the new urban poor.

At the level of leadership it is difficult to relate psychological arguments to personalities and experiences. Gandhi is a quite different figure from Nehru;[26] the stridency of Nkrumah contrasts sharply with the reflective, reasoned stance of Nyerere, and that in turn with the self-confident and intellectually opportunist position of Kenyatta. Of course, one can argue that the forms assumed by an identity crisis are varied and that what matters is the appeal of nationalism in coping with this crisis, whatever psychological symptons might accompany it. But this tends to deprive one of indices of this identity crisis or need other than the nationalist response itself, which is both indicative of as well as an answer to that identity crisis. But if one can plausibly portray nationalism as an answer to other, more specific problems which can be established independently of nationalism itself, such alternative explanations will obviously be superior to the psychological argument.

For example, Gellner, in addition to advancing an argument about the relationship between nationalism and 'culture as identity', also argues that such identities can be used to good effect in competitions over scarce resources such as jobs, housing and education in urban settings.[27] It is worth noting that the inter-ethnic conflicts to which this can give rise go rather against yet another argument of Gellner's about the way in which urban-industrial society and the modern state tend to fashion standard national cultures, an homogenous 'cultural zone' within which members of a modern society act. However, the point is that in this case the use of identity is related to specific problems in very specific settings. One may wish to retain the general argument about identity as an essential part of the background, but the argument which will convince through its specificity, its direct connection to a particular pattern of action, is that concerned with conflict over scarce resources.

Another major problem is that of testing such arguments. The historian of sentiments or politics will know little about the experiences and perceptions of most of those under investigation. Some leading figures, such as nationalist writers, will perhaps have left some evidence behind about their problems as 'marginal' men, but it is doubtful that one will

417

have much more than that.

Even when one does, for example through the use of questionnaires, it is clear that basic psychological categories of perception or commitment which might be thought to be indices of responses to modernisation tell us little about nationalism as politics.[28] At best, as with the communications approach, I would suggest that these ideas can tell us about the changing meanings which concepts such as culture and identity could have under certain modern conditions; that nationalism, amongst other doctrines or sentiments, can build upon these changed meanings; and that such doctrines or sentiments might be used by political movements. However, each stage of the argument can be detached from the other stages. The first level is so general as to be difficult to relate to any specific historical development. Furthermore, we can observe traditional societies, which do not yet appear to have been subjected to such changes, which provide support for nationalism.[29]

6 Functional approaches

Many of the approaches I have so far discussed can be given a functional form. Nationalism can 'function' as an instrument of class interest, or it can function to furnish an identity need. It is clear that the notion of class or identity need or some equivalent to these provides the causal element of the explanation. Functionalism itself describes rather than explains; it points to the role that something performs in a certain routine operation. This is not a task to be dismissed. If one really can show that 'x' constantly serves a function for 'y': first, one knows more than one did before this account was provided; and second, one can assume that in the absence of 'x' there will be problems about achieving 'y'. Functionalist accounts therefore often complement accounts which refer to some purpose. There are close links, for example, between functionalist and psychological accounts of nationalism. Functionalist sociology often works with a dichotomy between tradition and modernity, community and society, and tends to perceive rapid change as a breakdown of the relationships and values of the first of these, leading to the establishment of relationships and values characteristic of the second.[30] Such a notion of a transitional period of upheaval between two more stable states obviously links to the psychological arguments discussed above. The major implication is that rapid change precipitates a breakdown of traditional identity and the coming of modernity points to the shape a new identity could take. Within such an approach functionalism could try to account for the effects of a particular practice (here the function of nationalism in aiding the transition to modernity) but not why it appealed, while the psychological approach could account for the appeal of nationalism but not why it had a particular effect.

The main functional account is in terms of modernisation. National-

418

ism can help provide identity in a time of rapid change; it can motivate people to work for further change; it can guide action in such fields as the creation of a modern educational system and the raising of literacy standards – all of which help create a 'standard national culture'.[31] This all can look fairly plausible, although different notions of nationalism (a motivating ideology, a cultural consequence, and so on) are used in rather different ways.

Nevertheless there are four crippling defects in the deployment of functional accounts of nationalism.

First, there is a tendency to provide too large or holistic an account of that for which nationalism serves a function. If it is argued that nationalism functions to maintain social solidarity or to promote wholesale modernisation, the problem is that solidarity or modernisation are such large terms that it is difficult to know how one can connect anything as specific as nationalism to them. Is one suggesting that without nationalism these things could not be achieved? Hardly anyone would advance such an argument, first because the achievement can be so variously understood, and secondly because clearly something like solidarity or some kind of modernisation has taken place without nationalism seeming to be of central importance.

Second, there are a multitude of functions which it is suggested nationalism can serve. For some nationalism helps in the process of modernisation[32]; for others it helps maintain traditional identities and structures.[33] For some it is a function of class interest; for others of identity need. It is clear that there is no possibility of an agreed interpretation, and that nationalism is indeed associated with one or other of these consequences in different situations.

Third, one is still left asking why nationalism serves the function it does. For example, the argument that nationalism helps in the process of modernisation does not explain why nationalism helps in this way. For such an account we would have to ask questions such as why nationalist leaders use nationalism to justify modernisation politics and why supporters accept such arguments. In other words we have to introduce intentionality. Alternatively we can try to identify some routine social process by means of which nationalism 'selects' from a range of possible outcomes and thereby pushes events in a particular direction. By analogy, for example, one can say that in systems of free market competition the mechanism of bankruptcy serves the function of 'selecting' which firms can continue in a given situation. So far as I know, no one has ever offered such an account of nationalism.

Finally, functionalist accounts tend to focus on nationalism as ideology and understand ideology in the rather crude sense of motivating people to act. Generally, as I have argued in chapter 2, nationalist ideologies cannot easily be detached from the settings in which they are found,

419

and stand in a variety of relationships to those settings. Motivating people to act is only one function they might play.

7 Concluding comments

Each of the approaches that have been briefly described and criticised point to some important feature of modern times with which nationalism can be associated. Nationalism clearly builds upon some sense of cultural identity, even if it is the major creator of that sense. It is clearly connected with new and extended systems of communication, although these cannot account for the development of specific nationalisms. The growth of capitalism has created new social classes with new objectives and ways of seeking those objectives which nationalism might help serve. The creation of a genuine world-wide economic and political system has been marked by enormous disparities in wealth, power and values. These disparities have provoked attempts to get rid of subordination and exploitation or to sustain dominance and economic advantage. They have also involved painful adjustments to rapidly changing situations and attempts to realise new objectives in ways which call for directed social change. All these responses have, to some extent, been related to nationalism. Clearly the plausibility of relating these concerns to nationalism reflects their importance in modern times and the fact that they all, at times, intersect with nationalism.

The problem is that it soon proves very difficult to move beyond very general statements to make more specific connections to nationalism. Sometimes the arguments have to be made even looser in order to cover all cases. Imperialism becomes uneven development; modernisation turns out to have an almost infinite variety of characteristics; cultural identity becomes whatever nationalists say it is. Alternatively, the hypothesis is put more clearly and then can be falsified in numerous cases. Nationalism cannot be linked to any particular type of cultural attribute or social arrangement; or to any particular structure of communications; or to any particular class interest; or to any particular economic relationship; or to any particular psychological state or need; or to any particular social function or objective. It is therefore impossible to construct any acceptable theory of nationalism upon such bases.

These problems partly arise because the different concerns are themselves so various. Partly it is because some of the terms themselves are difficult to define precisely. But above all it is because the term 'nationalism' is used too widely and covers many and different kinds of things. It is used to refer to ideas, sentiments and politics, yet these are distinct kinds of things which do not stand in any necessary relationship to one another.

First, I advocate restricting the term to politics. In any case there tends only to be an interest in nationalist ideas or sentiments in so far as they are taken up in political movements. Furthermore, political action usually has the effect of selecting from a range of sentiments and giving focus to particular ideas which otherwise remain rather diffuse.

Second, even then I would restrict the term to political movements which aim to take state power on the basis of a nationalist programme or which use state power in certain, specifically nationalist ways (to destroy 'sub-national' identity, to make irredentist claims beyond present state borders). This then excludes inter-ethnic conflicts which do not produce movements or organisations aiming to take state power as well as any assertive foreign or domestic policies pursued by governments of nation-states.

Finally, I should stress that what should be sought is not some mono-causal theory of nationalism. Rather one should seek to establish the specific contexts in which nationalism arises. This is best achieved through systematic comparative history. On the basis of the results of such comparison one might be able to identify certain features which commonly accompany nationalism.

Notes

1   For a good survey of different approaches to nationalism see Anthony D. Smith, *Theories of Nationalism* (London, 1971). I consider the subject at greater length in an essay 'Approaches to Nationalism' in *Formen des nationalen Bewußtseins im Lichte zeitgenössischer Nationalismustheorien*, ed. B. Hartmann (Munich, 1993).

2   This is the procedure adopted by Anthony D. Smith in *The Ethnic Origins of Nations* (Oxford, 1986). I deal with this argument at some length in my essay, 'Approaches to Nationalism' cited in note 1.

3   The pioneer of this approach was Karl Deutsch. See his book *Nationalism and Social Communication* (New York, 1966).

4   In different ways Benedict Anderson and Ernest Gellner put forward powerful arguments about changing patterns of communication and the development of nationalism. Anderson in *Imagined Communities: reflections on the origins and spread of nationalism* (London, 1983) focuses upon the ways in which a more extensive print media could alter the sense of community amongst literate elites. Gellner in *Nations and nationalism* (Oxford, 1983) focuses upon the way in which greater social and geographical mobility within urban-industrial societies could make modes of communication increasingly central to social identity. Yet though both show how a sense of a new kind of shared culture could come about, neither in my view can show from this basis alone how and why that should take the assertive form of nationalism. I argue these points at greater length in an extended review of Anderson and Gellner, 'Reflections on nationalism', *Philosophy of the Social Sciences* 15 (1985), pp. 65–75.

5   For a very clear if crude view of such class alliances see the 'Address of the Central Committee to the Communist League' (March 1850) written by

Marx and Engels, in Karl Marx, *The Revolutions of 1848: political writings*, vol. 1, edited and introduced by David Fernbach (Harmondsworth, 1973), pp. 318–30.

6   See the debates over the work of N. Poulantzas, *Political Power and Social Class* (London, 1973), and *Fascism and Dictatorship* (London, 1974) as presented in J. Kaplan, 'Theories of Fascism: Nicol Poulantzas as historian', *History Workshop*, 3 (1977), pp. 83–100, and R. Milliband, 'Poulantzas and the Capitalist State', *New Left Review*, 82 (1973), along with Poulantzas, 'The Capitalist State: a reply to Milliband and Laclau', *New Left Review*, 95 (1976).

7   For example, the response of Hobsbawm to the arguments of Nairn (see below, 11) in *New Left Review*, 105 (1977), 'Some reflections on the break-up of Britain', which seems to me to typify this refusal although the negative points Hobsbawm makes and the brief descriptions he offers of particular sorts of nationalism are penetrating. A similar criticism could be made of his book, *Nations and nationalism since 1789: programme, myth, reality* (Cambridge, 1991). I do not consider here the important pre-1914 attempts to construct a general theory of nationalism by Marxists, but see above, pp. 39–42 for a consideration of the most important theorist, Otto Bauer.

8   For the divided and tentative character of Marxist thinking about politics generally see R. Milliband, *Marxism and Politics* (Oxford, 1977).

9   A case argued with great force by Barrington Moore in *Injustice: the social origins of obedience and revolt* (London, 1978).

10   I have also considered some of these issues in the section on economic approaches to imperialism in chapter 7.

11   Tom Nairn, 'Marxism and the modern Janus', *New Left Review*, 94 (1975), pp. 3–29. Some reviewers criticised me for attributing a theory of imperialism to Nairn which he did not propose. I accept the justice of this criticism, though it seems to me that Nairn's account of nationalism in less developed societies only really makes sense within some such imperialist framework. However, it is the particular attention to the quality and appeal of nationalism that is original and important.

12   Nairn does not define nationalism. He might, of course, argued that he does not consider these early nineteenth-century movements in Europe to be properly nationalist. I cannot work out what reasonable definition of nationalism would support such an argument, so in the absence of such a one on his part I will simply assume that his argument does not fit the evidence about the timing and location of the initial phases of nationalism.

13   See above, pp. 125–31. One might wish to advance the claims of the Polish or Italian movements as the 'first', but the general arguments about the lack of economic backwardness and the privileged position both of the nationality and of the leading groups involved in nationalism would continue to apply.

14   See above, pp. 135–9, on the Rumanians and the Serbians.

15   On the slow and halting way such a perception could develop, see now R. Boch, *Grenzenloses Wachstum? Das rheinische Wirtshcaftsbürgertum und seine Industrialisierungsdebatte 1814–1857* (Göttingen, 1991).

16 On nationalism, political order and economic stagnation see G. Heeger, *The Politics of Underdevelopment* (London, 1974), especially pp. 15–46. Indian and Chinese nationalism (considered in chapters 8 and 11 respectively) are cases where the main parts of the nationalist movement avoided making radical economic claims.

17 See, for example, L. Doob, *Patriotism and Nationalism* (London, 1964).

18 On the attractions of populism and socialism to nineteenth-century Russian intellectuals see the various studies by Isaiah Berlin collected in *Russian Thinkers* (Harmondsworth, 1979). I deal with other issues of the intelligentsia and nationalism in chapter 1.

19 A valuable argument to this effect, with a useful collection of statements by nationalist intellectuals, is E. Kedourie (edited and introduction), *Nationalism in Africa and Asia* (London, 1971). Kedourie makes out a similar case for European intellectuals in his book *Nationalism* (London, 1960), as does L. B. Namier, in a much more specific way, in *1848: the revolution of the intellectuals* (London, 1944).

20 This passage is, I hope, written rather more positively than in the first edition where I was not sufficiently sensitive to the harsh impact of western cultural presumptuousness and the role of cultural activity in combatting those presumptions. Nevertheless, I would still argue that much of what is involved is invention rather than discovery, and that in any case it is usually of only minor importance in the development of significant nationalist movements.

21 This concern in modern social thought is examined in R. Nisbet, *The Sociological Tradition* (London, 1976), pp. 47–106. It is, of course, embodied in the romantic critique of industrialisation already in nineteenth century Europe, though it has a longer tradition in a pastoral, anti-urban discourse. See, for example, R. Williams, *The Country and the City* (London, 1973).

22 The classic statement of this view was made at the end of the nineteenth-century by Ferdinand Tönnies in his book *Community and Society* (Gemeinschaft und Gesellschaft), translated and edited by C. P. Loomis (New York, 1963).

23 On the actual close relationship between images of small-town life and nationalism see the fascinating argument of Mack Walker, *German Home Towns: community, state and general estate, 1648–1871* (London, 1971), pp. 425–31, where he argues that National Socialist rhetoric created some connection between '. . . the longings of intellectuals for national community and hometownsmen's parochial values' (p. 427).

24 He first developed the case in *Thought and Change* (London, 1964), pp. 147–78. The argument (along with others) was elaborated further in *Nations and Nationalism* (Oxford, 1983). It is now part of a large framework of interpretation which sees 'culture' as having a different role and significance under conditions of modernity compared to earlier epochs. See *Plough, Sword, Book: the Structure of Human History* (London, 1988).

25 O. Mannoni, *Prospero and Caliban* (London, 1956); F. Fanon, *The Wretched of the Earth* (London, 1965).

26 I find persuasive Chatterjee's distinctions between different kinds of nation-

alism which includes an analysis of Gandhi and Nehru. But even if one could relate this argument (which I doubt) to pyschological questions, it sharply points to the changing meanings of nationalism and the kinds of identities it offers. See Partha Chatterjee, *Nationalist Thought and the Colonial World: a derivative discourse?* (London, 1986).

27 Gellner, *Thought and Change*, pp. 164–9.

28 See for example the argument developed in relation to Turkey in chapter 13 above.

29 This is a less dismissive treatment than in the first edition of the book, one reason being my subsequent appreciation of useful studies which provide careful and persuasive arguments utilising concepts from psychology and relating these to notions of national identity, if not nationalism. See, for example, W. Bloom, *Personal Identity, National Identity and International Relations* (Cambridge, 1990).

30 I am indebted to Anthony Smith for making this point clear to me in comments on a first draft of this section of the book.

31 A major argument used by Gellner.

32 See, for example, David Apter, *The Politics of Modernisation* (Chicago, 1965), and *idem* , 'Political religion in the new nations', in *Old Societies and New States*, ed. C. Geertz (New York, 1963), pp. 57–104. Smith in *Theories of Nationalism*, uses the phrase 'religion of modernisation' (p. 41).

33 See Heeger, *The Politics of Underdevelopment*, especially pp. 15–46, where nationalism as a device for maintaining order (rather than tradition) is stressed.

Chronologies

Not every reader will be well acquainted with all the case studies considered in this book. To help follow the argument I provide a list of dates of major events of relevance within the various cases. Apart from my own notes I found two historical chronologies useful in compiling these lists. These were: N. Williams, *Chronology of the Modern World – 1763 to the present time* (1966); and B. Green *The Timetables of History* (1975). For the chronologies for the USSR and east-central Europe I also used a chronology published by the German government and one compiled by J. Grotzky, *Konflikt im Vielvölkerstaat* (Munich, 1991), pp. 172–93.

England

1531 Henry VIII recognised as supreme head of the church in England; the Reformation programme carried out with the assistance of a number of parliaments in 1530s
1588 Defeat of the first Spanish Armada
1601 Earl of Essex leads revolt against Elizabeth I; tried for treason and executed
1603 James VI of Scotland succeeds Elizabeth as James I of England
1606 James I's proclamation of a national flag
1614 James I's second parliament, the 'Addled Parliament', meets, refuses to discuss financial matters and is dismissed
1622 James I dismisses another parliament
1623 James I's favourite, George Villiers, raised to rank of Duke of Buckingham
1624 James I's last parliament: monopolies declared illegal
1625 Charles I succeeds to the throne
1629 Charles I dissolves his third parliament; parliament not to meet again until April 1640
1639 First Bishops' War in Scotland
1640 Charles I calls parliament for assistance in the Scottish war. Short Parliament (April-May 1640); Long Parliament (November 1640 -1653)
1641 Execution of Strafford

1642 Start of civil war

1645 Cromwell made Lieutenant General of the New Model Army

1648 Parliamentary victory concluded with surrender of Oxford to the Round-heads

1649 3 January: execution of Charles I

1653 Oliver Cromwell becomes Lord Protector

1659 Cromwell dies; his son Richard assumes the title of Lord Protector

1660 Charles II enters London

1685 James II succeeds as king

1688 William of Orange arrives in England at the invitation of some English lords

1689 Parliament confirms the abdication of James II; Declaration of Rights; William and Mary proclaimed king and queen for life

France

1516 Concordat of Bologna between Pope Leo X and Francis I

1560 Huguenot conspiracy at Amboise; liberty of worship promised; Charles IX king, with his mother Catherine de Medici as regent

1560–98 A series of wars known collectively as the Wars of Religion, pitting Huguenots against Catholics

1572 St Bartholomew's Day massacre of the Huguenots and beginning of the fourth war of religion

1589 Assassination of Henry III; Henry of Navarre, leader of the Huguenot party, succeeds to the throne as the first Bourbon, but rejected by many Catholics

1593 Henry IV converts to Catholicism

1594 Henry IV enters Paris

1598 Civil war in France is brought to an end

1610 Assassination of Henry IV: Louis XIII succeeds to the throne (dies 1643)

1614–15 Meeting of Estates General; another one does not meet until 1789

1624 Richelieu becomes first minister

1629 Huguenot resistance brought to an end

1642 Mazarin succeeds Richelieu as first minister

1643 Louis XIV succeeds to the throne although supreme power vested in Anne of Austria, the queen mother

1648 Outbreak of the Fronde revolts; Peace of Westphalia ends Thirty Years War

1652 Provisional Fronde government set up in Paris; but Mazarin re-established in power with support of Louis XIV

1661 Louis XIV commences personal rule following death of Mazarin

1701–14 War of Spanish Succession

1715 Louis XV succeeds to the throne (dies 1774)

1756–63 Seven Years War: part of a world conflict between England and France which also extends to North America

1774 Louis XVI succeeds to the throne

1776 Outbreak of American War of Independence, which France supports;

Necker made Minister of Finance

1787 Following upon proposed fiscal measures of the crown the Parlement of Paris demands an Estates General be called

1788 Assembly of Notables meets but fails to come to agreement with crown

1789 Estates General called; Third Estate declares itself the National Assembly; Declaration of the Rights of Man

1792 Establishment of Commune and of First Republic

1793 Execution of Louis XVI

1799 Napoleon becomes Consul

1804 Napoleon proclaimed Emperor

Germany

1804 Creation of emperorship of Austria

1806 French defeat of Prussia; official end of Holy Roman Empire; formation of the Confederation of the Rhine

1813–14 War of Liberation

1814–15 Congress of Vienna; creation of the German Confederation with Austria as President

1834 German Zollverein (customs union) starts to operate under Prussian leadership and without the membership of Austria

1840 Frederick William IV becomes king of Prussia

1848 Revolution; a German National Assembly meets in Frankfurt am Main

1849 Frederick William IV rejects offer of Emperorship of Germany by the National Assembly; success of counter-revolution

1850 Prussian efforts at limited German unity brought to an end by Austria

1858 Liberal victories in elections to the Prussian lower House inaugurate the 'New Era'

1862 Bismarck appointed Minister President of Prussia

1864 War between Germany and Denmark: Austrian and Prussian troops occupy Schleswig and Holstein

1866 War between Austria (with most German states) and Prussia

1867 Establishment of the North German Confederation

1870–71 War between Prussia (allied with other German states) and France

1871 Declaration of the German Empire at Versailles; King William I of Prussia becomes Emperor William I of Germany

Italy

1796 Beginning in this year Italy reorganised in a variety of ways by Napoleon, first as a series of republics, later as a series of monarchies

1815 Congress of Vienna restores Papal temporal power in Italy; grants Lombardy and Venetia to Austria

1821 Austrian intervention in Naples and Piedmont to restore order

1831 Charles Albert becomes king of Piedmont

1832 Mazzini founds Young Italy

1848 Revolutions throughout Italy

1849 Charles Albert abdicates in favour of Victor Emmanuel I, following defeats by Austria; Venice falls to Austria; Pius IX restored to power in Rome
1852 Cavour becomes Prime Minister of Piedmont
1857 Garibaldi forms the Italian National Association
1859 Treaty of Alliance between Piedmont and France; war with Austria; Parma and Lombardy ceded to Piedmont
1860 Plebiscites in Tuscany, Emilia, Parma, Modena and Romagna favour union with Piedmont; meeting of first Italian parliament in Turin; Garibaldi enters Naples; Piedmont invades the Papal States
1861 Italian parliament proclaims Victor Emmanuel king; later the kingdom of Italy is proclaimed
1866 Venetia joins Italy following Austrian defeats in war with Prussia
1870 Italian troops enter Rome

Poland

1772 First partition of Poland
1793 Second partition of Poland
1794 Rising in the rump state of Poland
1795 Third partition of Poland ends independent existence of a Polish state
1807 Creation of the Grand Duchy of Warsaw
1815 Congress of Vienna settlement: parts of Poland incorporated directly into western Russia; another part organised as the kingdom of Poland (Congress Poland) bound by personal union to Russia; other parts organised as the Grand Duchy of Posen in Prussia and the kingdom of Galicia in the Habsburg Empire
1830–31 Polish revolt in Congress Poland
1846 Revolts in Poland; peasant *jacquerie* in Galicia; Austria annexes the Free City of Cracow
1848 Revolts in Poland suppressed by Austrian and Prussian troops
1863 Polish insurrection in Congress Poland is suppressed and leads to end of the special constitutional status of the area and a radical land reform programme

The Habsburg empire

1780 Joseph II becomes emperor
1783 Enforcement of the use of German as official language in Bohemia
1784 Abrogation of Hungarian constitution; suppression of feudal rights
1790–92 Leopold II undoes many of the reforms of Joseph II
1792 Francis II: Holy Roman Emperor to 1806, Austrian emperor 1804–35; petition from Greek Orthodox and Uniate church leaders in Rumania on behalf of the 'Rumanian nation'
1809 Metternich becomes chief minister following defeat by France
1813 Austria declares war on France for the fifth time since 1789
1815 Congress of Vienna settlement: Austria retains or acquires territories in northern Italy, Hungary and Transylvania, south-east Europe, Galicia, as well

as occupying dominant position in the German Confederation

1825 Opening of the Hungarian Diet after thirteen years; Francis I agrees to triennial meetings

1835 Ferdinand I becomes emperor

1841 Kossuth emerges as a leading Hungarian politician at the Diet

1847 Liberal majority in the lower chamber of the Hungarian Diet

1848 Revolution: April laws in Hungary; Pan-Slav congress in Prague; Serbian, Croatian, Slovak and, later, Rumanian military action against Magyars; October: Kossuth proclaims Hungary in open revolt

1849 April: Hungarian Diet declares Hungary independent under regency of Kossuth; August: surrender of Hungarian forces

1851 Abrogation of Austrian constitution

1854 Austrian occupation of Danubian principalities

1856 Amnesty for Hungarian insurgents of 1848–49

1859 Austrian forces defeated by French and Piedmontese; Lombardy ceded

1861 Centralisation of Austrian constitutional system by February patent; dissolution of Hungarian Diet

1864 Austrian and Prussian troops occupy Schleswig-Holstein

1866 Defeat in war with Prussia; end of German Confederation; loss of Venetia

1867 Creation of Austro-Hungarian dual monarchy

1868 Completion of incorporation of Transylvania into Hungary

1873 Reform of Austrian franchise in favour of Germans; Croatia granted internal self-government

1879 Taafe ministry in Austria (to 1893) ends German predominance in Austria in favour of Slavs

1897 Czech language granted equality with German in Bohemia; German opposition leads to resignation of Count Badeni

1898 Bohemia divided into Czech, German and mixed districts

1899 Bohemian language ordinance of 1897 repealed

1906 Universal suffrage bill introduced in Hungary; never implemented

1907 Universal direct suffrage introduced into Austria

1908 Austrian annexation of Bosnia and Herzegovina

1914 28 June: assassination of Archduke Franz Ferdinand, heir to the Austrian throne, sets in train the events leading to the First World War

1916 Death of Francis Joseph; succeeded by the last Habsburg emperor, Charles

1918 End of war and of the Habsburg empire

1919 The Peace Conference at Versailles divides the Habsburg Empire into a series of 'nation-states'

The Ottoman empire, Turkey, and the Middle East

1801 The Ottoman empire formally recovers Egypt

1804 Austria and Russia declare they will preserve the Ottoman empire against French expansion; peasant revolt in Serbia

1805 Egypt becomes virtually independent with proclamation of Mehemet Ali as Pasha

1806 Russian occupies the Danubian Principalities

1807 Serbian alliance with Russia
1809 Defeats at the hands of Russia
1811 Massacre of Mamelukes in Cairo; Rumanians take Belgrade
1812 Peace with Russia leaves the empire with Moldavia and Wallachia but cedes Bessarabia
1813 Serbian revolt suppressed
1814–15 Renewed revolt in Serbia
1817 Serbia granted partial autonomy
1821 Revolts in the Danubian Principalities lead to outbreak of revolts in Greek peninsula
1822 Greek declaration of independence
1823 Britain recognises Greeks as belligerents in war
1824 Death of Byron at Missolonghi
1826 Russian ultimatum over Serbia and Danubian Principalities; the Sultan decrees the dissolution of the janissaries
1827 Russia, France and Britain intervene in support of Greeks; destroy the joint Turkish-Egyptian fleet
1828 Russia declares war on Ottoman empire; Ottoman troops leave Greece
1829 End of war with Russia; Greek independence recognised; autonomy of Danubian Principalities and of Serbia recognised
1830 Serbia becomes fully autonomous
1831 Egypt conquers Syria
1832 Greek National Assembly elects Prince Otto of Bavaria as King Otto I (-1862)
1833 Sultan recognises independence of Egypt and cedes Syria and Aden to Mehemet Ali; Prussia, Austria and Russia agree to support integrity of Ottoman empire
1839–1 War with Mehemet Ali in Syria; Reform Decree in Ottoman empire guarantees life, liberty and property for all subjects
1840 British pressure on Egypt to withdraw from most of Syria
1841 The European powers guarantee Ottoman independence; Mehemet Ali recognised as hereditary ruler of Egypt
1848 Russia invades Danubian Principalities at Ottoman invitation in order to put down revolts
1853 Crimean war (-1856) with Britain and France supporting the empire against Russia
1856 Reform Edict in Ottoman empire; Peace of Paris recognises integrity of empire
1858 Great powers and Ottoman empire agree to unite Moldavia and Wallachia
1861 Sultan agrees to unification of Moldavia and Wallachia as Rumania
1875 Risings in Bosnia and Herzegovina; Sultan promises reforms
1876 Massacre of Bulgarians by Ottoman troops; two Sultans deposed in quick succession, followed by Abdul Hamid II (-1909); war with Serbia and Montenegro; new constitution proclaimed embodying parliamentary government, freedom of worship and a free press
1877 War with Russia
1878 Treaty of Berlin: part of Bulgaria becomes autonomous Montenegro, Rumania and Serbia become independent states

1891 Formation of the Young Turk movement
1906 Young Turk revolt in Macedonia; constitution of 1876 restored; first meeting of Ottoman parliament, with large Young Turk majority
1909 Young Turks depose Sultan; succeeded by his brother Mohammed V (-1918)
1912 General war in the Balkans
1913 Renewed war in Balkans
1914 At war with Germany and Austria-Hungary against France, Britain and Russia
1916 Arab revolts against empire
1917 Balfour Declaration on a Jewish homeland
1918 Defeat; the Allies occupy Constantinople
1919 Mustafa Kemal at Turkish National Congress declares himself independent of government in Istanbul
1920 British and French mandates granted in the Arab parts of the former Ottoman Empire; Greek offensive in Asia Minor against Turkish nationalists; government signs Treaty of Sevres, which is unacceptable to Turkish nationalists
1922 Mustafa Kemal proclaims Turkey a republic; an Arab congress rejects the Palestine mandate
1923 Mustafa Kemal elected President of Turkey; makes peace treaty of Lausanne with Greece and the Allies
1924 Turkish National Assembly abolishes the caliphate
1926 New code of laws in Turkey, and establishment of civil marriage
1928 Islam no longer recognised as state religion in Turkey
1929 Arabs attack Jews in Palestine over use of the Wailing Wall
1929 Name of Serbo-Croat-Slovene kingdom changed to Yugoslavia; Jewish Agency becomes representative of both Zionist and non-Zionist Jews; Female suffrage in Turkey
1930 Name of Constantinople changed to Istanbul
1932 Turkey admitted to the League of Nations
1935 Mustafa Kemal adopts name of Kemal Ataturk when National Assembly makes family names obligatory
1936 Arab High Committee formed to combat Jewish claims
1937 British royal commission on Palestine recommends establishment of Jewish and Arab states
1938 Ataturk dies
1939 Westminster approves British plan for an independent Palestine by 1947; this denounced by both Jews and Arabs in Palestine
1941 Iraq sides with Germany and demands withdrawal of British troops from Middle East
1942 Egypt cleared of Germans
1945 Arab League formed to oppose establishment of Jewish state
1947 British proposal to divide Palestine rejected by both Arabs and Jews; the question is referred to the United Nations, which announces plan for partition
1948 Jewish state comes into existence and repels Arab attacks
1949 Israel admitted to the United Nations
1956 Suez crisis: Anglo-French force lands in Egypt; Sudan declared a republic

and joins Arab League as ninth member
1958 Union between Egypt and Syria to form United Arab Republic, with Nasser as President
1961 Syria leaves United Arab Republic
1967 Six Day War
1969 Yasser Arafat elected chairman of executive committee of the Palestine Liberation Organisation
1970 Death of Nasser
1973 Renewed Israel-Arab war; moves by Arab oil-producing countries to embargo shipments of oil to the Western world
1978 Camp David accord signals withdrawal of Egypt from united Arab opposition to Israel

India

1793 East India Company introduces the Permanent Settlement
1802 Peshaw of Poona surrenders independence to Company
1803 Sindhia of Gwalior finally submits to British
1804 Company defeats Holkar of Indore
1818 Dominions of Holdar of Indore, the Rajput states and Poona come under British control
1846 Sikhs defeated by Company
1849 Annexation of the Punjab
1856 Annexation of Oudh
1857 Indian Mutiny
1858 Powers of Company transferred to British crown
1877 Queen Victoria declared Empress of India
1886 First Indian National Congress meets
1906 All India Moslem League founded
1909 Indian Councils Act gives greater power to legislative councils and ensures appointment of an Indian to the Viceroy's executive council
1918 Montagu-Chelmsford report on constitution of India published
1919 Constitutional reforms increase Indian participation in government and widen franchises to local legislative councils; troops fire on demonstrators in Jallianwala Bagh, martial law declared in Punjab; Gandhi starts first non-co-operation campaign
1921 First Indian parliament meets
1922 Gandhi sentenced to six years' imprisonment for civil disobedience
1926 Simon Commission on India appointed
1928 Large-scale strikes
1929 Round Table Conference between Viceroy and Indian leaders on dominion status
1930 Gandhi opens civil disobedience campaign; Simon report on India published
1931 Dehli Pact : civil disobedience campaign suspended, Congress promises to recognise Round Table Conference, political prisoners released
1932 Indian Congress declared illegal; Gandhi arrested; third India Conference

in London
1934 Gandhi suspends civil disobedience campaign
1935 Government of India Act reforms government system; separates Burma and Aden from India; grants provinces greater self-government and creates central legislature in Delhi (to come into effect 1 April 1937)
1937 All India Congress Party wins elections to provincial governments. Indian constitution in force; Congress Party abstains from forming a government, demanding complete independence
1940 Congress Party rejects Viceroy's invitation to serve on War Advisory Council
1942 Gandhi demands independence for India and is arrested
1945 All India Congress Committee, led by Gandhi and Nehru, rejects British proposals for self-government and calls on Britain to quit India; Congress Party and Muslim League win most seats in elections for Central Legislative Assembly
1946 Constituent Assembly, boycotted by Muslim League, discusses independence
1947 India proclaimed independent and partitioned into India and Pakistan

Kenya

1886 Anglo-German agreement delimiting respective spheres of influence in east Africa
1895 Creation of East Africa Protectorate
1896 Kenya incorporated into East Africa Protectorate
1910 Native Authority system in operation
1920 Creation of colony of Kenya
1924 Introduction of Local Native Councils
1921 Formation of Kikuyu Central Association (KCA) (first called Young Kikuyu Association) by Harry Thuku
1922 Harry Thuku deported
1928 Kenyatta becomes secretary-general of KCA
1929 The female circumcision controversy begins
1931 Kenyatta leaves Kenya and comes to Britain; not to return until 1946
1938 The KCA is banned; publication of Kenyatta's book, *Facing Mount Kenya*
1944 First African (Mathu) nominated to Legislative Council
1946 Kenyatta returns to Kenya; onset of a 'development' policy by Britain; Kenya African Union (KAU) founded; Kenyatta becomes President of KAU in 1947
1952 State of emergency declared following various murders by Africans who come to be known as the Mau Mau
1953 Kenyatta and five other Kikuyu convicted of managing the Mau Mau
1954 Executive Council turned into Council of Ministers
1957 Africans elected to Legislative Council
1958 African representation upon Legislative Council is expanded
1961 Kenyatta released from prison to lead independence negotiations
1963 Kenyatta and the Kenya African Union win elections to internal govern-

ment (May); full independence achieved in December

Africa (for chapters 4–8 and 10–12)

1806 British occupy Cape of Good Hope
1814 Cape of Good Hope province becomes British colony
1836 Beginning of the 'Great Trek'
1838 Battle of Blood River: Boers defeat Zulus
1852 South African Republic (Transvaal) established
1856 Natal established as crown colony
1862 Britain and France recognise independence of Zanzibar
1869 Opening of Suez Canal
1870 Diamonds discovered in Orange Free State
1873 Ashanti war breaks out
1875 Britain purchases 176,602 Suez Canal shares from Khedive of Egypt
1879 British-Zulu war; Transvaal Republic proclaimed
1880 Cape parliament rejects scheme for South African Federation; Transvaal declares itself independent of Britain
1881 Nationalist rising in Egypt under Arabi Pasha; Britain recognises independence of Transvaal
1882 British forces occupy Cairo; French-British dual control established
1883 Germany begins settlements in South West Africa; France begins to take over the upper Niger
1884 Berlin Conference of fourteen nations on African affairs
1885 Death of Gordon at Khartoum; Congo becomes personal possession of King Leopold of Belgium; Germany annexes Tanganyika and Zanzibar; Britain establishes protectorates over North Bechuanaland and the Niger river region
1886 Anglo-German agreement on frontiers of Gold Coast and Togoland and on respective spheres of influence in east Africa; German-Portugese agreement on boundaries between Angola and German South West Africa
1887 First colonial conference in London; Britain annexes Zululand; British East African Company chartered
1889 Rhodes's British South Africa Company granted mining rights
1890 Rhodes Premier of Cape Colony; Anglo-German convention defines various spheres of influence in Africa; Lugard occupies Uganda for British East Africa Company
1892 First trains arrive at Johannesburg from Cape
1893 Jameson crushes Matabele revolt for British South Africa Company and occupies Bulawayo
1894 Uganda becomes a British protectorate
1895 Creation of Rhodesia; Jameson raid; creation of East African Protectorate
1896 Jameson surrenders; Rhodes resigns premiership of Cape Colony; Ethiopians defeat Italian forces at Adowa
1898 French forced by Britain to evacuate Fashoda (Sudan)
1899 Beginning of first Boer war
1900 Uganda agreement establishes major role for the Baganda in British ad-

ministration
1901 Ashanti kingdom annexed to Gold Coast colony
1902 End of Boer war; Orange Free State becomes British crown colony
1905 First Moroccan crisis
1906 Self-government granted to Transvaal and Orange River colonies
1907 Governorship of Uganda established
1908 Union of South Africa established; Leopold transfers Congo to Belgium
1910 Union of South Africa becomes dominion within British Empire
1914 British protectorate proclaimed in Egypt
1919 Nationalist revolts in Egypt; Britain takes over Germany's east African territories; in Uganda a Native Laws Ordinance and Councils Ordinance establishes a type of indirect rule
1922 Britain recognises kingdom of Egypt
1936 Italy annexes Abyssynia
1945 First parties formed in Uganda and first African nominated to Legislative Council
1946 New constitution in Gold Coast which becomes the first British African colony with a majority of Africans in the legislature
1947 Nigeria acquires modified self-government
1948 Afrikaner nationalist victory in general election in South Africa
1949 Ugandan parties proscribed after riots; apartheid programme begins in South Africa
1952 Anti-British riots in Egypt; Farouk abdicates in favour of his son, Fuad; formation of Uganda National Congress
1953 Federal constitution of Rhodesia and Nyasaland comes into force; in Uganda African participation in colonial institutions extended; Kabaka deported
1954 Nasser takes power in Egypt; state of emergency in Uganda; Convention People's Party wins Gold Coast elections and Nkrumah forms government; outbreaks of terrorism in Algeria lead to dissolution of Algerian Nationalist Movement for the Triumph of Democratic Liberties
1955 First meeting of Federal Council of Nigeria; new constitution in force in Tanganyika; Buganda transitional agreement signed in Kampala; the Kabaka returns to Buganda and the Progressive Party is formed
1956 Suez crisis
1957 Ghana becomes independent
1958 Nkrumah sets up foundation for mutual assistance in Africa south of the Sahara; Algerian crisis helps bring down the French Fourth Republic; in Uganda, first direct elections to the Legislative Council: Buganda refuses to take part
1959 Belgium grants reforms in the Congo
1960 Belgian Congo granted full independence; Tshombe declares Katanga independent; France agrees to independence of Dahomey, Niger, Upper Volta, Chad, Ivory Coast, Central Africa and the French Congo; independence of the Nigerian Federation; Macmillan makes his 'wind of change' speech in Cape Town; Sharpeville shootings in South Africa; creation of the Uganda People's Congress as the main nationalist party in Uganda, headed by Obote
1961 Sierra Leone becomes independent within the Commonwealth; collapse of

army revolt in Algeria; South Africa becomes an independent republic outside the Commonwealth; general election for a new national assembly in Uganda boycotted by Baganda, but compromise between Uganda People's Congress and Buganda against Democratic Party

1962 Ben Bella becomes premier of Algeria; Uganda and Tanganyika become independent

1963 Kenya becomes independent; Nyasaland becomes self-governing: Kabaka of Buganda becomes first President of Uganda; Zanzibar becomes independent

1964 Kaunda becomes President of Northern Rhodesia, which goes on to become independent as Zambia; Ian Smith elected Prime Minister of Southern Rhodesia; Nyasaland becomes independent as Malawi; creation of Tanzania; Kenya becomes a republic; renewed rebellions in Congo (Zaire)

1965 Southern Rhodesia unilaterally declares independence

1966 Military coup in Nigeria; Obote ends special status of Buganda; Mobutu restoring control in Zaire

1967 Beginning of civil war in Nigeria

1970 Biafra capitulates to federal (Nigerian) troops

1971 Amin overthrows government of Obote in Uganda

1974 Revolution in Portugal weakens Portuguese colonial authority in Africa

1975 Angola, Mozambique and other Portugese African colonies become independent

1979 Amin overthrown after intervention by Tanzanian troops; Southern Rhodesia becomes independent state of Zimbabwe under system of majority rule

1980 Milton Obote becomes first leader of a new state to regain power after being overthrown; his party wins elections in Uganda

China

1839–42 First Opium War; at end of war ports opened to Britain

1850–55 Taiping rebellion

1857 Royal Navy destroys Chinese fleet; British and French forces take Canton

1858 End of Anglo-Chinese war; further ports opened to Britain and France and the opium trade is legalised

1860 Anglo-French troops defeat Chinese at Pa Li Chau

1887 Portugal secures cession of Macoa from China

1893 War with Japan

1895 Japan gains port facilities and ceded areas at end of war

1897 German and Russian occupations in China

1898 'The Boxers', an anti-Western organisation, is formed; Emperor begins extensive reform programme but removed from power by the dowager empress, who revokes reforms

1900 Boxer uprising

1901 Rising ended; China to pay indemnity to the great powers

1905 Sun Yat Sen founds union of secret societies to expel the Manchus from China

1908 Dowager Empress dies

1911 Establishment of Chinese republic; Sun Yat Sen is President and Chiang Kai Shek his military adviser
1913 Yam Shih Kai elected President of Chinese Republic
1922 Nine-power treaty in Washington preserves principle of 'open door' in trading relations with China; civil war in China
1924 First Kuomintang Congress admits communists to party and welcomes Russian advisers
1926 Chiang Kai Shek reaches Hankow in his northern campaign in the civil war
1927 National government established at Hankow; Chinese communists seize Nanking; Chiang Kai Shek organises government at Nanking; Chiang Kai Shek massacres communists in Shanghai
1928 Clashes between China and Japan; China annuls 'unequal treaties'; Chiang Kai Shek elected President of China
1933 Japan occupies China north of the Great Wall; Japan withdraws from the League of Nations
1934–35 The Long March led by Mao Tse Tung
1936 Chiang Kai Shek enters Canton; declares war on Japan
1937 Japanese seize Peking, Tienkin, Shanghai, Nanking and Hangchow; Chiang Kai Shek unites with communists led by Mao Tse Tung and Chou en Lai
1938 Japanese instal puppet government of Chinese Republic at Nanking
1941 China allied with the USA against Japan following Japanese attack on Pearl Harbour
1943 Churchill, Roosevelt and Chiang Kai Shek agree at Cairo on measures for defeating Japan
1945 Fighting breaks out between communists and nationalists in north China
1946 Chinese-US treaty of friendship and commerce
1947 US withdraws as mediator in China
1948 Chiang Kai Shek re-elected President by Nanking assembly and granted dictatorial powers; communists announce formation of North China People's Republic
1949 Chiang Kai Shek forced to withdraw to Formosa; Communist People's Republic proclaimed under Mao Tse Tung, with Chou en Lai as Premier

Japan

1854 US makes first trade treaty with Japan
1858 Anglo-Japanese commercial treaty providing for unsupervised trade and for the setting up of a British residency
1864 British, French and Dutch fleets attack Japan in reprisal for closing ports and expelling foreigners; Japan made to pay an indemnity
1868 Shogunate abolished; Meiji dynasty restored
1871 Abolition of domains and replacement by prefectures
1877 Satsuma rebellion crushed
1880 New penal code introduced, based on that of France
1881 Political parties formed following imperial decree that an assembly will be

convened in 1890

1889 Constitution granted in Japan with two-chamber Diet but emperor retains extensive powers

1890 First general election

1892 Prince Ito becomes Premier

1893 At war with China

1904 At war with Russia; substantial cessions made at end of war by Russia. (For subsequent Japanese actions in China see China chronology)

1941 Japan bombs Pearl Harbour and US enters war on side of Britain and the Commonwealth

1942 Major Japanese advances in Far East (including Singapore and Burma)

1945 US drops two atomic bombs on Japan; Japan surrenders a week later

Fascism in Germany, Italy and Rumania

1919 First *fascii* formed in Italy; Gabriele d'Annunzio seizes Fiume; Weimar constitution; foundation of the National Socialist Workers' Party; National Liberal regime in Rumania defeated in elections

1920 Failure of Kapp *putsch*; royal *coup d'état* restores National Liberals to power in Rumania

1921 Twenty-nine fascists returned to parliament in Italian elections; state of emergency declared in Germany

1922 Mussolini marches on Rome and forms a government

1923 French and Belgian troops occupy the Ruhr; failure of *putsch* in Munich led by Hitler; non-fascist parties dissolved in Italy

1924 Non-fascist trade unions abolished in Italy; Hitler sentenced to five years' imprisonment but released in December; May: nationalist and communist gains in German elections; murder of Italian socialist Matteoti leads to opposition leaving parliament; French and Belgian troops withdraw from Ruhr; December: socialist recovery against nationalists and communists in German elections

1925 Hindenburg elected President

1927 Codreanu and colleagues form League of Archangel Michael (known as Iron Guard)

1928 National Peasants' Party Congress in Rumania demands responsible government and later wins elections; socialists gain at expense of nationalists in German elections and social democrats re-enter a coalition government; Fascist Grand Council made part of Italian constitution with right of nominating candidates to the Chamber

1929 Onset of economic depression; Young Plan on reparations upheld in a referendum in Germany; fascists 'win' single-party elections in Italy

1930 Minority government in Germany under chancellorship of Bruning dependent on presidential decrees to get through some of its measures; in elections of September the Nazis win 107 seats

1932 In run-off presidential elections Hindenburg gets 19 million and Hitler 13 million votes; in July elections Nazis win 231 seats; Hitler refuses post of Vice-chancellor under Franz von Papen; deadlock maintained after elections of November; General von Schleicher becomes Chancellor in December

1933 January: Hitler appointed Chancellor; February: Reichstag fire leads to suspension of civil liberties and freedom of press; March: Nazis win 288 seats in elections; Enabling Law grants Hitler far-reaching powers for five years; May: trade unions suppressed; July: parties other than Nazis suppressed; November: Nazis gain 92 per cent of votes in elections

1934 August: following the death of Hindenburg a plebiscite approves vesting of sole executive power in Hitler as Fuhrer

1937 Iron Guard officially take 16 per cent of the votes in elections in Rumania

1938 King Carol II takes over direct power

1939 Carol II removed from power; in his place an alliance between the army and Iron Guard

1940 Anonescu, leader of the army in Rumania, destroys the Iron Guard and assumes complete control

Post-war separatism in the United Kingdom

1921 Creation of Northern Ireland parliament (Stormont) to govern the six counties of Ulster

1925 Formation of Plaid Genedlactrol Cymru [Welsh National(ist) Party]

1928 Formation of National Party of Scotland

1934 Formation of Scottish National Party (SNP)

1945 Welsh party changes its name to Plaid Cymru

1949 Covenant proposing Scottish parliament receives up to 2 million signatures

1963 The Prime Minister of Ulster, Terence O'Neill, begins a process of gradual reform

1964 Campaign for Democracy in Ulster established

1967 SNP victory in Hamilton by-election

1968 Rioting in Londonderry

1969 Following extensive rioting the British army moves into Belfast and Londonderry

1971 Introduction of internment in Ulster

1972 30 January: 'Bloody Sunday', thirteen people shot dead following civil rights march in Derry in defiance of government ban; under Northern Ireland (Temporary Provisions) Bill Stormont is prorogued and executive and legislative powers are transferred to London

1973 Publication of the Kilbrandon report on devolution; in Ulster, election held for a new assembly which should produce a power-sharing executive; in talks at Sunningdale, Dublin, London and the new Northern Ireland executive agree to the setting up of an All Ireland Council

1974 1 January: direct rule in Ulster comes to an end and government transferred to the new assembly and power-sharing executive; February general election: Conservative, 297; Labour, 301; Liberal, 14; Plaid Cymru, 2; SNP, 7; others (GB), 2; others (NI), 12. * (*Of the twelve MPs returned from Northern Ireland, eleven were anti-Sunningdale Unionists.); May: Northern Ireland executive falls following a general strike against the Sunningdale agreement; October general election: Conservative, 277; Labour, 319; Liberal,

13; Plaid Cymru, 3; SNP, 11; others (NI), 12
1974–5 Two White Papers on devolution
1975 Elections to a convention in Ireland won by Loyalists opposed to power-sharing; deadlock leads to reversion to direct rule from London
1976 Introduction of Scotland and Wales bill
1977 February: defeat of a timetable motion to limit debate at committee stage on the Scotland and Wales bill effectively kills the measure; November: government introduces two bills for devolution, one for Scotland and one for Wales
1978 The two bills become law; a referendum in Scotland and Wales on the bills planned for 1 March 1979; to come into effect the measures have to secure the support of 40 per cent of the total electorate
1979 General election: Conservative victory, SNP reduced to two MPs; in referendum on devolution Wales measure is heavily defeated and Scottish measure, although receiving majority support from those who voted, fails to secure the 40 per cent of the electorate required.

The break-up of the USSR

1982 Andropov new Soviet leader following Brezhnev's death.
1984 Chernenko new Soviet leader following Andropov's death.
1985 Gorbachev new Soviet leader following Chernenko's death.
1987 Gorbachev publishes his book *Perestroika*, warns of threat of nationalism in USSR.
1988 February: First large national demonstrations in the Baltic republics and Armenia.
1988 June/July: First CPSU party conference for 50 years.
1989 First contested elections to Congress of People's Deputies.
1989–90 Elections to republican parliamer.ts.
1989 April: Soviet troops kill demonstrators in Tblisi.
August: A huge human chain formed in 3 Baltic republics, demand Hitler-Stalin pact be declared void; Moldavian declared official language of the republic.
September: Ukrainian national movement 'Rukh' formed.
October: Ukrainian made official language of republic.
1990 February: CPSU gives up its 'leading' role in USSR.
March: Soviet Presidency established and Gorbachev elected to the post by Congress of People's Deputies; Congress strikes monopoly right of CPSU from constitution so new parties can start to form; Lithuania declares independence.
May: Yeltsin elected chairman of Russian Supreme Soviet.
June-December: All the republics and many autonomous areas declare their law takes precedence over Soviet law.
August: Armenia elects non-communist President (Petrosian).
October: Non-communist victories in Georgian elections.
November: Draft Union treaty published.
1991 January: Soviet military action against Lithuania and Latvia.
March: All-Union referendum on future of USSR.

June: Yeltsin elected President of Russia.

August: Attempted coup day before new Union Treaty due to signed; failure of coup; Yeltsin abolishes CPSU in Russia.

Aug-16 December: All republics except Russia declare independence.

September: USSR recognises independence of three Baltic states which are all admitted to the UN.

December: Establishment of Commonwealth of Independent States.

25 December: Gorbachev resigns his last public office.

The collapse of communism in east-central Europe

1985 Death of Enver Hoxha: dictator of Albania

1987 Slobodan Milosevic comes to power in Serbian League of Communists

1989 January: Erich Honecker declares Berlin Wall will, if need be, stand for another 100 years

June:Solidarity victories in controlled and partial elections in Poland.

July: Warsaw Pact meeting in Bucharest where USSR makes clear its abandonment of the 'Brehznev doctrine' of intervention in internal affairs of other states.

August: Solidarity activist Tadeusz Mazowiecki becomes Prime Minister in Poland.

September: Hungary completely opens borders with Austria: demonstrations start in Leipzig.

October: Gorbachev visits Berlin; Honecker removed from power and replaced by Egon Krenz; Hungary declares itself a multi-party republic.

November: East Germany revokes border controls with Czechoslovakia and then declares Berlin Wall open; demonstrations dispersed violently in Prague; general strike in Czechoslovakia; overthrow of Tudor Zhivkov, the Bulgarian dictator; disturbances begin in Rumania; West German Chancellor Kohl unveils his 10–point programme.

December: Havel elected interim president of Czecholslovakia; Ceasescu regime overthrown and Ceasescu and his wife executed.

1990 March: multi-party elections in East Germany; one week later, also in Hungary.

April: multi-party elections in Slovenia and Croatia; Albanian communist regime announces a few reforms.

June: multi-party elections in Czechoslovakia; also in Bulgaria.

July: Havel elected President of Czechoslovakia for 2–year period.

October: the restored Länder of East Germany accede to West Germany under Article 23 of the Basic Law of 1949.

December: first all-German general election returns Kohl and his coalition to power. Slovenian referendum supports declaration of independence.

1991–2 (Yugoslavia only)

1991 March: demonstrations in Belgrade fail to bring down Milosevic.

May: beginning of Croat-Serbian clashes in various parts of Croatia.

June: Slovenia and Croatia declare independence.

December: Milosevic wins Serbian elections.

1992 January: European Community recognises independence of Croatia. March: referendum in Bosnia-Herzegovina leads to declaration of independence. War begins in Bosnia-Herzegovina.

Bibliographical essay

Apart from the appendix, where I discuss some of the literature on nationalism, it did not seem appropriate to provide detailed references. In this bibliography I provide references for further reading on the various case studies as well as mentioning some items which have been of particular importance in the writing of this book. A complete bibliography of nationalism would be impossible to draw up, and it would not serve much purpose to note everything I have read in connection with the subject. For work up to the early 1970s the best bibliographical guide I know of is Anthony D. Smith, *Nationalism: Trend Report and Bibliography*, in *Current Sociology* (1973). A more recent bibliography is H. A. Winkler (ed.), *Bibliographie zum Nationalismus* (Göttingen, 1979). For a survey of current publications since 1990 one can now consult *The ASEN Bulletin*, published by the Association for the Study of Ethnicity and Nationalism which is based at the London School of Economics.

Unless otherwise stated, the place of publication is London.

Introduction

The older works by Hans Kohn, *The Idea of Nationalism* (New York, 1967), and Carlton Hayes, *The Historical Evolution of Nationalism* (New York, 1931), are still among the best historical treatments of the subject. More recent general historical works which provide a broad survey are Boyd C. Schafer, *Faces of Nationalism: New Realities and Old Myths* (New York, 1972), and Hugh Seton-Watson, *Nations and States: an inquiry into the origins of nations and the politics of nationalism* (1977). Yet both these books lack a clear focus which makes it difficult to discern nationalism as anything other than a series of particular histories or as some gradually unfolding development to which virtually everything is relevant. There is, by contrast, a very sharp focus in the work of Elie Kedourie, *Nationalism* (1960) and *Nationalism in Africa and Asia* (1971). The second of these is a collection of statements by various nationalists

443

edited and with an introduction by Kedourie which takes up the arguments of his first book and extends them beyond Europe. Kedourie places a much greater emphasis than I do upon the role of intellectuals and accordingly concentrates on nationalism as doctrine rather than as politics. Another book, written from a 'conservative' viewpoint and treating nationalism as doctrine is J. L. Talmon, *The Myth of the Nation and the Vision of Revolution* (1981).

Since the publication of the first edition of this book there have appeared a number of important general studies. I have already cited the work of Anthony D. Smith, *Theories of Nationalism* (1971) for a good introduction to various approaches to nationalism. Smith has published some further books of general importance including: *Nationalism in the Twentieth Century* (Oxford, 1979), *The Ethnic Origins of Nations* (Oxford, 1986); and *National Identity* (1991). More recent general studies are Peter Alter, *Nationalism* (1989), and E. Hobsbawn, *Nation and nationalism since 1789: programme, myth, reality* (Cambridge, 1991). Two outstanding books, each with a distinctive thesis about nationalism, are: Benedict Anderson, *Imagined Communities: reflections on the origins and spread of nationalism* (London, 1983); and Ernest Gellner, *Nations and nationalism* (Oxford, 1983). The rigorous comparative approach to European nationalism adopted by Miroslav Hroch can now be obtained in English: *Social Preconditions of National Revival in Europe: A Comparative Analysis of the Social Composition of Patriotic Groups among the Smaller European Nations* (Cambridge, 1985).

Chapter 1

I can think of nothing generally relevant on this subject. My own arguments were arrived at by piecing together material from a wide range of cases. All I can do is cite some literature which I found particularly suggestive. For the European working class and 'communal' nationalism I found very helpful Hans Mommsen, *Die Sozialdemokratie und die Nationalitätenfrage im habsburgischen Vielvölkerstaat* (Vienna, 1963), and P. Gibbon, *The Origins of Ulster Unionism* (see reading for chapter 16). For nineteenth-century central Europe see the work by Hroch cited in the previous section of this bibliography. For the early German nationalist movement see now D. Düding, 'The nineteenth-century German nationalist movement as a movement of societies', in *Nation-building in central Europe*, edited by H. Schulze (Leamington Spa, 1987). In the twentieth century support for fascism has attracted a good deal of study and comparison: see now Detlev Mühlberger, (ed.), *The social basis of European fascist movements* (London, 1987). The issue of links between fascism and big business has been studied in detail in H. A. Turner, *German Big Business and the rise of Hitler* (Oxford, 1985). An interesting attempt to link French nationalism to bourgeois interests is H. J. Haupt, *National-ismus und Demokratie. Zur Geschichte der Bourgeoisie im Frankreich der Restauration* (Frankfurt/M. , 1974). On the church and nationalism there is the work of E. Larkin, *The Historical Dimensions of Irish Catholicism* (New York, 1976), especially the essay 'Church, state and nation in modern Ireland', originally published in *American Historical Review*, LXXX, no. 5 (1975). On colonial nationalism and organised labour there are the conflicting views argued by E. J. Berg and J. Butler, 'Trade Unions', in *Political Parties and National Integration in Tropical Africa*, ed. J. S. Coleman and C. G. Rosberg (Berkeley and Los Angeles, 1964), and R. Cohen, *Labour and Politics in Nigeria, 1945–71* (1974), especially chapter 8, 'Labour and politics in Africa: a comparative perspective'. On peasant responses to nationalism there is the general work of E. Wolf, *Peasant Wars of the Twentieth Century* (1973) which deals with the question of how any peasants can be mobilised behind any mass political movement. A general attempt to analyse social class responses to nationalism in less developed societies is presented in P. Worsley, *The Third World* (1967). For more developed societies see *Mouvements Nationaux d'independence et classes populaires aux XIX et XX siècles en Occident et en Orient*, published under the auspices of the Commission Internationale d'histoire des mouvement sociaux et des structures sociales, Vol. 1 (Paris, 1971).

Chapter 2

There is a large literature dealing with nationalist ideology: indeed, for many writers this is what nationalism is. The general works by Kohn, Hayes and Kedourie cited in the further reading for the Introduction are all relevant. My original concern with the 'state-society' relationship was much influenced by S. Wolin, *Politics and vision: continuity and innova-tion in Western political thought* (1961). For references to important nationalist texts and general studies of nationalist ideology see Smith, *Nationalism: Trend Report and Bibliography*, items 6–26. Specifically on Herder whom I consider in this chapter see F. M. Barnard, *Herder's Social and Political Thought: from enlightenment to nationalism* (Oxford, 1965).

Chapter 3

On 'nationalism' before 1500 see the works cited in Smith, *Trend Report and Bibliography*, items 118–40. I found V. G. Kiernan, 'State and nation in western Europe', *Past and Present*, 31 (1965), particularly suggestive. See also now O. Dann (ed.), *Nationalismus in vorindustrieller Zeit* (Mu-nich, 1986), and J. A. Armstrong, *Nations before nationalism* (Chapel Hill, 1982).

On national(ist) sentiment in the early modern period see E. Marcu,

Sixteenth Century Nationalism (New York, 1976), and O. Ranum (ed.), *National Consciousness, History and Political Culture in Early Modern Europe* (Baltimore, 1975).

On the relationship between national sentiment and religion before and during the Reformation see G. Strauss (ed), *Manifestations of Discontent in Germany on the Eve of the Reformation* (Bloomington, Indiana, 1971), and A. G. Dickens, *The German Nation and Martin Luther* (1974). On the role of religion in new types of political opposition see H. G. Koenigsberger, 'The revolutionary parties of the sixteenth century', *Journal of Modern History* (1955).

General historical treatment of the early modern period and the development of strong monarchical government is provided in H. Kamen, *The Iron Century* (1971), and E. N. Williams, *The Ancien Régime in Europe, 1648–1789* (1970). Specifically on the subject of absolutism see P. Anderson, *Lineages of the Absolutist State* (1974), although I think this works better as comparative political description than as a demonstration of the class basis of absolutism. A descriptive political account of absolutism, using typologies derived from sociology and constitutional law is also offered by G. Poggi, *The Development of the Modern State: a sociological introduction* (1978), chapter 4. For the nature of power rather than a focus on state institutions see Michael Mann, *The Sources of Social Power* , vol. 1 (Cambridge, 1986). On the role of military development in promoting state development see G. Parker, *The military revolution: military innovation and the rise of the West 1500–1800* (Cambridge, 1988).

On religion and stronger government see generally, for Spain, J. H. Elliott, *Imperial Spain* (1963), and, for England, G. R. Elton, *England under the Tudors* (1956). For France see R. J. Knecht, 'The Concordat of 1516: a reassessment', *University of Birmingham Journal* (1963).

On patronage and monarchy I found useful J. Neale, 'The Elizabethan political scene', in his *Essays in Elizabethan History* (1958), and J. Salmon, 'Venality of office and popular sedition in seventeenth-century France', *Past and Present*, 37 (1967). Also useful is J. Hurstfield, 'Social structure, office holding and politics, chiefly in western Europe', in *The New Cambridge Modern History*, vol. III, *The Counter-Reformation and Price Revolution, 1559–1610* (1968).

Generally on representative institutions see A. R. Myers, *Parliaments and Estates in Europe up to 1789* (1975). For England see J. Neale, *Elizabeth I and her Parliaments* (1953, 1957), and W. Notestein, *The Winning of the Initiative by the House of Commons* (1924). Criticisms of these works are contained in the articles by Elton and Russell cited in note 10 to the Conclusion. The 'growth' of parliament as a national institution beyond Westminster is taken up in D. Hirst, *The Representative of the People? Voters and voting in England under the early Stuarts* (1975), and J. H. Plumb, 'The growth of the electorate in England, 1600–1715', *Past and Present*, 45 (2969). I also found useful Plumb's book, *The Growth of Political Stability in England, 1675–1725* (1967). Ever since Seeley published his book *The Expansion of England* over a century ago we have also needed historians to consider how English/British identity was shaped through the growth of state power and international conflict. Such work is now appearing, for example, J. Brewer, *The Sinews of Power: War, Money and the English state, 1688–1783* (1989); C. A. Bayly, *Imperial Meridian: the British Empire and the World, 1780–1830*; and the work of L. Colley: notably 'Britishness and Otherness: an argument', *Journal of British Studies* (October, 1992), and *Britons: Forging the Nation 1707–1837* (1992).

On France the various works by J. Russell Major on representative institutions have most influenced me. I would pick out as very suggestive his article 'The loss of royal initiative and the decay of the Estates General in France, 1421–1615', *International Commission for the History of Representative and Parliamentary Institutions*, XXIV (1961). For the sixteenth century there are useful essays in R. Hatton (ed.), *Louis XIV and Absolutism* (1976), and R. Kierstead (ed.), *State and Society in Seventeenth Century France* (New York, 1975).

There is an immense literature on the English and French revolutions. L. Stone, *The Causes of the English Revolution* (1972) has now been overhauled by C. Russell, *The Causes of the English Civil War* (Oxford, 1991), and A. Hughes, *The causes of the English civil war* (1991). For France there is still the fine introduction by G. Lefebvre, *The Coming of the French Revolution* (Princeton, 1967). Particularly important for my arguments are R. Palmer, *The Age of Democratic Revolution* (2 vols. , Princeton, 1959, 1964), and W. Doyle, 'The parlements of France and the breakdown of the Old Regime, 1771–1788', *French Historical Studies*, 6, no. 4 (1970). The bicentenary brought forth many books on the revolution but most of them eschewed broad political analysis for the more fashionable pursuits of narrative or culture. Of general use, however, is W. Doyle, *The Oxford History of the French Revolution* (Oxford, 1989). The best-selling narrative treatment by S. Schama, *Citizens* (1989) does, however, implicitly point to the construction of a national ideology of reform to be led by the monarchy as a key development up to 1789, and indeed through to 1792. On national sentiment just before and during the revolution see B. Schafer, 'Bourgeois nationalism in the pamphlets on the eve of the French revolution', *Journal of Modern History*, X (1938), and B. Hyslop, *French Nationalism in 1789 according to the General Cahiers* (New York, 1934).

Chapter 4

For the French revolutionary background we now have the very useful collection of essays edited by O. Dann and J. Dinwiddy under the title *Nationalism in the Age of the French Revolution* (1988). On the Napoleonic background see now S. J. Woolf, *Napoleon's Integration of Europe* (1991), and G. Ellis, *The Napoleonic Empire* (1991).

Much of the work on German nationalism has taken the form of intellectual history which tends to overemphasise the role of ideas and intellectuals, particularly those of a romantic and irrational slant. Typical for Germany is G. L. Mosse, *The Crisis of German Ideology* (1966), a book which at times reflects the incoherence of its subject matter. Hans Kohn, *The Mind of Germany* (1966), and F. Stern, *The Politics of Cultural Despair: a study in the rise of Germanic ideology* (Berkeley, 1967) are tighter studies but taken alone are still misleading. The more liberal and statist elements in German nationalist thought are brought out well in works such as F. Meinecke, *Cosmopolitanism and the National State* (Princeton, 1970), and W. Simon, 'Variations in nationalism during the great reform period in Prussia', *American Historical Review*, 59 (1954). Particularly valuable for the way it avoids reading the present back into the past is the trio of intellectual studies by Wilhelm Mommsen, *Stein, Ranke, Bismarck. Ein Beitrag zur politischen und sozialen Bewegung des 19. Jahrhunderts* (Munich, 1954).

Again there are many works on the Risorgimento as an intellectual movement. See, for example, E. Holt, *Risorgimento: the making of Italy, 1815–1870* (1970). Some useful extracts from contemporary writers are contained in D. Mack Smith (ed.), *The Making of Italy, 1796–1870* (1968).

It is the attempt to see how such sentiments translate into effective politics which principally concerns me. For Germany I found especially useful F. Eyck, *The Frankfurt Parliament, 1848–49* (1968), and O. Pflanze, *Bismarck and the Development of Germany* (3 vols, Princeton, 1990), especially vol. 1, *The Period of Unification, 1815–1871*. For liberal nationalism see J. Sheehan, *German Liberalism in the Nineteenth Century* (Chicago, 1978), and for a fine overview of the earlier period *idem*, *Germany 1770–1866* (Oxford, 1990). Of general use now is a book I have recently edited: *The State of Germany: the national idea in the making, unmaking and remaking of a nation-state* (1992) and also the study by M. Hughes, *Nationalism and Society: Germany 1800–1945* (1988).

For Italy I have been influenced above all by the work of D. Mack Smith. Apart from his general work *Italy: a modern history* (Michigan, 1969), there is *Cavour and Garibaldi, 1860: a study in political conflict* (Cambridge, 1954) and *Victor Emmanuel, Cavour and the Risorgimento* (1971). We are fortunate now to possess some recent fine studies of modern Italy. There are two books in the Longman History of Italy series: H. Hearder, *Italy in the Age of the Risorgimento, 1790–1870* (1983), and M. Clark, *Modern Italy 1871–1982* (1984). There is also S. J. Woolf, *A*

History of Italy 1700–1860: the social constraints of political change (1979). And for the role of elite liberal nationalism see R. Grew, *A sterner plan for Italian unity: the Italian National Society in the Risorgimento* (Princeton, 1963).

On Poland generally see O. Halecki, *A History of Poland* (1955) and N. Davies, *God's Playground: A History of Poland*, vol. 2, *1792 to present* (New York, 1982). My thinking has been particularly influenced by the work of R. F. Leslie: *Polish Politics and the Revolution of November 1830* (1956) and *Reform and Insurrection in Russian Poland, 1856–65* (1963). Also of use was A. Gill, *Die polnische Revolution, 1846* (Munich and Vienna, 1974), which deals with the uprising in Galicia. For Posen there is little in English though it is touched upon by W. Hagen, *Germans, Poles and Jews: the nationality conflict in the Prussian East, 1772–1914* (Chicago, 1980). The excesses of the account provided in L. B. Namier, *1848: the revolution of the intellectuals* (1944), are brought into perspective in Eyck, *The Frankfurt Parliament*, chapter 7.

Chapter 5

General works on Austria-Hungary are R. Kann, *The Multinational Empire: nationalism and national reform in the Habsburg monarchy, 1848–1918* (2 vols, New York, 1950), and A. J. P. Taylor, *The Habsburg Monarchy, 1809–1918* (1964). For the nationalist movements of subordinate groups (or 'small nations') there is the fine comparative study by M. Hroch, *Vorkämpfer der nationalen Bewegungen bei den kleinen Völkern Europas* (Prague, 1968). For an abridged English version see above, section on Introduction.

For Hungary I found four works of particular value: G. Barany, *Stephen Szechenyi and the Awakening of Hungarian Nationalism, 1791–1841* (Princeton, 1968); L. Deme, *The Radical Left in the Hungarian Revolution of 1848* (New York, 1976); G. Szabad, *Hungarian Political Trends between the Revolution and the Compromise, 1848–1867* (Budapest, 1977); and, above all, I. Deak, *The Lawful Revolution: Louis Kossuth and the Hungarians, 1848–49* (New York, 1979).

For the intellectual aspect of Czech nationalism the study by J. Zacek, *Palacky: the historian as scholar and nationalist* (The Hague, 1978), is useful. For the politics see S. Z. Pech, *The Czech Revolution of 1848* (Chapel Hill, 1969), and B. Garver, *The Young Czech Party, 1874–1901, and the Emergence of the Multi-party System* (New Haven, 1978). Since the publication of the first edition I have benefitted from discussions with Professor Jiri Korâlka who takes a similar approach to mine. See now his book *Tschechen im Habsburgerreich und in Europa 1815–1914. Sozialgeschichtliche Zusammenhänge der neuzeitlichen Nationsbildung und der Nationalitätenfrage in den böhmischen Ländern* (Munich and Vienna, 1991).

Bibliographical essay

For nationalism in the Balkans I found L. Stavrianos, *The Balkans since 1453* (New York, 1958) an invaluable introduction. E. Turcynski, *Konfession und Nation. Zur Frühgeschichte der serbischen und rumänischen Nationalbildung* (Düsseldorf, 1976) is a valuable comparative study. For the Rumanians of Transylvania I have been especially influenced by the work of K. Hitchins: *The Rumanian National Movement in Transylvania, 1780–1849* (Cambridge, Mass. , 1969) and *Orthodoxy and Nationality: Andreu Saguna and the Rumanians of Transylvania, 1846–1873* (Cambridge, Mass. , 1977)

Generally on the Ottoman empire see W. Haddad and W. Ochsenwald (eds), *Nationalism in a Non-national State: the dissolution of the Ottoman Empire* (Ohio, 1977). B. Lewis, *The Emergence of Modern Turkey* (1968) concentrates on the centre of the empire. An interesting article of general value is G. Stokes, 'Dependency and the rise of nationalism in south-east Europe', *International Journal of Turkish Studies*, 1, no. 1 (winter 1979–80).

On the Greek movement see D. Dakin, *The Unification of Greece, 1770–1923* (1972). For other movements in the European part of the Ottoman empire one can start with the various studies provided in P. Sugar and I. Lederer (eds), *Nationalism in Eastern Europe* (Seattle, 1969).

Chapter 6

Very different approaches to early Arab nationalism are presented in G. Antonius, *The Arab Awakening* (1938), and Z. Zeine, *The Emergence of Arab Nationalism* (Beirut, 1966). Also useful is C. Ernest Dawn, *From Ottomanism to Arabism: essays on the origins of Arab nationalism* (Urbanan, Ill. , 1973). A more recent study is F. Clements, *The Emergence of Arab Nationalism from the Nineteenth Century to 1921* (1976).

An immensely stimulating history of modern Egypt is J. Berque, *Egypt: imperialism and revolution* (1972). On Egyptian nationalist thought I was particularly influenced by N. Safran, *Egypt in Search of Political Community: an analysis of the intellectual and political evolution of Egypt, 1804–1952* (Cambridge, Mass. , 1961).

Chapter 7

A useful account of the historiography of colonial nationalism up to the mid-1960s is provided by J. Lonsdale, 'The emergence of African nations', *African Affairs*, 67 (1968). A classic general version of the 'westernisation' approach is R. Emerson, *From Empire to Nation* (Cambridge, Mass. , 1960). The works by Robinson and Ranger cited in the notes to chapter 7 provide an introduction to approaches which emphasise the role of either collaboration and/or resistance in shaping the colonial relationship and the

450

subsequent nationalist response.

On African nationalism generally see T. Hodgkin, *Nationalism in Africa* (1956), which is still of great value. Modern general accounts of Africa in the colonial and post-colonial period are B. Davidson, *Africa in Modern History* (1978), and H. S. Wilson, *The Imperial Experience in Sub-Saharan Africa since 1870* (Minnesota, 1977). A more recent book is A. Mazrui and M. Tidy, *Nationalism and the new states in Africa: from about 1935 to the present* (Nairobi, 1984), and see also Anthony D. Smith, *State and nation in the Third World: the western state and African nationalism* (New York, 1983). Generally on India see J. Masselos, *Nationalism on the Indian Subcontinent* (1972). Much further reading on nationalism in Africa and Asia can be found in Smith, *Nationalism: Trend Report and Bibliography*, items 287–496.

Chapter 8

There is a large literature on Indian nationalism. Apart from the good introductory study by Masselos cited in the previous section I found particularly valuable two collections of essays: J. Gallagher, G. Johnson, and A. Seal (eds), *Locality, Province and Nation: essays on Indian politics, 1870–1940* (1973), and D. A. Low (ed.), *Congress and the Raj: facets of the Indian struggle, 1917–1947* (Columbia, 1977), especially the opening essays by Seal and Low respectively. There is also now the general study by Judith Brown, *Modern India: the origins of Asian democracy* (Oxford, 1985). In writing these chapters on colonial nationalism for the first edition of this book I was, perhaps, unduly influenced by the 'Cambridge school', though I also criticised shortcomings of this approach. Thanks to Rudra Mukherjee I have had an opportunity to read some of the work by Indian historians critical of the Cambridge school and developing a distinctive approach of their own. Two works I found especially useful were: Sumit Surkar, *Modern India 1885–1947* (2nd. ed. , London, 1989), and Partha Chatterjee, *Nationalist Thought and the Colonial World: a derivative discourse?* (London, 1986). I have not read B. Chandra, *Nationalism and colonialism in modern India* (New Delhi, 1979)

For Kenya, as for East Africa generally, the best introduction is the three-volume *History of East Africa* published by Oxford University Press. Volume II (Oxford, 1965), edited by V. Harlow and E. M. Chilver deals largely with the colonial period before the rise of nationalist opposition. Volume III (Oxford, 1976), edited by D. A. Low and A. Smith, deals with the post-1945 period. For the political history of Kenya see the two essays by G. Bennett and J. Middleton in vol. II and the essay by G. Bennett and A. Smith in vol. III. On the Kikuyu, especially the Mau Mau episode, see C. G. Rosberg and J. Nottingham, *The Myth of the Mau Mau: nationalism in Kenya* (1966), and D. L. Barnett and K. Njama, *Mau Mau from within:*

451

autobiography and analysis of Kenya's peasant revolt (1966) which present rather different intepretations. On the Luo I have been greatly influenced by the work of J. Lonsdale, notably 'Political associations in western Kenya', in *Protest and Power*, ed. R. Rotberg and A. Mazrui (New York, 1970) and 'Some origins of nationalism in East Africa', *Journal of Modern History*, IX (1968). The latter, though general, draws especially on examples from western Kenya. On Kenyatta there is his own fascinating book *Facing Mount Kenya* (1938), and a good biography by J. Murray Brown, *Kenyatta* (1972).

Chapter 9

For Muslims in India see P. Hardy, *The Muslims of British India* (1972). For African cases see V. Oloronsola (ed.), *The Politics of Cultural Subnationalism in Africa* (New York, 1972), which has essays dealing with the cases analysed in this chapter as well as other cases. This book as well as the valuable work by C. Young, *The Politics of Cultural Pluralism* (Wisconsin, 1976), were essential both for this chapter and for chapter 12. For further details on Uganda see D. A. Low, *Buganda in Modern History* (1971), and the essays by D. A. Low and R. S. Pratt in vol. II of *The History of East Africa* and by C. Gertzel in vol. III. Apart from the fine essay by T. Turner on the Belgian Congo in the Oloronsola volume there is a useful monograph by H. Weiss, *Political Protest in the Congo* (Princeton, 1967), which deals with one of the main African parties.

Chapter 10

There is hardly anything of specific relevance to refer to for this chapter. The essay by Heesterman cited in the notes to the chapter was extremely valuable to me. Although I disagree with much of the argument, the article by J. Lonsdale and B. Berman, 'Coping with the contradictions: the development of the colonial state in Kenya, 1895–1914', *Journal of African History*, 20 (1979), has a significance which extends beyond the particular case with which it deals. The book by Chatterjee cited in the section on chapter 8 is valuable in showing the increasingly positive view of the colonial state taken by more 'advanced' nationalists like Nehru.

Chapter 11

There are a number of valuable comparative studies of relevance. Barrington Moore, *The Social Origins of Dictatorship and Democracy: lord and peasant in the making of the modern world* (1969) is especially useful in relating state development to class relations in the countryside. T. Skocpol, *States and Social Revolutions: a comparative analysis of France, Russia and China* (1979) is especially useful on state institutions and the international pressures to which they are subjected. A more specifically relevant comparative study, also for chapter 12, is R. Ward and D. Rustow (eds), *Political Modernisation in Japan and Turkey* (Princeton, 1964).

On early reform attempts in China see M. Wright, *The Last Stand of Chinese Conservatism: the T'ung Chih restoration, 1862–74* (Stanford, 1957). On the development of nationalist ideology see the superb study by J. R. Levenson, *Liang Ch'i-Ch'ao and the Mind of Modern China* (Berkeley and Los Angeles, 1959). On reform movements under Kuomintang and the character of the Kuomintang movement I found useful: J. Israel, 'Kuomintang policy and student politics, 1927–37', in *Approaches to Modern Chinese History*, ed. A. Feuerwerker *et. al.* (Los Angeles, 1967); P. Cavendish, 'The 'New China' of the Kuomintang', in *Modern China's Search for a Political Form*, ed. J. Gray (1969); and R. North and I. Pool, 'Kuomintang and Chinese communist elites', in *World Revolutionary Elites*, ed. H. Lasswell and D. Lerner (Cambridge, Mass. , 1960).

There is a very large literature on Chinese communism. For links with nationalism see C. Johnson, *Peasant Nationalism and Communist Power* (1963). A critical view of some of Johnson's arguments can be found in L. Bianco, *Origins of the Chinese Revolution, 1915–1949* (1971).

Nationalism has been well studied in the Japanese case. Smith, *Nationalism: Trend Report and Bibliography*, items 287–300, cites some of the most relevant material. Generally I found G. Sansom, *The Western World and Japan* (1950), of great value. On the crucial period of the 1860s and 1870s there is W. J. Beasley, *The Meiji Restoration* (1973). The role of the domains is brought out in the case study of A. Craig, *Choshu and the Meiji Restoration* (Cambridge, Mass. , 1967). On nationalist ideology, apart from the items cited in Smith, there is a useful essay by R. Scalapiro, 'Ideology and Modernisation: the Japanese case', in *Ideology and Discontent*, ed. D. Apter (New York, 1964).

On Turkey the best starting point is B. Lewis, *The Emergence of Modern Turkey* (1968). On the reform background see C. V. Findley, *Bureaucratic Reform in the Ottoman Empire: the Sublime Porte, 1789–1922* (Princeton, 1980). On the intellectual roots of Turkish nationalism see S. Mardon, *The Genesis of Young Ottoman Thought* (Princeton, 1962). The earlier period of Turkish nationalism is dealt with in D. Kushner, *The Rise of Turkish Nationalism, 1867–1908* (1977). For the period after 1918 one can focus on the figure of Ataturk as examined by Lord Kinross in *Ataturk: the rebirth of a nation* (1964). For examples of secular Turkish nationalist ideology see the writings of Ziya Gokalp such as *Principles of Turkism* (Leiden, Brill, 1968),and *Turkish Nationalism and Western Civilisation*, ed. N. Berkes (1959).

Chapters 12–14

These chapters cover such recent and unfinished subjects that it is difficult to recommend particular items. On the issue of separatism the various studies in the Oloronsola volume and the book by Young cited for chapter 9 are relevant. A well argued case for the firmness of sub-national identity which I criticise is C. Geertz, 'The integrative revolution: primordial sentiments and civil politics in the new states', in *Old Societies and New States*, ed. C. Geertz (New York, 1963).

A positive view of 'nation-building' or modernisation is argued in J. Kautsky (ed.), *Political Change in Underdeveloped Countries* (New York, 1967). American political science has produced a large literature on the subject. See, for example, K. Deutsch and W. J. Foltz (eds), *Nation Building* (New York, 1963). For a criticism of the way in which such literature employs the notion of political identiy see W. J. M. Mackenzie, *Political Identity* (1978). Since the 1960s, as the actual project of modernisation faltered, so did criticisms of the theory of modernisation increase. The works which have particularly shaped my own sceptical views about the impact of nationalism on 'nation-building' are G. Heeger, *The Politics of Underdevelopment* (1974), and A. Zolberg, *Creating Political Order: the party states of West Africa* (Chicago, 1966). I distinguish between the more limited project of political modernisation and the more general transformation which modernisation theorists employ. With the collapse of the USSR one can expect the more ambitious modernisation approaches to be revived as in F. Fukuyama, *The End of History and the Last Man* (London, 1992), though these have not yet been applied to 'Third World' as opposed to 'Second World' countries.

On the Pan-African movement up to 1945 see I. Geiss, *The Pan-African Movement* (New York, 1974). C. Legum, *Panafricanism: a short political guide* (1962), takes the story a little further.

On aspects of modern Arab nationalism see T. E. Farah (ed.), *Pan-Arabism and Arab nationalism* (Boulder, 1987). There are many studies of the politics of particular Arab countries and of Palestinian nationalism and Islamic movements. A relevant study in German is B. Tibi, *Nationalismus in die dritten Welt am arabischen Beispiel* (Frankfurt/M. , 1971) which I cited in the first edition. This is now available in English under the title *Arab nationalism: a critical inquiry* (New York, 1981). For an earlier general English introduction see G. Kirk, *Contemporary Arab politics: a concise history* (New York, 1961). Also of use is P. Mansfield, *Nasser's Egypt* (1969), chapter 3.

Chapter 15

The literature on fascism, even in English, is vast, especially on Germany.

A good place to begin is W. Laquer (ed.), *Fascism: a reader's guide* (1979), which has valuable national and comparative studies as well as comprehensive suggestions for further reading, but is now a little dated. For a comparison between the German and Italian cases I am particularly indebted to the brilliant article by W. S. Allen, 'The appeal of fascism and the problem of national disintegration', in *Reappraisals of Fascism*, ed. H. Turner (New York, 1975). Generally for Italy I would recommend A. Lyttleton, *The Seizure of Power: fascism in Italy, 1919–1929* (1975), and M. Clark, *Modern Italy* (see chapter four, above). For Germany, still useful is K. Bracher, *The German Dictatorship* (1975). For more recent considerations of the rise of Hitler to power see I. Kershaw (ed.), *Weimar: Why did German democracy fail?* (1990), and for the Third Reich see *idem, The Nazi Dictatorship: Problems and Perspectives of Interpretation* (2nd. ed. , London, 1989).

For general background to Rumania see H. L. Roberts, *Rumania: political problems of an agrarian state* (Yale, 1951). The right is dealt with in E. Weber, 'Rumania', in *The European Right*, edited by H. Rogger and E. Weber (Berkeley, 1965). More specific to fascism are S. Fischer-Galati, 'Fascism in Rumania', and E. Turcynski, 'The background to Rumanian fascism', both of which are to be found in *Native Fascism in the Successor States*, edited by P. Sugar (Santa Barbara, 1971). A good political study which places Rumania in its east European context is J. Rothschild, *East Central Europe between the two World Wars* (New York, 1974).

Chapter 16

There has been a good deal of work on this subject recently. A good place to begin is with Anthony D. Smith, *Nationalism in the Twentieth Century* (Oxford, 1979), chapter 6, 'Ethnic resurgence in the West'. Useful articles introducing the subject generally for Europe are: G. van Benthem van der Berghe, 'Contemporary nationalism in the Western world', *Daedalus*, 95 (1966); J. Krejci, 'Ethnic problems in Europe', in *Contemporary Europe: social structures and cultural patterns* (1978), ed. S. Giner and M. S. Archer; and W. Petersen, 'On the subnations of western Europe', in *Ethnicity: theory and experience*, ed. N. Glazer and D. Moynihan (Cambridge, Mass. , 1975). More recent is M. Keating, *State and regional nationalism: territorial politics and the European state* (New York, 1988).

For Britain there are the interesting though different views from the left provided by T. Nairn, *The Break-Up of Britain: crisis and neo-nationalism* (1977), and M. Hechter, *Internal Colonialism: the Celtic fringe in British national development, 1536–1966* (Berkeley, 1975).

On Scottish nationalism there is the older work of H. J. Hanham, *Scottish Nationalism* (1969), and the more recent studies of K. Webb, *The Growth of Nationalism in Scotland* (1978), and J. Brand, *The National*

Movement in Scotland. Not surprisingly, the subject has attracted rather less attention since 1979.

On Ireland as a background to the Ulster case see R. Kee, *The Green Flag: a history of Irish nationalism* (1972).

Specifically on Ulster I have found stimulating the short work by P. Gibbon, *The Origins of Ulster Unionism: the formation of popular Protestant politics and ideology in nineteenth-century Ireland* (Manchester, 1975). For a short argument about the 'rationality' of unionism see P. Buckland, 'The Unity of Ulster Unionism, 1886–1939', *History*, 60, no. 199 (1975). The post-war troubles have produced a spate of literature. From the perspective of this book of particular interest is R. Bew, P. Gibbon, and H. Patterson, *The State in Northern Ireland, 1921–72: political forces and social classes* (Manchester, 1979).

For post-war Welsh nationalism see A. B. Philip, *the Welsh Question: nationalism in Welsh politics, 1945–70* (Cardiff, 1975).

On Spain one can begin with R. Payne, 'Catalan and Basque nationalism', *Journal of Contemporary History*, 6/1 (1971). More specifically on the Basque case see J. Harrison, 'Big business and the rise of Basque nationalism', *European Studies Review*, 7 (1977), and J. Hollyman, 'Basque revolutionary separatism: ETA', in *Spain in Crisis*, ed. P. Preston (Sussex, 1976). More recent is J. L. Sullivan, *ETA and Basque nationalism: the fight for Euskadi 1890–1986* (1988).

On Canada a work on the historic roots of French-Canadian nationalism which rather dents the nationalist view is F. Oullet, *Social Change and Nationalism* (Toronto, 1980). On the earlier twentieth century see H. F. Quinn, *The Union Nationale: a study in Quebec nationalism* (Toronto, 1968). There is a large, mainly polemical literature on the more recent phase of nationalism. I have found useful R. Cook (ed.), *Canada and the French Canadian Question* (Toronto, 1967).

Chapter 17

For the contemporary history of the USSR I have found useful S. White, *Gorbachev and After* (Cambridge, 1992). A. Motyl, *Sovietology, Rationality, Nationality: Coming to Grips with Nationalism in the USSR* (New York, 1990) provides much conceptual help in trying to understand the subject. Like everything anyone writes on this subject, it is soon overtaken by events – in this case the relatively non-violent collapse of the USSR. A good collection of essays is provided in R. Denber (ed.), *The Soviet Nationality Reader: The Disintegration in Context* (Boulder, Colorado, 1992). I also have found useful J. Grotzky, *Konflikt im Vielvölkerstaat: Die Nationen der Sowjetunion im Aufbruch* (Zürich, 1991). For the Ukrainian background see J. A. Armstrong, *Ukrainian Nationalism* (3rd ed., Englewood, Colorado, 1990).

As historical background to the states of east-central Europe I have found most useful the two books by J. Rothschild, *East Central Europe Between the Two World Wars* (New York, 1974), and *Return to Diversity: A Political History of East Central Europe since World War II* (New York, 1989). On the revolutions of 1989 I found most helpful T. Garton Ash, *The Uses of Adversity: Essays on the Fate of Central Europe* (Cambridge, 1989); and M. Glenny, *The Rebirth of History: Eastern Europe in the Age of Democracy* (1990). On the conflict in Yugoslavia up to the middle of 1992 see also his book *The Fall of Yugoslavia: The Third Balkan War* (1992).

For the reunification of Germany see the most recent editions of W. Carr, *A History of Germany 1815–1945* (London, 1991) and M. Fulbrook, *A Concise History of Germany* (Cambridge, 1992). The subject is also considered in J. Breuilly (ed.), *The State of Germany: the national idea in the making, unmaking, and remaking of a nation-state* (1992), especially my essay 'Conclusion: nationalism and German reunification'. Also of interest is H. Zwahr, 'Die Revolution in der DDR', in *Revolution in Deutschland? 1789–1989*, edited by M. Hettling (Göttingen, 1991).

However, the principal sources of information for such recent and, in many cases, unfinished events, are not books but the work of journalists in newspapers, radio and television. Glenny's books, for example, are the work of an outstanding journalist, first for *The Guardian* and then for the BBC.

Conclusion

G. Poggi, *The Development of the Modern State: a sociological introduction* (1978) was extremely useful. For an up-to-date survey see R. Axtmann, 'The formation of the modern state: the debate in the social sciences', in *National Histories and European Perspectives*, ed. M. Fulbrook (1993). A valuable study of the medieval background is J. Strayer, *On the Medieval Origins of the Modern State* (Princeton, 1970). The distinction between public and private is dealt with acutely in J. Habermas, *Strukturwandel der Öffentlichkeit* (Neuwied and Berlin, 1969). A convenient English-language summary of his main ideas is 'The public sphere', *New German Critique*, III (1974). A detailed working-out of the implications of these ideas about public and private distinctions which I have found impressive is N. O. Keohane, *Philosophy and the State in France: Renaissance to Enlightenment* (Princeton, 1980). I have tried to develop some of these ideas in relation to nineteenth-century Germany in 'Sovereignty and boundaries: modern state formation and national identity in Germany', in *National Histories and European Perspectives*, ed. M. Fulbrook (London, 1993). See also now A. Giddens, *The Nation State and Violence* (Cambridge, 1985). A work of central importance is K. Dyson,

The State Tradition in Western Europe (Oxford, 1980).

My comments on the Third Reich relate to debates amongst historians. A convenient introduction is to contrast the two essays of H. Mommsen, 'National Socialism: continuity and change' and of K. Bracher, 'The role of Hitler: perspectives of interpretation', both in W. Laquer (ed.), *Fascism: a reader's guide* (1979). The best way of following the debate is to read I. Kershaw, *The Nazi Dictatorship* (see above chapter 15). For what Hitler meant to the German people see also his two studies: *The Hitler Myth* (Oxford, 1987), and *Popular Opinion and Political Dissent in the Third Reich: Bavaria 1933–1945* (Oxford, 1983).

Some of the final points about the erosion of public and private fit into 'crisis of liberalism' arguments for which see T. Lowi, *The End of Liberalism* (New York, 1969). The liberal idea of separating the purposes of the state from the character of communities is critically treated in M. J. Sandel, *Liberalism and the Limits of Justice* (Cambridge, 1982).

As for my comments about Ireland, despite a hostile review of the first edition of my book in an Irish republican journal, I still continue to find stimulating the book by Conor Cruise O'Brien, *States of Ireland* (1974).

Index

The index does not cover chronologies or the bibliographical essay. Authors' names appear only where their work is separately discussed in the text. Where names of countries have changed, the name given is that most commonly used in the text, which is usually contemporary usage in the period under discussion. Cross-references are provided where necessary. 'n.' after a page reference denotes the number of a note on that page.

in Egypt, 154, 159, 274
in India, 171-83, 208-14
in Kenya, 183
in Uganda, 205-6
Broederbond (Afrikaner society), 66
Brown Shirts (SA, Nazi paramilitary group), 44, 314, 317n.15
Bruning, H. (German Chancellor), 298
Buda (Hungarian city), 127
Budapest, 353
Buganda, *see* Baganda
Bulgaria, 143, 341, 351
bureaucracy, 21
Burke, Edmund (British conservative writer and politician), 56, 87
businessmen, 30-3
Butler, David, 320

Cairo, 274
Calcutta (India), 24, 172, 264
Caliphate, 153, 155n.6
  Khilafat movement, 175, 208
Calvinists, 78, 79
Campania, fascist success in, 299
Canada, 7, 332-3, 334-5, 338
  see also French-Canadian nationalism
Canton, 235, 237
capitalism
  class, 30-2
  print, 77
Carlism in Spain, 289, 309
Carol II, King of Rumania, 300, 301, 302, 305
Casino (political meeting in Hungary), 128
Catalan nationalism, 11, 32, 335, 336
Catholic League, 78
Catholicism, 371, 372
  Canada, 332
  communal conflict, 23, 24
  Czechoslovakia, 134
  early modern Europe, 76-8
  England, 86
  Germany, 34, 61, 100, 111-12
  Habsburg empire, 124, 144
  Ireland, 30, 329, 396-7
  Italy, 99, 102
  Magyars, 126

Poland, 29, 117, 341, 351
Rhineland, 337
Transylvania, 136
Cavour, C. (Prime Minister of Piedmont), 97, 112-14
Ceaucescu, Nicolae (Rumanian dictator), 351
Celtic voting patterns in UK, 320
centralisation of power, 81
ceremonies, 64-8
Cetnik movement, 358, 359
Chagga (Tanganyika), 45
Charles I, King of England, 86
Charles Albert, King of Piedmont, 102, 103
Chattopadhyay, Bankihchandra, 208-9
Chernenko (Soviet president), 344
Chiang Kai Shek (Chinese nationalist), 233, 234, 236, 239, 240
China, 158, 230, 231-40, 252, 273, 379
  and Japan, 20, 248-51
  peasants, 45, 46
  symbolism, 278
  and Turkey, 211, 248
Choshu (Japanese domain), 25, 242
Chou en Lai (Chinese communist), 233
Christianity
  colonial response to, 162, 166
  see also specific churches and sects
Church of Scotland, 324
Cilliers, S. (Afrikaner nationalist), 66
citizenship, 11
Civic Forum (Czechoslovakia), 351
class, 25-51
  alignment, 321
  fascism, 290, 309-10
  Marxism, 407-11
co-ordination, 93, 224, 240, 382-6
Code Napoléon, Poland, 115
Codreanu, Cornelius (Rumanian fascist), 301, 303-4, 305
Coke, Sir Edward (English parliamentarian), 85, 94n.8
Coligny, Gaspard de (French Huguenot), 78
collaboration, 81-2, 195-6, 216, 221-2, 224, 226-8, 383-4
  anti-colonialism, 158-64

461

472

361, 362
Tudor dynasty, 76
Tunisia, 42
Turkey, 9, 124, 142, 151, 230, 231,
    244-7, 252, 270-3, 276, 277
  and China, 236, 248
  class, 29
  and Japan, 248

Uganda, 21, 190, 191, 200, 204-6,
    214-15, 261-3, 267
Ukraine, 341, 347-8, 364n.8
Ukrainian language, 348
Ulster
  Catholics, 396
  class, 42
  comparison with Scotland, 326, 330-1
  see also Ireland
Ulster Unionist Party, 322, 326,
    339n.14, 399
  class, 409
  communal conflicts, 25
Uniate Church (Transylvania), 124,
    126, 136, 148n.1
unification nationalism, 9-10, 12, 255,
    378
  new nation-states, 281-7
  nineteenth-century Europe, 96-122
Union Nationale, Canada, 332
Union of Soviet Socialist Republics, *see*
    Soviet Union
United Arab Republic, 284
United Diet (Prussia, 1847), 101
United Kingdom, *see* England; Great
    Britain; Ireland; Scotland; Wales
United Nations, 185, 284
United Party, South Africa, 66
United Provinces (India), 180, 207, 210,
    211
United States of America, *see* America,
    United States of
universalism, 5-7
Untouchables, championed by Gandhi,
    179
Urdu, as official language in Pakistan,
    264
USSR, *see* Soviet Union
Ustaca (Croatian fascist movement), 359

Valois dynasty (France), 76
Venetia, 101, 102, 103, 108, 144
Venice, 102, 103, 144
Verdi, G. (Italian composer), 66
Vico, G. (Italian writer), 56
Victor Emmanuel, King of Italy, 97, 113
Vienna, 99, 122n.4, 125, 128, 129, 303
Voivodina, 137, 359
voluntarist view of nationality, 6
Voortrekker museum (Pretoria), 66

Wales, 13, 38, 84, 320, 326-31, 336
  see also Great Britain
Walesa, Lech (Polish president), 351
Walker, Peter, 331
Wallachia (province of Ottoman
    empire), 135, 136-7, 140, 141
Wang Ching-Wei (collaborator with
    Japanese), 238
Warsaw, Grand Duchy of, 116, 118
Weber, Max, 219, 279n.4
Welsh language, 323, 326, 328
Welsh nationalism, *see* Plaid Cymru
West Indies, support for Pan-Africanism
    281
westernisation, 157-8, 166, 227
Westphalia, political integration in
    nineteenth century, 338
Whampoa Military Academy (China),
    233
White Highlands (Kenya), 190
Wielopolski (Polish magnate), 119
William I, Emperor of Germany, 97
Wilson, Harold (British prime minister),
    321, 325, 330
Württemberg (German state), 99, 121
working class, 36-44

Yeltsin, Boris, 349
Yemen, in United Arab Republic, 284
Yenan (Chinese province), 237
Yoruba (Nigeria), 29, 263
Young, M. Crawford, 203-4
Young Turk movement, 246
Yugoslavia, 341, 350-1, 353, 357-62
Yugoslavism, 358